CW00322266

Remedial Secession

A Right to External Self-Determination
as a Remedy to Serious Injustices?

SCHOOL OF HUMAN RIGHTS RESEARCH SERIES, Volume 61

The titles published in this series are listed at the end of this volume.

Remedial Secession
A Right to External Self-Determination
as a Remedy to Serious Injustices?

SIMONE F. VAN DEN DRIEST

intersentia

Cambridge – Antwerp – Portland

Intersentia Ltd
Trinity House | Cambridge Business Park | Cowley Road
Cambridge | CB4 0WZ | United Kingdom
Tel.: +44 1223 393 753 | mail@intersentia.co.uk

Simone F. van den Driest
Remedial Secession: A Right to External Self-Determination as a Remedy to Serious
Injustices?

ISBN 978-1-78068-153-5
D/2013/7849/33
NUR 828

Cover image by Jeroen Brevet (www.jeroenbrevet.nl)
Editing and typesetting by Steve Lambley Information Design

© 2013 Simone F. van den Driest/Intersentia
www.intersentia.com I www.intersentia.co.uk

British Library Cataloguing in Publication Data. A catalogue record for this book is
available from the British Library.

No part of this book may be reproduced in any form, by print, photoprint, microfilm
or any other means, without written permission from the publisher.

To my parents

ACKNOWLEDGEMENTS

Writing a dissertation is a challenging endeavour, which requires a great deal of effort, commitment and perseverance. Over the last couple of years, Tilburg University has given me the opportunity to delve into a fascinating and much debated subject of international law and to develop and improve my academic skills. It has been a very interesting and valuable experience, which I would not have missed for anything. Therefore, I am thankful for many people in both my professional and personal life who have contributed – each in their own way – to bring this project to a successful conclusion. I would like to take this opportunity to express my gratitude to a number of them in particular.

First and foremost, I would like to thank my supervisors Willem van Genugten, Nicola Jägers and Anna Meijknecht. I honestly could not have wished for a better and more pleasant 'team' to guide me through the process of writing this dissertation. Your constructive criticism and support have been very valuable to me and I truly enjoyed working with the three of you. Willem, I am most grateful for the confidence you instilled in me and your continuous encouragement, which helped me to keep on going and stimulated me to develop myself within academia. Thank you for your guidance and the opportunities you have given me over the last couple of years. You are a true mentor to me. Nicola and Anna, I am very thankful that you have both been willing to act as my supervisors. Your continuing willingness to discuss difficult issues of my research, your eye for detail, and your kind support have helped me tremendously. On a more personal level, I have thoroughly enjoyed our many pleasant talks, both short and long, about work-related and other matters. Thank you so much.

In addition, I would like to take the opportunity to extend my gratitude to the further members of the reading committee: Professors James Crawford, André Nollkaemper, Cedric Ryngaert and Nico Schrijver. I am grateful that they were willing to take a seat on the committee and I very much appreciate that they took the time to read and comment upon my manuscript.

Furthermore, I would like to thank my colleagues – both past and present – as they created such a pleasant working environment at the Law School's fifth floor. Since mentioning some individuals also means excluding others, I wish to thank them all as a group. A special word of thanks, however, goes to Byung Sook, with whom I shared an office for several years and whose presence made the process of writing a dissertation so much more enjoyable. Thank you for being such a wonderful room-mate and friend.

I also wish to mention my dear friends: Angèle, Christophe and Stefania, Femke, Jerom, Maartje and Gary, Marjolein, and Michelle. Thank you for your support and understanding and thank you for taking my mind off things. Thanks for the many chats, lovely and funny messages, many cups of tea, delicious dinners, shopping dates, theatre visits, and other pleasant get-togethers. In short: thank you for being there for me – it means a lot to me.

In order to turn the manuscript into a publishable book, I have had the pleasure of working with Steve Lambley, Jeroen Brevet and Tom Scheirs. I would like to thank Steve for skilfully editing and typesetting the manuscript, and for his incredible flex-ibility in that respect. I thank Jeroen for designing the cover image of this book and Tom for providing me with the necessary support on behalf of Intersentia.

Finally, a special word of gratitude goes to my dear parents, who have supported and encouraged me throughout this project, who strongly believed in me and always were there for me. I cannot express how thankful I am for the part they play in my life. It is to them that I dedicate this book.

Simone van den Driest
Breda, January 2013

TABLE OF CONTENTS

LIST OF ABBREVIATIONS

ACHPR	African Commission on Human and Peoples' Rights
AU	African Union
CIS	Commonwealth of Independent States
CoE	Council of Europe
CSCE	Conference on Security and Co-operation in Europe
EEC	European Economic Community
EC	European Community
ECtHR	European Court of Human Rights
EU	European Union
ELF	Eritrean Liberation Front
EPLF	Eritrean Peoples Liberation Front
IACHR	Inter-American Court of Human Rights
ICCPR	International Covenant on Civil and Political Rights
ICERD	International Convention on the Elimination of all Forms of Racial Discrimination
ICESCR	International Covenant on Economic, Social and Cultural Rights
ICISS	International Commission on Intervention and State Sovereignty
ICJ	International Court of Justice
ICRC	International Committee of the Red Cross
ICTY	International Criminal Tribunal for the Former Yugoslavia
ILA	International Law Association
ILC	International Law Commission
ILO	International Labour Organization
NATO	North Atlantic Treaty Organization
OAU	Organization of African Unity
OSCE	Organization for Security and Co-operation in Europe
PCIJ	Permanent Court of International Justice
RtoP/R2P	Responsibility to Protect
SFRY	Socialist Federal Republic of Yugoslavia
TRNC	Turkish Republic of Northern Cyprus
UDHR	Universal Declaration on Human Rights
UN	United Nations

UNDRIP	United Nations Declaration on the Rights of Indigenous Peoples
UNESCO	United Nations Educational, Scientific and Cultural Organization
UNMIK	United Nations Interim Administration in Kosovo
UNWGIP	United Nations Working Group on Indigenous Populations
US(A)	United States (of America)
USSR	Union of Soviet Socialist Republics
YNA	Yugoslav National Army

CHAPTER I

INTRODUCTION

"Until recently in international practice the right to self-determination was in practical terms identical to, and indeed restricted to, a right to decolonisation. In recent years a consensus has seemed to emerge that peoples may also exercise a right of self-determination if their human rights are consistently and flagrantly violated or if they are without representation at all or are massively under-represented in an undemocratic and discriminatory way. If this description is correct, then the right to self-determination is a tool which may be used to re-establish international standards of human rights and democracy."

Judge Luzius Wildhaber*

1. BALANCING ORDER AND JUSTICE: EXTERNAL SELF-DETERMINATION AFTER SERIOUS INJUSTICES?

1.1. The Contentious Issue of Unilateral Secession

On 17 February 2008, Serbia's restive province of Kosovo declared itself "to be an independent and sovereign State", thus seceding from the sovereign State of Serbia in the absence of the consent of the latter.[1] Serbia strongly opposed Kosovo's declaration of independence by claiming that its territorial integrity had been violated. Kosovo's secession from Serbia marked the end of a turbulent era for Kosovo: an era in which ethnic violence ultimately triggered NATO bombings in order to put an end to the ethnic cleansing of civilians, and in which the territory was subsequently administered by the United Nations for many years.[2] A considerable number of States responded to Kosovo's unilateral declaration of independence by formally

---

*   European Court of Human Rights, *Loizidou v. Turkey*, Application No. 15318/89, Judgment (Merits), 18 December 1996, Concurring opinion of Judge Wildhaber joined by Judge Ryssdal, at para. 2.

[1]   Kosovo's declaration of independence can be consulted at the website of the Ministry of Foreign Affairs of the Republic of Kosovo, *Kosovo Declaration of Independence*, available at <http://www.mfa-ks.net/?page=2,25>, last consulted on 24 September 2012.

[2]   For an accessible account of the history and possible future of Kosovo, see T. Judah, *Kosovo: What Everyone Needs to Know* (Oxford University Press, New York: 2008). For a more critical analysis of a

recognizing the Republic of Kosovo as an independent State.[3] Yet, to date, approximately as many States remain reluctant to do so. Russia and Serbia, for instance, have reacted to Kosovo's declaration of independence with maximal restraint. The Serbian Minister of Foreign Affairs, Vuk Jeremić, even initiated a resolution for the United Nations General Assembly to seek an advisory opinion from the International Court of Justice on the legality of Kosovo's attempt to secede unilaterally. Sending the question to the International Court of Justice "would prevent the Kosovo crisis from serving as a deeply problematic precedent in any part of the globe where secessionist ambitions are harboured", the Serbian Minister explained in his introduction to the text of the draft resolution.[4] During its sixty-third session, the General Assembly adopted Resolution 63/3 with a slim majority.[5] The States participating in the advisory proceedings expressed "radically different views" on the question of Kosovo's declaration of independence and the question of whether the "law of self-determination confers upon part of the population of an existing State a right to separate from that State", as the Court observed.[6] While some States indeed contended that present-day international law acknowledges a right to secede as a remedy to serious injustices committed against a people, other States – most prominently Serbia – excluded this possibility by emphasizing the prevalence of the sovereign prerogatives of the State, primarily the principle of respect for the territorial integrity of States.

The controversy with respect to the specific case of Kosovo and the diverging views expressed following its proclaimed independence reflect well the debate surrounding claims to self-determination and accompanying more general attempts at unilateral secession. Kosovo is just one example of a territory on which its population has persistently called for self-determination. Today, dozens of secessionist movements and associated conflicts can be counted world-wide,[7] ranging from the Basque country to Abkhazia and South Ossetia and from Kurdistan to West Papua, to

---

prominent episode in Kosovo's history, i.e. its struggle for independence, see M. Weller, *Contested Statehood: Kosovo's Struggle for Independence* (Oxford University Press, Oxford 2009).

[3]   Before the International Court of Justice issued its Advisory Opinion on the matter, sixty-nine States had recognized Kosovo as a sovereign State. By December 2012, ninety-six States had formally recognized the Republic of Kosovo. For an updated list of recognitions, see the website of the Ministry of Foreign Affairs of the Republic of Kosovo, *Countries that have recognized the Republic of Kosova*, available at <www.mfa-ks.net/?page=2,33>, last consulted on 30 December 2012.

[4]   UN Press Release, *Backing Request by Serbia, General Assembly Decides to Seek International Court of Justice Ruling on Legality of Kosovo's Independence*, UN Doc. GA/10764, 8 October 2008.

[5]   UN General Assembly Resolution 63/3 (*Request for an Advisory Opinion of the International Court of Justice on Whether the Unilateral Declaration of Independence of Kosovo is in Accordance with International Law*), UN Doc. A/Res/63/3, 8 October 2008.

[6]   International Court of Justice, *Accordance with International Law of the Unilateral Declaration of Independence in Respect of Kosovo*, Advisory Opinion, ICJ Reports 2010, p. 403, at para. 82.

[7]   M. Weller, 'Settling Self-Determination Conflicts: Recent Developments' (2009) 20 *European Journal of International Law* 111 at p. 112.

mention a few.[8] Yet, since unilateral secession is generally seen to conflict with fundamental principles within international law, the international community of States has been extremely reluctant to consider and accept claims to unilateral secession.

1.2. Unilateral Secession and Self-Determination

Notwithstanding the controversy surrounding the issue, these days, it is generally contended that unilateral secession is an expression – albeit the most extreme expression – of the right to self-determination of peoples. This right became most prominently visible against the backdrop of the decolonization process, when self-determination was primarily realized through the emergence of sovereign and independent States, casting off the yoke of the colonial powers.[9] This approach has led to the conclusion that the right to self-determination of colonial peoples was attained as soon as a dependent territory achieved independence from the colonial power. Beyond decolonization, the right to self-determination continued. It became a right of all peoples rather than merely colonial ones, and is now generally seen to involve two dimensions: one internal, the other external.[10] The internal dimension implies that self-determination should be achieved within the framework of the existing State, in the relation between the population of a State and its authorities. It seems to imply that the people concerned are able to choose their legislators and political representatives, without third State intervention and without any manipulation or interference from the central authorities, in order to express the popular will. Moreover, it requires the equal participation of the peoples in the general political decision-making process within a State.[11] In contrast to this internal dimension, the external dimension of the right to self-determination was prominent during the post-World War II decolonization period. Beyond the context of decolonization, it is accepted that the right to external self-determination may be exercised through the peaceful dissolution of a State, through consensual merger or (re)union with another State, or through consensual or constitutional secession.[12]

---

[8]   For an overview of regions and groups with active secessionist movements, see A. Pavković and P. Radan, *Creating New States: Theory and Practice of Secession* (Ashgate Publishing, Aldershot 2007) at pp. 257-259 (Appendix). It is noteworthy that after a decades-long civil war, the Tamil Tigers (LTTE), a very active secessionist movement in Sri Lanka, was declared defeated by the national government on 19 May 2009. The government announced that the rebel leader Prabhakaran had been killed during the final offensive in May and the Tamil Tigers announced they would lay down their arms. For more information on the conflict in Sri Lanka, see 'Sri Lanka Conflict History', available at <http://www.crisisgroup.org>, last consulted on 24 September 2012.

[9]   International Court of Justice, *Western Sahara*, Advisory Opinion, ICJ Reports 1975, p. 12, at paras 54-59.

[10] See Chapter III of the present study.

[11] See Chapter III, Section 3 of the present study.

[12] See Chapter III, Section 4 of the present study.

As was already seen above, whether unilateral secession – i.e. without the consent of the parent State or constitutional authorization – is also included in these options, is more questionable. International law does not explicitly acknowledge this mode of exercising the right to self-determination. In fact, unilateral secession seems to be irreconcilable with the fundamental position within the international legal order of the principle of respect for the territorial integrity of States, which is aimed at maintaining the territorial *status quo* of sovereign States,[13] while (unilateral) secession is precisely aimed at territorial change by modifying the external boundaries of the existing State. It is in this respect that unilateral secession is seen to challenge the very foundations of the State and the international order in general. It is often feared that unilateral secession will lead to the fragmentation of States and as such, have severely disruptive effects on the international legal order, since a large number of States harbours groups with secessionist ambitions. Hence, it is not surprising that beyond the context of decolonization, the emphasis is generally put on the internal rather than the external dimension of the right to self-determination. Considering the high value attributed to the principle of respect for the territorial integrity of States within the system of international law, it seems that no general entitlement to unilateral secession can exist.

1.3. Unilateral Secession as a Remedial Right?

A different situation, however, may be seen to arise when a people is submitted to serious injustices on the part of the State in which it resides. One may think of the situation in which, for instance, a people is persistently oppressed by the State, or in which its fundamental human rights are grossly and systematically violated by the central authorities. In those circumstances, and when the possibilities for reaching a peaceful solution within the framework of the existing State are either denied or exhausted, taking territorial integrity as being absolute, no human and just solution seems possible. That point of departure, requiring a people to remain within the borders of a State whatever the circumstances, would possibly "erect a principle of tyranny without measure and without end".[14] With a view to balancing order and justice, one might therefore argue that considering the well-established right to self-determination of peoples, in those exceptional circumstances when a people is flagrantly denied its right to internal self-determination, it should be endowed with a right to external self-determination by means of unilateral secession as a remedy to such gross injustices. Put differently, under specific circumstances, a people's right to internal self-determination might arguably become a right to external self-determination in the

---

[13] The principle of respect for the territorial integrity of States is referred to in Article 2(4) of the United Nations Charter.

[14] A. Cobban, *The Nation State and National Self-Determination* (Collins, London 1969) at p. 138.

manifestation of a right to unilateral secession. Until this critical point is reached, the right to self-determination could only be exercised within the limits set by the principle of respect for the territorial integrity of States, i.e. internally. As will be seen in the present study, legal literature has increasingly presented such an outlook and a considerable number of scholars has even maintained that a right to remedial secession does already exist under international law.[15] When seen from a moral perspective, it may indeed be attractive to warrant such a right. The question however remains to what extent a legal entitlement to remedial secession has actually emerged under contemporary international law. The present study aims to shed light on this issue.

2. The Approach of this Study

Before embarking on the substance of the issue outlined above, the approach of this study merits some explanation. Since the concepts of (unilateral) secession and remedial secession are at the heart of this thesis, it is important to formulate definitions of these notions for the present purposes. Subsequently, the principal research question will be phrased, after which the methodology and structure of this study will be outlined.

2.1. Defining (Unilateral) Secession and Remedial Secession

Considering the Latin roots of the word secession,[16] it is apparent that the concept of secession is related to "leaving or withdrawing from some place".[17] However, when seeking to formulate the meaning of the concept in greater detail, one will discover that in literature, various definitions are used, and that there is only little consensus on a definition of secession. Some definitions propounded by authors are broad and included many situations, while others are narrow, only applying to a limited set of circumstances.[18] Peter Radan, to give an example, suggested that secession should be defined as "the creation of a new State upon territory previously forming part of, or being a colonial entity of, an existing State".[19] This broad definition makes clear that, in essence, secession is viewed as a process which enables the creation of a new State. A similar, process-oriented definition is used by Georg Nolte and Bruno Coppieters. Nolte contended that secession means "the – not necessarily forceful – breaking away of an integral part of the territory of a State and its subsequent establishment

---

[15]   See Chapter IV, Section 2.2 of the present study.
[16]   The Latin word '*se*' means 'apart', and the verb '*cedere*' means 'to go'.
[17]   P. Radan, 'The Definition of "Secession"' (2007) *Macquarie Law Working Paper Series* at p. 2.
[18]   See *ibid.* at pp. 5-15.
[19]   See *ibid.* at p. 2.

as a new State"[20] and Coppieters defined the concept as the "withdrawal from a State or society through the constitution of a new sovereign and independent State".[21] James R. Crawford, however, used a narrower definition as he describes secession as "the creation of a State by the use or threat of force without the consent of the former sovereign".[22] As such, Crawford emphasized that secession involves the process of State-creation, but implies that not all cases in which the creation of the State results from the decolonization process are included. Moreover, according to Crawford, secession involves opposition from the existing sovereign State (i.e. the parent State).

In the present study, a middle course is adopted, defining secession as follows:

> The establishment of a new independent State through the withdrawal of an integral part of the territory of an existing State from that State, carried out by the resident population of that part of the territory, either with or without the consent of the parent State or domestic constitutional authorization.

Thus, this definition first articulates that secession is a process, of which – if successful – a new independent State is the outcome. Furthermore, implicit in this definition of secession is that, since only an integral part of the territory withdraws, the remaining part of the State continues the legal personality of the already existing parent State.[23] It is to be emphasized that the definition formulated above covers both instances of secession with and instances of secession without the consent of the parent State or a domestic constitutional arrangement authorizing withdrawal. The first category is referred to as consensual or constitutional secession, while the latter category is generally labelled as *unilateral* secession. Since this unilateral mode of secession will be at the centre of the present study, it merits a definition:

> The establishment of a new independent State through the withdrawal of an integral part of the territory of an existing State from that State, carried out by the resident population of that part of the territory, without either the consent of the parent State or domestic constitutional authorization.

---

[20] G. Nolte, 'Secession and External Intervention' in M.G. Kohen (ed.) *Secession International Law Perspectives* (Cambridge University Press, Cambridge 2006) at p. 65.

[21] B. Coppieters, 'Introduction' in B. Coppieters and R. Sakwa (eds) *Contextualizing Secession Normative Studies in Comparative Perspective* (Oxford University Press, Oxford 2003) at p. 4.

[22] J.R. Crawford, *The Creation of States in International Law* (2nd revised edn, Clarendon Press, Oxford 2006) at p. 375.

[23] On this issue, see P. Radan, 'Post-Secession International Borders: A Critical Analysis of the Opinions of the Badinter Arbitration Commission' (2000) 24 *Melbourne University Law Review* 50 at p. 56; D. Raič, *Statehood and the Law of Self-Determination* (Kluwer Law International, The Hague 2002) at p. 359; M. Weller, 'The Self-Determination Trap' (2005) 4 *Ethnopolitics* 3 at p. 8.

This definition emphasizes the problematic one-sided character of unilateral secession and, hence, the difference to consensual or constitutional secession.[24] Similar to Nolte but in contrast to Crawford's definition, the label of unilateral secession as used in the present study does not necessarily involve the threat or use of forceful means. One could call such an element superfluous, since, as Michael Schoiswohl observed, "an element of force is already inherent in the lack of approval by the previous sovereign".[25] In other words, it can be assumed that, if the claim to statehood by the secessionist movement is opposed by the parent State, at least an implicit threat of the use of force must be present.

Embroidering on the definitions of both secession and unilateral secession as presented above, it now becomes possible to formulate a definition of the concept of remedial secession. For the present purposes, remedial secession is defined as follows:

> The establishment of a new independent State through the withdrawal of an integral part of the territory of an existing State from that State, carried out by the resident population of that part of the territory, without either the consent of the parent State or domestic constitutional authorization, yet as a remedy of last resort to the serious injustices which the resident population of that part of the territory has suffered at the hands of the authorities of the parent State.

It should be emphasized, however, that the above is a working definition. While this definition considers the presence of serious injustices and the absence of any other remedies as a justification for unilateral secession, it may well be that the substance of this study will reveal additional or more specific circumstances which are seen to be relevant in this respect.

---

[24] On unilateral secession and consensual or constitutional secession, see A. Buchanan, *Justice, Legitimacy, and Self-Determination. Moral Foundations for International Law* (Oxford University Press, Oxford 2004) at pp. 338-339; Raič, *Statehood and the Law of Self-Determination* at pp. 313-316. On constitutional secession, see Weller, 'The Self-Determination Trap' at pp. 16-23. However, some commentators refer to the term dissolution in instances of consensual or constitutional separation. See, for instance, J. Dugard, 'A Legal Basis for Secession: Relevant Principles and Rules' in J. Dahlitz (ed.) *Secession and International Law* (T.M.C. Asser Press, The Hague 2003) at p. 89. Yet, in this study, it is the continuation or discontinuation of the legal personality of the previous sovereign which is considered as the key distinguishing feature between secession and dissolution, even though it is to be pointed out that the contrast between the two concepts appears to be less strict as has been traditionally argued. See Radan, 'Post-Secession International Borders: A Critical Analysis of the Opinions of the Badinter Arbitration Commission' at p. 56; Raič, *Statehood and the Law of Self-Determination* at pp. 358-360. On this distinction, see Chapter III, Section 4.1.4.

[25] M. Schoiswohl, *Status and (Human Rights) Obligations of Non-Recognized De Facto Regimes in International Law: The Case of 'Somaliland'. The Resurrection of Somaliland Against All International 'Odds': State Collapse, Secession, Non-Recognition and Human Rights* (Martinus Nijhoff Publishers, Leiden 2005) at p. 48.

2.2. Principal Research Question

In view of the indeterminacy of the external dimension of the right to self-determination as touched upon previously in this Chapter, in particular with respect to the issue of remedial secession, the principal question of this study reads as follows:

> To what extent has a legal entitlement to 'remedial secession', i.e. a right to external self-determination as a remedy to serious injustices, emerged under contemporary international law?

The present study seeks to answer this question by dealing with three broad sub-questions: (1) What is the conventional meaning of the right to self-determination of peoples? (2) To what extent has a legal entitlement to 'remedial secession' emerged under the sources of international law other than custom? (3) To what extent has a legal entitlement to 'remedial secession' emerged under customary international law? As will be seen below, these sub-questions will guide the structure and methodology of the present study.

2.3. Structure and Methodology

In this study, the classical legal methodology will be adopted. In the field of international law, this involves an examination of the various sources of international law. These sources are enumerated in Article 38(1) of the Statute of the International Court of Justice and include international conventions, customary international law, general principles of (international) law, judicial decisions and opinions, and doctrine. In addition, the unilateral acts of States and acts of international organizations will also be examined in the present study. Although not listed in Article 38(1), over time, they have often been suggested as sources of international law and therefore deserve to be considered as well. While the classical legal methodology of studying the sources of international law will be most apparent in Chapter IV and Chapter VI, explicitly assessing these sources one by one, it is important to note that this methodology will act as a guide throughout the present study as a whole. It should be emphasized, however, that it is by no means a straitjacket, as the various sources of international law are sometimes connected. For instance, international conventions may include codified norms of customary international law, and judicial decisions and opinions as well as doctrine are often based on the other sources of international law. This makes it impossible to strictly distinguish between the different sources of international law impossible. Further methodological choices – for instance concerning the approach adopted towards ascertaining norms of customary international law – will be made and explained in the individual Chapters where necessary. At this stage, it may also be noted that this study will be merely consider legal literature. While much has been written on the issues of self-determination and secession from a non-legal perspective – for instance through a philosophical, international relations, or political science lens – no such literature will be included as that is beyond the scope of the present research.

For the purpose of providing good insight into the structure of the present study, this thesis is divided into three parts, each of them corresponding to one of the sub-questions posed above. First, a theoretical framework concerning the generally accepted, conventional meaning of the right to self-determination will be construed. For this purpose, an examination of its history and development up to the decolonization period and beyond is necessary, as this evolution to a large extent determined the shape and content of the contemporary right to self-determination. Chapter II will therefore be devoted to the development of the concept of self-determination from principle to right. Subsequently, Chapter III will assess the extension of the right to self-determination beyond decolonization, i.e. its contemporary meaning. In doing so, a close look will be taken at the conceptual split into the external and internal dimensions. The present-day interpretation of these dimensions will be elaborated upon by examining their respective content, legal status and subjects. It is against this background that the full extent of the indeterminacy and controversy as regards the right to self-determination and unilateral secession will become apparent.

Secondly, the question needs to be answered as to what extent a legal entitlement to remedial secession has emerged under the sources of international law *other than customary international law*.[26] To answer this question, the various sources of international law will be examined one by one. Article 38(1) of the Statute of the International Court of Justice and the sources listed therein will act as a guide in this respect. More specifically, Chapter IV will deal with international conventions, doctrine, judicial decisions and opinions, and general principles of (international) law, in order to scrutinize whether traces of a right to remedial secession are reflected. In addition to this, a couple of other sources which are not listed in Article 38(1) of the Statute of the International Court of Justice, but are often mentioned as additional sources of international law, will be addressed. These sources involve the unilateral acts of States and acts of international organizations. Where traces of the acknowledgement of a right to remedial secession are found, Chapter IV will also seek to identify the conditions for such an entitlement to arise.

Thirdly, the question arises as to what extent a right to remedial secession has emerged under *customary international law*. It is important to note that this question merits separate elaboration, as the law of self-determination is constantly moulded by international practice. Moreover, should it be found that no right to remedial secession has emerged under the other sources of international law, then the question of a customary right to remedial secession would become all the more important. All in all, a detailed examination of State practice and *opinio juris* is of great significance

---

[26] For reasons explained below, the source of customary international law will be dealt with separately.

for the present study. Before assessing these traditional constituents of custom against the backdrop of the question of remedial secession, however, the source of customary international law in general first merits elaboration. Chapter V will therefore elaborate on the two traditional constituents of custom and demonstrate how these elements have traditionally been interpreted in literature and jurisprudence. Over time, various approaches towards customary international law have been adopted. Chapter V will critically consider the conventional approach as well as some progressive methodologies, such as the so-called human rights method towards ascertaining customary international law. This critical appraisal will lead to some preliminary observations as regards assessing the existence of a customary right to remedial secession, i.e. the contemporary interpretation of the conventional approach towards custom, which will be utilized in the following Chapter.

Having made some preliminary observations in this respect, Chapter VI will be devoted to the exercise of examining the emergence of a right to remedial secession under customary international law. For this purpose, international responses to (successful) attempts at unilateral secession beyond the context of decolonization will be analysed. In doing so, a prominent role will be granted to Kosovo's relatively recent attempt to secede unilaterally from Serbia in 2008 and the international reactions in this respect. Two prominent reasons may be seen to justify this choice. First, in view of the background of the case and particularly its history of oppression and gross human rights violations by the Serbian authorities, Kosovo is frequently regarded as a test-case or experimental plot for the contemporary validity of an alleged right to remedial secession.[27] Secondly, the case of Kosovo offers an exceptional insight in the present-day views of the international community with respect to unilateral secession. This is the result of the large number of States having responded to the issuing of Kosovo's unilateral declaration of independence, within international fora such as the UN General Assembly and UN Security Council, as well as in formal recognition statements and during the advisory proceedings before the International Court of Justice.[28] In addition to Kosovo, some other cases which are sometimes suggested as supporting the existence of a right to remedial secession will be reviewed. The selection of cases in this respect is to a large extent founded on the international responses in the case of Kosovo and the references – or the apparent lack thereof – to other relevant instances in practice. The creation of Bangladesh and Croatia have sometimes

---

[27] See, for instance, A. Tancredi, 'A Normative "Due Process" in the Creation of States through Secession' in M.G. Kohen (ed.) *Secession International Law Perspectives* (Cambridge University Press, Cambridge 2006) at pp. 187-188.

[28] See UN General Assembly Resolution 63/3 (*Request for an Advisory Opinion of the International Court of Justice on Whether the Unilateral Declaration of Independence of Kosovo is in Accordance with International Law*), UN Doc. A/Res/63/3, 8 October 2008; International Court of Justice Press Release, *Accordance with International Law of the Unilateral Declaration of Independence by the Provisional Institutions of Self-Government of Kosovo (Request for Advisory Opinion). Public hearings to be held from 1 December 2009*, No. 2009/27, 29 July 2009.

been adduced as cases which reveal State practice on the matter of remedial secession. Such reference was also made during the advisory proceedings, although without further elaboration upon the relevance.[29] Other instances which have occasionally been referred to as situations endorsing the doctrine of remedial secession are the emergence of Eritrea, the independence of the Baltic States and the other successor States to the former Soviet Union, and – generally in connection with Slovenia – the creation of Croatia and the other successor States to the Socialist Federal Republic of Yugoslavia. These events will also be addressed to see whether they indeed present evidence for the thesis that a right to remedial secession does exist. Having dealt with these cases of State creation beyond the decolonization context, Chapter VI will subsequently turn to an appraisal of the international responses to attempts at unilateral secession. In doing so, the elements of State practice and *opinio juris* with respect to a right to remedial secession as reflected in the abovementioned responses will be reviewed. First and foremost, this will be done on the basis of the contemporary interpretation of the conventional approach towards ascertaining customary international law. To see whether adherence to a more liberal and progressive methodology will lead to different outcomes – as is sometimes contended – the progressive human rights approach will be applied on a subsidiary level. This review will lead to answering the question which is at issue in this third part of the study.

Finally, the threefold analysis as outlined above will logically culminate into an answer to the principal question of this study. Therefore, after having recapitulated the main findings in this respect, Chapter VII will present the general conclusions and offer some final reflections on the concept of remedial secession, its alleged effectuation through recognition value and its possible future development.

---

[29] See International Court of Justice, *Accordance with International Law of the Unilateral Declaration of Independence by the Provisional Institutions of Self-Government of Kosovo (Request for Advisory Opinion)*, Oral Statement of the Netherlands (Lijnzaad), CR 2009/32, 10 December 2009, at para. 10.

CHAPTER II
SELF-DETERMINATION:
THE DEVELOPMENT FROM
PRINCIPLE TO RIGHT

"[T]he countries of the world belong to the people who live in them, and [...] they have a right to determine their own destiny and their own form of government and their own policy, and [...] no body of statesmen, sitting anywhere, no matter whether they represent the overwhelming physical force of the world or not, has the right to assign any great people to a sovereignty under which it does not care to live."

T. Woodrow Wilson*

1. INTRODUCTION

Defining the principle of self-determination is far from being a simple matter. The principle is included in some of the most prominent international legal instruments, in which it is ascribed to be the basis for friendly relations amongst States, peace and development, and as a precondition for the enjoyment of human rights. In practice, the concept of self-determination is widely invoked by groups claiming political autonomy or even full independence. As such, it is simultaneously linked to nationalism, to political participation and democracy, and to secession as well as statehood. Yet, the precise content of the notion of self-determination, its subject and application are highly contested. Therefore, it is helpful to consider the historical roots of the concept to shed some light on this indeterminacy. To this end, the present Chapter will explore the historical development of the notion of self-determination, from theories and ideologies underlying and arising from the American and French Revolutions to the political ideas of Lenin and Wilson, and from the League of Nations' Mandate System to the United Nations Charter. Subsequently, this Chapter will deal with

---

*   T. Woodrow Wilson, speech at Billings (Montana) on 11 September 1919, quoted in: A. Cassese, *Self-Determination of Peoples. A Legal Reappraisal* (Cambridge University Press, Cambridge 1995) at p. 20, footnote 26.

what is often referred to as the traditional context of the right to self-determination: the decolonization process. In doing so, it will demonstrate how self-determination evolved from a political principle to a legal right.

2. THE EMERGENCE OF THE PRINCIPLE OF SELF-DETERMINATION

2.1. Democratic Political Theory

It is in the ideas underlying the American and French Revolutions in the eighteenth century that the roots of the notion of self-determination may be found. It is important to note that before these revolutionary ideas could flourish, States frequently did not respond to the needs and will of their populations. Gradually, these populations refused to accept the exercise of power by an authority which they experienced as 'alien'.[1] Against this background, the idea took root that (the legitimacy of) governmental power should depend on the will and consent of the people, rather than on the will of the monarch, aristocracy or privileged elite. In other words, peoples are not the subjects of States, but "can do their own State-making".[2]

In the case of the American Revolution, this line of thought resulted in American opposition to British rule. The claim of peoples to govern themselves was expressed in the Declaration of Independence of the United States of America of 4 July 1776. This declaration, written by Thomas Jefferson, proclaimed that:

> We hold these truths to be self-evident, that all men are created equal, that they are endowed by their Creator with certain unalienable Rights, that among these are Life, Liberty, and the pursuit of Happiness. That to secure these rights, Governments are instituted among Men, deriving their just powers from the consent of the governed. That whenever any Form of Government becomes destructive of these ends, it is the Right of the People to alter or abolish it, and to institute new Government, laying its foundation on such principles and organizing its powers in such form, as to them shall seem most likely to effect their Safety and Happiness.[3]

Similar views were also reflected in the French Revolution of 1789, during which the French population turned against the ruling monarch, leading to the fall of monarchical authority.[4] These revolutionary events were rooted in the rise of political-

---

[1]   D. Raič, *Statehood and the Law of Self-Determination* (Kluwer Law International, The Hague 2002) at p. 173.

[2]   A. Whelan, 'Wilsonian Self-Determination and the Versailles Settlement' (1994) 43 *International and Comparative Law Quarterly* 99 at p. 99.

[3]   Quoted in J. Summers, *Peoples and International Law: How Nationalism and Self-Determination Shape a Contemporary Law of Nations* (Martinus Nijhoff Publishers, Leiden/Boston 2007) at pp. 95-96.

[4]   See, for instance, N.G. Hansen, *Modern Territorial Statehood* (Doctoral Thesis, Leiden University 2008) at pp. 78-79; Raič, *Statehood and the Law of Self-Determination* at p. 74.

philosophical theories, such as Locke's theory of government with the consent of the governed,[5] and Rousseau's *contrat social* and *volontée générale*, which were aimed at protecting democratic order, freedom of the individual, and the exercise of legitimate governmental power.[6] The key notion in this respect was that of popular sovereignty: the idea that the people are the highest authority and, therefore, State authority should be founded on the free will of the people. As such, the ideas underlying both revolutions connect closely to the more contemporary conception of self-determination, namely that a people has the right to freely determine its political status and economic, social and cultural development. This does not imply, however, that the concept of self-determination can be equated with the driving forces underlying the two revolutions, such as the Enlightenment and the doctrine of liberalism. For, both emphasized individualism and equal rights rather than the rights and status of a collectivity, with which the concept of self-determination is concerned. But one cannot deny that "the substantive development of several aspects of the concept of self-determination is linked to primarily Western democratic political thought and ideology as expressed in the American and French Revolutions".[7]

2.2. Ethnic Nationalism

A second idea which is important in understanding the principle of self-determination also originated at the time of the French Revolution and is closely related to the notion of popular sovereignty, namely nationalism. Adherents of this theory assumed that the world community could be divided into different ethnicities, called nations or peoples. Moreover, they put forward the ideal of ethnicities functioning as the foundations of legitimate statehood, since nationalists believed that individuals could only achieve self-realization and freedom through their nation. In turn, only free nations could maintain peaceful and friendly relations and accomplish progress and development, so it was viewed.[8]

Consequently, a system was pursued in which the State and the ethnic 'nationality' living on the territory are congruent: the State in an ethnic sense.[9] As such, the

---

[5] See J. Locke, *Two Treatises of Government [1689]* (Thomas Hollis edn, A. Millar et al., London 1764). See also Summers, *Peoples and International Law: How Nationalism and Self-Determination Shape a Contemporary Law of Nations* at pp. 94-95.

[6] See J.-J. Rousseau, *The Social Contract and Discourses [1761]* (G.D.H. Cole edn, J.M. Dent and Sons, London/Toronto 1923), Book I, Chapter 6 ('The Social Compact'), pp. 43-44.

[7] Raič, *Statehood and the Law of Self-Determination* at p. 175.

[8] Summers, *Peoples and International Law: How Nationalism and Self-Determination Shape a Contemporary Law of Nations* at pp. 9-10.

[9] See A. Eide, 'The National Society, Peoples and Ethno-Nations: Semantic Confusions and Legal Consequences' (1995) 64 *Nordic Journal of International Law* 353 at p. 355; Raič, *Statehood and the Law of Self-Determination* at p.174; Summers, *Peoples and International Law: How Nationalism and Self-Determination Shape a Contemporary Law of Nations* at p. 9.

meaning of the term 'State' came to encompass more than just a legal and territorial concept, as it also added a social and cultural dimension to it.[10]

2.3. Liberal Nationalism

In the aftermath of the Revolutions, while democratic political thought and the ideology of ethnic nationalism developed further, both theories gradually converged. The merger of liberal and nationalist values created the view that, for popular sovereignty to be effective, a common identity to some extent, or at least a sense of solidarity amongst the members of the group was necessary. Put differently, to construct a system based on representative, democratic government, it was viewed that nationalist conceptions were to be taken into account,[11] possibly necessitating the break-up or merger of States for equating State and nation.

It is this ideology of liberal nationalism which reflects how the concept of self-determination was both nurtured by the call for representative government and popular self-rule on the one hand, and the claim of ethnic nationalities to independent statehood for the purpose of determining their own destiny on the other hand. This observation is particularly interesting since, as will be demonstrated in the following Chapter, the contemporary notion of self-determination is generally seen to be bipartite in character, as it has an internal dimension and an external one. In this respect, it will become apparent that liberal theory emphasized what is now considered the internal dimension of self-determination, while nationalist ideology was concerned with what is called the external dimension of self-determination.

3. SELF-DETERMINATION BEFORE THE SECOND WORLD WAR

Democratic political theory, the theory of ethnic nationalism, and compound liberal nationalist thought not only provided for the historical roots of what later became known as the principle of self-determination. In addition, it appears that both theories exerted considerable influence on the actual development of the principle of self-determination. Although it was only after the Second World War that it came into general acceptance, the principle of self-determination was brought to the attention of the international community in the early twentieth century. In this respect, an important part was played by Vladimir I. Lenin and T. Woodrow Wilson, both of whom also contributed to the development of the content of the concept of self-determination.

---

[10] This concept of ethnic nationalism can be contrasted with what is called civic nationalism, which holds that "everybody living within the state should be part of the nation on a basis of equality, irrespective of their ethnic background". See Eide, 'The National Society, Peoples and Ethno-Nations: Semantic Confusions and Legal Consequences' at p. 355.

[11] Summers, *Peoples and International Law: How Nationalism and Self-Determination Shape a Contemporary Law of Nations* at p. 110.

As will be demonstrated below, it is unsurprising to observe that in an era of competing political ideologies, Lenin and Wilson advocated distinct conceptions of self-determination. Nevertheless, in both perspectives, democratic political theory as well as the theory of ethnic nationalism is reflected in some way or other.

3.1. Lenin's Conception of Self-Determination

The Bolshevik Revolution of 1917 and Vladimir Ilyich Lenin's seizing of power made the concept of self-determination appear explicitly within international politics. Being one of the first to enunciate this right, in his 'Theses on the Socialist Revolution and the Right of Nations to Self-Determination' (1916) and in subsequent Soviet declarations, Lenin claimed that a right to self-determination was a general condition for the liberation of oppressed nations. To Lenin, self-determination signified a right for subjugated nations to break away from the oppressor and create a new, independent State. Thus, Lenin's conception of self-determination implied a right to secession. Yet, it should be noted that he viewed secession as a last resort option only, as he wrote that a nation should only proceed to secession:

> [w]hen national oppression and national friction make joint life absolutely intolerable and hinder any and all economic intercourse. In that case, the interest of capitalist development and of the freedom of class struggle will be best served by secession.[12]

Unsurprisingly, Lenin's argument arose from tactical considerations. As the excerpt above indicates, for Lenin, self-determination in the form of secession did not serve to protect the collective identity of the nation involved. Rather, Lenin believed that the concept of self-determination would serve as an instrument for the spread of socialist revolution throughout the world and creating a universal socialist community in the long run.[13] In this context, Hurst Hannum has aptly noted that "it should be underscored that self-determination in 1919 had little to do with the demands of the

---

[12] V.I. Lenin, 'The Right of Nations to Self-Determination', in: V.I. Lenin, *Collected Works* (Progress Publishers, Moscow 1964), at p. 146, quoted in: Raič, *Statehood and the Law of Self-Determination* at p. 186.

[13] See Cassese, *Self-Determination of Peoples. A Legal Reappraisal* at p. 15; Summers, *Peoples and International Law: How Nationalism and Self-Determination Shape a Contemporary Law of Nations* at p. 127; Raič, *Statehood and the Law of Self-Determination* at p. 186; P. Thornberry, 'The Democratic or Internal Aspect of Self-Determination with Some Remarks on Federalism' in C. Tomuschat (ed.) *Modern Law of Self-Determination* (Martinus Nijhoff Publishers, Dordrecht 1993) at pp. 106-107; D. Thürer and T. Burri, 'Self-Determination' in R. Wolfrum (ed.) *Max Planck Encyclopedia of Public International Law* (fully updated online edn, Oxford University Press, New York 2010) at para. 3.

peoples concerned, unless those demands were consistent with the geopolitical and strategic interests of the Great Powers".[14]

Notwithstanding his Bolshevik objectives, one cannot deny that Lenin managed to stimulate the international debate on the role of self-determination. Antonio Cassese has identified three meanings expressed in Lenin's formulation of self-determination. First, it was to serve as an instrument for ethnic and national groups to freely determine their own destiny. This aim could be realized by means of more autonomy while remaining within the existing borders of the State, but also by means of secession.[15] In this context, secession should be seen "as a necessary final guarantor of the existence of the right".[16] Secondly, self-determination was to function as a guiding principle for territorial ordering in the aftermath of military conflicts between sovereign States. As such, it prohibited territorial annexation contrary to the will of the peoples at issue. This meaning of self-determination was a reiteration of the ideas proclaimed after the French Revolution. Thirdly, self-determination was to provide for a measure for anti-colonialism, to be invoked by colonial peoples against their imperialist powers, leading to independence.[17] This final meaning should not be underestimated, since the Soviet Union's urge for the liberation of colonial peoples played an important part in the decolonization efforts initiated by the United Nations after its establishment.[18]

It follows from the Bolshevik leader's theory that he stressed an external dimension of self-determination as he defined it as the right of a nation to choose its political status in the international sphere by means of secession from the parent State. At the same time, however, one should bear in mind that, in essence, the core meaning of Lenin's conception of self-determination is concerned with an internal element. Lenin believed that the concept of self-determination enabled nations to freely determine their political destiny by means of 'self-government', thus affecting the internal relationship between the government and the governed within the borders of the State. In this respect, he viewed political separation of a collectivity, i.e. secession, as a remedy of last resort to effectuate internal self-determination.[19]

3.2. Wilson's Conception of Self-Determination

With his formulation of the United States' perspective of self-determination, the American President T. Woodrow Wilson provided a counterbalance to Lenin's

---

[14]   H. Hannum, *Autonomy, Sovereignty, and Self-Determination. The Accommodation of Conflicting Rights* (2nd revised edn, University of Pennsylvania Press, Philadelphia 1996) at p. 28.
[15]   Cassese, *Self-Determination of Peoples. A Legal Reappraisal* at p. 16.
[16]   Hansen, *Modern Territorial Statehood* at p. 80.
[17]   Cassese, *Self-Determination of Peoples. A Legal Reappraisal* at p. 16.
[18]   *Ibid.* at p. 19.
[19]   Raič, *Statehood and the Law of Self-Determination* at pp. 187-188.

conception of self-determination. In contrast to Lenin, for Wilson, self-determination signified true self-government, rather than "incorporation in a larger, centralized communist State".[20] As such, the origins of Wilson's conception of self-determination can be traced back to democratic political thought as developed in the era of the American and French Revolutions.[21] More specifically, Wilson linked a democratic governmental system with a peaceful society. He argued that only a democratic form of government would offer an ethnically identifiable people or nation the opportunity to both choose its own government as well as control the actions of the government, thus ensuring that it would not lose track of the rights and interests of its population. According to Wilson, only this form of government could be the foundation for a lasting world peace.[22]

It was from this conviction that Wilson, in his famous Fourteen Points Address of 8 January 1918,[23] proposed a post-war settlement taking his point of departure from the idea that each people or nation has the right to determine the system of government under which it would live. This implied the division of the Ottoman and Austro-Hungarian Empires and the restructuring of Europe in accordance with the interests of the populations involved.[24] In his Fourteen Points Address, Wilson did not explicitly mention the term self-determination. Yet, it is broadly accepted that six of the fourteen points implicitly concern the concept of self-determination. Wilson himself confirmed that his proposed post-war settlement was founded upon the idea of self-determination in his address to the Congress on 11 February 1918, which became known as the Four Principles Address. In this speech, he explicitly dealt with the concept of self-determination by stating that "[s]elf-determination is not a mere phrase. It is an imperative principle of action, which statesmen will henceforth ignore at their peril".[25]

Analysing Wilson's theory, two dimensions of self-determination can be distinguished.[26] The first dimension is internal, requiring a continuing democratic relationship between the government and its people. In contrast, the second dimension is external, claiming that ethnic groups should have the opportunity to govern their own territory. In other words, this theory opened doors to the establishment of ethnically

---

[20]   Hansen, *Modern Territorial Statehood* at p. 81.

[21]   Raič, *Statehood and the Law of Self-Determination* at p. 177-178.

[22]   See *ibid.* at p. 178. See also Whelan, 'Wilsonian Self-Determination and the Versailles Settlement' at p. 100.

[23]   The speech was delivered to a joint session of the United States Congress. See T.W. Wilson, 'An Address to a Joint Session of Congress' in A.S. Link (ed.) *The Papers of Woodrow Wilson* (Princeton University Press, Princeton 1984).

[24]   Cassese, *Self-Determination of Peoples. A Legal Reappraisal* at pp. 20-21.

[25]   Quoted in: Raič, *Statehood and the Law of Self-Determination* at p. 182.

[26]   Compare to Cassesse, who provides for a brief analysis of Wilson's ideas by distinguishing four elements of self-determination. See Cassese, *Self-Determination of Peoples. A Legal Reappraisal* at pp. 20-21.

homogeneous States.[27] It should be noted that Wilson's perception of self-determination did not entail a norm of international law, meaning "a right, that is, with verifiable bearers ('peoples') and corresponding duties owed by other parties (States)".[28] Rather, as a result of Wilson's efforts, self-determination had evolved into a political principle in the international political arena.

Notwithstanding the fact that Wilson paved the way for the development of self-determination within international law, his theory was heavily criticized as well. First, Wilson's theory was phrased generally and remained rather indeterminate since significant questions as to, for instance, the subjects or 'units' of a right to self-determination remained unanswered.[29] Secondly, perhaps somewhat naively, Wilson underestimated the consequences of his words on the world stage when giving utterance to his ideas. Again, an illustrative extract in this respect comes from Lansing, who wrote:

> The more I think about the President's declaration as to the right of 'self-determination', the more convinced I am of the danger of putting such ideas into the minds of certain races. It is bound to be the basis of impossible demands on the Peace Congress and create trouble in many lands.
>
> What effect will it have on the Irish, the Indians, the Egyptians, and the nationalists among the Boers? Will it not breed discontent, disorder, and rebellion? Will not the Mohammedans of Syria and Palestine and possibly of Morocco and Tripoli rely on it? How can it be harmonized with Zionism, to which the President is practically committed?
>
> The phrase is simply loaded with dynamite. It will raise hopes which can never be realized. It will, I fear, cost thousands of lives. In the end, it is bound to be discredited, to be called the dream of an idealist who failed to realize the danger until too late to check those who attempt to put the principle in force. What a calamity that the phrase was ever uttered! What a misery it will cause![30]

A third drawback of Wilson's theory which should be noted here is that it was not meant to be applied internally, in the United States itself. What is more, Wilson rejected the concept of self-determination which was aimed at the protection of American minorities and ethnic groups. Rather, Wilson's concept of self-determination was designed to function internationally – in particular on the European continent. Finally, it must

---

[27] Hannum, *Autonomy, Sovereignty, and Self-Determination. The Accommodation of Conflicting Rights* at pp. 30-31. See also Raič, *Statehood and the Law of Self-Determination* at p. 183.

[28] Whelan, 'Wilsonian Self-Determination and the Versailles Settlement' at p. 105.

[29] Secretary of State Robert Lansing wrote: "When the President talks of "self-determination" what unit has he in mind? Does he mean a race, a territorial area, or a community? Without a definite unit which is practical, application of this principle to dangerous to peace and stability". See R. Lansing, *The Peace Negotiations. A Personal Narrative* (Constable and Company, London 1921) at p. 86.

[30] *Ibid.* at p. 87.

be pointed out that Wilson's theory remained largely unadopted on the international level due to its incoherence, which will be touched upon below.[31]

3.3. Self-Determination in the Wake of the First World War

Approximately one year after Wilson delivered his famous speeches, he had the opportunity to enunciate his theory of self-determination at the Paris Peace Conference, which was held from 18 January to 21 January 1919. The Allied victors of World War I had assembled at Versailles to design a post-war settlement and create the League of Nations.[32] Most of them agreed that a re-division of Europe was necessary to create a lasting peace, and the Allies had advocated the formation of new States and made promises as regards self-government for oppressed populations at various occasions during the war. As a consequence, however, the nationalities concerned had already started to form their own States – a process which was not executed consistently and did not correspond to the ideas of the Allies.[33] Furthermore, competing interests among the Allies forced Wilson to depart from his bold demands and make concessions. In both respects, Wilson failed to live up to the expectations raised as a result of his pleas for self-determination.

Eventually, the Paris Peace Conference resulted in the application of the concept of self-determination by the allied powers, albeit rather arbitrarily: groups which had been allegiant to the victors were granted the opportunity to create their own, independent State, whereas claims made by other, less loyal communities fell on deaf ears. It goes without saying that political, strategic and economic interests of the allies often were of overriding importance.[34] Yet, practical obstacles occurred as well, since it appeared to be simply unattainable to apply the principle of self-determination without any limitations whatsoever, thus dividing Europe into ethnically homogeneous nation States.[35]

As already mentioned above, the victors of World War I did not merely assemble in Versailles to design a post-war peace settlement. They also aimed at establishing

---

[31]   Cassese, *Self-Determination of Peoples. A Legal Reappraisal* at p. 23.
[32]   For a discussion of power relations at Versailles, see G. Simpson, *Great Powers and Outlaw States. Unequal Sovereigns in the International Legal Order* (Cambridge University Press, Cambridge 2004) at pp. 154-159.
[33]   Raič, *Statehood and the Law of Self-Determination* at pp. 188-189.
[34]   Cassese, *Self-Determination of Peoples. A Legal Reappraisal* at p. 25; Raič, *Statehood and the Law of Self-Determination* at p. 190.
[35]   See L.C. Buchheit, *Secession: The Legitimacy of Self-Determination* (Yale University Press, New Haven 1978) at p. 64, quoting C. Webster, *The League of Nations in Theory and Practice* (Allen and Unwin, London 1933) at p. 206, and explaining that if self-determination would be applied without any restraint, the inescapable consequence would be that "[t]he solution of one set of minority problems [would] involve the creation of another set, with the dismal prospect of the commencement of a fresh cycle of conflict, revolt and war".

an international alliance of States which was dedicated to, *inter alia*, the promotion of international co-operation, the settlement of disputes among States, and achieving international peace and security: the League of Nations.[36] In drawing up the League of Nations Covenant, however, the failure of the Wilsonian concept of self-determination became unpleasantly apparent again. Wilson's draft provision on self-determination remained unenshrined in the Covenant, despite his efforts. Although he aimed at including the concept as a basis for potential territorial adjustments "by reason of changes in present racial conditions and aspirations or present social and political relationships",[37] the final version of the Covenant made no reference to self-determination at all. A general fear for disintegration must be considered as the preliminary reason for this exclusion.[38]

Despite of this lack of explicitly mentioning self-determination, the concept of self-determination is generally viewed as the main idea behind the so-called Mandate System of the League of Nations, which was provided for in Article 22 of the Covenant. The Mandate System was established in order to solve the problem of the colonies of the defeated powers which – after the war and collapse of the empires of old – no longer fell under the sovereignty of an existing, independent State.[39] Instead of "distributing" these formerly colonized territories among the victors of the war, they were placed under supervision of the League of Nations and governed on a day-to-day basis by so-called mandatory powers, while the territories themselves only had a limited degree of autonomy as they were not yet conceived to be ready to govern themselves.[40]

The Mandate System created three categories of mandate, with a decreasing level of self-administration in accordance with their degree of advancement – or what this degree was conceived to be. First, so-called 'A' mandates encompassed the highest level of autonomous administration. The former Turkish Empire territories were placed under this mandate, and were expected to be independent rather soon. Secondly, the former German territories in Central Africa were categorized as 'B' mandates. Thirdly, 'C' mandates related to territories which required governance by more "advanced nations", and applied to South-West Africa and several South Pacific Islands.[41] Although this system might convey the impression of disguised

---

[36]   See P. Sands and P. Klein, *Bowett's Law of International Institutions* (5th edn, Sweet & Maxwell, London 2001) at pp. 9-13 for an introduction to the League of Nations system.

[37]   D.H. Miller, *The Drafting of the Covenant* (Putnam's, New York 1928), quoted in: Raič, *Statehood and the Law of Self-Determination* at p. 194.

[38]   See S. Smis, *A Western Approach to the International Law of Self-Determination: Theory and Practice* (Doctoral Thesis, Vrije Universiteit Brussel 2001) at p. 58.

[39]   Raič, *Statehood and the Law of Self-Determination* at p. 194.

[40]   A. Anghie, *Imperialism, Sovereignty and the Making of International Law* (Cambridge University Press, Cambridge 2007) at p. 116.

[41]   See Article 22 of the Covenant of the League of Nations. For an overview of the territories under the Mandate System, see J.R. Crawford, *The Creation of States in International Law* (2nd revised edn,

colonialism,[42] it was established for the purpose of achieving exactly the opposite, as it attempted to "protect the interests of backward people, to promote their welfare and development and to guide them toward self-government and, in certain cases, independence".[43] One might argue that by stressing these benevolent aims of the Mandate System, the League of Nations sought to justify the administration of formerly colonized peoples, which would otherwise strongly hint at neo-imperialism.[44] Yet, the Mandate System can also be viewed as an important shift in the international legal realm, for it introduced a new approach to the management of 'backward' territories. Governing these territories was no longer conducted by colonial powers which were driven by pure self-interest, but rather by administrators who aimed at collecting detailed knowledge of these backward societies and economies for the purpose of outlining policies needed to guide the native peoples involved to development and self-government.[45]

In addition to the Mandate System, the League of Nations also provided for a settlement for those minorities or ethnic groups which could not – out of fear of the disintegration of Europe – exercise a right to self-determination by forming their own State. For these communities, the founding States of the League of Nations came up with international guarantees for national minorities,[46] which were intended to ensure the preservation of their racial, national and cultural peculiarities and to "place them on a footing of perfect equality" with the other communities within the State.[47] This was not implemented by means of the development of a universal instrument, but rather by means of a system based on individual minority treaties. These treaties were concluded between the allies on the one hand, and the individual State in which minority protection was needed on the other. As such, minority treaties were signed primarily with Central and Eastern European States. Since it was aimed to draw identical treaties, the treaty with Poland was used as a basis for the system.[48]

The League of Nations was involved in the supervision of the minority protection system. Special committees, each composed of three members of the Council, were created to monitor compliance with the obligations concerning the protection of

---

Clarendon Press, Oxford 2006) Appendix 2, at pp. 741-745.

[42] See *ibid.* at p. 568.

[43] Anghie, *Imperialism, Sovereignty and the Making of International Law* at p. 120.

[44] *Ibid.* at p. 140.

[45] *Ibid.* at p. 185 and p. 195.

[46] On this topic, see A.K. Meijknecht, 'Minority Protection System between World War I and World War II' in R. Wolfrum (ed.) *Max Planck Encyclopedia of Public International Law* (fully updated online edn, Oxford University Press, New York 2010).

[47] Permanent Court of International Justice, *Minority Schools in Albania*, Advisory Opinion, PCIJ Series A/B, No. 64, (1935), at p. 17.

[48] See Smis, *A Western Approach to the International Law of Self-Determination: Theory and Practice* at pp. 58-59. On the content of the treaty with Poland, see A.K. Meijknecht, *Towards International Personality: The Position of Minorities and Indigenous Peoples in International Law* (School of Human Rights Research Series, Intersentia/Hart, Antwerp/Groningen/Oxford 2001) at pp. 124-127.

minorities as conferred by the treaties. A significant element in the supervision was the petition procedure. Aggrieved minorities could file a petition with the League of Nations regarding a minority's issue, which was forwarded to both the authorities at issue and the members of the Council. If one of the members drew attention to the alleged (risk of) violation of the obligations as stipulated in the relevant treaty, the petition could be examined by one of the special committees. The petition system, however, became an ineffective instrument. Although hundreds of petitions were filed and found admissible, only a few were eventually addressed by the Council.[49] In the League's minority protection system, the Permanent Court of International Justice played an indirect yet important role. Minorities themselves had no standing before the Court, but the case law and advisory opinions it issued can be said to have contributed considerably to the development of minority rights law.[50]

With World War II, the minority system of the League of Nations collapsed. The United Nations succeeded the League, but its system of minority protection was discontinued. Not only did the minorities in Europe almost vanish as a result of the genocide during the war, but the United Nations also opted for a different approach. No special protection for minorities was deemed necessary, as the principle of non-discrimination and the concept of universal human rights were found to provide for sufficient protection to everyone, including minorities.[51] It was not until 1966 with the inclusion of Article 27 in the ICCPR that the United Nations explicitly made reference to special minority rights.[52]

3.4. The *Åland Islands* Case

As demonstrated above, the notion of self-determination was used in a somewhat haphazard manner in the aftermath of World War I. It was only through its invocation in the *Åland Islands* case in 1920 that the notion acquired significance in a legal context. What is more, it is said that what would later be labelled as a remedial right to secession has its origins in this case.[53] In this connection, the *Åland Islands* case and its background will be further elaborated upon elsewhere in this study.[54] For the purpose of this Chapter, the case will only be dealt with briefly at this point.

---

[49] Meijknecht, 'Minority Protection System between World War I and World War II' at paras 18-23.

[50] See *ibid.* at paras 24-25.

[51] See A. Eide, 'The Non-Inclusion of Minority Rights: Resolution 217C (III)' in G. Alfredsson and A. Eide (eds) *The Universal Declaration of Human Rights: A Common Standard of Achievement* (Martinus Nijhoff Publishers, The Hague 1999).

[52] Smis, *A Western Approach to the International Law of Self-Determination: Theory and Practice* at p. 61. See also Meijknecht, 'Minority Protection System between World War I and World War II' at para. 31.

[53] See M. Sterio, *On the Right to External Self-Determination: "Selfistans", Secession and the Great Powers' Rule* (Working Paper, Cleveland State University 2009) at p. 5.

[54] See Chapter IV, Section 2.3.1.

In short, the *Åland Islands* case dealt with a legal dispute between Sweden and Finland. It involved, *inter alia*, the question of whether the inhabitants of the Åland Islands – an archipelago situated in the Baltic Sea, between Finland and Sweden – were allowed to secede from Finland and subsequently attach themselves to Sweden.[55] An International Commission of Jurists and a Committee of Rapporteurs, both established by the Council of the League of Nations for the purpose of this very case, were seized to write an advisory opinion on the matter. The report by the Commission of Jurists (hereafter: Jurists) was supposed to clarify the question of whether the League of Nations Council was entitled to exercise jurisdiction regarding the Åland Islands dispute. In this context, the relationship between self-determination and State sovereignty was explored, which gave the Jurists occasion to express their view on the status of self-determination within international law. It appeared that the Jurists did not consider self-determination, interpreted as secession, to be a legal right under positive international law:

> Although the principle of self-determination of peoples plays an important part in modern political thought, especially since the Great War, it must be pointed out that there is no mention of it in the Covenant of the League of Nations. The recognition of this principle in a certain number of international treaties cannot be considered as sufficient to put it upon the same footing as a positive rule of the Law of Nations. On the contrary, in the absence of express provisions in international treaties, the right of disposing of national territory is essentially an attribute of the sovereignty of every State. Positive International Law does not recognize the right of national groups, as such, to separate themselves from the State of which they form part by the simple expression of a wish, any more than it recognizes the right of other States to claim such a separation. Generally speaking, the grant or the refusal of such a right to a portion of its population of determining its own political fate by plebiscite or by some other method is, exclusively, an attribute of the sovereignty of every State which is definitely constituted.[56]

In other words, although the Jurists denied self-determination by means of the separation of part of a territory as being a right under positive international law, that thesis only applied to States which were definitively constituted.

After the opinion of the Jurists had made the Åland Islands dispute subject to international jurisdiction by the League of Nations, a Committee of Rapporteurs (hereafter: Rapporteurs) was set up so as to analyze the matter and formulate a solution. In this connection, the Rapporteurs made some general remarks on self-determination as well. It stated that:

---

[55] See, generally, J. Barros, *The Aland Islands Question: Its Settlement by the League of Nations* (Yale University Press, New Haven 1968).

[56] *Report of the International Commission of Jurists (Larnaude, Huber, Struycken)*, LNOJ Special Supplement No. 3 (October 1920), at para. 5.

[t]his principle is not, properly speaking a rule of international law and the League of Nations has not entered it in its Covenant. [...] It is a principle of justice and of liberty, expressed by a vague and general formula which has given rise to most varied interpretations and differences of opinion. [...] Is it possible to admit as an absolute rule that a minority of the population of a State, which is definitely constituted and perfectly capable of fulfilling its duties as such, has the right of separating itself from her in order to be incorporated in another State or to declare independence? The answer can only be in the negative. To concede minorities, either of language or religion, or to any fraction of a population the right of withdrawing from the community to which they belong, because it is their wish or their good pleasure, would be to destroy order and stability within States and to inaugurate anarchy in international life; it would be to uphold a theory incompatible with the very idea of the State as a territorial and political unity. [...] The separation of a minority from the State can only be considered as an altogether exceptional solution, a last resort when the State lacks either the will or the power to enact and apply just and effective guarantees.[57]

As the Rapporteurs were of the opinion that the language and culture of the Ålanders could be safeguarded through the introduction of political autonomy under Finnish sovereignty, secession of the Åland Islands was out of the question. Only if Finland would manifestly fail to meet the proposed standards, would the breaking-away of the islands be an alternative supported by the Rapporteurs.[58]

In conclusion, it can be said that although both the Commission of Jurists and the Committee of Rapporteurs denied the existence of self-determination as an absolute right for minorities and national groups to separate unilaterally, the possible resort to secession was acknowledged for cases where no alternative solution would be reasonably expected as a result of extreme oppression. Moreover, the political importance of the concept was recognized. All in all, the *Åland Islands* case can be viewed as a landmark in the history of self-determination. As Cassese put it: "a *policy line* was put forward which the world community, to some extent, took up and, indeed, which might yield even more fruit in the future".[59]

4. SELF-DETERMINATION IN THE POST-WAR ERA

With the entry into force of the Charter of the United Nations in 1945, the notion of self-determination entered the second stage of its evolution, as the principle was now codified in an international legal document. It was further crystallized against the backdrop of the decolonization process – a process in which the concept of

---

[57]   *Report of the International Committee of Rapporteurs (Beyens, Calonder, Elkens)*, 16 April 1921, LN Council Document B7/2I/68/106 [VII], at paras 22-23.

[58]   *Ibid.*, at paras 33-34.

[59]   Cassese, *Self-Determination of Peoples. A Legal Reappraisal* at p. 33 (emphasis added).

self-determination was explicitly applied in practice for the very first time. Both contexts of self-determination will be discussed in the following sub-sections.

4.1. The Charter of the United Nations

Already towards the end of the Second World War, in 1944, various draft proposals were made for a charter of a new world organization. In these initial Dumbarton Oaks proposals, no mention was made of self-determination or any peoples' rights whatsoever. However, when the United Nations Conference on International Organization assembled in San Francisco, a provision regarding the principle of self-determination was presented. Pressure from the Soviet Union was the principal cause for reconsidering the matter. The provision proposed by the Soviet Union expressed the organization's purpose "to develop friendly relations among nations based on respect for the principle of equal rights and self-determination of peoples, and to take other appropriate measures to strengthen universal peace".[60] What followed was a laborious process in the relevant bodies of the San Francisco Conference, during which it became apparent that not all of the States present were receptive to the proposed charter provision. Most objections stemmed from fear that a provision regarding self-determination would encourage civil strife and secessionist movements, having destabilizing effects. Moreover, it was stipulated that the concept of self-determination is prone to misuse, for example as a justification for intervention and annexation.[61] As the Sixth Committee specified in its final report:

> [c]oncerning the principle of self-determination, it was strongly emphasized on the one side that this principle corresponds closely to the will and desires of peoples everywhere and should be clearly enunciated in the Charter; on the other side, it was stated that the principle conformed to the purposes of the Charter only insofar as it implied the right of self-government of peoples and not the right of secession.[62]

At last, the participating States managed to agree on the matter. The final text of the United Nations Charter, which entered into force in October 1945, explicitly refers to the notion of self-determination twice. First, Article 1(2) of the Charter designates "respect for the principle of equal rights and self-determination of peoples" as one of the purposes of the organization, with a view to the development of "friendly relations among nations". Secondly, reference to self-determination is made in Article 55, this time against the backdrop of international economic and social cooperation and respect for human rights.

---

[60] *Ibid.* at p. 38.
[61] *Ibid.* at pp. 39-40.
[62] UN Conference on International Organization, UNCIO Doc. 343, I/1/16, Vol. VI (1945), at p. 296.

In sum, the codification of the principle of self-determination in the Charter is important for the reason that it placed self-determination in context. Yet, at the same time, the codification led to questions concerning the content of self-determination, as the Charter did not provide a definition of the notion and the references concerned were rather cryptic. Who were to be regarded as 'peoples'? Was the provision intended to refer to States, or also to the inhabitants of a territory? Was it meant to be an anti-colonial principle only? Did it apply to groups with secessionist ambitions as well? Unfortunately, the *travaux préparatoires* of the Charter offer little guidance in this respect.[63] On this matter, Helen Quane noted that in 1945, the term 'secession' could refer to two types of situation. On the one hand, "[i]t could refer to colonial peoples demanding independence", while on the other hand, it could refer "to claims by national groups within the continuous boundaries of independent States to break away from these States". Although the latter is the meaning which is generally attributed to the term 'secession' today, Quane contended that no support for such interpretation can be found in the drafting history of the Charter.[64] Furthermore, the codification of the principle of self-determination gave rise to questions concerning its legal status. Was the principle to be regarded as a binding right at that time? The majority view held that the general terms employed in the Charter are insufficient to conclude so.[65] As Malcolm N. Shaw pointed out, "[n]ot every statement of a political aim in the Charter can be regarded as automatically creative of legal obligations".[66] While in this respect, the Charter may be called a *lex imperfecta*, and although Articles 1(2) and 55 of the Charter provided neither for the firm establishment of a positive legal right, nor for an expansion of the notion of self-determination, or an account of how to deal with it in practice, it was an important step in the evolution of self-determination, as the Charter introduced self-determination as one of the principal aims of the new world organization.[67] The subsequent major step in this evolution was taken in the context of the decolonization process, when various resolutions dealing with self-determination were adopted, in particular by the General Assembly. This will be elaborated upon below.

---

[63]   For an elaborate review of the *travaux préparatoires*, see H. Quane, 'The United Nations and the Evolving Right to Self-Determination' (1998) 47 *International and Comparative Law Quarterly* 537 at pp. 541-544. See also Cassese, *Self-Determination of Peoples. A Legal Reappraisal* at pp. 37-43.

[64]   See H. Quane, 'The United Nations and the Evolving Right to Self-Determination' at p. 547.

[65]   See Thürer and Burri, 'Self-Determination' at para. 8.

[66]   M.N. Shaw, *International Law* (5th edn, Cambridge University Press, Cambridge 2003) at p. 226.

[67]   See Cassese, *Self-Determination of Peoples. A Legal Reappraisal* at p. 43; Raič, *Statehood and the Law of Self-Determination* at p. 200; Thornberry, 'The Democratic or Internal Aspect of Self-Determination with Some Remarks on Federalism' at p. 109.

4.2. The Decolonization Process

4.2.1. The Meaning of Self-Determination in the Context of Decolonization

Although the notion of self-determination was not explicitly mentioned in Chapter XI or Chapter XII of the Charter, these chapters played an important part in the development of the notion. At this point, the Declaration Regarding Non-Self-Governing Territories and the International Trusteeship System of the United Nations, as provided for in Chapter XI and Chapter XII respectively, need to be addressed. The theoretical roots of the Trusteeship System can be found in the Mandate System of the League of Nations,[68] as the "entrusted powers"[69] were obliged to guide the peoples of trust territories[70] towards independence as appropriate, thereby fortifying self-determination of these groups. As such, the Trusteeship System can be viewed as a tool to bring about decolonization. Chapter XI applies to non-self-governing territories other than trust territories[71] and requires that on these territories administered by UN Member States, self-government will be developed progressively, thereby taking "due account of the political aspirations of the peoples".[72]

In the early 1950s, however, this aspiration of the *gradual* development towards self-government and independence was put under pressure in practice. Communist States within the General Assembly – in particular the Soviet Union – urged *immediate* decolonization by the Western powers.[73] Unsurprisingly, East-European and Asian-African countries supported the idea of decolonization, the latter group of countries demanding a speedy end to colonialism during the Bandung Conference in 1955.[74] In the course of time, the General Assembly adopted a number of resolu-

---

[68]   See Section 3.3 of this Chapter.

[69]   Hansen, *Modern Territorial Statehood* at p. 89.

[70]   According to Article 77, such territories were to consist of territories held under mandate, areas detached from enemy States responsible for their administration. Nowadays, there are no trust territories left.

[71]   UN General Assembly Resolution 1514 (XV) (*Declaration on the Granting of Independence to Colonial Countries and Peoples*), UN Doc. A/Res/1514, 14 December 1960, states that it is presumed that Article 73 of Chapter XI is applicable to every territory "which is geographically separate and is distinct ethnically and/or culturally from the country administering it". For a large part, such territories have gained independence during the decolonization period. See, for instance, P. Malanczuk, *Akehurst's Modern Introduction to International Law* (7th revised edn, Routledge, London/New York 1997) at pp. 329-332.

[72]   Article 73(b) of the UN Charter.

[73]   See Raič, *Statehood and the Law of Self-Determination* at pp. 203-204; Cassese, *Self-Determination of Peoples. A Legal Reappraisal* at p. 44.

[74]   During this conference in Bandung (Indonesia) in April 1955, representatives from twenty-nine governments of both Asian and African States assembled for the purpose of discussing the issue of peace and the role of the Third World as regards the Cold War, economic development and decolonization. The final resolution drafted at the close of the Bandung Conference provided for a number of objectives, such as the promotion of economic and cultural cooperation, the protection of human rights and the principle

tions concerning decolonization, non-self-governing territories and self-determination in order to clarify and supplement the Charter provisions. Resolution 1514 (XV) is generally viewed as one of the most important contributions in this regard, setting the terms for the debate. The Resolution proclaimed "the necessity of bringing to a speedy and unconditional end colonialism in all its forms and manifestations"[75] and stated that "[a]ll peoples have the right to self-determination; by virtue of that right they freely determine their political status and freely pursue their economic, social and cultural development".[76] More specifically, independence was the principal goal of the Resolution, and it even stated that lack of sufficient political, economic, social or educational attentiveness cannot be an excuse for delaying independence.[77] Further, the Resolution declared that:

> [i]mmediate steps shall be taken, in Trust and Non-Self-Governing Territories or all other territories which have not yet attained independence, to transfer all powers to the peoples of those territories, without any conditions or reservations, in accordance with their freely expressed will and desire, without any distinction as to race, creed or colour, in order to enable them to enjoy complete independence and freedom.[78]

Yet, it is important to note that the following paragraph of the Resolution set forth another fundamental principle of international law, namely that of territorial integrity. By stressing that "[a]ny attempt aimed at the partial or total disruption of the national unity and the territorial integrity of a country is incompatible with the purposes and principles of the Charter of the United Nations", the scope of the reference to self-determination was mitigated.[79] In addition, from the general language employed one can deduce that, although from the perspective of trust, independence is the preferred outcome of the right to self-determination, other outcomes are not ruled out either.[80]

---

of self-determination, and the ending of racial discrimination. Moreover, it emphasized the importance of peaceful coexistence of States. See U.S. Department of State, Timeline of U.S. Diplomatic History, *Bandung Conference (Asian-African Conference), 1955*, available at <http://history.state.gov/>, last consulted on 24 September 2012.

[75] UN General Assembly Resolution 1514 (XV) (*Declaration on the Granting of Independence to Colonial Countries and Peoples*), UN Doc. A/Res/1514, 14 December 1960, preamble.

[76] *Ibid.*, at para. 2.

[77] *Ibid.*, at para. 3.

[78] *Ibid.*, at para. 5.

[79] See Hannum, *Autonomy, Sovereignty, and Self-Determination. The Accommodation of Conflicting Rights* at p. 34.

[80] The United Nations agreed with the integration of twelve territories, namely the Netherlands Antilles and Surinam, Alaska, Hawaii, Tokelau, Wallis and Futuna Islands, British Togoland, northern British Cameroons, southern British Cameroons, North Borneo and Sarawak, West Irian, the Mariana Islands and the Cocos Islands. Moreover, seven colonial territories integrated with independent States, namely Puerto Rico, Greenland, Cook Islands, Niue, the Marshall Islands, the Federated States of Micronesia and Palau. See Quane, 'The United Nations and the Evolving Right to Self-Determination' at p. 550 and p. 553.

4.2.2. The Subjects and Legal Status of Self-Determination in the Context of Decolonization

Having determined what can be called the core meaning of self-determination during the decolonization period, questions arise regarding the subject and legal status of the right to self-determination in this context. When it comes to the subject of self-determination, one might think that the terms "all peoples" in Resolution 1514 (XV) suggests universal applicability of the 'right' to self-determination. State practice, however, demonstrates that application of the right was primarily restricted to the colonial context. Furthermore, attempts to exercise self-determination on an ethnic, linguistic or religious basis were by and large unsuccessful, indicating that, at that time, the concept of "peoples" was conceived to be a territorial one.[81]

In this respect, the advisory opinion of the International Court of Justice in the *Namibia (South West Africa)* case should be pointed out as well.[82] In considering the legality of the presence of South Africa in Namibia, the Court stressed that:

> the subsequent development of international law in regard to non-self-governing territories as enshrined in the Charter of the United Nations made the principle of self-determination applicable to all of them. […] These developments leave little doubt that the ultimate objective of the sacred trust was the self-determination and independence of the peoples concerned.[83]

Accordingly, self-determination was viewed as a right for both trust territories and non-self-governing territories.[84] As was explained in Resolution 1541 (XV),

---

[81] Hannum, *Autonomy, Sovereignty, and Self-Determination. The Accommodation of Conflicting Rights* at p. 36. Over time, some exceptions have been made to this tendency. These concern the reunification of a pre-colonial entity, the opposition of the inhabitants to maintain the colonial entity, or the voluntary union of two separate colonies. See Quane, 'The United Nations and the Evolving Right to Self-Determination' at p. 552.

[82] This advisory opinion emanated from a request of the UN Security Council, and was the fourth interference of the International Court of Justice on the status of Namibia, a former German colony which was administered by South Africa. This complex relationship had caused a long-lasting dispute between South Africa and the UN. In the present advisory opinion, the request by the Security Council concerned the following question: What are the legal consequences for States of the continued presence of South Africa in Namibia notwithstanding Security Council Resolution 276 (1970)?

[83] International Court of Justice, *Legal Consequences for States of the Continued Presence of South Africa in Namibia (South West Africa) notwithstanding Security Council Resolution 276 (1970)*, Advisory Opinion, ICJ Reports 1971, p. 31, paras 52-53.

[84] For a clear discussion of the contribution of this advisory opinion to the clarification of the right to self-determination, see, for instance, A. Cassese, 'The International Court of Justice and the Right of Peoples to Self-Determination' in V. Lowe and M. Fitzmaurice (eds) *Fifty Years of the International Court of Justice Essays in Honour of Sir Robert Jennings* (Cambridge University Press, Cambridge 1996) at pp. 353-356; G. Zyberi, 'Self-Determination through the Lens of the International Court of Justice' (2009) 56 *Netherlands International Law Review* 429 at pp. 435-437.

Principle VI, a non-self-governing territory is a "territory which is geographically separate and is distinct ethnically and/or culturally from the country administering it".[85] This theory is frequently referred to as the 'salt water barrier'.[86] Subsequently, the Resolution listed three modes of effectuating self-determination. According to Principle VI, full self-government can be attained by (a) emergence as a sovereign independent State; (b) free association with an independent State; or (c) integration with an independent State. Principles VII and IX of the Resolution stipulate that "free association" should be achieved by a "free and voluntary choice by the peoples of the territory concerned", and that "integration" is to be based on "the freely expressed wishes of the territory's peoples". As such, democratic processes seem to be required for realizing the right to (external) self-determination.

Another issue which needs to be addressed is that of the legal status of self-determination in the context of the decolonization process. The explicit reference to a 'right' to self-determination rather than a 'principle' of self-determination in Resolution 1514 (XV) suggests that, by adopting this document, a positive legal right was created. In this respect, a remark should be made. Although General Assembly resolutions are recommendatory in nature, they might contribute to the development of international (customary) law, depending on, *inter alia*, the voting record at the time of adoption and the subsequent State practice.[87] Resolution 1514 (XV) was adopted by 89 votes to none. Nine States, all colonial powers, abstained from voting. These abstentions and their dissent on fundamental provisions may prevent the conclusion that the Resolution mirrored rules of general international law. In addition, statements made at the time of adoption of Resolution 1514 (XV) reveal that it was generally not considered to be legally binding.[88] By contrast, some legal scholars find it plausible that the General Assembly considered self-determination as a right under customary international law at the time of the adoption of Resolution 1514 (XV). To underpin this argument, they point to a number of General Assembly resolutions which were already adopted in the 1950s, and in which reference was made to the "right" of peoples to self-determination.[89] Moreover, these scholars emphasize the fact that

---

[85]   UN General Assembly Resolution 1541 (XV) (*Principles Which Should Guide Members in Determining Whether or Not an Obligation Exists to Transmit the Information Called for Under Article 73(e) of the Charter*), UN Doc. A/Res/1541 (XV), 15 December 1960.

[86]   Raič, *Statehood and the Law of Self-Determination* at pp. 206-207.

[87]   Shaw, *International Law* at pp. 106-110.

[88]   Quane, 'The United Nations and the Evolving Right to Self-Determination' at p. 551.

[89]   UN General Assembly Resolution 637 A-B-C (*The Right of Peoples and Nations to Self-Determination*), UN Doc. A/Res/637, 16 December 1952; UN General Assembly Resolution 742 (VIII) (*Factors Which Should be Taken into Account in Deciding Whether a Territory Is or Is not a Territory Whose People No Yet Attained a Full Measure of Self-Government*), UN Doc. A/Res/742 (VIII), 27 November 1953; UN General Assembly Resolution 1188 (XII) (*Recommendations Concerning International Respect for the Right of Peoples and Nations to Self-Determination*), UN Doc. A/Res/1188 (XII), 11 December 1957.

approximately thirty Non-Self-Governing Territories and Trust Territories became independent prior to December 1960, when the Resolution was adopted.[90]

In sum, it is difficult to ascertain whether Resolution 1514 (XV) created a positive, legal right to self-determination, or merely mirrored a political obligation. Despite this uncertainty and despite the limitations discussed above, Resolution 1514 (XV) and Resolution 1541 (XV) are regarded as marking an important change in the approach to self-determination. Whereas the notion of self-determination first served to authorize the actions of colonizers and mandatory powers, with the adoption of Resolution 1514 (XV) in particular, the emphasis then shifted to the inhabitants of the territories concerned.[91]

Even so, the development of the principle of self-determination continued. In its advisory opinion on the *Western Sahara* case, the International Court of Justice affirmed the importance of the right of peoples to self-determination in the decolonization context. It stressed that the "essential feature of the right of self-determination" is that its "application requires a free and genuine expression of the will of the peoples concerned".[92] The case concerned the decolonization of the territory of Western Sahara. This territory was controlled by Spain, the colonial power. It was the irredentism of Morocco and Mauritania, however, which caused the dispute. The Court, therefore, was requested to give its opinion with regard to two questions. The first concerned the question of whether Western Sahara was a territory that belonged to no-one (*terra nullius*) at the time of colonization by Spain.[93] The second question – and more important in this context – concerned the legal ties between Western Sahara and Morocco on the one hand, and between the Western Sahara and the Mauritanian entity on the other hand. In its discussion of the merits of the case, the Court analysed the provisions of the UN Charter and the relevant resolutions of the General Assembly. Subsequently, it reached the conclusion that the legal ties which had existed between the territory of Western Sahara and both claimants during the

---

[90] Raič, *Statehood and the Law of Self-Determination* at pp. 215-217.

[91] Hansen, *Modern Territorial Statehood* at pp. 92-92; Raič, *Statehood and the Law of Self-Determination* at p. 204.

[92] International Court of Justice, *Western Sahara*, Advisory Opinion, ICJ Reports 1975, p. 12, at para. 55.

[93] The Court unanimously answered this first question in the negative: at the time of colonization by Spain – the period beginning in 1884 – Western Sahara was not *terra nullius*. The term *terra nullius* is considered to be "a legal term of art employed in connection with 'occupation' as one of the accepted legal methods of acquiring sovereignty over territory" (para. 79). For an occupation to be legally valid, the given territory should be *terra nullius* at the time of the commencement of the occupation. Therefore, the Court was of the opinion that it could only be determined that Western Sahara was *terra nullius* if it was established that at the time of colonization, "the territory belonged to no-one in the sense that it was then open to acquisition through the legal process of 'occupation'" (para. 79). In this period, State practice demonstrated that territories which were inhabited by tribes or peoples having a social and political organization, were not conceived to be *terrae nullius*. Since at the time of colonization, Western Sahara was this kind of territory, the Court concluded that the territory was not *terra nullius* (paras 80-83).

relevant period did not affect the application of either Resolution 1514 (XV) in the decolonization of Western Sahara or "the principle of self-determination through the free and genuine expression of the will of the peoples of the Territory" in particular.[94] Furthermore, the Court noted that some discretion was left to the Court concerning the forms and procedures for realizing self-determination.[95] From this, it can be derived that the Court considered self-determination to be a legal principle in the context of decolonization.[96] Even if one would question the legal status of self-determination under international law in the early decolonization period, this authoritative judgment indicates that by 1975, self-determination was to be regarded as a legal entitlement rather than a mere political principle. This conclusion seems to be corroborated by the Declaration on Principles of International Law Concerning Friendly Relations and Co-operation Among States in Accordance with the Charter of the United Nations (also abbreviated to the Friendly Relations Declaration), which was adopted by the General Assembly in 1970. It refers to the 'principle of equal rights and self-determination of peoples' and in this respect imposes upon States "the duty to respect this right".[97] As the scope of this document extends beyond the decolonization context, it will be elaborated upon in the following Chapter.[98]

The status of self-determination in the context of decolonization was put on a higher plane with the judgment of the International Court of Justice in the *East Timor* case.[99] In its judgment, by considering the UN Charter and relevant previous judgments of the Court in the cases of *Namibia (South West Africa)* and *Western Sahara* respectively, the Court emphasized the elementary and special character of the right to self-determination. It observed that this right is "one of the essential principles of

---

[94] International Court of Justice, *Western Sahara*, Advisory Opinion, ICJ Reports 1975, p. 12, at para. 162 (cfm. paras 54-59).

[95] International Court of Justice, *Western Sahara*, Advisory Opinion, ICJ Reports 1975, p. 12, at para. 71.

[96] See, for instance, Shaw, *International Law* at p. 229; Zyberi, 'Self-Determination Through the Lens of the International Court of Justice' at pp. 437-438.

[97] UN General Assembly Resolution 2625 (XXV) (*Declaration on Principles of International Law Concerning Friendly Relations and Co-Operation Among States in Accordance with the Charter of the United Nations*), UN Doc. A/Res/2625 (XXV), 24 October 1970.

[98] See Chapter III, Section 2.2 of the present study.

[99] International Court of Justice, *East Timor (Portugal v. Australia)*, Judgment, ICJ Reports 1995, p. 90. This case addressed a dispute between Portugal as the administering power of East Timor and Australia. Portugal and Australia had negotiated and concluded the Treaty of 11 December 1989, thus creating a "Zone of Cooperation [...] in an area between the Indonesian Province of East Timor and Northern Australia" (para. 18). In the proceedings, Portugal maintained that Australia, as a consequence, "in initiating performance of the Treaty, in taking internal legislative measures for its application, and in continuing to negotiate with Indonesia, ha[d] acted unlawfully, in that it ha[d] infringed the rights of the people of East Timor to self-determination" (para. 19).

contemporary international law"[100] and determined that the right to self-determination had irreproachably evolved into a norm *erga omnes*.[101]

In the *East Timor* case, the International Court of Justice did not (expressly) note that self-determination had become a norm of *jus cogens*.[102] Nevertheless, the International Law Commission referred to this judgment and other judgments of the Court in order to confirm its qualification of the obligation to respect the right to self-determination of dependent territories as a peremptory norm of international law, having the status of *jus cogens*.[103] This opinion is also supported by a substantial number of prominent legal scholars.[104]

5. CONCLUSIONS

This Chapter has outlined the historical development of the notion of self-determination, the origins of which may be traced back to the theories and ideologies underlying and arising from the American and French Revolutions. It was seen how the phrase of self-determination was embedded in the political ideas of both Lenin and Wilson, each in their own way, and how eventually, the League of Nations' Mandate System may be said to be founded on the notion of self-determination, albeit as a justification for the administration of formerly colonized territories. Moreover, it was demonstrated that in the *Åland Islands* case, self-determination first gained

---

[100]   International Court of Justice, *East Timor (Portugal v. Australia)*, Judgment, ICJ Reports 1995, p. 90, at para. 29.

[101]   *Ibid*. In short, the *erga omnes* character of a norm indicates that the norm concerned applies to the international community as a whole and that all States can be said to have a legal interest in its protection. See also International Court of Justice, *Barcelona Traction, Light and Power Company, Limited (Belgium v. Spain)*, Second Phase, Judgment, ICJ Reports 1970, p. 3, at para. 33. As will be seen in the next Chapter of the present study, the Court classified the right to self-determination as a norm *erga omnes* beyond the context of decolonization as well. See International Court of Justice, *Legal Consequences of the Construction of a Wall in the Occupied Palestinian Territory*, Advisory Opinion, ICJ Reports 2004, p. 136 at paras 155-156.

[102]   In its final draft on the Law of Treaties (1966), Article 50, the International Law Commission accepted the concept of *jus cogens* as involving "peremptory norm[s] of general international law from which no derogation is permitted and which can be modified only by a subsequent norm of general international law having the same character".

[103]   International Law Commission, 53rd session, 23 April – 1 June and 2 July – 10 August 2001, UN GAOR, 56th session, Suppl. No.10, A/56/10, *Draft Articles on Responsibility of States for International Wrongful Acts, with Commentaries*, UN Doc. A/CN.4/L.602/Rev.1, 26 July 2001, Chapter III at p. 113. See also Raič, *Statehood and the Law of Self-Determination* at p. 219.

[104]   See, for instance, UN Commission on Human Rights, Sub-Commission on Prevention of Discrimination and Protection of Minorities, *The Right to Self-Determination: Implementation of United Nations Resolutions. Study Prepared by Héctor Gros-Espiell*, UN Doc. E/CN.4/Sub.2/405/Rev.1 (1980); I. Brownlie, *Principles of Public International Law* (6th edn, Oxford University Press, Oxford 2003) at p. 511; Cassese, *Self-Determination of Peoples. A Legal Reappraisal* at pp. 133-140; J.R. Crawford, *The International Law Commission's Articles on State Responsibility. Introduction, Text and Commentaries* (Cambridge University Press, Cambridge 2002) at p. 38.

significance in a legal context. In painting this historical picture, it was seen how self-determination evolved from a mere political principle into a legal entitlement. The inclusion of the notion of self-determination in the Charter of the United Nations in 1945 was an important step in this particular development. Despite the explicit reference to self-determination in the Charter, the precise legal status and content of the notion remained ambiguous at that time. Against the backdrop of the decolonization process, with the issuing of UN General Assembly Resolution 1514 (XV) and Resolution 1541 (XV), light was shed on these issues. In these documents, the need to end colonialism was expressed and all (colonial) peoples were granted the right to self-determination. In this context, the right to self-determination first and foremost implied the right to establish a sovereign and independent State, thus enabling the people at hand to "freely determine their political status and freely pursue their economic, social and cultural development". When a colonial territory became independent from its colonizer, the right to self-determination was considered to be realized.

In its judgment in the *East Timor* case, the International Court of Justice stressed the elementary and unique character of the right to self-determination by concluding that it had developed into a norm *erga omnes*. While not confirmed by the International Court of Justice, it is often argued that with regard to dependent territories, the right to self-determination has also attained the status of *jus cogens*. In the context of decolonization as well, the International Court of Justice observed that the core element of the right to self-determination involves the "free and genuine expression of the will of the peoples concerned". As will be seen in the following Chapter, the phrasing of this very essence may be seen to have enabled the further development of the right to self-determination beyond the decolonization process.

CHAPTER III
THE CONTEMPORARY MEANING OF THE RIGHT TO SELF-DETERMINATION

"Self-determination has never simply meant independence. It has meant the free choice of peoples."

Rosalyn Higgins*

1. INTRODUCTION

Having traced the roots of the concept of self-determination, its role beyond decolonization shall be examined. In the post-decolonization era, two important developments with regard to self-determination can be discerned. The first development is the continuing evolution of the legal status of self-determination. What was once nothing more than a political principle had gradually grown into a valuable positive legal right as a result of several new international legal documents elaborating on the notion of self-determination. The second development relates to the crystallization and acknowledgement of the two previously mentioned dimensions of self-determination. During the post-war decolonization period, emphasis was placed primarily on the external dimension of self-determination. In this context, the right to self-determination could be realized through the formation of independent States. Here, the Wilsonian concept of self-government is reflected: it is only by giving colonial people the opportunity to choose their external political status within the international community that the 'consent of the governed' could be realized. This approach has led to the conclusion that the right to self-determination was attained as soon as a dependent territory achieved independence.[1]

---

*   R. Higgins, *Problems and Process: International Law and How We Use It* (Oxford University Press, New York 1994) at p. 119.
[1]   D. Raič, *Statehood and the Law of Self-Determination* (Kluwer Law International, The Hague 2002) at p. 226. Yet, one might also perceive the external dimension of self-determination "as continuous defence against external subversion or intervention". In that line of thought, the continuous character is not exclusively reserved for the internal dimension of the right to self-determination. See P. Thornberry, 'The Democratic or Internal Aspect of Self-Determination with Some Remarks on Federalism' in

Over recent decades, however, State practice and international legal and political documents began to reflect that, in addition, self-determination has an internal dimension, related to the relationship between a people and its government and accompanied by a continuing character.[2] This development accords with what may be called a "general trend" concerning the decrease of the absolute nature of State sovereignty in favour of human rights,[3] popular sovereignty and a democratic governmental system.[4] In a statement by UNESCO to the UN Sub-Commission on the Prevention of Discrimination and Protection of Minorities, it was aptly expressed that the right to self-determination is "a reminder of the ultimate accountability of every State and every political system of the peoples who live under its legal jurisdiction".[5] Thus,

---

C. Tomuschat (ed.) *Modern Law of Self-Determination* (Martinus Nijhoff Publishers, Dordrecht 1993) at p. 101.

[2] See A. Rosas, 'Internal Self-Determination' in C. Tomuschat (ed.) *Modern Law of Self-Determination* (Martinus Nijhoff Publishers, Dordrecht 1993) at p. 229.

[3] See, for instance, K. Mills, *Human Rights in the Emerging Global Order. A New Sovereignty?* (Palgrave Macmillan, New York 1998); W.M. Reisman, 'Sovereignty and Human Rights in Contemporary International Law' in G.H. Fox and B.R. Roth (eds) *Democratic Governance and International Law* (Cambridge University Press, Cambridge 2000).

[4] Some legal scholars have even argued that a *right* to democratic governance is emerging. With his well-known article 'The Emerging Right to Democratic Governance', Thomas M. Franck initiated the discussion on the question of whether an international legal right to representative government is coming into existence. Franck holds that the provisions in the Universal Declaration on Human Rights (UDHR), the major human rights conventions and several regional instruments constitute "a net of participatory entitlements" (p. 79). In addition, an important role is attributed to the Organization for Security and Co-operation in Europe (OSCE) in specifying the elements of democratic government. As a result, Franck argues, democracy is no longer a moral prescription, but is "while not yet fully word made law, [...] rapidly becoming in our time, a normative rule of the international system" (p. 46). To support his proposition, Franck discerns three overlapping stages in the evolution of the gradually augmenting entitlement. First, the internal dimension of the right to self-determination is the oldest aspect of the right to democratic governance, as "self-determination postulates the right of a people organized in an established territory to determine its political destiny in a democratic fashion" (p. 52). Secondly, Franck presents the right to free political expression, found in common Article 1(1) of the international human rights covenants of 1966 and Articles 18, 19, and 22 UDHR, as a building block of a legal right to democracy. The third and newest aspect of the democratic entitlement is the "emerging normative requirement of a participatory electoral process" (p. 63). Article 25 ICCPR extends this right to every citizen, as does Article 21 UDHR. See T.M. Franck, 'The Emerging Right to Democratic Governance' (1992) 86 *American Journal of International Law* 46. On this topic, see also G.H. Fox, 'The Right to Political Participation in International Law' (1992) 17 *Yale Journal of International Law* 539; G.H. Fox and B.R. Roth (eds), *Democratic Governance and International Law* (Cambridge University Press, Cambridge 2000); C.M. Cerna, 'Universal Democracy: An International Legal Right or a Pipe Dream of the West?' (1995) 86 *NYU Journal of International Law and Politics* 289; S. Smis, *A Western Approach to the International Law of Self-Determination: Theory and Practice* (Doctoral Thesis, Vrije Universiteit Brussel 2001) at pp. 259-330; S. Wheatley, 'Democracy in International Law: A European Perspective' (2002) 51 *International and Comparative Law Quarterly*.

[5] UN Sub-Commission on the Prevention of Discrimination and Protection of Minorities, *UNESCO activities concerning prevention of discrimination and protection of minorities*, UN Doc. E/CN.4/Sub.2/1992/6, 24 July 1992.

self-determination is not merely realized through the formation of new States, but also requires a *continuous* implementation of the people's self-determination *within* States.[6] As such, a different mode of implementation of the right to self-determination has become increasingly relevant, which may even be said to constitute the focus of most contemporary instruments including this right. This will be expounded in the present Chapter.

2. SELF-DETERMINATION AS A CONTINUOUS ENTITLEMENT

Although initially, the right to self-determination was intended to be applicable to a colonial context only, the right underwent further development and the field of application changed with the creation of several new international legal instruments. While some of these instruments were drafted and adopted during the decolonization era, as will be demonstrated below, their interpretation of the right to self-determination extends beyond the context of decolonization. In fact, they were intended to be universally applicable. In view of this, the 1966 international human rights covenants as well as the 1970 Friendly Relations Declaration will be addressed below and not, as their dates of origin may suggest, in the previous Chapter.[7]

2.1. The International Human Rights Covenants of 1966

For an understanding of the present-day significance of the right to self-determination, it is important to address the International Covenant on Civil and Political Rights (ICCPR) and the International Covenant on Economic, Social and Cultural Rights (ICESCR) in the first place. Both Covenants were adopted by the General Assembly in 1966 and are international treaties which have to date been ratified by a large majority of States.[8]

The right to self-determination can be found in Article 1 of both Covenants. Most important is the first paragraph of common Article 1, which reads as follows:

> All peoples have the right to self-determination. By virtue of that right they freely determine their political status and freely pursue their economic, social and cultural development.

---

[6] Raič, *Statehood and the Law of Self-Determination* at p. 234.

[7] In view of this, the Covenants of 1966 were not addressed in Chapter II, in the context of the decolonization process, but rather they will be addressed in the present Chapter, where the contemporary meaning of the right to self-determination is central.

[8] In October 2012, 167 States were party to the ICCPR, while the ICESCR had 160 State parties. See the website of the United Nations High Commissioner for Human Rights, *Ratifications and Reservations*, updates available at <http://treaties.un.org/Pages/Treaties.aspx?id=4&subid=A&lang=en>, last consulted on 5 October 2012.

With the introduction of this article, both the content and mode of application of the right to self-determination and its field of application shifted. A significant element of common Article 1(1) is the phrase "freely determine their political status". Although not explicitly stated, it requires that the people concerned are able to choose their legislators and political representatives, without third State intervention and without any manipulation or interference from the current authorities, in order to express their popular will.[9] In this respect, an internal dimension of the right to self-determination manifests itself,[10] as well as a continuing entitlement to self-determination. The latter implies that, unlike the external dimension which ceases to exist as soon as independence is achieved, the internal dimension of the right to self-determination "is neither destroyed nor diminished by its having already been evoked or put into effect",[11] but should be pursued continuously.

Focusing on the content of this internal dimension of the right to self-determination, one may take issue with Antonio Cassese that this concept is, in fact, a manifestation of the various civil and political rights and freedoms as provided for in the ICCPR, such as freedom of expression, the right of peaceful assembly, the right to freedom of association, the right to vote and the right to take part in the conduct of public affairs, for the exercise of these rights and freedoms enables expression of popular will.[12] Or one might take issue, slightly differently, with James R. Crawford, who conceives internal self-determination as "essentially a summary of other rights".[13] Be that as it may, it should be emphasized that the right to self-determination is not limited to the freedom of peoples to determine their political status. It also includes peoples' freedom to pursue their desired economic, social and cultural development. It is clear that these latter goals are, in essence, achieved by participation of a people in the general political decision-making process within a State.[14] In this context, Article

---

[9]   Antonio Cassese even calls this the "primary significance" of common Article 1(1). See A. Cassese, *Self-Determination of Peoples. A Legal Reappraisal* (Cambridge University Press, Cambridge 1995) at p. 53.

[10]   As Allan Rosas rightly noted, since this provision is part of a human rights convention, it should be read in this context as well. Accordingly, it goes without saying that the provision on self-determination addresses the relation between citizens and their own government. See Rosas, 'Internal Self-Determination' at p. 243.

[11]   Cassese, *Self-Determination of Peoples. A Legal Reappraisal* at p. 101.

[12]   *Ibid.* at p. 53; S. Joseph, J. Schultz and M. Castan, *The International Covenant on Civil and Political Rights: Cases, Materials, and Commentary* (Oxford University Press, Oxford 2000) at p. 103.

[13]   J.R. Crawford, 'The Right to Self-Determination in International Law: Its Development and Future' in P. Alston (ed.) *Peoples' Rights* (Oxford University Press, Oxford 2001) at p. 25.

[14]   For a similar argument, see A. Xanthaki, *Indigenous Rights and United Nations Standards. Self-Determination, Culture and Land* (Cambridge University Press, New York 2007) at pp. 158-159: "Pursuing [economic, social, and cultural] development essentially involves establishing policy priorities and trade-offs in policy allocations and benefits; this is political in nature. Political, but also economic and social policies can only be decided and implemented through a political process, where the state and its institutions are involved."

25 ICCPR is of particular importance, as this provision seems to touch upon the core of the rights guaranteed in Article 1(1).[15] Article 25 ICCPR[16] states that:

> [e]very citizen shall have the right and the opportunity [...] (a) to take part in the conduct of public affairs, directly or through freely chosen representatives; (b) to vote and to be elected at genuine periodic elections which shall be by universal and equal suffrage and shall be held by secret ballot, guaranteeing the free expression of the will of the electors; (c) to have access, on general terms of equality, to public service in his country.

Thus, (political) self-determination functions as a tool to attain self-determination – politically, economically, socially and culturally – in general,[17] and Article 25 ICCPR can play an important role in this respect. Common Article 1(3) of the human rights covenants of 1966 may illustrate this interrelationship of the various aspects of self-determination. By virtue of this provision, the inhabitants of a territory are granted the right to control and benefit from the natural wealth and resources of that territory. This facet of the right to self-determination can be viewed as a logical consequence of the political one, for it implies a duty for the authorities chosen to divert the natural wealth and resources in conformity with the interests of the people as reflected when participating in the political sphere.[18]

---

[15] Cassese, *Self-Determination of Peoples. A Legal Reappraisal* at p. 54; Raič, *Statehood and the Law of Self-Determination* at p. 239. See also the Committee on the Elimination of Racial Discrimination (CERD) in its General Recommendation No. 21 on the right to self-determination, stressing the link between the internal aspect of the right to self-determination and "the right of every citizen to take part in the conduct of public affairs at any level" and referring to Article 5(c) of the Convention on the Elimination of All Forms of Racial Discrimination. See Committee on the Elimination of Racial Discrimination, *General Recommendation No. 21: Right to Self-Determination*, UN Doc. A/51/18 (1996), Annex VIII, at para. 4. Words to that effect were also used by the Human Rights Committee in its General Comment on common Article 1 of the human rights covenants of 1966. See Human Rights Committee, *General Comment No. 12: Article 1 (Right to Self-Determination), The Right to Self-Determination of Peoples*, UN Doc. HRI/GEN/1/Rev.1 (1994), 13 March 1984.

[16] For a rather detailed commentary on this article, see Joseph, Schultz and Castan, *The International Covenant on Civil and Political Rights: Cases, Materials, and Commentary* at pp. 497-511.

[17] Although the use of the term 'political self-determination' is obvious, strictly speaking, it is not necessary. The general interpretation of self-determination stresses a people's freedom to determine its political status (both externally and internally), but simultaneously is an instrument to enable the achievement of self-determination in an economic, social and cultural context. As a result, the use of the general term 'self-determination' suffices as well.

[18] Although an elaborate discussion of this resource dimension of the right to self-determination is beyond the scope of this Study, which focuses mainly on the political dimension of self-determination, it must not go unrecorded that disregard of this aspect of self-determination can represent serious obstruction in the enjoyment of other human rights, for example the right to adequate food. For a brief discussion of this resource dimension of the right to self-determination and the corresponding duties for States, see Cassese, *Self-Determination of Peoples. A Legal Reappraisal* at pp. 55-57. For a comprehensive analysis of the evolution and content of the underlying principle of sovereignty over natural resources

As was already mentioned, not only the content and mode of application of the right to self-determination shifted with the adoption of the human rights covenants of 1966, in addition, the field of application of the right to self-determination changed. In contrast to the conception of self-determination in General Assembly Resolution 1514 (XV), the phrase "all peoples" suggests universal applicability of the principle. Put differently, it appears that the international human rights covenants do not merely apply to colonial peoples or other specific categories of peoples. This notion is also reflected in the *travaux préparatoires* of the ICCPR.[19] Yet, formulating a definition of 'peoples' remained challenging. Various suggestions were made, but none of the proposals were adopted. In the end, it was agreed upon that the term 'peoples' was to be understood "in its most general sense and that no definition was necessary".[20]

Nevertheless, restraint should be exercised with regard to conclusions drawn from this open concept of 'peoples', since a substantial number of States emphasized that this did not imply the existence of a right to secede. This is noteworthy, for Article 1(1) ICCPR does not provide for explicit restrictions as to the different modes available for 'peoples' to exercise the right to freely determine their political status, for instance by excluding the possibility of establishing a new, independent State. Hence, as Helen Quane aptly noted, "the blanket denial of a right to secession suggests that groups within States or colonial territories cannot be regarded as peoples for the purpose of Article 1".[21] The *travaux préparatoires* of the ICCPR indicate that proposals were made to include reference to a right to "establish an independent State", to "choose its own form of government", or to "secede from or unite with another people".[22] These suggestions, however, remained unadopted, since it was found that listing the components of the right to self-determination would probably be incomplete. Accordingly, preference was given rather to sketch the right in the abstract.[23] This resulted in continuing uncertainties as regards the scope of common Article 1(1): even though it was clear that the term "all peoples" in the international human rights covenants

---

and its relationship with other branches of international law, see N.J. Schrijver, *Sovereignty over Natural Resources: Balancing Rights and Duties* (Cambridge University Press, Cambridge 2008).

[19] See M.J. Bossuyt, *Guide to the "Travaux Préparatoires" of the International Covenant on Civil and Political Rights* (Martinus Nijhoff Publishers, Dordrecht 1987) at pp. 32, 44-45. For an account of preliminary discussions leading to the codification of common Article 1(1), see also Cassese, *Self-Determination of Peoples. A Legal Reappraisal* at pp. 52-62; J.R. Crawford, 'The Right of Self-Determination in International Law: Its Development and Future' in P. Alston (ed.) *Peoples' Rights* (Oxford University Press, Oxford 2001) at pp. 28-29; H. Hannum, 'Rethinking Self-Determination' (1993) 34 *Virginia Journal of International Law* 1 at pp. 18-25.

[20] Cited in Bossuyt, *Guide to the "Travaux Préparatoires" of the International Covenant on Civil and Political Rights* at p. 32.

[21] H. Quane, 'The United Nations and the Evolving Right to Self-Determination' (1998) 47 *International and Comparative Law Quarterly* 537 at p. 560.

[22] See Bossuyt, *Guide to the "Travaux Préparatoires" of the International Covenant on Civil and Political Rights* at p. 34.

[23] *Ibid.* at p. 34.

of 1966 was no longer limited to colonial peoples or the inhabitants of Trust or Non-Self-Governing Territories, it remained questionable which 'peoples' were entitled to which manifestation of self-determination.[24] For, it appears that not all 'peoples' are permitted to exercise all levels of self-determination under all circumstances.

2.2. The Friendly Relations Declaration

An additional document which has been essential for the development of the right to self-determination was adopted four years after the ICCPR and ICESCR. In 1962, the General Assembly had authorized a study of the principles of the United Nations and the duties these principles imposed on the Member States.[25] For this purpose, a committee was established,[26] which drafted the 1970 Declaration on Principles of International Law Concerning Friendly Relations and Co-operation Among States in Accordance with the Charter of the United Nations (hereafter: Friendly Relations Declaration). The General Assembly adopted this Declaration almost unanimously[27] as Resolution 2625 (XXV).[28] Notwithstanding its legally non-binding status, the Friendly Relations Declaration is nowadays commonly viewed as the most authoritative expression of the scope and meaning of the basic principles of the international legal order.[29] It endeavours to be more explicit on the implications of self-determination than previous texts have been.[30] The reference to '[t]he principle of equal rights and self-determination of peoples' (Principle V) provides as follows:

> By virtue of the principle of equal rights and self-determination of peoples enshrined in the Charter of the United Nations, all peoples have the right to freely determine, without external interference, their political status and pursue their economic, social and

---

[24] This issue will be dealt with in Sections 3.3 and 4.2 of the present Chapter.

[25] UN General Assembly Resolution 1815 (XVII) (*Consideration of Principles of International Law Concerning Friendly Relations and Co-operation Among States in Accordance with the Charter of the United Nations*), UN Doc. A/Res/1815 (XVII), 18 December 1962.

[26] UN General Assembly Resolution 1966 (XVIII) (*Consideration of Principles of International Law Concerning Friendly Relations and Co-operation Among States in Accordance with the Charter of the United Nations*), UN Doc. A/Res/1966 (XVIII), 16 December 1963.

[27] See General Assembly Official Records, *25th Session: 1883th Plenary Meeting*, UN Doc. A/PV.1883, 24 October 1970, and the official records of the 1872th-1879th plenary meetings, and the 1881th-1882th plenary meetings.

[28] UN General Assembly Resolution 2625 (XXV) (*Declaration on Principles of International Law Concerning Friendly Relations and Co-operation Among States in Accordance with the Charter of the United Nations*), UN Doc. A/Res/2625 (XXV), 24 October 1970.

[29] International Court of Justice, *Case Concerning Military and Paramilitary Activities in and against Nicaragua (Nicaragua v. United States of America)*, Merits, Judgment, ICJ Reports 1986, p. 14, at paras 100-103.

[30] See Crawford, 'The Right of Self-Determination in International Law: Its Development and Future' at p. 30.

cultural development, and every State has the duty to respect this right in accordance with the provisions of the Charter.

Every State has the duty to promote [...] realization of the principle of equal rights and self-determination of peoples [...] in order:
(a) To promote friendly relations and co-operation among States; and
(b) To bring a speedy end to colonialism, having due regard to the freely expressed will of the peoples concerned; and bearing in mind that subjection of peoples to alien subjugation, domination and exploitation constitutes a violation of the principle [of self-determination], as well as denial of fundamental rights, and is contrary to the Charter [...]

The establishment of a sovereign and independent State, the free association or integration with an independent State or the emergence into any other political status freely determined by a people constitute modes of implementing the right of self-determination by that people.

Every State has the duty to refrain from any forcible action which deprives peoples referred to above in the elaboration of the present principle of their right to self-determination and freedom and independence. In their actions against, and resistance to, such forcible action in pursuit of the exercise of their right to self-determination, such peoples are entitled to seek and to receive support in accordance with the purposes and principles of the Charter.

The territory of a colony or other Non-Self-Governing Territory has, under the Charter, a status separate and distinct from the territory of the State administering it; and such separate and distinct status under the Charter shall exist until the people of the colony or Non-Self-Governing Territory have exercised their right of self-determination in accordance with the Charter, and particularly its purposes and principles.

Nothing in the foregoing paragraph shall be construed as authorizing or encouraging any action which would dismember or impair, totally or in part, the territorial integrity or political unity of sovereign and independent States conducting themselves in compliance with the principle of equal rights and self-determination of peoples as described above and thus possessed of a government representing the whole people belonging to the territory without distinction as to race, creed or colour.

Every State shall refrain from any action aimed at the partial or total disruption of the national unity and territorial integrity of any other State or country.

It needs little explanation that, in view of the above, the Friendly Relations Declaration contains a reference to the existence of both an external and internal dimension of the right to self-determination. Principle V states that self-determination may be exercised through the formation of an independent State, or the association or integration with an independent State. Since these modes of implementation of the right to self-determination by a people result in the alteration of the boundaries of the State of which that people are inhabitants, this reference to the right to self-determination concerns the external dimension of the right.[31] In addition, Principle V clearly implies that a right to self-determination does not cease to exist as soon as independence has been achieved, since it links self-determination with the internal commitment to "a government representing the whole people belonging to the territory without distinction as to race, creed or colour". The inclusion of this phrase may be explained by the concern of the international community at the time of drafting the Declaration, which involved the Apartheid regime in South Africa and white minority rule in Southern Rhodesia (now Zimbabwe), both in which the non-white majority of the population was denied a representative government.[32] Nonetheless, taking into account the abovementioned phrase and the *travaux préparatoires* of the Declaration, it appears that, similar to the international human rights covenants of 1966, the Declaration was intended to be universally applicable, rather than applicable to colonial situations only.[33] Furthermore, Principle V addresses all States – not merely colonial powers – as a consequence of which every State is obliged to live up to the requirements set by the right to self-determination.[34] Despite this broad scope of application and reference to the external dimension of the right, it is questionable whether the right to self-determination as embodied in the Friendly Relations Declaration should be interpreted as either prohibiting or allowing a people to determine their external political status by means of secession. The *travaux préparatoires* disclose that some States were rather hesitant about the inclusion of the penultimate paragraph of Principle V. They feared that it would contribute to the progressive development of the right to self-determination and could hence be invoked to legitimize secession.[35] Consequently, the final text of the Declaration attributes considerable weight to the principle of territorial integrity and political unity of sovereign and independent States. At the same time, however, secession is not explicitly ruled out either. As will be seen elsewhere in the present study, this has led a considerable number of authors to argue that the text of the Declaration opens up the possibility for unilateral secession.[36]

---

[31] See, for instance, Raič, *Statehood and the Law of Self-Determination* at p. 289.

[32] See, for instance, Cassese, *Self-Determination of Peoples. A Legal Reappraisal* at pp. 119-121; Xanthaki, *Indigenous Rights and United Nations Standards. Self-Determination, Culture and Land* at p. 147.

[33] Quane, 'The United Nations and the Evolving Right to Self-Determination' at pp. 562-563.

[34] Raič, *Statehood and the Law of Self-Determination* at p. 231.

[35] See Quane, 'The United Nations and the Evolving Right to Self-Determination' at p. 564. See also Cassese, *Self-Determination of Peoples. A Legal Reappraisal* at pp. 115-118.

[36] The academic debate on this issue will be dealt with in Chapter IV, Section 2.2 of the present study.

2.3. Subsequent Documents

In addition to the Friendly Relations Declaration, evidence for the suggestion that the right to self-determination transcends colonialism can also be found in the Helsinki Final Act,[37] as this document was adopted during the Conference on Security and Co-operation in Europe (CSCE) in 1975.[38] By that time, there were no longer colonial situations in Europe and Northern America. The fact that the States participating to the Helsinki Conference explicitly rejected the argument that, because of the end of the decolonization process, no reference to self-determination was needed makes the inclusion of Principle VIII of the Helsinki Final Act even more telling.[39] It states that:

> [b]y virtue of the principle of equal rights and self-determination of peoples, all peoples always have the rights, in full freedom, to determine, when and as they wish, their internal and external political status, without external interference, and to pursue as they wish their political, economic, social and cultural development.

Several legal scholars have even called the Helsinki Final Act innovative, arguing that the aforementioned excerpt is much less restrained than previous references to self-determination.[40] Whereas the Friendly Relations Declaration does not explicitly grant the right to self-determination to "all peoples", the Helsinki Final Act does so. The *travaux préparatoires* reveal that it was intended to refer to peoples organized as nations in the first place.[41] Moreover, it uses the specific terms "always" and "when and as they wish" to emphasize that it concerns an ongoing (internal) right, which continues to exist even after a people has determined its internal and external political status.[42] Yet, this broad scope of application of the right to self-determi-

---

[37]   Conference on Security and Co-operation in Europe, *Conference on Security and Co-operation in Europe Final Act*, Helsinki, 1 August 1975, available at <http://www.osce.org/mc/39501?download=true>, last consulted on 20 September 2012.

[38]   As from 1 January 1995, the Conference on Security and Co-operation in Europe (CSCE) was renamed the Organization for Security and Co-operation in Europe (OSCE). Participating States of the OSCE are not merely European States, but cover a geographical area "from Vancouver to Vladivostok" as North America and Central Asia are also involved. The OSCE conducts a wide range of activities which are all related to three 'dimensions of security': the politico-military, the economic-environmental, and the human dimension.

[39]   See Raič, *Statehood and the Law of Self-Determination* at p. 231.

[40]   See, for instance, Cassese, *Self-Determination of Peoples. A Legal Reappraisal* at pp. 285-288.

[41]   See *ibid.* at pp. 285-286.

[42]   See *ibid.* at p. 285. Against this backdrop, it is interesting to note that the so-called Copenhagen Document, which was also adopted by the CSCE, affirmed that "democracy is an inherent element of the rule of law" (para. 3) and declared "that the will of the people, freely and fairly expressed through periodic and genuine elections, is the basis of the authority and legitimacy of all government. The participating States will accordingly respect the right of their citizens to take part in the governing of their country, either directly or through representatives freely chosen by them through fair electoral processes" (para. 6). In addition, the Copenhagen Document spelled out the contents of the rights of political participation

nation should be viewed against the backdrop of two important principles, i.e. the inviolability of frontiers (Principle III) and the territorial integrity of States (Principle IV).[43] Moreover, it should be noted that the Helsinki Final Act is a political document rather than a document to which the States involved are legally bound. In addition, it does not concern a universal document, but a regional one. Nonetheless, the Helsinki Final Act is considered to be important with respect to an understanding of the development and content of the right to self-determination – not only because of its innovative language used, but also because it reflected concurrence between the Western and Soviet powers on the very topic of self-determination and other matters, while the Cold War was in full swing.[44]

More recently, the Charter of Paris was adopted during the CSCE summit meeting in November 1990.[45] The reference to self-determination in this document:

> reaffirm[ed] the equal rights of peoples and their right to self-determination in conformity with the Charter of the United Nations and with the relevant norms of international law, including those relating to the territorial integrity of States.

Here as well, the point was made that the right to self-determination excluded the justification of secession, since this mode of implementation would violate the territorial integrity of States.[46]

Subsequently, the Vienna Declaration and Programme of Action, adopted during the 1993 World Conference on Human Rights, strongly reflected the importance of the internal dimension of the right to self-determination. The Vienna Declaration and Programme of Action even considered "the denial of self-determination as a violation of human rights", and required that there be a government which effectively represents the entire population of the territory concerned, "without distinction of any

---

in more concrete terms – to ensure that the will of the people serves as the basis of the authority of government. See Conference on Security and Co-operation in Europe, *Document of the Copenhagen Meeting of the Conference on the Human Dimension*, Copenhagen, 29 June 1990, available at <http://www.osce. org/odihr/elections/14304>, last consulted on 20 September 2012. Drafted in reaction to the events in the former Soviet Union, the Moscow Document subsequently expressed in a very clear way the value of representative government by strongly condemning the attempted Soviet coup of 1991. One may argue that this document substitutes the Wilsonian notion of popular sovereignty, as it called on participating States not to recognize "unreservedly forces which seek to take power from a representative government [...] against the will of the people as expressed in free and fair elections" (para. 17.1). See Conference on Security and Co-operation in Europe, *Document of the Moscow Meeting on the Human Dimension, Emphasizing Respect for Human Rights, Pluralistic Democracy, the Rule of Law, and Procedures for Fact-Finding*, Moscow, 3 October 1991, available at <http://www.osce.org/odihr/elections/14310>, last consulted on 20 September 2012.

43   Hannum, 'Rethinking Self-Determination' at p. 29.
44   See *ibid.* at p. 28.
45   Conference on Security and Co-operation in Europe, *Charter of Paris for a New Europe*, Paris, 21 November 1990, available at <http://www.osce.org/mc/39516>, last consulted on 20 September 2012.
46   Hannum, 'Rethinking Self-Determination' at p. 29.

kind".[47] Similar to the Helsinki Final Act, the Vienna Declaration and Programme of Action concerns a political document rather than a legally binding one. But in contrast to the Helsinki Final Act, the Vienna Declaration and Programme of Action can be viewed as a universal document, since it was adopted by consensus by 171 States. Moreover, during the preparatory process leading to the World Conference, three regional meetings had been organized in Tunis, San José and Bangkok, contributions and suggestions had been made by governments, intergovernmental and non-governmental organizations, and various studies had been prepared by independent experts. This input was all taken into account when drafting the declaration.[48]

In addition, support for the proposition that the right to self-determination goes beyond the context of decolonization can also be found in the African Charter on Human and Peoples' Rights. This document was adopted by the Assembly of Heads of States and Government of the Organization of African Unity (OAU) in 1981, by which time colonialism had almost vanished on the continent. Article 20 provides for the right to self-determination:

> 1. All peoples shall have the right to existence. They shall have the unquestionable and inalienable right to self-determination. They shall freely determine their political status and shall pursue their economic and social development according to the policy they have freely chosen.

> 2. Colonized or oppressed peoples shall have the right to free themselves from the bonds of domination by resorting to any means recognized by the international community.

> 3. All peoples shall have the right to the assistance of the States parties to the present Charter in their liberation struggle against foreign domination, be it political, economic or cultural.

The first paragraph of this provision demonstrates some similarities with common Article 1 of the Covenants of 1966, as it grants all peoples the right to self-determination, which the text of the paragraph seems to interpret as having the right to choose political status and economic and social development. However, as the second and third paragraphs of Article 20 seem to indicate, in certain situations, a right to external self-determination was also envisaged. Even so, the communication of the African Commission on Human and Peoples' Rights concerning *Katangese Peoples' Congress v. Zaire*[49] imposed some restraints on such an extensive interpretation of

---

[47] World Conference on Human Rights, *Vienna Declaration and Programme of Action*, adopted on 25 June 1993, UN Doc. A/CONF.157/23, 12 July 1993, at para. 2.

[48] *Ibid.*, preamble.

[49] See African Commission on Human and Peoples' Rights, *Katangese Peoples' Congress v. Zaire*, Comm. No. 75/92, 1995 (not dated). For a more elaborate account of this case, see Chapter IV, Section 2.3.2.

the right to self-determination. It was emphasized that the right to self-determination as reflected in Article 20 should be implemented "in any [...] form of relations that accords with the wishes of the people but fully cognisant of other recognised principles such as sovereignty and territorial integrity". In view of the above, it may be concluded that the right to self-determination under the African Charter should be interpreted as first and foremost including a right to internal self-determination.

Finally, reference should be made to the UN Declaration on the Rights of Indigenous Peoples (UNDRIP), which was adopted by the General Assembly in 2007.[50] While this document and its legal status will be discussed in more detail elsewhere in the present Chapter,[51] at this point, it is important to note that the Declaration explicitly provides a right to self-determination for indigenous peoples, thus extending the right to self-determination beyond decolonization. In addition, the Declaration demonstrates a clear focus on the internal dimension of the right. In express terms, Article 3 UNDRIP grants indigenous peoples the right to self-determination, as it provides:

> Indigenous peoples have the right to self-determination. By virtue of that right they freely determine their political status and freely pursue their economic, social and cultural development.

Since this phrasing is almost identical to that of common Article 1 of the Covenants of 1966, it seems that an internal right to self-determination was envisaged. This assumption is confirmed by subsequent provisions in the Declaration. First, Articles 4, 18, and 31 UNDRIP positively refer to and elaborate on autonomy rights for indigenous peoples. Secondly, Article 46(1) UNDRIP limits the modes of exercising the right to self-determination as it emphasizes the need for upholding the right to territorial integrity when interpreting the rights granted in the Declaration. As such, interpreting the right to self-determination as including a right to secession seems out of the question.

Having outlined the development of the right to self-determination beyond the context of decolonization, two dimensions of self-determination have become apparent: the continuous, internal dimension and the traditional, external dimension. Subsequently, the question arises as to what the implications of this development of the concept are with regard to the present-day interpretation of self-determination. In view of this, the contemporary meaning of both modes of self-determination will be discussed below.

---

[50] UN General Assembly Resolution 61/295 (*United Nations Declaration on the Rights of Indigenous Peoples*), UN Doc. A/Res/61/295, 13 September 2007.
[51] See Section 3.3.4 of the present Chapter, considering indigenous peoples as subjects of the right to internal self-determination.

3. INTERNAL SELF-DETERMINATION

While in essence, the principal question of this study concerns external self-determination, the internal mode also should be assessed for the present purposes. First, elaboration of the internal dimension of the right to self-determination is vital for the purpose of understanding the present-day meaning of the right to self-determination. As has become apparent above and will also be seen below, contemporary international law seems to emphasize internal rather then external self-determination, hence explaining (part of) the controversy surrounding the latter dimension. In addition to this, it has sometimes been argued that the persistent denial of the right to internal self-determination may, at a certain point, convert into a right to external self-determination. For this reason as well, it is important to shed light on the contemporary meaning of the internal dimension. In this respect, the status, content and subjects of the right to internal self-determination are to be determined in order to know who is entitled to it, who is to observe it, and when it has been violated.

3.1. The Content of the Right to Internal Self-Determination

As has been outlined in the previous Chapter, the notion of self-determination has evolved from a political principle to a legal right under international law. Above, it was seen that in this capacity, the development of the right to self-determination continued beyond the context of decolonization. The analysis of these developments enables painting a more detailed picture of the contemporary core meaning of the right to internal self-determination.

The essence of the contemporary meaning of the right to internal self-determination can be said to have been introduced by the International Court of Justice in the *Western Sahara* case and was "defined as the need to pay regard to the freely expressed will" of the peoples at issue.[52] This core meaning may be specified by adding a context in which the political status or political interests of a people are at stake. In these instances, a decision on the matter at hand needs to result from the "free and genuine expression of the will of the peoples concerned".[53]

The above formulated core meaning, however, does not reveal the rationale of the right to internal self-determination. Hence, the question left is as to why, according to the concept of self-determination, there is a need to found decisions affecting the political status or interests of what may be called a 'people' on the freely and

---

[52] International Court of Justice, *Western Sahara*, Advisory Opinion, ICJ Reports 1975, p. 12, at para. 59. However, it should be noted that this remark was made in the context of dependent territories. See also Cassese, *Self-Determination of Peoples. A Legal Reappraisal* at pp. 319-320; Rosas, 'Internal Self-Determination' at pp. 232-236.

[53] See Raič, *Statehood and the Law of Self-Determination* at p. 223, cf. International Court of Justice, *Western Sahara*, Advisory Opinion, ICJ Reports 1975, p. 12, at para. 55.

genuinely expressed will of these people. As the Commission of Jurists observed in its report concerning the *Åland Islands* case, the purpose of the concept of self-determination is "to assure some group the maintenance and free development of its social, ethnical or religious characteristics".[54] What is more, Dietrich Murswiek has argued that the rationale is that a group can inhabit its traditional territory and, in this environment, is enabled to "cultivate, preserve, and develop the specific character-istics determining its identity".[55] All in all, it can be alleged that the rationale of the notion of self-determination is:

[t]he protection, preservation, strengthening and development of the cultural, ethnic and/or historical identity or individuality (the 'self') of a collectivity, that is, of a 'people', and thus guaranteeing a people's freedom and existence.[56]

Put differently, it may be suggested that the objective of the principle of self-determi-nation to protect, preserve, strengthen and develop the 'collective identity'.

3.1.1. Implementation of the Right to Internal Self-Determination

Having touched upon the purpose of the concept of self-determination, the question arises as to the more practical implications of the core meaning of the right to self-determination. In the words of Antonio Cassese, the right to internal self-determi-nation presumes that all peoples are "allowed to exercise those rights and freedoms which permit the expression of the popular will".[57] That popular participation in the political decision-making process of the State plays a key role in achieving self-deter-mination is also emphasized by various other scholars, international bodies and judi-cial organs.[58] Political participation in public affairs can be exercised either directly

---

[54] *Report of Commission of Jurists (Larnaude, Huber, Struycken)*, LNOJ Special Supplement No. 3 (October 1920), at para. 6.

[55] D. Murswiek, 'The Issue of a Right of Secession – Reconsidered' in C. Tomuschat (ed.) *Modern Law of Self-Determination* (Martinus Nijhoff Publishers, Dordrecht 1993) at p. 27.

[56] Raič, *Statehood and the Law of Self-Determination* at p. 223.

[57] Accordingly, Antonio Cassese has pointed out that the right to internal self-determination is to be viewed as a "manifestation of the totality of rights embodied in the [ICCPR]". See Cassese, *Self-Deter-mination of Peoples. A Legal Reappraisal* at p. 53.

[58] See, for instance, L.C. Buchheit, *Secession: The Legitimacy of Self-Determination* (Yale Univer-sity Press, New Haven 1978) at p. 16; A Eide, *Second Progress Report on 'Possible Ways and Means of Facilitating the Peaceful and Constructive Solution of Problems Involving Minorities*, UN Doc. E/CN.4/Sub.2/1992/37, at para. 165; Hannum, 'Rethinking Self-Determination' at pp. 33-35; Franck, 'The Emerging Right to Democratic Governance' at pp. 58-59; See also Rosas, 'Internal Self-Determination' at p. 249. Likewise, the Human Rights Committee has explained the connection between the right of peoples to self-determination and the right of citizens to political participation. See UN Human Rights Committee, *General Comment No. 25: Article 25 (Participation in Public Affairs and the Right to Vote), The Right to Participate in Public Affairs, Voting Rights and the Right to Equal Access to Public Service*, UN Doc. CCPR/C/21/Rev.1/Add.7 (1996), 12 July 1996, at paras 1-2. See also Raič, *Statehood and the*

or indirectly. Although plebiscites or referenda as regards public matters[59] may function as avenues for direct participation of citizens, in most societies, it is practically impossible to provide for direct participation in public affairs by all citizens in view of the large number of peoples involved. Therefore, indirect participation by means of a representative government is generally accepted to be an acceptable and workable alternative. Against this backdrop, the notion of direct participation primarily refers to the right to stand for election for the purpose of creating a representative government, while the notion of indirect participation generally refers to periodic voting processes in order to elect the political representatives of the people.[60]

As was expressed in the preparatory debates of the adoption of the Friendly Relations Declaration,[61] in the Friendly Relations Declaration itself and in the Vienna

---

Law of Self-Determination at pp. 237-238, sources referred to in footnote 42. To that effect, several judicial decisions have proclaimed that political participation of the entire population is essential with regard to the exercise of the internal aspect of self-determination. See Supreme Court of Canada, *Reference re Secession of Quebec*, [1998] 2 S.C.R. 217; Constitutional Court of the Russian Federation, *Republic of Tatarstan*, 13 March 1992, Decision No. 671; African Commission on Human and Peoples' Rights, *Katangese Peoples' Congress v. Zaire*, Comm. No. 75/92, 1995 (not dated). For a consideration of these cases against the background of the right to self-determination, see J. Summers, *Peoples and International Law: How Nationalism and Self-Determination Shape a Contemporary Law of Nations* (Martinus Nijhoff Publishers, Leiden/Boston 2007) at pp. 265-267, 274-278, 293-301; M. Suski, 'Keeping the Lid on the Secession Kettle: A Review of Legal Interpretations Concerning Claims of Self-Determination by Minority Peoples' (2005) 12 *International Journal on Minority and Group Rights* 189 at pp. 207-216.

[59] Plebiscites and referenda may be defined as J. Patrick Boyer did: "The referendum is generally an established procedure provided or by existing constitutional or legislative provisions, while a plebiscite arises either by a special legislative Act providing for it or by a special initiative of a government, utilizing procedures already provided by statutes […] The main difference between the two voting devices is therefore that a plebiscite is essentially a public opinion poll but a referendum automatically binds a government to enact a law (or to refrain from doing so) according to the voters' wishes." See R.A. Miller, 'Self-Determination in International Law and the Demise of Democracy?' (2003) 41 *Columbia Journal of Transnational Law* 601 at p. 626, quoting J. Patrick Boyer.

[60] See Joseph, Schultz and Castan, *The International Covenant on Civil and Political Rights: Cases, Materials, and Commentary* at pp. 501-511.

[61] Concerning the provision dealing with self-determination of peoples which, in the end, was determined as Paragraph 7 of Principle V of this document, the United Kingdom submitted a proposal which stated under (4): "States enjoying full sovereignty and independence, and possessed of a representative government, effectively functioning as such to all distinct peoples within their territory, shall be considered to be conducting themselves in conformity with the principle as regards those peoples". See UN Doc. A/Ac.125/L44, 19 July 1967. This proposal bears likeness to the proposal which had been made by the United States, which read as follows: "[t]he existence of a sovereign and independent State possessing a representative Government, effectively functioning as such to all distinct peoples within its territory, is presumed to satisfy the principle of equal rights and self-determination as regards these peoples". See UN Doc. A/AC.125/L32, 12 April 1966, at para. B. Finally, the Italian proposal can be seen as both confirming and refining the abovementioned proposals: "States enjoying full sovereignty and independence, and possessed of a government representing the whole of their population, shall be considered to be conducting themselves in conformity with the principle of equal rights and self-determination of peoples as regards that population. Nothing in the foregoing paragraphs shall be construed as authorizing any action which would impair, totally or in part, the territorial integrity, or political unity, of such States". See UN

Declaration and Programme of Action, the presence of a representative government is vital for the exercise of the right to internal self-determination. Hence, it is helpful to consider what exactly should be understood by this important concept of representative government. In general, such a government claims to represent the authority or will of its people.[62] More specifically, when a government claims to represent its people, this implies that it represents the population as a whole. Thus, the implementation of the right to internal self-determination is inextricably linked to the principle of equal rights of peoples and, in particular, the principle of non-discrimination. The government should be seen to represent all inhabitants of its territory without any distinction.[63] This aspect can also be found in the UN Charter (Article 2(1)), in the Friendly Relations Declaration (Principle V, paragraph 7), and in the Vienna Declaration and Programme of Action (Part I, Article 2).

Above, it was argued that, for a political system to qualify as representative and participatory, open electoral processes, by means of which the people's representatives are chosen, and continuing possibilities to participate in the decision-making process, are of vital importance. An additional – in fact preceding – aspect facilitates the people to constitute its own political system, in this way acting as a so-called *pouvoir constituant*.[64] As the right to self-determination is often characterized as inalienable and ongoing,[65] this also implies that at any moment in time, the people can change or re-create the manifestation of their system of government and administration.[66] Furthermore, a representative government should allow its people to participate in the general decision-making process of the State, in this way effectively – not merely formally – determining not only its political, but also its economic, social and cultural development. Put differently, governmental responsiveness is essential. In this regard, policy outcomes may function as a continuous measuring instrument

---

Doc. A/AC.125/L80, 1969. For an elaborate account of the preparatory works to the Friendly Relations Declaration, see Cassese, *Self-Determination of Peoples. A Legal Reappraisal* at pp. 115-118.

[62]   Raič, *Statehood and the Law of Self-Determination* at p. 273.

[63]   In order to ensure such government without distinction, "measures in favour of the minority group, such as autonomy" might be required. See J. Wright, 'Minority Groups, Autonomy, and Self-Determination' (1999) 19 *Oxford Journal of Legal Studies* 605 at p. 618.

[64]   Rosas, 'Internal Self-Determination' at pp. 230, 249. See also Suski, 'Keeping the Lid on the Secession Kettle: A Review of Legal Interpretations Concerning Claims of Self-Determination by Minority Peoples' at p. 201, referring to M. Suski, 'On Mechanisms of Decision-Making in the Creation (and the Re-Creation) of States – with Special Reference to the Relationship between the Right to Self-Determination, the Sovereignty of the People and the *pouvoir constituant*' (1997) 3 *Tidsskrift for Rettsvitenskap* 426.

[65]   See, for instance, UN Human Rights Committee, *General Comment No. 12: Article 1 (Right to Self-Determination), The Right to Self-Determination of Peoples*, UN Doc. HRI/GEN/1/Rev.1 (1994), 13 March 1984.

[66]   Raič, *Statehood and the Law of Self-Determination* at p. 238. In this respect, plebiscites or referenda may be viewed as appropriate avenues for allowing the people to act as a *pouvoir constituant*.

for qualifying a political system as participatory and representative, and for checking whether the core meaning of the right to internal self-determination is complied with.

3.1.2. Internal Self-Determination and Democratic Governance?

When considering the relevant human rights instruments, it might appear that recognition of the right to internal self-determination requires the creation and upholding of a democratic governmental system as perceived by the West, albeit implicitly. Whether this is true or not, it is indeed the view of the Human Rights Committee.[67] When considering the net of political entitlements provided for in the ICCPR and explained in the context of this Covenant,[68] the Western conception of representative democratic government is mirrored. What is more, the Human Rights Committee has stressed that the (individual) rights of political participation as provided for in Article 25 ICCPR[69] are related to, yet distinct from, the right to self-determination of peoples. The Committee contended that the rights to political participation enable "individuals to participate in those processes which constitute the conduct of public affairs" and stressed that these rights lie "at the core of democratic government based on the consent of the people".[70] One of the former members of the Committee, Dame Rosalyn Higgins, has explained that "Article 25 is concerned with the *detail* of how free choice (necessarily implied in Article 1) is to be provided – by periodic elections, on the basis of universal suffrage".[71] From this outlook, ultimately, the conclusion may be drawn that some of these details from Article 25 are a *conditio sine qua non* for observance of the internal dimension of the right to self-determination. The reason behind this conclusion is that without ensuring rights to both direct and indirect participation no free choice is possible, as a result of which there can be no

---

[67] See J.R. Crawford, 'Democracy and International Law' (1993) 64 *British Yearbook of International Law* 113 at p. 114. See also J.R. Crawford, 'Democracy and the Body of International Law' in G.H. Fox and B.R. Roth (eds) *Democratic Governance and International Law* (Cambridge University Press, Cambridge 2000) at pp. 94-95.

[68] See, in general, Joseph, Schultz and Castan, *The International Covenant on Civil and Political Rights: Cases, Materials, and Commentary*; Bossuyt, *Guide to the "Travaux Préparatoires" of the International Covenant on Civil and Political Rights*.

[69] Article 25 ICCPR shows that the rights of political participation, attributed to every citizen, can be divided into rights to indirect participation in public affairs, and rights to direct participation in public affairs (Article 25(a)). The first is exercised through periodic voting processes freely electing the political representatives of the people (Article 25(b)); the latter requires that citizens have the right to stand for election (Article 25(b)) and equal access to the public service (Article 25(c)). See Joseph, Schultz and Castan, *The International Covenant on Civil and Political Rights: Cases, Materials, and Commentary* at pp. 501-511. See also Fox, 'The Right to Political Participation in International Law' at pp. 553-560.

[70] UN Human Rights Committee, *General Comment No. 25: Article 25 (Participation in Public Affairs and the Right to Vote), The Right to Participate in Public Affairs, Voting Rights and the Right to Equal Access to Public Service*, UN Doc. CCPR/C/21/Rev.1/Add.7 (1996), 12 July 1996, at paras 1-2.

[71] Dame Rosalyn Higgins, quoted in Raič, *Statehood and the Law of Self-Determination* at p. 274.

genuine exercise of internal self-determination either.[72] As a logical consequence, it might even be argued that the internal aspect of the right to self-determination implies that the right to freedom of thought (Article 18 ICCPR), the right of peaceful assembly (Article 21 ICCPR), the right to freedom of association (Article 22 ICCPR) and the right to freedom of expression (Article 19 ICCPR) need to be safeguarded,[73] for compliance with these political rights is presupposed for the effectuation of true political participation.[74] That the effective implementation of the internal dimension of the right to self-determination necessitates, in one way or another, democratic governance is also acknowledged in several State reports to the Human Rights Committee.[75] From the relevant paragraphs in these reports, ostensibly, the argument may be derived "that the only form of government compatible with the right to internal self-determination is a democratic one: a regime in which political power is based on the will of the people, and which provides all citizens the opportunity to participate equally in the political life of their societies".[76]

In sum, the argument that the internal aspect of the right to self-determination can be equated with the Western-style concept of democratic governance would be an argument too drastic for a number of interrelated reasons. First, *communis opinio* as regards the interpretation of the concept 'representative government' is lacking

---

[72] *Ibid.* at p. 274.

[73] See also UN General Assembly Resolution 217 (III) (*Universal Declaration on Human Rights*), UN Doc. A/Res/217, 10 December 1948, Articles 19 (right to freedom of opinion and expression) and 20 (right to peaceful assembly and association).

[74] See Cassese, *Self-Determination of Peoples. A Legal Reappraisal* at p. 54. In reaction to Cassese, it has been argued by one commentator that, "[i]n this way, the concept of self-determination becomes the mirror image of the human rights situation in that area of the public sector that in a large sense is commonly associated with the political life of a society". See P. Hilpold, 'Self-Determination in the 21st Century: Modern Perspectives for an Old Concept' in Y. Dinstein (ed.) *Israel Yearbook on Human Rights* (Nijhoff, Dordrecht 2006) at p. 263.

[75] In this respect, reference can be made to the following reports: Second periodic report (Bolivia), UN Doc. CCPR/C/63/Add 4, para. 2; Second periodic report (Cameroon), UN Doc. CCPR/C/63/Add 1, para. 26; Initial report (Croatia), UN Doc. CCPR/C/HRV/99/1, para. 10; Fourth periodic report (Ecuador), UN Doc. CCPR/C/84/Add 6, para. 11; Third periodic report (India), UN Doc. CCPR/C/76/Add 6, para. 32; Second periodic report (Jamaica), UN Doc. CCPR/C/42/Add 15, para. 2; Second periodic report (Republic of Korea), UN Doc. CCPR/C/114/Add 1, para. 18; Second periodic report (Lebanon), UN Doc. CCPR/C/42/Add 14, para. 2; Initial report (Lesotho), UN Doc. CCPR/C/81/Add 14, paras 4-8; Third periodic report (Mauritius), UN Doc. CCPR/C/64/Add 12, para. 5; Initial report (Nepal), UN Doc. CCPR/C/74/Add 2, para. 1; Fourth periodic report – Addendum (Peru), UN Doc. CCPR/C/PER/98/4, para. 3; Fourth periodic report (Romania), UN Doc. CCPR/C/95/Add 7, paras 6-7; Second periodic report (Sudan), UN Doc. CCPR/C/75/Add 2, para. 22; Third and Fourth periodic report (Trinidad and Tobago), UN Doc. CCPR/C/TTO/99/3, paras 20-21; Second periodic report (Zambia), UN Doc. CPR/C/75/Add 2, para. 22.

[76] Wheatley, 'Democracy in International Law: A European Perspective' at p. 232. Yet, if the ICCPR would indeed require the introduction of a Western democratic system, this would raise the question of whether this implies that States which are not party to the Covenant are under the obligation to introduce a democratic governmental system as well. See *ibid.* at p. 233.

on the international level.[77] What is more, even though some contend that a right to democratic governance is emerging,[78] under contemporary international law, an obligation to democratic governance does not exist (yet).[79] To put it even more strongly, there is no single mould of democracy either.[80] In the words of the then UN Secretary-General, Kofi A. Annan, democracy is "not a model to be copied but a goal to be attained".[81] Rather, many manifestations of a democratic system can be discerned, differing from society to society and depending on their particular characteristics and circumstances.[82] These various manifestations of democracy may involve various senses – stronger and weaker – of political representation and participation.[83] As such, it can be argued that the notion of democracy operates on a sliding scale.[84] All in all, the concept of democracy is both adaptable and evolutionary. As a result of this lack of clarity, accepting an international legal entitlement to or obligation for democratic government would even lead to a meaningless term, prone to political misuse. The second objection follows naturally from the previous line of argument: by equating internal self-determination with the Western idea of representative democratic government, hardly any room would be left "for a population's *own* perception of the representative character of its government and for a people's own (traditional) procedures".[85] It should be remembered that, as Jean Salmon observed,

---

[77] During the drafting process of the Friendly Relations Declaration, Third World States pronounced that their interpretation of the phrase "a government representing the whole population belonging to the territory without distinction as to race, creed or colour" mainly concerns the requirement of a non-racist government. See T.D. Musgrave, *Self-Determination and National Minorities* (Oxford University Press, Oxford 1997) at pp. 100-101; M. Pomerance, *Self-Determination in Law and Practice* (Martinus Nijhoff Publishers, Dordrecht 1982) at p. 39. See also Raič, *Statehood and the Law of Self-Determination* at p. 276.

[78] See footnote 4 *supra*, referring to the famous article by Thomas M. Frank. See also Cerna, 'Universal Democracy: An International Legal Right or a Pipe Dream of the West?'.

[79] For a substantiated argument, see J. Wouters, B. De Meester and C. Ryngaert, 'Democracy and International Law' in I.F. Dekker and E. Hey (eds) *Netherlands Yearbook of International Law* (T.M.C. Asser Press, The Hague 2003) at pp. 155-156.

[80] Political scientists generally discern four main approaches in conceptualizing democracy: constitutional, procedural, substantive and process-oriented. See C. Tilly, *Democracy* (Cambridge University Press, Cambridge 2007) at p. 7. Likewise, the UN Commission on Human Rights has recognized the "rich and diverse nature of the community of the world's democracies". See Commission on Human Rights, *Promotion of the Right to Democracy*, UN Doc. E/CN4/Res/1999/57, 28 April 1999. For an elaborate discussion of different theoretical approaches to democracy, see, for instance, F. Cunningham, *Theories of Democracy: A Critical Introduction* (Routledge, London/New York 2002).

[81] UN Secretary-General, *Support by the United Nations System of the Efforts of Governments to Promote and Consolidate New or Restored Democracies*, UN Doc. A/2/513, 21 October 1997, para. 27.

[82] UN Secretary-General, *Supplement to Reports on Democratization*, UN Doc. A/51/761, 20 December 1996, para. 1.

[83] See Thornberry, 'The Democratic or Internal Aspect of Self-Determination with Some Remarks on Federalism' at p. 116.

[84] Wheatley, 'Democracy in International Law: A European Perspective' at p. 235

[85] Raič, *Statehood and the Law of Self-Determination* at p. 277.

there are many regimes in the world which are not similar to Western parliamentarism and which may, however, be viewed as truly representative of the peoples concerned according to their own social and historic traditions. Furthermore, the Western democracies do not all present the same features. It is also an historical fact that authoritarian governments may turn out from ballot-boxes. The concepts of democracy and representation are therefore to be handled with care. It seems indispensable to advocate a concept of democracy sufficiently wide to encompass the diversity of forms of representation rooted in the culture and the history of peoples, provided their genuine will is ascertained.[86]

As such, the automatic and necessary linking of internal self-determination with the Western notion of democracy, thus imposing a particular political model on a population, would be incompatible with the core meaning of the right to self-determination itself, which involves the principle of free choice. In sum, to a certain extent, one can agree with writers who have contended that "there is no self-determination without democratic decision-making"[87] or that the internal dimension of the right to self-determination necessitates the introduction and maintenance of some form of democratic government.[88] However, it is to be emphasized that the notion of democracy involves more than just the classical Western conception, focusing on "representative legislative bodies acting under procedures of majority rule, freely elected under universal suffrage, competition for office, periodic elections and the rule of law".[89] This necessarily implies that other forms of government which are conceived as being representative and participatory by the people at issue, may also ensure respect for the right to internal self-determination. The basic principle for observance of this right and, hence, for governance, should be the freely expressed will of the people concerned.[90] As such, full respect for the political rights as granted by the ICCPR should be seen as a possible means of implementing the internal aspect of the right to self-determination. Yet, it is not the sole means towards observance of this right.

In view of the above, a caveat is appropriate here. A governmental system which entitles the people to participate in the political decision-making process by means of organizing elections, on the basis of which representatives of the population are chosen, is not necessarily a guarantee for respecting the right to internal self-determination of a people constituting a (numerical) minority group within a State.

---

[86] J. Salmon, 'Internal Aspects of the Right to Self-Determination: Towards a Democratic Legitimacy Principle?' in C. Tomuschat (ed.) *Modern Law of Self-Determination* (Martinus Nijhoff Publishers, Dordrecht/Boston/London 1993) at p. 280. In this respect, reference can be made to the constitutional structures of the Marshall Islands, Palau, the Cook Islands, Vanuatu and Fiji, where governance is based upon traditional social structures, but is nonetheless in conformity with democratic structures. See Wheatley, 'Democracy in International Law: A European Perspective' at p. 233, footnote 59.

[87] Cassese, *Self-Determination of Peoples. A Legal Reappraisal* at p. 54.

[88] Wheatley, 'Democracy in International Law: A European Perspective' at pp. 231-233.

[89] Raič, *Statehood and the Law of Self-Determination* at p. 275.

[90] *Ibid.* at p. 279.

Put differently, an electoral system which is based upon simple majoritarianism may not be said to ensure observance of the core meaning of the right to self-determination of minority groups, since the formal procedures of majority rule adhered to may be used as a cover for unequal treatment and discrimination in substance.[91] This may result in a threat to the collective identity of the people at issue.[92] While it is true that, generally, the internal dimension of the right to self-determination does not require any particular organizational outcome, in plural societies, the introduction of specific structures of participation may be instrumental in achieving and ensuring that the possibilities for effective and ongoing participation and true representation may be better achieved.[93] In this respect, arrangements such as autonomy,[94] federalism[95] or

---

[91]   Wright, 'Minority Groups, Autonomy, and Self-Determination' at pp. 616-617; Xanthaki, *Indigenous Rights and United Nations Standards. Self-Determination, Culture and Land* at pp. 160-161. This was also acknowledged by the Human Rights Committee in its General Comment on Article 25 ICCPR. See Human Rights Committee, *General Comment No. 25, Article 25: Participation in Public Affairs and the Right to Vote*, UN Doc. CCPR/C/21/Rev.1/Add.7 (1996), 12 July 1996, at para. 7.

[92]   Raič, *Statehood and the Law of Self-Determination* at p. 281.

[93]   See, for instance, K. Henrard, *Devising an Adequate System of Minority Protection: Individual Human Rights, Minority Rights and the Right to Self-Determination* (Martinus Nijhoff Publishers, The Hague 2000) at p. 315; Raič, *Statehood and the Law of Self-Determination* at p. 281; Summers, *Peoples and International Law: How Nationalism and Self-Determination Shape a Contemporary Law of Nations* at pp. 342-343; Thornberry, 'The Democratic or Internal Aspect of Self-Determination with Some Remarks on Federalism' at p. 133; Wright, 'Minority Groups, Autonomy, and Self-Determination' at pp. 608, 614.

[94]   Although there is little agreement on the precise meaning of the term, the concept of autonomy is generally understood to refer to self-government or self-rule in relation to devolved competences. As autonomy provides local actors with the competence to take decisions which concern themselves, autonomy has been the classical means of settling self-determination disputes beyond the context of decolonization. Examples in this respect are the settlement for the Åland Islands, the arrangement for the Azores in relation to Portugal, and arrangements for Aceh and West Papua in Indonesia. Autonomy can be operationalized in various ways: it may be restricted to certain issues concerning a (numerical) minority, such as their cultural matters, natural resources, and education, but it may also be extended to refer to complete self-government of a certain territory. The extent of autonomy which is granted in a particular situation is usually established in the constitution or in an autonomy statute. See, in general, Henrard, *Devising an Adequate System of Minority Protection: Individual Human Rights, Minority Rights and the Right to Self-Determination* at pp. 311-313; R. Lapidoth, *Autonomy: Flexible Solutions to Ethnic Conflicts* (United States Institute of Peace Press, Washington D.C. 1997); M. Weller, *Escaping the Self-Determination Trap* (Martinus Nijhoff Publishers, Leiden 2009) at pp. 78-90. See also J. Rehman, 'The Concept of Autonomy and Minority Rights in Europe' in P. Cumper and S. Wheatley (eds) *Minority Rights in the 'New' Europe* (Martinus Nijhoff Publishers, The Hague/London/Boston 1999) at pp. 218-219; Wright, 'Minority Groups, Autonomy, and Self-Determination' at p. 614. On the 'legal notion' of autonomy (and its different manifestations), see H. Hannum and R.B. Lillich, 'The Concept of Autonomy in International Law' (1980) 74 *American Journal of International Law* 858.

[95]   Federalism is a more symmetrical mode of organization than autonomy arrangements. The core of a federal structure, which is laid down in a constitution or basic law, is twofold. First, the territory of the State is divided into multiple components ('cantons'). Secondly, the powers within the State are divided between the government at a central level having authority within the entire State territory on the one hand, and a number of cantonal governments with authority within their demarcated territory on the other.

complex power-sharing[96] should be mentioned, as these offer enhanced self-govern-ment. Moreover, in view of the opportunities which these organizational structures offer to (minority) groups seeking to assert their separate identity, autonomy, fed-eralism and complex power-sharing are frequently seen as instruments to mediate secessionist claims or even as alternatives to secession.[97] At the same time, however, it cannot be denied that this kind of arrangement does not always prove capable of

---

With regard to the distribution of powers, subsidiarity principles are incorporated. As such, federalism provides for a balanced division of competences and, in addition, enables the development of a separate identity without obtaining a sovereign status, such a structure may indicate and simultaneously promote mutuality among the various groups residing within the State. An example of a federal-type arrangement is the United Cyprus Republic, which consists of a federal government and two equal constituent States, that is the Greek Cypriot State and the Turkish Cypriot State. See, for instance, Y. Dinstein, 'The Degree of Self-Rule of Minorities in Unitarian and Federal States' in C. Brölmann, R. Lefeber and M. Zieck (eds) *Peoples and Minorities in International Law* (Martinus Nijhoff Publishers, Dordrecht 1993); Henrard, *Devising an Adequate System of Minority Protection: Individual Human Rights, Minority Rights and the Right to Self-Determination* at pp. 308-309; Suski, 'Keeping the Lid on the Secession Kettle: A Review of Legal Interpretations Concerning Claims of Self-Determination by Minority Peoples' at pp. 193-194; Thornberry, 'The Democratic or Internal Aspect of Self-Determination with Some Remarks on Federal-ism' at pp. 133-134; Weller, *Escaping the Self-Determination Trap* at pp. 91-112.

[96]   Complex power-sharing arrangements consider a broad range of issues and do so at different levels of government. As such, complex power-sharing is a multi-dimensional system in which both horizon-tal and vertical layers of public authority are created. In the words of Marc Weller, "[t]his will include autonomous structures [and] is matched by the application of consociationalist techniques, such as gov-ernmental power-sharing, guaranteed parliamentary representation for the minority, veto rights for ethnic communities or ethno-territorial entities, the granting of minority rights and agreements on the transfer of economic resources. In addition, there is an element of international involvement in the negotiation and implementation of the settlement, and in post-conflict governance". Complex power-sharing was deployed, for instance, in relation to Bosnia and Herzegovina. See M. Weller, 'Settling Self-Determina-tion Conflicts: An Introduction' in M. Weller and B. Metzger (eds) *Settling Self-Determination Dispute: Complex Power-Sharing in Theory and Practice* (Martinus Nijhoff Publishers, Leiden/Boston 2008) at pp. xiii-xiv. Notwithstanding the positive influence the introduction of complex power-sharing arrange-ments may exert on the implementation of the right to self-determination, Steven Wheatley notes that, since internal self-determination is an ongoing right, "[a]ny proposed scheme which provides for consti-tutionally entrenched [arrangements], substitutes self-determination for pre-determination, and is unac-ceptable". See S. Wheatley, 'Minority Rights, Power Sharing and the Modern Democratic State' in P. Cumper and S. Wheatley (eds) *Minority Rights in the 'New' Europe* (Martinus Nijhoff Publishers, The Hague/London/Boston 1999) at p. 202.

[97]   See, for instance, Suski, 'Keeping the Lid on the Secession Kettle: A Review of Legal Interpretations Concerning Claims of Self-Determination by Minority Peoples'; Weller, 'Settling Self-Determination Conflicts: An Introduction' at p. xiii; M. Weller, 'Why the Legal Rules on Self-Determination Do Not Resolve Self-Determination Disputes' in M. Weller and B. Metzger (eds) *Settling Self-Determination Disputes: Complex Power-Sharing in Theory and Practice* (Martinus Nijhoff Publishers, Leiden/Boston 2008) at pp. 18-19. Weller, however, refers to these settlements as "circumven[ing] the underlying self-determination issue". See M. Weller, 'The Self-Determination Trap' (2005) 4 *Ethnopolitics* 3 at p. 27.

settling conflicts. Rather, it may even promote ethnic self-awareness while failing to accommodate grievances,[98] which might result in increased clamour for secession.[99]

In summary, the core meaning of the right to internal self-determination concerns the need to pay regard to the freely expressed will of the peoples at issue. Observance of this right is vital, since the principal aim of the right to internal self-determination boils down to the protection, preservation, strengthening and development of the 'collective identity' of a people. Above, it was demonstrated that against this background, international law appears to require a representative government and, as a consequence, political participation. From these strict prerequisites, some presuppositions naturally follow. These should be viewed as possible means of ensuring that the popular will can be freely and genuinely expressed. Subsequently, it was emphasized that although the internal dimension of the right to self-determination requires some kind of democracy in both procedure and substance, the Western-style representative democracy is by no means the sole governmental model which can meet the standard set by the right to self-determination of peoples.

3.2. The Status of the Right to Internal Self-Determination

Above, the analysis of the development of the concept of self-determination has already dealt with the shift of its status from mere political principle to legal right. Since it became apparent that the content of the internal dimension of the right to self-determination differs from that of the external dimension, it is helpful to consider the legal status of both aspects separately. For this purpose, the various sources of international law will be touched upon: international instruments, State practice, jurisprudence and legal doctrine.

As has already been demonstrated in previous sections, self-determination beyond decolonization has been acknowledged as a right of peoples in various international legal and political instruments, such as the International Human Rights Covenants of 1966, the Friendly Relations Declaration, the Helsinki Final Act and the African Charter.[100] In view of their phrasing, these relevant documents denote that even beyond the colonial context, the right to self-determination is a right of all peoples which should be observed by all States, and evidence the existence of an internal dimension to self-determination, as they indicate that self-determination primarily involves the relationship between the State and its population. As such, this internal

---

[98]   In this respect, the ethnic federalist structures in Ethiopia may serve as an example. See International Crisis Group, *Ethiopia: Ethnic Federalism and its Discontents* (2009), in particular at pp. 22-29.

[99]   See S. Wheatley, *Democracy, Minorities and International Law* (Cambridge University Press, Cambridge 2005) at p. 84.

[100]   See Section 2 of this Chapter.

dimension of self-determination cannot be excluded from self-determination as a positive legal right.[101]

This conclusion is confirmed by State practice. Today, no less than 167 States are party to the ICCPR,[102] which grants the right of peoples to internal self-determination as was demonstrated previously. States which are not party to this Covenant are in many cases party to another legal instrument which provides for the right to internal self-determination, such as the African Charter.[103] Moreover, State reports demonstrate that the internal aspect of the right to self-determination is considered to be a legal entitlement under positive international law. As was already touched upon previously in this Chapter, in their reports to the Human Rights Committee, the majority of States account – both implicitly and explicitly – for their implementation of the right to self-determination within the borders of the State, particularly in the relationship between the government and the governed.[104] In this respect, the general tendency of 'democratization' in the sense of providing for a representative government and enabling political participation of citizens should be recalled here as well.[105] Despite these developments, it cannot be denied that the legal character of the right to internal self-determination is disputed by some States. Nonetheless, as David Raič has argued, considering "the opposition by clearly oppressive regimes as evidence of the absence of a customary rule of internal self-determination is unacceptable".[106] Such an argument is in line with the position of Judge Tanaka, who in his dissenting opinion to the *South West Africa* cases wrote that a few 'dissidents' do not prohibit the possibility of creating a norm of customary international law.[107]

Furthermore, reference must be made to jurisprudence. Several judicial decisions have shown that the peoples' right to self-determination is to be qualified as a legal right under positive international law. What is more, the International Court of Justice has even declared it to have an *erga omnes* character.[108] Although this characterization

---

[101]   Rosas, 'Internal Self-Determination' at p. 239.
[102]   For the up-to-date status of this Covenant, see Office of the United Nations High Commissioner for Human Rights, *Human Rights Committee, Status of Ratification, Reservations, Declarations*, available at <http://treaties.un.org/Pages/Treaties.aspx?id=4&subid=A&lang=en>, last consulted on 5 October 2012.
[103]   Raič, *Statehood and the Law of Self-Determination* at p. 288, footnote 251.
[104]   For an analysis of this State practice, based on State reports submitted under Article 40 ICCPR, see H. Quane, 'A Right to Self-Determination for the Kosovo Albanians?' (2000) 13 *Leiden Journal of International Law* 219 at pp. 221-222. Quane conducted a survey of the periodic reports of 97 States. Of these States, 87 reports amplified on the right to self-determination. Of these reports, 69 States referred to the internal dimension of self-determination either directly or indirectly.
[105]   See Section 3.1.2 of this Chapter.
[106]   Raič, *Statehood and the Law of Self-Determination* at p. 288.
[107]   International Court of Justice, *South West Africa cases (Ethiopia v. South Africa; Liberia v. South Africa)*, Second Phase, Judgment, ICJ Reports 1966, p. 6, at p. 291, Dissenting Opinion of Judge Tanaka.
[108]   International Court of Justice, *East Timor (Portugal v. Australia)*, Judgment, ICJ Reports 1995, p. 90, at para. 29.

was made against the background of decolonization,[109] it also applies beyond this context for, in 2004, the Court underpinned this classification in the *Construction of a Wall* advisory opinion. It stated the following:

> The Court would observe that the obligations violated by Israel include certain obligations *erga omnes*. As the Court indicated in the *Barcelona Traction* case, such obligations are by their very nature "the concern of all States" and, "In view of the importance of the rights involved, all States can be held to have a legal interest in their protection" (*Barcelona Traction, Light and Power Company, Limited, Second Phase, Judgment,* ICJ Reports 1970, p. 32, para. 33). The obligations *erga omnes* violated by Israel are the obligation to respect the right of the Palestinian people to self-determination, and certain of its obligations under international humanitarian law.
>
> As regards the first of these, the Court has already observed [...] that in the *East Timor* case, it described as "irreproachable" the assertion that "the right of peoples to self-determination, as it evolved from the Charter and from United Nations practice, has an *erga omnes* character" (ICJ Reports 1995, p. 102, para. 29). The Court would also recall that under the terms of General Assembly resolution 2625 (XXV) [...], "Every State has the duty to promote, through joint and separate action, realization of the principle of equal rights and self-determination of peoples, in accordance with the provisions of the Charter, and to render assistance to the United Nations in carrying out the responsibilities entrusted to it by the Charter regarding the implementation of the principle."[110]

From the context of the above cited case and from the Court's reference to the particular phrasing of the Friendly Relations Declaration, it can be deduced that the internal dimension of the right to self-determination beyond decolonization should also be viewed as a right with an *erga omnes* character.

The proposition of internal self-determination as imposing obligations towards all members of the international community has been adopted by legal doctrine as well.[111] What is more, some authors have gone so far as to contend that internal self-determination has, in addition, become a peremptory norm of international law from which no derogation is possible, otherwise known as a norm of *jus cogens*.[112] Whether such an argument is correct is by no means undisputed. As endorsed in

---

[109] See also Chapter II, Section 4.2.2 of the present study.

[110] International Court of Justice, *Legal Consequences of the Construction of a Wall in the Occupied Palestinian Territory*, Advisory Opinion, ICJ Reports 2004, p. 136, at paras 155-156.

[111] See, for instance, Cassese, *Self-Determination of Peoples. A Legal Reappraisal* at pp. 133-134.

[112] On the concept of *jus cogens*, see I. Brownlie, *Principles of Public International Law* (6th edn, Oxford University Press, Oxford 2003) at pp. 510-512; P. Malanczuk, *Akehurst's Modern Introduction to International Law* (7th revised edn, Routledge, London/New York 1997) at pp. 57-58; M.N. Shaw, *International Law* (5th edn, Cambridge University Press, Cambridge 2003) at pp. 115-119; H. Thirlway, 'The Sources of International Law' in M.D. Evans (ed.) *International Law* (Oxford University Press, Oxford 2003) at pp. 141-142.

Article 53 of the 1969 Vienna Convention on the Law of Treaties, a rule cannot become a peremptory norm unless it is "accepted and recognized [as such] by the international community of States as a whole".[113] Although this notion of *jus cogens* appears to be generally accepted, the content of this category of norms remains rather obscure to date.[114] Consequently, it seems that there are only few rules which seem to pass this stringent test. The prohibition of the use of force, genocide, slavery and racial discrimination may be mentioned in this respect, although these examples are not uncontested either.[115] According to some writers, the right to self-determination should be added to this enumeration as well.[116] Indeed, there are signs that such a position may be correct. For instance, one might argue that the *jus cogens* character of the internal dimension of self-determination may be derived from custom.[117] Moreover, the sweeping consequences stemming from a violation of the internal aspect of the right to self-determination[118] appear to support a *jus cogens* character.[119] Nonetheless, it is to be emphasized that it is highly questionable whether the right to internal self-determination has evolved into a norm of *jus cogens* and if so, whether all elements of this right can be considered as such. Antonio Cassese, for instance, held the opinion that only particular aspects of the right to internal self-determination belong

---

[113] Texts adopted subsequently to the 1969 Vienna Convention on the Law of Treaties have employed similar language. See *Vienna Convention on the Law of Treaties Between States and International Organizations or between International Organizations*, 21 March 1986, A/Conf.129/15, Art. 53 (not entered into force). Moreover, nowadays, the concept of peremptory norms is applied outside the context of treaty law as well. See International Law Commission, 53rd session, 23 April – 1 June and 2 July – 10 August 2001, UN GAOR, 56th session, Suppl. No.10, A/56/10, *Draft Articles on Responsibility of States for International Wrongful Acts, with Commentaries*, UN Doc. A/CN.4/L.602/Rev.1, 26 July 2001, Arts 26, 40, 50(1)(d).

[114] J.R. Crawford, *The Creation of States in International Law* (2nd revised edn, Clarendon Press, Oxford 2006) at p. 101.

[115] See *ibid.* at p. 101; Shaw, *International Law* at pp. 117-118.

[116] See, for instance, Brownlie, *Principles of Public International Law* at p. 511; Cassese, *Self-Determination of Peoples. A Legal Reappraisal* at pp. 133-140; K. Doehring, 'Self-Determination' in B. Simma (ed.) *The Charter of the United Nations A Commentary* (2nd edn, Oxford University Press, Oxford 2002) at p. 62; J.A. Frowein, 'Self-Determination as a Limit to Obligations Under International Law' in C. Tomuschat (ed.) *Modern Law of Self-Determination* (Martinus Nijhoff Publishers, Dordrecht 1993) at pp. 218-221; Malanczuk, *Akehurst's Modern Introduction to International Law* at p. 327; Rosas, 'Internal Self-Determination' at p. 247. In contrast, others have denied that internal self-determination has become a norm of *jus cogens*. See, for instance, Crawford, *The Creation of States in International Law* at p. 101; Pomerance, *Self-Determination in Law and Practice* at pp. 70-72.

[117] Malanczuk, *Akehurst's Modern Introduction to International Law* at p. 58.

[118] For instance, the violation of internal self-determination may lead to an obligation of non-recognition, as happened in the case *inter alia* of Southern Rhodesia. On this issue, see Chapter VI, Section 2.1 of the present study.

[119] See Raič, *Statehood and the Law of Self-Determination* at p. 289, footnote 254. Likewise, Hugh Thirlway has argued that "it is accepted that the status of peremptory norm derives from the importance of the *content* of the norm to the international community". See Thirlway, 'The Sources of International Law' at p. 141.

to the body of *jus cogens*, specifically the right of a people to freely choose its rulers and the right of ethnic groups to have access to government.[120] In view of these uncertainties, this study will not regard the internal dimension of the right to self-determination as a norm of *jus cogens*, but merely as an obligation *erga omnes*. This finding is relevant for the purposes of the present study, as the *jus cogens* status of the right to internal self-determination could have added to the argument that the violation of this norm constitutes a breach of international law so serious that it warrants the extreme measure of unilateral secession as a remedy.

3.3. The Subjects of the Right to Internal Self-Determination

In previous sections, it has been demonstrated that self-determination extends beyond the colonial context in the form of a continuous entitlement concerning the internal relation between 'peoples' and their State. Accordingly, the subject of the right cannot be limited to ethnicities or populations of colonies and dependent territories.[121] Hence, the question arises as to what collectivities can be considered as 'peoples' holding a right to internal self-determination. Phrased differently: who are the 'self' to which the right to internal self-determination attaches?

International law does not offer an authoritative definition of who or what constitutes a 'people'.[122] Several attempts at formulating a definition have been made, but no consensus has been reached to date. The main reason for this seems to be that States fear for the proliferation of claims by 'peoples' once agreement exists on what constitutes a 'people'. The lack of definition, however, has made some commentators rather cynical about the right to self-determination. Already in 1956, W. Ivor Jennings noted:

> Nearly forty years ago a Professor of Political Science who was also President of the United States, President Wilson, enunciated a doctrine which was ridiculous, but which was widely accepted as a sensible proposition, the doctrine of self-determination. On the surface, it seemed reasonable: let the people decide. It was in fact ridiculous because the people cannot decide until someone decides who are the people.[123]

Similarly, in his comment on the Friendly Relations Declaration, Sir Gerald Fitzmaurice criticized the idea of a right to self-determination as 'nonsense', wondering

---

[120] Cassese, *Self-Determination of Peoples. A Legal Reappraisal* at pp. 133-140.

[121] See, for instance, Thornberry, 'The Democratic or Internal Aspect of Self-Determination with Some Remarks on Federalism' at pp. 119-120; UN Human Rights Committee, *Concluding Observations on Azerbaijan*, UN Doc. A/49/40, 3 August 1994, at para. 296.

[122] On the notion of a 'people' more in general, see, for instance, J.R. Crawford (ed.), *The Rights of Peoples* (Clarendon Press, Oxford 1988).

[123] W.I. Jennings, *The Approach of Self-Government* (Cambridge University Press, Cambridge 1956) at pp. 55-56.

how a legally non-existent entity could possibly be the holder of a legal right.[124] Nonetheless, there is a diversity of viewpoints on the concept of 'peoples' in the specific context of self-determination and more generally. A group of UNESCO experts, for instance, envisaged the term 'peoples' as a concept which is dynamic and might imply a different scope for different rights.[125] It does not require explanation that such a specification is not particularly helpful in seeking to determine who are the holders of the internal dimension of the right to self-determination. Therefore, the views most often presented on this issue will be discussed below.

3.3.1. All Inhabitants of a State

The first understanding of the term 'peoples' is territorial in nature: entire populations of existing States are viewed as subjects of, and hence having a right to, internal self-determination.[126] When defining 'peoples' in this fashion, neither ethnic considerations nor a colonial context are relevant. In fact, this understanding refers to the nation as the subject of the right to internal self-determination. According to Asbjørn Eide, this view is a sound one, since "[f]rom the standpoint of international law, the 'permanent population' is identical to the nation".[127] Support for this position can be found in international legal documents concerning self-determination.

First, although Article 1 ICCPR does not mention the term 'nations' and the drafting history reveals that the emphasis of the right to self-determination was on the external dimension, it has become clear that the phrase "all peoples" at least refers to people organized as States. Both Western and non-Western States agreed that self-determination should "afford a right to be free from an authoritarian regime" to all inhabitants of a State.[128] What is more, the Human Rights Committee has confirmed that the term 'peoples' is not restricted to colonial peoples, but refers to the populations of sovereign and independent States.[129] State reports submitted to the Human Rights Committee also reflect the fact that internal self-determination is primarily

---

[124] I. Sinclair, 'The Significance of the Friendly Relations Declaration' in V. Lowe and C. Warbrick (eds) *The United Nations and the Principles of International Law* (Routledge, London/New York 1994) at pp. 7- 8.

[125] UNESCO, *International Meeting of Experts on Further Study of the Concept of the Rights of Peoples. Final Report and Recommendations*, Paris, 22 February 1990, SHS-89/CONF.602/7, at paras 19, 24. See also J. Dugard, 'Secession: Is the Case of Yugoslavia a Precedent for Africa?' (1993) 5 *African Journal of International and Comparative Law* 163 at p. 171, referring to the concept of 'peoples' as being variable.

[126] See Raič, *Statehood and the Law of Self-Determination* at p. 244; Musgrave, *Self-Determination and National Minorities* at pp. 151-154 (calling this approach the "representative government definition").

[127] A. Eide, 'Territorial Integrity of States, Minority Protection, and Guarantees for Autonomy Arrangements: Approaches and Roles of the United Nations' (Local Self-Government, Territorial Integrity and Protection of Minorities 1996) at para. 2.2.

[128] See Cassese, *Self-Determination of Peoples. A Legal Reappraisal* at pp. 50-51, 59-60.

[129] See Wheatley, *Democracy, Minorities and International Law* at p. 80.

implemented as being a right for the entire population of a territory.[130] Such an interpretation is also endorsed by judicial decision of the Supreme Court of Canada in the case *Reference re Secession of Quebec*, although the Supreme Court argued that the subjects of the right cannot be restricted to "the entirety of a State's population" only.[131] Furthermore, the Friendly Relations Declaration more explicitly states that the right to self-determination is complied with when States provide for a government which represents "the whole people belonging to the territory".[132] The Vienna Declaration and Programme of Action contains a similarly phrased statement.[133] Finally, the Helsinki Final Act should be mentioned here, as its *travaux préparatoires* make clear that the term 'peoples' was intended to refer to peoples organized as nations in the first place.[134] In sum, it can be concluded that evidence exists for the view that nations are subjects of the right to internal self-determination under international law.

3.3.2. Subgroups within States

A question which has yet remained unanswered is whether – in addition to the entire population of a State – certain subgroups within States may also be considered as subjects of the right to internal self-determination. This issue will be touched upon below. As already noted, the Friendly Relations Declaration stresses that the right to self-determination requires "a government representing the whole people to the territory"; a phrase which is supplemented with the words "without distinction as to race, creed or colour".[135] This addition, which can be found in the Vienna Declaration and Programme of Action in similar wording,[136] appears to provide an argument for extending the applicability of internal self-determination to separate groups within

---

[130] Quane, 'A Right to Self-Determination for the Kosovo Albanians?' at pp. 221-222.

[131] Supreme Court of Canada, *Reference re Secession of Quebec*, 20 August 1998, [1998] 2 S.C.R. 217, at para. 124. For an examination and discussion of this case from the perspective of international law, see P. Dumberry, 'Lessons Learned from the *Quebec Secession Reference* before the Supreme Court of Canada' in M.G. Kohen (ed.) *Secession International Law Perspectives* (Cambridge University Press, Cambridge 2006). See also Section of Chapter IV, Section 2.3.4 of this study.

[132] UN General Assembly Resolution 2625 (XXV) (*Declaration on Principles of International Law Concerning Friendly Relations and Co-operation Among States in Accordance with the Charter of the United Nations*), UN Doc. A/Res/2625 (XXV), 24 October 1970, Principle V, at para. 7.

[133] World Conference on Human Rights, *Vienna Declaration and Programme of Action*, adopted on 25 June 1993, UN Doc. A/CONF.157/23, 12 July 1993, at para. 2.

[134] See Cassese, *Self-Determination of Peoples. A Legal Reappraisal* at pp. 265-266.

[135] UN General Assembly Resolution 2625 (XXV) (*Declaration on Principles of International Law Concerning Friendly Relations and Co-operation Among States in Accordance with the Charter of the United Nations*), UN Doc. A/Res/2625 (XXV), 24 October 1970, Principle V, at para. 7.

[136] The Vienna Declaration and Programme of Action stipulates that States conduct themselves in compliance with the principle of equal rights and self-determination if they provide for "a government representing the whole people belonging to the territory *without distinction of any kind*" (emphasis added). See World Conference on Human Rights, *Vienna Declaration and Programme of Action*, adopted on 25 June 1993, UN Doc. A/CONF.157/23, 12 July 1993, at para. 2.

a State.[137] Yet, several other arguments can be mentioned for broadening the field of application of the right. First of all, in the international instruments containing references to self-determination, the term 'peoples' is often used simultaneously with words such as 'nations' or 'States', which seems to be indicative of a difference in meaning between these two terms.[138] An additional argument for assuming that not only entire populations of a State are subjects of the right to self-determination can be found in the fact that international documents emphasize that the right to self-determination may only be exercised within the limits of the principle of territorial integrity of States. This caveat can only imply that distinct divisions of the State are holders of the right to self-determination as well, since, in the words of Erica-Irene Daes:

> It would have been unnecessary to make such a qualification unless it was understood that the population of a State could consist of a number of 'peoples', each possessing the right of self-determination.[139]

The Supreme Court of Canada held the same view, as it concluded in its judgment that:

> [t]o restrict the definition of the term to the population of existing States would render the granting of a right to self-determination largely duplicative, given the parallel emphasis within the majority of the source documents on the need to protect the territorial integrity of existing States, and would frustrate its remedial purpose.[140]

Finally, David Raič has added an argument derived from a theoretical point of view. He aptly noted that broadening the field of application of the right to internal self-determination to subgroups seems to be "a logical and necessary consequence of the *raison d'être* of self-determination", which involves, *inter alia*, the promotion and protection of the collective identity of a group. The majority of States are not ethnically homogeneous territories, but rather accommodate more than one ethnic group. Considering the fact that these ethnic groups are often in a non-dominant position within the State, it can be contended that with respect to these (ethnic) subgroups, the

---

[137] See, for instance, Quane, 'A Right to Self-Determination for the Kosovo Albanians?' at p. 223; Raič, *Statehood and the Law of Self-Determination* at p. 255.

[138] Supreme Court of Canada, *Reference re Secession of Quebec*, 20 August 1998, [1998] 2 S.C.R. 217, at para. 124. See also Raič, *Statehood and the Law of Self-Determination* at p. 249.

[139] UN Commission on Human Rights, Sub-Commission on Prevention of Discrimination and Protection of Minorities, Working Group on Indigenous Populations, *Standard-Setting Activities: Evolution of Standards Concerning the Rights of Indigenous Peoples. Working Paper by the Chairperson-Rapporteur, Mrs. Erica-Irene A. Daes, on the concept of "indigenous people"*, UN Doc. E/CN.4/Sub.2-AC.4/1996/2 (1996), at para. 19.

[140] Supreme Court of Canada, *Reference re Secession of Quebec*, [1998] 2 S.C.R. 217, at para. 124.

protection of collective identity is more vital than with regard to nations as a whole, for their position is more vulnerable.[141]

Obviously, identifying subgroups within a State as the subjects of the right to internal self-determination is much more difficult than indicating nations as the subjects of this right. In order to justify a claim for internal self-determination, it is often argued that a subgroup needs to satisfy the criterion of collective individuality, as not every social or political group constitutes a 'people'.[142] Collective individuality is generally seen to determine the 'peoplehood' of a group and is based on the idea that "there can be no 'me' if there is no 'you', so there can be no 'us' if there is no 'them'".[143] In essence, it concerns a factual question rather than a legal one. Yet, since the identification of collective individuality may have significant implications for the application of international law, it is important to phrase the relevant criteria as accurately as possible.

First, an objective element can be discerned in the concept of collective individuality: the members of the group concerned share objectively identifiable common features, which distinguishes them from other groups which do not share these common features. In this respect, this may concern some or all or the following features: "(a) a (historical) territorial connection, on which territory the group forms a majority; (b) a common history; (c) a common ethnic identity or origin; (d) a common language; (e) a common culture; (f) a common religion or ideology".[144] The term 'objective' does not imply that the features referred to cannot change over time or that these features exist completely independent from the decisions and opinions of the subgroup itself. Rather, it refers to those features which are 'objectively' perceptible for outside observers and which are often associated with an ethnic group.[145] While it usually depends on the specific context which of the features present themselves as regards a particular group,[146] the territorial connection is often referred to as a

---

[141] Raič, *Statehood and the Law of Self-Determination* at p. 248.

[142] See J. Wilson, 'Ethnic Groups and the Right to Self-Determination' (1996) 11 *Connecticut Journal of International Law* 433 at p. 440; Hannum, 'Rethinking Self-Determination' at pp. 35-36.

[143] Wilson, 'Ethnic Groups and the Right to Self-Determination' at p. 440.

[144] Raič, *Statehood and the Law of Self-Determination* at p. 262. For a similar enumeration, see UNESCO, *International Meeting of Experts on Further Study of the Concept of the Rights of Peoples. Final Report and Recommendations*, Paris, 22 February 1990, SHS-89/CONF.602/7, at para. 22; UN Commission on Human Rights, Sub-Commission on the Prevention of Discrimination and Protection of Minorities, *The Right to Self-Determination: Historical and Current Development on the Basis of United Nations Instruments. Study Prepared by A. Cristescu*, UN Doc. E/CN.4/Sub.2/404/Rev.1 (1981), at pp. 40-41.

[145] Raič, *Statehood and the Law of Self-Determination* at p. 263.

[146] See J. Klabbers and R. Lefeber, 'Africa: Lost Between Self-Determination and *Uti Possidetis*' in C. Brölmann, R. Lefeber and M. Zieck (eds) *Peoples and Minorities in International Law* (Martinus Nijhoff Publishers, Dordrecht 1993) at p. 39.

necessary condition for collective individuality. It should be stressed, however, that this criterion *an sich* is insufficient in this respect.[147]

Secondly, a subjective element is present in the criterion of collective individuality:

> the belief of being a distinct people distinguishable from any other people inhabiting the globe, and the wish to be recognized as such, as well as the wish to maintain, strengthen and develop the group's identity.[148]

Considering the aforementioned elements, in essence, the 'peoplehood' of a group is determined by a combination of objective and subjective features.[149] This is not to say, however, that determining whether a particular subgroup actually meets the requirements of collective individuality and can thus be identified as a subject of the right to (internal) self-determination is without any difficulties. Since the concept of collective individuality is a relative one, which merely determines the 'peoplehood' of a subgroup in comparison with other subgroups, it may be complicated to clearly distinguish between these groups for the purpose of delimiting the 'people' at hand.[150] Furthermore, as the subjective element concerns the internal perception of the subgroup itself, this feature may not always be visible. Consequently, it may be difficult for outside observers to ascertain whether the subjective element is present.[151] At the same time, however, it is often contended that the subjective element is the most important criterion for 'peoplehood'. For, the objective characteristics will only be maintained as long as the members of the group actually have the will to preserve these objective features which distinguish them from any other people.[152] All in all, it can be concluded that while the practical application ma be rather complicated, those subgroups within States which satisfy the criterion of collective individuality may also be seen as the subjects of the right to internal self-determination under international law.

---

[147] See Murswiek, 'The Issue of a Right of Secession – Reconsidered' at p. 37; Raič, *Statehood and the Law of Self-Determination* at pp. 263-264.

[148] *Ibid.*, at pp. 262-263. See also Thornberry, 'The Democratic or Internal Aspect of Self-Determination with Some Remarks on Federalism' at p. 124.

[149] Wilson, 'Ethnic Groups and the Right to Self-Determination' at p. 440.

[150] See K. Knop, *Diversity and Self-Determination in International Law* (Cambridge University Press, Cambridge 2002) at p. 80,

[151] For a similar argument in the context of identifying minorities and indigenous peoples, and for several suggestions to overcome this problem, see A.K. Meijknecht, *Towards International Personality: The Position of Minorities and Indigenous Peoples in International Law* (School of Human Rights Research Series, Intersentia/Hart, Antwerp/Groningen/Oxford 2001) at pp. 86-93.

[152] See K. Knop, *Diversity and Self-Determination in International Law* at p. 80,

3.3.3. Minorities

The relevant international documents on self-determination seem to point towards a difference between the concept of 'people' and that of 'minority'. For, the international instruments dealing with the right to self-determination do not explicitly include minorities as bearers of the right. Moreover, the international instruments dealing with the rights of minorities do not include any express reference to the right of self-determination of these groups.[153] Yet, a subsequent question which may arise is whether minorities are also meant to refer to 'peoples' as subgroups within a State, hence bearing a right to internal self-determination as well.

Although minorities are recognized as a set of 'groups' within international human rights law,[154] and although various (working) definitions of the term 'minority' have been formulated by various authors,[155] no legal definition has been formally accepted yet.[156] States are generally unwilling to accept such a definition as they are aware and afraid of the risk that groups on their territory will lay claims, including secessionist demands. Moreover, it should be borne in mind that a great variety of minority groups exists worldwide, as a result of which it is complicated to subsume all these groups with their particular characteristics under one and the same abstract 'heading'. Nonetheless, the (working) definitions which have been proposed over time do reveal some recurring elements, some of which are objective, while others are subjective in nature. With respect to the objective elements, a numerical factor is often included, requiring that the group concerned constitutes less than half of the population of the State. A related component is that of non-dominance, which demands that the group concerned is in a non-dominant position within society. Even when a group constitutes a numerical minority within the State, this element would preclude that group from being a minority under international law if it holds a dominant position within

---

[153] Raič, *Statehood and the Law of Self-Determination* at p. 265.

[154] See Wilson, 'Ethnic Groups and the Right to Self-Determination' at pp. 465-468.

[155] See UN Commission on Human Rights, Sub-Commission on the Prevention of Discrimination and Protection of Minorities, *Study on the Rights of Persons Belonging to Ethnic, Religious and Linguistic Minorities. Study Prepared by F. Capotorti*, UN Doc. E/CN.4/Sub.2/384/Add.1-7 (1991) at para. 568; UN Commission on Human Rights, Sub-Commission on the Prevention of Discrimination and Protection of Minorities, *United Nations Sub-Commission on the Prevention of Discrimination and Protection of Minorities. Proposal Concerning a Definition of the Term 'Minority'. Report Submitted by Mr Jules Deschênes*, UN Doc. E/CN.4/Sub.2/1985/31 (1985) at para. 181; UN Commission on Human Rights, Sub-Commission on the Prevention of Discrimination and Protection of Minorities, *Protection of Minorities, Possible Ways and Means of Facilitating the Peaceful and Constructive Solution of Problems Involving Minorities. Report Submitted by Asbjørn Eide*, UN Doc. E/CN.4/Sub.2/1993/34 (1993) at para. 29. See also Henrard, *Devising an Adequate System of Minority Protection: Individual Human Rights, Minority Rights and the Right to Self-Determination* at pp. 21-24, discussing the definitions proposed by Capotorti, Deschênes and Eide.

[156] See, for instance, Meijknecht, *Towards International Personality: The Position of Minorities and Indigenous Peoples in International Law* at pp. 70-71.

society. The rationale of this feature is that dominant minorities would not need the special protection which minorities are granted. A third recurring objective component is that of nationality. This element implies that only those groups composed of individuals who are nationals or citizens of the State can be considered to form a minority, thus excluding people temporarily residing in a country, such as immigrants and migrant workers,[157] refugees and nomads.[158] Whatever the accuracy of these recurring elements, it appears that the core features of a minority are a certain (objective) distinctiveness of the group from the rest of the population and the (subjective) will to be recognized as a separate entity.[159] The objective feature requires that the group has certain ethnic, religious or linguistic characteristics which distinguish it from the rest of the population of the State. The subjective element demands some kind of self-identification on the part of the minority. It is vital for its status as a minority that the group has the wish to exist and to be recognized as an entity with a distinct identity, and to preserve this distinctiveness.[160]

Having established that minority groups are generally characterized by this combination of objective and subjective features, it is to be noted that the aim of (the various systems of) minority protection is generally twofold. On the one hand, it is to ensure that minorities are placed on an equal footing with other nationals of the State, thus implementing the principle of non-discrimination. On the other hand, it is to protect and promote the separate identity of minorities, including for instance their ethnic, religious and linguistic characteristics.[161] In view of these objectives, including minority groups within the set of subjects of the right to internal self-determination would not seem incongruous considering the *raison d'être* of the right, which

---

[157] It should be noted, however, that immigrant communities and migrant workers cannot be excluded from the rights enshrined in Article 27 of the ICCPR. See Henrard, *Devising an Adequate System of Minority Protection: Individual Human Rights, Minority Rights and the Right to Self-Determination* at pp. 37-42. Moreover, immigrant communities and migrant workers are sometimes suggested to form a category of 'new' minorities. On this issue, see, for instance, R.M. Letschert, 'Successful Integration While Respecting Diversity: 'Old' Minorities Versus 'New' Minorities' (2007) 18 *Helsinki Monitor* 46.

[158] See Henrard, *Devising an Adequate System of Minority Protection: Individual Human Rights, Minority Rights and the Right to Self-Determination* at pp. 30-42; Meijknecht, *Towards International Personality: The Position of Minorities and Indigenous Peoples in International Law* at pp. 77-85.

[159] See Henrard, *Devising an Adequate System of Minority Protection: Individual Human Rights, Minority Rights and the Right to Self-Determination* at pp. 43-45; Meijknecht, *Towards International Personality: The Position of Minorities and Indigenous Peoples in International Law* at p. 70; M.N. Shaw, 'The Definition of Minorities in International Law' in Y. Dinstein (ed.) *The Protection of Minorities and Human Rights* (Martinus Nijhoff Publishers, Dordrecht/Boston/London 1992) at pp. 23-31.

[160] See M. van den Bosch and W.J.M. van Genugten, 'International Protection of Migrant Workers, National Minorities and Indigenous Peoples – Comparing Underlying Concepts' (2002) 9 *International Journal on Minority and Group Rights* 195 at pp. 198-199; Meijknecht, *Towards International Personality: The Position of Minorities and Indigenous Peoples in International Law* at p. 87.

[161] See Henrard, *Devising an Adequate System of Minority Protection: Individual Human Rights, Minority Rights and the Right to Self-Determination* at pp. 8-11.

concerns, amongst other things, the protection of the collective (or, separate) identity of a group.[162] As Dietrich Murswiek put it:

> The intrinsic idea of the right to self-determination is to provide every people with the possibility to live under those political, social and cultural conditions that correspond best with its characteristic singularity, and above all to protect and develop its own identity.[163]

Indeed, various international instruments have recognized the importance of political participation by subgroups within a State, including minorities.[164] In Article 27 of the ICCPR, it was stipulated that (persons belonging to) ethnic, religious or linguistic minorities have the collective right "to enjoy their own culture, to profess and practice their own religion, or to use their own language". In this respect, it may be contended that:

> there seems to be no reason, in law, why a minority cannot constitute a 'people'. There may be strong political objections to this position, but those objections stem from fears regarding the concept of self-determination, particularly the equating of a right of self-determination with a right to secede.[165]

Although it is true that the aforementioned core features of a minority (i.e. distinctiveness and self-identification) bear a resemblance to some important characteristics of subgroups constituting a 'people' as was discussed previously,[166] minority groups

---

[162] This was also concluded by the Commission of Jurists in the *Åland Islands* case, as it noted that the principle of self-determination and the protection of minorities "have a common object – to assure some national groups the maintenance and free development of its social, ethnical or religious characteristics". See *Report of the International Commission of Jurists (Larnaude, Huber, Struycken)*, LNOJ Special Supplement No. 3 (October 1920), at para. 3. See also Henrard, *Devising an Adequate System of Minority Protection: Individual Human Rights, Minority Rights and the Right to Self-Determination* at pp. 315-316, and Chapter IV, Section 2.3.1 of the present study.

[163] Murswiek, 'The Issue of a Right of Secession – Reconsidered' at p. 38.

[164] See Thornberry, 'The Democratic or Internal Aspect of Self-Determination with Some Remarks on Federalism' at p. 127, referring to, *inter alia*, the Helsinki Final Act and the Copenhagen Document, both drafted by the Conference on Security and Co-operation in Europe. See also Section 2.3 of the present Chapter, elaborating on these documents. More specifically, reference can be made to discussions on the report of Iraq which was submitted to the Human Rights Committee. One of the Committee members argued that everyone "including minorities, had the right to take part in the political system and social destiny; if that was not the case, they did not enjoy their right to self-determination". See Rosalyn Higgins on the third periodic report of Iraq, UN Doc. CCPR/C/SR.1108 at para. 65, quoted in Thornberry, 'The Democratic or Internal Aspect of Self-Determination with Some Remarks on Federalism' at p. 127. Yet, it was not made explicit that the references to internal self-determination for minorities do include ethnic and national minorities as well.

[165] Wright, 'Minority Groups, Autonomy, and Self-Determination' at p. 627.

[166] This was also observed by Patrick Thornberry, who aptly noted that the descriptions of 'people' and of 'minority' "can be compared (and confused) [...] since they revolve around essentially the same

do not necessarily constitute subgroups in the sense of 'peoples' enjoying a right to internal self-determination. First, it should be noted that international law generally does not consider minority groups as right bearers, but rather, rights are granted to 'persons belonging' to minorities. Thus, these persons bear individual rights as a consequence of their belonging to a minority, while eventually it is the minority group which exercises the right.[167] This idea has been referred to as concept of 'in-community-with-others-rights': individual human rights which can be exercised in community with other members of a certain group.[168] Article 27 ICCPR is an example in this respect. Furthermore, the feature of collective individuality, reflecting the 'people-hood' of a group that makes one particular group discernible from others, may operate as an important distinguishing aspect between the concepts of 'people' (including subgroups) and 'minority'. It has been argued by David Raič that not all minority groups seem to possess this characteristic of collective individuality. His argument stems from the observation that the distinctiveness of a minority, as referred to in various working definitions,

> essentially concern[s] the distinctiveness of a 'minority' in relation to the rest of the population (the majority) of the State wherein such a 'minority' resides. Thus, the characteristic of distinctiveness in the case of 'minorities' (which do not constitute a 'people' in an anthropological sense) does not relate to communities beyond the external borders of that State.[169]

In this connection, it is important to elaborate on the term 'ethnic' or 'national minority', which is often included in documents on the rights of minorities. This term is most commonly used to refer to collectivities inhabiting one particular State, while their kith and kin have created their own State. The Serb minority in Croatia, for instance, exemplifies this respect.[170] Even though these groups do have a 'sense of community',[171] ethnic or national minorities generally do not satisfy the subjective criterion of collective individuality,[172] as they "cannot (apart from the geographical

---

characteristics". See Thornberry, 'The Democratic or Internal Aspect of Self-Determination with Some Remarks on Federalism' at p. 125. See also Section 3.3.2 of this Chapter.

[167] See Meijknecht, *Towards International Personality: The Position of Minorities and Indigenous Peoples in International Law* at p. 171.

[168] On this category of rights in the context of migrant workers, national minorities and indigenous peoples, see Van den Bosch and Van Genugten, 'International Protection of Migrant Workers, National Minorities and Indigenous Peoples – Comparing Underlying Concepts' at pp. 216-225.

[169] Raič, *Statehood and the Law of Self-Determination* at p. 267.

[170] See *ibid.* at p. 268.

[171] See Shaw, 'The Definition of Minorities in International Law' at pp. 27-28.

[172] As was noted previously, both objective and subjective criteria are to be met before a group can be said to possess a collective individuality. The objective elements involve (a) a (historical) territorial connection, on which territory the group forms a majority; (b) a common history; (c) a common ethnic identity or origin; (d) a common language; (e) a common culture; (f) a common religion or ideology. The

factor) and, indeed, do not wish to be distinguished from their kith and kin residing in the kin State".[173] Consequently, it appears that ethnic or national minorities do not constitute peoples as subgroups within the State which are considered to be subjects of the right to internal self-determination.[174] Rather, the members of these minority groups may claim minority rights only.[175] As Raič aptly noted, although such a distinction may be morally reprehensible, it seems that this is the way things are under contemporary international law.[176]

The exclusion of ethnic or national minorities as subjects of the right to internal self-determination, however, is not to say that a minority can never and will never in the future qualify as a 'people' within the meaning of that concept. First, it should be emphasized that, in some instances, minority groups can possess the characteristic of collective individuality and, hence, at the same time constitute a 'people' as the subject of the right to internal self-determination. As such, reference can be made to ethnic groups which constitute a numerical minority in relation to the other the inhabitants of the State in which they reside, which can and wish to be distinguished from the rest of the population of that State as well as from those residing in the kin State.[177]

Secondly, it might be argued that contemporary international practice reveals a careful tendency towards extending the scope of the right to internal self-determination to ethnic or national minorities.[178] This seems to be suggested by the international response to the Kosovo crisis. From the support for substantial autonomy for

---

subjective element concerns the wish of the group to exist and to be recognized as an entity with a distinct identity. See Section 3.3.2 of the present Chapter.

[173] Raič, *Statehood and the Law of Self-Determination* at p. 269.

[174] See also C. Ryngaert and C.W. Griffioen, 'The Relevance of the Right to Self-Determination in the Kosovo Matter: In Partial Response to the Agora Papers' (2009) *Chinese Journal of International Law – Advance Access* at paras 11-12.

[175] For members of a minority, a right comparable to the people's right to self-determination can be found in Article 27 ICCPR.

[176] Raič, *Statehood and the Law of Self-Determination* at p. 270.

[177] See *ibid.* at p. 269. See also Ryngaert and Griffioen, 'The Relevance of the Right to Self-Determination in the Kosovo Matter: In Partial Response to the Agora Papers' at para. 12, contending that "minorities and peoples are no mutually exclusive terms". But see Rosalyn Higgins, who was of the opinion that minorities are under no circumstances entitled to self-determination since the rights of people belonging to minorities are contained in Article 27 ICCPR. Higgins maintained that "one cannot [...] assert that minorities are *peoples* and therefore minorities are entitled to the right of self-determination. This is simply to ignore the fact that the Political Covenant provides for two discrete rights". See R. Higgins, 'Postmodern Tribalism and the Right to Secession. Comments' in C. Brölmann, R. Lefeber and M. Zieck (eds) *Peoples and Minorities in International Law* (Martinus Nijhoff Publishers, Dordrecht 1993) at p. 32.

[178] See, for instance, Henrard, *Devising an Adequate System of Minority Protection: Individual Human Rights, Minority Rights and the Right to Self-Determination* at pp. 315-316; Raič, *Statehood and the Law of Self-Determination* at pp. 270-271; P. Thornberry, *International Law and the Rights of Minorities* (Clarendon Press, Oxford 2001) at pp. 14-15.

the Kosovo Albanians as expressed in several texts elaborating on the future political status of Kosovo, one might deduce that ethnic or national minorities can be considered to constitute peoples for the purpose of the right to internal self-determination.[179] However, one should be cautious in drawing (far-reaching) conclusions. Although the UN Security Council has on several occasions unambiguously commented that the future status of Kosovo should be based on a "substantially greater degree of autonomy and meaningful self-administration",[180] it is to be noted that reference to the concept of self-determination in this context remained forthcoming. Rather, it appears that the support for autonomy arrangements with respect to Kosovo was expressed against the backdrop of minority rights and minority protection. And even though the opinion concerning the right to self-determination as drafted by the Arbitration Committee[181] may invoke the impression that ethnic groups within States, such as the Kosovo Albanians, do possess a confined right to internal self-determination, the juridical importance of this opinion may be subverted for several reasons. Generally, the weight of the opinion is undermined because the European Commission did not always consider the Committee's opinions to be binding. More specifically, in this particular opinion on self-determination,[182] the Committee provided few arguments underpinning its conclusion, despite the fact that this conclusion was not in line with State practice on the matter.[183] As such, for the time being, conclusions to

---

[179] See Quane, 'A Right to Self-Determination for the Kosovo Albanians?' at pp. 219-220; Ryngaert and Griffioen, 'The Relevance of the Right to Self-Determination in the Kosovo Matter: In Partial Response to the Agora Papers' at para. 12. But see G. Lauwers and S. Smis, 'New Dimensions of the Right to Self-Determination: A Study of the International Response to the Kosovo Crisis' (2000) 6 *Nationalism and Ethnic Politics* 43 at pp. 55-57.

[180] UN Security Council Resolution 1160 (1998) (*On the letters from the United Kingdom (S/1998/223) and the United States (S/1998/272)*), UN Doc. S/Res/1160, 31 March 1998, at para. 5. See also UN Security Council Resolution 1199(1998) (*On the situation in Kosovo (FRY)*), UN Doc. S/Res/1199, 23 September 1998, Preamble, at para. 12; UN Security Council Resolution 1203 (1999) (*On the situation in Kosovo*), UN Doc. S/Res/1203, 24 October 1998, Preamble, at para. 8; UN Security Council Resolution 1244 (1999) (*On the situation relating Kosovo*), UN Doc. S/Res/1244, 10 June 1999, Preamble, at para. 11.

[181] In August 1991, during a peace conference on Yugoslavia, the Arbitration Committee was created by the European Economic Community (EEC) and its Member States. This Committee is better known as the Badinter Arbitration Committee, named after its chairman Robert Badinter, who was President of the French Constitutional Council. Other members of the Committee were the Presidents of the German and Italian Constitutional Courts, the Belgian Court of Arbitration and the Spanish Constitutional Tribunal. The Badinter Arbitration Committee was given the mandate to issue binding decisions upon request from "valid Yugoslavian authorities". See A. Pellet, 'The Opinions of the Badinter Arbitration Committee: A Second Breath for the Self-Determination of Peoples' (1992) 3 *European Journal of International Law* 178 at p. 178.

[182] Arbitration Committee of the Conference on Yugoslavia, *Opinion No. 2 (Self-Determination)*, 11 January 1992. See International Conference on the Former Yugoslavia, 'Opinions No. 1-3 of the Arbitration Commission of the International Conference on Yugoslavia' (1992) 3 *European Journal of International Law* 182 at pp. 183-184.

[183] See Quane, 'A Right to Self-Determination for the Kosovo Albanians?' at p. 225.

the extent that the international response to the events in Kosovo have contributed to the evolution of the right to self-determination, in the sense that its internal dimension can also be invoked by ethnic and national minorities, seem premature.[184] Nonetheless, these responses do not preclude future developments as regards extending the right to internal self-determination to ethnic and national minorities. More than that, they may even have laid the foundations for such developments.

In conclusion, so far, two categories of subjects of the right to internal self-determination can be identified beyond the colonial context: entire populations of existing sovereign States and subgroups within such States. Minority groups may only be viewed as subgroups covered by the second category if they possess collective individuality. The aforementioned findings justify adding another feature to the internal right to self-determination: the group characteristic. After all, it has emerged that international law does not recognize individual human beings as holders of the right to self-determination, but merely groups. This may be called the 'surplus value' of the right to self-determination,[185] or simply what sets this particular right apart from the collection of individual rights and freedoms as provided for in the ICCPR and ICESCR.

3.3.4. Indigenous Peoples

Having considered whether subgroups within States and minorities are subjects of the internal dimension of the right to self-determination of peoples, one may wonder whether indigenous peoples are viewed to be subjects of this right as well. To answer this question, the notion of indigenous peoples merits some explanation first. Over time, various (working) definitions and sets of criteria have been proposed. The term indigenous peoples was initially used to refer to the descendants of the inhabitants of a territory prior to its Western colonization.[186] In this respect, the definition used in the study conducted by Special Rapporteur José R. Martínez Cobo is relevant:

> Indigenous communities, peoples and nations are those which, *having a historical continuity with pre-invasion and pre-colonial societies* that developed on their territories, consider themselves distinct from other sectors of the societies now prevailing in those territories, or parts of them. They form at present non-dominant sectors of society and are determined to preserve, develop and transmit to future generations their ancestral territories, and their ethnic identity, as the basis of their continued existence as peoples, in accordance with their own cultural patterns, social institutions and legal systems.[187]

---

[184] See *ibid.* at p. 227; Raič, *Statehood and the Law of Self-Determination* at p. 272.

[185] See, for instance, *ibid.* at pp. 239-240.

[186] See International Law Association, Committee on the Rights of Indigenous Peoples, *Interim Report*, The Hague Conference (2010), at p. 7.

[187] UN Commission on Human Rights, Sub-Commission on Prevention of Discrimination and Protection of Minorities, *Study of the Problem of Discrimination Against Indigenous Populations, Final Report*,

Consequently, this definition covers well-known communities such as the Aborigines, Inuit, and Maori, but excludes other groups, such as the Saami people, who had not suffered from colonial oppression. As a result of the adoption of ILO Convention No. 169 on Indigenous and Tribal Peoples,[188] which contains a slightly broader definition, these communities were also included.[189] Article 1.2 of ILO Convention No. 169 describes indigenous peoples as follows:

> Peoples in independent countries who are regarded as indigenous on account of their descent from the populations which inhabited the country, or a geographical region to which the country belongs, at the time of conquest or colonization or the establishment of present State boundaries and who, irrespective of their legal status, retain some or all of their own social, economic, cultural and political institutions.

So far, this Convention has been ratified by twenty States only, as a consequence of which the abovementioned definition cannot be seen to be universally accepted.[190] Despite sustained efforts, it has proved difficult to formulate a definition which meets with general approval. Nonetheless, a number of core elements can be derived from the various attempts to define the notion of 'indigenous peoples'. As Asbjørn Eide aptly noted, while "controversial in its boundaries", "[t]he definition of indigenous peoples is clear enough at its core".[191] The International Law Association's Committee on the Rights of Indigenous Peoples suggested the following indicia for ascertaining whether a certain community can be considered as an indigenous people: self-identification, historical continuity, special relationship with ancestral lands, distinctiveness, non-dominance and perpetuation.[192] According to the Committee, merely two of these indicia are crucial, that is the special relationship with ancestral lands, and the self-identification as both indigenous and as a people.[193] This approach reflects the well-known combination of an objective and a subjective element respectively.[194]

---

submitted by the Special Rapporteur Mr. José R. Martínez Cobo, UN Doc. E/CN.4/Sub.2/1986/7 and Add. 1-4, at para. 379 (emphasis added).

[188] International Labour Organization, *Convention Concerning Indigenous and Tribal Peoples in Independent Countries*, ILO Convention C169, adopted 27 June 1989, entered into force 5 September 1991.

[189] See A. Eide, 'Rights of Indigenous Peoples. Achievements in International Law During the Last Quarter of a Century' (2006) 37 *Netherlands Yearbook of International Law* 155 at p. 187.

[190] See International Labour Organization, *Indigenous and Tribal Peoples*, <http://www.ilo.org/indigenous/lang--en/index.htm>, last consulted on 24 September 2012.

[191] Eide, 'Rights of Indigenous Peoples. Achievements in International Law During the Last Quarter of a Century' at p. 186.

[192] International Law Association, Committee on the Rights of Indigenous Peoples, *Interim Report*, The Hague Conference (2010), at pp. 7-8.

[193] International Law Association, Committee on the Rights of Indigenous Peoples, *Final Report*, Sofia Conference (2012), at p. 3.

[194] International Law Association, Committee on the Rights of Indigenous Peoples, *Final Report*, Sofia Conference (2012), at pp. 2-3. See also Section 3.3.2 and 3.3.3 of the present Chapter.

Over the last two decades, the attention for the position of indigenous peoples under international law has increased significantly.[195] This development was highlighted by the adoption of the UN Declaration on the Rights of Indigenous Peoples (UNDRIP) in 2007.[196] Being a General Assembly resolution, the Declaration concerns a legally non-binding document *per se* and its content as a whole cannot yet be seen to constitute customary international law. Nonetheless, it should be noted that some of its key provisions do reflect general principles of international law or even existing customary rules.[197] Moreover, it seems that those provisions not yet corresponding to customary norms may be seen as emerging customary law as they "express the aspirations of the world's indigenous peoples, as well as of States, in their move to improve existing standard for the safeguarding of indigenous peoples' human rights".[198]

Yet, it should not go by unrecorded that the drafting of this Declaration was a long-term and intricate process,[199] during which indigenous peoples have dedicated

---

[195] See, for instance, Eide, 'Rights of Indigenous Peoples. Achievements in International Law During the Last Quarter of a Century'; Wheatley, *Democracy, Minorities and International Law* at pp. 109-123; Xanthaki, *Indigenous Rights and United Nations Standards. Self-Determination, Culture and Land* at pp. 47-127.

[196] UN General Assembly Resolution 61/295 (*United Nations Declaration on the Rights of Indigenous Peoples*), UN Doc. A/Res/61/295, 13 September 2007. The Declaration was adopted by a majority of 144 states in favour, 4 votes against (Australia, Canada, New Zealand and the United States), and 11 abstentions (Azerbaijan, Bangladesh, Bhutan, Burundi, Colombia, Georgia, Kenya, Nigeria, Russian Federation, Samoa and Ukraine).

[197] International Law Association, Committee on the Rights of Indigenous Peoples, *Resolution No. 5/2012, Rights of Indigenous Peoples*, 75th Conference of the International Law Association held in Sofia, Bulgaria, 26-30 August 2012, at para. 2. See also International Law Association, Committee on the Rights of Indigenous Peoples, *Interim Report*, The Hague Conference (2010), at pp. 51-52; International Law Association, Committee on the Rights of Indigenous Peoples, *Final Report*, Sofia Conference (2012), at p. 28.

[198] International Law Association, Committee on the Rights of Indigenous Peoples, *Resolution No. 5/2012, Rights of Indigenous Peoples*, 75th Conference of the International Law Association held in Sofia, Bulgaria, 26-30 August 2012, at para. 3.

[199] The Declaration was drafted by the United Nations Working Group on Indigenous Populations (UNWGIP), which was established in 1982 as a subsidiary UN body. It was one of the six working groups supervised by the Sub-Commission on the Prevention of Discrimination and the Protection of Minorities (as of 1999 known as the Sub-Commission on the Promotion and Protection of Human Rights), which at the time was the main subsidiary body of the United Nations Commission on Human Rights. The UNWGIP's mandate was twofold: "to review developments pertaining the promotion and protection of human rights and fundamental freedoms of indigenous peoples" and "to give attention to the evolution of international standards concerning indigenous rights". Within this mandate, the UNWGIP developed the draft Declaration on the Rights of Indigenous Peoples upon request by the Sub-Commission. Its drafting was a protracted process. A draft Declaration was first completed in 1993, but lingered for years. It was not before June 2006 that a revised text of the Declaration was adopted during the very first session of the new Human Rights Council. Subsequently, the Declaration was submitted to the General Assembly for its final approval. On the drafting process, see E.I.A. Daes, 'The Spirit and Letter of the Right to Self-Determination of Indigenous Peoples: Reflections on the Making of the United Nations Draft Declaration' in

themselves to, *inter alia*, the inclusion of an express and unlimited right to self-determination. Most States, however, remained reluctant in considering such an indigenous right, as they valued traditional concepts such as State sovereignty and territorial integrity highly, and feared indigenous claims for separate statehood, based on an interpretation of self-determination, as including the right to secede. One may question whether this fear is realistic, as only few indigenous communities, if any, desire full independence. Rather, most indigenous groups have stressed that the creation of a sovereign State is neither what they aim for, nor what seems to be viable:

> Indigenous peoples are not geographically or economically situated in a way that makes independence particularly attractive. Most, if not all indigenous peoples are constantly seeking democratic reforms and power sharing within existing states.[200]

It seems inconsistent that, notwithstanding these exclusively internal aspirations, indigenous communities have strongly opposed a restricted understanding of the right to self-determination. This stance may be seen as an attempt to leave open the possibility for demands of full independence in case the government of the State refuses to grant an apposite degree of internal self-determination.[201] States, however, were only willing to accept the inclusion of the right to self-determination on the condition of the insertion of Article 46(1), affirming that:

> [n]othing in this Declaration may be interpreted as implying for any State, people, group or person any right to engage in any activity to perform any act contrary to the Charter of the United Nations or construed as authorizing or encouraging any action which would dismember or impair, totally or in part, the territorial integrity or political unity of sovereign and independent States.

P. Aikio and M. Scheinin (eds) *Operationalizing the Right of Indigenous Peoples to Self-Determination* (Institute for Human Rights, Åbo Akademi University, Turku/Åbo 2000); Eide, 'Rights of Indigenous Peoples. Achievements in International Law During the Last Quarter of a Century'; Xanthaki, *Indigenous Rights and United Nations Standards. Self-Determination, Culture and Land* at pp. 102-121.

[200] Statement of the Four Directions Council distributed during the 1995 Commission Working Group, quoted in Xanthaki, *Indigenous Rights and United Nations Standards. Self-Determination, Culture and Land* at p. 168. See also UN Commission on Human Rights, Sub-Commission on Prevention of Discrimination and Protection of Minorities (by E.-I.A. Daes, Chairperson of the Working Group on Indigenous Populations), *Discrimination against Indigenous Peoples: Explanatory Note Concerning the Draft Declaration on the Rights of Indigenous Peoples*, UN Doc. E/CN.4/Sub.2/1993/26/Add.1 (1993), at para. 28: "Most indigenous peoples also acknowledge the benefits of a partnership with existing states, in view of their small size, limited resources and vulnerability. It is not realistic to fear indigenous peoples' exercise of the right to self-determination. It is far more realistic to fear that the denial of indigenous' rights to self-determination will leave the most marginalised and excluded of all the world's peoples without a legal, peaceful weapon to press for genuine democracy in the states in which they live."

[201] Eide, 'Rights of Indigenous Peoples. Achievements in International Law During the Last Quarter of a Century' at pp. 198-199.

As this provision confirms that the Declaration does not involve a general right for indigenous peoples to unilaterally create their own State, it cleared the way for the acknowledgement of a right to self-determination.[202] Most explicitly, this right is enshrined in Article 3 UNDRIP, which states:

> Indigenous peoples have the right to self-determination. By virtue of that right they freely determine their political status and freely pursue their economic, social and cultural development.

This phrasing is identical to that of common Article 1 of the ICCPR and ICESCR, with the replacements of the term 'all peoples' by 'indigenous peoples'.[203] Connected to Article 3 is Article 4 UNDRIP, which may be read as a possible limitation to the modes of exercising the right to self-determination, as it stipulates that in exercising this right, indigenous peoples "have the right to autonomy or self-government in matters relating to their internal and local affairs". Both provisions of the Declaration are seen to reflect existing norms of customary international law.[204]

In view of the provisions addressed above, it appears that the right to self-determination for indigenous peoples is restricted to the internal dimension of the right and by no means includes a right to unilateral secession. As such, the right to self-determination may be seen to focus on two aspects: the free determination of a people's political status and representation on the one hand, and autonomy on the other. The first aspect is referred to in Article 18 UNDRIP, which stipulates that:

> [i]ndigenous peoples have the right to participate in decision-making in matters which would affect their rights, through representatives chosen by themselves in accordance with their own procedures, as well as to maintain and develop their own indigenous decision-making institutions.

The aspect of autonomy is elaborated upon in Article 31 UNDRIP, providing that:

> [i]ndigenous peoples have the right to maintain, control, protect and develop their cultural heritage, traditional knowledge and traditional cultural expressions, as well as

---

[202] See International Law Association, Committee on the Rights of Indigenous Peoples, *Interim Report*, The Hague Conference (2010), at p. 9.

[203] This is not to say, however, that the application of common Article 1 of the 1966 International Covenants in the context of indigenous peoples is undisputed. On the contrary: since its adoption, the question has been raised as to whether indigenous peoples can be considered as 'peoples' for the purpose of Article 1 of the ICCPR and ICESCR. The Human Rights Committee was requested to address this issue twice, but it declared the communications concerned inadmissible for other reasons. See, for instance, Xanthaki, *Indigenous Rights and United Nations Standards. Self-Determination, Culture and Land* at pp. 133-134. See also Chapter IV, Section 2.3 of the present study.

[204] See International Law Association, Committee on the Rights of Indigenous Peoples, *Interim Report*, The Hague Conference (2010), at p. 51.

the manifestations of their sciences, technologies and cultures, including human and genetic resources, seeds, medicines, knowledge of the properties of fauna and flora, oral traditions, literatures, designs, sports and traditional games and visual and performing arts. They also have the right to maintain, control, protect and develop their intellectual property over such cultural heritage, traditional knowledge, and traditional cultural expressions.

In addition to the Declaration, doctrine also recognizes that indigenous peoples are subjects of the right to self-determination, although *prima facie* limited to the internal aspect of the right.[205] Erica-Irene A. Daes, for instance, has argued that the meaning of the right to self-determination for indigenous peoples should be understood in accordance with what she – in the early 1990s – called the "new meaning" of the right, i.e. its internal dimension. More specifically, the right to self-determination should allow indigenous peoples "to negotiate freely their political status and representation in the States in which they live".[206] Similar remarks have been made by other commentators. S. James Anaya, for instance, maintained that self-determination for indigenous peoples is to be regarded "in relation to the institutions of government under which they live".[207]

Having established the (internal) core of the right to self-determination for indigenous peoples, the question presents itself as to how this right may be implemented in this specific and relatively new context. Unfortunately, there is no unequivocal answer to this question, since appropriate measures will differ from case to case. Nevertheless, some general remarks can be made in this respect. As was explained previously, the internal dimension of the right to self-determination generally requires a participatory and representative political system. In the present context, it is to be recalled that an electoral system based upon simple majoritarianism may be inadequate to achieve the indigenous peoples' self-determination within the political structures of the State.[208] As indigenous peoples are usually non-dominant groups, they are likely

---

[205] *Ibid.*, at pp. 9-12.

[206] E.-I.A. Daes, 'Some Considerations on the Right of Indigenous Peoples to Self-Determination' (1993) 3 *Transnational Law and Contemporary Problems* 1 at pp. 8-9.

[207] S.J. Anaya, *Indigenous Peoples in International Law* (2nd edn, Oxford University Press, Oxford 2004) at p. 104. See also G. Alfredsson, 'The Right to Self-Determination and Indigenous Peoples' in C. Tomuschat (ed.) *Modern Law of Self-Determination* (Martinus Nijhoff Publishers, Dordrecht 1993) at pp. 50-53; Eide, 'Rights of Indigenous Peoples. Achievements in International Law During the Last Quarter of a Century' at pp. 196-199; C.E. Foster, 'Articulating Self-Determination in the Draft Declaration on the Rights of Indigenous Peoples' (2001) 12 *European Journal of International Law* 141 at pp. 150-156; B. Kingsbury, 'Reconstructing Self-Determination: A Relational Approach' in P. Aikio and M. Scheinin (eds) *Operationalizing the Right of Indigenous Peoples to Self-Determination* (Institute for Human Rights, Åbo Akademi University, Turku/Åbo 2000) at pp. 23-27; D. Sanders, 'Self-Determination and Indigenous Peoples' in C. Tomuschat (ed.) *Modern Law of Self-Determination* (Martinus Nijhoff Publishers, Dordrecht 1993) at pp. 79-80.

[208] This was already noted in Section 3.1.1 of the present Chapter.

to be overruled by the majority. Additional measures may therefore be necessary to include and reflect indigenous voices in the political decision-making process. In this respect, some States have adopted special arrangements, such as designated parliamentary seats for indigenous representatives and the introduction of so-called tribal delegates in parliament, who are neither elected, nor members of the parliament.[209] In addition, as the twofold focus in the Declaration on the Rights of Indigenous Peoples indicated, autonomy arrangements may be introduced for meeting the demands for the right to internal self-determination. Such arrangements can take various forms. They can be territorial in character, involving autonomy for indigenous peoples over their traditional lands and accompanying natural resources. An alternative is to extend autonomy arrangements to certain matters which are of special concern to indigenous peoples, for instance culture.[210] As such, autonomy may not only be instrumental in implementing indigenous peoples' right to self-determination; it may be a tool for protecting the distinct identity of an indigenous population as well. However, as Alexandra Xanthaki cautioned, "autonomy is not a panacea for indigenous problems around the world. It also has disadvantages, not least that it promotes segregation and separation and fails to encourage dialogue".[211]

In this connection, a relatively recent development should be addressed. The principle of 'free, prior and informed consent' is increasingly considered to be connected to the right to self-determination in the context of indigenous rights.[212] More than that, it arguably is the most far-reaching corollary of the internal dimension of the right to self-determination for indigenous peoples. The concept has been discussed and debated in both national and international fora, such as the UN Permanent Forum on Indigenous Issues. This UN body views 'free, prior and informed consent' as a participatory process which implies and requires free discussions, consultations, meetings and agreements between the indigenous peoples, States, intergovernmental organizations and the private sector in matters affecting the indigenous peoples' land, territories, resources and their way of life, in order to protect their rights.[213] Put differently, for indigenous peoples, the concept of 'free, prior and informed consent' appears to

---

[209] See Xanthaki, *Indigenous Rights and United Nations Standards. Self-Determination, Culture and Land* at pp. 160-161.

[210] See Eide, 'Rights of Indigenous Peoples. Achievements in International Law During the Last Quarter of a Century' at p. 197; Sanders, 'Self-Determination and Indigenous Peoples' at pp. 70-71; Xanthaki, *Indigenous Rights and United Nations Standards. Self-Determination, Culture and Land* at pp. 163-165.

[211] *Ibid.*, at pp. 165-166.

[212] See T. Ward, 'The Right to Free, Prior and Informed Consent: Indigenous Peoples Participation Rights within International Law' (2011) 10 *Northwestern Journal of International Human Rights* 54. See also International Law Association, Committee on the Rights of Indigenous Peoples, *Interim Report*, The Hague Conference (2010), at pp. 14-15; International Law Association, Committee on the Rights of Indigenous Peoples, *Final Report*, Sofia Conference (2012), at pp. 3-4.

[213] See Permanent Forum on Indigenous Issues, *Report on the International Workshop on Methodologies Regarding Free, Prior and Informed Consent and Indigenous Peoples*, UN Doc. E/C.19/2005/3, 17 February 2005, at para. 43.

be a prerequisite and manifestation of the exercise of the right to self-determination as it is defined under international law. Although the Declaration both implicitly and explicitly affirms the concept of 'free, prior and informed consent' in its provisions,[214] the precise scope of the requirements has not yet been clarified entirely. It seems that this elucidation is reserved for the Inter-American Human Rights System, which has developed an advanced body of jurisprudence on the rights of indigenous peoples.[215]

All in all, it can be concluded that in addition to the entire populations of existing sovereign States and subgroups within such States, indigenous peoples are subjects of the right of internal self-determination as well. The right to indigenous peoples to self-determination involves a norm of customary international law and focuses on the free determination of a people's political status and representation, and on forms of autonomy to implement this. However, the right to self-determination for indigenous peoples clearly excludes a general right to unilateral secession.[216]

3.4. Conclusions on Internal Self-Determination

Above, the internal dimension of the right to self-determination was scrutinized. As explained at the outset, the purpose of this section was twofold. First, elaboration on internal self-determination is necessary in order to fully understand the contemporary meaning of the right to self-determination, with its emphasis on the internal dimension. Secondly, it is important to assess the content, status, and subjects of the right to internal self-determination as it is sometimes contended that the persistent denial of this right may trigger a right to external self-determination through unilateral secession.

---

[214] Implicit references to the concept of free, prior and informed consent can be found in, for instance, Articles 10, 11, 28, and 29 UNDRIP. Article 19 UNDRIP contains an explicit reference to the concept, which holds that "States shall consult and cooperate in good faith with the indigenous peoples concerned through their own representative institutions in order to obtain their free, prior and informed consent before adopting and implementing legislative or administrative measures that may affect them."

[215] The *Saramaka* case before the Inter-American Court of Human Rights (IACHR) is often considered to be a landmark case in this respect. See Inter-American Court of Human Rights, *Case of the Saramaka People v. Suriname*, Series C No. 172, Judgment, 28 November 2007, at paras 134-137. For an exploration of the content and requirements of the concept of 'free, prior and informed consent', thereby also considering the decisions and opinions of the Inter-American Court of Human Rights, see Ward, 'The Right to Free, Prior and Informed Consent: Indigenous Peoples Participation Rights within International Law'.

[216] It is striking, however, that while the International Law Association's Committee on the Rights of Indigenous Peoples focused on the internal implementation of the right to self-determination and excluded a general right to unilateral secession, it left open the possibility of unilateral secession in what it termed as "appropriate cases", i.e. when they are denied meaningful access to government to pursue their political, economic, social and cultural development. According to the Committee, "under general international law indigenous peoples who find themselves in such a condition have the right to pursue secession". See International Law Association, Committee on the Rights of Indigenous Peoples, *Interim Report*, The Hague Conference (2010), at p. 10.

It was demonstrated above that the internal dimension of the right to self-determination has become increasingly important after the decolonization process. It became clear that today, the right to self-determination cannot be seen to be realized as soon as an independent State is created, but instead involves a continuous entitlement of all peoples. As such, the right to internal self-determination requires the free and genuine expression of the will of a people, so as to enable a people to determine its political, economic, social, and cultural development. More specifically, it demands free popular participation in the political decision-making process and a representative government. While its *erga omnes* character is undisputed, it remains uncertain whether the internal dimension of the right to self-determination has also attained the status of *jus cogens*. Having established the core meaning and status, the question was raised as to which entities are considered to be the subjects of this internal dimension of the right to self-determination. It was found that, at present, entire populations of existing States are bearers of this right, as well as those subgroups within States who constitute a 'people', and indigenous peoples. Minorities may only be subjects of the right to internal self-determination if they have collective individuality and, hence, can be considered as subgroups constituting a people.

4. EXTERNAL SELF-DETERMINATION

It was seen in the previous Chapter that the traditional context in which the external dimension of the right to self-determination was exercised was that of the decolonization process. Whereas in due course, both international legal and political documents have increasingly focused on the internal dimension of the concept of self-determination, official legal documents have not paid much attention to the content of the external dimension beyond the context of decolonization. Nonetheless, in both scholarly literature and practice, this aspect of self-determination has been addressed and invoked frequently. This section will deal with the meaning, status and subjects of the contemporary external dimension of the right to self-determination rather briefly, while the following Chapter will elaborate upon the most controversial issue as regards the right, i.e. the concept of secession.

4.1. The Content of the Right to External Self-Determination

The text of the Friendly Relations Declaration is regarded as including the principal reference to the external dimension of the right to self-determination outside the colonial context.[217] After phrasing a general right for all peoples to freely determine

---

[217] See Section 2.2 of this Chapter.

their political status and development,[218] it expresses that this right to self-determination may be implemented through the "establishment of a sovereign and independent State, the free association or integration with an independent State, or the emergence into any other political status freely determined by a people".[219] More specifically, the external dimension of the right to self-determination is viewed as being exercised through the peaceful dissolution of a State, through the (re)union or merger of one State with another State, or though secession.[220] The different modes of implementing the external dimension of the right to self-determination will be addressed hereafter, although it is to be emphasized that these are not mutually exclusive concepts. Rather, it appears that the distinctions between the different concepts are blurred. This point will be made below.

4.1.1. Dissolution

To start with, dissolution refers to the establishment of a new independent State through the separation of one or more integral parts of the territory of an existing State from that State, resulting in the discontinuation of the legal personality of the previous sovereign.[221] Commonly, dissolution occurs in the context of federal-type territorial units. In these instances, the possibility of dissolution is often provided for in the constitution by confirming a right to self-determination for the constituent units.[222] In this respect, the break-up of the Socialist Federal Republic of Yugoslavia

---

[218]   See also Committee on the Elimination of Racial Discrimination, *General Recommendation No. 21: Right to Self-Determination*, UN Doc. A/51/18 (1996), Annex VIII, at para. 4.

[219]   UN General Assembly Resolution 2625 (XXV) (*Declaration on Principles of International Law Concerning Friendly Relations and Co-operation Among States in Accordance with the Charter of the United Nations*), UN Doc. A/Res/2625 (XXV), 24 October 1970, Principle V, at para. 4.

[220]   See Raič, *Statehood and the Law of Self-Determination* at p. 289. In addition to these modes of implementing the right to external self-determination, the text of the Friendly Relations Declaration concerning the right to self-determination is generally seen to give rise to a right to independence for the population of a State whose territory has been annexed or occupied by foreign powers as well (Principle V, para. 5). As such, it is not quite proper to speak about the exercise of the right to self-determination by means of the creation of a new, independent State, but rather by means of the *de facto* re-establishment of the independence of a State. In this respect, reference may be made to Iraq's annexation of Kuwait in 1990. See also Cassese, *Self-Determination of Peoples. A Legal Reappraisal* at pp. 90-99.

[221]   See P. Radan, 'Post-Secession International Borders: A Critical Analysis of the Opinions of the Badinter Arbitration Commission' (2000) 24 *Melbourne University Law Review* 50 at p. 56; Raič, *Statehood and the Law of Self-Determination* at pp. 358-360.

[222]   See Weller, 'The Self-Determination Trap' at pp. 20-22.

(SFRY)[223] and of the Union of Soviet Socialist Republics (USSR)[224] in 1990 and 1991 respectively are frequently mentioned as examples.[225] Both instances will be elaborated upon elsewhere in the present study.[226]

4.1.2. (Re)union or Merger

Secondly, and in addition to dissolution as a mode of exercising the external dimension of the right to self-determination, the possibility of (re)union or merger is to be noted. As such, the right to external self-determination is exercised by the consolidation of two or more States – whether or not they had previously existed as one State – thereby creating a new sovereign State. Although instances of (re)union or merger occur only infrequently, there are some examples in this respect. Most commonly known is probably the reunification of East and West Germany in 1990 after the fall

---

[223] The break-up of the Socialist Federal Republic of Yugoslavia was the result of a complex and violent process, which started late 1990 and can be said to have reached a conclusion in December 1995 with the Dayton-Paris Peace Agreement. The Socialist Federal Republic of Yugoslavia consisted of six republics (Slovenia, Croatia, Serbia, Bosnia-Herzegovina, Montenegro and Macedonia) and two autonomous regions (Kosovo and Vojvodina). In short, four of the six constituent republics attempted to break away by proclaiming their independence. Subsequently, in April 1992, Serbia and Montenegro proclaimed the establishment of a new Federal Republic of Yugoslavia (FRY), composed of the territories and populations of both republics. The United Nations, however, did not recognize the newly proclaimed FRY as a continuation of the legal personality of the old Socialist Federal Republic. In view of this, labeling the fragmentation of Yugoslavia as dissolution rather than secession seems to be the most obvious conclusion. See Raič, *Statehood and the Law of Self-Determination* at pp. 290-291; M. Weller, 'The International Response to the Dissolution of the Socialist Federal Republic of Yugoslavia' (1992) 86 *American Journal of International Law* 569.

[224] In the case of the Soviet Union, prior to the declaration of independence, referenda were held as regards this issue. Thereupon, a tripartite meeting of Russia, Ukraine and Belarus was held in Minsk on 8 December 1991 and subsequently, eleven of the fourteen republics participated in the Alma Ata conference of 21 December 1991. During both meetings, declarations were adopted with the tenor of forming the Commonwealth of Independent States and hence making the USSR extinct. Moreover, it was declared that the eleven newly established States would support Russia taking over the membership of the Soviet Union within the United Nations. In this respect, one may argue that with this declaration, State continuity was recognized and, as such, that the republics had seceded from the Soviet Union. See Y.Z. Blum, 'Russia Takes Over the Soviet Union's Seat at the United Nations' (1992) 3 *European Journal of International Law* 354 at p. 355 and pp. 357-360. However, as Raič explains, "[i]f Russia continued the legal personality of the Soviet Union, this would mean that the Republics, except for Russia, had seceded from the Soviet Union. For reasons of Soviet domestic politics, this position was not feasible. Therefore, and although legitimized through recognition, the continuity of the legal personality of the Soviet Union by Russia should essentially be explained in political terms". As such, it seems more appropriate to speak of dissolution than of secession. See Raič, *Statehood and the Law of Self-Determination* at pp. 290-291.

[225] On both the cases of the Soviet Union and Yugoslavia, see R. Müllerson, 'The Continuity and Succession of States by Reference to the Former USSR and Yugoslavia' (1993) 42 *International and Comparative Law Quarterly* 473; Weller, 'The Self-Determination Trap' at pp. 17-20.

[226] See Section 4.1.4 of the present Chapter and Chapter VI, Section 3.2.3 and Section 3.2.4.

of the Berlin Wall.[227] Moreover, the establishment of the United Arab Republic by the sovereign States of Egypt and Syria in 1958 may be mentioned in this context.[228]

4 1.3. Secession

A third mode of implementing external self-determination is secession. As was already expounded in Chapter I, secession generally refers to the establishment of a new independent State through the withdrawal of an integral part of the territory of an existing State from that State, carried out by the resident population of that part of the territory, either with or without the consent of the parent State or domestic constitutional authorization.[229] In cases of secession, the legal personality of the previous sovereign is continued.[230] This kind of withdrawal by a subgroup on the territory may occur with the consent of the parent State or as a result of a clause in the domestic constitution enabling separation.[231] If secession occurs in absence of consent or a constitutional provision, reference is generally made to the term unilateral secession. The two first-mentioned manifestations of secession will be addressed below, whereas the issue of unilateral secession will be examined in detail separately in view of its controversial and complex character on the one hand, and the fact that it constitutes the very core of the present study on the other.

The concept of consensual secession does not require much explanation. It refers to the separation of part of the territory with prior consent of the central government.[232] Secession by agreement has only occurred in a few instances, such as the

---

[227] After World War II, the defeated German State was divided into different sections and placed under quadripartite government by the Allied powers, i.e. France, the United Kingdom, the United States, and the Union of Soviet Socialist Republics. Subsequently, in 1949, the sections ruled by the Western Allies were merged into the Bundesrepublik Deutschland (BDR), while the Soviet zone became the Deutsche Demokratische Republik (DDR). By 1973, these territories were both recognized as States. The fall of the Berlin Wall finally enabled the reunification of Germany, which was concluded on 3 October 1990. See Crawford, *The Creation of States in International Law* at pp. 452-466.

[228] The United Arab Republic was created by the union of Egypt and Syria in 1958, but dissolved in 1961 when Syria withdrew from the union. See *ibid.* at p. 489.

[229] See Chapter I, Section 2.1.

[230] See, for instance, Raič, *Statehood and the Law of Self-Determination* at p. 359; Weller, 'The Self-Determination Trap' at p. 8.

[231] On constitutional secession, see, for instance, A. Pavković and P. Radan, *Creating New States: Theory and Practice of Secession* (Ashgate Publishing, Aldershot 2007) at pp. 221-232; Weller, 'The Self-Determination Trap' at pp. 16-23. For a critical view of constitutional secession, see D. Philpott, 'Self-Determination in Practice' in M. Moore (ed.) *National Self-Determination and Secession* (Oxford University Press, Oxford 2003) at pp. 93-98.

[232] Some authors have labeled this manifestation of secession as implied constitutional secession. According to Marc Weller, this would be the case "where a distinct 'nation' or 'people' inhabit a clearly constitutionally defined territory. Where the central government consents to the holding of a referendum on the issue of secession, or where such provision exists according to the constitution in the absence of

separation of Singapore from Malaysia,[233] and, more recently, the separation of Southern Sudan from Sudan.[234]

The concept of constitutional secession refers to constitutions which, in a clear and unambiguous fashion, determine that specific constituent entities enjoy a right to external self-determination, provided that particular procedural conditions are met.[235] A clear example in this respect is the Ethiopian constitution from 1994, declaring that "[e]very Nation, Nationality and People in Ethiopia has an unconditional right to self-determination, including the right to secession".[236] The possibility of secession provided for in the constitution is generally restricted to federal-type entities, since these usually have a clearly defined territory.[237] Nonetheless, the constitution of the Principality of Liechtenstein may also be mentioned here, as it authorizes every municipality to "remove itself from the state-community".[238] As will be pointed out in the following sub-section, the constitutions of the former Soviet Union and Yugoslavia have sometimes been suggested in the context of constitutional secession as well.

---

an express reference to self-determination, there is an expectation that such a referendum would need to be respected by the central authorities". See Weller, 'The Self-Determination Trap' at p. 22.

[233] After becoming independent from its colonial power Great Britain in 1963, Singapore merged with three other territories to form Malaysia. This federation, however, did not prove successful and on 9 August 1965, Singapore seceded from the federation by means of a Separation Agreement, which was signed by both Singapore and Malaysia. It provided that "it has been agreed by the parties thereto that fresh arrangements should be made for the order and good government of the territories comprised in Malaysia by the separation of Singapore from Malaysia upon which Singapore shall become an independent and sovereign state and nation separate from and independent of Malaysia and so recognized by the Government of Malaysia". As such, Singapore became independent while Malaysia retained its international legal personality. See Crawford, *The Creation of States in International Law* at pp. 392-393.

[234] From 9 to 15 January 2011, a referendum was held in Sudan on the question whether the Southern part of the country should separate from the North. An overwhelming majority of 98.83 percent voted in favour of secession. The 2005 Comprehensive Peace Agreement determined that the ten regions of Southern Sudan may secede from Sudan if the voter turnout for the referendum is no less than 60 percent and, in addition, 50 percent of the voters vote in favour of independence. Moreover, following the announcement of the official results of the referendum, President Omar Al-Bashir promulgated a formal decree acknowledging the outcome. In a speech on State television, Al-Bashir noted that he welcomes the results of the referendum as they reflect the will of the people in Southern Sudan. On 9 July 2011, the Republic of South Sudan, the newest African State, was announced. For more information on the referendum, see *Southern Sudan Referendum Commission*, available at <http://southernsudan2011.com/>, last consulted on 24 September 2012.

[235] Weller, 'The Self-Determination Trap' at p. 16 and p. 19.

[236] Constitution of the Federal Democratic Republic of Ethiopia, adopted on 8 December 1994, Article 39(5).

[237] See Pavković and Radan, *Creating New States: Theory and Practice of Secession* at p. 221; Weller, 'The Self-Determination Trap' at p. 17.

[238] Constitution of the Principality of Liechtenstein, published on 15 September 2003, Article 4(2).

4.1.4. Dissolution and Secession: A Blurred Distinction

In addition to being mentioned as examples of constitutional secession, the demise of both the Union of Soviet Socialist Republics (USSR) and the Socialist Federal Republic of Yugoslavia (SFRY), also illustrate that the various concepts concerning the exercise of the right to external self-determination cannot be strictly distinguished. Both matters will be elaborated on below.

The Constitution of the former Soviet Union provided – in conformity with Lenin's ideas – that the Union is "an integral, federal, multinational state formed on the principle of socialist federalism as a result of the free self-determination of nations and the voluntary association of equal Soviet Socialist Republics".[239] More specifically, it stated that "[e]ach Union Republic shall retain the right freely to secede from the USSR".[240] Indeed, as was already touched upon previously, the Baltic republics asserted this constitutional right to self-determination and announced their intent to move towards full independence. This triggered strong opposition by the Soviet authorities, which pointed at a constitutional provision regulating that the territory of a Union Republic may not be altered in absence of mutual agreement.[241] Obviously, such an interpretation of the provision at issue would counteract the right to unilateral secession as granted elsewhere in the Constitution. The rigid stance of the Soviet authorities not only led to a legal tussle on the issue between the Baltic republics and Moscow, but also between Moscow and some Western States, such as the United States and Germany, which were of the opinion that the Baltic republics were never lawfully incorporated into the Soviet Union, since this inclusion was the result of forceful annexation.[242]

It is notable that three different views on or characterizations of the relevant events have been expressed as regards the separation of the Baltic republics from the Soviet Union. First, the Baltic republics themselves considered their move towards independence as the exercise of their constitutional right to secession. In contrast, the Soviet authorities viewed the events as an act of (illegitimate) unilateral secession, while some Western States represented the third view, as they regarded all this as annexed territories regaining independence. The separation of the Baltic republics set in train the demise of the Soviet Union,[243] and as such, the case of the Soviet Union is generally referred to as one of the principal examples of absolute dissolution of

---

[239] Constitution of the Union of Soviet Socialist Republics, adopted on 7 October 1977, Article 70.
[240] *Ibid.*, Article 72.
[241] *Ibid.* Article 78.
[242] See, for instance, Crawford, *The Creation of States in International Law* at pp. 394-395; Murswiek, 'The Issue of a Right of Secession – Reconsidered' at pp. 31-32; Weller, 'The Self-Determination Trap' at p. 17.
[243] See, for instance, Pavković and Radan, *Creating New States: Theory and Practice of Secession* at pp. 138-141. See also Chapter VI, Section 3.2.3.

a federal-type entity. Accordingly, the doctrine of express constitutional secession cannot be said to have been tested completely.

In this respect, the example of the former Yugoslavia deserves some elaboration as well. This case also demonstrated that the distinctions between the concepts addressed above are indefinite. The Constitution of the SFRY, in a clear and unambiguous phrasing, granted the right to self-determination, including the right to secession, to all 'nations', i.e. federal republics, within the federation.[244] This constitutional clause was challenged in 1991, when, in response to changes in power relations, Croatia and Slovenia were the first republics attempting to break away from the federation by declaring their independence.[245] As it took the line that the doctrine of territorial integrity prohibited the declarations of independence, the central government in Belgrade responded to these acts with the use of force. The European Community (EC), being the principal mediator in the Yugoslav crisis, took a different view: it was of the opinion that Croatia and Slovenia had already become States or were entitled to become States and, hence, that they enjoyed the right to territorial integrity and unity and the protection against the use of force. Against this backdrop, the EC sought to provide for a well-ordered and peaceful secession, whereby the legal personality of the SFRY was continued. However, this attempt failed.[246]

In response to the continuing crisis, the Peace Conference on Yugoslavia was established by the EC. In turn, the Peace Conference on Yugoslavia created an Arbitration Committee, presided by Robert Badinter, for the purpose of giving the EC advice on legal issues in the context of the Yugoslav crisis.[247] This Committee reported on its first findings in its Opinion No. 1 of 29 November 1991. This report was written at the request of Lord Carrington, President of the Peace Conference on Yugoslavia, who had addressed a letter to the Arbitration Committee, questioning whether the declarations of independence by the Yugoslav republics which had

---

[244] See Constitution of the Socialist Federal Republic of Yugoslavia, adopted on 21 February 1974, Section I.

[245] See Weller, 'The Self-Determination Trap' at p. 18l; Weller, 'The International Response to the Dissolution of the Socialist Federal Republic of Yugoslavia' at pp. 569-570. For a more elaborate discussion of the separation of Croatia and Slovenia, see Chapter VI, Section 3.2.4.

[246] Weller, 'The Self-Determination Trap' at p. 19.

[247] The Committee was chaired by the President of the French Constitutional Court and further comprised of the Presidents of the German and Italian Constitutional Courts, the Belgian Court of Arbitration and the Spanish Constitutional Tribunal. The mandate of the Committee was rather obscure, as it was envisaged that it would rule at the request of 'valid Yugoslavian authorities' and that its decisions would be binding. Nonetheless, the Committee issued no less than fifteen opinions between late 1991 and the middle of 1993, of which several were handed down in response to requests by Lord Carrington. For general information on the Badinter Arbitration Committee, see: M.C.R. Craven, 'The European Community Arbitration Commission on Yugoslavia' (1995) 66 *British Yearbook of International Law* 222; Pellet, 'The Opinions of the Badinter Arbitration Committee: A Second Breath for the Self-Determination of Peoples' at pp. 178-179; Radan, 'Post-Secession International Borders: A Critical Analysis of the Opinions of the Badinter Arbitration Commission' at pp. 50-53.

already been issued or which would be issued in the future, should be regarded as States established as a consequence of secession or as a consequence of the dissolution of the SFRY. The letter made clear that the request ensued from the differing views in this respect as presented by Serbia and Montenegro on the one hand and the other former republics on the other hand. In response to Lord Carrington's request, the Committee stated that the Yugoslav federation was in the process of dissolution, involving the emergence of its constituent republics as independent States, although that process was still ongoing.[248]

An important point should be made here. Both the Committee's opinions and the declarations of independence of Croatia and Slovenia indicate that the traditionally strict distinction between dissolution and secession is inaccurate. For, the Committee first stated that the SFRY had "retained its international personality [even though] the Republics have expressed their desire for independence". As such, the Committee seemed to implicitly label the declarations of independence by Croatia and Slovenia as acts of (unilateral) secession.[249] In spite of this observation, the Committee referred to the events in Yugoslavia as being a "process of dissolution". In its Opinion No. 8, the Committee expressed the view that this process was to be completed. It reiterated what the Security Council had uttered previously, namely that the "claim by the Federal Republic of Yugoslavia (Serbia and Montenegro) to continue automatically (the membership) of the former Socialist Federal Republic of Yugoslavia (in the United Nations) has not been generally accepted".[250] In addition, it was noted that Croatia, Slovenia and Bosnia and Herzegovina had been recognized as newly established, independent States, and that Serbia and Montenegro had adopted a new constitution for the Federal Republic of Yugoslavia.[251] Consequently, the Committee concluded that the SFRY had ceased to exist.[252] In Opinion No. 11, the Committee stated that the process of dissolution in the SFRY had commenced on 29 November 1991,[253] so before the republics of Croatia and Slovenia had proclaimed independence.

---

[248] Conference on Yugoslavia, Arbitration Commission, *Opinion No. 1*, 29 November 1991, reprinted as: International Conference on the Former Yugoslavia, 'Opinions No. 1-3 of the Arbitration Commission of the International Conference on Yugoslavia' at pp. 182-183, at para. 3.

[249] *Ibid.* at pp. 182-183, at para. 2(a).

[250] See UN Security Council Resolution 757 (1992) (*Bosnia and Herzegovina*), UN Doc. S/Res/757 (1992), 30 May 1992, Preamble; see also UN Security Council Resolution 777 (1992) (*Federal Republic of Yugoslavia*), 19 September 1992. This statement was recalled in: Conference on Yugoslavia, Arbitration Commission, *Opinion No. 8*, 4 July 1992, reprinted as: International Conference on the Former Yugoslavia, 'Opinions No. 4-10 of the Arbitration Commission of the International Conference on Yugoslavia' (1993) 4 *European Journal of International Law* 74 at pp. 87-88, at para. 3.

[251] *Ibid.* at pp. 87-88, at para. 3.

[252] *Ibid.* at pp. 87-88, at para. 4.

[253] Conference on Yugoslavia, Arbitration Commission, *Opinion No. 11*, 16 July 1993, reprinted in: International Conference on the Former Yugoslavia, 'Advisory Opinions No. 11-15 of the Arbitration Commission of the International Conference on Yugoslavia' (1993) 32 *International Legal Materials: Current Documents* 1586 at pp. 1587-1589, at para. 2.

Hence, from the statements of the Committee, it may be inferred that the acts of Croatia and Slovenia actuated the process of dismemberment of the SFRY, which ultimately resulted in the demise of the Yugoslav Republic.[254] Accordingly, as was aptly formulated by one commentator, "the proclamations of independence by the two republics must be seen as acts of *unilateral secession* which, in combination with other factors, led to the *dissolution* of the SFRY".[255] This particular outlook is not only reflected in the declarations of independence of the Croatia and Slovenia,[256] but is also confirmed in scholarly literature.[257] In view of this blurred distinction between the concepts of dissolution and secession, it should be concluded that considering the break-up of a State requires a phased approach, judging the separation of entities one by one, in order to correctly link the situation to one of the concepts concerning the exercise of external self-determination.

4.2. The Status and Subjects of the Right to External Self-Determination

As was pointed out above, there is no single mode of implementation of the external dimension of the right to self-determination beyond decolonization. Rather, several means have been discerned – from consensual or constitutional modes to the much more drastic unilateral act of secession. It may therefore not come as a surprise that this range of applications of the contemporary concept of external self-determination brings along nuances as regards the status and subject of the right. Yet, it is rather difficult to determine which position external self-determination beyond decolonization has attained within international law. This indistinctness appears to have its roots in the fact that the implementation of external self-determination inevitably leads to the modification of borders of an existing State, which is a far-reaching effect. In this respect, a group of UNESCO experts noted that when the exercise of the right to

---

[254] See, generally, P. Radan, *The Break-Up of Yugoslavia and International Law* (Routledge, London/New York 2002).

[255] Raič, *Statehood and the Law of Self-Determination* at p. 360 (emphasis included). For a discussion of the role of nationalism in the break-up of the SFRY (and the Soviet Union), see Musgrave, *Self-Determination and National Minorities* at pp. 108-124.

[256] Both proclamations emphasized that the republics of Croatia and Slovenia disassociated from the SFRY by establishing independent States, which implied that, in principle, these acts would leave the SFRY intact.

[257] See, for instance, Murswiek, 'The Issue of a Right of Secession – Reconsidered' at pp. 30-33; Radan, 'Post-Secession International Borders: A Critical Analysis of the Opinions of the Badinter Arbitration Commission' at pp. 54-55; Weller, 'The International Response to the Dissolution of the Socialist Federal Republic of Yugoslavia' at p. 606; Weller, 'The Self-Determination Trap' A. Whelan, 'Wilsonian Self-Determination and the Versailles Settlement' (1994) 43 *International and Comparative Law Quarterly* 99 at pp. 114-115. Likewise, Malcolm Shaw observed that "[w]hether the federation dissolves into two or more states also brings into focus the doctrine of self-determination in the form of secession. Such *dissolution* may be the result of an amicable and constitutional arrangement or may occur pursuant to a forceful exercise of *secession*". See Shaw, *International Law* at p. 196 (emphasis added).

self-determination comes into conflict with the principles of territorial integrity and State sovereignty, "[t]here is an understandable fear that, understood in one way, the peoples' right to self-determination might lead to the fragmentation of States, the disruption of settled international boundaries, the breakdown of governmental authority and even manipulation of peoples for the purpose of disrupting the internal affairs of States".[258] Consequently, the sources of international law (other than doctrine) tend not to focus on the external dimension of self-determination as a right of peoples beyond the context of decolonization. Rather, they emphasize the internal – and less problematic – dimension of the right and stress its importance and special legal status.

Nonetheless, it cannot be denied that the Friendly Relations Declaration in its clear phrasing proclaimed that non-violent dissolution, merger or (re)union are lawful modes of implementing the right to external self-determination.[259] There is no rule or principle of international law prohibiting the creation of new States by these means – neither the principle of territorial integrity, nor the principle of State sovereignty. The rationale behind it is that in these instances, the right to self-determination is understood to be implemented by all inhabitants of a State, regardless of ethnic or other considerations.[260] In real terms, this usually implies that such a decision is based on majority rule. The holding of a referendum or the use of any other procedure so as to determine and reflect the genuine will of the people at issue seems appropriate here.[261] In cases of consensual or constitutional separation, the right to secession underlying this act is based in national rather than international law. To put it even more strongly, international law is not concerned with these kinds of arrangements, for it considers these types of secession to be exclusively within the domestic realm.

More uncertain, however, is the question of the exercise of external self-determination by a portion of the population – i.e. subgroup – of an existing State, which is neither based on consent nor on a constitutional clause. In these instances, there appears to be a clear conflict between the exercise of this right, which is aimed at territorial change, on the one hand, and the principles of territorial integrity and *uti possidetis juris*, which are aimed at maintaining the territorial *status quo*, on the other hand. Most controversial is the issue of unilateral secession and its contemporary status under international law. International legal documents do not explicitly acknowledge a right to unilateral secession, nor do they explicitly deny such a right. Nonetheless, as will be demonstrated hereafter, various (ethnic) subgroups

---

[258] UNESCO, *International Meeting of Experts on Further Study of the Concept of the Rights of Peoples. Final Report and Recommendations*, Paris, 22 February 1990, SHS-89/CONF.602/7, at para. 5.

[259] UN General Assembly Resolution 2625 (XXV) (*Declaration on Principles of International Law Concerning Friendly Relations and Co-operation Among States in Accordance with the Charter of the United Nations*), UN Doc. A/Res/2625 (XXV), 24 October 1970, Principle V, para. 4.

[260] In this respect, reference should be made to Section 3.3.1 of the present Chapter, which elaborated upon this territorial interpretation of the subject of a right to (internal) self-determination.

[261] See Raič, *Statehood and the Law of Self-Determination* at pp. 292-293.

within States have claimed the existence of a right to unilateral secession and several legal scholars have argued in favour of it. Hence, the question of a right of peoples to unilateral secession comes to mind. This issue will be addressed in the following Chapter.

4.3. Conclusions on External Self-Determination

This section has dealt with the right to external self-determination beyond the decolonization context. In contrast to the internal dimension, the external dimension inevitably leads to the alteration of borders of an existing State. While it was seen that there is no single mode of implementation of this right, it is generally acknowledged that this right may be realized through the peaceful dissolution of a State, and the (re)union or merger of one State with another State. Secession is another means of exercising the right to external self-determination. It was explained that in practice, the distinction between dissolution and secession is not always as clear as may be suggested in theory.

As non-violent dissolution, (re)union or merger are generally seen to be exercised by all inhabitants of the State, these arrangements are uncontested under international law. Usually, referenda or other techniques are used to determine the will of the nation as a whole. Acts of secession which have been approved by the parent State or are based on a constitutional arrangement do not pose specific international legal questions either. In fact, these manifestations of secession are considered to be matters concerning domestic rather than international law. Controversial, however, is the establishment of a new State following an act of unilateral secession by a subgroup within the State, as this is often seen to conflict with other fundamental principles of international law, such as that of respect for the territorial integrity of the State. The question thus arises as to whether unilateral secession is a lawful mode of exercising the external dimension of the right to self-determination.

5. CONCLUSIONS

In this Chapter, the development of the right to self-determination beyond the context of decolonization and hence its contemporary meaning were expounded. In doing so, two dimensions of the right to self-determination have become apparent: an external and an internal dimension. It is this latter element of the right to self-determination which has come to play an important role in contemporary international law. It was expounded that the internal dimension of the right to self-determination basically presumes that all peoples are "allowed to exercise those rights and freedoms which permit the expression of the popular will".[262] In this respect, it was emphasized that

---

[262] Cassese, *Self-Determination of Peoples. A Legal Reappraisal* at p. 53.

both popular participation in the political decision-making process of a State and a government representing the people play a key role in implementing self-determination, as these concepts allow a people to freely determine its political, economic, social and cultural development. In order to ensure this, arrangements such as autonomy, federalism or complex power-sharing may be necessary, especially in a multi-ethnic State. For, not only entire populations of existing sovereign States, but also subgroups within such States and indigenous peoples can be viewed as subjects of the right to internal self-determination. All in all, this examination of the further development of the concept of self-determination beyond decolonization has shown that the contemporary right to self-determination is not attained when a new, independent State is created, but rather, that the right to self-determination is an ongoing right of all peoples, which should be respected continuously.

Nonetheless, the more traditional dimension of the right to self-determination, i.e. external self-determination is still relevant today. It is generally considered to be exercised through the dissolution of a State, (re)union or merger, or through secession. When exercised by the nation as a whole, the claim of external self-determination is undisputed under international law. As it was pointed out in this Chapter, there is no rule of international law which proscribes the creation of new States as a result of these actions, since in these cases self-determination is presumed to be either an expression of the entire population of a State, or a consensual or constitutional separation. Yet, the creation of a new State as a result of unilateral secession is much more controversial and contested. It appears that this – disputed – mode of exercising the right to self-determination is at odds with the prominent international legal principles of State sovereignty and territorial integrity, as already briefly touched upon in the present Chapter. This perceived field of tension between preserving the territorial *status quo* on the one hand, and effectuating territorial change on the other hand, however, has not prevented various subgroups within States to claim a right to external self-determination in the form of unilateral secession. It also leaves unanswered the main question of this study, i.e. the question of unilateral secession as a remedy to serious injustices. Against this backdrop, the following Chapter will examine the state of the art as regards the emergence of a (remedial) right to unilateral secession under international law.

CHAPTER IV
TRACES OF A (REMEDIAL) RIGHT TO UNILATERAL SECESSION IN CONTEMPORARY INTERNATIONAL LAW?

> *"In the present stage of evolution of the law of nations (*le droit des gens*) it is unsustainable that a people should be forced to live under oppression, or that control of territory could be used as a means for conducting State-planned and perpetrated oppression. That would amount to a gross and flagrant reversal of the ends of the State, as a promoter of the common good."*

> Judge Antônio Augusto Cançado Trindade*

1. INTRODUCTION

As was noted in the previous Chapter, despite the emphasis on the internal dimension of the right to self-determination outside the context of decolonization, the external aspect of self-determination is still applicable today. It may be exercised through the dissolution of a State, merger or (re)union with another State, or through secession. With respect to secession, the constitutional and consensual modes do not raise any pressing international legal questions. In contrast, the exercise of the right to self-determination by means of secession absent of constitutional authorization or prior consent of the parent State is certainly not uncontested under international law. This controversy is due to several circumstances. First of all, neither an explicit right to unilateral secession, nor an express proscription of unilateral secession can be found in the written sources of international law. Some authors, such as James R. Crawford, have even contended that "secession is neither legal nor illegal in international law, but a legally neutral act the consequences of which are, or may be regulated

---

* International Court of Justice, *Accordance with International Law of the Unilateral Declaration of Independence by the Provisional Institutions of Self-Government of Kosovo (Request for Advisory Opinion)*, Advisory Opinion, ICJ Reports 2010, p. 403, Separate Opinion of Judge Antônio Augusto Cançado Trindade, at para. 137.

internationally".[1] In this respect, he has argued that "unilateral secession [does] not involve the exercise of any right conferred by international law".[2] Secondly, the potential "deeply subversive and disruptive" effect of the concept of self-determination is to be mentioned.[3] Conventional international law generally gives priority to the traditional principles of State sovereignty and territorial integrity, which seem to cause a field of tension with the unilateral withdrawal of an integral part of the territory of an existing State from that State, carried out by the resident population of that part of the territory. Furthermore, as UN Secretary-General Boutros Boutros-Ghali noted,

> [i]f every ethnic, religious or linguistic group [could claim] statehood, there would be no limit to fragmentation, and peace, security, and well-being for all would become even more difficult to achieve.[4]

In spite of the controversy touched upon above, it appears elsewhere in this Chapter that the possibility of resorting to external self-determination by means of unilateral secession is not excluded completely, judging by, *inter alia*, the phrasing used in the Friendly Relations Declaration. Consequently, the question presents itself as to whether unilateral secession can currently be regarded as the lawful exercise of the right to self-determination. Phrased differently, does modern international law recognize a right to unilateral secession for subgroups constituting peoples within sovereign States? And if so, is this right absolute or does it arise under certain circumstances only? Does it arise as a remedy to persistent oppression and gross human rights violations? In order to paint a clear picture as regards the acknowledgement or otherwise of a (remedial) right to unilateral secession under current international law, the present Chapter will consider the sources of international law other than custom. As the law of self-determination "is continuously shaped by the realities of practice",[5] thoroughly examining State practice and *opinio juris* is of great importance for the

---

[1]   J.R. Crawford, *The Creation of States in International Law* (2nd revised edn, Clarendon Press, Oxford 2006) at p. 390. See also P. Hilpold, 'The Kosovo Case and International Law: Looking for Applicable Theories' (2009) 8 *Chinese Journal of International Law* 47 at p. 55; T.D. Musgrave, *Self-Determination and National Minorities* (Oxford University Press, Oxford 1997) at p. 210; J. Vidmar, 'Explaining the Legal Effects of Recognition' (2012) 61 *International and Comparative Law Quarterly* 361 at p. 375.

[2]   Crawford, *The Creation of States in International Law* at p. 388.

[3]   A. Cassese, 'The International Court of Justice and the Right of Peoples to Self-Determination' in V. Lowe and M. Fitzmaurice (eds) *Fifty Years of the International Court of Justice Essays in Honour of Sir Robert Jennings* (Cambridge University Press, Cambridge 1996) at p. 351.

[4]   UN Secretary-General, *An Agenda for Peace. Preventive Diplomacy, Peacemaking and Peace-keeping. Report of the Secretary-General pursuant to the statement adopted by the Summit Meeting of the Security Council on 31 January 1992*, UN Doc. A/47/277 – S/24111, 17 June 1992, at para. 17.

[5]   L.M. Graham, 'Self-Determination for Indigenous Peoples After Kosovo: Translating Self-Determination "Into Practice" and "Into Peace"' (2000) 6 *ILSA Journal of International and Comparative Law* 455 at p. 457.

purpose of this study. Before assessing these traditional constituents of custom against the backdrop of the question of remedial secession, the source of customary international law first merits some elaboration. Over time, various approaches towards ascertaining customary international law have been adopted, as a consequence of which it becomes necessary to critically consider the various relevant theories and argue which approach will be utilized in this study. In view of this, the question of whether customary international law recognizes a (remedial) right to unilateral secession merits separate elaboration. This will be done in Chapters V and VI.

2. RECOGNIZING A (REMEDIAL) RIGHT TO UNILATERAL SECESSION?

The question of whether a right to unilateral secession does, in fact, exist as a means of exercising the right to external self-determination of peoples under contemporary international law will be answered by examining the sources of international law[6] as identified in Article 38(1) of the Statute of the International Court of Justice and some possible other sources. As such, international conventions will serve as a starting point for searching traces of a right to unilateral secession, followed by a review of doctrine, judicial decisions and opinions, general principles of (international) law and, finally, unilateral acts of States and acts of international organizations.

2.1. Traces of a (Remedial) Right to Unilateral Secession in International Conventions

Although Article 38 of the Statute of the International Court of Justice does not explicitly reflect a hierarchy of sources, international conventions are generally seen as the most important source of international law.[7] Their importance is highlighted by the observation that they "are the only way states can create international law consciously",[8] since they are the result of a voluntary and deliberate act. Moreover, the legally binding force of this source of international law is clear: State parties are bound by the terms of conventions and treaties *vis-à-vis* the other parties to that particular instrument.[9] As a consequence of these characteristics, international conventions are more likely to be complied with than other sources of international law.[10]

---

[6]   On this topic, see generally H. Thirlway, 'The Sources of International Law' in M.D. Evans (ed.) *International Law* (Oxford University Press, Oxford 2003).

[7]   There is no set nomenclature for this source of law. Treaties may also be referred to as conventions, covenants, acts, charters, statutes or protocols. See M. Dixon, *Textbook on International Law* (6th edn, Oxford University Press, Oxford 2007) at p. 55.

[8]   See *ibid.* at p. 26.

[9]   In contrast to the obvious legally binding character of treaties, the binding force of other international instruments often is more obscure. As will be expounded in Section 2.5.2 of the present Chapter, the binding force of acts of international organizations, for instance, is ambiguous and largely depends upon the circumstances.

[10]   Dixon, *Textbook on International Law* at p. 27.

The above explains the relevance of a reference to a right to post-decolonization unilateral secession as part of the peoples' right to self-determination in international conventions. Yet, as was already briefly noted in Chapter I, international conventions lack such an explicit reference. In these international legal instruments, merely general references to a right to self-determination of peoples can be found. At the same time, weighty references to the principle of territorial integrity of States seem to delimit the meaning of the right to self-determination beyond the context of decolonization, resulting in great obscurity as regards the issue of unilateral secession. Indeed, the text of the UN Charter, which can be regarded as the cornerstone of international law, does not provide much clarity, since its Articles 1(2) and 55 only refer to a right to self-determination of peoples in fairly general terms, without expounding whether this right also includes unilateral secession. Although neither offering a conclusive answer, the *travaux préparatoires* demonstrate that some debate was devoted to the question of unilateral secession. The preparatory works disclose two opposite approaches to the matter of unilateral secession shown during the drafting process at the San Francisco Conference:

> Concerning the principle of self-determination, it was strongly emphasised on the one side that this principle corresponds closely to the will and desires of peoples everywhere and should be clearly enunciated in the Charter; on the other side, it was stated that the principle conformed to the purposes of the Charter only insofar as it implied the right of self-government of peoples and not the right of secession.[11]

From this, some commentators derived that the drafters of the UN Charter had no intention of establishing a right to unilateral secession,[12] while others carefully concluded that the *travaux préparatoires* of the UN Charter remain neutral on the question of whether unilateral secession is considered to be part of the general right to self-determination.[13]

Similar comments can be made with regard to the International Covenants of 1966, since both the texts of these documents and the preparatory works are quite inconclusive on the matter. Common Article 1 of the Covenants does not make

---

[11] N.G. Hansen, *Modern Territorial Statehood* (Doctoral Thesis, Leiden University 2008) at p. 87, quoting the *Final Report of the Sixth Committee*, San Francisco 1945, UNCIO, doc. 343, I/1/16, Vol. 6 296 (1945).

[12] See, for instance, D. Murswiek, 'The Issue of a Right of Secession – Reconsidered' in C. Tomuschat (ed.) *Modern Law of Self-Determination* (Martinus Nijhoff Publishers, Dordrecht 1993) at pp. 34-35; G. Lauwers and S. Smis, 'New Dimensions of the Right to Self-Determination: A Study of the International Response to the Kosovo Crisis' (2000) 6 *Nationalism and Ethnic Politics* 43 at p. 62; S. Smis, *A Western Approach to the International Law of Self-Determination: Theory and Practice* (Doctoral Thesis, Vrije Universiteit Brussel 2001) at p. 204.

[13] See, for instance, Musgrave, *Self-Determination and National Minorities* at pp. 181-182; L.C. Buchheit, *Secession: The Legitimacy of Self-Determination* (Yale University Press, New Haven 1978) at p. 73.

reference to secession. Nonetheless, the issue was debated extensively during the drafting process of the ICCPR. Some States opposed the legal recognition of self-determination as they viewed secession as a possible mode of exercising self-determination and, hence, feared that inclusion of an article on the matter would trigger secessionist claims. Other States expressly turned against the acceptance of unilateral secession as an inherent form of asserting self-determination. Nonetheless, it should be emphasized that no State initiated a draft of Article 1 which explicitly prohibited or acknowledged secession.[14] Besides, the State reports submitted to the Human Rights Committee only rarely refer to a right to secession and where they do so, reference is generally made to cases of constitutional secession, which is not very relevant to international law.[15]

In addition, the 1978 Vienna Convention on Succession of States in Respect of Treaties is relevant when seeking traces of a right to unilateral secession. Article 34 of this Convention regulates issues regarding the "succession of States in cases of separation of parts of a State". Although not mentioned explicitly, the first paragraph of this Article refers to both instances of dissolution and secession, and regulates the consequences of these modalities of separation.[16] From this, one may deduce that this Convention did not view secession as an infringement of international law. Such a conclusion seems to be confirmed by Article 6 of this Convention, which expresses that the treaty is merely applicable to the effects of a succession which occurred in conformity with international law. Accordingly, it may even be inferred that some forms of secession are in compliance with international law.[17]

In the context of analysing international (legal) documents in search of traces of a right to unilateral secession, the International Convention on the Elimination of all Forms of Racial Discrimination (ICERD)[18] should be addressed as well. Despite the

---

[14] See Buchheit, *Secession: The Legitimacy of Self-Determination* at pp. 79-83; Smis, *A Western Approach to the International Law of Self-Determination: Theory and Practice* at pp. 209-210; C. Tomuschat, 'Secession and Self-Determination' in M.G. Kohen (ed.) *Secession International Law Perspectives* (Cambridge University Press, Cambridge 2006) at pp. 26-27. For the drafting history of Article 1(1) of the ICCPR, see M.J. Bossuyt, *Guide to the "Travaux Préparatoires" of the International Covenant on Civil and Political Rights* (Martinus Nijhoff Publishers, Dordrecht 1987) at pp. 32-37.

[15] Smis, *A Western Approach to the International Law of Self-Determination: Theory and Practice* at p. 209.

[16] The text of Article 34(1) reads as follows: "When a part or parts of the territory of a State separate to form one or more States *whether or not the predecessor State continues to exist*: (a) any treaty in force at the date of the succession of States in respect of the entire territory of the predecessor State continues in force in respect of each successor State so formed; (b) any treaty in force at the date of the succession of States in respect only of that part of the territory of the predecessor State which has become a successor State continues in force in respect of that successor State alone" (emphasis added).

[17] See Smis, *A Western Approach to the International Law of Self-Determination: Theory and Practice* at pp. 208-209.

[18] International Convention on the Elimination of all Forms of Racial Discrimination, 660 UNTS 195, adopted on 21 December 1965.

fact that this Convention does not deal with self-determination explicitly, it is closely linked to this concept, since it was drafted against the background of anti-colonialism and anti-apartheid. As such, this Convention may also be relevant in the context of self-determination. In one of its General Recommendations, the Committee on the Elimination of Racial Discrimination focused on self-determination, thereby elaborating on both the internal and external dimensions of the concept. With regard to the latter dimension, General Recommendation XXI stated:

> In accordance with the Declaration of the General Assembly on Friendly Relations, none of the Committee's actions shall be construed as authorizing or encouraging any action which would dismember or impair, totally or in part, the territorial or political unity of sovereign and independent states conducting themselves in compliance with the principle of equal rights and self-determination of peoples and possessing a government representing the whole people belonging to the territory without distinction as to race, creed or colour. In the view of the Committee international law has not recognized a general right of peoples to unilaterally declare secession from a State. In this respect, the Committee follows the views expressed in the Agenda for Peace (paras 17 et seq.), namely that a fragmentation of States may be detrimental to the protection of human rights as well as to the preservation of peace and security. This does not, however, exclude the possibility of arrangements reached by free agreements of all parties concerned.[19]

That the above should not be read as outlawing secession, but rather allows for secession in three exceptional situations, was expressed by one of the Committee members, who stated the following:

> If a part of the population of a particular country wanted to change their status, there were three contexts in which this could be achieved: when the constitution established a right to self-determination; when all parties concerned agreed to secession; and when that part of the population was denied the right to participate freely in the conduct of public affairs or if their civil and political as well as economic, social and cultural rights were denied.[20]

In view of this, the General Recommendation of the Committee on the Elimination of Racial Discrimination can be said to be progressive, for it adduces that under certain circumstances, unilateral secession as a remedy may be legal.[21]

---

[19] UN Committee on the Elimination of Racial Discrimination, *General Recommendation No. 21: Right to Self-Determination*, UN Doc. A/51/18 (1996), Annex VIII.

[20] Commission on Human Rights, *Report of the United Nations seminar to access the implementation of the International Convention on the Elimination of All Forms of Racial Discrimination with particular reference to articles 4 and 6*, UN Doc. E/CN.4/1997/68/Add.1, para. 27.

[21] See Smis, *A Western Approach to the International Law of Self-Determination: Theory and Practice* at p. 211.

In sum, it is to be concluded that conventions and treaties offer only little guidance as regards the possible existence of a right to unilateral secession. No clear traces of such a right can be found in conventional treaty law. As will be demonstrated hereafter, it is sometimes contended that the Friendly Relations Declaration contains the very first reference to a right to unilateral secession, albeit still implicitly.

2.2. Traces of a (Remedial) Right to Unilateral Secession in Doctrine

Doctrine has provided substantial support for the thesis that a qualified right to unilateral secession does exist under contemporary international law. In this respect, two international instruments have proved particularly significant: the Friendly Relations Declaration and the Vienna Declaration and Programme of Action. Both instruments were already touched upon in the context of the contemporary meaning of the right to self-determination.[22] It should be emphasized that technically speaking, these instruments ought to be addressed in the context of other (possible) sources of international law, i.e. the acts of international organizations. However, since doctrine heavily relies on the Friendly Relations Declaration and Vienna Declaration and Programme of Action, the relevant paragraphs deserve to be considered before addressing the viewpoints of various eminent scholars on the existence of a (remedial) right to unilateral secession. Therefore, the content of both instruments will already be touched upon in the present Section.[23]

The Friendly Relations Declaration has been characterized as "the most authoritative statement of the principles of international law relevant to the questions of self-determination and territorial integrity",[24] as it appears to balance the right to self-determination with the territorial integrity of a sovereign State. Hence, unsurprisingly, the Friendly Relations Declaration is frequently cited in the context of unilateral secession. After having endorsed that all peoples have a right to self-determination, it stipulates that:

> [n]othing in the foregoing paragraphs shall be construed as authorizing or encouraging any action which would dismember or impair, totally or in part, the territorial integrity or political unity of sovereign and independent States conducting themselves in compliance with the principle of equal rights and self-determination of peoples as described above and thus possessed of a government representing the whole people of belonging to the territory without distinction as to race, creed or colour.[25]

---

[22] See Chapter III, Section 2.2 and 2.3.

[23] The legal value of these documents will be discussed in Section 2.5.2 of the present Chapter, in the context of the acts of international organizations.

[24] International Commission of Jurists, 'East Pakistan Staff Study' (1972) 8 *International Commission of Jurists Review* 23 at p. 44.

[25] UN General Assembly Resolution 2625 (XXV) (*Declaration on Principles of International Law Concerning Friendly Relations and Co-Operation Among States in Accordance with the Charter of the*

This so-called 'safeguard clause'[26] was reiterated in the Vienna Declaration and Programme of Action, albeit phrased somewhat differently. The relevant paragraph in this document provides:

> In accordance with the Declaration on Principles of International Law concerning Friendly Relations and Cooperation Among States in accordance with the Charter of the United Nations, this [i.e. the right to self-determination] shall not be construed as authorizing or encouraging any action which would dismember or impair, totally or in part, the territorial integrity or political unity of sovereign and independent States conducting themselves in compliance with the principle of equal rights and self-determination of peoples and thus possessed of a Government representing the whole people belonging to the territory without distinction of any kind.[27]

Affirming respect for the territorial integrity of States complying with the right to internal self-determination, and thus possessing a representative government, the phrasing of these 'safeguard clauses' suggests that a State is entitled to the protection of territorial integrity as long as its government represents the whole people of the territory without distinction of any kind. The core of this argument consists of the words 'without distinction', which is interpreted in human rights terminology as the principle of equality and non-discrimination.[28] Reasoning *a contrario*, one might contend that lack of such representative, non-discriminatory government would negate a State's right to territorial integrity. It is plain that, interpreting the phrase as such, this clause would not rule out the existence of a right to external self-determination in the form of secession. Accordingly, it has been argued that the paragraph in the Friendly Relations Declaration and the one in the Vienna Declaration and Programme

---

United Nations), UN Doc. A/Res/2625 (XXV), 24 October 1970, Principle V, Para. 7.

[26] This formula is frequently referred to as 'safeguard clause' or 'saving clause' since it can be interpreted as a safeguard against secession for States complying with the principle of self-determination. This was the viewpoint of the Government of Canada in the case before the Supreme Court of Canada, *Reference re Secession of Quebec*, 20 August 1998, [1998] 2 S.C.R. 217, at paras 133-134.

[27] World Conference on Human Rights, *Vienna Declaration and Programme of Action*, adopted on 25 June 1993, UN Doc. A/CONF.157/23, 12 July 1993, Part I, Para. 2. It was reaffirmed in the UN General Assembly, *Declaration on the Occasion of the Fiftieth Anniversary of the UN*, UN Doc. A/Res/50/49, 24 October 1995, para. 1. The relevant paragraph declares that the United Nations will "[c]ontinue to reaffirm the right to self-determination of all peoples, taking into account the particular situation of peoples under colonial or other forms of alien domination or foreign occupation, and recognize the right of peoples to take legitimate action in accordance with the Charter of the United Nations to realize their inalienable right of self-determination. This shall not be construed as authorizing or encouraging any action that would dismember or impair, totally or in part, the territorial integrity or political unity of sovereign and independent States conducting themselves in compliance with the principle of equal rights and self-determination of peoples and thus possessed of a Government representing the whole people belonging to the territory without distinction of any kind."

[28] Smis, *A Western Approach to the International Law of Self-Determination: Theory and Practice* at p. 141.

of Action remain neutral as regards the possibility of secession, while others have asserted that the 'safeguard clauses' implicitly recognize the lawfulness of secession, albeit in specific situations only, such as in the absence of representative government or respect for a peoples' right to internal self-determination. This position is taken by, *inter alia*, Lee C. Buchheit and Antonio Cassese.[29]

The preparatory works of the Friendly Relations Declaration may be said to include some support for the argument made by Buchheit, Cassese and others. Presenting their views in the Special Committee on Principles of International Law Concerning Friendly Relations,[30] the Western States articulated their ideology of popular and national sovereignty, hence emphasizing support for internal self-determination for peoples of sovereign States.[31] By contrast, socialist and developing States viewed the right to self-determination first and foremost as a right to free colonial territories from alien rule, while they considered the Western focus on internal self-determination as a threat to their autocratic tool.[32] Both extreme positions, however, did not gain sufficient support in order to be included in the Declaration. Consequently, clarity was to be forfeited to bring the divergent viewpoints together in a consensus

---

[29] Buchheit, *Secession: The Legitimacy of Self-Determination* at pp. 221-222; A. Cassese, *Self-Determination of Peoples. A Legal Reappraisal* (Cambridge University Press, Cambridge 1995) at p. 118. These and other doctrinal visions will be dealt with hereinafter.

[30] The Special Committee on Principles of International Law Concerning Friendly Relations and Co-operation Among States was established in 1963 by the UN General Assembly and composed of thirty-one 'jurists' – eminent or otherwise – representing the Member States, thereby taking into consideration "the principle of equitable geographical representation and the necessity that the principal legal systems of the world should be represented". The Special Committee was initially asked to study four essential principles of international law, i.e. the prohibition of the use of force, the principle of peaceful dispute settlement, that of non-intervention and that of sovereign equality of States. See UN General Assembly Resolution 1966 (XVIII) (*Consideration of Principles of International Law Concerning Friendly Relations and Co-operation Among States in Accordance with the Charter of the United Nations*), UN Doc. A/Res/1966 (XVIII), 16 December 1966. Later, three other principles were added to the mandate of the Special Committee: the principle of equal rights and self-determination of peoples, the duty to co-operate, and the principle of good faith. After having issued five reports on these seven principles, the Special Committee was requested to finish its work and provide the General Assembly with a full draft Declaration. The debates leading to this draft are summarized in the Special Committee's sixth and final report: Special Committee on Principles of International Law Concerning Friendly Relations and Co-operation Among States, *Report 6*, UN Doc. A/8018 (XXV).

[31] See, for instance, UN Doc. A/AC/125/SR.44, 27 July 1966, para. 12 (United States): "no rational international legal order could exist if the Charter were taken to sanction an unlimited right of secession by indigenous peoples from sovereign and independent States"; UN Doc. A/AC.125/SR.69, 4 December 1967, p. 19 (United Kingdom): "in the language of the Charter [nothing can be found] about the principle of equal rights and self-determination to support the claim that part of a sovereign independent State was entitled to secede".

[32] See, for instance, UN Doc. A/AC.125/S.106, 5 November 1969, p. 62 (Soviet Union); UN Doc. A/AC.125/SR.40, 27 July 1966, p. 10 (Yugoslavia).

text.[33] In this respect, several other statements reflected a more moderate attitude. The statement made by the Netherlands, for instance, reads as follows:

> The real problem [is] whether the firm determination to safeguard the concept of territorial integrity of sovereign States should go so far as to exclude under all circumstances the possibility of the existence or emergence of the right to self-determination [i.e. a right to unilateral secession] on the part of a given people within a given State [...]. So long as adequate provision was made against abuse, the Committee would not serve the cause of justice by excluding the possibility that a people within an existing or future State would possess sufficient individual identity to exercise the right of self-determination. If, for example – in the opinion of the world community – basic human rights and fundamental freedoms which imposed obligations on all States, irrespective of their sovereign will, were not being respected by a certain State *vis-à-vis* one of the peoples living within its territory, would one in such an instance – whatever the human implications – wish to prevent the people that was fundamentally discriminated against from invoking its right to self-determination? [...] The concept of self-determination was based on the right of collective self-expression and it was conceivable that there were cases, albeit exceptional, where a people within a State had, or might have in the future, the right of self-determination.[34]

On the basis of this and some other moderate statements pointing at the acceptance of unilateral secession under certain circumstances,[35] it has been argued that the safeguard clause from the Friendly Relations Declaration may be interpreted as reconciling these conflicting views on the matter of a right to unilateral secession.[36]

If this argumentation is indeed correct, then the Friendly Relations Declaration may be said to recognize a qualified right to unilateral secession which subjects the lawfulness of acts of secession to both the legitimacy and performance of the

---

[33] See Smis, *A Western Approach to the International Law of Self-Determination: Theory and Practice* at p. 138.

[34] UN Doc. A/AC.125/SR.107, 5 November 1969, pp. 85-86 (the Netherlands).

[35] See, *inter alia*, UN Doc. A/AC/125/SR.69, 4 December 1967, pp. 22-23 (Kenya); UN Doc. A/AC/125/SR.68, 3 August 1967, p. 12 (Ghana); UN Doc. A/AC.125/SR44, 27 July 1966, para. 12, (United States), referred to in D. Raič, *Statehood and the Law of Self-Determination* (Kluwer Law International, The Hague 2002) at p. 320.

[36] See Buchheit, *Secession: The Legitimacy of Self-Determination* at pp. 88-97; Cassese, *Self-Determination of Peoples. A Legal Reappraisal* at pp. 115-120; H. Hannum, 'Rethinking Self-Determination' (1993) 34 *Virginia Journal of International Law* 1 at pp. 17; J. Summers, *Peoples and International Law: How Nationalism and Self-Determination Shape a Contemporary Law of Nations* (Martinus Nijhoff Publishers, Leiden/Boston 2007) at pp. 218-222; Raič, *Statehood and the Law of Self-Determination* at pp. 319-320; Smis, *A Western Approach to the International Law of Self-Determination: Theory and Practice* at p. 138. Yet, it is to be noted that the *travaux préparatoires* have also been used to conclude that the Friendly Relations Declaration does not imply a right to unilateral secession. See D. Thürer, *Das Selbstbestimmungsrecht der Völker: mit einem Exkurs zur Jurafrage* (Stämpfli, Bern 1976) at pp. 186-189, referred to in Smis, *A Western Approach to the International Law of Self-Determination: Theory and Practice* at p. 143.

government of the parent State.[37] More precisely, in this line of reasoning, unilateral secession may be justified when the parent State does not act in conformity with the right to internal self-determination, which requires representative, non-discriminatory government. As such, a link between the internal dimension and external dimension of the right to self-determination presents itself. In case a State seriously and persistently violates the right to *internal* self-determination, it forfeits its right to territorial integrity and, hence, a right to *external* self-determination by means of unilateral secession may be exercised.[38] This relationship may even be pursued by arguing that under certain extreme circumstances, the internal dimension of the right to self-determination turns into a right to external self-determination. Until this critical point has been reached, the right to self-determination might only be implemented within the framework of the existing State, thus internally.[39]

In conclusion, the safeguard clauses of the Friendly Relations Declaration and the Vienna Declaration and Programme of Action seem to have become the "interpretative touchstone" for a qualified or remedial right to unilateral secession in doctrine, as they arguably make an exception to the right to territorial integrity under specific circumstances.[40] The significance and scope of the safeguard clauses will become even more apparent below, where the viewpoints of Buchheit and Cassese will be elaborated upon and the opinions of other scholars on this matter will be explored.

2.2.1. The Content of a (Remedial) Right to Unilateral Secession

Buchheit's argument originates from the broad acceptance on the international level of "the State as a privileged but not absolutely unassailable entity". According to Buchheit, this development is reflected in the reluctance of the UN General Assembly to ensure in the Friendly Relations Declaration the territorial integrity of a State which does not possess a government representing the inhabitants of the territory. In addition, he considered the international response to the events in Bangladesh – and to a lesser degree Biafra – as confirming the thesis that the international community of States "has accepted the legitimacy of secession as a self-help remedy in cases of extreme oppression".[41] In this connection, Buchheit contended that:

---

[37] See Raič, *Statehood and the Law of Self-Determination* at p. 321.
[38] See Cassese, *Self-Determination of Peoples. A Legal Reappraisal* at p. 120; J. Dugard and D. Raič, 'The Role of Recognition in the Law and Practice of Self-Determination' in M.G. Kohen (ed.) *Secession International Law Perspectives* (Cambridge University Press, Cambridge 2006) at pp. 103-104, 137; Raič, *Statehood and the Law of Self-Determination* at p. 321.
[39] See Raič, *Statehood and the Law of Self-Determination* at pp. 321-322.
[40] K. Knop, *Diversity and Self-Determination in International Law* (Cambridge University Press, Cambridge 2002) at p. 74.
[41] Buchheit, *Secession: The Legitimacy of Self-Determination* at pp. 221-222.

[t]he focus of attention here is on the condition of the group making the claim. Remedial secession envisions a scheme by which, corresponding to the various degrees of oppression inflicted upon a particular group by its governing State, international law recognizes a continuum of remedies ranging from protection of individual rights, to minority rights, and ending with secession as the *ultimate level*. At a certain point, the severity of a State's treatment of its minorities becomes a matter of international concern. This concern [...] may finally involve an international legitimation of a right to secessionist self-determination as self-help remedy by the aggrieved group (which seems to have been the approach of the General Assembly in its 1970 declaration).[42]

It is clear from this paragraph that Buchheit considered a right to unilateral secession as a remedy of last resort only. Until this point is reached, less extreme remedies from the continuum, such as regional or economic autonomy, are to be applied. Buchheit's plea, however, fails to specify exactly which groups can invoke a right to 'remedial secession'. It remains unclear whether minorities are the legal subjects of this right, or whether it applies more generally to "any segment of [the State's] population".[43]

In the vein of Buchheit, Antonio Cassese has elaborated on the question of a right to unilateral secession as well. In doing so, he granted a prominent role the safeguard clause of the Friendly Relations Declaration, as he contended that, in view of the preparatory works and the text of the document, the safeguard clause implicitly authorizes unilateral secession. Subsequently, the question was raised as to under which circumstances the Friendly Relations Declaration allows the right to self-determination to violate the territorial integrity of a State.[44] Cassese did not go into details before stressing that the safeguard clause should be interpreted restrictively, since "the reference to the requirement of not disrupting the territorial integrity of States was placed at the beginning of the clause, in order to underscore that territorial integrity should be the paramount value for States to respect". Accordingly, he suggested that the safeguard clause merely permits secession when strict conditions are met.[45] The mere lack of a representative government is insufficient to warrant a right to unilateral secession. In addition, flagrant violations of fundamental human rights are necessary to reach the threshold and a peaceful solution within the framework of the existing State must have been excluded.[46] In the opinion of Cassese, a situation legitimizing unilateral secession may only arise:

when the central authorities of a sovereign State persistently refuse to grant participatory rights to a religious or racial group, grossly and systematically trample upon their

---

[42] *Ibid.* at p. 222 (emphasis original).
[43] *Ibid.* at pp. 222-223.
[44] Cassese, *Self-Determination of Peoples. A Legal Reappraisal* at p. 118.
[45] See *ibid.* at p. 118. Likewise, see Buchheit, *Secession: The Legitimacy of Self-Determination* at p. 222.
[46] Cassese, *Self-Determination of Peoples. A Legal Reappraisal* at pp. 119-120.

fundamental rights, and deny the possibility of reaching a peaceful settlement within the framework of the State structure.[47]

In addition to Buchheit and Cassese, a vast number of other authors have alleged that a qualified right to unilateral secession does exist under contemporary international law and have touched upon circumstances under which such a right may be warranted.[48] Christian Tomuschat, for example, has conceived the question of a right to

---

[47]   *Ibid.* at p. 119.

[48]   See for instance S.V. Chernichenko and V.S. Kotliar, 'Ongoing Global Debate on Self-Determination and Secession: Main Trends' in J. Dahlitz (ed.) *Secession and International Law* (T.M.C. Asser Press, The Hague 2003) at pp. 78-79; Dugard and Raič, 'The Role of Recognition in the Law and Practice of Self-Determination' at pp. 103-104; R. Emerson, 'The Logic of Secession' (1980) 89 *Yale Law Journal* 802 at pp. 807-809; T.M. Franck, 'Postmodern Tribalism and the Right to Secession' in C. Brölmann, R. Lefeber and M. Zieck (eds) *Peoples and Minorities in International Law* (Martinus Nijhoff Publishers, Dordrecht 1993) at pp. 13-14; J.A. Frowein, 'Self-Determination as a Limit to Obligations Under International Law' in C. Tomuschat (ed.) *Modern Law of Self-Determination* (Martinus Nijhoff Publishers, Dordrecht 1993) at p. 213; Hansen, *Modern Territorial Statehood* at p. 105; O.S. Kamenu, 'Secession and the Right of Self-Determination: An OAU Dilemma' (1974) 12 *Journal of Modern African Studies* 355 at p. 361; F.L. Kirgis Jr, 'The Degrees of Self-Determination in the United Nations Era' (1994) 88 *American Journal of International Law* 304 at p. 306; J. Klabbers and R. Lefeber, 'Africa: Lost Between Self-Determination and *Uti Possidetis*' in C. Brölmann, R. Lefeber and M. Zieck (eds) *Peoples and Minorities in International Law* (Martinus Nijhoff Publishers, Dordrecht 1993) at pp. 47-48; Knop, *Diversity and Self-Determination in International Law* at pp. 74-77; P.H. Kooijmans, 'Tolerance, Sovereignty and Self-Determination' (1996) 43 *Netherlands International Law Review* 211 at p. 215; D. Kumbaro, *The Kosovo Crisis in an International Law Perspective: Self-Determination, Territorial Integrity and the NATO Intervention* (2001) at pp. 18-19, 29; R. McCorquodale, 'Self-Determination: A Human Rights Approach' (1994) 43 *International and Comparative Law Quarterly* 857 at pp. 879-880; Murswiek, 'The Issue of a Right of Secession – Reconsidered' at pp. 26-27; Musgrave, *Self-Determination and National Minorities* at pp. 188-192; V.P. Nanda, 'Self-Determination Outside the Colonial Context: The Birth of Bangladesh in Retrospect' (1979) 1 *Houston Journal of International Law* 71 at p. 85; F. Ouguergouz and D.L. Tehindrazanarivelo, 'The Question of Secession in Africa' in M.G. Kohen (ed.) *Secession International Law Perspectives* (Cambridge University Press, Cambridge 2006) at pp. 288-289; A. Peters, 'Does Kosovo Lie in the *Lotus*-Land of Freedom?' (2011) 24 *Leiden Journal of International Law* 95 at pp. 102-103; H. Quane, 'A Right to Self-Determination for the Kosovo Albanians?' (2000) 13 *Leiden Journal of International Law* 219 at p. 223; Raič, *Statehood and the Law of Self-Determination* at pp. 324-328; C. Ryngaert and C.W. Griffioen, 'The Relevance of the Right to Self-Determination in the Kosovo Matter: In Partial Response to the Agora Papers' (2009) *Chinese Journal of International Law – Advance Access* at para. 14; M.P. Scharf, 'Earned Sovereignty. Juridical Underpinnings' (2004) 31 *Denver Journal of International Law and Policy* 373 at pp. 381-385; M.N. Shaw, 'Peoples, Territorialism and Boundaries' (1997) 8 *European Journal of International Law* 478 at p. 483; Smis, *A Western Approach to the International Law of Self-Determination: Theory and Practice* at pp. 154-156, 257-258; L.-A. Thio, 'International Law and Secession in the Asia and Pacific Regions' in M.G. Kohen (ed.) *Secession International Law Perspectives* (Cambridge University Press, Cambridge 2006) at pp. 299-300; C. Tomuschat, 'Self-Determination in a Post-Colonial World' in C. Tomuschat (ed.) *Modern Law of Self-Determination* (Martinus Nijhoff Publishers, Dordrecht 1993) at pp. 9-11; Tomuschat, 'Secession and Self-Determination' at p. 42; L. Wildhaber, 'Territorial Modifications and Breakups in Federal States' (1995) 33 *Canadian Yearbook of International Law* 41 at p. 71; R.C.A. White, 'Self-Determination: Time for a Re-Assessment?' (1981) 28 *Netherlands International Law Review* 147 at pp. 160-166; G. Wilson, 'Self-Determination, Recognition

unilateral secession in the perspective of the developments as regards the relationship between a State and its citizens. States are no longer unassailable, but rather have a specific *raison d'être*. By implication, if States radically fail to meet their most elementary obligations, their legitimacy will fade and eventually their rationale can be disputed.[49] Against this background, Tomuschat has argued that the concept of "remedial secession should be acknowledged as part and parcel of positive law, notwithstanding the fact that its empirical basis is fairly thin, but not totally lacking".[50] In this regard, this scholar has perceived evidence for a conditional right to unilateral secession in the events leading to the creation of Bangladesh and the events leading to the autonomous position of Kosovo under international administration.[51]

To the same effect, Michael P. Scharf has pointed at "the modern trend", evidenced by most sources of international law, of support for the right of peoples to secede unilaterally in exceptional cases. Following Buchheit, he refers to this concept as the "remedial right to secession".[52] More specifically, Scharf has contended that:

> if a government is at the high end of the scale of representative government, the only modes of self-determination that will be given international backing are those with minimal destabilizing effect and achieved by consent of all parties. If a government

---

and the Problem of Kosovo' (2009) 56 *Netherlands International Law Review* 455 at pp. 467-472. It should be noted, however, that the argument that present-day international law includes a qualified to unilateral secession is not well argued by all writers, as a result of which the underlying considerations sometimes remain obscure. See, for instance, Karl Doehring, who acknowledges that a right to unilateral secession may arise "if the minority discriminated against is exposed to actions by the sovereign State power which consist in an evident and brutal violation of fundamental human rights, e.g. through killing or unlimited imprisonment without legal protection, destroying family relations, expropriation without any regard for the necessities of life, though special prohibitions against the following religious professions or using one's own language, and, lastly, through executing all these prohibitions with brutal methods and measures", but does not substantiate his argument. See K. Doehring, 'Self-Determination' in B. Simma (ed.) *The Charter of the United Nations A Commentary* (2nd edn, Oxford University Press, Oxford 2002) at p. 58. See also UN Commission on Human Rights, Sub-Commission on the Prevention of Discrimination and Protection of Minorities, *The Right to Self-Determination: Historicaland Current Development on the Basis of United Nations Instruments. Study Prepared by A. Cristescu*, UN Doc. E/CN.4/Sub.2/404/Rev.1 (1981) at para. 173 (holding that a "right to secession unquestionably exists, however, in a special but very important case: that of peoples, territories and entities subjugated in violation of international law. In such cases, the people have the right to regain their freedom and constitute themselves independent sovereign States").

49 Tomuschat, 'Self-Determination in a Post-Colonial World' at p. 9. In this connection, it may be noted that similar arguments have been put forward to raise the principle of non-intervention in domestic affairs in cases of gross violations of human rights. See Smis, *A Western Approach to the International Law of Self-Determination: Theory and Practice* at p. 143.

50 Tomuschat, 'Secession and Self-Determination' at p. 42.

51 *Ibid.* at p. 42.

52 Scharf, 'Earned Sovereignty. Juridical Underpinnings' at pp. 381-385. His claim is based on an examination of "the writings of numerous scholars, UN General Assembly resolutions, declarations of international conferences, judicial pronouncements, decisions of international arbitral tribunals, and some state practice".

is extremely unrepresentative and abusive, then much more potentially destabilizing modes of self-determination, including independence, may be recognized as legitimate.[53]

With this phrasing, Scharf seems to link the internal dimension of the right to self-determination to the external dimension: denial of the meaningful exercise of the right to internal self-determination may lead to a right to external self-determination by means of unilateral secession. A considerable number of other commentators have discerned a similar connection, while in addition indicating discriminatory treatment of a people[54] and serious breaches of fundamental human rights[55] as constitutive parameters for a right to unilateral secession. It appears that these three factors should not be regarded separately, but rather as being interrelated. The point of departure in this respect is the deprival of internal self-determination, either directly or indirectly. Thus, a people may not only be formally denied this right by the central authorities, but in addition, other governmental acts may qualify as a violation of the right to internal self-determination as well. A people formally granted this right may be denied the practical exercise of that right as a result of a persistent campaign of discrimination.[56] But not only are the parameters of the denial of internal self-determination and of discriminatory treatment strongly linked, what is more, discriminatory practices by the central authorities often violate the enjoyment of other fundamental human rights.[57] As Tomuschat observed, "discrimination in the political field is often co-terminous with discrimination and even persecution over the whole breadth of human activities".[58] In

---

[53] *Ibid.* at p. 385.

[54] See, for instance, Doehring, 'The Charter of the United Nations. A Commentary' at p. 66; Emerson, 'The Logic of Secession' at pp. 808-809; Knop, *Diversity and Self-Determination in International Law* at pp. 75-77; Kooijmans, 'Tolerance, Sovereignty and Self-Determination' at pp. 214-216; McCorquodale, 'Self-Determination: A Human Rights Approach' at pp. 879-880; Murswiek, 'The Issue of a Right of Secession – Reconsidered' at pp. 26-27; Raič, *Statehood and the Law of Self-Determination* at p. 332; Ryngaert and Griffioen, 'The Relevance of the Right to Self-Determination in the Kosovo Matter: In Partial Response to the Agora Papers' at para. 6; Smis, *A Western Approach to the International Law of Self-Determination: Theory and Practice* at p. 207; White, 'Self-Determination: Time for a Re-Assessment?' at pp. 160-161, 164; Wilson, 'Self-Determination, Recognition and the Problem of Kosovo' at p. 467.

[55] See, for instance, Cassese, *Self-Determination of Peoples. A Legal Reappraisal* at pp. 118-119; Dugard and Raič, 'The Role of Recognition in the Law and Practice of Self-Determination' at pp. 103-104; Klabbers and Lefeber, 'Africa: Lost Between Self-Determination and *Uti Possidetis*' at pp. 47-48; Kooijmans, 'Tolerance, Sovereignty and Self-Determination' at pp. 214-215; Kumbaro, *The Kosovo Crisis in an International Law Perspective: Self-Determination, Territorial Integrity and the NATO Intervention* at p. 19; Ouguergouz and Tehindrazanarivelo, 'The Question of Secession in Africa' at pp. 288-295; Ryngaert and Griffioen, 'The Relevance of the Right to Self-Determination in the Kosovo Matter: In Partial Response to the Agora Papers' at para. 6; Wilson, 'Self-Determination, Recognition and the Problem of Kosovo' at p. 467.

[56] See, for instance, Raič, *Statehood and the Law of Self-Determination* at p. 368; White, 'Self-Determination: Time for a Re-Assessment?' at p. 161.

[57] See, for instance, Kooijmans, 'Tolerance, Sovereignty and Self-Determination' at pp. 214-215.

[58] Tomuschat, 'Secession and Self-Determination' at p. 39.

turn, obvious and grave violations of the fundamental human rights of the members of a certain people may arguably amount to a denial of internal self-determination and as such, may warrant unilateral secession. This is particularly true for serious and widespread violations of the right to life, such as genocide or ethnic cleansing, but less excessive situations may also qualify. An example in this respect would be the massive and arbitrary use of armed force against a people, for this may constitute a threat to a people's existence and the maintenance of its collective identity.[59]

All in all, the parameters of serious and persistent denial of the right to internal self-determination, discriminatory treatment and violations of fundamental human rights appear to be interrelated. For some scholars, it seems that the essential touchstone is that of discrimination.[60] This reference point is not limited to discrimination on grounds of race, creed or colour, as was formulated in the safeguard clause of the Friendly Relations Declaration. Rather, as the relevant paragraph of the 1993 Vienna Declaration and Programme of Action indicates, it is suggested that it concerns discrimination of any kind.[61] It is to be noted, however, that the touchstone of discriminatory treatment does not imply that unilateral secession is warranted in all instances of discrimination. Particularly when there is no clear evidence of a high level of discrimination against the people at issue[62] and when chances are that the central government may stop the discrimination when called for or when legal remedies are provided, no right to unilateral secession can be claimed.[63]

Most scholars regard a conditional right to unilateral secession as a way of exercising the right to self-determination. In fact, Raič has expressed the view that the former is even an *integral* and *essential* component of the right to self-determination:

> Given the fact that self-determination is, firstly, recognized as a legal right by the international community, secondly, that its principal objective is to guarantee the effective development and preservation of the collective identity of a people as well as the effective enjoyment of the individual human rights of its members, and thirdly, that the guarantee of the right to self-determination logically implies the guarantee of that people's freedom and existence, it is difficult to accept that self-determination would not encompass a conditional right of unilateral secession.[64]

---

[59] Raič, *Statehood and the Law of Self-Determination* at pp. 368-369.
[60] See, for instance, Murswiek, 'The Issue of a Right of Secession – Reconsidered' at p. 26; White, 'Self-Determination: Time for a Re-Assessment?' at p. 164.
[61] For an argument in the same vein, see, for instance, Raič, *Statehood and the Law of Self-Determination* at p. 255.
[62] In this regard, White has emphasized that the "assertion of a high level of discrimination reflects the status of secession as a remedy of last resort assailing the territorial integrity of states. Low levels of discriminatory activity should be processed through the existing machinery for the international protection of human rights, imperfect though the available procedures may be". See White, 'Self-Determination: Time for a Re-Assessment?' at p. 164.
[63] Murswiek, 'The Issue of a Right of Secession – Reconsidered' at p. 26.
[64] Raič, *Statehood and the Law of Self-Determination* at p. 326.

In this regard, Raič recalls that international law does not provide for remedies which may enforce a peoples' right to self-determination. Accordingly, only little would remain of the rationale and objective of the right to self-determination if the right is seriously infringed by the authorities of the State while no effective and realistic remedy for a peaceful settlement would be available within the framework of that State. In such situations, a right to unilateral secession is a last resort response to serious injustices. An argument of similar purport has been made by Dietrich Murswiek, who noted that, without a right to unilateral secession in exceptional situations, the people's right to self-determination would be but a hollow shell.[65] Admittedly, not all writers accepting a right to unilateral secession explicitly consider such a right to be an intrinsic element of the right to self-determination as Raič and Murswiek do. Nevertheless, most of those writers do share the view that the existence of a situation in which a right to secede unilaterally arises cannot be assumed lightly. They contend that unilateral secession may only be permitted as an *ultimum remedium*,[66] that is when all adequate settlements within the legal and political system of the parent State have failed or cannot be reasonably expected. In other words, a claim to unilateral secession may only be legitimate if it is established that all other legal and political options for effectively ensuring the people at issue their right to self-determination internally have been exhausted or rejected by the majority of the population of the parent State.[67] As such, this high threshold can arguably be seen as an additional yet fundamental condition for the legitimate exercise of a right to unilateral secession. According to Raič, however, it may not always be required to have exhausted all reasonable and effective remedies before unilateral secession may be warranted. He submitted that "in cases of widespread and serious violations of fundamental human rights" this condition may be deemed to be fulfilled, in addition to that of the violation of the right to internal self-determination. As such, the argument would be that the cruelties committed by the authorities may not only have amounted to a denial

---

[65]   Murswiek, 'The Issue of a Right of Secession – Reconsidered' at p. 26.
[66]   This terminology is used by, for instance, Pieter H. Kooijmans and David Raič. See Kooijmans, 'Tolerance, Sovereignty and Self-Determination' at p. 216; Raič, *Statehood and the Law of Self-Determination* at p. 326. In this respect, Christian Tomuschat uses the term *ultima ratio*. See Tomuschat, 'Secession and Self-Determination' at pp. 35, 41.
[67]   See, *inter alia*, Cassese, *Self-Determination of Peoples. A Legal Reappraisal* at pp. 119-120; Dugard and Raič, 'The Role of Recognition in the Law and Practice of Self-Determination' at p. 109; Kamenu, 'Secession and the Right of Self-Determination: An OAU Dilemma' at p. 361; Klabbers and Lefeber, 'Africa: Lost Between Self-Determination and *Uti Possidetis*' at pp. 47-48; Kooijmans, 'Tolerance, Sovereignty and Self-Determination' at pp. 215-216; Lauwers and Smis, 'New Dimensions of the Right to Self-Determination: A Study of the International Response to the Kosovo Crisis' at p. 66; Ouguergouz and Tehindrazanarivelo, 'The Question of Secession in Africa' at p. 288-289; Raič, *Statehood and the Law of Self-Determination* at pp. 370-371; Ryngaert and Griffioen, 'The Relevance of the Right to Self-Determination in the Kosovo Matter: In Partial Response to the Agora Papers' at para. 14; Tomuschat, 'Self-Determination in a Post-Colonial World' at p. 11; White, 'Self-Determination: Time for a Re-Assessment?' at pp. 161, 164.

of the people's right to internal self-determination as was noted above, but they may also have caused feelings of hatred and distrust to such an extent that it would be unreasonable and even futile to require further negotiations to reach a peaceful settlement within the framework of the existing State. Under those circumstances, secession would be the only reasonable and realistic option left for protecting the human rights of the members of the people concerned and simultaneously safeguarding their collective right to self-determination.[68]

Some writers have taken a slightly different approach than those described above. They link the justifiability of unilateral secession to some elements of the traditional notion of colonialism, without making reference to unilateral secession as being a contemporary component of the peoples' right to self-determination. This so-called internal colonialism doctrine holds that the characteristics and consequences of colonialism are applicable to peoples on the territory of non-colonial States under certain circumstances. Thomas M. Franck, for example, has contended that:

> when a minority within a sovereign State – especially if it occupies a discrete territory within that State – persistently and egregiously is denied political and social equality and the opportunity to retain its cultural identity [...] it is conceivable that international law will define such repression, prohibited by the [ICCPR], as coming within a somewhat stretched definition of colonialism. Such repression, even by an independent State not normally thought to be "imperial" would then give rise to a right of "decolonization".[69]

This approach is also advocated by James R. Crawford, who noted that a central government may treat a people inhabiting a demarcated territory within the State in such a way that, in effect, it becomes a non-self-governing territory with respect to the rest of that State. To put it in the words of Crawford, such territories are subject to *carence de souveraineté*.[70] Although he considered Bangladesh, Kosovo and possibly Eritrea to present cases of internal colonialism, Crawford emphasized that those situations are exceptional.[71] It is noteworthy to point out that the essence of both the internal colonialism doctrine and the doctrine of a qualified right to unilateral secession is that they require a serious and persistent deprivation of the right to internal self-determination, possibly accompanied by widespread violations of fundamental human rights before the people at issue are allowed to break away from the State. As such, it can be argued that the internal colonialism approach underpins the existence of a conditional right to unilateral secession. What is more, it seems that the critical point is not

---

[68] Raič, *Statehood and the Law of Self-Determination* at p. 372.
[69] Franck, 'Postmodern Tribalism and the Right to Secession' at pp. 13-14.
[70] Crawford, *The Creation of States in International Law* at p. 126.
[71] J.R. Crawford, 'Outside the Colonial Context' in W.J.A. Macartney (ed.) *Self-Determination in the Commonwealth* (Aberdeen University Press, Aberdeen 1988) at pp. 13-14; Crawford, *The Creation of States in International Law* at p. 126.

whether a situation can be labelled as colonialism, but whether the preconditions of a grave and enduring violation of the right to internal self-determination, discriminatory treatment and/or massive violations of basic human rights have been met.[72]

2.2.2. The Subjects of a (Remedial) Right to Unilateral Secession

Having found that the idea of a remedial right to unilateral secession is broadly supported in scholarly literature and having identified some widely accepted constitutive parameters for its exercise, the question arises as to which collectivities may arguably be entitled to appeal to such a right. Evidently, as (unilateral) secession is generally considered to be a means of exercising the right to external self-determination, the subject of a qualified right to unilateral secession is a 'people'. And in contrast to the subjects of the right to internal self-determination, a 'people' in the context of secession is not understood to refer to the population of a State as a whole, but rather to a numerical minority in relation to the rest of the population of the State, since secession concerns the separation of only a part of a State's territory.

Regrettably, only few commentators have elaborated on the issue of the beneficiaries of a right to unilateral secession and sought to elucidate the meaning of the term 'peoples' in this context.[73] Since it was seen above that in scholarly literature the safeguard clauses of the Friendly Relations Declaration and the Vienna Declaration and Programme of Action are generally viewed as the "interpretative touchstone" for a qualified right to secession,[74] the question as to the beneficiaries of such a right may be considered in light of the texts of these clauses. It was already pointed out previously that when reading the safeguard clauses *a contrario*, denial of the meaningful exercise of the peoples' right to internal self-determination arguably triggers a right to external self-determination by means of unilateral secession. Pursuing this argument further, it seems that infra-State groups entitled to internal self-determination should be regarded as the subjects of a qualified right to unilateral secession as well.[75] Put differently, in absence of internal self-determination, peoples entitled to this

---

[72]   In this connection, David Raič has observed that "the attempts [...] to defend a qualified right of territorial separation through the 'stretching' of concepts and definitions appears to be somewhat artificial". See Raič, *Statehood and the Law of Self-Determination* at p. 328.

[73]   A number of authors do not specify which collectivities they consider to be the subjects of a right to unilateral secession. Those who do particularize this issue often just use notions as 'minority', 'people' or 'group' with no further detail.

[74]   See also Knop, *Diversity and Self-Determination in International Law* at p. 74.

[75]   In the previous Chapter, two categories of subjects of the right to internal self-determination were identified: entire populations of existing sovereign States and subgroups within such States. Here, it is to be emphasized that entire populations of existing sovereign States are obviously not entitled to a right to unilateral secession, for, by definition, secession concerns the breaking away of only a segment of the population and territory of a sovereign State.

dimension of the right to self-determination may likewise be entitled to a right to secession by way of a remedy as well.

In this connection, Cassese has argued that a right to unilateral secession can only be invoked by religious and racial groups, while this right is to be withheld from linguistic and national groups.[76] This interpretation is based on the fact that nowhere in the Friendly Relations Declaration is reference made to ethnic or linguistic minorities as subgroups to which this document is addressed. In fact, it merely emphasizes that discrimination on the basis of race, creed or colour is contrary to the principle of equal rights and self-determination.[77] Cassese's restrictive interpretation of the safeguard clause from the Friendly Relations Declaration has been criticized by David Raič, arguing that the subgroups entitled to internal self-determination are not restricted to religious and racial groups, but also include ethnic groups.[78] His position is substantiated by various arguments.[79] Amongst others, Raič asserted that considering the *travaux préparatoires*, the motivation underlying the safeguard clause of the Friendly Relations Declaration appears to aim towards broad application of the provision rather than application to specific situations only, such as the situation in South Africa and Southern Rhodesia at that time.[80] Moreover, he argues that this broad interpretation of the safeguard clause is confirmed by the text of the Vienna Declaration and Programme of Action of 1993, which stipulates that States conduct themselves in compliance with the principles of equal rights and self-determination if possessing "a Government representing the whole people to the territory *without distinction of any kind*".[81] This phrasing arguably includes peoples – or more specifically: subgroups possessing peoplehood – of any kind as bearers of the right to self-determination.[82] As such, Raič suggested that a people constituting a numerical minority in relation to the rest of the population of the parent State may invoke a right to unilateral secession in certain situations, provided that this people comprises a

---

[76] Cassese, *Self-Determination of Peoples. A Legal Reappraisal* at pp. 114, 119.

[77] See *ibid.* at pp. 112-121. This line of reasoning is adopted by, for instance, Smis, *A Western Approach to the International Law of Self-Determination: Theory and Practice* at pp. 141-142.

[78] Raič, *Statehood and the Law of Self-Determination* at pp. 251, 257-258.

[79] *Ibid.* at pp. 251-258.

[80] *Ibid.* at pp. 253-254.

[81] World Conference on Human Rights, *Vienna Declaration and Programme of Action*, adopted on 25 June 1993, UN Doc. A/CONF.157/23, 12 July 1993, at para. 2 (emphasis added). In this connection, Frederic L. Kirgis Jr held that "from about 1970 on, there could be a right of 'peoples' [...] to secede from an established state that does not have a fully representative form of government, or at least to secede from a state whose government excludes people of any race, creed or colour from political representation when those people are the ones asserting the right and they have a claim to a defined territory. By 1993, the right had arguably expanded to be assertable against a government that is unrepresentative of people who are defined by characteristics *not limited to race, creed or colour*" (emphasis added). See Kirgis Jr, 'The Degrees of Self-Determination in the United Nations Era' at p. 306.

[82] See also Smis, *A Western Approach to the International Law of Self-Determination: Theory and Practice* at pp. 145-146.

majority possessing collective individuality within an identifiable part of the territory of that State. In this respect, it is important to realize that national or ethnic minorities are generally seen to be excluded as subjects of a right to unilateral secession. They do not constitute a 'people' under contemporary international law as a result of their lack of 'collective individuality'. This distinction between peoples which are warranted the right to self-determination and members of national or ethnic minorities which are merely entitled to minority rights was already elaborated upon previously in this study.[83] Further, the requirement of a bond between the people concerned and an identifiable territorial unit implies that the people are entitled to exercise their right to external self-determination with regard to that particular territorial unit on which they represent a clear majority.[84] While, in addition to Raič, the above reading[85] has been adopted by some other writers as well[86] and some corresponding interpretations have been suggested,[87] it appears that there is no consensus in literature on the issue of the beneficiaries of a qualified right to unilateral secession.[88]

2.2.3. Contraindications

Although doctrine shows considerable support for a right to unilateral secession as a remedy for serious injustices, admittedly, various authors remain hesitant in this

---

[83] See Chapter II, Section 3.3.3.

[84] See Raič, *Statehood and the Law of Self-Determination* at p. 367; Murswiek, 'The Issue of a Right of Secession – Reconsidered' at p. 37.

[85] See Raič, *Statehood and the Law of Self-Determination* at p. 332.

[86] See Dugard and Raič, 'The Role of Recognition in the Law and Practice of Self-Determination' at p. 109; Ryngaert and Griffioen, 'The Relevance of the Right to Self-Determination in the Kosovo Matter: In Partial Response to the Agora Papers' at para. 6; G. Zyberi, 'Self-Determination through the Lens of the International Court of Justice' (2009) 56 *Netherlands International Law Review* 429 at p. 447.

[87] Robin C.A. White has noted that "there must be a 'self' or people who for a cohesive unit which is distinct from the main population of the State by reason of its ethnic, religious or national origins". See White, 'Self-Determination: Time for a Re-Assessment?' at p. 161. In addition, Pieter H. Kooijmans has emphasized that the group concerned should possess "a definite territorial base". See Kooijmans, 'Tolerance, Sovereignty and Self-Determination' at p. 216. Combining both views, Dietrich Murswiek has contended that the people is to be "distinguished from other peoples by objective ethnic criteria, particularly by culture, language, birth or history. Secondly, a people must settle on a coherent territory, on which it forms at least a clear majority". See Murswiek, 'The Issue of a Right of Secession – Reconsidered' at p. 37.

[88] See, for instance, Kooijmans, 'Tolerance, Sovereignty and Self-Determination' at pp. 213-215; Lauwers and Smis, 'New Dimensions of the Right to Self-Determination: A Study of the International Response to the Kosovo Crisis' at p. 63; Wilson, 'Self-Determination, Recognition and the Problem of Kosovo' at p. 471. More than that, some authors have even contended that, since the safeguard clauses use the phrase "the whole people" rather than "all the distinct peoples", subgroups within States cannot claim a right to unilateral secession, for this right is reserved for the population of the State as a whole. See, for instance, C.J. Iorns, 'Indigenous Peoples and Self-Determination: Challenging State Sovereignty' (1992) 24 *Case Western Reserve Journal of International Law* 199 at p. 261.

respect. Malcolm N. Shaw, for instance, has contended that a theory of remedial secession based on an *a contrario* reading of the safeguard clause is troublesome:

> Such a major change in legal principle cannot be introduced by way of an ambiguous subordinate clause, especially when the principle of territorial integrity has always been accepted and proclaimed as a core principle of international law, and is indeed placed before the qualifying clause in the provision in question.[89]

Moreover, Shaw has put forward a practically oriented argument, which is that "no mechanism really exists to determine whether a particular State may be the subject of secession on the basis of nonconformity with the [safeguard clause]".[90] With his observation, Shaw seems to point at the problem of determining the (human rights) situations under which a State may be said to have violated the safeguard clause, hence warranting unilateral secession, and the risk of arbitrariness in this respect. Alexandra Xanthaki has raised a similar objection, as she wondered "[w]ho would be the interpreter of the law of self-determination" and determine whether a certain people has a right to secession in view of the circumstances?[91] Since a qualified right to unilateral secession would generally arise as a remedy for the (in)actions of the State, the government of the State in which the people live would not be a very reliable interpreter in this respect. According to Xanthaki, the international community as represented by the UN General Assembly would be a more dependable body. Yet, she admitted that, being a political body, it is more than likely that the General Assembly will exercise restraint in assessing whether particular situations involve a right to secession.[92] This seems to be demonstrated by the case of Kosovo.[93]

While these are indeed pertinent remarks, most commentators who remain cautious with regard to the recognition of a qualified right to unilateral secession advance the argument that scholarly writings do not provide for sufficient and compelling

---

[89] Shaw, 'Peoples, Territorialism and Boundaries' at p. 483. This stance was also reflected in M.N. Shaw, 'Report by Malcolm N. Shaw: "Re: Order in Council P.C. 1996-1497 of 30 September 1996"' in A.F. Bayefsky (ed.) *Self-Determination in International Law. Quebec and Lessons Learned* (Kluwer Law International, The Hague 2000) at p. 138.

[90] M.N. Shaw, 'The Role of Recognition and Non-Recognition with Respect to Secession: Notes on Some Relevant Issues' in J. Dahlitz (ed.) *Secession and International Law* (T.M.C. Asser Press, The Hague 2003) at p. 248.

[91] A. Xanthaki, *Indigenous Rights and United Nations Standards. Self-Determination, Culture and Land* (Cambridge University Press, New York 2007) at p. 144. Likewise, Robin C.A. White has drawn attention to the need for international institutions competent to assess claims to self-determination. See White, 'Self-Determination: Time for a Re-Assessment?' at p. 169 (citing Hans Blix).

[92] Xanthaki, *Indigenous Rights and United Nations Standards. Self-Determination, Culture and Land* at pp. 144-145.

[93] See Section 2.3.6 of the present Chapter.

evidence for the practical existence of a remedial right to unilateral secession.[94] As Antonello Tancredi aptly stated:

> it is to be stressed that the remedial secession thesis has generated considerable litera-
> ture during the last twenty years. It may be correctly affirmed that today most writers
> uphold this theory, at least form a *de lege ferenda* perspective. Notwithstanding its
> popularity among legal scholars, its correspondence to positive international law can
> still be doubted with good reason. The theory's main flaw is the lack of a sufficient
> basis in State practice. Putting aside the Bangladesh case, whose exceptional character
> has been widely underscored, one can barely cite a case in which the scheme of reme-
> dial secession has been concretely applied.[95]

Thus, while the concept of remedial secession is accepted from a *de lege ferenda* viewpoint, modern practice does not lend support for the view that peoples have a (qualified) right to unilateral secession, Tancredi contended.

In this connection, it is worth briefly touching upon scholarly writings in reaction to the events in Kosovo as well.[96] Unsurprisingly, Kosovo's contested declaration of independence in February 2008 generated a substantial amount of literature. Before the International Court of Justice issued its Advisory Opinion on the matter,[97] most commentators remained relatively hesitant to argue in favour of a right to unilat-eral secession for the Kosovo Albanians. It appears that this reluctance is primarily due to the indefinite status of such a right in general. In the words of Bing Bing Jia, "[i]t is felt, in any case, that more is required to clarify the existing law of seces-sion before it can be suitably applied to such a situation like Kosovo".[98] Against this

---

[94] Peter Hilpold, for example, has argued that although "international lawyers are trying hard to make theory fit with reality [...] no convincing proof for the existence of [a qualified right to unilateral seces-sion] has been given". See Hilpold, 'The Kosovo Case and International Law: Looking for Applicable Theories' at pp. 47, 55-56. See also J.R. Crawford, 'Report by James Crawford: "Response to Experts Reports of the *Amicus Curiae*"' in A.F. Bayefsky (ed.) *Self-Determination in International Law. Quebec and Lessons Learned Legal Opinions Selected and Introduced* (Kluwer Law International, The Hague 2000) at pp. 59-61; Hannum, 'Rethinking Self-Determination' at pp. 42-43; M.G. Kohen, 'Introduction' in M.G. Kohen (ed.) *Secession International Law Perspectives* (Cambridge University Press, Cambridge 2006) at pp. 10-11; Shaw, 'Secession and International Law' at pp. 247-248; A. Tancredi, 'A Normative "Due Process" in the Creation of States through Secession' in M.G. Kohen (ed.) *Secession International Law Perspectives* (Cambridge University Press, Cambridge 2006) at pp. 184-188; D. Thürer and T. Burri, 'Secession' in R. Wolfrum (ed.) *Max Planck Encyclopedia of Public International Law* (fully updated online edn, Oxford University Press, New York 2009) at para. 17.

[95] Tancredi, 'A Normative "Due Process" in the Creation of States through Secession' at p. 184.

[96] These events will be touched upon in Section 2.3.6.1 of the present Chapter.

[97] International Court of Justice, *Accordance with International Law of the Unilateral Declaration of Independence in Respect of Kosovo*, Advisory Opinion, ICJ Reports 2010, p. 403.

[98] B.B. Jia, 'The Independence of Kosovo: A Unique Case of Secession?' (2009) 8 *Chinese Journal of International Law* 27 at p. 42.

backdrop, reference has been made to the lack of clear State practice in support of that doctrine.[99] Therefore, although many scholars agreed that Kosovo's self-proclaimed independence might have a significant impact on the development of international law as regards the existence of a qualified or remedial right to unilateral secession,[100] and some even referred to the Kosovo case as the "ideal test-case for the current validity of the remedial secession theory",[101] most writers in this context refrained from providing conclusive answers as to the existence of such a theory or right under contemporary international law.[102] Moreover, it is to be noted that various writers referred to the uniqueness or *sui generis* character of the Kosovo case.[103] The extraordinary concurrence of circumstances has often been put forward, including Kosovo's history as an autonomous province, the background of the disintegration of the Socialist Republic of Yugoslavia, the atrocities committed against the civilians in Kosovo, the military intervention by NATO, and the subsequent intensive international involvement on the territory, in particular by means of UN administration.[104]

---

[99] See, for instance, *ibid.* at p. 42; Tancredi, 'A Normative "Due Process" in the Creation of States through Secession' at pp. 187-188; J. Vidmar, 'International Legal Responses to Kosovo's Declaration of Independence' (2009) 42 *Vanderbilt Journal of Transnational Law* 779 at pp. 814-818.

[100] See, for instance, C.J. Borgen, 'Kosovo's Declaration of Independence: Self-Determination, Secession and Recognition' (2008) 12/2 *ASIL Insights*; Hilpold, 'The Kosovo Case and International Law: Looking for Applicable Theories' at pp. 54-56, 60-61; Jia, 'The Independence of Kosovo: A Unique Case of Secession?' at p. 29; R. Muharremi, 'Kosovo's Declaration of Independence: Self-Determination and Sovereignty Revisited' (2008) 33 *Review of Central and East European Law* 401 at pp. 432-435; Tomuschat, 'Secession and Self-Determination' at p. 38; Wilson, 'Self-Determination, Recognition and the Problem of Kosovo' at pp. 480-481; Zyberi, 'Self-Determination Through the Lens of the International Court of Justice' at pp. 442-444, 451.

[101] Tancredi, 'A Normative "Due Process" in the Creation of States through Secession' at pp. 187-188.

[102] An exception is to be mentioned in this respect. Against the backdrop of Kosovo's declaration of independence, Cedric Ryngaert and Christine Griffioen have determinedly contended that contemporary international law does accept a remedial right to unilateral secession. They have argued that a modern interpretation of customary international law provides for the basis of such a right, and that State practice and institutional practice support this view. See Ryngaert and Griffioen, 'The Relevance of the Right to Self-Determination in the Kosovo Matter: In Partial Response to the Agora Papers' at paras 14-30; C.W. Griffioen, *Self-Determination as a Human Right. The Emergency Exit of Remedial Secession* (Master's Thesis, Utrecht University 2009) at pp. 126-130.

[103] See, for example, Jia, 'The Independence of Kosovo: A Unique Case of Secession?' at pp. 29-31; Muharremi, 'Kosovo's Declaration of Independence: Self-Determination and Sovereignty Revisited' at p. 435; Wilson, 'Self-Determination, Recognition and the Problem of Kosovo' at pp. 477-480; Zyberi, 'Self-Determination Through the Lens of the International Court of Justice' at p. 443.

[104] In addition to the sources referred to above, see also C. Warbrick, 'Kosovo: the Declaration of Independence' (2008) 57 *International and Comparative Law Quarterly* at pp. 679-680. The arguments put forward in this respect will be discussed in more detail in Chapter VI of this study. For a critical consideration of the uniqueness argument, see R. Müllerson, 'Precedents in the Mountains: On the Parallels and Uniqueness of the Cases of Kosovo, South Ossetia and Abkhazia' (2009) 8 *Chinese Journal of International Law* 2, contending that uniqueness, "or the parallels for that matter, are in the eye of the beholder. Whether certain situations, facts or acts can serve as precedents depends to a great extent on whether one is interested in seeing them as precedents or not" (para. 5).

Consequently, it has been argued that Kosovo cannot serve as a precedent for other sub-State groups with secessionist intensions. This emphasis on the singularity of the Kosovo case may be interpreted as a rejection of the argument that serious injustices may justify unilateral secession as a remedy. To quote Robert Muharremi, "[o]therwise, what sense would it make to qualify the Kosovo case as *sui generis?*"[105]

2.2.4. Conclusions on Doctrine

In view of the foregoing, it can be concluded that, while there is a clear trend towards the acceptance of a remedial right to unilateral secession, scholarship is not conclusive on this issue. Writings on the case of Kosovo issued shortly after its declaration of independence seem to support this conclusion. It is, therefore, important to consider other sources of international law and their attitude towards the concept of unilateral secession as a qualified right and its interpretation. As the criticism towards the recognition of such a right already indicated, examining the status of State practice will be of great significance for this purpose. After all, as one commentator noted, "the development of self-determination as a legal construct is continuously shaped by the realities of practice".[106] But before turning to a review of State practice and *opinio juris* as elements of customary international law, judicial decisions and opinions, general principles of (international) law, and some possible additional sources of international law will be explored first.

2.3. Traces of a (Remedial) Right to Unilateral Secession in Judicial Decisions and Opinions

Although the right to self-determination as it has developed under international law has generated a vast amount of literature, it is frequently conceived as a right which is left aside or even avoided by judicial bodies, both on the national and the international level. Arguably, the practice of the UN Human Rights Committee has contributed to this image of the issue. This Committee, which is entrusted with the task of considering individual petitions on human rights violations under the Optional Protocol to the ICCPR, has repeatedly rejected appeals on the right to self-determination under Article 1 of the ICCPR. The line of argument generally presented by the Committee is that the complaints procedure established under the Optional Protocol is reserved for individuals, as a consequence of which merely the individual rights enshrined in

---

[105] Muharremi, 'Kosovo's Declaration of Independence: Self-Determination and Sovereignty Revisited' at p. 435.

[106] Graham, 'Self-Determination for Indigenous Peoples After Kosovo: Translating Self-Determination "Into Practice" and "Into Peace"' at p. 457.

Part III of the ICCPR (i.e. Article 6 to Article 27 inclusive) can be invoked.[107] This is remarkable, since it not only has the competence to deal with communications on all rights protected under the ICCPR,[108] but more specifically, it has insisted on the obligation of State parties to include information on their implementation of both paragraphs of Article 1 in their reports submitted to the Committee.[109] In more recent cases, the Committee has shown a reserved acknowledgement of the right by noting that it may be taken into account when interpreting other human rights enshrined in the Covenant.[110] The International Court of Justice has been very cautious as well when commenting on self-determination. Over time, however, a number of judicial decisions and opinions dealing with the right to self-determination beyond the colonial context have emerged, both on the international, regional, and national level. Interestingly, some of these judgments touch upon the question of a right to unilateral secession as well. In search of traces of such a right in judicial decisions and

---

[107] In this connection, mention may be made of the case of *A.D. v. Canada*. In this case, the Grand Captain of the Mikmaq Tribal Society brought a claim before the Human Rights Committee, alleging that Canada had deprived the Mikmaq people of their right to self-determination and that the Mikmaq nation should be recognized as a State. The Committee dismissed the petition on the basis of the argument that the Grand Captain had not demonstrated that he was the authorized representative of the Mikmaq Tribal Society. Moreover, the Committee observed that he had failed "to advance any pertinent facts supporting his claim that he is personally a victim of a violation of any rights contained in the Covenant". See UN Human Rights Committee, *A.D. (the Mikmaq Tribal Society) v. Canada*, Communication No. 78/1980, UN Doc. Supp. No. 40 (A/39/40) at p. 200 (1984), at para. 8.2. In the case of *Kitok v. Sweden*, the Committee held that an individual "could not claim to be the victim of a violation of the right of self-determination enshrined in [A]rticle 1 of the Covenant". See UN Human Rights Committee, *Kitok v. Sweden*, Communication No. 197/1985, UN Doc. CCPR/C/33/D/197/1985 (1988) at para. 6.3. The Committee maintained a similar position in the case of *Ominayak and the Lubicon Lake Band v. Canada*. It further stressed that "[w]hile all peoples have the right of self-determination and the right freely to determine their political status, pursue their economic, social and cultural development and dispose of their natural wealth and resources, as stipulated in Article 1 of the Covenant, the question whether the Lubicon Lake Band constitutes a 'people' is not an issue for the Committee to address under the Optional Protocol to the Covenant. The Optional Protocol provides a procedure under which individuals can claim that their individual rights have been violated". See UN Human Rights Committee, *Ominayak and the Lubicon Lake Band v. Canada*, Communication No. 167/1984, UN Doc. Supp. No. 40 (A/45/40) at p. 1 (1990), at paras 13.3 and 32.1.

[108] Article 2 of the Optional Protocol to the ICCPR stipulates that "individuals who claim that any of their rights enumerated in the Covenant have been violated and who have exhausted all available domestic remedies may submit a written communication to the Committee for consideration."

[109] UN Human Rights Committee, *General Comment No. 12: Article 1 (Right to Self-Determination), The Right to Self-Determination of Peoples*, UN Doc. HRI/GEN/1/Rev.1 (1994), 13 March 1984, at paras 3-6.

[110] See, for instance, UN Human Rights Committee, *J.G.A. Diergaardt et al. v. Namibia*, Communication No. 760/1997, UN Doc. CCPR/C/69/D/760/1997 (2000), at para. 10.3; UN Human Rights Committee, *Apirana Mahuika et al. v. New Zealand*, Communication No. 547/1993, UN Doc. CCPR/C/70/D/547/1993 (2000), at para. 9.2; UN Human Rights Committee, *Gillot v. France*, Communication No. 932/2000, UN Doc. A/57/40 at p. 270 (2002), at para. 13.4.

opinions, this section will address those cases in which a (remedial) right to unilateral secession is considered.[111] The relevant cases will be presented here chronologically.

2.3.1. The Åland Islands Case

The *Åland Islands* case was already briefly touched upon in the context of the development of self-determination from principle to right.[112] The present section, however, will elaborate on the case against the backdrop of the question of the existence of a (remedial) right to unilateral secession, as it is sometimes argued that such an entitlement finds its origins in the *Åland Islands* case.[113]

The *Åland Islands* case dealt with a legal dispute between Sweden and Finland in 1920.[114] It concerned the question whether the inhabitants of the Åland Islands – an archipelago located in the Baltic Sea, between Finland and Sweden – were allowed to secede from Finland and subsequently attach themselves to Sweden. It is important to note that the Åland Islands had been under Swedish control from the twelfth to the early nineteenth century. Consequently, in large measure, the inhabitants of the archipelago were Swedish in language and culture. As such, Sweden remained the "cultural motherland" of the Ålanders.[115] When Sweden was defeated by the Russian Empire in 1809, Finland – including the Aland Islands – was surrendered to Russia. Subsequently, Finland became an autonomous Grand Duchy within the Russian Empire. Following the Russian Revolution, Finland declared its independence in December 1917. Hence, the question presented itself as to whether the Åland Islands had become part of the new and sovereign Finnish State, or whether they were allowed to reunite with Sweden. In June 1919, a plebiscite was held on the Åland Islands, which resulted in a vote of 96.4 per cent in favour of association of the archipelago with the Swedish territory. Unsurprisingly, proposals by Finland to offer the islands autonomy were rejected by the Ålanders. When in June 1920, Finland

---

[111] As such, the jurisprudence from the Inter-American Human Rights System will not be included, since to date, it has merely focused on the right to self-determination through land and resource rights rather than through unilateral secession. Likewise, those cases from the African Commission on Human and Peoples' Rights merely dealing with the internal dimension of the right to self-determination will be omitted here. For a concise discussion of regional jurisprudence with regard to the right to self-determination in general, see, for instance, D. Shelton, 'Self-Determination in Regional Human Rights Law: From Kosovo to Cameroon' (2011) 105 *American Journal of International Law* 60.

[112] See Chapter II, Section 3.4.

[113] M. Sterio, *On the Right to External Self-Determination: "Selfistans", Secession and the Great Powers' Rule* (Working Paper, Cleveland State University 2009) at p. 5. See also Raič, *Statehood and the Law of Self-Determination* at pp. 328-330; Summers, *Peoples and International Law: How Nationalism and Self-Determination Shape a Contemporary Law of Nations* at pp. 285-293; Tancredi, 'A Normative "Due Process" in the Creation of States through Secession' at pp. 177-178.

[114] See, generally, J. Barros, *The Aland Islands Question: Its Settlement by the League of Nations* (Yale University Press, New Haven 1968).

[115] Hannum, 'Rethinking Self-Determination' at p. 8.

sent military troops to the archipelago and detained two leaders of the Åland separatist movement as they were allegedly guilty of treason, Great Britain intervened by referring the dispute to the League of Nations.[116]

Subsequently, the Council of the League of Nations established two expert bodies in order to give an advisory opinion on the matter: an International Commission of Jurists and a Committee of Rapporteurs. The mandate of the Commission of Jurists (hereafter: Jurists) was primarily concerned with the question of whether, under Article 15(8) of the Covenant of the League of Nations, the Åland Islands dispute was to be left within the domestic jurisdiction of Finland, or whether the League Council was entitled to exercise jurisdiction. As such, the mandate of the Jurists did not specifically address the question of a right to self-determination for the inhabitants of the Åland Islands. Nonetheless, the Jurists dealt with the issue of domestic jurisdiction by elaborating upon the relationship between self-determination on the one hand, and the principles of State sovereignty and minority rights on the other.[117] It was in connection with the balance between self-determination and State sovereignty[118] that the Jurists dismissed the assumption of self-determination as a legal right within international law:

> Although the principle of self-determination of peoples plays an important part in modern political thought, especially since the Great War, it must be pointed out that there is no mention of it in the Covenant of the League of Nations. The recognition of this principle in a certain number of international treaties cannot be considered as sufficient to put it upon the same footing as a positive rule of the Law of Nations. On the contrary, in the absence of express provisions in international treaties, the right of disposing of national territory is essentially an attribute of the sovereignty of every State. Positive International Law does not recognize the right of national groups, as such, to separate themselves from the State of which they form part by the simple expression of a wish, any more than it recognizes the right of other States to claim such a separation. Generally speaking, the grant or the refusal of such a right to a portion of its population of determining its own political fate by plebiscite or by some other method is, exclusively, an attribute of the sovereignty of every State which is definitely constituted.[119]

---

[116] See *ibid.* at pp. 8-9; Summers, *Peoples and International Law: How Nationalism and Self-Determination Shape a Contemporary Law of Nations* at p. 279.

[117] See Summers, *Peoples and International Law: How Nationalism and Self-Determination Shape a Contemporary Law of Nations* at p. 280.

[118] With respect to the relationship between self-determination and minority rights, the Commission observed, *inter alia*, that the two concepts have a common goal, i.e. "to assure to some national Group the maintenance and free development of its social, ethnical or religious characteristics". As such, the Commission considered self-determination and minority rights as being two distinct methods for achieving that goal. See *Report of the International Commission of Jurists (Larnaude, Huber, Struycken)*, LNOJ Special Supplement No. 3 (October 1920), at para. 6.

[119] *Ibid.*, at paras 5-6.

In short, State sovereignty prevailed for the Jurists, as it considered the question of self-determination in the form of secession to be a matter which should be – in general – left exclusively to the domestic jurisdiction of the State(s) concerned. The Jurists, however, touched upon circumstances which may shift the jurisdiction from the national to the international plane by stating that:

> [t]he Commission, in affirming these principles, does not give an opinion concerning the question as to whether a manifest and continued abuse of sovereign power, to the detriment of a section of the population of a State, would, if such circumstances arose, give to an international dispute, arising therefrom, such a character that its object should be considered as one which is not confined to the domestic jurisdiction of the State concerned, but comes within the sphere of action of the League of Nations.[120]

As regards the specific case under consideration, the Jurists reported that such a situation was not applicable to the Åland Islands question.[121] Yet, they considered that Finland was not yet a definitively established sovereign State in 1917, since at that time Finland itself was breaking away from the Russian Empire and establishing its independence. Consequently, the matter did not exclusive involve Finland and, hence, the League of Nations Council was authorized to come up with recommendations for a settlement of the dispute under Article 15(8) of the Covenant of the League of Nations, the Jurists argued.[122]

After the report by the Jurists was submitted to open the Åland Islands dispute to international jurisdiction, a Committee of Rapporteurs (hereafter: Rapporteurs) was created for the purpose of examining the matter and formulating a solution. Similar to the report of the Jurists, the relationship between self-determination and State sovereignty formed the basis for the Rapporteurs' reflections. The question the Rapporteurs asked themselves concerned "that of Finland's right of sovereignty with regard to the Åland Islands".[123] Was Finland a sovereign State after its declaration of independence from Russia and did Finland have sovereignty over the Åland Islands? In contrast to the Jurists, the Rapporteurs did not consider Finland to be a new sovereign State. Having considered both historical and geographical factors, the Rapporteurs concluded that "the right of sovereignty of the Finnish State over the Åland Islands is, in our view, incontestable and their present legal status is that they form part of Finland".[124] Despite this sovereignty, the Rapporteurs held the view that the Åland Islands question surpassed the domestic jurisdiction of Finland.[125] Consequently, it

---

[120] *Ibid.*

[121] *Ibid.*, at para. 5.

[122] *Ibid.*, at para. 14.

[123] *Report of the International Committee of Rapporteurs (Beyens, Calonder, Elkens)*, 16 April 1921, LN Council Document B7/21/68/106 [VII], at para. 22.

[124] *Ibid.*, at para. 25.

[125] *Ibid.*, at para. 22.

considered whether "adequate reasons" and "sufficiently weighty considerations" were present to organize a plebiscite for the Ålanders and to alter their situation.[126] In this connection, the relationship between self-determination and minority rights was explored. The Rapporteurs agreed with the Jurists that self-determination was:

> not, properly speaking a rule of international law and the League of Nations has not entered it in its Covenant. [...] It is a principle of justice and of liberty, expressed by a vague and general formula which has given rise to most varied interpretations and differences of opinion.[127]

In addition, the Rapporteurs stressed that minority rights should be seen as means of justice and liberty as well. Whether justice and liberty should be obtained through self-determination or through minority rights depended on two factors, i.e. stability and oppression. The Rapporteurs considered the following:

> Is it possible to admit as an absolute rule that a minority of the population of a State, which is definitely constituted and perfectly capable of fulfilling its duties as such, has the right of separating itself from her in order to be incorporated in another State or to declare independence? The answer can only be in the negative. To concede minorities, either of language or religion, or to any fraction of a population the right of withdrawing from the community to which they belong, because it is their wish or their good pleasure, would be to destroy order and stability within States and to inaugurate anarchy in international life; it would be to uphold a theory incompatible with the very idea of the State as a territorial and political unity.[128]

With this statement on the importance of stability, the Rapporteurs seemed to repudiate the existence of an absolute right to secede unilaterally. At the same time, the Rapporteurs expressed their awareness of situations in which justice and liberty are not served by forcing a minority to stay within the borders of a State. Hence, the Rapporteurs deliberately left open the possibility of secession as a last resort, for instance in cases of persistent and extreme oppression of a group:[129]

> The separation of a minority from the State can only be considered as an altogether exceptional solution, a last resort when the State lacks either the will or the power to enact and apply just and effective guarantees.[130]

---

[126] *Ibid.*, at para. 25.

[127] *Ibid.*, at para. 27.

[128] *Ibid.*, at paras 27-28.

[129] Thomas D. Musgrave referred to this concept as the 'right of reversion'. See Musgrave, *Self-Determination and National Minorities* at p. 171.

[130] *Report of the Committee of Rapporteurs (Beyens, Calonder, Elkens)*, 16 April 1921, LN Council Document B7/2I/68/106 [VII], at para. 28.

According to the Rapporteurs, this special case did not apply to the Ålanders. In this respect, it considered that although the Ålanders were threatened in their language and culture, and although two of their leaders had been arrested, no evidence of oppression could be found. Accordingly, the Rapporteurs deemed it possible to come to a settlement which would guarantee the cultural identity of the Ålanders, but short of separation.[131]

Ultimately, the Rapporteurs concluded that, in principle, the Åland Islands dispute was to be settled by granting the archipelago political autonomy under Finnish sovereignty. More specifically, the proposed settlement entailed the extension of the 1920 Autonomy Act with several measures concerning education, migration and property rights. This conclusion, however, was followed by a caveat, noting that if Finland would fail to grant the Ålanders the guarantees which the Rapporteurs deemed necessary, they would recommend another solution, which was exactly the one which they wished to preclude:

> The interest of the Ålanders, the interests of a durable peace in the Baltic, would then force us to advise the separation of the islands from Finland, based on the wishes of the inhabitants which would be freely expressed by means of a plebiscite.[132]

In sum, it can be concluded that both the report by the Commission of Jurists and the report by the Committee of Rapporteurs rejected self-determination to be a right for minorities or national groups to secede unilaterally from the sovereign State they belong to. At the heart of this conclusion were considerations of stability. Simultaneously, both reports admitted the option of application of the principle of self-determination by means of territorial separation for sub-State groups which are subjected to extreme misgovernment and oppression by the parent State.[133] In this connection however, the Committee of Rapporteurs stressed that initially, the parties involved should seek to negotiate a settlement within the framework of the existing State, for instance through the granting of minority rights. Put differently, unilateral secession was seen as a last resort option. Arguably, the origins of the concept of remedial secession may be found here.[134]

---

[131]   *Ibid.*

[132]   *Ibid.*, at para. 34.

[133]   This is what James R. Crawford termed *carence de souveraineté*. See Crawford, *The Creation of States in International Law* at p. 111.

[134]   See Sterio, *On the Right to External Self-Determination: "Selfistans", Secession and the Great Powers' Rule* at p. 5.

2.3.2. Katangese Peoples' Congress v. Zaire

The Kantangese Peoples' Congress was a political organization claiming to represent the population of Katanga, a region of Zaire (as the Democratic Republic of Congo was then called) which had attempted to separate from that country in 1960. In 1992, the President of the Katangese Peoples' Congress submitted a communication to the African Commission on Human and Peoples' Rights (ACHPR) on behalf of the organization, involving a claim of denial of self-determination. The complaint aimed, *inter alia*, at gaining recognition of the Katangese Peoples' Congress as a liberation movement, at obtaining recognition of the right of the Kantagese people to secede from Zaire, and at safeguarding the withdrawal of Zaire from the territory.[135]

The African Commission responded to these claims by stating that the right to self-determination as expressed in Article 20(1) of the African Charter on Human and Peoples' Rights[136] (hereafter: African Charter) was, indeed, applicable to the circumstances at issue. Subsequently, it explained that the right to self-determination might be exercised by means of, for instance, "independence, self-government, federalism, confederalism, unitarism or any other form of relations that accords with the wishes of the people".[137] With this phrase, the African Commission recognized the existence of the external dimension of self-determination as well as the internal one. In this connection, the African Commission expressed its awareness of the principles of State sovereignty and territorial integrity, and observed that it had an obligation to support the sovereignty and territorial integrity of Zaire, which was a member of the Organization of African Unity (today: African Union) and a party to the African Charter.[138] The African Commission proceeded by stating:

> In the absence of concrete evidence of violations of human rights to the point that the territorial integrity of Zaire should be called into question and in the absence of evidence that the people of Katanga are denied the right to participate in government as guaranteed by Article 13(1) of the African Charter, the Commission holds the view that Katanga is obliged to exercise a variant of self-determination that is compatible with the sovereignty and territorial integrity of Zaire.[139]

---

[135] African Commission on Human and Peoples' Rights, *Katangese Peoples' Congress v. Zaire*, Comm. No. 75/92, 1995 (not dated), at para. 1.

[136] Article 20(1) of the African Charter on Human and Peoples' Rights reads as follows: "All peoples shall have the right to existence. They shall have the unquestionable and inalienable right to self-determination. They shall freely determine their political status and shall pursue their economic and social development according to the policy they have freely chosen."

[137] African Commission on Human and Peoples' Rights, *Katangese Peoples' Congress v. Zaire*, Comm. No. 75/92, 1995 (not dated), at para. 4.

[138] *Ibid.*, at para. 5.

[139] *Ibid.*, at para. 6.

Thus, since the Katangese Peoples had merely complained of a violation of the right to self-determination without substantiating that other human rights guaranteed in the African Charter had been infringed, their right to self-determination was to be exercised within the framework of the existing State rather than by means of independence. Consequently, the claim by the Katangese Peoples' Congress was rejected.

When reading the above reasoning *a contrario*, arguably, the African Commission took the view that under certain circumstances, the Katangese people would be allowed to exercise a modality of self-determination which would infringe the territorial integrity of Zaire, i.e. by means of unilateral secession. The first situation indicated was that of severe human rights violations; the second was that of lack of internal self-determination. Since evidence for such circumstances was not presented in this case, the African Commission ruled that the people of Katanga were compelled to implement their right to self-determination within the framework of the State they belonged to, so internally.[140] Perhaps even more importantly, it should be emphasized that the African Commission did not refer to the notion of remedial secession explicitly, but rather an *a contrario* reading is needed for such an interpretation.

It may be noted that, with respect to the issues underlying the decision, the African Commission remained obscure. For example, although it noted that "whether the Katangese consist of one or more ethnic groups is, for this purpose immaterial",[141] the African Commission did not take a clear standpoint as regards the question of whether the inhabitants of the Katanga region were to be viewed as a people. The fact that it recognized that Katanga was entitled to "a variant of self-determination", which is generally considered to be a right of peoples, possibly implied that the African Commission considered the inhabitants of the territory to constitute a people.[142]

2.3.3. Loizidou v. Turkey

In the case of *Loizidou v. Turkey*,[143] the European Court of Human Rights (ECtHR) was not explicitly asked to comment on the issue of self-determination of peoples. Rather, *Loizidou v. Turkey* is generally considered to involve a landmark decision concerning the rights of refugees who wish to return to their former homes and properties. The applicant in the case, Mrs Titina Loizidou, was a Cypriot national who was

---

[140] See, for instance, Raič, *Statehood and the Law of Self-Determination* at p. 330; D. Shelton, 'Self-Determination in Regional Human Rights Law: From Kosovo to Cameroon' (2011) 105 *American Journal of International Law* 60 at p. 66; Summers, *Peoples and International Law: How Nationalism and Self-Determination Shape a Contemporary Law of Nations* at p. 266.

[141] African Commission on Human and Peoples' Rights, *Katangese Peoples' Congress v. Zaire*, Comm. No. 75/92, 1995 (not dated), at para. 3.

[142] See Summers, *Peoples and International Law: How Nationalism and Self-Determination Shape a Contemporary Law of Nations* at pp. 266-267.

[143] European Court of Human Rights, *Loizidou v. Turkey*, Application No. 15318/89, Judgment (Merits), 18 December 1996.

dispelled from her home in Kyrenia when Turkey invaded the Republic of Cyprus in 1974. For years, she attempted to return to her properties, but being a Greek Cypriot, she was denied access to the northern part of Cyprus which was occupied by Turkish forces. As a result of the application by Mrs Loizidou, the European Court of Human Rights held Turkey responsible for violations of property rights in the northern part of Cyprus, since Turkish forces exercised effective overall control over this territory.[144]

It is to be noted that, as such, neither the facts of the case, nor the judgment itself is of great relevance to this Chapter. Yet, what is pertinent is the separate opinion of Judge Wildhaber, joined by Judge Ryssdal. This opinion was phrased against the backdrop of the circumstances of the case, which will only be highlighted here.[145] After nearly a decade of fierce bi-communal strife between the Turkish and Greek inhabitants of Cyprus, Turkish forces invaded Cyprus to occupy the Northern part of the island following a coup in 1974. When negotiations between the Greek and Turkish Cypriots proved unsuccessful, the Turkish area declared itself the Turkish Republic of Northern Cyprus (TRNC). The UN Security Council subsequently adopted Resolution 541 (1983), which, *inter alia*, condemned the declaration establishing the TRNC and required that all foreign troops would be withdrawn from the Republic of Cyprus.[146] Again, with the adoption of Resolution 550 (1984), the UN Security Council condemned "all secessionist actions", incited States not to recognize the TRNC, and called upon them "to respect the sovereignty, independence, territorial integrity, unity and non-alignment of the Republic of Cyprus".[147] However, the UN peace proposal efforts failed and in May 1985, the Turkish Cypriots approved a constitution for the TRNC by means of a referendum. Nonetheless, the independent status of this entity was recognized only by Turkey, which still deploys about 30,000 troops on the territory.

It was in light of the events set forth above that Judge Wildhaber attached a separate opinion to the judgment in the case of *Loizidou v. Turkey*. In his concurring opinion, Judge Wildhaber found that Turkey could not legitimately claim "that the 'TRNC' was established by the Turkish Cypriot people in pursuance of their right to self-determination", as it did not meet the conditions to warrant this right.[148] In this respect, he observed that:

---

[144] *Ibid.*, at paras 39-64.

[145] For a more elaborate overview of this historical background, see, generally, F. Hoffmeister, 'Cyprus' in R. Wolfrum (ed.) *Max Planck Encyclopedia of Public International Law* (fully updated online edn, Oxford University Press, New York 2010). See also European Court of Human Rights, *Loizidou v. Turkey*, Application No. 15318/89, Judgment (Merits), 18 December 1996, at paras 16-25.

[146] UN Security Council Resolution 541 (1983) *(On Cyprus)* UN Doc. S/Res/541 (1983), 18 November 1983.

[147] UN Security Council Resolution 550 (1984) *(On Cyprus)*, UN Doc. S/Res/550 (1984), 11 May 1984.

[148] European Court of Human Rights, *Loizidou v. Turkey*, Application No. 15318/89, Judgment (Merits), 18 December 1996, Concurring opinion of Judge Wildhaber joined by Judge Ryssdal, at para. 1.

[u]ntil recently in international practice the right to self-determination was in practical terms identical to, and indeed restricted to, a right to decolonisation. In recent years a consensus has seemed to emerge that peoples may also exercise a right of [external] self-determination if their human rights are consistently and flagrantly violated or if they are without representation at all or are massively under-represented in an undemocratic and discriminatory way. If this description is correct, then the right to self-determination is a tool which may be used to re-establish international standards of human rights and democracy.[149]

Regrettably for the purpose of the present study, Judge Wildhaber did not elaborate on the grounds on which he reached this conclusion. The context suggests that he identified an emerging agreement amongst scholars that the right to self-determination – more specifically its external dimension by means of secession – is to be interpreted as a remedy to a people whose rights have been abused by the State in a consistent and severe manner. At the same time, however, it seems that Judge Wildhaber himself was not fully convinced of the correctness of this observation, as he phrased the latter sentence using rather careful language. Consequently, one needs to be cautious with drawing far-reaching conclusions from this extract.

2.3.4. Reference re Secession of Quebec

The decision of the Supreme Court of Canada in the famous *Reference re Secession of Quebec* is generally viewed to provide guidance for the recognition of secessionist claims beyond colonization.[150] It may be said that the Canadian Supreme Court showed a more considerate view of the right to self-determination than the African Commission on Human and Peoples' Rights did in the case of the *Katangese Peoples' Congress v. Zaire*. In *Reference re Secession of Quebec*, the Canadian Supreme Court framed its view on the issues of self-determination and secession in very cautious language, thereby indicating a duty for all parties involved to negotiate a settlement and emphasizing that outside the colonial context, unilateral secession may only be permitted in exceptional and defined circumstances. What is more, in this case before

---

[149] *Ibid.*, at para. 2.
[150] See, for instance, A.F. Bayefsky, 'Introduction' in A.F. Bayefsky (ed.) *Self-Determination in International Law. Quebec and Lessons Learned* (Kluwer Law International, The Hague 2000), for example at p. 4; P. Dumberry, 'Lessons Learned from the *Quebec Secession Reference* before the Supreme Court of Canada' in M.G. Kohen (ed.) *Secession International Law Perspectives* (Cambridge University Press, Cambridge 2006) at pp. 416-452; Hansen, *Modern Territorial Statehood* at pp. 128-136; P. Oliver, 'Canada's Two Solitudes: Constitutional and International Law in *Reference re Secession of Quebec*' (1999) 6 *International Journal on Minority and Group Rights* 65; Raič, *Statehood and the Law of Self-Determination* at pp. 331-332; Summers, *Peoples and International Law: How Nationalism and Self-Determination Shape a Contemporary Law of Nations* at pp. 293-301; M. Suski, 'Keeping the Lid on the Secession Kettle: A Review of Legal Interpretations Concerning Claims of Self-Determination by Minority Peoples' (2005) 12 *International Journal on Minority and Group Rights* 189 at pp. 214-216.

the Canadian Supreme Court, international legal experts from around the world were invited to prepare written opinions on the questions at hand.[151] These expert opinions should not only be viewed as useful insights into the ongoing scholarly debate concerning the right to self-determination,[152] but also as important input in the Supreme Court's considerations.

The case before the Canadian Supreme Court may be traced back to November 1976, when the separatist *Parti Québécois* was elected into office in the Province of Quebec[153] for the first time. The *Parti Québécois* capitalized on the sense of discontent amongst the French-Canadians, who form the majority in Quebec but are a minority in Canada as a whole, and have a distinct language and culture. In order to protect this special identity, the *Parti Québécois* presented a plan of sovereignty association for Quebec, which essentially encompassed the secession of Quebec combined with an economic association and monetary union with Canada. This option was put before the enfranchised citizens of Quebec in a referendum in the spring of 1980, during which it was declined by almost 60 per cent of the votes.[154] In response to the outcome of the referendum, expectations of constitutional change were created by the federal government. The negotiations, however, did not satisfy the concerns of Quebec. Yet, after being re-elected in 1994, the *Parti Québécois* presented a draft bill to the Quebec National Assembly, which set out a proposal for Quebec's transition to sovereignty. According to this draft bill, which was first to be approved by the Quebec National Assembly, a referendum on the matter was to be held to consult the entire population of Quebec. Following a positive outcome of the referendum, negotiations on an economic and political partnership with Canada were to be initiated. Only if these negotiations would fail, could the National Assembly proclaim the independence of Quebec.[155] Consequently, three separatist parties, i.e. the *Parti Québécois*, *Bloc Québécois* and *Action Démocratique du Québec*, concluded a Tripartite Agreement in 1995, in which they anticipated an economic partnership with

---

[151] The experts involved were Georges Abi-Saab, Christine Chinkin, James R. Crawford, Thomas M. Franck, Alain Pellet, Malcolm N. Shaw and Luzius Wildhaber. Crawford and Wildhaber were asked to write opinions for the Attorney General, while the other experts were nominated as *Amicus Curiae* to present arguments on behalf of the secessionist entity, for the government of Quebec refused to participate in the proceedings. The expert reports are documented in A.F. Bayefsky (ed.), *Self-Determination in International Law. Quebec and Lessons Learned* (Kluwer Law International, The Hague 2000).

[152] For an outline of the scholarly debate on this matter, see Section 2.2 of the present Chapter.

[153] Quebec is the largest Canadian province by area and the second largest in population. See M.D. Behiels, 'Quebec' *Encyclopædia Britannica* (Encyclopædia Britannica Online edn, 2010).

[154] See, for instance, Bayefsky (ed.), *Self-Determination in International Law. Quebec and Lessons Learned* at pp. 5-6; Oliver, 'Canada's Two Solitudes: Constitutional and International Law in *Reference re Secession of Quebec*' at pp. 71-72; Summers, *Peoples and International Law: How Nationalism and Self-Determination Shape a Contemporary Law of Nations* at p. 418.

[155] Draft Bill, *An Act Respecting the Sovereignty of Quebec*, tabled at the National Assembly on 6 December 1994.

Canada and the (unilateral) proclamation of Quebec's sovereignty after one year.[156] It is noteworthy that a lawyer from the city of Quebec, Mr Bertrand, initiated proceedings before the Quebec Superior Court aimed at preventing the referendum. He adduced that the draft bill and the proposal for Quebec's transition to sovereignty were constitutionally invalid. Although the Court found that the constitutional rights of Mr Bertrand were indeed threatened by the draft bill since it intended to declare the independence of Quebec unilaterally, it deemed the issuing of an injunction as a means to prevent the referendum improper.[157]

Ultimately, the referendum was held on 30 October 1995 and resulted in a rejection of Quebec's move towards sovereignty with 50.58 per cent of the votes.[158] After the alarming outcome of the referendum and bearing in mind the pending renewed litigation initiated by Mr Bertrand, the federal government changed to a strategy of opposition to the sentiment of separatism within Quebec. This policy involved, *inter alia*, the submission of a reference to the Supreme Court of Canada as regards a number of legal issues in the event of a future attempt by Quebec to secede from Canada unilaterally. Under Section 53 of the Supreme Court Act, the following (hypothetical) questions were referred to the Court:

1. Under the Constitution of Canada, can the National Assembly, legislature or Government of Quebec effect the secession of Quebec from Canada unilaterally?
2. Does international law give the National Assembly, legislature or Government of Quebec the right to effect the secession of Quebec from Canada unilaterally? In this regard, is there a right to self-determination under international law that would give the National Assembly, legislature or Government of Quebec the right to effect the secession of Quebec from Canada unilaterally?
3. In the event of a conflict between domestic and international law on the right of the National Assembly, legislature or Government of Quebec to effect the secession of Quebec from Canada unilaterally, which would take precedence in Canada?[159]

It is understood that the second question is most relevant for the purpose of this study. This question will therefore be examined before briefly touching upon the first and

---

[156] Bill 1, *An Act Respecting the Sovereignty of Quebec*, 1st Sess., 35th Leg., Quebec. The Tripartite Agreement of 12 June 1995 was included as a schedule within Bill 1.

[157] See, for instance, Bayefsky (ed.), *Self-Determination in International Law. Quebec and Lessons Learned* at pp. 10-12.

[158] The question put before the enfranchised citizens read as follows: "Do you agree that Quebec should become sovereign, after having made a formal offer to Canada for a new economic and political partnership, within the scope of the bill respecting the future of Quebec and of the agreement signed on June 12, 1995 (i.e. the 'Tripartite Agreement')?"

[159] Supreme Court of Canada, *Reference re Secession of Quebec*, [1998], 2 S.C.R. 217. As the government of Quebec declined the opportunity to participate in the proceedings before the Court, the Court assigned – in conformity with the Statute of the Supreme Court – an *amicus curiae* so as to defend the position of Quebec.

third question. In approaching the second questions, the Supreme Court started by observing that:

> [i]nternational law contains neither a right of unilateral secession nor the explicit denial of such a right, although such a denial is, to some extent, implicit in the exceptional circumstances required for secession to be permitted under the right of a people to self-determination.[160]

Subsequently, the Supreme Court explored the substance of this right to self-determination. In this respect, it noted that today, the existence of such a right is so widely accepted in various international legal documents that "the principle has acquired a status beyond 'convention' and is considered a general principle of international law".[161] The Supreme Court continued by exploring the relationship between self-determination and territorial integrity and found that:

> international law expects that the right to self-determination will be exercised by peoples within the framework of existing sovereign states and consistently with the maintenance of the territorial integrity of those states.[162]

Thus, according to the Supreme Court, self-determination was effectively restricted by the prevailing right to territorial integrity. In this connection, a second balance was applied. In the *Åland Islands* case, the Committee of Rapporteurs had struck a balance between self-determination on the one hand and minority rights on the other. In the present case, the Supreme Court balanced the internal dimension and the external dimension of self-determination. The Supreme Court interpreted the internal dimension as "a people's pursuit of its political, economic, social and cultural development within the framework of an existing state", while the external dimension was defined by using the wording of the Friendly Relations Declaration: "[t]he establishment of a sovereign and independent State, the free association or integration with an independent State or the emergence into any other political status freely determined by a people".[163] On the basis of the sources of international law, the Supreme Court concluded that, in principle, the right to self-determination is exercised through internal self-determination.[164] Considerations of threats to the territorial integrity of and the stability of international relations among States were at the basis of this finding.[165]

Nonetheless, the Supreme Court admitted that in exceptional circumstances, the peoples' right to self-determination may be exercised externally, which would

---

[160] *Ibid.*, at para. 112.
[161] *Ibid.*, at para. 114.
[162] *Ibid.*, at para. 122.
[163] *Ibid.*, at para. 126.
[164] *Ibid.*, at para. 126.
[165] *Ibid.*, at para. 127.

presumably include the means of secession. This only applies to "the most extreme of cases and, even then, under carefully defined circumstances".[166] More specifically, the Supreme Court noted that the first context in which a right to external self-determination was certainly applicable was that of colonial people. Another undisputed and related context was that of a "people which is subject to alien subjugation, domination or exploitation outside a colonial context".[167] Subsequently, the Supreme Court argued that several scholars – whom it did not mention by name – have advanced an additional circumstance under which external self-determination would be applicable:

> Although this third circumstance has been described in several ways, the underlying proposition is that, when a people is blocked from the meaningful exercise of its right to self-determination internally, it is entitled, as a last resort, to exercise it by secession.[168]

In the opinion of the Supreme Court, the text of the Vienna Declaration and Programme of Action – more specifically, its safeguard clause – added credence to this assertion. Nonetheless, it continued with the caveat that it "remains unclear whether this third proposition actually reflects an established international law standard", but the Supreme Court did not find it necessary for the purpose of the reference to elaborate on that issue.[169] In sum, the three circumstances phrased all point at the precondition of a denial of internal self-determination. As such, the Supreme Court deemed the exceptional circumstances "manifestly inapplicable" to the case of Quebec. It therefore concluded that, under contemporary international law, Quebec did not possess a right to secede unilaterally from Canada.[170] Notwithstanding this view, the Supreme Court remained ambiguous as regards the question of whether the inhabitants of Quebec constituted a 'people' according to international law. Although it acknowledged that characterization as a 'people' was the "threshold step" for the entitlement to self-determination,[171] it refrained from determining whether the population of Quebec would actually qualify as such. It merely noted that while for a large part the inhabitants of Quebec had common characteristics, which is important in considering whether a certain group constitutes a 'people', "it is not necessary to explore this legal characterization to resolve Question 2 appropriately".[172]

With regard to the first question of the reference, the Supreme Court acknowledged that "the legality of unilateral secession must be evaluated [...] from the perspective

---

[166] *Ibid.*, at para. 126.
[167] *Ibid.*, at paras 131-133.
[168] *Ibid.*, at para. 134.
[169] *Ibid.*, at para. 135.
[170] *Ibid.*, at para. 138.
[171] *Ibid.*, at para. 123.
[172] *Ibid.*, at para. 125.

of the domestic legal order of the state from which the unit seeks to withdraw".[173]
It may be recalled in this respect that when dealing with the second question of the
reference, it observed that "[i]nternational law contains neither a right of unilateral
secession nor the explicit denial of such a right". Rather, in large measure, "it leaves
the creation of a new state to be determined by the domestic law of the existing state
of which the seceding entity presently forms a part".[174] Exploring domestic law, the
Supreme Court found that the Canadian Constitution remains silent on the matter of
unilateral secession: it is neither expressly permitted nor prohibited. Nevertheless, it
took the view that an act of secession would "alter the governance of Canadian territory in a manner which undoubtedly is inconsistent with our current constitutional
arrangements" and as such, it deemed unilateral secession to be illegal.[175] As regards
the effect of a referendum, the Supreme Court rejected the claim that an outcome in
favour of secession would immediately exclude Quebec from domestic jurisdiction,
as a result of which the case would be governed by international law. Accordingly, it
considered that:

> the clear repudiation of the existing constitutional order and the clear expression of the
> desire to pursue secession by the population of a province would give rise to a recipro-
> cal obligation on all parties to the Confederation to negotiate constitutional changes to
> respond to that desire.[176]

Thus, the Supreme Court imposed a duty on the parties involved to negotiate in good
faith about the possibility and terms of secession. These negotiations should be conducted in conformity with the constitutional principles of federalism, democracy,
constitutionalism and the rule of law, and respect for minorities,[177] and should include
all matters, ranging from borders to economic issues.[178] In this connection, the importance of the popular will was emphasized and limited at the same time, since it was
noted that the right to self-determination could not be invoked in order to impose
the terms of the proposed secession to the other parties in question. For, "that would
not be a negotiation at all".[179] Furthermore, attention was drawn to the relationship
between the domestic and the international realms, as the Supreme Court held that the
ultimate success of secession would depend on the recognition by the international
community of the newly proclaimed State. Whether either of the parties involved has
been unwilling to enter into negotiations might influence the process of international

---

[173] *Ibid.*, at para. 83.
[174] *Ibid.*, at para. 112.
[175] *Ibid.*, at para. 84.
[176] *Ibid.*, at para. 88.
[177] *Ibid.*, at paras 87-91, 149.
[178] *Ibid.*, at para. 96.
[179] *Ibid.*, at para. 91.

recognition following an act of unilateral secession.[180] Yet, it stressed that international recognition could not provide for a justification of the secession in retroaction, neither under Canadian constitutional law nor under international law.[181] Finally, considering the answers formulated to the first and second questions of the reference, the Supreme Court did not elaborate on the third question. It was merely noted that *in casu*, there was no conflict between domestic and international law.[182]

In sum, it is to be noted that although the Canadian Supreme Court did not clearly express its own views as regards the existence of a right to unilateral secession under contemporary international law, it appears that it tended to recognize the existence of such a qualified right rather than to repudiate it.[183] Yet, it should be kept in mind that the Supreme Court used very careful language, which conveys the impression that it sought to avoid attaching far-reaching consequences to its decision. First, it denied the existence of a constitutional right to secede and identified a constitutional obligation for all parties involved to enter into negotiations in case a majority expresses the wish to secede. Subsequently, with respect to the international legal perspective, the Supreme Court emphasized that, outside the colonial context, external self-determination could only be exercised in exceptional and defined situations. In addition, it remained rather indistinct as to the precise circumstances required to trigger a right to unilateral secession beyond colonialism, as it merely noted the situations of alien subjugation, domination or exploitation and that of the denial of the meaningful exercise of internal self-determination. What is more, the Supreme Court immediately mitigated its proposition by noting that it remains questionable whether such a right to unilateral secession is an established norm under contemporary international law. Likewise, it seemed to avoid the contentious issue of whether the inhabitants of Quebec constituted a 'people' under international law.[184] Finally, it is to be emphasized that the acknowledgement of a right to remedial secession in this very case remained confined to an *obiter dictum*, which means that it concerns a comment by the Court which was not required for reaching a decision on the matter at hand and, therefore, is not binding.[185] In view of the foregoing, although the Canadian Supreme Court's decision certainly shows some support for the existence of a right to unilateral secession, one should be cautious drawing extensive conclusions from it.

---

[180] *Ibid.*, at paras 103, 142-143, 155.

[181] *Ibid.*, at para. 155.

[182] *Ibid.*, at para. 147.

[183] Raič, *Statehood and the Law of Self-Determination* at pp. 331-332.

[184] See also Dumberry, 'Lessons Learned from the *Quebec Secession Reference* before the Supreme Court of Canada' at p. 436; Summers, *Peoples and International Law: How Nationalism and Self-Determination Shape a Contemporary Law of Nations* at pp. 295-296.

[185] This remark was also made by Jure Vidmar. See J. Vidmar, 'Remedial Secession in International Law: Theory and (Lack of) Practice' (2010) 6 *St Antony's International Review* 37 at p. 39.

2.3.5. *Kevin Ngwanga Gumne et al. v. Cameroon*

Years after having addressed the peoples' right to self-determination in its decision regarding *Katangese Peoples' Congress v. Zaire*, the African Commission on Human and Peoples' Rights was requested to deal with that right once again in the case of *Kevin Ngwanga Gumne et al. v. Cameroon*.[186] In doing so, the African Commission reiterated the conditions for unilateral secession it had formulated in *Katangese Peoples' Congress v. Zaire*, as will be demonstrated below.

In the case of *Kevin Ngwanga Gumne et al. v. Cameroon*, fourteen individuals had brought a communication against the Republic of Cameroon before the African Commission on their behalf and on behalf of the population of the Southern Cameroon region. After World War I, this part of the Republic of Cameroon became a territory administered by the British under the League of Nations Mandate System, while the remainder of the territory was placed under French rule. At the end of World War II, both territories converted into trust territories under the UN Trusteeship System. Subsequent to the independence of the Republic of Cameroon in 1960, a UN plebiscite was held, offering the Southern Cameroonians two options, i.e. joining Nigeria or joining Cameroon. Although they voted for the latter option, the communication submitted to the African Commission alleged that the UN plebiscite disregarded a third alternative, that is, independent and sovereign statehood for Southern Cameroon. According to the complainants, a vast majority of 99 per cent of the region's inhabitants preferred independence over the two options which were presented in the plebiscite. The failure of the Republic of Cameroon to exercise that "third alternative" impacted negatively on the right of the people of Southern Cameroon to self-determination, so it was asserted.[187] Furthermore, the complainants asserted that the Republic of Cameroon has systematically violated the human rights of several individuals.[188]

For the purpose of this study, most relevant are the paragraphs of the African Commission's decision considering the alleged violation of the right to self-determination under Article 20 of the African Charter.[189] In this respect, the complainants claimed that the "alleged unlawful and forced annexation and colonial occupation" of Southern Cameroon by the Republic of Cameroon constituted a violation of this provision.[190] In addition, it was asserted that the Southern Cameroonians were a "separate

---

[186] African Commission on Human and Peoples' Rights, *Kevin Ngwanga Gumne et al. v. Cameroon*, Comm. No. 266/2003, 2009 (not dated).

[187] *Ibid.*, at paras 1-6. For an elaborate account of the history of Cameroon, see M.W. DeLancey, 'Cameroon' *Encyclopædia Britannica* (Encyclopædia Britannica Online edn, 2010).

[188] African Commission on Human and Peoples' Rights, *Kevin Ngwanga Gumne et al. v. Cameroon*, Comm. No. 266/2003, 2009 (not dated), at para. 18. More specifically, in addition to violation of the right to self-determination, the complainants asserted that Articles 2, 3, 4, 5, 6, 7(1), 9, 10, 11, 12, 13, 17(1), 19, 20, 21, 22, 23(1), and 24 of the African Charter had been violated.

[189] *Ibid.*, at paras 163-203.

[190] *Ibid.*, at para. 163.

and distinct people" as a result of the British administration over the territory. This had led to the use of the English language, the common law legal tradition and a distinct educational and governmental system. Moreover, the inhabitants of Southern Cameroon were said to have their own traditional cultures.[191]

In response to these claims, the African Commission first sought to elucidate the meaning of the term 'peoples' under the African Charter. It started by acknowledging the "controversial nature of the issue, due to the political connotation that it carries".[192] Although to date, international law has not been able to define the notion, a number of objective characteristics which are attributable to a collectivity of people and may qualify them as a 'people' have been recognized. Reference was made, *inter alia*, to the UNESCO group of experts, which in this respect listed a common historical tradition, a racial or ethnic identity, cultural homogeneity, linguistic unity, religious and ideological affinities, territorial connection and a common economic life.[193] Having analysed literature on the matter and having reflected upon the arguments put forward by the parties involved, the African Commission concluded that the population of Southern Cameroon can be viewed as a 'people' under international law, since:

> they manifest numerous characteristics and affinities, which include a common history, linguistic tradition, territorial connection, and political outlook. More importantly, they identify themselves as a people with a separate and distinct identity.[194]

Subsequently, the question raised whether the people of Southern Cameroon may claim the right to self-determination. In answering this question, the African Commission granted a prominent position to its considerations in *Katangese Peoples' Congress v. Zaire*. In conformity with its reasoning in the latter case, it noted that the African Commission is required to uphold the territorial integrity of State Parties to the African Charter and accordingly, cannot allow or promote an act of secession by the Southern Cameroonians.[195] In this connection, it expressed the view that the right to self-determination may only be exercised externally, through unilateral secession, if the test as phrased in *Katangese Peoples' Congress v. Zaire* is met. That is to say, there must be:

> concrete evidence of violations of human rights to the point that the territorial integrity of the State Party should be called to question, coupled with the denial of the people, their right to participate in the government as guaranteed by Article 13(1).[196]

---

[191] *Ibid.*, at paras 167-168.
[192] *Ibid.*, at para. 169.
[193] *Ibid.*, at paras 169-170.
[194] *Ibid.*, at paras 178-179.
[195] *Ibid.*, at para. 190.
[196] *Ibid.*, at para. 194.

Since the African Commission found that, *in casu*, the complainants had neither demonstrated proof of massive human rights violations, nor that their right to participate in the government had been violated, it concluded that the people of Southern Cameroon were not entitled to secede unilaterally.[197] Yet, as the African Commission recalled, secession is not the only means of exercising the right to self-determination. Autonomy arrangements within the framework of the existing State were also possible means for the people of Southern Cameroon to exercise their right to self-determination.[198] Finally, the African Commission stated the conviction that resolving the grievances of the Southern Cameroons did not require secession, but would rather call for a "comprehensive national dialogue".[199]

Summarizing, it may be said that in *Kevin Ngwanga Gumne et al. v. Cameroon*, the African Commission showed some traces of a qualified right to unilateral secession. It seems that it recognized the existence of such a right with more conviction than in *Katangese Peoples' Congress v. Zaire*. This time, no *a contrario* reasoning is needed to reveal the support for a right to unilateral secession, for the African Commission put the basis for the justified exercise of secession in more positive phraseology:

> in order for [human rights] violations to constitute the basis for the exercise of the right to [external] self-determination under the African Charter, they must meet the test set out in the Katanga case.[200]

As such, it appears that the African Commission not only reiterated the view expressed in *Katangese Peoples' Congress v. Zaire*, but also convincingly reinforced that outlook by establishing a touchstone in this respect. In sum, although the African Commission generally gives precedence to the principle of territorial integrity of States and focuses on internal self-determination, it grants an important role to the political rights embodied in Article 13 of the African Charter in assessing whether or not a people is oppressed to the extent that their right to internal self-determination converts into an entitlement to secede from the existing State.[201]

2.3.6. Accordance with International Law of the Unilateral Declaration of Independence by the Provisional Institutions of Self-Government of Kosovo

The International Court of Justice's Advisory Opinion regarding Kosovo's unilateral declaration of independence was long-awaited by many people. From the Serb

---

[197] *Ibid.*, at paras 195-200.
[198] *Ibid.*, at para. 191.
[199] *Ibid.*, at para. 203.
[200] *Ibid.*, at para. 194.
[201] See Shelton, 'Self-Determination in Regional Human Rights Law: From Kosovo to Cameroon' at pp. 4-6.

government and the Kosovo Albanian population to academics and the community of States, many expected this ruling to shed some light on important (legal) questions, including that of the (il)legality of Kosovo's attempt to secede by declaring itself independent from Serbia on 17 February 2008. Although it may be said that the Court failed to live up to these high expectations, its Advisory Opinion is relevant when searching for traces of a right to unilateral secession. Therefore, the background of the case, the Advisory Opinion itself and some individual opinions by Judges attached to it will be scrutinized below.

2.3.6.1. Background of the Case

Within the Former Socialist Federal Republic of Yugoslavia, Kosovo had been an autonomous province of the Republic of Serbia.[202] The ethnic make-up of Kosovo is majority Albanian with a Serb minority. In 1989, President Slobodan Milošević withdrew Kosovo's special autonomy.[203] This decision seems to stem from fear of ethnic dominance of the Serb minority by the Albanian majority, while the Serbs considered Kosovo to be the cradle of their culture. Under Serb rule, the Albanian population was oppressed and discriminated against: the Kosovo parliament was dissolved, Kosovo Albanians lost their jobs to Serb fellow citizens, restraints were imposed on the Albanian media, and reports concerning abuse and even torture of detained Kosovo Albanians were reported.[204] Consequently, an underground movement led by Ibrahim Rugova was established, which created a shadow society. After years of peaceful yet unsuccessful resistance by Rugova and his followers, in 1996, a radicalized part of the Albanian population founded the Kosovo Liberation Army UÇK, which called for the restoration of Kosovo's autonomy. When they felt that their wishes were ignored, the UÇK shifted to an armed campaign. Attacks on primarily Serbian military targets followed, but assaults were also committed on Albanians suspected of collaboration. In turn, the Serb government responded with police and military action, resulting in widespread violence which was not only aimed at the UÇK, but also at Kosovo's civilian population. These events are to be seen against the background of great unrest in the Balkans. Four of the six republics of the Social-

---

[202] For a brief history of Kosovo, see, for instance, J.B. Allcock, 'Kosovo' *Encyclopædia Britannica* (Encyclopædia Britannica Online edn, 2010); T. Judah, *Kosovo: What Everyone Needs to Know* (Oxford University Press, New York: 2008); J. Summers, 'Kosovo: From Yugoslav Province to Disputed Independence' in J. Summers (ed.) *Kosovo: A Precedent? The Declaration of Independence, the Advisory Opinion and Implications for Statehood, Self-Determination and Minority Rights* (Martinus Nijhoff Publishers, Leiden/Boston 2011) at pp. 3-51; M. Weller, *Contested Statehood: Kosovo's Struggle for Independence* (Oxford University Press, Oxford 2009) at pp. 25-40.

[203] See International Criminal Tribunal for the Former Yugoslavia, *Prosecutor v. Milutinović et al.*, Judgment (vol. 1), ICTY-IT-05-87-T, 26 February 2009, at paras 213-222.

[204] *Ibid.*, at paras 223-230. See also UN General Assembly Resolution 48/153 (*Situation of human rights in the territory of the former Yugoslavia*), UN Doc. A/Res/48/153, 20 December 1993, at paras 17-19.

ist Federal Republic of Yugoslavia declared independence, which set off the break-up of the Republic.[205]

The UN Security Council adopted a couple of resolutions condemning the excessive use of force by both Serbian troops and the UÇK, and calling on the parties involved to seek a political solution.[206] Regrettably, these resolutions had no result. When reports concerning forced expulsion, streams of refugees, mass graves and ethnic cleansing were reported, the international community intervened.[207] Initially, diplomatic means were employed, but the agreements reached were not complied with and the atrocities continued. Therefore, a special conference was organized in Rambouillet for the purpose of resolving the status of Kosovo and the rights of the Kosovo Albanians. In this context, in early 1999, a plan was drafted. This plan was signed by the Kosovo Albanians, but turned down by the Serbs: a three-year period of self-government for Kosovo and the presence of NATO forces on the territory appeared to be unacceptable to Serbia. Even when NATO Member States threatened air attacks, the Serb government did not waver. Eventually, without prior UN authorization, NATO launched an air campaign in order to compel the Serb government to withdraw its forces.[208] At first, the gross human rights violations committed by the Serb authorities continued: torture, rape, homicide and expulsion of the Albanian population from Kosovo continued to occur on a large scale.[209] Seventy-eight days after the start of the air campaign, the Serb government signed an agreement and withdrew its military and police forces from Kosovo.

---

[205] See also Chapter III, Section 4.1.4.

[206] UN Security Council Resolution 1160 (1998) (*On the letters from the United Kingdom (S/1998/223) and the United States (S/1998/272)*), UN Doc. S/Res/1160 (1998), 31 March 1998; UN Security Council Resolution 1199 (1998) (*On the situation in Kosovo (FRY)*), UN Doc. S/Res/1199 (1998), 23 September 1998.

[207] See, for instance, Independent International Commission on Kosovo, *The Kosovo Report. Conflict, International Response, Lessons Learned*, available at <http://reliefweb.int>, last consulted on 5 October 2012; Human Rights Watch, *Under Orders: War Crimes in Kosovo*, available at <http://www.hrw.org/reports/2001/kosovo/>, last consulted 5 October 2012, at pp. 38-58; International Criminal Tribunal for the Former Yugoslavia, *Prosecutor v. Milutinović et al.*, Judgment (vol. 1), ICTY-IT-05-87-T, 26 February 2009, at paras 842-920. See also UN Security Council, *Report of the Secretary-General pursuant to resolutions 1160 (1998) and 1199 (1998) of the Security Council*, UN Doc. S/1998/912, 3 October 1998, at paras 7-9.

[208] It is to be noted, however, that the legality of NATO's actions is highly contested. NATO started an air campaign without an explicit prior authorization by the UN Security Council, which is needed on the basis of the prohibition of the use of force and the formal exceptions as formulated in the UN Charter. See, for instance, S. Chesterman, *Just War or Just Peace? Humanitarian Intervention and International Law* (Oxford University Press, Oxford 2001); B. Simma, 'NATO, the UN and the Use of Force: Legal Aspects' (1999) 10 *European Journal of International Law* 1.

[209] See, for instance, Human Rights Watch, *Under Orders: War Crimes in Kosovo*, available at <http://www.hrw.org/reports/2001/kosovo/>, last consulted 5 October 2012, pp. 109-154.

The UN Security Council subsequently adopted Resolution 1244 (1999),[210] which authorized a United Nations Interim Administration in Kosovo (UNMIK), a UN administration with far-reaching competences.[211] The object of UNMIK was not just to execute administrative functions temporarily, but in addition to advance substantial autonomy and self-government in Kosovo, to facilitate a political process to determine Kosovo's future status, to promote human rights, and to support the restoration of the general infrastructure on the territory. In 2006, the international process for resolving the issue of Kosovo's final status started. The Kosovo population, in the main, aspired to independence, but Serbia stuck to its guns and invoked its sovereign rights. Although agreement was reached on certain matters, the parties were diametrically opposed in this respect. In 2007, UN Special Envoy for Kosovo Martti Ahtisaari submitted a plan which envisioned 'supervised independence' for Kosovo after a period of international administration.[212] The plan was rejected by Serbia, but accepted by the Kosovo authorities.

About one year after the Ahtisaari Plan was submitted, in February 2008, the "democratically elected leaders" of Kosovo issued their declaration of independence. In this declaration, they proclaimed, *inter alia*, that the Republic of Kosovo was an "independent and sovereign State".[213] Although a significant number of States recognized Kosovo's claim to sovereign statehood,[214] various States refused to recognize an independent Kosovo. Some States, including Serbia, even asserted the illegality of Kosovo's declaration of independence. What is more, the Serbian Minister of Foreign Affairs initiated a resolution for the United Nations General Assembly to seek an advisory opinion from the International Court of Justice (ICJ), which led to the following question: is the unilateral declaration of independence by the Provisional Institutions of Self-Government of Kosovo in accordance with international law? In early October 2008, the General Assembly adopted the resolution with a slim majority.[215] Following the request by the General Assembly, the Court decided that

---

[210] UN Security Council Resolution 1244 (1999) (*Kosovo*), UN Doc. S/Res/1244 (1999), 10 June 1999.

[211] On the issue of temporary UN administration in post-conflict situations, see S. Chesterman, *You, the People. The United Nations, Transitional Administration, and State-Building* (Oxford University Press, Oxford 2004).

[212] See 'Report of the Special Envoy of the Secretary-General on Kosovo's Future Status'and 'Main Provisions of the Comprehensive Proposal for the Kosovo Status Settlement', both available in: *Letter dated 26 March 2007 from the Secretary-General addressed to the President of the Security Council*, UN Doc. S/2007/168, 26 March 2007.

[213] See Ministry of Foreign Affairs of Kosovo, *Kosovo Declaration of Independence*, available at <http://www.mfa-ks.net/?page=2,25>, last consulted 1 October 2012.

[214] For an up to date overview of States which have recognized Kosovo, see Ministry of Foreign Affairs of Kosovo, *Countries that have recognized the Republic of Kosova*, available on <http://www.mfa-ks.net/?page=2,33>, last consulted 30 December 2012.

[215] UN General Assembly Resolution 63/3 (*Request for an Advisory Opinion of the International Court of Justice on Whether the Unilateral Declaration of Independence of Kosovo is in Accordance with International Law*), UN Doc. A/Res/63/3, 8 October 2008. The resolution was adopted by a recorded vote

"the United Nations and its Member States are considered likely to be able to furnish information on the question submitted to the Court for an advisory opinion".[216] Consequently, thirty-six UN Member States filed written statements on the question before the Court and after having held public hearings,[217] the Court started its deliberations.[218]

2.3.6.2. The Advisory Opinion

It was not until 22 July 2010 that the International Court of Justice issued its Advisory Opinion on the matter, concluding by ten votes to four that Kosovo's declaration of independence did not violate international law.[219] To arrive at this conclusion, first, the Court had to clear several jurisdictional hurdles which had been raised by States during the proceedings. It was alleged, for instance, that the request by the General Assembly was beyond the scope of its competences under the UN Charter, since the Security Council was already seized of the situation in Kosovo. Further, it was argued that the question phrased by the General Assembly was political in nature rather than legal, which was adduced as a reason for the Court to refuse rendering an opinion.[220]

---

of 77 in favour to 6 against (Albania, Marshall Islands, Federated States of Micronesia, Nauru, Palau, United States), and with 74 abstentions. See UN Press Release, *Backing Request by Serbia, General Assembly Decides to Seek International Court of Justice Ruling on Legality of Kosovo's Independence*, UN Doc. GA/10764, 8 October 2008. It is noteworthy that the draft resolution submitted by Serbia (UN Doc. A/63/L.2) contained a question which was phrased with slightly different wording to the question which the General Assembly eventually included in its resolution. The original text included a request for an advisory opinion of the ICJ on "whether the 17 February 2008 unilateral declaration of independence in Kosovo is in accordance with international law".

[216] International Court of Justice Press Release, *Accordance with International Law of the Unilateral Declaration of Independence by the Provisional Institutions of Self-Government of Kosovo (Request for Advisory Opinion). Filing of written statements and of a written contribution*, No. 2009/17, 21 April 2009. As was observed by Sienho Yee, it should be mentioned that it was the first time that all of the permanent members of the UN Security Council participated in the written as well as the oral proceedings. See S. Yee, 'Notes on the International Court of Justice (Part 4): The *Kosovo* Advisory Opinion' (2010) 9 *Chinese Journal of International Law* 763 at para. 1.

[217] International Court of Justice Press Release, *Accordance with International Law of the Unilateral Declaration of Independence by the Provisional Institutions of Self-Government of Kosovo (Request for Advisory Opinion). Public hearings to be held from 1 December 2009*, No. 2009/27, 29 July 2009.

[218] International Court of Justice Press Release, *Accordance with International Law of the Unilateral Declaration of Independence by the Provisional Institutions of Self-Government of Kosovo (Request for Advisory Opinion). Conclusion of public hearings. Court ready to begin its deliberation*, No. 2009/34, 11 December 2009.

[219] International Court of Justice, *Accordance with International Law of the Unilateral Declaration of Independence in Respect of Kosovo*, Advisory Opinion, ICJ Reports 2010, p. 403.

[220] *Ibid.*, at paras 24-26. It may be interesting to note that a recent article called upon the Court to "exercise its discretion and refuse a request for an advisory opinion when the underlying problem can be resolved only by lengthy and difficult political negotiations", such as the case of Kosovo. See A. Aust, 'Advisory Opinions' (2010) 1 *Journal of International Dispute Settlement* 123.

After a lengthy and formal assessment, the Court unanimously found that it had juris-diction and that no compelling reasons were present not to respond to the question.[221] The Court subsequently decided to focus on the scope and meaning of the question put before it. According to the Court,

> [t]he question is narrow and specific; it asks for the Court's opinion on whether or not the declaration of independence is in accordance with international law. It does not ask about the legal consequences of that declaration. In particular, it does not ask whether or not Kosovo has achieved statehood. Nor does it ask about the validity or legal effects of the recognition of Kosovo by those States which have recognized it as an independent State.[222]

Thus, in the Court's reasoning, it was not requested to decide whether international law confers a *positive* right or entitlement upon entities within a State to separate unilaterally from their parent State and create a new sovereign State – neither in the specific case of Kosovo, nor in general. In this respect, the Court distinguished the question at issue from the one submitted to the Canadian Supreme Court in the *Refer-ence re. Secession of Quebec*, which was discussed above.[223] The Court likewise left aside the right to self-determination and the concept of remedial secession; it found that those issues were not covered by the question which was put before it.[224]

In addressing the substance of this question, the Court first considered the lawful-ness of declarations of independence under general international law (*lex generalis*).[225] In this context, it observed that declarations of independence have been issued for centuries and have only led to international recognition and actual independence in some instances. Nonetheless, State practice does not suggest that the issuing of these declarations was in violation of international law. Moreover, during the second half of the twentieth century, the right to self-determination evolved into a right to inde-pendence for the peoples of colonial and non-self-governing territories. Although a great number of new States have come into existence by means of this right, beyond the context of decolonization, States have been created as well. In this respect, State practice does not point to the existence of a prohibition of declarations of independ-ence, the Court considered.[226] Yet, during the proceedings, several States had argued that such a prohibition is implicit in the principle of territorial integrity of States. As will be expounded elsewhere in the present Chapter, this principle protecting the bor-ders of States is deeply rooted in international law and reflected in the UN Charter and

---

[221] International Court of Justice, *Accordance with International Law of the Unilateral Declaration of Independence in Respect of Kosovo*, Advisory Opinion, ICJ Reports 2010, p. 403, at paras 29-48.

[222] *Ibid.*, at para. 51.

[223] *Ibid.*, at para. 56.

[224] *Ibid.*, at para. 51.

[225] *Ibid.*, at paras 78-84.

[226] *Ibid.*, at para. 79.

other international legal and political instruments. The Court found that "the scope of the principle of territorial integrity is confined to the sphere of relations between States".[227] Thus, in the present case, Serbia's territorial integrity was not violated, since Kosovo's independence was declared by a non-State entity within the borders of the State. Anticipating a more elaborate review of this conclusion elsewhere in this study,[228] it may be noted here that one may question the appropriateness of the Court's statement. On the one hand, the Court's statement may be called conservative, considering the emerging role of non-State actors within contemporary international law. Yet simultaneously, the Court's finding that the acts of sub-State entities are not restricted by the principle of territorial integrity may be deemed remarkably progressive as well, as it appears to lift what has traditionally been regarded as the primary obstacle to unilateral secession. During the proceedings, a number of States had contended that in its resolutions, the UN Security Council has condemned several declarations of independence, for instance in the cases of Southern Rhodesia and Northern Cyprus. In response to this observation, the Court noted that these condemnations were unrelated to the unilateral character of the declarations of independence issued in those instances. According to the Court,

> the illegality attached to the declarations of independence thus stemmed [...] from the fact that they were, or would have been, connected with the unlawful use of force or other egregious violations of norms of general international law, in particular those of a peremptory character (*jus cogens*).[229]

Considering the exceptional character of the Security Council resolutions referred to, the Court concluded that no general prohibition of unilateral declarations of independence can be inferred from this.[230] A number of States, including the Netherlands, alleged that the population of Kosovo could claim the right to self-determination and a right to remedial secession ensuing from this, as a result of which Kosovo was entitled to separate itself from Serbia and to create an independent State. As to the question of the extent of the right to self-determination beyond the context of decolonization, the Court merely noted that the States taking part in the proceedings showed "radically different views" on the matter and that:

> [s]imilar differences existed regarding whether international law provides for a right of "remedial secession" and, if so, in what circumstances. There was also a sharp

---

[227] *Ibid.*, at para. 80.

[228] The Court's statement regarding the principle of territorial integrity will be further considered in Section 2.4.1 of the present Chapter.

[229] International Court of Justice, *Accordance with International Law of the Unilateral Declaration of Independence in Respect of Kosovo*, Advisory Opinion, ICJ Reports 2010, p. 403, at para. 81.

[230] *Ibid.*

difference of views as to whether the circumstances which some participants maintained would give rise to a right of "remedial secession" were actually present in Kosovo.[231]

From this, one may deduce that the Court found that no *opinio juris* was reflected[232] on the contemporary scope of the right to self-determination and the existence of a remedial right to unilateral secession.[233] Furthermore, the Court observed that the argument in favour of a right to remedial secession was in virtually every instance made as a secondary argument only.[234] The Court accordingly considered it "not necessary to resolve such questions in the present case" as it deemed those issues being "beyond the scope of the question" which was before it.[235]

The Court subsequently examined whether Security Council Resolution 1244 (1999) had created special rules or measures, particularly the UNMIK Constitutional Framework, which affected the lawfulness of Kosovo's declaration of independence.[236] According to the Court, these regulations merely aimed at creating an interim regime for the purpose of stabilizing Kosovo and restoring basic public order and did not determine Kosovo's final status or the preconditions for that status.[237] In this connection, the Court also examined the identity of the authors of the declaration.[238] From the phrasing of the declaration and the conditions under which it was adopted, the Court inferred that these authors should not be regarded as the Provisional Institutions of Self-Government as established under the Constitutional Framework, but rather as an assembly of persons acting "as representatives of the people of Kosovo outside the framework of the interim administration".[239] According to the Court, a

---

[231] *Ibid.*, at para. 82.

[232] It may be interesting to note that the Court took a comparable approach in its *Nuclear Weapons* Advisory Opinion, where the observation that "the members of the international community [were] profoundly divided on the matter of whether non-recourse to nuclear weapons of the past 50 years constitutes the expression of an *opinio juris*" led the Court to conclude that no such *opinio juris* existed. See International Court of Justice, *Legality of the Threat or Use of Nuclear Weapons*, Advisory Opinion, ICJ Reports 1996, p. 226, at para. 67.

[233] For a similar conclusion, see Yee, 'Notes on the International Court of Justice (Part 4): The *Kosovo* Advisory Opinion' at para. 39. As Yee rightly observes, "[i]f one is to follow the normal method of finding customary international law as required by Article 38(1)(b) of the ICJ Statute, no custom regarding such a right can be found here". Whether such a conclusion should indeed be drawn with respect to the question of remedial secession will be considered in the following Chapters of this study.

[234] International Court of Justice, *Accordance with International Law of the Unilateral Declaration of Independence in Respect of Kosovo*, Advisory Opinion, ICJ Reports 2010, p. 403, at para. 82.

[235] *Ibid.*, at para. 83.

[236] *Ibid.*, at paras 94-121.

[237] *Ibid.*, at para. 98.

[238] *Ibid.*, at paras 102-109. This approach was criticized by Vice-President Tomka in his declaration attached to the Advisory Opinion. See *ibid.*, Declaration of Vice-President Tomka, paras 10-21.

[239] International Court of Justice, *Accordance with International Law of the Unilateral Declaration of Independence in Respect of Kosovo*, Advisory Opinion, ICJ Reports 2010, p. 403, at para. 109.

prohibition of declarations of independence can neither be derived from Security Council Resolution 1244 (1999) nor the Constitutional Framework, as these merely determined Kosovo's interim political structures, nor do these documents contain any legal obligation binding upon the authors of Kosovo's declaration of independence.[240] Considering the foregoing, the Court ultimately came to the conclusion that the adoption of the declaration of independence of 17 February 2008 "did not violate any applicable rule of international law".[241]

The Court's approach as outlined above has been criticized by commentators for various reasons.[242] Moreover, it has led several judges to attach a separate opinion to the decision, dissociating themselves from the Court's narrow and restrictive reading.[243] Indeed, the question which was put before the Court concerned the "accordance with international law of the action undertaken by the representatives of the people of Kosovo with the aim of establishing such a new State without the consent of the parent State". The question as to the legality of Kosovo's attempt to secede unilaterally from Serbia, however, logically flows from this. In the words of Judge Yusuf:

---

[240] *Ibid.*, at paras 118-121.

[241] *Ibid.*, at para. 122.

[242] For a criticism on (primarily) the Court's limited approach, see, for instance, B. Arp, 'The ICJ Advisory Opinion on the Accordance with International Law of the Unilateral Declaration of Independence in Respect of Kosovo and the International Protection of Minorities' (2010) 11 *German Law Journal* 847; T. Burri, 'The Kosovo Opinion and Secession: The Sounds of Silence and Missing Links' (2010) 11 *German Law Journal* 881; T. Christakis, 'The ICJ Advisory Opinion on Kosovo: Has International Law Something to Say about Secession?' (2011) 24 *Leiden Journal of International Law* 73; R. Falk, 'The Kosovo Advisory Opinion: Conflict Resolution and Precedent' (2011) 105 *American Journal of International Law* 50; H. Hannum, 'The Advisory Opinion on Kosovo: An Opportunity Lost, or a Poisoned Chalice Refused?' (2011) 24 *Leiden Journal of International Law* 155; M.G. Kohen and K. Del Mar, 'The Kosovo Advisory Opinion and UNSCR 1244 (1999): A Declaration of 'Independence from International Law'?' (2011) 24 *Leiden Journal of International Law* 109; R. Muharremi, 'A Note on the ICJ Advisory Opinion on Kosovo' (2010) 11 *German Law Journal* 867; C. Ryngaert, 'The ICJ's Advisory Opinion on Kosovo's Declaration of Independence: A Missed Opportunity?' (2010) 57 *Netherlands International Law Review* 481; N.J. Schrijver, 'Kosovo: dynamiek of dynamiet?' (2010) 85 *Nederlands Juristenblad* 1737; M. Vashakmadze and M. Lippold, '"Nothing But a Road Towards Secession"? The International Court of Justice's Advisory Opinion on Accordance with International Law of the Unilateral Declaration of Independence in Respect of Kosovo' (2010) 2 *Goettingen Journal of International Law* 619; R. Wilde, 'International Decisions – Accordance with International Law of the Unilateral Declaration of Independence in Respect of Kosovo' (2011) 105 *American Journal of International Law* 301; Yee, 'Notes on the International Court of Justice (Part 4): The *Kosovo* Advisory Opinion'.

[243] See International Court of Justice, *Accordance with International Law of the Unilateral Declaration of Independence in Respect of Kosovo*, Advisory Opinion, ICJ Reports 2010, p. 403, Separate Opinion of Judge Sepúlveda-Amor, at paras 33-35; *ibid.*, Separate Opinion of Judge Yusuf, at paras 2, 5, 17; *ibid.*, Dissenting Opinion of Judge Koroma, at paras 4, 20; *ibid.*, Declaration of Judge Simma, at paras 1, 6-7. For a more indirect criticism, see *ibid.*, Separate Opinion of Judge A.A. Cançado Trindade. In total, nine judges appended a declaration or separate opinion.

the Court was asked to assess whether or not the process by which the people of Kosovo were seeking to establish their own State involved a violation of international law, or whether that process could be considered consistent with international law in view of the possible existence of a positive right of the people of Kosovo in the specific circumstances which prevailed in that territory. Thus, the restriction of the scope of the question to whether international law prohibited the declaration of independence as such voids it of much of its substance.[244]

Viewed from this perspective, the request by the General Assembly deserved a more comprehensive assessment than the Court provided for.[245] In sum, although the circumstances of the case seem to be of great relevance to this Chapter and several States participating in the proceedings explicitly invoked arguments relating to the right to self-determination and the concept of remedial secession,[246] unfortunately, the majority opinion does not provide for much clarity with regard to the question of the existence of a (qualified) right to unilateral secession. Only implicitly, the Court noted that no *opinio juris* was shown on the scope of the right to self-determination beyond decolonization and the existence of a remedial right to unilateral secession. Yet, the Declaration of Judge Simma and the Separate Opinions of Judge Yusuf, Judge Cançado Trindade and Judge Koroma are significant in this respect. Their views will be discussed below.

2.3.6.3. Individual Opinions of Judges on a Right to Remedial Secession

In his Declaration attached to the Advisory Opinion, Judge Simma criticized the "unnecessarily limited" and "potentially misguiding" analysis of the Court.[247] According to Judge Simma, the Court's interpretation of the question before it showed an outdated view of international law, as it seemed to apply the so-called '*Lotus* principle'[248] by merely considering rules possibly prohibiting the promulga-

---

[244] *Ibid.*, Separate Opinion Judge Yusuf, at para. 2.

[245] But see Marc Weller, arguing that "it seems strange to criticize the Court for not answering the questions it was – with great deliberation – not asked. Having failed to frame the question differently may have been a miscalculation on the part of Serbia, but this failing is hardly attributable to the Court". M. Weller, 'Modesty Can Be a Virtue: Judicial Economy in the ICJ Kosovo Opinion?' (2011) 24 *Leiden Journal of International Law* 127 at p. 132.

[246] See, for instance, the submissions by Albania, Estonia, Finland, Germany, Ireland, Jordan, the Netherlands, Poland, Russia, and Switzerland. Their views will be elaborated upon in Chapter VI, Section 3.1.2.1.

[247] International Court of Justice, *Accordance with International Law of the Unilateral Declaration of Independence in Respect of Kosovo*, Advisory Opinion, ICJ Reports 2010, p. 403, Declaration Judge Simma, at paras 1-5.

[248] The '*Lotus* principle' flows from *The Case of the SS Lotus* and boils down to the proposition that what is not explicitly prohibited under international law is permitted for States. *The Case of the SS Lotus* concerned a dispute between France and Turkey following the collision of two ships on the high seas on 2 August 1926. In this accident between a French mail steamer (*Lotus*) and the Turkish collier

tion of a unilateral declaration of independence.[249] Moreover, he observed that both the authors of this declaration and some of the States participating in the proceedings made reference to the exercise of a right to self-determination.[250] In view of this, Judge Simma contended that the question phrased by the General Assembly:

> deserve[d] a more comprehensive answer, assessing both permissive and prohibitive rules of international law. This would have included a deeper analysis of whether the principle of self-determination or any other rule (perhaps expressly mentioning remedial secession) permit or even warrant independence (via secession) of certain peoples/territories.[251]

Judge Simma did not scrutinize these issues in his Declaration, as he considered that it would be an inappropriate exercise of his judicial role.[252] Yet, reading between the

---

(*Boz-Kourt*), eight Turkish persons on board died. The Turkish authorities subsequently started criminal proceedings against a number of persons, including Lieutenant Demons, a French citizen who was the officer of the watch on the *Lotus*. Although Lieutenant Demons contended that Turkey had no jurisdiction on the matter, he was sentenced for involuntary manslaughter by the Criminal Court of Istanbul. These actions triggered diplomatic representations aimed at transferring the case to the French courts. Accordingly, the Turkish government declared its willingness to bring the dispute before the Permanent Court of International Justice (PCIJ), which had to rule on the question of whether the prosecution of Lieutenant Demons was inconsistent with the Article 15 of the Convention of Lausanne. This provision held that "all questions of jurisdiction shall, as between Turkey and the other contracting Powers, be decided in accordance with the principles of international law". According to the French government, for Turkey to have criminal jurisdiction, an explicit international legal entitlement was needed. In the opinion of the Turkish government, however, it had jurisdiction unless it was prohibited under international law. In this respect, the Court considered, *inter alia*, that "[f]ar from laying down a general prohibition to the effect that States may not extend the application of their laws and the jurisdiction of their courts to persons, property and acts outside their territory, it leaves them in this respect with *a wide measure of discretion which is only limited in certain cases by prohibitive rules*" (emphasis added). In absence of such prohibitive rules, the Court concluded that Turkey had not acted in violation of the principles of international law when instigating the criminal proceedings against Lieutenant Demons. See Permanent Court of International Justice, *The Case of the SS Lotus (France v. Turkey)*, Judgment, PCIJ Series A, No. 10 (1927). One may criticize the highly positivistic approach which the PCIJ took in this case. Moreover, it is to be noted that the relevance of the *Lotus* principle for today's international legal system is disputed due to various developments in international law. See, for instance, A. von Bogdandy and M. Rau, 'The Lotus' in R. Wolfrum (ed.) *Max Planck Encyclopedia of Public International Law* (fully updated online edn, Oxford University Press, New York 2010).

[249] Théodore Christakis, however, has qualified Judge Simma's argument that the Court applied the *Lotus* principle in its Advisory Opinion. See Christakis, 'The ICJ Advisory Opinion on Kosovo: Has International Law Something to Say about Secession?' at pp. 78-80.

[250] International Court of Justice, *Accordance with International Law of the Unilateral Declaration of Independence in Respect of Kosovo*, Advisory Opinion, ICJ Reports 2010, p. 403, Declaration Judge Simma, at para. 6.

[251] *Ibid.*, at para. 7.

[252] *Ibid.*

lines, one may discern his implicit support for the acknowledgement of a right to remedial secession.

Similar to Judge Simma, Judge Yusuf found it regrettable that the Court decided not to pronounce on the question of whether international law acknowledged a right to self-determination in the case of Kosovo. In his Concurring Opinion, he first enumerated four arguments in this respect. First, Judge Yusuf noted that although declarations of independence as such are not regulated by international law, the latter is relevant when considering the aim and claim of the declaration:

> If such claim meets the conditions prescribed by international law, particularly in situations of decolonization or of peoples subject to alien subjugation, domination and exploitation, the law may encourage it; but if it violates international law, the latter can discourage it or even declare it illegal.[253]

Secondly, Judge Yusuf articulated that the Court could have contributed to a better understanding of the scope and legal content of the right to self-determination, both beyond the colonial context in general, and in the specific situation of Kosovo.[254] Thirdly, he feared that the restrictive approach by the Court may be misinterpreted as legitimizing attempts to secede by separatist groups. Fourthly and finally, Judge Yusuf observed that the Court's remark that "the declaration of independence is an attempt to determine finally the status of Kosovo" (para. 114) is inconsistent with the Court's failure to assess whether the final status aimed at, i.e. separate statehood, is in accordance with international law.[255] Subsequently, Judge Yusuf turned to the substance of the issue of self-determination itself. He recalled the internal dimension of the right to self-determination beyond decolonization[256] and continued by pointing at the challenge which claims to external self-determination pose to international law as well as to States. He admitted that, in contrast to the generally accepted right to external self-determination for inhabitants of non-self-governing territories and peoples under alien subjugation, domination or exploitation, contemporary international law does not grant a "general positive right" to all ethnically or racially distinct groups or entities within States to claim sovereign statehood.[257] According to Judge Yusuf,

> [t]his does not, however, mean that international law turns a blind eye to the plight of such groups, particularly in those cases where the State not only denies the exercise of their internal right of self-determination [...], but also subjects them to discrimination,

---

[253] International Court of Justice, *Accordance with International Law of the Unilateral Declaration of Independence in Respect of Kosovo*, Advisory Opinion, ICJ Reports 2010, p. 403, Separate Opinion Judge Yusuf, at para. 5.

[254] *Ibid.*

[255] *Ibid.*, at para. 6.

[256] *Ibid.*, at paras 8-9.

[257] *Ibid.*, at para. 10.

persecution and egregious violations of human rights or humanitarian law. Under such exceptional circumstances, the right of peoples to self-determination may support a claim to separate statehood provided that it meets the conditions prescribed by international law, in a specific situation, taking into account the historical context.[258]

Judge Yusuf derived the acknowledgement of such a qualified right to unilateral secession from "various international instruments", in particular from the Friendly Relations Declaration with its safeguard clause.[259] To strengthen his argument, he referred to some phrases by the African Commission of Human and Peoples' Rights in the *Katangese Peoples' Congress v. Zaire* and the Canadian Supreme Court in the *Reference re. Secession of Quebec*.[260] He continued by noting that,

> [t]o determine whether a specific situation constitutes an exceptional case which may legitimize a claim to external self-determination, certain criteria have to be considered, such as the existence of discrimination against a people, its persecution due to its racial or ethnic characteristics, and the denial of autonomous political structures and access to government. A decision by the Security Council to intervene could also be an additional criterion for assessing the exceptional circumstances which might confer legitimacy on demands for external self-determination by a people denied the exercise of its right to internal self-determination. Nevertheless, even where such exceptional circumstances exist, it does not necessarily follow that the concerned people has an automatic right to separate statehood. All possible remedies for the realization of internal self-determination must be exhausted before the issue is removed from the domestic jurisdiction of the State which had hitherto exercised sovereignty over the territory inhabited by the people making the claim. In this context, the role of the international community, and in particular of the Security Council and the General Assembly, is of paramount importance.[261]

Given the special context of the events in Kosovo, Judge Yusuf wrote, there was sufficient reason for the Court to consider whether the situation reflected the type of exceptional circumstances which may convert a right to internal self-determination into a right to secede unilaterally from the parent State.[262] While Judge Yusuf – in contrast to the majority of judges – appeared to be convinced of the existence of a right to self-determination which may support a claim to separate statehood under certain circumstances, it should be noted that he ventured no opinion on the question of whether such a right could legitimately be invoked in the case of Kosovo. Neither

---

[258] *Ibid.*, at para. 11.

[259] *Ibid.*, at paras 11-12.

[260] *Ibid.*, at paras 14-15.

[261] *Ibid.*, at para. 16.

[262] *Ibid.*, at para. 13. For an argument in the same vein, see International Court of Justice, *Accordance with International Law of the Unilateral Declaration of Independence in Respect of Kosovo*, Advisory Opinion, ICJ Reports 2010, p. 403, Separate Decision of Judge A.A. Cançado Trindade, at para. 179.

did he refer to other specific cases to which such a right would have applied. As such, his argument in favour of a right to remedial secession remains rather theoretical only.

The Separate Opinion of Judge Cançado Trindade should be addressed when looking for traces of a (qualified) right to unilateral secession. Although less explicit than Judge Yusuf, he made reference to such a right as well. Throughout his seventy-page account, Judge Cançado Trindade emphasized the humane ends of international law and the responsibility which States bear for human beings on their territory. From that perspective, he recalled that the principle of self-determination of peoples was widely applied in the decolonization process and contended that today, the notion "applies in new situations of systematic oppression, subjugation and tyranny".[263] He continued by arguing that:

> [n]o State can invoke territorial integrity in order to commit atrocities (such as the practices of torture, and ethnic cleansing, and massive forced displacement of the population), nor perpetrate them on the assumption of State sovereignty, nor commit atrocities and then rely on a claim of territorial integrity notwithstanding the sentiments and ineluctable resentments of the "people" or "population" victimized. What has happened in Kosovo is that the victimized "people" or "population" has sought independence, in reaction against systematic and long-lasting terror and oppression, perpetrated in flagrant breach of the fundamental principle of equality and non-discrimination [...]. The basis lesson is clear: no State can use territory to destroy the population. Such atrocities amount to an absurd reversal of the ends of the State, which was created and exists for human beings, and not *vice-versa*.[264]

Thus, although Judge Cançado Trindade did not expressly refer to the concept of remedial secession, the phrasing of his argument clearly discloses support for the existence of such a right under contemporary international law. Besides taking a general humanist vision of international law,[265] it appears that Judge Cançado Trindade considered the safeguard clause from the Friendly Relations Declaration and its reiteration in the Vienna Declaration and Programme of Action to be the primary basis for this right, both in general[266] and in the specific event of Kosovo.[267]

---

[263] *Ibid.*, at para. 175. See also *ibid.*, at para. 184.

[264] *Ibid.*, at para. 176.

[265] See, in particular, *ibid.*, at paras 75-96 ('The Contemporaneity of the '*Droit des Gens*': The Humanist Vision of the International Legal Order').

[266] *Ibid.*, at paras 177-181.

[267] *Ibid.*, at para. 181: "The massive violations of human rights and international humanitarian law to which the Kosovar Albanians were subjected in the nineties met the basic criterion set forth in the 1970 U.N. Declaration of Principles [i.e. Friendly Relations Declaration], and enlarged in scope in the 1993 final document of the U.N.'s II World Conference on Human Rights [i.e. Vienna Declaration and Programme of Action]. The entitlement to self-determination of the victimized population emerged, as the claim to territorial integrity could no longer be relied upon by the willing victimizers."

Finally, the Dissenting Opinion of Judge Koroma merits brief discussion. In contrast to the opinions of the three Judges referred to above, Judge Koroma rejected the existence of a (remedial) right to unilateral secession under international law. Judge Koroma first contended that the question which was put before the Court concerned "a legal question requiring a legal response", and hence, the Court should have answered it instead of avoiding it. According to Judge Koroma,

> the unilateral declaration of independence by the Provisional Institutions of Self-Government of Kosovo amounted to secession and was not in accordance with international law. A unilateral secession of a territory from an existing State without its consent, as in this case under consideration, is a matter of international law.[268]

In this respect, Judge Koroma strongly emphasized that international law upholds respect for the territorial integrity of States, being one of the fundamental principles of the international legal order. To substantiate his argument, Judge Koroma *inter alia* referred to this principle as enshrined in Principle V, paragraph 7 of the Friendly Relations Declaration, which stipulates that:

> [n]othing in the foregoing paragraphs shall be construed as authorizing or encouraging any action which would dismember or impair, totally or in part, the territorial integrity or political unity of sovereign and independent States [...][269]

However, it is striking that Judge Koroma omitted to include the remaining phrase of the safeguard clause,[270] which concerns precisely that part of the clause upon which Judge Yusuf and Judge Cançado Trindade – along with many legal scholars[271] – had founded the existence of a right to remedial secession.

In sum, it can be concluded that, whereas some individual Judges expressly or implicitly acknowledged the existence of a qualified right to unilateral secession and one Judge rejected this outlook, the Court's majority opinion on the legality of Kosovo's unilateral declaration of independence did not reveal support for such a thesis. Rather, the Court determinedly remained silent as regards the issues of self-determination and remedial secession, as it found that these matters were beyond the scope

---

[268] International Court of Justice, *Accordance with International Law of the Unilateral Declaration of Independence in Respect of Kosovo*, Advisory Opinion, ICJ Reports 2010, p. 403, Dissenting Opinion of Judge Koroma, at para. 20.

[269] UN General Assembly Resolution 2625 (XXV) (*Declaration on Principles of International Law Concerning Friendly Relations and Co-Operation Among States in Accordance with the Charter of the United Nations*), UN Doc. A/Res/2625 (XXV), 24 October 1970, Principle V, Para. 7.

[270] International Court of Justice, *Accordance with International Law of the Unilateral Declaration of Independence in Respect of Kosovo*, Advisory Opinion, ICJ Reports 2010, p. 403, Dissenting Opinion of Judge Koroma, at para. 22.

[271] See Section 2.2. of the present Chapter.

of the question which was put before it. The Court nevertheless emphasized that the declarations of the States participating in the advisory proceedings reflected widely differing opinions on these matters. In view of the above, it may at best be said that the Court's Advisory Opinion indicates that 'there is something brewing' when it comes to the existence of a right to unilateral secession.

2.3.7. Conclusions on Judicial Decisions and Opinions

This section has demonstrated that over the last two decades, judicial decisions and opinions have shown some support for the thesis that the peoples' right to self-determination includes a qualified right to unilateral secession. Although most decisions did not enlarge in great detail on the circumstances in which such a right to unilateral secession may be warranted, evidence of massive human rights violations and the denial of the meaningful exercise of the right to internal self-determination are generally mentioned as conditions for reaching the threshold.

However, some remarks are called for. First, it is to be noted that the judiciary sometimes relied on trends it had identified in scholarly literature rather than expressing its own views as regards the existence of a (qualified) right to unilateral secession under contemporary international law. This was clearly the case in the *Reference re Secession of Quebec*. Also, it is to be admitted that the acknowledgement of such a right has so far remained hypothetical, as no judicial decision or opinion has actually granted a people a right to secede unilaterally in view of the circumstances of the specific case at issue.[272] Even in the case of Kosovo, which had frequently been referred to as the ultimate test case for the existence of a right to unilateral secession, the Court ventured no (majority) opinion on this question. Finally, it was seen that most courts were very cautious with respect to acknowledging the existence of a right to unilateral secession under contemporary international law.

In light of the above, although the existence of a conditional right to unilateral secession has been acknowledged in some instances, it may be concluded that the judiciary remains rather ambiguous on the matter. One should therefore be cautious in drawing conclusions from the judicial decisions and opinions regarding the existence of such a right.

2.4. Traces of a (Remedial) Right to Unilateral Secession in General Principles of (International) Law

Article 38(1)(c) of the Statute of the International Court of Justice identifies "the general principles of law recognized by civilized nations" as one of the sources

---

[272] A similar conclusion was reached by Jure Vidmar. See Vidmar, 'Remedial Secession in International Law: Theory and (Lack of) Practice' at p. 40.

of international law. Although it is generally agreed that today, the term 'civilized nations' no longer attains a special meaning,[273] opinions differ as regards the understanding of the concept of general principles of law in the main.[274] Broadly speaking, two diverging interpretations can be discerned. The one interpretation considers general principles of law to be principles which appear in the majority of the various systems of municipal law and are necessary for the proper implementation of international law. These principles, such as the principle of good faith, proportionality, equity and *pacta sunt servanda* may be referred to as 'general principles of law'. The alternative interpretation considers general principles of law to be principles which have been developed within the international legal realm and which are applicable to the relations among States. Such 'general principles of international law' are different from customary rules or norms codified in treaties in that they are – as the concept itself already suggests – "more general and less precise".[275] As Antonio Cassese explained, they are often "the expression and result of conflicting views of States on matters of crucial importance".[276] The principle of self-determination of peoples is a prominent example in this respect.[277] In practice, both approaches seem to have been adopted: principles stemming from domestic law as well as principles finding their origin on the international level are used as a source of international law.[278]

Since general principles of (international) law are often loose, multifaceted, and even ambiguous it may be argued that they can be used for various applications which might even be contradictory. While these characteristics may be seen as weaknesses, at the same time, they provide general principles with their dynamic nature and normative potential.[279] As such, general principles of (international) law may be said to play a twofold role in the main. First, they may be seen as a basic standard for interpreting international law where specific norms codified in treaties or developed through custom are obscure or ambiguous. Secondly, they may prove helpful in cases

---

[273] The new term applied is 'peace-loving nations', as is also stated in Article 4 of the UN Charter. See P. Malanczuk, *Akehurst's Modern Introduction to International Law* (7th revised edn, Routledge, London/ New York 1997) at p. 48.

[274] It is even said that there was consensus neither among the drafters of the Statute of the Permanent Court of International Justice nor among of the Statute of the International Court of Justice as to the exact import of the phrase. See I. Brownlie, *Principles of Public International Law* (7th edn, Oxford University Press, Oxford 2008) at p. 16; G. Gaja, 'General Principles of Law' in R. Wolfrum (ed.) *Max Planck Encyclopedia of Public International Law* (fully updated online edn, Oxford University Press, New York 2010) at paras 1-6.

[275] Cassese, *Self-Determination of Peoples. A Legal Reappraisal* at p. 128.

[276] *Ibid.* at p. 128.

[277] See, for instance, Gaja, 'General Principles of Law' at paras 1-6; Malanczuk, *Akehurst's Modern Introduction to International Law* at p. 48; M.N. Shaw, *International Law* (5th edn, Cambridge University Press, Cambridge 2003) at pp. 93-94; Thirlway, 'The Sources of International Law' at pp. 130-132.

[278] See Gaja, 'General Principles of Law' at paras 7-20; Thirlway, 'The Sources of International Law' at pp. 131-132.

[279] Cassese, *Self-Determination of Peoples. A Legal Reappraisal* at pp. 128-129.

which are not covered by specific rules of international law at all.[280] In both respects, general principles of (international) law can provide a guideline for judges when positive international law does not provide a clear-cut answer,[281] and simultaneously, they may confine the discretionary powers of both the judiciary and the executive branch with regard to decisions in individual cases.[282]

Yet, as Hugh Thirlway noted, there is "a striking lack of evidence in international practice and jurisprudence of claims to a specific right of a concrete nature being asserted or upheld on the basis simply of the general principles of law".[283] This makes it difficult to identify a fixed set of general principles of law and to consider this array against the background of the issue of a (qualified) right to unilateral secession. Nonetheless, as was observed above, some principles seem to be broadly recognized as general principles of law. General principles common in municipal laws, such as good faith and proportionality, may certainly be taken into account when adducing arguments in support of the existence of a right to unilateral secession. For instance, it might be argued that in case of gross and systematic human rights violations, the principle of proportionality requires that the peoples' right to self-determination will prevail over the sovereign rights of States rather then *vice versa*. Such principles may, however, play a marginal role only as they are background principles "informing and shaping the observance of existing rules of international law and in addition constraining the manner in which those rules may legitimately be exercised".[284] When it comes to general principles which are relevant only under international law, the principles of respect for the territorial integrity of States and *uti possidetis juris* should be recalled in the present context, as it is often argued that these principles collide with the right to (external) self-determination. These principles will be addressed below. Moreover, self-determination of peoples will be considered in its quality of principle, thereby demonstrating the distinct role of the principle and its inaptitude in providing clarity as regards the existence of a right to remedial secession.

2.4.1. The Principle of Respect for the Territorial Integrity of States

The principle of respect for the territorial integrity of States is considered to be one of the fundamental principles of the State-centred system on which international law is built.[285] It is contained in Article 2(4) of the Charter of the United Nations, which

---

[280] See *ibid.* at pp. 132-133.

[281] International law refers to this problem as *non liquet*. See Shaw, *International Law* at p. 93.

[282] See M. Sepúlveda *et al.*, *Human Rights Reference Handbook* (3rd revised edn, University for Peace, Ciudad Colon 2004) at p. 24.

[283] Thirlway, 'The Sources of International Law' at p. 132.

[284] Shaw, *International Law* at p. 98.

[285] See, for instance, S.K.N. Blay, 'Territorial Integrity and Political Independence' in R. Wolfrum (ed.) *Max Planck Encyclopedia of Public International Law* (fully updated online edn, Oxford University Press, New York 2010) at para. 1.

articulates it as one of the organization's principles and links it to the prohibition of the threat or use of force. Moreover, the principle of territorial integrity is set forth in other regional legal and political documents, such as the Charter of the Organization of American States (Articles 1, 12 and 20), the Charter of the Organization of African Union (Preamble), the Helsinki Final Act (Principles I, II, IV and VIII), and the Charter of Paris (Principle III: Friendly Relations among Participating States). Further, the principle of territorial integrity is included in the Friendly Relations Declaration (Principle I, Principle V, paragraphs 7 and 8, and Principle VI(d)), where it is conceived as one of the elements of the principle of sovereign equality. In addition to being included in these abovementioned international instruments, the principle of territorial integrity has been affirmed by the International Court of Justice on various occasions. Already in the 1949 *Corfu Channel* case, the Court highlighted the value of this principle by noting that "[b]etween independent States, respect for territorial sovereignty is an essential foundation of international relations".[286] In its famous case on the *Military and Paramilitary Activities in and against Nicaragua*, the Court emphasized "the duty of every State to respect the territorial sovereignty of others".[287] More recently, the International Court of Justice recalled the "central importance in international law and relations of State sovereignty over territory and of the stability and certainty of that sovereignty".[288] So, the doctrine of the stability of borders also reflects the importance which international law attaches to preserving the territorial *status quo*.[289]

2.4.1.1. The Content of the Principle of Territorial Integrity

It has already been indicated that the principle of respect for the territorial integrity of States is firmly rooted in international law and is often referred to in connection with related concepts such as State sovereignty, political independence and the stability of borders. To put it even more strongly, the principle of territorial integrity can hardly be detached from these notions. Although the territory of a State may be defined as "the material elements of the State, namely the physical and demographic resources that lie within its territory (land, sea and airspace) and are delimited by the State's frontiers",[290] the principle of respect for the territorial integrity encompasses more

---

[286] International Court of Justice, *Corfu Channel (United Kingdom of Great Britain and Northern Ireland v. Albania)*, Merits, Judgment, ICJ Reports 1949, p. 4, at para. 35.

[287] International Court of Justice, *Military and Paramilitary Activities in and against Nicaragua (Nicaragua v. United States of America)*, Merits, Judgment, ICJ Reports 1986, p. 14, at para. 213.

[288] International Court of Justice, *Sovereignty over Pedra Branca/Pulau Batu Puteh, Middle Rocks and South Ledge (Malaysia v. the Republic of Singapore)*, Judgment, ICJ Reports 2008, p. 1, at para. 122.

[289] This was also stressed in International Court of Justice, *Case Concerning the Temple of Preah Vihear (Cambodia v. Thailand)*, Merits, Judgment, ICJ Reports 1962, p. 6, at p. 32.

[290] C.L. Rozakis, 'Territorial Integrity and Political Independence' in R. Bernhardt (ed.) *Encyclopedia of Public International Law* (Elsevier, Amsterdam 2000) at p. 813.

than merely the protection of a State's possession of these resources situated within its borders. In addition to this inviolability of the territory, the principle includes the capacity of a State to exercise and control all State functions over its territory, which logically implies that no other State may interfere or exercise its power over (part of) a territory of another State without the consent of the latter.[291] As such, the principle of respect for territorial integrity is intertwined with the idea of political independence. In sum, the principle of respect for the territorial integrity of States is generally seen to be infringed when a part of a State's territory is being dismembered or when a State forcibly loses control – either directly or indirectly – over its territory or a part thereof. For the purpose of upholding its territorial integrity, a State is entitled to protect itself from illegal interventions and to preserve the unity of its territory by all lawful means.[292]

As one of the core elements of statehood and as a corollary of State sovereignty, international law attaches great importance to protecting the territorial integrity of sovereign States, in particular since it interacts with other principles of international law. In this respect, the interrelationship with the prohibition of the use or threat of force, the principle of non-intervention in the internal affairs of other States, the protection of human rights and the right to self-determination of peoples can be mentioned.[293] As Antonio Cassese felicitously noted, these principles:

> supplement and support one another and also condition each other's application. International subjects must comply with all of them. Also, in the application of any one of the principles, all the others must simultaneously be borne in mind.[294]

2.4.1.2. The Principle of Territorial Integrity and the Right to Self-Determination

The meaning and content of the principle of territorial integrity as dealt with above raise questions as to how this principle and the right to self-determination of peoples relate to each other. At first sight, the right to territorial integrity of States and the right to self-determination of peoples seem to sit together uncomfortably when it comes to external self-determination by means of unilateral secession.[295] For, the first concept aims to maintain the territorial *status quo*, while the latter inevitably leads to unwished-for alterations in territory and loss of control over a part thereof. In other words, the express acceptance of the principle of territorial integrity and

---

[291] This capacity to exercise and control all State functions over a territory may be restricted by resolutions adopted by the UN Security Council under Chapter VII of the UN Charter.

[292] Raič, *Statehood and the Law of Self-Determination* at p. 294.

[293] See, for instance, W.E. Butler, 'Territorial Integrity and Secession: The Dialectics of International Order' in J. Dahlitz (ed.) *Secession and International Law* (T.M.C. Asser Press, The Hague 2003) at pp. 112-113.

[294] A. Cassese, *International Law* (Oxford University Press, Oxford 2001) at p. 112.

[295] See, for instance, Hannum, 'Rethinking Self-Determination' at p. 42.

the express prohibition of the partial or total disruption of the national unity and territorial integrity of a State[296] appear to imply the non-recognition of a right to unilateral secession. Various writers have noted this (ostensible) tension,[297] which is frequently seen as one of the principal obstacles for acknowledging unilateral secession. In order to paint a more complete picture of the relationship between the principle of territorial integrity and the external dimension of the right to self-determination, some approaches towards the matter will be dealt with below.

The question of the addressees of the principle of territorial integrity should be touched upon first. While it is beyond question that the principle of territorial integrity generally applies to inter-State relations, in the context of the right to unilateral secession, the question has been raised whether the principle is relevant to peoples with secessionist ambitions (i.e. sub-State groups) to the same extent. This matter was discussed quite extensively in the expert reports prepared for the Canadian Supreme Court's *Reference re Secession of Quebec*. In general, the experts shared the opinion that seceding groups within the State are not bound by the principle of territorial integrity. While this argument was presented in various ways and with differing nuances, the international law specialists involved agreed that the principle of territorial integrity does not apply to seceding groups since:

> such groups are not subjects of international law at all, in the way that states are. A group does not become a subject of international law simply by expressing its wish to secede. Until an advanced stage in the process, secession is a matter within the domestic jurisdiction of the affected state.[298]

---

[296] UN General Assembly Resolution 2625 (XXV) (*Declaration on Principles of International Law Concerning Friendly Relations and Co-Operation Among States in Accordance with the Charter of the United Nations*), UN Doc. A/Res/2625 (XXV), 24 October 1970, Principle V, Para. 7. See also UN General Assembly Resolution 1514 (XV) (*Declaration on the Granting of Independence to Colonial Countries and Peoples*), UN Doc. A/Res/1514, 14 December 1960, Para. 6.

[297] See, *inter alia*, Blay, 'Territorial Integrity and Political Independence' at para. 40; L. Brilmayer, 'Secession: A Theoretical Interpretation' (1991) 16 *Yale Journal of International Law* 177 at p. 178; Buchheit, *Secession: The Legitimacy of Self-Determination* at p. 95; J.C. Duursma, *Fragmentation and the International Relations of Micro-States: Self-Determination and Statehood* (Cambridge University Press, Cambridge 1996) at pp. 77-79; Emerson, 'The Logic of Secession' at p. 809; McCorquodale, 'Self-Determination: A Human Rights Approach' at p. 879; Muharremi, 'Kosovo's Declaration of Independence: Self-Determination and Sovereignty Revisited' at p. 403; Murswiek, 'The Issue of a Right of Secession – Reconsidered' at pp. 22-23, 35; Peters, 'Does Kosovo Lie in the *Lotus*-Land of Freedom?' at pp. 102-103; M. Pomerance, *Self-Determination in Law and Practice* (Martinus Nijhoff Publishers, Dordrecht 1982) at p. 12; Raič, *Statehood and the Law of Self-Determination* at p. 293; Shaw, 'Peoples, Territorialism and Boundaries' at pp. 478-479; Tancredi, 'A Normative "Due Process" in the Creation of States through Secession' at p. 176; Thürer and Burri, 'Secession' at para. 14; Vidmar, 'Remedial Secession in International Law: Theory and (Lack of) Practice' at pp. 37-38.

[298] Crawford, 'Report by James Crawford: "Response to Experts Reports of the *Amicus Curiae*"' at p. 157. See also G. Abi-Saab, 'Report by George Abi-Saab: "The Effectivity Required of an Entity that Declares its Independence in Order for it to be Considered a State in International Law"' in A.F. Bayefsky

Thus, according to the experts, the principle of territorial integrity is generally irrelevant in those situations. Yet, two exceptions were made in this respect. First, it follows from the above that if the attempt to secede would be actively supported by another State or even carried out by foreign authorities in the sense that these invade a territory with the object of separating it from its parent State, the events would constitute a violation of the principle of territorial integrity. Secondly, it was emphasized that the State "is entitled to resist challenges to its territorial integrity, whether these challenges are internal (e.g. secession) or external".[299]

More recently, reasoning similar to that of the expert reports for the *Reference re Secession of Quebec* appeared to be applied by the International Court of Justice in its Advisory Opinion on Kosovo's unilateral declaration of independence. According to the Court, "the scope of the principle of territorial integrity is confined to the sphere of relations between States".[300] The Court's statement concerned the issuing of unilateral declarations of independence, but in view of its general phrasing and reasoning by analogy, it may be argued that it also applies to situations of unilateral secession.[301] Being non-State actors, seceding groups are thus not bound by the principle of territorial integrity, the Court seemed to imply. Therefore, the issuing of a unilateral declaration of independence by such an entity by no means violates the principle of territorial integrity. In this respect, the Court recalled the inclusion of this principle in several provisions which all related to the principle of territorial integrity against the background of the threat or use of force between States rather than between States and non-State entities.[302] The Court did not provide further foundations for its argument.

This lack of clarification is unfortunate, since it may be questioned whether the outlook of the Court with respect to the principle of territorial integrity and, likewise,

---

(ed.) *Self-Determination in International Law. Quebec and Lessons Learned* (Kluwer Law International, The Hague 2000) at pp. 72-73; A. Pellet, 'Report by Alain Pellet: "Legal Opinion on Certain Questions of International Law Raised by the Reference"' in A.F. Bayefsky (ed.) *Self-Determination in International Law. Quebec and Lessons Learned* (Kluwer Law International, The Hague 2000) at para. 19; Shaw, 'Report by Malcolm N. Shaw: "Re: Order in Council P.C. 1996-1497 of 30 September 1996"' at paras 39-41.

[299] Crawford, 'Report by James Crawford: "Response to Experts Reports of the *Amicus Curiae*"' at p. 158. See further T.M. Franck, 'Report by Thomas M. Franck: "Opinion Directed at Question 2 of the Reference"' in A.F. Bayefsky (ed.) *Self-Determination in International Law. Quebec and Lessons Learned* (Kluwer Law International, The Hague 2000) at para. 3.3; Pellet, 'Report by Alain Pellet: "Legal Opinion on Certain Questions of International Law Raised by the Reference"' at para. 7; Shaw, 'Report by Malcolm N. Shaw: "Re: Order in Council P.C. 1996-1497 of 30 September 1996"' at para. 44.

[300] See International Court of Justice, *Accordance with International Law of the Unilateral Declaration of Independence in Respect of Kosovo*, Advisory Opinion, ICJ Reports 2010, p. 403, at para. 80.

[301] Ryngaert, 'The ICJ's Advisory Opinion on Kosovo's Declaration of Independence: A Missed Opportunity?' at p. 491.

[302] The Court referred to Article 2(4) of the UN Charter, Principle I of the Friendly Relations Declaration and Principle IV of the Helsinki Final Act.

the view commonly presented in the expert reports drafted for the Canadian Supreme Court in the *Reference re Secession of Quebec* can actually be maintained. The finding that the actions of sub-State entities are not restricted by the principle of territorial integrity seems rather conservative, considering the emerging role of non-State actors within contemporary international relations, the belief that not all of these entities should and do operate in a legal vacuum, and relevant practice in this regard.[303] In the present context, it may be illustrative to note that the classical conception that the prohibition of the use of force is restricted to the acts of States has been challenged over the last decade as well. There is a growing body of opinion arguing that this norm extends to terrorists and other non-State actors in addition to the traditional category of States.[304] As such, reference can be made to national liberation movements, which are seen to be subjects of international law to a certain extent.[305]

What is more, it is to be noted that opinions expressed by the States participating in the Kosovo advisory proceedings did not reflect consensus as to the issue of the applicability of territorial integrity to non-State entities.[306] Whereas some States held on to the idea that international law remains neutral as to the matter of unilateral secession, implying that the principle of territorial integrity is inapplicable in this context, other States maintained that under contemporary international law, non-State actors as well as States are bound by the principle of territorial integrity. Serbia, for instance, alleged that "[t]he classical structure of international law has changed and no State or other entity may seek now to cling to it in the face of established

---

[303] For a comparable observation, see I. Cismas, 'Secession in Theory and Practice: the Case of Kosovo and Beyond' (2010) 2 *Goettingen Journal of International Law* 531 at p. 550, footnote 81. See also Vashakmadze and Lippold, '"Nothing But a Road Towards Secession"? The International Court of Justice's Advisory Opinion on Accordance with International Law of the Unilateral Declaration of Independence in Respect of Kosovo' at p. 632. A brief and general overview of the rising relevance of non-State actors is provided by M. Wagner, 'Non-State Actors' in R. Wolfrum (ed.) *Max Planck Encyclopedia of Public International Law* (fully updated online edn, Oxford University Press, New York 2010). For a more encompassing account of this matter, see A. Bianchi (ed.), *Non-State Actors and International Law* (Ashgate, Farnham 2009).

[304] See O. Corten, 'Territorial Integrity Narrowly Interpreted: Reasserting the Classical Inter-State Paradigm of International Law' (2011) 24 *Leiden Journal of International Law* 87 at pp. 90-91. See also O. Corten, *The Law against War* (Hart Publishing, Oxford 2010) at Chapter 3.

[305] On this topic, see M.N. Shaw, 'The International Status of National Liberation Movements' (1983) 5 *Liverpool Law Review* 19. It is to be noted that the concept of national liberation movements generally excludes today's secessionist entities, since merely three categories of States are considered to be 'candidate States' for national liberation movements, that is colonial powers, occupying powers and racist regimes. See, for instance, D.W. Glazier, 'Wars of National Liberation' in R. Wolfrum (ed.) *Max Planck Encyclopedia of Public International Law* (Oxford University Press, New York 2010) at paras 17-19; Shaw, *International Law* at pp. 220-223.

[306] See also Corten, 'Territorial Integrity Narrowly Interpreted: Reasserting the Classical Inter-State Paradigm of International Law' at p. 89, footnote 7; Vashakmadze and Lippold, '"Nothing But a Road Towards Secession"? The International Court of Justice's Advisory Opinion on Accordance with International Law of the Unilateral Declaration of Independence in Respect of Kosovo' at pp. 631-632, footnote 60.

evolution" and that "recent practice has shown a number of examples where non-State entities within an existing State are directly addressed in the context of internal conflict and with regard to territorial integrity".[307] In this respect, reference was made to a number of Security Council resolutions reaffirming the significance of the sovereignty and territorial integrity of States which were confronted with situations of internal conflict and secessionist attempts, such as Bosnia-Herzegovina, Croatia, Georgia, Somalia and Sudan.[308] Further, some international and regional instruments dealing with the protection of minorities and indigenous peoples were recalled, such as the European Framework Convention for the Protection of National Minorities and the United Nations Declaration on the Rights of Indigenous Peoples. These documents emphasize that the rights of these groups are to be achieved in accordance with the sovereign equality, territorial integrity and political independence of States, which seems to imply that these non-State actors are also bound by this principle.[309] Most recently, this outlook was acknowledged by the Independent International Fact-Finding Mission on the Conflict in Georgia, a body established by the Council of the European Union.[310] In its Report, it was noted that the argument that the principle of respect for the territorial integrity of States is not directed against sub-State groups is "not fully persuasive, especially as international law increasingly addresses situations within the territory of states".[311] In addition to Serbia, various other States made similar arguments, thus extending the scope of the principle of territorial integrity to include entities within States.[312]

---

[307] See International Court of Justice, *Accordance with International Law of the Unilateral Declaration of Independence by the Provisional Institutions of Self-Government of Kosovo (Request for Advisory Opinion)*, Oral Statement of Serbia (Shaw), CR 2009/24, 1 December 2009, at para. 10. For a more detailed presentation of this argument, see *ibid.*, Written Statement of Serbia, 17 April 2009, at paras 440-491.

[308] See the Security Council Resolutions recalled in *ibid.*

[309] See International Court of Justice, *Accordance with International Law of the Unilateral Declaration of Independence by the Provisional Institutions of Self-Government of Kosovo (Request for Advisory Opinion)*, Oral Statement of Serbia (Shaw), CR 2009/24, 1 December 2009, at paras 11-12.

[310] The Mission was established by Council Decision 2008/901/CFSP of 2 December 2008. It should be noted that this was the first time since its creation that the European Union decided to actively intervene in armed conflict. Moreover, it was the first time that the European Union formed a Fact-Finding Mission for the purpose of giving a political and diplomatic follow-up to a conflict in which a ceasefire has been reached. On 30 September 2009, the Mission presented its Report to the Council of the European Union, the Organization for Security and Co-operation in Europe, the United Nations, and the conflicting parties. See Independent International Fact-Finding Mission on the Conflict in Georgia, *Report of the Independent International Fact-Finding Mission on the Conflict in Georgia* (2009), available at <http://www.ceiig.ch/Index.html>.

[311] Independent International Fact-Finding Mission on the Conflict in Georgia, *Report of the Independent International Fact-Finding Mission on the Conflict in Georgia* at pp. 136-137.

[312] See, for instance, International Court of Justice, *Accordance with International Law of the Unilateral Declaration of Independence by the Provisional Institutions of Self-Government of Kosovo (Request for Advisory Opinion)*, Written Statement of Argentina, at paras 75-82, para. 121; *ibid.*, Written Comment of Argentina, at para. 39; *ibid.*, Oral Statement of Argentina (Ruiz Cerutti), CR 2009/26, 2 December 2009,

Besides these arguments presented during the proceedings, the narrow outlook of the Court as regards the principle of territorial integrity does not seem to be justified when carefully reading the Friendly Relations Declaration. Not only does it confirm a people's right to self-determination, it does so in connection to the principle of respect for the territorial integrity of States and emphasizes that the right to self-determination may not be construed as "authorizing or encouraging any action which would dismember or impair, totally or in part, the territorial integrity or political unity of sovereign and independent States".[313] Thus, in addition to addressing the relationships between States, the Declaration encompasses what may be called an intra-State dimension of the principle of territorial integrity, as it prohibits peoples from infringing the territorial integrity of the State.[314] The safeguard clause of the Declaration also seems to indicate that the principle of territorial integrity does have an intra-State dimension as well.[315] In this connection, one commentator observed that the Friendly Relations Declaration "confers some measure of international legal personality on non-state actors active *within* a state".[316] This outlook seems to be confirmed by the *Reference re Secession of Quebec*, in which the Canadian Supreme Court considered the question of secession against the backdrop of the principle of territorial integrity of States,[317] and by the *Western Sahara* case, where it was observed that territorial integrity could affect the implementation of the right to self-determination.[318]

Considering the above, it appears that opinions are divided on whether or not the principle of respect for the territorial integrity of States is applicable to non-State actors in the context of attempts at unilateral secession. Strong arguments supporting the thesis that these non-State entities are also bound by this principle have been presented. As a result, one may at least question whether the thesis that respect for the principle of territorial integrity is confined to the sphere of relations between States does justice to the fundamental character which international law attributes to territorial integrity and the purpose of this principle, which seems to be to provide

---

at paras 18-20; *ibid.*, Written Statement of Azerbaijan, paras 26-27; *ibid.*, Oral Statement of Azerbaijan (Mehdiyev), CR 2009/27, 3 December 2009, at paras 20-27; *ibid.*, Oral Statement of Bolivia (Calzadilla Sarmiento), CR 2009/28, 4 December 2009, paras 6-7; *ibid.*, Oral Statement of China (Xue), CR 2009/29, 7 December 2009, at paras 14-17; *ibid.*, Written Statement of the Islamic Republic of Iran, paras 3.1-3.6; *ibid.*, Written Comments of Cyprus, at para. 18; *ibid.*, Written Statement of Spain, at paras 29-34; *ibid.*, Written Comments of Spain, at paras 4-5; *ibid.*, Oral Statement of Venezuela (Fleming), CR 2009/33, 11 December 2009, at paras 18-19.

[313] UN General Assembly Resolution 2625 (XXV) (*Declaration on Principles of International Law Concerning Friendly Relations and Co-Operation Among States in Accordance with the Charter of the United Nations*), UN Doc. A/Res/2625 (XXV), 24 October 1970, Principle V, Para. 7.

[314] Ryngaert, 'The ICJ's Advisory Opinion on Kosovo's Declaration of Independence: A Missed Opportunity?' at p. 491.

[315] See *ibid.* at pp. 491-492.

[316] *Ibid.* at p. 491 (emphasis original).

[317] Supreme Court of Canada, *Reference re Secession of Quebec*, [1998], 2 S.C.R. 217, at para. 122.

[318] International Court of Justice, *Western Sahara*, Advisory Opinion, ICJ Reports 1975, p. 12, at para. 162.

protection against challenges of the State's territory, whether or not these are initiated externally or internally. What is more, it seems that at present, secessionist groups can indeed be regarded as (additional) addressees of the principle of territorial integrity. Viewed at from that perspective, an attempt at unilateral secession may constitute a violation of this principle. In this respect, a second differentiation concerning the relationship between the principle of territorial integrity and the (external dimension of the) right to self-determination should be addressed at this point.

2.4.1.3. A Balancing Approach

This second line bears upon the absolute character or otherwise of the norms of territorial integrity and self-determination. It is contended that there is an interaction between the right to self-determination of peoples and the principle of territorial integrity of States. This mutual relationship will be expounded below. As was seen elsewhere in the present Chapter, the relevant instruments on the right to self-determination link this right to the principle of territorial integrity in the sense that they prohibit the partial or total disruption of the territorial integrity of independent States in the exercise of the right to self-determination.[319] An illustrative example in this respect is the Charter of Paris, which noted that the participating States:

> reaffirm the equal rights of peoples and their right to self-determination in conformity with the Charter of the United Nations and with the relevant norms of international law, including those relating to the territorial integrity of States.[320]

In view of this, the scope of application and implementation of the right to (external) self-determination are to be interpreted in light of the principle of territorial integrity of States.[321] Such an interpretation implies upholding the territorial integrity of States, thus logically eliminating the idea of self-determination as encompassing an unconditional entitlement to unilateral secession, i.e. a right applicable to all peoples, under all circumstances.[322] At the same time, however, it should be emphasized that

---

[319] Shaw, 'Peoples, Territorialism and Boundaries' at p. 482. See also Section 4.1 of the present Chapter.

[320] Conference on Security and Co-operation in Europe, *Charter of Paris for a New Europe*, Paris, 21 November 1990, available at <http://www.osce.org/mc/39516>, last consulted on 20 September 2012.

[321] See, *inter alia*, Cassese, *International Law* at p. 112; Dugard and Raič, 'The Role of Recognition in the Law and Practice of Self-Determination' at pp. 105-106; Duursma, *Fragmentation and the International Relations of Micro-States: Self-Determination and Statehood* at pp. 80-81; Murswiek, 'The Issue of a Right of Secession – Reconsidered' at p. 35; Peters, 'Does Kosovo Lie in the *Lotus*-Land of Freedom?' at pp. 102-103; Raič, *Statehood and the Law of Self-Determination* at pp. 296.

[322] Raič, *Statehood and the Law of Self-Determination* at pp. 322-323. See also Butler, 'Secession and International Law' at pp. 112-113; Murswiek, 'The Issue of a Right of Secession – Reconsidered' at p. 35; A. Cobban, *The Nation State and National Self-Determination* (Collins, London 1969) at p. 138; Raič, *Statehood and the Law of Self-Determination* at p. 312.

in exercising their right to territorial integrity, States are not immune to the application of other legal obligations under international law either. It is generally agreed that today, the right to territorial integrity may be limited by other international legal norms, such as the fundamental rules and principles of human rights law, the basic norms of international humanitarian law, and the (external dimension of the) right to self-determination.[323] To put it even more strongly, without external self-determination as an *ultimum remedium*, practically nothing would be left of peoples' right to self-determination.[324] Considering the above, it may be concluded that neither self-determination nor territorial integrity is an absolute norm, but rather a principle which can be applied to a greater or lesser extent. Accordingly, the ostensible conflict existing between these norms can be resolved through what may be called a balancing approach.[325] As one commentator pertinently noted,

> [b]alancing requires the jurist to assess the importance of the conflicting legally protected interests and to strike a fair balance according to their respective weight. One of the objectives of balancing is to reconcile these interests to the largest extent possible by defining a compromise solution.[326]

Such an approach appears to leave the door open to a right of remedial secession, as the balance may be tilted towards the (external dimension of the) right to self-determination in extreme situations if separation of the mother State is the only remedy to the persistent denial of internal self-determination and other gross human rights violations. If such exceptional circumstances do not present themselves, the balance will tilt to the preservation of the State's territorial integrity, for the maintenance of the territorial *status quo* is generally considered to serve peace and stability. This then implies that the right to self-determination is to be exercised internally, so within the framework of the existing sovereign State. Phrased differently, until the circumstances at issue are so grave that the right to internal self-determination converts into a right to secession, the scope and implementation of the right to self-determination are restricted – or, balanced – by the principle of territorial integrity.[327] Whether such

---

[323] See Blay, 'Territorial Integrity and Political Independence' at para. 35; Butler, 'Secession and International Law' at p. 112; Raič, *Statehood and the Law of Self-Determination* at pp. 295-296; Vidmar, 'Remedial Secession in International Law: Theory and (Lack of) Practice' at p 38.

[324] See also Murswiek, 'The Issue of a Right of Secession – Reconsidered' at p. 35.

[325] Needless to say, the balancing technique can only be applied when it comes to legal norms which are not absolute and which are in a non-hierarchical relationship, such as norms having a peremptory character (*jus cogens*). Thus, for instance the right to life and the prohibition of torture are excluded from a balancing exercise.

[326] Peters, 'Does Kosovo Lie in the *Lotus*-Land of Freedom?' at p. 102. For a similar line of reasoning, see Murswiek, 'The Issue of a Right of Secession – Reconsidered' at p. 35.

[327] See Dugard and Raič, 'The Role of Recognition in the Law and Practice of Self-Determination' at p. 104; Peters, 'Does Kosovo Lie in the *Lotus*-Land of Freedom?' at pp. 102-103.

grave circumstances actually present themselves and which principle deserves priority is to be decided on a case-by-case basis.

According to some commentators, this balancing approach is implicitly acknowledged in the safeguard clause of the Friendly Relations Declaration, which is often put forward as implying a conditional right to unilateral secession.[328] Further, despite the expert opinions presented before it, the Canadian Supreme Court seems to have applied the balancing technique as well. It declared that "international law expects that the right to self-determination will be exercised by peoples within the framework of the existing sovereign States and consistently with the maintenance of the territorial integrity of those States", but at the same time acknowledged that a right to unilateral secession may arise, that is "only in the most extreme of cases and, even then, under carefully defined circumstances".[329] Both the *a contrario* interpretation of the Friendly Relations Declaration's safeguard clause and the judgment of the Canadian Supreme Court have been expounded upon elsewhere in the present Chapter.[330]

2.4.1.4. Conclusions on the Principle of Territorial Integrity

The foregoing assessment of the principle of respect for the territorial integrity of States leads to the conclusion that, despite the ostensible tension between the principle of territorial integrity on the one hand and attempts at unilateral secession on the other, the differentiations set forth above do not necessarily preclude the existence of a right to remedial secession. To put it even more strongly, even when regarding non-State entities as additional addressees of the principle of territorial integrity – as was submitted above – and simultaneously balancing the demands of the concepts of territorial integrity and self-determination, some room appears to be left for a right to remedial secession. Yet, it would go too far to contend that the principle of respect for the territorial integrity of States reveals clear traces of a qualified right to secession. All in all, the principle of territorial integrity does not provide for a decisive answer to the question of whether or not a right to remedial secession does exist under contemporary international law.

---

[328] See, for instance, Cassese, *Self-Determination of Peoples. A Legal Reappraisal* at pp. 118-120; Dugard and Raič, 'The Role of Recognition in the Law and Practice of Self-Determination' at pp. 103-104, 137; Raič, *Statehood and the Law of Self-Determination* at p. 321.

[329] Supreme Court of Canada, *Reference re Secession of Quebec*, [1998], 2 S.C.R. 217, at paras 122 and 126.

[330] See Sections 3.2 and 3.3.4 of the present Chapter.

2.4.2. The Principle of Uti Possidetis Juris

Against the backdrop of the right to territorial integrity and in relation to the right to self-determination of peoples, it is relevant to address the principle of *uti possidetis juris*. While linked to the concept of territorial integrity, the principle of *uti possidetis juris* should not be equated with this notion.[331] The principal difference between the concepts lies in the time of application. Territorial integrity becomes relevant once a territory is established as an independent State in conformity with international law. In contrast, the principle of *uti possidetis juris* only applies at the very moment of transition to independence. As such, it is of a temporary character, whereas the right to territorial integrity is continuing in nature. This will become clear below. In order to answer the question of whether this principle is permissive or prohibitive of a right to unilateral secession, its historical development and rationale of the principle must be discussed.

2.4.2.1. The Content of the Principle of *Uti Possidetis Juris*

The principle of *uti possidetis juris* originates from Roman law, where it served as one of a series of edicts that the praetor could issue in disputes concerning ownership of (private) real property.[332] Gradually, it developed into a concept applied in international law. It appears to have been first invoked and implemented in Latin America, where the administrative borders of the Spanish empire were converted into borders of the newly established, independent successor States. In these matters, the

---

[331] See Raič, *Statehood and the Law of Self-Determination* at p. 303; Shaw, 'Report by Malcolm N. Shaw: "Re: Order in Council P.C. 1996-1497 of 30 September 1996"' at paras 78-79. Conversely, Thomas M. Franck has used the concepts of *uti possidetis juris* and territorial integrity interchangeably; an approach which has been criticized by Dame Rosalyn Higgins. See Franck, 'Postmodern Tribalism and the Right to Secession' at p. 4; R. Higgins, 'Postmodern Tribalism and the Right to Secession. Comments' in C. Brölmann, R. Lefeber and M. Zieck (eds) *Peoples and Minorities in International Law* (Martinus Nijhoff Publishers, Dordrecht 1993) at p. 34.

[332] The edict '*uti possidetis, ita possidetis*', meaning as much as 'as you possess, so you may possess', was applied by the praetor when possession of the land was achieved in good faith. The edict was used to grant provisional possession to the party possessing the property during the proceedings. As such, application of this rule did not simultaneously imply ownership, but rather shifted the burden of proof during the litigation. Whether a person could claim ownership as well was decided before the courts of law. See J. Castellino, *International Law and Self-Determination: The Interplay of the Politics of Territorial Possession with Formulations of Post-Colonial 'National' Identity* (Martinus Nijhoff Publishers, The Hague 2000) at pp. 111-112; E. Hasani, '*Uti Possidetis Juris*: From Rome to Kosovo' (2003) 27 *Fletcher Forum of World Affairs* 85 at p. 86; H. Post, 'International Law Between Dominium and Imperium: Some Reflections on the Foundations of the International Law on Territorial Acquisition' in T.D. Gill and W.P. Heere (eds) *Reflections on Principles and Practices of International Law Essays in Honour of Leo J Bouchez* (Martinus Nijhoff Publishers, The Hague 2000) at pp. 161-172; S.R. Ratner, 'Drawing a Better Line: *Uti Possidetis* and the Borders of New States' (1996) 90 *American Journal of International Law* 590 at pp. 592-593.

concept of *uti possidetis juris* was used in order to preclude gaps in sovereignty, at least theoretically. Subsequently, after the Organization of African Unity had adopted the concept, it became a well-established principle which was generally applied on the African continent during the decolonization period.[333] Essentially, the concept of *uti possidetis juris* determined that new independent States would come into existence with the same borders as they had when they were units under colonial rule, "no matter how arbitrarily those boundaries may have been drawn".[334] More specifically, as a consequence of this principle, the administrative boundaries created under colonial power were transformed into external frontiers protected by international law.[335] In effect, *uti possidetis juris* produced a "photograph of the territory", thus freezing the borders as they were at the moment independence was achieved.[336] As already mentioned, it is important to stress that despite its linkages with the concept of territorial integrity, the principle of *uti possidetis juris* should not be equated with the former notion. In the previous Section, it was seen that territorial integrity is applicable once a territory is established as an independent State in conformity with international law. In contrast with this continuing character, the principle of *uti possidetis juris* is of a temporary nature, being merely applicable at the moment of the changeover to independence.[337] The rationale of the principle of *uti possidetis juris*

---

[333] According to Christian Tomuschat, the principle of *uti possidetis juris* had even become "the leading maxim for the territorial delimitation of Africa". See Tomuschat, 'Secession and Self-Determination' at p. 27. For an overview of the historical roots of the concept of *uti possidetis juris* and its modern-day application, see Castellino, *International Law and Self-Determination: The Interplay of the Politics of Territorial Possession with Formulations of Post-Colonial 'National' Identity* at pp. 114-144; Hasani, 'Uti Possidetis Juris: From Rome to Kosovo'; Klabbers and Lefeber, 'Africa: Lost Between Self-Determination and *Uti Possidetis*' at pp. 54-65; P. Radan, *The Break-Up of Yugoslavia and International Law* (Routledge, London/New York 2002) at pp. 69-134; Ratner, 'Drawing a Better Line: *Uti Possidetis* and the Boders of New States' at pp. 592-601; Shaw, 'Peoples, Territorialism and Boundaries' at pp. 492-496.

[334] Klabbers and Lefeber, 'Africa: Lost Between Self-Determination and *Uti Possidetis*' at p. 54. This problem has led Joshua Castellino to conclude that the principle of *uti possidetis juris* appears to "allow stronger [colonial] powers to use force and then legitimise it by preventing retaliation". See Castellino, *International Law and Self-Determination: The Interplay of the Politics of Territorial Possession with Formulations of Post-Colonial 'National' Identity* at p. 132.

[335] See International Court of Justice, *Case Concerning the Frontier Dispute (Burkina Faso v. Republic of Mali)*, Judgment, ICJ Reports 1986, p. 554, at para. 23. For a description of the distinction between administrative or internal boundaries and international frontiers, see Shaw, 'Peoples, Territorialism and Boundaries' at p. 490. According to Shaw, international frontiers "fix permanent lines, both geographically and legally, with full effect within the international system, and can only be changed through the consent of the relevant states". In contrast, internal borders possess none of these characteristics.

[336] International Court of Justice, *Case Concerning the Frontier Dispute (Burkina Faso v. Republic of Mali)*, Judgment, ICJ Reports 1986, p. 554, para. 30.

[337] See Raič, *Statehood and the Law of Self-Determination* at p. 303. Conversely, Thomas M. Franck has used the concepts of *uti possidetis juris* and territorial integrity interchangeably; an approach which has been criticized by Dame Rosalyn Higgins. See Franck, 'Postmodern Tribalism and the Right to Secession' at p. 4; Higgins, 'Postmodern Tribalism and the Right to Secession. Comments' at p. 34.

was twofold. First, it served as a tool to prevent (internal) conflicts over borders, thus protecting stability; secondly, implementation of the principle avoided the creation of *terra nullius*, which frequently served as an alleged reason for Western occupation.[338]

2.4.2.2. The Applicability of the Principle of *Uti Possidetis Juris*

In the 1964 Cairo Declaration, the Heads of States and Governments of the Organization of African Unity implicitly adopted the principle of *uti possidetis juris* by stipulating that "all Member States pledge themselves to respect the borders existing on their achievement of their national independence".[339] This political document, however, did not alter the legal status of the principle of *uti possidetis juris*, of which its legally binding character had long been subject to a specific stipulation concerning the resolution of border disputes in a treaty between the relevant States. In the absence of such an explicit reference, the principle was not applicable in the conflict at issue.[340] It was not before 1986 that specific treaty provisions on *uti possidetis juris* were no longer needed for that principle to apply to a certain case. In the *Case Concerning the Frontier Dispute*,[341] a Chamber of the ICJ[342] not only referred to the principle of *uti possidetis juris*' "exceptional importance for the African

---

[338] See Castellino, *International Law and Self-Determination: The Interplay of the Politics of Territorial Possession with Formulations of Post-Colonial 'National' Identity* at p. 115; Hasani, 'Uti Possidetis Juris: From Rome to Kosovo' at pp. 89-90; Klabbers and Lefeber, 'Africa: Lost Between Self-Determination and *Uti Possidetis*' at p. 55.

[339] Organization of African Unity, *Resolution adopted by the first ordinary session of the Assembly of the Heads of State and Government held in Cairo, U.A.R., from 17 to 21 July 1964*, AHG Res. 1 – AHG. Res. 24 (1).

[340] P. Radan, 'Post-Secession International Borders: A Critical Analysis of the Opinions of the Badinter Arbitration Commission' (2000) 24 *Melbourne University Law Review* 50 at pp. 59-60.

[341] International Court of Justice, *Case Concerning the Frontier Dispute (Burkina Faso v. Republic of Mali)*, Judgment, ICJ Reports 1986, p. 554. This case addressed a frontier dispute between Burkina Faso and Mali. The Chamber of the ICJ was asked to indicate the line of the frontier between the two States in a disputed area. Subsequent to serious incidents between the armed forces of both States late 1985, both Burkina Faso and Mali submitted a request to the Chamber of the ICJ for the indication of interim protective measures. The Chamber, in its judgment, first determined the source of the rights claimed by Burkina Faso and Mali. In this respect, it stated that the applicable principles were that of the intangibility of frontiers inherited from colonization (para. 19), the principle of *uti possidetis juris* (paras 20-26), and the principle of equity *infra legem* (paras 27-28). Burkina Faso and Mali had put forward several types of evidence in support of their positions, such as French legislative and regulative texts, administrative documents, and cartographic materials (paras 51-111). After having considered these sources of evidence, the Chamber fixed the boundary between the two States in the disputed area (paras 112-174).

[342] The ICJ has dealt with the principle of *uti possidetis juris* in numerous contentious cases. For a list of cases, see J. Castellino, 'Territorial Integrity and the "Right" to Self-Determination: An Examination of the Conceptual Tools' (2008) 33 *Brooklyn Journal of International Law* 503 at pp. 509-510 (footnote 34).

continent", but also emphasized that it was "a firmly established principle of international law where decolonization is concerned".[343] According to the Chamber,

> [t]he principle is not a special rule which pertains solely to one specific system of international law. It is a general principle, which is logically connected with the phenomenon of the obtaining of independence wherever it occurs. Its obvious purpose is to prevent the independence and stability of new States being endangered by fratricidal struggles provoked by the challenging of frontiers following the withdrawal of the administering power. [...] The fact that the new African States have respected the administrative boundaries and frontiers established by the colonial powers must be seen not as a mere practice contributing to the gradual emergence of a principle of customary international law, limited in its impact to the African continent as it had previously been to Spanish America, but as the application in Africa of a rule of general scope.[344]

When considering the principle of *uti possidetis juris* as a norm of "general scope" – as the Chamber suggested – a question which naturally follows is whether it may be argued that it is a principle with universal application. Phrased differently, is the principle of *uti possidetis juris* – by analogy – applicable to all situations involving the establishment of new, independent States? This question was addressed by the Badinter Arbitration Committee against the backdrop of the dissolution of the SFRY. In response to the questions of whether the internal boundaries between Croatia and Serbia and between Bosnia-Herzegovina and Serbia could be regarded as frontiers in terms of public international law, the Committee contended that the issue of borders in the SFRY should be resolved in accordance with the principle of, *inter alia*, territorial integrity. It took the view that:

> [e]xcept where otherwise agreed, the former boundaries become frontiers protected by international law. This conclusion follows from the principle of respect for the territorial *status quo* and, in particular, from the principle of *uti possidetis*. *Uti possidetis* [...] is today recognized as a general principle, as stated by the International Court of Justice in its Judgment of 22 December 1986 in the case between Burkina Faso and Mali [...].[345]

This ruling, referred to as the Badinter Borders Principle and reflecting the notion of respect for the territorial *status quo*, seems to accept the applicability of the principle

---

[343] International Court of Justice, *Case Concerning the Frontier Dispute (Burkina Faso v. Republic of Mali)*, Judgment, ICJ Reports 1986, p. 554, at para. 20.

[344] International Court of Justice, *Case Concerning the Frontier Dispute (Burkina Faso v. Republic of Mali)*, Judgment, ICJ Reports 1986, p. 554, at paras 20-21.

[345] See International Conference on the Former Yugoslavia, 'Opinions No. 1-3 of the Arbitration Commission of the International Conference on Yugoslavia' (1992) 3 *European Journal of International Law* 182 at pp. 184-185.

of *uti possidetis juris* beyond decolonization. In addition, it assumed that territorial conflicts among newly established independent States arising from the SFRY could be prevented by transforming former administrative borders into international frontiers which are protected under international law. It has been contended that the Committee's ruling reflected political aims of European leaders who insisted that only the constituent (federal) republics of the SFRY could claim a right to self-determination in the form of full independence.[346]

The opinion of the Badinter Arbitration Committee has been challenged by various legal scholars.[347] At this stage, it is worth noting two principal objections. First, it may be questioned whether the interpretation of Chamber's decision in the *Case Concerning the Frontier Dispute* can actually be maintained, for the Badinter Arbitration Committee quoted only selectively from the Chamber's decision. More than that, the omitted phrase and other parts of the judgment clearly indicate that the Chamber considered the principle of *uti possidetis juris* to be applicable in the context of decolonization. The Chamber's reference to the general scope of the principle seems to be intended to state that *uti possidetis juris* is not confined to application in "one specific system of international law", that is that of Latin America only, but rather that it applied to cases of decolonization wherever it occurs, including on the African and Asian continents. In addition, it may be noted that nothing in the Chamber's decision is suggestive of the principle of *uti possidetis juris* applying to cases concerning the dissolution of or secession from independent States, so beyond the context

---

[346] As such, Enver Hasani argued, the ruling of the Committee "reflected 'balance of power' politics and the desire to balance forces within multinational republics that existed at the time of independence." See Hasani, 'Uti Possidetis Juris: From Rome to Kosovo' at p. 92. See also Chapter III, Section 4.1.4 of this study.

[347] See, *inter alia*, Hannum, 'Rethinking Self-Determination' at p. 55; Radan, 'Post-Secession International Borders: A Critical Analysis of the Opinions of the Badinter Arbitration Commission' at pp. 61-62; Ratner, 'Drawing a Better Line: *Uti Possidetis* and the Boders of New States' at pp. 613-615. Malcolm N. Shaw offers an opposing view, as he supports the opinion of the Badinter Arbitration Committee concerning the applicability of the principle of *uti possidetis juris* beyond the context of decolonization. According to Shaw, when carefully reading the reasoning of the Chamber in the *Case Concerning the Frontier Dispute* and paying particular attention to the wording used, it seems "that the Chamber was seeking to underline that behind the application of *uti possidetis [juris]* to all decolonization situations lay a more general principle which relates to all independence processes". See Shaw, 'Peoples, Territorialism and Boundaries' at pp. 496-498. See also T.M. Franck and others, 'Expert Opinion Prepared in 1992 by T.M. Franck, R. Higgins, A. Pellet, M.N. Shaw and C. Tomuschat, "The Territorial Integrity of Québec in the Event of the Attainment of Sovereignty"' in A.F. Bayefsky (ed.) *Self-Determinaiton in International Law. Quebec and Lessons Learned* (Kluwer Law International, The Hague 1992), at paras 2.44-2.50 and para. 4.01. For disproof of Shaw's point of view, see Radan, 'Post-Secession International Borders: A Critical Analysis of the Opinions of the Badinter Arbitration Commission' at pp. 62-65. More in general, Jochen A. Frowein has expressed his astonishment about the conciseness and "boldness with which very difficult issues of public international law are being decided [by the Badinter Arbitration Committee] in a clear-cut manner without much argument". See Frowein, 'Self-Determination as a Limit to Obligations Under International Law' at p. 216.

of decolonization. The second important objection to the opinion of the Badinter Arbitration Committee as reflected in literature concerns the argument that acceptance of *uti possidetis juris* as a principle of general applicability would offend other principles of international law. This objection to the expansion of the principle of *uti possidetis juris* as a general principle of international law, to which the Badinter Arbitration Committee took the first step, is related to the (ostensible) tension between that concept and the right to self-determination of peoples. Implementation of the right to self-determination requires that new frontiers in one way or another reflect the will of the people at issue, rather than being created pursuant to former internal boundaries, so in accordance with the principle of *uti possidetis juris*. In this respect, Steven Ratner noted that "when a new state is formed, its territory ought not to be irretrievably predetermined but should form an element in the goal of maximal internal self-determination". In contrast, the principle of *uti possidetis juris* presupposes that any changes in borders for the purpose of furthering self-determination are always counterbalanced by the risk of conflict.[348] Considering this tension, it has been argued that (external) self-determination and the principle of *uti possidetis juris* are irreconcilable.[349]

Despite these (theoretical) objections, admittedly, practice does seem to support the view that the principle of *uti possidetis juris* applies beyond the decolonization context, at least to a certain extent. In addition to the ruling by the Badinter Arbitration Committee which deemed the principle applicable to the collapse of Yugoslavia,[350] the Guidelines on Recognition of New States in Eastern Europe and the Soviet Union, adopted by the European Community (now European Union) and its Member States, applied *uti possidetis juris* to the dissolution of the Soviet Union as well. It required, *inter alia*, "respect for the inviolability of all frontiers which can only be changed by peaceful means and by common agreement".[351] Moreover, with

---

[348] Ratner, 'Drawing a Better Line: *Uti Possidetis* and the Boders of New States' at p. 612.

[349] See, for instance, Castellino, *International Law and Self-Determination: The Interplay of the Politics of Territorial Possession with Formulations of Post-Colonial 'National' Identity* at pp. 132-133; V. Epps, *Evolving Concepts of Self-Determination and Autonomy in International Law: The Legal Status of Tibet* (Suffolk University Law School 2008) at p. 8; Ratner, 'Drawing a Better Line: *Uti Possidetis* and the Boders of New States' at pp. 614-615. Shaw terms this as the contrast between the "self-determination and the 'Peoples' approach" on the one hand and the "territorialist approach" on the other hand. See Shaw, 'Peoples, Territorialism and Boundaries' at pp. 479, 501-503.

[350] Joshua Castellino emphasizes two important differences in the application of the principle of *uit possidetis juris* between this case and the decolonization process. First, the people of Yugoslavia were strictly speaking not under colonial rule and, secondly, the internal borders of the State did have "a certain historical legitimacy (pre-1918)", whereas this element was absent in most (African) decolonizations. See Castellino, *International Law and Self-Determination: The Interplay of the Politics of Territorial Possession with Formulations of Post-Colonial 'National' Identity* at p. 118.

[351] European Community, 'Declaration on Yugoslavia and on the "Guidelines on the Recognition of New States in Eastern Europe and in the Soviet Union in Eastern Europe and in the Soviet Union"', 16 December 1991, 31 *International Legal Materials* 1485 (1992).

the Charter of the Commonwealth of Independent States, the signatory States agreed to preserve the internal borders of the republics as they existed at the time that they were part of the Soviet Union.[352] This reasoning on the basis of the principle of *uti possidetis juris* was furthermore applied in the case of the dissolution of Czechoslovakia in 1993, since the two republics involved agreed that the administrative boundary between the Czech and the Slovak parts of the former State would become an international frontier.[353] In addition to this practice, it is noteworthy that the principle of *uti possidetis juris* is included in various national constitutions.[354] From this practice, it may thus be derived that *uti possidetis juris* does apply beyond the context of decolonization, at least to the extent that it concerns situations of the break-up of federal States and situations where the application of the principle is constitutionally established or mutually agreed upon by the parties concerned. It remains to be determined, however, whether the principle applies to all scenarios of independence.

2.4.2.3. The Principle of *Uti Possidetis Juris* and the Right to Self-Determination

The perceived tension between the principle of *uti possidetis juris* and the right to self-determination may be refuted as well. For, it should be recalled that in the *Case Concerning the Frontier Dispute*, the Chamber noted "to take account of [*uti possidetis juris*] in the interpretation of the principle of self-determination of peoples", except where the parties concerned agree otherwise.[355] Thus, when using the principle as a mode of interpreting the external dimension of the right to self-determination, in the end, the conflict between the two norms would be counterbalanced. As such, applying the principle of *uti possidetis juris* in this context would entail "that a collectivity which constitutes a majority within a certain administrative unit of a State and which is entitled to external self-determination [...] has the right to exercise its right to external self-determination with regard to that administrative unit", to the effect that the borders of that administrative unit become frontiers protected by international law.[356] Put differently, *uti possidetis juris* imposes geographical restrictions to the scope of implementation of the right to self-determination.[357]

---

[352] Commonwealth of Independent States, *Charter of the Commonwealth of Independent States*, 22 June 1993.

[353] See Shaw, 'Peoples, Territorialism and Boundaries' at p. 500.

[354] See Castellino, *International Law and Self-Determination: The Interplay of the Politics of Territorial Possession with Formulations of Post-Colonial 'National' Identity* at p. 122.

[355] International Court of Justice, *Case Concerning the Frontier Dispute (Burkina Faso v. Republic of Mali)*, Judgment, ICJ Reports 1986, p. 554, at para. 25.

[356] Raič, *Statehood and the Law of Self-Determination* at pp. 303-304 (original emphasis omitted).

[357] See *ibid.* at p. 304. See also Franck, 'Report by Thomas M. Franck: "Opinion Directed at Question 2 of the Reference"' at p. 84.

2.4.2.4. Conclusions on the Principle of *Uti Possidetis Juris*

From the above, it follows that the principle of *uti possidetis juris* does not generally preclude the acknowledgement or exercise of a right to external self-determination by means of unilateral secession. First and foremost, it remains questionable whether the principle actually pertains to situations other than those pointed out above, for instance situations in which an ethnic minority attempting to secede does not correlate to internal borders or administrative lines of the State.[358] In addition, in cases where the principle is relevant, it was seen that it sets the geographical conditions under which independence – by means of exercising the right to external self-determination – may be achieved, rather than prohibiting it.

2.4.3. *The Principle of Self-Determination*

Finally, reference must be made to self-determination, which not only plays a part in international law as a fully fledged right of peoples, but also as a more general principle.[359] This was already demonstrated in outlining the historical development of the concept of self-determination.[360] So far, this study has primarily focused on the concept of self-determination as a legal entitlement under modern international law. At this stage, however, its contemporary manifestation and content as a general principle merit some elaboration.

The concept of self-determination was included in the UN Charter and has been confirmed on various occasions since. For instance, it was embodied in the Friendly Relations Declaration as one of the seven basic principles of international law and recognized by the International Court of Justice on various occasions with reference to the principle's elementary and special character.[361] In the *East Timor* case, for one,

---

[358] See Crawford, 'Report by James Crawford: "Response to Experts Reports of the *Amicus Curiae*"' at p. 169.

[359] See, for instance, Crawford, *The Creation of States in International Law* at pp. 122-128; Gaja, 'General Principles of Law' at paras 1-6; Malanczuk, *Akehurst's Modern Introduction to International Law* at p. 48; Thirlway, 'The Sources of International Law' at pp. 130-132. See also Cassese, *Self-Determination of Peoples. A Legal Reappraisal* at pp. 126-127 and the references made in that respect. It may be interesting to note that self-determination of peoples has also been regarded as a 'global value'. In this respect, see O. Spijkers, *The United Nations, the Evolution of Global Values and International Law* (School of Human Rights Research Series, Intersentia, Cambridge/Antwerp/Portland 2011) at pp. 355-445.

[360] See Chapter II of the present study.

[361] See International Court of Justice, *Legal Consequences for States of the Continued Presence of South Africa in Namibia (South West Africa) notwithstanding Security Council Resolution 276 (1970)*, Advisory Opinion, ICJ Reports 1971, p. 31, at para. 53; International Court of Justice, *Western Sahara*, Advisory Opinion, ICJ Reports 1975, p. 12, at paras 54-59; International Court of Justice, *East Timor (Portugal v. Australia)*, Judgment, ICJ Reports 1995, p. 90, at para. 29; International Court of Justice, *Legal Consequences of the Construction of a Wall in the Occupied Palestinian Territory*, Advisory Opinion, ICJ Reports 2004, p. 136 at paras 155-156.

the Court emphasized that "[t]he principle of self-determination […] is one of the essential principles of contemporary international law".[362] This principle appears to encompass the core meaning of self-determination, i.e. the "need to pay regard to the freely expressed will of peoples" each time the interests of peoples are at stake, as was expressed by the International Court of Justice in its Advisory Opinion in the *Western Sahara* case.[363] It expounds a rather general yet fundamental norm for the performance of governments, requiring them to enable peoples to freely express their wishes whenever their interests may be affected. As such, it may be seen as implicitly protecting peoples from oppression in the broadest sense of the word. However, as Antonio Cassese observed,

> this principle poses a very loose standard; it does not define either the *units of self-determination* or *areas or matters* to which it applies, or the *means or methods* of its implementation. In particular, it does not specify whether self-determination should have an *internal* or *external* dimension, nor does it point to the *objective* of self-determination (independent statehood, integration or association with another State, self-government, secession form an existing State, etc.). The principle simply sets out general guidelines for State behaviour and therefore acts as a sort of overarching standard for international relations.[364]

Those issues not defined or specified by the principle have – at least to a certain extent – been explicated in other sources of international law, such as treaties, judicial decisions and custom.[365] It was seen previously in the present study that these rules set forth the scope of application, modes of implementation, and the subjects (or: units) of self-determination. This may explain why, despite its recognition as a general principle of (international) law, only little reference is made to self-determination in this capacity, and the concept of self-determination mainly operates as a right in contemporary international law. It is in this latter capacity that the concept of self-determination and, more specifically, its external dimension, has been invoked as the root from which a (remedial) right to unilateral secession may be derived. Against this background, Antonio Cassese found the principle of self-determination to play a threefold role. First, it may indicate the method of exercising self-determination, i.e. through the free and genuine expression of the will of the people. This means it pertains to both internal and external self-determination. Secondly, the principle of self-determination may serve as a basic standard of interpretation in cases where the

---

[362] International Court of Justice, *East Timor (Portugal v. Australia)*, Judgment, ICJ Reports 1995, p. 90, at para. 29.
[363] International Court of Justice, *Western Sahara*, Advisory Opinion, ICJ Reports 1975, p. 12, at para. 59. See also Cassese, *Self-Determination of Peoples. A Legal Reappraisal* at p. 128.
[364] *Ibid.* at p. 128.
[365] *Ibid.* at p. 129.

treaty rule or customary norm is unclear or ambiguous. Thirdly and finally, it may be of use in those cases which are not covered by specific rules at all.[366]

In this connection, the question arises as to whether self-determination as a general principle of (international) law can prove helpful in determining whether or not a right to remedial secession exists. The general meaning of this principle as was phrased above does not seem to preclude the acknowledgement of a right to remedial secession, as long as secession is in conformity with the will of the people. Yet, since the principle of self-determination entails a positive obligation for States, a kind of reversed reading would be needed to interpret it as encompassing (traces of) a right to remedial secession. Whether that would be appropriate is highly questionable, particularly in view of the very role which the principle of self-determination plays in international law. As noted above, the principle should be seen as a rather flexible, coordinating standard, while further interpretation is provided for by other sources of international law. Therefore, it is submitted that no drastic conclusions as regards an extensive interpretation of the concept of self-determination, its scope of application, modes of application, subjects and preconditions should be drawn on the basis of this principle. Thus, in its capacity as general principle of international law, self-determination is of little use to resolving the question of a right to remedial secession.

2.4.4. Conclusions on General Principles of (International) Law

What can be concluded at this stage is that general principles of international law do not provide for a conclusive answer as regards the question of whether a right to unilateral secession exists under international law. They neither reveal clear traces of a right to unilateral secession nor an unambiguous prohibition thereof either. First, it was argued that general principles common in municipal laws can play a subsidiary role only, since they may be used in the interpretation of existing rules of international law. Subsequently, some general principles relevant under international law were considered. It was seen that, although there is an ostensible tension between the principles of respect for the territorial integrity of States and *uti possidetis juris* on the one hand and the exercise of the external dimension of the right to self-determination by means of unilateral secession on the other, these concepts do not appear to be irreconcilable.

More than that, on a couple of occasions, it has been contended that non-State entities are not bound by the principle of respect for the territorial integrity of States in the first place. In this line of reasoning, this latter principle would be irrelevant in the situation of secessionist groups attempting to break away from a sovereign State. However, this assertion does not seem tenable today. It appears that secessionist entities should indeed be viewed as (additional) addressees of the principle of territorial

---

[366] See *ibid.* at pp. 131-132.

integrity. If an attempt at unilateral secession does constitute a violation of this principle, then it becomes relevant to note that both territorial integrity and the right to self-
determination are not absolute. The principle of territorial integrity is to be taken into
account in the interpretation of the scope and implementation of the right to (external)
self-determination, and *vice versa*. Such a balancing exercise appears to leave room
for the acceptance of a right to unilateral secession under exceptional circumstances.
This involves a delicate process, however, in which not only the territorial integrity
of the State and the right to self-determination of the people are weighed, but also the
importance of international or regional peace, security and stability.

With respect to the principle of *uti possidetis juris*, it remains questionable
whether it is applicable to all situations of independence, including cases where the
sub-State entity attempting to secede is not connected to a territory which is demarcated by internal borders or administrative lines. In situations in which the principle
is clearly applicable, however, it was found that *uti possidetis juris* determines the
geographical restrictions of the implementation of the right to (external) self-determination rather than restricting the actual exercise of this right. Thus, the principle of
uti possidetis juris does not preclude the recognition of a qualified right to unilateral
secession either.

Although the principle of self-determination of peoples encompasses the very
essence of self-determination, it was contended that its role as a general principle
is distinct from rules concerning this concept. The principle merely operates as a
loose and overarching standard, as a result of which only modest significance is to be
attached to the principle of self-determination when it comes to sweeping questions
such as that of a right to remedial secession. In this connection as well, it remains
pertinent to assess whether contemporary customary international law acknowledges
such a right as a corollary of the concept of self-determination. This will be carried
out in the following Chapter.

2.5. Traces of a (Remedial) Right to Unilateral Secession in Other Possible Sources of International Law

The enumeration of sources of international law in Article 38 of the Statute of the
International Court of Justice suggests that this list is exhaustive. Although this
was most probably true for the time the Statute was drafted, in addition to these
sources listed, over time, some other (quasi-)sources of international law have been
suggested.[367] In this respect, unilateral acts of States and acts of international organizations will be considered.[368]

---

[367] See, generally, Malanczuk, *Akehurst's Modern Introduction to International Law* at pp. 52-56; Shaw,
International Law at pp. 107-115; Thirlway, 'The Sources of International Law' at pp. 138-142.
[368] In addition to these supplementary sources of international law, some authors also mention equity.
Although a clear definition of this notion is lacking, in the present context, equity is often used in

2.5.1. Unilateral Acts of States

First, unilateral acts of States need to be addressed. Such acts might cover, for instance, international recognition of newly established States and objections aiming to limit or prevent the formation of new customary international law. For a long time, unilateral acts were generally viewed as playing a very confined role only within the system of international law. This perception, however, seems to have changed with the *Nuclear Tests* cases,[369] in which the International Court of Justice noticed the

---

connection with considerations of fairness, reasonableness and justness. As such, the concept is closely linked to general principles of international law. It is nevertheless highly questionable whether equity in itself can be considered as a formal source of international law today. See, for instance, Brownlie, *Principles of Public International Law* at pp. 25-26; F. Francioni, 'Equity in International Law' in R. Wolfrum (ed.) *Max Planck Encyclopedia of Public International Law* (fully updated online edn, Oxford University Press, New York 2010) at para. 4; Malanczuk, *Akehurst's Modern Introduction to International Law* at p. 55; Thirlway, 'The Sources of International Law' at p. 140. Admittedly, equity may be an important factor in judgments and advisory opinions of international judicial bodies such as the International Court of Justice. It may introduce some concerns of fairness and justice into the general structure of the law, in order to accommodate the general rules of international law to the circumstances of a specific case. Moreover, equity may be used to fill the gaps in international law by means of invoking general principles of law as referred to in Article 38(1)(c) of the Statute of the International Court of Justice. In addition, equity may function as a catalyst for the alteration and modernization of the law, as it may supplement or support the transformation of custom. See Francioni, 'Equity in International Law' at paras 5-7, 26. Nonetheless, as the Court acknowledged, equity is "not in itself a source of obligation where none would otherwise exist". See International Court of Justice, *Border and Transborder Armed Actions (Nicaragua v. Honduras)*, Jurisdiction and Admissibility, Judgment, ICJ Reports 1988, p. 12, at para. 94. Rather, as Hugh Thirlway noted, equity may probably best be regarded as "one of the basic principles governing the creation and performance of legal obligations". See Thirlway, 'The Sources of International Law' at p. 140. In view of this, the present study will not consider equity in the context of finding traces of a right to unilateral secession within the sources of international law.

[369] International Court of Justice, *Nuclear Tests (Australia v. France)*, Judgment, ICJ Reports 1974, p. 253. This is one of a pair of cases in which a dispute with France concerning the conduct of nuclear tests was brought before the Court. Being a State possessing nuclear weapons, France performed periodical nuclear weapons tests. From 1966 to 1972, France carried out such tests on the territory of French Polynesia. Conducting nuclear tests above ground (i.e. atmospheric testing), however involves a high risk of radioactive material being dispersed in the atmosphere, which would eventually fall to the surface. Situated in the South Pacific region, Australia and New Zealand considered themselves to be vulnerable to the dangers of this possible radioactive fall-out resulting from the French nuclear tests. Consequently, Australia and New Zealand instituted proceedings before the Court against France, claiming that carrying out further atmospheric nuclear weapons tests is inconsistent with international law (para. 11). From the applications and from further statements, the Court concluded that both Australia and New Zealand aimed at obtaining an assurance from the French government that no further nuclear tests would be conducted above ground (para. 30). The Court made reference to, *inter alia*, several statements made by the French government, which displayed the intention to unconditionally cease the atmospheric nuclear testing following the conclusion of the 1974 series of tests (paras 31-41). In this connection, the Court held that legal obligations may arise from unilateral acts in case the State making the statement intends to become bound by it (para. 43). For a more elaborate description of the two *Nuclear Tests* cases, see for instance, A. Watts QC, 'Nuclear Tests Cases' in R. Wolfrum (ed.) *Max Planck Encyclopedia of Public International Law* (fully updated online edn, Oxford University Press, New York 2010).

'strictly unilateral nature' of certain legal acts.[370] As a general rule, the Court stipulated the following:

> It is well recognized that declarations made by way of unilateral acts, concerning legal or factual situations, may have the effect of creating legal obligations. [...] When it is the intention of the State making the declaration that it should become bound according to its terms, that intention confers on the declaration the character of a legal undertaking, the State being henceforth legally required to follow a course of conduct consistent with the declaration.[371]

Nonetheless, the Court acknowledged that not all unilateral acts constitute international obligations. Two elements are of vital importance for the binding force of a unilateral act. First, the State making the declaration should express the intention to be bound. Secondly, the declaration is to be brought to the notice of the international legal subject at issue. The first element has to be determined on the basis of the circumstances of the particular case, thereby considering the place, type, manner and form of the declaration.[372] Yet, when statements are made which limit the State's freedom of action, a restrictive interpretation is called for.[373] In this connection, it is to be noted that unilateral acts are closely connected to another source of international law, namely general principles of (international) law. It may be argued that in accepting a unilateral act as creating a legally binding obligation, the Court has applied the principle of good faith. For, it would be contrary to this principle if a State would be able to retract a declaration which was clearly intended to be binding and which would cause harm to a third party.[374] In view of this strong relationship with one of the general principles as referred to in Article 38 of the Statute of the International Court of Justice, some authors have rejected the argument that unilateral acts are to be treated as a new source of law.[375]

Having touched upon the concept of unilateral acts of States, the question as to their effects arises. As Wilfried Fiedler aptly noted,

---

[370] Notwithstanding this pronouncement, a uniform and accurate definition of unilateral acts is lacking. See W. Fiedler, 'Unilateral Acts in International Law' in R. Bernhardt (ed.) *Encyclopedia of Public International Law* (Elsevier, Amsterdam 2000) at pp. 1018-1019.

[371] International Court of Justice, *Nuclear Tests (Australia v. France)*, Judgment, ICJ Reports 1974, p. 253, at para. 43.

[372] See V. Rodriguez Cedeno and M.I. Torres Cazorla, 'Unilateral Acts of States in International Law' in R. Wolfrum (ed.) *Max Planck Encyclopedia of Public International Law* (fully updated online edn, Oxford University Press, New York 2010) at paras 25-27.

[373] See Fiedler, 'Unilateral Acts in International Law' at pp. 1021-1022; Shaw, *International Law* at p. 115.

[374] See, for instance, Rodriguez Cedeno and Torres Cazorla, 'Unilateral Acts of States in International Law' at paras 34-39.

[375] See, for example, Thirlway, 'The Sources of International Law' at pp. 139-140.

[t]hrough the binding force of the declaration the declaring subject of international law undertakes a unilateral obligation to act in compliance with its declaration. The individual State is therefore in a position to unilaterally create law under certain circumstances and on the basis of valid customary law.[376]

As such, unilateral acts may contribute to the development of international law and the limitation or prevention of new norms of customary international law. Moreover, by means of corresponding State practice, unilateral acts may even alter the interpretation of international treaties which already exist, hence affecting and complementing international law.[377]

In search of traces of a right to unilateral secession, unilateral acts seem to be primarily relevant as a possible source of international law when done as declarations concerning the recognition (or non-recognition) of newly proclaimed States following an attempt to secede. Such declarations, however, will be dealt with elsewhere in the present study, in the context of *opinio juris* and State practice as the preconditions for customary international law.[378] For, unilateral declarations of recognition or non-recognition and possibly corresponding State practice may show how States perceive the right to self-determination and whether they acknowledge a right to unilateral secession under certain circumstances. As such, unilateral acts may indeed influence the interpretation of international law.

2.5.2. Acts of International Organizations

Having touched upon unilateral acts as possible sources of international law, the acts of international organizations are to be addressed. The increasing number of international organizations following the First World War has led to suggestions that the acts of these organizations should be regarded as a source of international law as well. In this respect, it should be mentioned that despite this emergence, States have exercised restraint in allotting bodies of international organizations the competence to issue decisions which are binding upon all member States. Only in a very limited number of cases have States been willing to grant such extensive competences to an international organization. The principal example in this regard is that of the European Union.[379] The only example arising from the Charter of the United Nations is the

---

[376] Fiedler, 'Unilateral Acts in International Law' at p. 1022.

[377] See *ibid*.

[378] See Chapter VI of this study.

[379] Initially, competences were attributed to the European Economic Community (EEC). With the 1993 Treaty of Maastricht, the EEC as an organization merged into the European Union and turned into one of its three pillars. With the Treaty of Lisbon, which entered into force on 1 December 2009, the pillar structure was dissolved. Hence, a single European Union was established, which has both replaced and succeeded the EEC. See, for instance, J. Fairhurst, *Law of the European Union* (8th edn, Pearson, Harlow 2010) at pp. 3-55.

UN Security Council, which is empowered to issue orders which are binding upon all UN member States in the context of its competence to deal with threats to international peace and security.[380]

On the international plane, decisions and resolutions of the UN General Assembly have particularly been suggested as a formal source of international law.[381] This might seem striking, as the General Assembly is a political organ which is competent to issue decisions and resolutions that are recommendatory in nature rather than legally binding, apart from a few exceptions.[382] Yet, when these 'recommendations' are concerned with substantive questions of international law, they may have great legal value as well, since an interplay exists between these decisions and resolutions on the one hand and customary international law on the other. When they claim to articulate binding rules – either explicitly or impliedly – the decisions and resolutions of the General Assembly may be seen as 'legal pronouncements' which can be relevant in the sense of customary law. Such pronouncements may, for instance, declare what is existing customary international law (i.e. *lex lata*). In addition to evidencing the law, decisions and resolutions of the General Assembly may also state legal wishes or aspirations (i.e. *lex ferenda*). When adopted unanimously or by a vast majority, the latter category of pronouncements may contribute to *opinio juris* on a certain matter. If this *opinio juris* is in turn reiterated and reflected within State practice as well, General Assembly resolutions may even give rise to the emergence of a new norm of customary international law, binding upon all States.[383] This outlook seems to be affirmed by the ICJ in its Advisory Opinion on the *Legality of the Threat or Use of Nuclear Weapons* as well.[384] Further, it may be observed that the decisions and resolutions of the General Assembly raise the political pressure on States. As Martin

---

[380] Malanczuk, *Akehurst's Modern Introduction to International Law* at pp. 52-53; Shaw, *International Law* at p. 108.

[381] See, for example, Malanczuk, *Akehurst's Modern Introduction to International Law* at pp. 52-54; Thirlway, 'The Sources of International Law' at p. 141, who only addresses General Assembly resolutions in the context of acts of international organizations. It is to be noted, however, that other international organizations may also issue decisions and resolutions which may have a similar effect. Examples in this respect are the Organization of American States and the Organization of African Unity, as well as some specialized organizations such as the International Labour Organization and the International Atomic Energy Agency. See Dixon, *Textbook on International Law* at p. 49.

[382] The main exception in this respect is that General Assembly resolutions which concern the internal working of the United Nations are legally binding for all members of the organization. See Dixon, *Textbook on International Law* at p. 48.

[383] See, for instance, Brownlie, *Principles of Public International Law* at p. 15; Dixon, *Textbook on International Law* at pp. 48-49; International Law Association, Committee on the Formation of Customary (General) International Law, *Statement of Principles Applicable to the Formation of General Customary International Law*, London Conference (2000), at pp. 55-65; Malanczuk, *Akehurst's Modern Introduction to International Law* at pp. 52-53; Shaw, *International Law* at pp. 108-109; Thirlway, 'The Sources of International Law' at p. 141.

[384] International Court of Justice, *Legality of the Threat or Use of Nuclear Weapons*, Advisory Opinion, ICJ Rep. 1996, p. 226, at paras 70-73.

Dixon aptly noted, "the political expectation raised by a positive vote will have considerable impact on the behaviour of states and, therefore, on the development of customary law".[385] In connection to the above, however, it is to be emphasized that the mere acceptance of a decision or resolution during a meeting of an international organization *ipso facto* is insufficient for those acts being legally binding upon all States. Rather, the legally binding character of such acts may merely ensue from the fact that they meet the requirements of customary international law, i.e. at least in the conventional view, the existence of State practice and *opinio juris*. As will be submitted in the following Chapter of this study,[386] both constituents should not be assumed too easily.[387]

A similar effect as was outlined in the context of General Assembly resolutions may be attributed to the conclusions of international intergovernmental conferences, for instance so-called final acts. When adopted unanimously or by a substantial majority, such conclusions may evidence the existence of *opinio juris* on the subject matter concerned and may, as such, contribute to the creation of a customary norm, which is legally binding upon all States.[388] Moreover, these documents may – due to their political significance – also have considerable impact on the practice of States, thus adding to the development of custom.[389]

Although the foregoing explicates why some acts of international organizations have been suggested as an independent source of law and are sometimes referred to as generating "soft law",[390] the interplay with customary international law reveals why some authors remain hesitant in accepting such a position.[391] For the sake of completeness, however, both resolutions issued by the UN General Assembly and the conclusions of international conferences deserve consideration when seeking traces of a right to unilateral secession. As has been demonstrated previously in this study,

---

[385] Dixon, *Textbook on International Law* at p. 49.

[386] See Chapter V, in particular Sections 3 and 4.

[387] In this respect, an observation by the International Court of Justice in its Advisory Opinion on the *Legality of the Threat or Use of Nuclear Weapons* is illustrative. The Court found that in view of the "substantial numbers of negative votes and abstentions" with which the resolutions under consideration had been adopted, "they still fall short of establishing the existence of an *opinio juris*". See International Court of Justice, *Legality of the Threat or Use of Nuclear Weapons*, Advisory Opinion, ICJ Rep. 1996, p. 226, at para. 71. See also the Dissenting Opinion of Judge Schwebel attached to the case.

[388] Brownlie, *Principles of Public International Law* at pp. 14-15; International Law Association, Committee on the Formation of Customary (General) International Law, *Statement of Principles Applicable to the Formation of General Customary International Law*, London Conference (2000), at pp. 65-66.

[389] Dixon, *Textbook on International Law* at p. 49.

[390] As observed by Martin Dixon, the term 'soft law' is used to refer to two phenomena in international law. First, it is used to denote norms of international law which do not prescribe clear rights or obligations to the addressees, due to the flexibility or ambiguity of its content. In this respect, one may think of Article 2 ICESCR. Secondly, the term 'soft law' is used to indicate those principles which may grow into international legal rules, but have not yet achieved this status. Put differently, the concept of 'soft law' may be used to refer to *lex ferenda*. See *ibid*. at p. 50.

[391] See, for example, Thirlway, 'The Sources of International Law' at p. 141.

in the context of the historical development of the notion of self-determination, the General Assembly has promulgated a number of resolutions which have been important for the evolution of the notion of self-determination against the backdrop of decolonization.[392] It was shown already that in the context of the question of a unilateral right to secession, the Friendly Relations Declaration is considered to be crucial. For proponents of a (qualified) right to unilateral secession, the safeguard clause of this document has been at the basis of their thesis.[393] That said, questions may arise as regards the legal status of the most prominent sources providing an argument for existence of a qualified right to unilateral secession as discussed above.

As far as the Friendly Relations Declaration is concerned, it is to be emphasized that this document was adopted by the General Assembly with no opposition.[394] Therefore, this document can be said to reflect at least strong *opinio juris*.[395] That the Friendly Relations Declaration mirrors substantial *opinio juris* was also suggested by the International Court of Justice in the *Nicaragua* case, as it stated that:

> [t]he effect of consent to the text of such resolutions cannot be understood as merely that of a 'reiteration or elucidation' of the treaty commitment undertaken in the Charter. On the contrary, it may be understood as an acceptance of the validity of the rule or set of rules declared by the resolution by themselves.[396]

Whether this has indeed led to the existence of a customary norm regarding a right to unilateral secession will be scrutinized in the following Chapter. In addition, as has been demonstrated previously in this Chapter, the Friendly Relations Declaration has been frequently used by both the International Court of Justice[397] and national courts[398] when analysing the condition of international law.[399]

---

[392] The principle of self-determination as enshrined in the UN Charter evolved into a right to self-determination for colonial peoples by means of UN General Assembly Resolution 1514 (XV) and Resolution 1541 (XV). See Chapter II, Section 4.2 of the present study.

[393] See Section 2.2 of the present Chapter.

[394] UN General Assembly Resolution 2625 (XXV) was adopted without vote.

[395] Ryngaert and Griffioen, 'The Relevance of the Right to Self-Determination in the Kosovo Matter: In Partial Response to the Agora Papers' at para. 19.

[396] International Court of Justice, *Military and Paramilitary Activities in and Against Nicaragua (Nicaragua v. United States of America)*, Merits, Judgment, ICJ Reports 1986, p. 14, at para. 188.

[397] International Court of Justice, *Western Sahara*, Advisory Opinion, ICJ Reports 1975, at para. 58; International Court of Justice, *Case Concerning Military and Paramilitary Activities in and against Nicaragua (Nicaragua v. United States of America)*, Merits, Judgment, ICJ Reports 1986, p. 14, at paras 188, 191; International Court of Justice, *Legal Consequences of the Construction of a Wall in the Occupied Palestinian Territory*, Advisory Opinion, ICJ Reports 2004, p. 136, at paras 87-88, 156.

[398] See, for instance, Supreme Court of Canada, *Reference re Secession of Quebec*, [1998], 2 S.C.R. 217; African Commission on Human and Peoples' Rights, *Katangese Peoples' Congress v. Zaire*, Comm. No. 75/92, 1995 (not dated).

[399] See Summers, *Peoples and International Law: How Nationalism and Self-Determination Shape a Contemporary Law of Nations* at pp. 255-317; Suski, 'Keeping the Lid on the Secession Kettle: A Review

The same line of reasoning may hold for the Vienna Declaration and Programme of Action, which contains a significant reaffirmation of the safeguard clause from the Friendly Relations Declaration. In June 1993, the Vienna Declaration and Programme of Action was adopted by consensus of 171 States during the UN World Conference on Human Rights in Vienna. Subsequently, the General Assembly adopted the Declaration as part of General Assembly Resolution 48/121.[400] As one commentator noted, the reaffirmation of the safeguard clause in the Vienna Declaration and Programme of Action "arguably strengthens any argument that it has come to form part of customary international law".[401] Nonetheless, restraint is to be exercised with regard to the legal value attributed to resolutions emanating from the General Assembly and conclusions resulting from international conferences. As Malcolm N. Shaw rightly pointed out, these documents "are often the result of political compromises and arrangements and, comprehended in that sense, never intended to constitute binding norms".[402] One must therefore be prudent when identifying legal norms from *opinio juris* and State practice in connection to these acts of international organizations. Although the relevant General Assembly resolutions and final acts can certainly be said to have legal value, before drawing far reaching conclusions as to the existence of a right to unilateral secession ensuing from an *a contrario* interpretation of those instruments, State practice needs to be scrutinized first. This will be done in Chapter VI.

2.5.3. Conclusions on Other Possible Sources of International Law

After having scrutinized the sources of international law as listed in Article 38 of the Statute of the International Court of Justice, this section considered some additional sources, i.e. unilateral acts of States and acts of international organizations. It was found that when seeking traces of a right to unilateral secession, unilateral acts are mainly of interest in their manifestation as declarations regarding the (non-)recognition of new States which are proclaimed after an attempted secession. As such, unilateral acts of States will be addressed elsewhere in the present study, against the background of *opinio juris* and State practice being the materials of customary international law.

Also with respect to the acts of international organizations, an important connection with custom as a formal source of international law may be established. It was noted that General Assembly resolutions which are adopted unanimously or by a vast

---

of Legal Interpretations Concerning Claims of Self-Determination by Minority Peoples' at pp. 205-226.

[400] See World Conference on Human Rights, *Vienna Declaration and Programme of Action*, adopted on 25 June 1993, UN Doc. A/CONF.157/23, 12 July 1993, at para. 2.

[401] See Wilson, 'Self-Determination, Recognition and the Problem of Kosovo' at p. 467.

[402] Shaw, *International Law* at p. 110. That the Friendly Relations Declaration was created as a result of political compromises has been demonstrated in Section 2.2 of the present Chapter.

majority and final acts of international conferences may constitute a source of international law as well. For attaining this status, however, these acts are first to fulfil the conditions of customary international law. That is to say that they need to reflect *opinio juris* on the matter and that equivalent State practice should be present. So, although it has been determined previously that some acts of international organizations are highly relevant when searching for traces of a (qualified) right to unilateral secession, State practice should be examined before one may conclude that a perceived right to unilateral secession follows from these acts.

3. CONCLUSIONS

This Chapter has addressed the questions of whether contemporary international law recognizes a right to unilateral secession for subgroups constituting peoples within sovereign States, and if so, whether this right is absolute or conditional in character. For the purpose of addressing that matter, the sources of international law other than custom were scrutinized one by one. First, international treaties were examined in search of traces of a right to unilateral secession. The UN Charter, the 1966 International Covenants, the 1978 Vienna Convention on Succession of States in Respect of Treaties, and the International Convention on the Elimination of All Forms of Racial Discrimination were considered, but no conclusive evidence of such a right was found in conventional treaty law. Secondly, a close look was taken at scholarly literature. It seems that as a result of the writings of Lee C. Buchheit and Antonio Cassese, a remedial right to unilateral secession became accepted by many legal scholars. Yet, the caveat was made that scholarship is not decisive on the matter. This was most prominently reflected in scholarly writings following Kosovo's unilaterally proclaimed independence. In that context, most authors were rather reticent in providing conclusive answers as to the existence of a (qualified) right to unilateral secession under modern international law. Thirdly, decisions and opinions from both national and international judicial bodies were dealt with in order to find elements of such a right. It was demonstrated that although the theory of remedial secession has some support in jurisprudence, to date, no judicial body has accepted a (qualified) right to unilateral secession as an entitlement of a particular people in a specific case. Also in its Advisory Opinion on Kosovo's unilateral declaration of independence, the International Court of Justice refused to take a clear position on this matter. Fourthly, some general principles of law were considered. While general principles common in municipal laws, such as good faith and proportionality, may indeed be taken into account when arguing in favour of the existence of a right to unilateral secession, it was found that general principles which are merely relevant under international law do not seem to reveal clear traces of such a right. More than that, the principles of respect for the territorial integrity of States and *uti possidetis juris* ostensibly conflict with the thesis that a (qualified) right to unilateral secession does exist under contemporary international law. Close scrutiny of those principles, however, has demonstrated that these concepts are not irreconcilable. Thus, although general principles of international law do not support the existence of a qualified right to unilateral secession, they do not preclude it either and seem to leave some scope for the acknowledgement of such a right. Fifthly and finally, some possible sources of international law beyond the scope of Article 38 of the Statute of the ICJ were addressed, namely unilateral acts of States and acts of international organizations. Both types of acts will be further considered hereinafter in the context of customary international law.

From the analysis in the present Chapter, it may be inferred that (theoretical) support for the existence of a right to remedial secession is mainly found in doctrinal writings and, to a limited extent, in jurisprudence. In this respect, it is important to bear in mind that it is particularly these sources which Article 38(1)(d) of the Statute of the ICJ lists as "subsidiary means for the determination of law", as a result of which they should be seen to have supplementary value rather than principal importance. Moreover, it seems that both scholars and judicial bodies primarily base the thesis of such a right on a progressive, *a contrario* reading of the safeguard clause of the Friendly Relations Declaration. As was demonstrated, however, such an interpretation is not uncontested. Not only since it concerns an indeterminate clause, but also considering the rather vacillating relationship with a principle which is firmly rooted in international law, i.e. that of territorial integrity. In sum, it may even be said, as Daniel Thürer and Thomas Burri aptly observed, that deducing a qualified right to secession from the safeguard clause is "on the fringes of legal analysis and is strongly inspired by legitimacy considerations".[403] While the doctrine of remedial secession might indeed be attractive, it may be concluded here that its theoretical foundations are rather fragile and it remains to be seen whether international practice shows sufficient and compelling support for it. To shed some light on this latter issue, the following Chapter will present some preliminary remarks for the ascertainment of customary international law, after which Chapter VI will scrutinize State practice and *opinio juris* as being the classical elements of international customary law.

---

[403]   Thürer and Burri, 'Secession' at para. 17.

CHAPTER V
CUSTOMARY INTERNATIONAL LAW: PRELIMINARY REMARKS ON ASSESSING THE EXISTENCE OF A CUSTOMARY RIGHT TO REMEDIAL SECESSION

"[M]ost of what we perversely persist in calling customary international law is not only not *customary law: it does not even faintly resemble a customary law."*

Sir Robert Y. Jennings*

1. INTRODUCTION

Examining the sources of international law other than custom has led to the conclusion that (theoretical) support for the existence of a right to remedial secession can be found in doctrinal writings and, to a limited extent, in jurisprudence. It seems that both scholars and judicial bodies primarily base the thesis of such a right on a progressive, *a contrario* reading of the safeguard clause of the Friendly Relations Declaration. In this regard, the lack of a representative government, serious and widespread violations of fundamental human rights, structural discriminatory treatment and the exhaustion of peaceful remedies have generally been adduced as indicia for a right to remedial secession. However, as was demonstrated, such an interpretation is not uncontested. It was contended that, while the doctrine of remedial secession might indeed be attractive from a moral perspective, its theoretical foundations are rather fragile and it remains to be seen whether it has a sufficient and compelling empirical basis. As was observed previously, the development of the law of self-determination is to a large extent determined by the realities of practice.[1] Therefore, it should be assessed whether the theoretical concept and its specific interpretation are being reflected in practice. Put differently, it is to be scrutinized to what extent a customary

---

*   R.Y. Jennings, 'The Identification of International Law' in B. Cheng (ed.) *International Law: Teaching and Practice* (Stevens, London 1982) at p. 5.
[1]   See Chapter IV, Section 1.

right to unilateral secession has emerged under contemporary international law. Before proceeding to such exercise, first, the present Chapter will introduce the concept of customary international law.

While this Chapter will elaborate on customary international law in detail, it should be emphasized that this Chapter does not intend to substantially contribute to the development of theories with respect to the formation of customary international law. Such a comprehensive approach would go beyond the scope of the present research, which in essence focuses on the question of the emergence of a right to unilateral secession under modern international law. Rather, the purpose of this Chapter is primarily instrumental. In this regard, it will first present the two well-known elements of customary international law, i.e. State practice and *opinio juris sive necessitatis*, and elaborate on how these have been interpreted by the International Court of Justice and in doctrine. Secondly, the present Chapter will map out and appraise some relevant models of ascertaining customary norms. In this respect, conventional approaches towards this subject matter as well as some – more or less – progressive views will be discussed and criticized. Thirdly and finally, based on the foregoing, this Chapter will present the approach towards customary international law – by no means an unambiguous or comprehensive checklist – which will be utilized in the assessment regarding a customary right to unilateral secession. All in all, the present Chapter will serve as an important starting point and account for the subsequent exercise, as the theory of custom one adheres to will determine the approach of and possibly even the answer to the question of whether or not a customary norm with respect to a right to unilateral secession actually does exist today.

2. THE TWO CONVENTIONAL ELEMENTS OF CUSTOMARY INTERNATIONAL LAW

The previous Chapter took Article 38(1) of the Statute of the International Court of Justice as a point of departure for examining the sources of international law, as this provision is frequently seen as a (non-exhaustive) catalogue of these sources. Likewise, this provision serves as the starting point for describing the notion of customary international law.[2] In sub-paragraph (b), it prescribes that the Court shall apply

---

[2] The term 'customary international law' is often used to address different notions. One the one hand, it refers to a complex and often obscure process through which particular norms of international law are created. On the other hand, it concerns the substantive rules which have been materialized through this process and which are binding upon all States (see, for instance, T. Treves, 'Customary International Law' in R. Wolfrum (ed.) *Max Planck Encyclopedia of Public International law* (fully updated online edn, Oxford University Press, New York 2010) at para. 1). Moreover, the expression 'customary international law' is sometimes used to denote the principles governing the process of creating or finding law, which can be applied on the specific process of determining customary law as well and may be part of customary law on their own, rather than merely being general principles of law (see N.J. Arajärvi, *The Changing Nature of Customary International Law: Methods of Interpreting the Concept of Custom in International*

"international custom, as evidence of a general practice accepted as law". As such, the formation process of customary international law is an ongoing process which "enables international law to develop in line with the needs of the time".[3] In addition to its flexible nature, customary law has other advantages. For example, even where norms have been restated in international legal instruments, customary rules have added value as they also bind States which are not party to the instrument at hand. Moreover, State parties cannot terminate their obligations stemming from customary international law by withdrawal.[4] Customary norms may also provide for a clarification or elaboration of the rules included in treaty provisions and, as such, contribute to the evolution of international legal norms.[5] This again emphasizes the flexibility of customary international law.

From the wording of Article 38(1)(b) of the Statute of the International Court of Justice, it is possible to discern two elements in the materialization of a norm of customary international law: an objective element referring to the actual behaviour of States (State practice) and a subjective, psychological element which concerns the belief of States that such behaviour – either by action or omission – is a legal obligation (*opinio juris sive necessitatis*,[6] generally abbreviated as *opinio juris*).[7] As will be expounded elsewhere in this Chapter, the conventional view holds that both these constituents are required for the creation of customary international law. In 1929, the two-element theory was reflected by the Permanent Court of International Justice in the *Lotus* case, as it noted that only if certain conduct was based on the consciousness of States of a legal obligation to act accordingly would it be possible to speak of

---

Criminal Tribunals (European University Institute 2011) at p. 20). For the purpose of the present study, the term 'customary international law' will be used to refer to substantive rules of international law which are customary in nature, except where explicitly noted otherwise.

[3]   M. Dixon, *Textbook on International Law* (6th edn, Oxford University Press, Oxford 2007) at pp. 30-31.

[4]   See International Court of Justice, *Military and Paramilitary Activities in and Against Nicaragua (Nicaragua v. United States of America)*, Merits, Judgment, ICJ Reports 1986, p. 14, at paras 113-114.

[5]   T. Meron, *The Humanization of International Law* (Martinus Nijhoff Publishers, Leiden/Boston 2006) at pp. 357-358.

[6]   Despite the Latin phraseology, the concept does not find its origin in Roman law. According to Maurice H. Mendelson, François Gény was the first author who used the phrase *opinio juris sive necessitatis* in 1919 in the context of municipal law. See M.H. Mendelson, 'The Formation of Customary International Law' (1998) 272 *Collected Courses of the Hague Academy of International Law (Recueil des Cours)* 155 at p. 268.

[7]   See, for instance, I. Brownlie, *Principles of Public International Law* (7th edn, Oxford University Press, Oxford 2008) at p. 6; P. Malanczuk, *Akehurst's Modern Introduction to International Law* (7th revised edn, Routledge, London/New York 1997) at p. 44; M.N. Shaw, *International Law* (5th edn, Cambridge University Press, Cambridge 2003) at p. 70; H. Thirlway, 'The Sources of International Law' in M.D. Evans (ed.) *International Law* (Oxford University Press, Oxford 2003) at p. 125; Treves, 'Customary International Law' at para. 8.

customary international law.[8] Consequently, in the absence of this subjective belief of obligation, the State practice concerned was considered to be nothing more than usage. The International Court of Justice further developed this approach of customary law in the well-known *North Sea Continental Shelf* case, in which it considered the process by which a treaty provision could generate a customary norm. In this respect, the Court discerned the two elements required for the creation of customary international law more explicitly:

> [I]n order to achieve this result, two conditions must be fulfilled. Not only must the acts concerned amount to a settled practice, but they must also be such, or be carried out in such a way, as to be evidence of a belief that this practice is rendered obligatory by the existence of a rule of law requiring it. The need for such a belief, i.e. the existence of a subjective element, is implicit in the very notion of the *opinio juris sive necessitatis*. The States concerned must therefore feel that they are conforming to what amounts to a legal obligation.[9]

Throughout its decision, the Court clearly considered State practice to be the core element in the formation of a customary norm, which is to be confirmed by the reflection of *opinio juris*. In addition to the landmark decision in the *North Sea Continental Shelf* case, the *Nicaragua* case has become an important decision concerning the two-element theory and is frequently quoted by scholars and judges in the context of determining and interpreting customary international law. Here, the Court stated – *inter alia* – that "[f]or a new customary norm to be formed not only must the acts concerned 'amount to settled practice' but they must be accompanied by the *opinio juris sive necessitatis*".[10] While the two-element theory is confirmed in this passage of the ruling, other parts of this decision are generally seen as reflecting a differentiation of the rule flowing from the *North Sea Continental Shelf* case. This will be demonstrated hereafter.

Numerous scholars have also endorsed the two-element theory of customary international law. Today, it is still considered to be the dominant view.[11] It should be

---

[8]   Permanent Court of International Justice, *The Case of the SS Lotus (France v. Turkey)*, Judgment, PCIJ Series A No. 10 (1927), at p. 28.

[9]   International Court of Justice, *North Sea Continental Shelf (Federal Republic of Germany/Denmark; Federal Republic of Germany/Netherlands)*, Judgment, ICJ Reports 1969, p. 3, at para. 77.

[10]   International Court of Justice, *Military and Paramilitary Activities in and Against Nicaragua (Nicaragua v. United States of America)*, Merits, Judgment, ICJ Reports 1986, p. 14, at para. 207. See also para. 183, where the Court referred to one of its considerations in the *Libya/Malta* case (International Court of Justice, *Continental Shelf (Libyan Arab Jamahiriya/Malta)*, Judgment, ICJ Reports 1985, p. 13, at para. 27).

[11]   See, for instance, Brownlie, *Principles of Public International Law* at pp. 7-10; J.-M. Henckaerts and L. Doswald-Beck, *Customary International Humanitarian Law* (International Committee of the Red Cross/ Cambridge University Press, Cambridge 2005) at pp. xxxvii-xxxviii; International Law Association, Committee on the Formation of Customary (General) International Law, *Statement of Principles Applicable to the Formation of General Customary International Law*, London Conference (2000) at pp. 6-7; F.L. Kirgis

emphasized, however, that the concept of customary international law is not as unambiguous as it might ostensibly seem in view of the above. Therefore, the generally accepted understanding of the elements of State practice and *opinio juris* should be specified, thereby highlighting the complexity of the matter and revealing the subtle shades and increased interrelatedness of the two elements, as a result of which the strict distinction between the two elements has become theoretical to a certain extent.

2.1. State Practice

As has become clear from the above, State practice is one of the two elements of customary international law. Even more so, it is traditionally considered to be the key component in the formation process of customary law. In this respect, it needs to be emphasized that not all behaviour of States automatically leads to the establishment of such norms. The question thus arises as to which activities do constitute practice for the purpose of contributing to the creation of customary international law. When conceived narrowly, as Anthony A. D'Amato did, merely the physical acts of States (i.e. what States actually do and omit to do) in the international sphere are covered.[12] Examples in this respect are the establishment of international relations, battlefield conduct, the use of military means either collectively or unilaterally, the seizure of property, the arresting of individuals and economic measures or otherwise taken by way of countermeasures.[13] However, merely focusing on these physical acts as was traditionally done appears to be a view that has been superseded. Today, the notion of State practice is generally considered to be much more inclusive.[14] Judicial opinions[15]

Jr, 'Custom on a Sliding Scale' (1987) 81 *American Journal of International Law* 146 at p. 146; Malanczuk, *Akehurst's Modern Introduction to International Law* at p. 39; A. Orakhelashvili, *The Interpretation of Acts and Rules in Public International Law* (Oxford University Press, Oxford 2008) at pp. 79-80; Shaw, *International Law* at pp. 70-71; Thirlway, 'The Sources of International Law' at pp. 125-127; Treves, 'Customary International Law' at para. 8. However, as will be demonstrated in Section 3 of the present Chapter, more progressive approaches towards ascertaining customary international law are on the rise.

[12] According to Anthony A. D'Amato, State practice is established by acts and omissions, whereas *opinio juris* is materialized by statements. See A.A. D'Amato, *The Concept of Custom in International Law* (Cornell University Press, London 1971) at pp. 89-90.

[13] See, for instance, Henckaerts and Doswald-Beck, *Customary International Humanitarian Law* at p. xxxviii; International Law Association, Committee on the Formation of Customary (General) International Law, *Statement of Principles Applicable to the Formation of General Customary International Law*, London Conference (2000) at p. 14; Treves, 'Customary International Law' at para. 27.

[14] See, for instance, M. Byers, *Custom, Power and the Power of Rules. International Relations and Customary International Law* (Cambridge University Press, Cambridge 1999) at p. 134; Dixon, *Textbook on International Law* at p. 31; Meron, *The Humanization of International Law* at p. 361.

[15] See, for instance, International Court of Justice, *Military and Paramilitary Activities in and Against Nicaragua (Nicaragua v. United States of America)*, Merits, Judgment, ICJ Reports 1986, p. 14, at para. 190, in which the Court acknowledged the customary nature of the prohibition of the use of force on the basis of, *inter alia*, the fact that it was "frequently referred to in statements by State representatives". See also International International Criminal Tribunal for the Former Yugoslavia, *Prosecutor v. Tadić*,

and the reports of authoritative legal bodies such as the International Law Association[16] have demonstrated that evidence of what a State does can also be derived from verbal acts.[17] These acts are more common manifestations of State practice than the physical behaviour of States. On the domestic level, governmental declarations made in parliament are examples of relevant sources from which evidence of State practice may be deduced, as well as *inter alia* internal memoranda, official manuals concerning legal issues, diplomatic correspondence, national legislation and decisions of national courts and executive authorities. At the international stage, official statements, reactions or declarations presented by the delegates of States in international organizations or conferences are seen to reflect State practice,[18] as well as pleadings before and submissions to international courts and tribunals. In particular, governmental positions *vis-à-vis* written texts, such as draft proposals of treaties and other international legal instruments are viewed to be significant, for "they may contribute to the formation of precise and detailed customary international rules".[19] For those verbal acts to count as State practice, however, they need to be public. That is to say that these pronouncements are to be communicated to at least one other State.[20] Maurice H. Mendelson refers to this as the "claim and response" element of practice.[21]

Decision on the defence motion for interlocutory appeal on jurisdiction, ICTY-IT-94-AR72, 2 October 1995, at para. 99, where it was noted that in determining customary norms of international humanitarian law, "reliance must primarily be placed on such elements as official pronouncements of States, military manuals and judicial decisions."

[16] See International Law Association, Committee on the Formation of Customary (General) International Law, *Statement of Principles Applicable to the Formation of General Customary International Law*, London Conference (2000) at pp. 14-15. See also International Law Commission, 'Draft Articles on State Responsibility', *Yearbook of the International Law Commission*, 1980, Vol. II, Part 2, UN Doc. A/CN.4/SER.A/1980/Add.1 (Part 2), 29 February, 10 and 19 June 1980, pp. 34-52. The ILC scrutinized the concept of 'state of necessity' and in this connection, referred to and heavily relied on the statements of government representatives and scholars.

[17] See Henckaerts and Doswald-Beck, *Customary International Humanitarian Law* at pp. xxxviii-xl; Mendelson, 'The Formation of Customary International Law' at pp. 204-207; Shaw, *International Law* at pp. 77-78.

[18] In his separate opinion attached to the *Barcelona Traction* case, Judge Ammoun noted that "it cannot be denied, with regard to the resolutions which emerge therefrom, or better, with regard to the votes expressed therein in the name of States, that these amount to precedents contributing to the formation of custom". See International Court of Justice, *Barcelona Traction, Light and Power Company, Limited (Belgium v. Spain)*, Judgment, ICJ Reports 1970, p. 3, at pp. 302-303.

[19] Treves, 'Customary International Law' at para. 26. See also Brownlie, *Principles of Public International Law* at pp. 6-7; Henckaerts and Doswald-Beck, *Customary International Humanitarian Law* at p. xxxviii; Shaw, *International Law* at p. 78.

[20] International Law Association, Committee on the Formation of Customary (General) International Law, *Statement of Principles Applicable to the Formation of General Customary International Law*, London Conference (2000) at p. 15.

[21] M.H. Mendelson, 'The Subjective Element in Customary International Law' (1996) 66 *British Yearbook of International Law* 177 at p. 204; Mendelson, 'The Formation of Customary International Law' at p. 204.

This inclusive approach towards identifying State practice seems to soften the distinction traditionally made between State practice and *opinio juris*. Not merely what States actually do, but also what States say is considered to contribute to the establishment of State practice. Yet, such verbal State practice may include subjective elements and does not always correspond with the physical actions of States. The classical example in this respect concerns States which formally uphold the prohibition of torture and deny that they are involved in such malpractices, while in fact, they do engage in torture. What is more, verbal State practice is closely linked to the notion of *opinio juris*, since the content of such verbal acts often simultaneously expresses the legal conviction of the State.[22] Consequently, it is "often difficult or even impossible to disentangle the two elements",[23] as a result of which it is "largely theoretical to strictly separate elements of practice and legal conviction".[24] This position will be elaborated upon in the context of the subjective element of custom.[25]

In the context of the above, it should be emphasized that although the behaviour of actors other than States – that is to say their legislative, executive and judicial branches[26] – cannot be regarded as practice which directly contributes to the crystallization of customary norms,[27] indirectly, international organizations and other

---

[22]   Henckaerts and Doswald-Beck, *Customary International Humanitarian Law* at p. xlvi; Mendelson, 'The Formation of Customary International Law' at p. 206.

[23]   International Law Association, Committee on the Formation of Customary (General) International Law, *Statement of Principles Applicable to the Formation of General Customary International Law*, London Conference (2000) at p. 7.

[24]   Henckaerts and Doswald-Beck, *Customary International Humanitarian Law* at p. xlvi.

[25]   See Section 2.2 of the present Chapter.

[26]   On this topic, see Mendelson, 'The Formation of Customary International Law' at pp. 198-200.

[27]   However, given that international law increasingly regulates the rights and obligations of actors other than States, several authors have suggested to reformulate understandings of customary international law so as allow non-State actors to contribute more directly to the formation of customary norms. Anthea E. Roberts and Sandesh Sivakumaran, for instance, have proposed a theory of "quasi-custom" in this respect. See A.E. Roberts and S. Sivakumaran, 'Lawmaking by Nonstate Actors: Engaging Armed Groups in the Creation of International Humanitarian Law' (2012) 37 *Yale Journal of International Law* 107, at pp. 149-151. By taking the example of armed groups and their influence on the creation of customary international humanitarian law, Roberts and Sivakumaran suggest "to develop a theory of quasi-customary international law that would be based on the practices and views of states plus actors other than states" (p. 150). This does neither imply that non-State actors acting alone would have the power to create new customary norms, nor that they are in the position to amend existing customary norms. According to Roberts and Sivakumaran, the actions and views of State should also be weighted and should even be given more weight in order to safeguard the vital role of States in the formation or changing of customary international law. Moreover, they stress that non-State actors should remain bound by existing customary international law (p. 151). Similar proposals have been made by other authors, *inter alia*, by Robert McCorquodale. See R. McCorquodale, 'An Inclusive International Legal System' (2004) 17 *Leiden Journal of International Law* 477, at pp. 498-499. While it is beyond the scope of the present study to elaborate on these theories and critically consider them, it deserves to be emphasized that at present, suggestions to allow non-State actors to play a role in the creation of customary international law are by no means generally accepted.

non-State actors (e.g. political movements and armed opposition groups) have become progressively more involved in this process. Not only may the perceptions of these entities influence the practice of States at both the national and international level,[28] over recent decades, international organizations have provided a forum for States to deliberate and to act. As such, international organizations may even be viewed as "instrumental" in the formation process of custom.[29] For, as the International Law Commission has noted, "records of the cumulative practice of international organizations may be regarded as evidence of customary international law with reference to States' relations to the organizations".[30]

Having addressed the manifestations of State practice, questions arise as to the interpretation of this objective constituent of customary international law. State practice is generally seen to be based on three factors determining its 'denseness': uniformity (*ratione materiae*), extensiveness and representativeness (*ratione loci*), and duration (*ratione temporis*).[31] These factors merit some clarification.

2.1.1. Uniformity

It is commonly accepted that relevant practice need not be absolutely consistent in order to contribute to the formation of a customary norm. Rather, as the International Court of Justice held in the *North Sea Continental Shelf* case, practice is to be "virtually uniform".[32] This basically means that the States involved must not have engaged in significantly different behaviour.[33] Nevertheless, in the *Fisheries* case, the Court held that in assessing State practice, one need not attach too much value to "a few uncertainties or contradictions, real or apparent".[34] The practice at hand merely needs to be sufficiently similar, so it seems. From this case, it also follows that the degree of consistency that is required may depend upon the subject matter of the norm at issue. More specifically, positive obligations for the State call for a greater degree of

---

[28]   Treves, 'Customary International Law' at para. 33. See also Arajärvi, *The Changing Nature of Customary International Law: Methods of Interpreting the Concept of Custom in International Criminal Tribunals* at p. 23.

[29]   See Shaw, *International Law* at p. 78.

[30]   International Law Commission, 'Ways and means for making the evidence of customary international law more readily available', *Yearbook of the ILC*, 1950, vol. II, pp. 367-374, at para. 78.

[31]   See, for instance, Henckaerts and Doswald-Beck, *Customary International Humanitarian Law* at p. xlii; International Law Association, Committee on the Formation of Customary (General) International Law, *Statement of Principles Applicable to the Formation of General Customary International Law*, London Conference (2000) at p. 20.

[32]   International Court of Justice, *North Sea Continental Shelf (Federal Republic of Germany/Denmark; Federal Republic of Germany/Netherlands)*, Judgment, ICJ Reports 1969, p. 3, at para. 74.

[33]   See, for instance, International Court of Justice, *Asylum (Colombia v. Peru)*, Judgment, ICJ Reports 1950, p. 266, at p. 15.

[34]   International Court of Justice, *Fisheries (United Kingdom v. Norway)*, Judgment, ICJ Reports 1951, p. 116, at p. 138.

uniformity than negative obligations. The same goes for proposed customary rules which affect the sovereign rights of States rather than confirm or even increase those privileges. Yet, modifying a customary norm which has a *jus cogens* character does require the presence of almost absolute uniform State practice before it may be effectuated, "at least where it is claimed that the 'new' rule now allows that which was previously prohibited".[35] While contrary practice ostensibly challenges the uniformity of State practice, it does not necessarily preclude the materialization of a customary norm, as Court stressed in the *Nicaragua* case:

> The Court does not consider that, for a rule to be established as customary, the corresponding practice must be in absolute rigorous conformity with the rule. In order to deduce the existence of customary rules, the Court deems it sufficient that the conduct of States should, in general, be consistent with such rules, and that instances of State conduct inconsistent with a given rule should generally have been treated as breaches of that rule, not as indications of the recognition of a new rule. If a State acts in a way *prima facie* incompatible with a recognized rule, but defends its conduct by appealing to exceptions or justifications contained within the rule itself, then whether or not the State's conduct is in fact justifiable on that basis, the significance of that attitude is to confirm rather than to weaken the rule.[36]

Thus, if the contrary conduct is condemned by third States or denied by the government of the acting State as being its official practice, the rule at hand may be seen to be confirmed. The same goes for State practice which appears inconsistent with a rule, but is upheld by the State by invoking exceptions or justifications which are part of that rule. This finding is particularly relevant for some human rights and international humanitarian norms, which are strongly confirmed by verbal State practice, yet simultaneously contradicted by violations of the rule at issue. In sum, due to the ambiguity of this requirement, opinions still differ as to the precise extent of uniformity that is required.[37]

2.1.2. Extensiveness and Representativeness

With regard to the need for extensiveness and representativeness, it is important to note that the State practice does not need to be universal. Rather, 'general' practice is sufficient.[38] There is no precise number of States which should be involved in order

---

[35] See Dixon, *Textbook on International Law* at p. 39. See also pp. 31-32.

[36] International Court of Justice, *Military and Paramilitary Activities in and Against Nicaragua (Nicaragua v. United States of America)*, Merits, Judgment, ICJ Reports 1986, p. 14, at para. 186.

[37] See A.T. Guzman, 'Saving Customary International Law' (2005) 27 *Michigan Journal of International Law* 115 at p. 124.

[38] Henckaerts and Doswald-Beck, *Customary International Humanitarian Law* at p. xliv; International Law Association, Committee on the Formation of Customary (General) International Law, *Statement of Principles Applicable to the Formation of General Customary International Law*, London Conference (2000) at p. 24.

to classify practice as such for the purpose of creating customary international law. Neither is a certain degree of consensus or majority voting required in this respect. According to some commentators, a possible explanation for this is that the requirement of extensiveness is "*qualitative* rather than quantitative". Put differently, it is not merely a matter of the number of States that are involved in the practice at hand, but in addition and perhaps even more importantly, which States.[39] As the Court expressed in the *North Sea Continental Shelf* case, it must at least include the practice of "States whose interests are specially affected".[40] Which States are 'specially affected' by the subject matter of the rule will, of course, depend on the circumstances. For example, to determine the existence of a customary rule concerning the law of the sea, the relevant State practice of the principal maritime powers seems indispensable. Conversely, it may be concluded that the lack of practice by some less involved States does not necessarily stand in the way of ascertaining State practice in a certain field.[41] Thus, the above does not necessarily imply that some States are more important or more powerful than others, but rather, that the practice of some States is considered to be more relevant as these States are directly affected by a certain norm.[42] At the same time, however, it should be noted that particularly those States which are 'specially affected' may have an interest in securing certain outcomes in the formation process of customary international law. As such, it seems appropriate to critically consider the role of 'specially affected States' on a case-by-case basis.[43] In addition to the criterion of extensiveness, the accompanying element of representativeness is qualitative in character as well. It calls for taking into account the practice a variety of States, including non-Western States and preferably representing a broad range of cultures, social and economic systems, as a result of which the practice at hand can at least be presumed to be representative for the community of States as a whole.[44] If practice merely involves a particular region, this may point at the emergence or existence of rules of customary *regional* law rather than customary *international* law.[45]

Since no universal practice is required for the crystallization of customary norms, it follows that a State can be bound by the general practice of other States even against its will. The only exception to this could be a situation in which a State has

---

[39] Dixon, *Textbook on International Law* at p. 32; Henckaerts and Doswald-Beck, *Customary International Humanitarian Law* at p. xliv (emphasis in original); International Law Association, Committee on the Formation of Customary (General) International Law, *Statement of Principles Applicable to the Formation of General Customary International Law*, London Conference (2000) at p. 26.

[40] International Court of Justice, *North Sea Continental Shelf (Federal Republic of Germany/Denmark; Federal Republic of Germany/Netherlands)*, Judgment, ICJ Reports 1969, p. 3, at para. 74.

[41] See Treves, 'Customary International Law' at para. 36.

[42] See Dixon, *Textbook on International Law* at p. 32.

[43] See B.D. Lepard, *Customary International Law. A New Theory with Practical Applications* (Cambridge University Press, Cambridge 2010) at p. 28, citing W. Michael Reisman.

[44] See *ibid.* at pp. 153-154.

[45] See, for instance, Shaw, *International Law* at pp. 87-88.

explicitly expressed its opposition to the development of the customary rule at issue from the outset and persistently continues to do so after its crystallization.[46] Put differently, "initial and sustained objection"[47] may prevent a State from being bound by a new or changed norm of customary international law. This is generally referred to as the 'persistent objector' rule. In connection to the required involvement of 'specially affected States', it is interesting to note that:

> while it is generally true that an objection from one state will not prevent the formation of customary law for other, non-objecting states, in some cases it may be that the persistent objector is such an important operator in a particular field that its continued objection prevents customary law developing for all states.[48]

The acceptance of the persistent objector exception, however, remains disputed, particularly when it comes to fundamental principles of international (human rights) law.[49] Moreover, practice has shown that objecting States generally do not manage to remain unaffected by the new customary norm for very long, due to (peer) pressure to act in conformity with this newly established standard and disadvantages of acting contrary to the accepted view.[50]

2.1.3. Duration

In addition to the above, the duration of practice has sometimes been mentioned as a relevant factor in the creation of custom (*ratione temporis*).[51] The time factor, however, should not be seen in isolation, but rather in connection with the requirements concerning the uniformity, extensiveness and representativeness of the practice. On the one hand, some passage of time is usually needed in order to satisfy these criteria.[52] On the other, as the International Court of Justice held in the *North Sea Continental Shelf* case:

---

[46]   On the (disputed) acceptance of this rule, see Mendelson, 'The Formation of Customary International Law' at pp. 227-244.

[47]   Dixon, *Textbook on International Law* at p. 33.

[48]   *Ibid.* at p. 33.

[49]   See, for instance, International Law Association, Committee on the Formation of Customary (General) International Law, *Statement of Principles Applicable to the Formation of General Customary International Law*, London Conference (2000) at pp. 27-29; Malanczuk, *Akehurst's Modern Introduction to International Law* at pp. 47-48; Thirlway, 'The Sources of International Law' at pp. 128-130.

[50]   See Dixon, *Textbook on International Law* at p. 33.

[51]   As noted by Maurice H. Mendelson, the time factor was particularly important for the formation of customary law for the Romans and in the English common law system. See Mendelson, 'The Formation of Customary International Law' at p. 209.

[52]   Henckaerts and Doswald-Beck, *Customary International Humanitarian Law* at p. xlv.

> Although the passage of only a short period of time is not necessarily, as of itself, a bar to the formation of a new rule of customary international law [...], an indispensable requirement would be that within the period in question, short though it might be, State practice [...] should have been both extensive and virtually uniform in the sense of the provision invoked.[53]

Thus, it is basically a matter of establishing a dense practice: as long as uniformity, extensiveness and representativeness are manifested, no specific duration of the relevant State practice is demanded.[54] What is more, it has become generally accepted that customary norms may emerge rapidly. In response to new technological developments and accompanying new legal subject matters, Bin Cheng was the first to propose the notion of 'instant custom' already in 1965. He argued that a rule could emerge into customary law in the absence of protracted State practice provided that general and representative *opinio juris* would be present as regards the existence of such a norm. Subsequent practice would then only be necessary to confirm the existence of this customary rule. As such, Cheng advanced that customary norms can – in appropriate circumstances – be deduced from General Assembly resolutions, as these may reflect evidence of *opinio juris* and State practice simultaneously.[55] Cheng's theory on this matter, however, has never been fully endorsed and may even be said to have been rejected by the International Court of Justice, as it considers General Assembly resolutions as reflecting *opinio juris*, but not as acts providing evidence of State practice.[56] As one author concluded from the Court's reasoning, "[t]he position appears to be that in a field of activity in which there has not yet been an opportunity for State practice, there is no customary law in existence".[57] Admittedly, some developments have indeed contributed to the acceleration of the materialization of customary norms. For example, the increased role of international organizations and conferences within international society and the augmented conclusion of multilateral treaties have brought about the increased involvement of States in the formation process of customary international law, as a result of which verbal State practice and *opinio juris* can be manifested more swiftly.[58] This is not to say, however, that the traditional model considers the presence of physical State practice to be redundant.

---

[53] International Court of Justice, *North Sea Continental Shelf (Federal Republic of Germany/Denmark; Federal Republic of Germany/Netherlands)*, Judgment, ICJ Reports 1969, p. 3, at para. 74.

[54] International Law Association, Committee on the Formation of Customary (General) International Law, *Statement of Principles Applicable to the Formation of General Customary International Law*, London Conference (2000) at p. 20.

[55] See B. Cheng, 'United Nations Resolutions on Outer Space: "Instant" International Customary Law?' (1965) 5 *Indian Journal of International Law* 23.

[56] International Court of Justice, *Military and Paramilitary Activities in and Against Nicaragua (Nicaragua v. United States of America)*, Merits, Judgment, ICJ Reports 1986, p. 14, at paras 184, 188.

[57] Thirlway, 'The Sources of International Law' at p. 127.

[58] Treves, 'Customary International Law' at para. 25.

Rather, in this view, proof of the objective element of custom is still essential to determine the existence of a norm of customary international law.

2.1.4. The Interrelationship of the Three Factors

With regard to the three factors addressed – uniformity, extensiveness and representativeness, and duration – it should be emphasized that they should be considered in connection with each other, as inadequacies with respect to one factor may be counterbalanced by the strength of the other two. Such interplay not only exists concerning the requirement of duration on the one hand, and those of uniformity, extensiveness and representativeness on the other. Such interrelationship may also exist between the latter factors: "a more pronounced generality of the practice could cure some weaknesses in its uniformity, or vice versa".[59] Yet, even when all three factors are sufficiently present, usage does not necessarily lead to the crystallization of a norm of customary international law. As the International Court of Justice aptly expressed in the *North Sea Continental Shelf* case, actions by States can also be dictated "only by considerations of courtesy, convenience or tradition, and not by any sense of legal duty".[60] This is where the subjective or psychological element of *opinio juris*, which will be discussed below, becomes relevant.[61]

2.2. Opinio Juris

When seeking to determine the existence of norms of customary international law, it is conventionally contended that examining the physical actions of States is insufficient. As the International Court of Justice explained:

Not only must the acts concerned amount to a settled practice, but they must also be such, or be carried out in such a way, as to be *evidence of a belief that this practice is rendered obligatory by the existence of a rule of law requiring it.* The need for such a belief, i.e. the existence of a subjective element, is implicit in the very notion of the *opinio juris sive necessitatis. The States concerned must therefore feel that they are conforming to what amounts to a legal obligation.*[62]

---

[59] R. Kolb, 'Selected Problems in the Theory of Customary International Law' (2003) 50 *Netherlands International Law Review* 119 at p. 133.

[60] International Court of Justice, *North Sea Continental Shelf (Federal Republic of Germany/Denmark; Federal Republic of Germany/Netherlands)*, Judgment, ICJ Reports 1969, p. 3, at para. 77.

[61] See also International Law Association, Committee on the Formation of Customary (General) International Law, *Statement of Principles Applicable to the Formation of General Customary International Law*, London Conference (2000) at p. 34: "It is for the purpose of distinguishing practices which generate customary rules from those that do not that *opinio juris* is most useful."

[62] International Court of Justice, *North Sea Continental Shelf (Federal Republic of Germany/Denmark; Federal Republic of Germany/Netherlands)*, Judgment, ICJ Reports 1969, p. 3, at para. 77 (emphasis added).

Put differently, in addition to *how* States act, it is important to see *why* States act in a certain way. It is this subjective element rising from an internal belief and usually referred to as *opinio juris*, which is traditionally seen to mark the distinction between mere usage and practice contributing to the crystallization of a binding norm of customary international law and therefore is traditionally seen as indispensable for the establishment of custom.[63]

In addition to the phrase from the *North Sea Continental Shelf* case, the necessity of this psychological element in the formation of customary international law has been emphasized in other judgments of the Permanent Court of Justice and the International Court of Justice.[64] Moreover, commentators have sought to explain why the element of *opinio juris* is generally considered to be essential for the transformation from usage to customary international law. Generally speaking, two approaches may be discerned in this respect. Some scholars have taken the position that *opinio juris* is principally an expression of State consent to a certain norm, just like the signing and ratification of treaties are written expressions of the State's will to obey a set of rules. This position, which reflects the consensual or voluntary character of international law, seems to be supported by, for instance, Anthony A. D'Amato. For him, *opinio juris* is the articulation of the legal character of the practice at hand, which is a precondition for a norm of customary international law to arise: [65]

> The articulation of a rule of international law [...] in advance of or concurrently with a positive act (or omission) of a state gives a state notice that its action or decision will have legal implications. In other words, given such notice, statesman will be able freely to decide whether or not to pursue various policies, knowing that their acts may create or modify international law.[66]

Most commentators, however, adhere to the opposite approach, contending that the legally binding force of custom simply ensues from the belief of States that the

---

[63] See, for instance, Brownlie, *Principles of Public International Law* at p. 6; Malanczuk, *Akehurst's Modern Introduction to International Law* at p. 44; Mendelson, 'The Formation of Customary International Law' at p. 245; Meron, *The Humanization of International Law* at p. 366; Orakhelashvili, *The Interpretation of Acts and Rules in Public International Law* at pp. 79-80; Shaw, *International Law* at pp. 70, 80; Thirlway, 'The Sources of International Law' at p. 125; Treves, 'Customary International Law' at para. 8.

[64] See, for instance, Permanent Court of International Justice, *The Case of the SS Lotus (France v. Turkey)*, Judgment, PCIJ Series A No. 10, at p. 28; International Court of Justice, *Military and Paramilitary Activities in and Against Nicaragua (Nicaragua v. United States of America)*, Merits, Judgment, ICJ Reports 1986, p. 14, at paras 183-185.

[65] D'Amato, *The Concept of Custom in International Law* at p. 74. For a more contemporary plea for the consensualist approach, see Orakhelashvili, *The Interpretation of Acts and Rules in Public International Law* at pp. 71-75.

[66] D'Amato, *The Concept of Custom in International Law* at p. 75.

behaviour at issue is called for by a legal norm.[67] As Maurice H. Mendelson submitted, the consensualist approach is unable to provide for a cogent reason why States which have not participated in the formation process of a customary norm are legally bound by it, while it is beyond dispute that they are.[68]

The question now arises as to how to determine *opinio juris* or, put differently, how this element of custom manifests itself.[69] Since *opinio juris* concerns a state of mind, obvious difficulties occur in this respect. First, it may be noted that "[t]here is clearly something artificial about trying to analyse the psychology of collective entities such as states".[70] As States are institutions, it is submitted that one cannot know what States truly believe, but merely what States claim to believe.[71] Secondly, and even more importantly, it is hard to ascertain whether a State acted because it considered itself bound by a rule of customary international law, or whether the State would have acted similarly in the absence of such an alleged norm. Irrespective of these difficulties, the traditional view holds that this psychological component of custom can be detected from official pronouncements by various 'agents' of the State, such a heads of States, heads of government, members of government, members of parliament and national judicial bodies. Their pronouncements on both the national and international level, for instance governmental statements made in parliament, declarations presented by the representatives of States in international organizations, governmental positions concerning draft proposals of treaties and resolutions, and judicial decisions, can be seen as sources of *opinio juris*.[72] Moreover, it should be recalled that (legally non-binding) resolutions of the UN General Assembly resolutions may under

---

[67]   See Mendelson, 'The Formation of Customary International Law' at p. 246 (and the references mentioned there). In this connection, it may be noted that some scholars have proposed a slightly different definition of *opinio juris*, including the belief that the practice is required by a norm which *should* become law. A definition of this kind differs from the traditional understanding of the concept and has not (yet) been generally accepted, but seems more appropriate for explaining how new norms of custom can come into existence, while simultaneously avoiding the so-called paradox connected with *opinio juris*. This paradox refers to the chronological problem that the generally accepted understanding of *opinio juris* seems to require a State to believe that a norm is law for it to become law. Put differently, how can a rule of customary international law be created if in order to create such a rule, States need to act from the belief that the law already necessitates that behaviour? See Lepard, *Customary International Law. A New Theory with Practical Applications* at pp. 22-23 and pp. 118-121. See also Kolb, 'Selected Problems in the Theory of Customary International Law' at pp. 137-141.

[68]   Mendelson, 'The Formation of Customary International Law' at p. 292.

[69]   See Brownlie, *Principles of Public International Law* at p. 8; Malanczuk, *Akehurst's Modern Introduction to International Law* at p. 44.

[70]   Malanczuk, *Akehurst's Modern Introduction to International Law* at p. 44. See also Thirlway, 'The Sources of International Law' at p. 126.

[71]   See Mendelson, 'The Formation of Customary International Law' at p. 269.

[72]   See, for instance, Brownlie, *Principles of Public International Law* at pp. 6-7.

certain circumstances be seen to reflect *opinio juris*. This subject has been expounded elsewhere in the present study.[73]

As was already pointed out in the previous section, however, the pronouncements reflecting *opinio juris* may often be seen as the evidence of verbal State practice as well. In this connection, Jan Wouters and Cedric Ryngaert have noted that "[a] n analysis of such statements may kill two birds with one stone: it may satisfy the requirement of *opinio juris* and the requirement of State practice at the same time".[74] Consequently, strictly distinguishing between (verbal) State practice and *opinio juris* becomes problematic. Taking this entanglement of the two elements of customary international law one step further is to infer *opinio juris* indirectly from what States actually do or omit to do and, in addition, how other States react to this. In this respect, it is sometimes argued that the general practice of States may constitute the principal evidence of *opinio juris*. Put differently, when there is a sufficiently dense practice of States on a certain issue (as was explained in the previous section), it may be assumed that *opinio juris* does exist. As a consequence of this trend, in many cases it would become superfluous to distinctly demonstrate the existence of *opinio juris*.[75] Provided that it can be shown that State practice is sufficiently dense and unequivocal, and no precedential value of this conduct is precluded by the States involved,[76]

> it is not necessary to prove the existence of an *opinio juris*. It may often be present, or it may be possible to infer it; but it is not a requirement that its existence be demonstrated.[77]

Such a view, allegedly blurring a strict distinction between the two traditional elements of customary international law,[78] was reflected by for instance Judge Lachs

---

[73] This was discussed already in the context of the acts of international organizations as a possible source of international law. See Chapter III, Section 3.5.2.

[74] J. Wouters and C. Ryngaert, 'Impact on the Process of the Formation of Customary International Law' in M.T. Kamminga and M. Scheinin (eds) *The Impact of Human Rights Law on General International Law* (Oxford University Press, Oxford 2009) at p. 115.

[75] See, for instance, Henckaerts and Doswald-Beck, *Customary International Humanitarian Law* at p. xlvi; International Law Association, Committee on the Formation of Customary (General) International Law, *Statement of Principles Applicable to the Formation of General Customary International Law*, London Conference (2000) at pp. 30-32; Kirgis Jr, 'Custom on a Sliding Scale' at p. 148; H. Lauterpacht, *The Development of International Law by the International Court* (Cambridge University Press, Cambridge 1982) at p. 380; Malanczuk, *Akehurst's Modern Introduction to International Law* at p. 44; Mendelson, 'The Formation of Customary International Law' at pp. 289-290.

[76] It is to be noted that when there is a settled State practice, but the States involved emphasize that their conduct does not have any precedential value, no *opinio juris* can be ascertained.

[77] International Law Association, Committee on the Formation of Customary (General) International Law, *Statement of Principles Applicable to the Formation of General Customary International Law*, London Conference (2000) at p. 31.

[78] According to the International Law Association, it may well be that the statements of the International Court of Justice concerning the two constituents of custom have been taken out of their context:

in his dissenting opinion attached to the *North Sea Continental Shelf* case.[79] The international criminal tribunals tend to take a similarly loose approach towards determining *opinio juris*, as they often assume its existence on the basis of extensive State practice, general agreement in doctrine, or previous assessments of international tribunals.[80] The International Court of Justice has been willing to adopt such an approach in various cases as well.[81] Yet, in some cases, the International Court of Justice has applied a more rigorous and strict method, requiring isolated evidence for the existence of *opinio juris* rather than presuming this from the practice of States. The first example in this respect was the judgment in the *Lotus* case, in which the Court's predecessor held that:

> [e]ven if the rarity of the judicial decisions to be found among the reported cases were sufficient to prove in point of fact the circumstances alleged by the Agent for the French Government, it would merely show that States had often, in practice, abstained from instituting criminal proceedings, and not that they recognized themselves as being obliged to do so; for only if such abstention were based on their being conscious of a duty to abstain would it be possible to speak of an international custom. The alleged fact does not allow one to infer that States have been conscious of having such a duty; on the other hand [...] there are other circumstances calculated to show that the contrary is true.[82]

A similar view was expressed by the majority of the Court in the *North Sea Continental Shelf* case, where it was noted that the "frequency, or even habitual character" of State practice is insufficient to determine the presence of *opinio juris*.[83] This stance appears to imply that *opinio juris* cannot be inferred from the availability of State practice.

"[t]he Court has not in fact said in so may words that just because there are (allegedly) distinct elements in customary law the same conduct cannot manifest both". See *ibid.* at p. 7.

[79] See International Court of Justice, *North Sea Continental Shelf (Federal Republic of Germany/Denmark; Federal Republic of Germany/Netherlands)*, Merits, Judgment, ICJ Reports 1969, p. 219, at pp. 231-232, Dissenting Opinion of Judge Lachs.

[80] On this topic, see Arajärvi, *The Changing Nature of Customary International Law: Methods of Interpreting the Concept of Custom in International Criminal Tribunals.*

[81] See, for instance, International Court of Justice, *Fisheries (United Kingdom v. Norway)*, Judgment, ICJ Reports 1951, p. 116, at p. 128; International Court of Justice, *Barcelona Traction, Light and Power Company Limited (Belgium v. Spain)*, Judgment, ICJ Reports 1970, p. 3, at para. 70; International Court of Justice, *Continental Shelf (Libyan Arab Jamahiriya/Malta)*, Judgment, ICJ Reports 1985, p. 13, at para. 34. See also Brownlie, *Principles of Public International Law* at pp. 8-9; Mendelson, 'The Formation of Customary International Law' at pp. 289-290.

[82] Permanent Court of International Justice, *The Case of the SS Lotus (France v. Turkey)*, Judgment, PCIJ Series A, No. 10, at p. 28.

[83] International Court of Justice, *North Sea Continental Shelf (Federal Republic of Germany/Denmark; Federal Republic of Germany/Netherlands)*, Merits, Judgment, ICJ Reports 1969, p. 3, at para. 77.

As suggested by, for instance, Maurice H. Mendelson, it seems that the choice of methodology in this respect partly depends upon the presence of unequivocal and dense State practice. When such practice is available, no separate proof for the existence of *opinio juris* may be needed. But when uncertainties as regards the practice present themselves, *opinio juris* serves as a "necessary tool in resolving the uncertainty". [84] What is more, the subject matter of the alleged customary norm appears to be relevant for the choice of approach towards *opinio juris*. As was likewise noted in the context of the objective constituent of customary international law, where the rule involves a positive obligation for States, where the sovereign rights of States are affected, or where a *jus cogens* norm is concerned, a high degree of proof will be required. In such circumstances, simply inferring *opinio juris* from the availability of State practice will not suffice, but rather, clear and distinct evidence of *opinio juris* will be required.[85] This line of reasoning also applies to situations in which States omit to act.[86] All in all, it appears that there is no exclusive methodology for the determination of *opinio juris*. It may even be contended that "[i]n essence, the matter is one of judgment", since "international law might require different levels of *opinio juris* and different degrees of proof for different substantive rules of customary law".[87]

3. CUSTOMARY INTERNATIONAL LAW BEYOND THE CONVENTIONAL MODEL?

Above, the two classical constituents of customary international law have been considered. At first sight, the elements of State practice and *opinio juris* seemed to be two clearly distinctive concepts which are both required for ascertaining customary international law but have different features: the former being an objective constituent which is reflected in what States actually do, while the latter concerns a subjective constituent covering the legal convictions of States. In the previous section, however, the necessary differentiations were made, thereby revealing the intricacy of the matter and demonstrating that in the contemporary formation process of customary

---

[84] See Mendelson, 'The Formation of Customary International Law' at pp. 285-286. See also Henckaerts and Doswald-Beck, *Customary International Humanitarian Law* at p. xlvi.

[85] See Dixon, *Textbook on International Law* at p. 35. See also Ian Brownlie, who noted that the choice of approach depends "upon the nature of the issues (that is, the state of the law may be a primary point in contention)". In addition, Brownlie found that it also depends upon the "discretion of the Court". See Brownlie, *Principles of Public International Law* at p. 9.

[86] See Henckaerts and Doswald-Beck, *Customary International Humanitarian Law* at p. xlvi, recalling an example from the *Lotus* case, in which the Court refused to qualify the absence of certain prosecutions as evidence of a customary prohibition to prosecute. The Court stated that is remained unclear whether States had refrained from prosecutions because of the belief that it was unlawful to do so, or whether their omissions were due to other reasons. According to the Court, there was no proof of any "conscious[ness] of having a duty to abstain". See Permanent Court of International Justice, *The Case of the SS Lotus (France v. Turkey)*, Judgment, PCIJ Series A, No. 10, at p. 28.

[87] Dixon, *Textbook on International Law* at p. 35.

international law, State practice and *opinio juris* have increasingly grown towards one another and even overlap to a certain extent.

Against this background, it was already obliquely noted that the conventional approach towards custom, which is generally set forth in reference books on international law, consistently requires the presence of both State practice and *opinio juris* for the creation of customary norms.[88] This is not to say, however, that this traditional model considers both elements to be equally important. Rather, it views State practice to be the key element of custom, while *opinio juris* is deemed necessary as it reflects the belief of the legally binding nature of the practice. This might explain why the conventional approach – even though it has become generally accepted that in addition to the physical acts of States, verbal acts may also reflect evidence of the objective element of custom – still emphasizes physical State practice over verbal acts of States, as the latter category seems to include some subjective elements as well.[89]

When considering the (relative) importance of the elements of State practice and *opinio juris* in the formation process of customary international law, more progressive – yet more contentious – approaches towards the matter have also been suggested. Particularly in those fields of international law where State practice is generally scant or sometimes even lacking, innovative methodologies regarding custom have been proposed so as to meet the changing concerns and demands of the international community. Whether or not one of the classical elements of custom is to be prioritized over the other and whether one of these constituents may be glossed over under circumstances are prominent questions within these approaches. While it is beyond the scope of this research to analyse and categorize the whole spectrum of theoretical positions on the matter, the two models or approaches are relevant in the context of the quest for a customary right to unilateral secession, since the question of whether one adheres to the conventional or progressive model might be of influence in the outcome of this assessment due to different approaches towards the elements which are required for the ascertainment of customary rules and how those elements may be evidenced.[90] The following sections will therefore expound and appraise some

---

[88] See, for instance, Brownlie, *Principles of Public International Law* at p. 6; Dixon, *Textbook on International Law* at p. 31; Dixon, *Textbook on International Law* Malanczuk, *Akehurst's Modern Introduction to International Law* at p. 44; Shaw, *International Law* at p. 70; Thirlway, 'The Sources of International Law' at p. 125; Treves, 'Customary International Law' at para. 8.

[89] The traditional model is generally viewed to be reflected in the writings of, for instance, Anthony A. D'Amato (although his definition of *opinio juris* is slightly different). See D'Amato, *The Concept of Custom in International Law*.

[90] For example, Cedric Ryngaert and Christine Griffioen alleged that a right to remedial secession does exist on the basis of a progressive interpretation of customary international law. See C. Ryngaert and C.W. Griffioen, 'The Relevance of the Right to Self-Determination in the Kosovo Matter: In Partial Response to the Agora Papers' (2009) *Chinese Journal of International Law – Advance Access* at para. 27.

progressive approaches towards customary international law, eventually enabling to take a position on the matter to be taken.

3.1. Progressive Approaches towards Customary International Law

Besides the conventional model of customary international law some more progressive approaches towards the matter have been proposed over time. The judgment of the International Court of Justice in the *Nicaragua* case is widely referred to as the basis for these rather progressive approaches, since in that particular case the Court stressed *opinio juris* to the detriment of State practice when considering norms of customary law on the use of force. More specifically, the Court noted that existence of a certain rule "in the *opinio juris* of States" is to be confirmed by practice[91] and subsequently did not pay much attention to discrepancies as regards State practice.[92] It considered the inconsistent conduct of States as the violation of an established norm, rather than as evidence of a newly emerging customary rule. As such, the Court conveyed the impression that provided that strong *opinio juris* is present, defects in the physical practice of States may be overlooked, possibly resulting in the materialization of a norm of customary international law. This method seems to be contradictory to the conventional approach to customary law, which prioritizes (physical) State practice over *opinio juris*.[93]

The approach taken in the *Nicaragua* case has arguably been endorsed by several other authoritative international legal bodies as well. For instance, the *Tadić* case before the International Criminal Tribunal for the Former Yugoslavia (ICTY) is considered to be relevant in this respect. In this case, the ICTY strongly mitigated the importance of (battlefield) practice in the formation process of customary international law due to untrustworthiness and held that emphasis is to be put on verbal State practice:

> not only is access to the theatre of military operations normally refused to independent observers (often even to the ICRC) but what is worse, often recourse is had to misinformation with a view to misleading the enemy as well as public opinion and foreign Governments. In appraising the formation of customary rules or general principles

---

[91] International Court of Justice, *Military and Paramilitary Activities in and Against Nicaragua (Nicaragua v. United States of America)*, Merits, Judgment, ICJ Reports 1986, p. 14, at para. 184.

[92] International Court of Justice, *Military and Paramilitary Activities in and Against Nicaragua (Nicaragua v. United States of America)*, Merits, Judgment, ICJ Reports 1986, p. 14, at para. 186.

[93] It should be noted, however, that the Court itself did not refer to its approach as being innovative. Rather, it alleged that it was applying the standard method of ascertaining customary international law. International Court of Justice, *Military and Paramilitary Activities in and Against Nicaragua (Nicaragua v. United States of America)*, Merits, Judgment, ICJ Reports 1986, p. 14, at paras 97-98. See also A.E. Roberts, 'Traditional and Modern Approaches to Customary International Law: A Reconciliation' (2001) 95 *American Journal of International Law* 757 at p. 768.

one should therefore be aware that, on account of the inherent nature of this subject-matter, reliance must be primarily placed on such elements as official pronouncements of States, military manuals and judicial decisions.[94]

As a consequence of the line of reasoning in the *Tadić* case, the existence of customary international humanitarian norms will be accepted more easily, since (often inhumane) battlefield practice is overlooked or even deemed completely irrelevant due to untrustworthiness.[95] A similar approach was taken by the ICTY in the *Kupreškić* case, in which it held that scant or inconsistent State practice does not bar the emergence of norms of customary international humanitarian law when "the demands of humanity or the dictates of public conscience" demand the materialization of such norms.[96]

These approaches may be said to be reflected as well by the International Law Association's Committee on the Formation of Customary (General) International Law, as it held that "a substantial manifestation of acceptance (consent or belief) by States that a customary rule exists may compensate for a relative lack of practice, and vice versa".[97] In this respect, a caveat was made requiring that *opinio juris* must be "clear-cut and unequivocal" before it can be considered as the principal constituent of a new norm of customary international law.[98] In its study on customary international humanitarian law, the International Committee of the Red Cross (ICRC) appears to have endorsed a similar method of ascertaining customary international law. It was noted that international courts and tribunals occasionally hold that a customary norm does exist if that particular norm is desirable in view of international peace and security or the protection of humanity, on condition that there are no significant indications of contrary *opinio juris*.[99] Moreover, the ICRC identified a vast amount of rules of customary humanitarian international law primarily on the basis of *opinio juris* combined with verbal acts rather than physical (battlefield) practice.[100]

It should be mentioned, however, that in response to the study of the ICRC, the United States' Government raised its concerns about the methodology applied by the authors. Several serious objections were lodged in an open letter to the President

---

[94] International Criminal Tribunal for the Former Yugoslavia, *Prosecutor v. Tadić*, Decision on the defence motion for interlocutory appeal on jurisdiction, ICTY-IT-94-AR72, 2 October 1995, at para. 99.

[95] Wouters and Ryngaert, 'Impact on the Process of the Formation of Customary International Law' at p. 116. See also Meron, *The Humanization of International Law* at p. 367.

[96] International Criminal Tribunal for the Former Yugoslavia, *Prosecutor v. Kupreškić*, Trial Chamber Judgment, ICTY-IT-95-16-T, 14 January 2000, at para. 527.

[97] International Law Association, Committee on the Formation of Customary (General) International Law, *Statement of Principles Applicable to the Formation of General Customary International Law*, London Conference (2000) at p. 40.

[98] See *ibid.* at p. 42.

[99] Henckaerts and Doswald-Beck, *Customary International Humanitarian Law* at p. xlviii.

[100] See, for instance, Rule 157 on universal jurisdiction over war crimes. See J.B. Bellinger and W.J. Haynes, 'A US Government Response to the International Committee of the Red Cross study *Customary International Humanitarian Law*' (2007) 89 *International Review of the Red Cross* 443 at pp. 465-471.

of the ICRC. The US Government argued, *inter alia*, that the State practice which was cited by the ICRC was "insufficiently dense to meet the 'extensive and virtually uniform' standard generally required to demonstrate the existence of a customary rule".[101] It further found that the ICRC attributed too much weight to verbal acts, such as military manuals, UN General Assembly Resolutions and statements of non-governmental organizations (including the ICRC itself), while disregarding the actual practice of 'specially affected States' during armed conflicts.[102] The US Government contended that no *opinio juris* was to be determined if a State's legal conviction is reflected in military manuals for the most part and expressed its concern regarding the merger of the two elements of State practice and *opinio juris* into one single element.[103] Although the content of the letter obviously aimed to serve the national interests of the United States,[104] this response to the study of the ICRC does demonstrate that the human rights methodology is debatable and may be seen as an indication that the conventional approach towards customary international law cannot be abandoned.

Following the allegedly innovative approach of the Court in the *Nicaragua* case and subsequent developments, various scholars have proposed – more or less – progressive views on the formation of customary international law.[105] As a result, the spectrum of theoretical positions on this process has broadened significantly, ranging from the strictly traditional model of custom on the one extreme to the modern approach as ostensibly applied the *Nicaragua* case on the other. Some scholars have advanced what may be labelled as an intermediate conception, bringing together those divergent lines as outlined above. In 1987, Frederic Kirgis was one of the first scholars – if not the very first – who sought to reconcile the two extreme models

---

[101] *Ibid.* at pp. 444-445. See also Wouters and Ryngaert, 'Impact on the Process of the Formation of Customary International Law' at p. 117.

[102] Bellinger and Haynes, 'A US Government Response to the International Committee of the Red Cross Study *Customary International Humanitarian Law*' at pp. 445-446.

[103] See *ibid.* at pp. 446-447.

[104] Not only the methodology applied, but also some specific rules ascertained by the ICRC were criticized in the letter. For instance, the existence of a customary rule on universal jurisdiction over war crimes (referred to as Rule 157) was questioned because of lack of sufficient physical State practice. See *ibid.* at pp. 465-471.

[105] See, for instance, Guzman, 'Saving Customary International Law'; Kirgis Jr, 'Custom on a Sliding Scale'; Lepard, *Customary International Law. A New Theory with Practical Applications*; Meron, *The Humanization of International Law*; Roberts, 'Traditional and Modern Approaches to Customary International Law: A Reconciliation'; O. Schachter, 'Entangled Treaty and Custom' in Y. Dinstein (ed.) *International Law at a Time of Perplexity: Essays in Honour of Shabtai Rosenne* (Martinus Nijhoff Publishers, Dordrecht 1989); J. Tasioulas, 'Customary International Law and the Quest for Global Justice' in A. Perreau-Saussine and J.B. Murphy (eds) *The Nature of Customary Law: Philosophical, Historical and Legal Perspectives* (Cambridge University Press, Cambridge 2007); C Tomuschat, 'Obligations Arising for States Without or Against their Will' (1993) 241 *Collected Courses of the Hague Academy of International Law (Recueil des Cours)*.

of customary international law.[106] According to Kirgis, such reconciliation becomes possible "if one views the elements of custom not as fixed and mutually exclusive, but as interchangeable along a sliding scale".[107] Customary international law based on highly consistent State practice but with scant *opinio juris* is positioned at the one extreme of the sliding scale, whereas custom based on strong *opinio juris* in the absence of consistent State practice is positioned at the other extreme. As the availability of consistent State practice declines, the need for evidence of *opinio juris* increases in order to ascertain a norm of customary international law and vice versa. For Kirgis, the relative importance of the constituents of customary international law depends on the activity at issue and the desirability of the norm asserted. Involving considerations of, for instance, humanity, peace and security, this premise enables the materialization of customary norms even when one of the two constituents is scant or even absent. In essence, Kirgis' sliding scale theory reflects the idea that "the more destabilizing or morally distasteful the activity", the more easily one element of customary international law will be substituted for the other.[108]

Other scholars have advanced even more progressive ideas, contending that the methodology of determining custom in some fields of international law, such as human rights law and humanitarian law, necessitates an approach which is different from the conventional approach towards customary international law. In this respect, their conceptions demonstrate a clear relationship between the substantive significance of the norm on the one hand and the willingness to overlook inadequacies in the traditional elements for the establishment of custom – primarily physical State practice – on the other.[109] As such, the progressive approaches seem to be strongly inspired by considerations of morality and may even be said to aim at "the strengthening of norms with moral impact", since the official pronouncements of States and their practice on the ground often do not correspond in the field of human rights law

---

[106] Building upon the work of Kirgis and some other authors, Anthea E. Roberts has also attempted to combine both methods of ascertaining customary international law by proposing a 'reflective interpretive approach'. This theory does not exclude either State practice or *opinio juris*. Rather, Roberts proposed two dimensions which are linked to the traditional constituents of customary international law and are to be balanced against one another in order to achieve a 'reflective equilibrium'. First, the dimension of 'fit' provides for descriptive accuracy based on State practice. Secondly, a dimension of 'substance' is introduced, referring to both substantive and procedural normativity based on moral and political ideals. These ideals can often be found in pronouncements of *opinio juris*. According to Roberts, the balancing of 'fit' and 'substance' allows for the creation of customary norms with strong moral footings, while avoiding the materialization of laws which appear utopian as they are incapable of regulating reality. Although this model may be attractive in theory, it has not (yet) been implemented in practice. See Roberts, 'Traditional and Modern Approaches to Customary International Law: A Reconciliation' at pp. 774-781.

[107] Kirgis Jr, 'Custom on a Sliding Scale' at p. 149.

[108] See *ibid.* at p. 149.

[109] See Meron, *The Humanization of International Law* at p. 369.

and humanitarian law.[110] Oscar Schachter, for example, has noted that international (Courts and) tribunals as well as States do not contest the customary nature of norms which "express deeply-held and widely shared convictions about the unacceptability of the proscribed conduct" because of inconsistent or even scarce State practice. Although his observation was initially made in the context of rules on the use of force, Schachter has argued that his conclusion also applies to "rules that have outlawed genocide, the killing of prisoners of war, torture, and large-scale discrimination".[111] Christian Tomuschat, for his part, has distinguished different classes or categories of customary international law, including a class encompassing constitutional foundations of the international community and a class covering rules stemming from these foundations and common values of mankind. With respect to the first class, he refers to the core principle of sovereign equality.[112] The second class comprises those rules which flow from this principle, as sovereign equality imposes certain duties and responsibilities on States and other subjects of international law.[113] In this respect, the ban on the use of force, principles of environmental law, and humanitarian law are mentioned. According to Tomuschat, the customary principles of these two categories can be ascertained through a deductive process, thus departing from the traditional method by deriving custom primarily from the articulation of *opinio juris* while assigning a secondary role only to general State practice.[114] In a similar vein, Brian D. Lepard has advanced a theory which, in essence, reduces the two elements of custom to one constituent only, i.e. *opinio juris*. As such, *opinio juris* is interpreted as the belief of States "that it is desirable now or in the near future to have an authoritative legal principle or rule prescribing, permitting, or prohibiting certain state conduct".[115] Accordingly, State practice is no longer viewed as a necessary element, but rather serves as evidence for this belief.[116]

Since these progressive approaches towards customary international law have particularly been proposed in the field of human rights law and humanitarian law, they are sometimes referred to as the 'human rights method'. [117] As Jan Wouters and Cedric Ryngaert recapitulated, the 'human rights method' implies that:

---

[110] See N. Petersen, 'Customary International Law. A New Theory with Practical Applications' (2010) 21 *European Journal of International Law* 795 at p. 795.

[111] Schachter, 'Entangled Treaty and Custom' at p. 734.

[112] C. Tomuschat, 'Obligations Arising for States Without or Against their Will' (1993) 241 *Collected Courses of the Hague Academy of International Law (Recueil des Cours)* at pp. 292-293.

[113] *Ibid.* at p. 293.

[114] *Ibid.* at pp. 293-303.

[115] Lepard, *Customary International Law. A New Theory with Practical Applications* at pp. 97-98.

[116] See *ibid.* at p. 98.

[117] Alexander Orakhelashvili has identified a similar tendency which he calls the 'sociological approach' and noting that "the mere *social interest* behind the rule can justify its binding force at the expense of the formal elements of law-making". See Orakhelashvili, *The Interpretation of Acts and Rules in Public International Law* at p. 85 (emphasis added).

the more important the common interests of the states or humanity are, the greater the weight that might be attached to *opinio juris* as opposed to state practice. If the stakes are high, inconsistent state practice may be glossed over, and a high premium may be put on states's statements and declarations, *inter alia* in multilateral fora, in identifying customary international law combined with general principles of law.[118]

It should be noted that, even under this approach, *opinio juris* is still to be confirmed by State practice. Yet, as in the field of human rights law and humanitarian law,[119] as the physical acts of States with respect to a particular norm are often inconsistent, untrustworthy, or even lacking at all (due to the involvement of a prohibitive norm), the focus may be on verbal State practice.[120] In this connection, the difficulty of distinguishing verbal State practice from evidence of *opinio juris* is to be recalled. Consequently, if verbal State practice is consistently emphasized over the physical actions of States, establishing State practice as an indispensable constituent of customary international law seems to become redundant.[121]

3.2. A Critical Appraisal

From the various perspectives outlined above, it follows that there is an apparent trend to progressively reinterpret the notion of customary international law. When viewed from a moral perspective and bearing in mind the development which is sometimes referred to as the 'humanization of international law',[122] the idea that a substantial manifestation of *opinio juris* on the existence of a certain customary norm may compensate for deficiencies in the actual practice of States or the complete lack thereof is highly attractive indeed. Since this methodology lowers the burden of proof which is required for the establishment of norms with a generally binding, customary status it has the capacity to widen the 'protective net' which positive international law provides to human beings.[123] As such, more progressive methods may be said to be

---

[118] Wouters and Ryngaert, 'Impact on the Process of the Formation of Customary International Law' at p. 112.

[119] For the presentation and application of this method for ascertaining customary norms in the field of humanitarian law, see the influential International Committee of the Red Cross study on customary international humanitarian law: Henckaerts and Doswald-Beck, *Customary International Humanitarian Law*, in particular at pp. xxxi-li.

[120] Wouters and Ryngaert, 'Impact on the Process of the Formation of Customary International Law' at p. 115.

[121] *Ibid.*

[122] In brief, this development encompasses a shift of focus from a State-centred system to a system in which human beings are at the forefront. On this topic, see, for instance, A.A. Cançado Trindade, *International Law for Humankind. Towards a New Jus Gentium* (Martinus Nijhoff Publishers, Leiden 2010); Meron, *The Humanization of International Law*.

[123] Wouters and Ryngaert, 'Impact on the Process of the Formation of Customary International Law' at p. 111.

better able to protect and promote human rights and other significant moral concerns compared to the traditional method of ascertaining customary international law.[124] Focusing on these benevolent results, the (primarily scholarly) inclination to adhere to a progressive interpretation of custom is understandable, as was also observed by Bruno Simma and Philip Alston:

> Given the fundamental importance of the human rights component of a just world order, the temptation to adapt or re-interpret the concept of customary law in such a way as to ensure that it provides the 'right' answers is strong, and at least to some, irresistible. It is thus unsurprising that some of the recent literature in this field, especially but not exclusively coming out of the United States, is moving with increasing enthusiasm in that direction. But while largely endorsing the result that is thereby sought to be achieved, we have considerable misgivings about the means being used.[125]

Indeed, a critical appraisal is needed. In addition to the response by the US Government to the study of the ICRC as touched upon above, the progressive methods of ascertaining customary international law have been disputed on various grounds – conceptual, methodological and substantive – in scholarly literature as well.[126] It should be emphasized that those objections particularly hold for those approaches which completely overlook the element of State practice and, thus, are situated at the extreme end of the spectrum of progressive models, such as the human rights method. The most prominent critiques in this respect will be addressed below.

A conceptual objection which has been raised is that customary international law cannot exist in absence of custom, as that would be a *contradictio in terminis*.[127] In view of the definition provided in Article 38(1)(b) of the ICJ Statute, a general practice of States constitutes the core root of this source of international law, as it is conduct which brings about custom. Ascertaining customary international law in absence of State practice thus "counteracts the very essence of custom".[128]

---

[124] *Ibid.* at p. 118. See also Roberts, 'Traditional and Modern Approaches to Customary International Law: A Reconciliation' at p. 766: "The reduced focus on state practice in the modern approach is explained by its use to create generally binding laws on important moral issues".

[125] B. Simma and P. Alston, 'The Sources of Human Rights Law: Custom, Jus Cogens, and General Principles' (1988-1989) 12 *Australian Year Book of International Law* at p. 83.

[126] This is not to say, however, that the traditional methodology is immune to criticism. Anthea E. Roberts, for instance, has argued that traditional custom suffers from a democratic deficit as it is often based on the practice of a selection of (Western) States only, while all States are considered to be bound by it. See Roberts, 'Traditional and Modern Approaches to Customary International Law: A Reconciliation' at pp. 767-768.

[127] International Law Association, Committee on the Formation of Customary (General) International Law, *Statement of Principles Applicable to the Formation of General Customary International Law*, London Conference (2000) at p. 41.

[128] N.J. Arajärvi, 'The Lines Begin to Blur? Opinio Juris and the Moralisation of Customary International Law' (2011) *SSRN Working Paper Series* at p. 19.

More importantly, several methodological weaknesses of very progressive approaches have been noted as well. First, it is to be emphasized that no clear and detailed criteria for the formation of customary international law under the progressive view have been stipulated in the case law of the International Criminal Court. To put it even more strongly, in the *Nicaragua* case, the Court first recalled the conventional outlook,[129] before focusing on *opinio juris* and only cursorily considering State practice – thus arguably applying the modern methodology.[130] So although this judgment is now considered by many as the foundation of progressive approaches towards custom, this basis remains questionable.[131] Moreover, adopting a methodology for establishing customary international law which leaves such a broad margin of appreciation for considerations of humanity and morality does raise some concerns. Considering the absence of a central authority within the international system, one may wonder who is to determine the 'moral distastefulness' of a certain conduct or the 'common interests of humankind' which may justify ignoring inconsistent State practice and establishing a customary rule on the mere basis of *opinio juris*. It thus appears that the progressive approaches allow more subjectivity to seep into the formation process of customary international law,[132] which arguably erodes the integrity of custom as one of the two principal sources of international law. In the words of J. Patrick Kelly, customary international law may become "indeterminate and manipulable", simply "a matter of taste".[133] A further methodological critique is that it implies the involvement of normative elements in the creation of customary international law. This objection merits some explanation. The conventional methodology of ascertaining custom is to a large extent descriptive, as it is first and foremost based on State practice. In contrast, progressive approaches rely heavily on *opinio juris*, which is more ambiguous as the pronouncements evidencing this psychological element may represent *lex lata* (what is the law) or *lex ferenda* (what should be the law), the latter being a normative characteristic rather than a descriptive one.[134] It has even

---

[129] See International Court of Justice, *Military and Paramilitary Activities in and Against Nicaragua (Nicaragua v. United States of America)*, Merits, Judgment, ICJ Reports 1986, p. 14, at para. 183: "to consider what are the rules of customary international law applicable to the present dispute [the Court] has to direct its attention to the practice and *opinio juris* of States."

[130] *Ibid.*, at paras 184-186.

[131] See, for instance, Meron, *The Humanization of International Law* at p. 362; Roberts, 'Traditional and Modern Approaches to Customary International Law: A Reconciliation' at p. 768.

[132] See, for instance, Arajärvi, *The Changing Nature of Customary International Law: Methods of Interpreting the Concept of Custom in International Criminal Tribunals* at p. 30; Mendelson, 'The Formation of Customary International Law' at p. 385. Whether this approach is actually less rigorous and less objective is questioned by Jan Wouters and Cedric Ryngaert. See Wouters and Ryngaert, 'Impact on the Process of the Formation of Customary International Law' at p. 119.

[133] J.P. Kelly, 'The Twilight of Customary International Law' (2000) 40 *Virginia Journal of International Law* 448 at p. 451.

[134] Roberts, 'Traditional and Modern Approaches to Customary International Law: A Reconciliation' at pp. 762-763, citing Martti Koskenniemi.

been alleged that "modern custom seems to be based on normative statements of *lex ferenda* cloaked as *lex lata*".[135] Considering the fundamental difference in nature as stipulated above, *opinio juris* cannot simply be used as a substitute for State practice.

The normative nature of the most progressive approaches towards customary international law leads to significant objections on the more substantive level as well, which may even be said to constitute the principal criticism of this method. It is argued that the very progressive approaches to customary international law may produce morally or politically desired outcomes instead of reflecting contemporary social realities. Such approaches may even be viewed as an escape if the conventional track does not lead to the determination of customary norms as wished for.[136] As Anthea E. Roberts observed, they appear to formulate "aspirational aims rather than realistic requirements about action".[137] In the same vein, Bruno Simma and Philip Alston perceptively remarked that the formation process of customary international law has "thus turned into a self-contained exercise in rhetoric".[138] Consequently, these most progressive approaches would create a gap between what is claimed to be custom on the one hand and the practice of States on the other. This would be a highly undesirable development, as it undermines the consistency and foreseeability and, thus, the authority of new norms of customary international law.[139] As such, it would pose problems as regards the acceptability and the regulatory function of these norms.

Considering the above, despite the manifestations of support for the human rights methodology and other very progressive approaches towards ascertaining customary international law and its morally attractive outcomes, it is emphasized here that the traditional model still prevails and that international legal norms do not arise simply whenever that is considered to be desirable.[140] To put it even more strongly, it is argued here with Anthony A. D'Amato that legal norms are distinct from purely "moral requirements".[141] With respect to customary law in particular, Sir Robert Y. Jennings observed that "most of what we perversely persist in calling customary international law is not only *not* customary law: it does not even faintly resemble a

---

[135]   *Ibid.* at p. 763.
[136]   See Simma and Alston, 'The Sources of Human Rights Law: Custom, Jus Cogens, and General Principles' at p. 83: "Caution is far from being a characteristic of much of the contemporary human rights literature. Perhaps this has to do with the fact that 'human rights lawyers are notoriously wishful thinkers', as John Humphrey once observed" (p. 84).
[137]   Roberts, 'Traditional and Modern Approaches to Customary International Law: A Reconciliation' at p. 769.
[138]   *Ibid.* at p. 89.
[139]   In the field of international criminal law, there seems to be a (conceptual) tension between the progressive approaches towards customary international law and the principle of legality as well. On this topic, see Arajärvi, *The Changing Nature of Customary International Law: Methods of Interpreting the Concept of Custom in International Criminal Tribunals* at pp. 151-196 (Chapter 4: Principle of Legality, Customary International Law and Individual Criminal Responsibility – Conceptual Tensions).
[140]   See *ibid.* at p. 32.
[141]   D'Amato, *The Concept of Custom in International Law* at p. 76.

customary law".[142] Such a state of affairs, however, is highly objectionable. Some caution is thus required in assuming the existence of new customary norms, as these are binding upon all States (apart from persistent objectors) and custom is considered to be one of the two principal sources of international law.

The objections lodged with respect to the most progressive approaches towards determining customary international law are not to say, however, that moral norms bear no legal value at all. Admittedly, non-legal considerations may influence the international law-making process[143] and morality may on occasion call for the expansion of the scope of protection which international legal norms offer, particularly when it comes to human rights and humanitarian law. If such development is not (yet) reflected in the legal practice of States, however, it is questionable whether stretching the nature of customary international law through the progressive human rights method is the appropriate means of accommodating these ends.[144]

4. PRELIMINARY REMARKS ON ASSESSING THE EXISTENCE OF A CUSTOMARY RIGHT TO REMEDIAL SECESSION

Before proceeding to an analysis of State practice and *opinio juris* for the purpose of assessing the existence of a customary right to remedial secession, it should be explained which method of ascertaining customary international law will be applied

---

[142] Jennings, 'The Identification of International Law' at p. 5.

[143] See Orakhelashvili, *The Interpretation of Acts and Rules in Public International Law* at p. 85.

[144] In view of the reservations expressed above, some fundamental questions concerning the sources of international law arise. While it is beyond the scope of the present study to consider these issues, two relevant theoretical approaches may be briefly noted. First, one may wonder whether sources of international law other than custom may be exerted for the purpose of giving legal expression to moral considerations. For instance, Bruno Simma and Philip Alston have proposed the use of general principles as sources of fundamental human rights. They put forward the idea that such general principles would emerge as a result of the general acceptance or recognition of fundamental human rights norms by States – i.e. *opinio juris*, for instance as expressed in resolutions of the UN General Assembly – notwithstanding the lack of State practice. According to these scholars, such principles seem "to conform more closely than the concept of custom to the situation where a norm invested with strong inherent authority is widely accepted even though widely violated". See Simma and Alston, 'The Sources of Human Rights Law: Custom, Jus Cogens, and General Principles' at pp. 102-106. For a similar argument, see T. Meron, *Human Rights and Humanitarian Norms as Customary Law* (Clarendon Press, Oxford 1989) at pp. 88-89. A further relevant question against the backdrop of the foregoing is whether contemporary international law is perhaps moving towards the acceptance of another new source of international law beyond the (non-exhaustive) catalogue from Article 38(1) of the Statute of the International Court of Justice. These questions touch upon a fundamental and lively debate on the need for revising the traditional doctrine of sources. Several writers have scrutinized this issue and even proposed new theories in this respect. For discussions and suggestions, see for instance, Arajärvi, *The Changing Nature of Customary International Law: Methods of Interpreting the Concept of Custom in International Criminal Tribunals* at pp. 218-222; H.E. Chodosh, 'Neither Treaty nor Custom: The Emergence of Declarative International Law' (1991) 26 *Texas International Law Journal* 87; H.G. Cohen, 'Finding International Law: Rethinking the Doctrine of Sources' (2007) 93 *Iowa Law Review* 65; Thirlway, 'The Sources of International Law' at pp. 138-142.

for this purpose and which framework is relevant in this respect. In view of the critique on the very progressive approaches as discussed above, yet simultaneously bearing in mind the evolution which the traditional model has seen, the present study will give priority to what may be called a contemporary interpretation of the conventional approach towards customary international law.

It has been explained before that this approach first and foremost requires the presence of both State practice and *opinio juris* for the creation of traditional customary international law. Whereas the traditional approach prioritizes State practice over *opinio juris*, the contemporary interpretation of this approach generally considers both constituents to be equally important. Further, the contemporary interpretation involves an inclusive understanding of the objective element of custom, which encompasses both physical and verbal acts of States. As such, the importance of these two manifestations of practice may be seen as relative, meaning that a shortage with regard to the one manifestation may be counterbalanced by the strength of the other. To be specific, in instances in which there is little activity by States in a certain matter – for instance due to the character or subject matter of the alleged norm at issue – the weight attributed to verbal acts compared to physical acts may increase. This is, however, not to say that the physical and verbal manifestations of State practice are fully interchangeable as a consequence of which physical acts may be completely absent. As contended before, such interpretation would allow customary international law to materialize without the presence of any actual practice whatsoever and would lead to a situation in which norms of customary international law may become purely theoretical. Rather, the importance of physical and verbal practice is to be seen in relation to the level of activity in the matter. In addition to this understanding of the objective constituent of custom, the contemporary interpretation implies that where sufficiently unequivocal and dense State practice is present and depending upon the subject matter of the norm, *opinio juris* might be seen to be contained within that practice, as a result of which it is not always necessary to provide for separate proof of the existence of this subjective element of custom.

One might find the approach presented here too strict and orthodox because of its allegiance to both the objective and the subjective constituents of customary international law. Yet, it is submitted here that it is the strength of the contemporary interpretation of the conventional approach that it does not purposively lower the burden for the creation of customary norms, simply because those norms are attractive. By requiring the availability of State practice as well as *opinio juris*, this model seeks to uphold the distinction between *lex lata* and *lex ferenda* and assure that customary international law continues to reflect legal realities rather than producing outcomes which are particularly morally or politically attractive. As was contended before, this is important for maintaining the acceptance and regulatory function of customary international law. At the same time, the present interpretation allows for a certain degree of flexibility so as to enable the materialization of customary norms in those branches of international law where – due to the character or subject matter of these norms – there is relatively little activity by States in the phenomenon. Furthermore, the approach prioritized here has kept up with the times as a result of the contemporary interpretation of the objective element of custom, i.e. State practice. As such, the contemporary interpretation of the conventional approach reflects well the interrelationship between State practice – particularly its verbal manifestation – and *opinio juris*.

Bearing in mind the question of a remedial right to unilateral secession, it now becomes possible to enunciate the approach to assessing the existence of a customary norm in this respect. As to the interpretation of the element of State practice, it has been explained that the denseness of the practice may be determined on the basis of the factors of uniformity, extensiveness and representativeness, and possibly duration. It was emphasized that these factors should be considered in connection to each other, as a strong manifestation of the one factor may compensate deficiencies as regards the other. Further, it was observed that the threshold for meeting these factors may depend upon the subject matter of the alleged customary norm. For example, rules which involve a positive obligation for States will require a higher degree of uniformity and extensiveness of the practice at hand than rules encompassing a negative obligation for States. With respect to an alleged customary right to remedial secession, it seems that a high threshold is set. Given the fact that such a right would restrict the sovereign rights of States, such as territorial integrity, it can be argued that a high level of uniformity, extensiveness and representativeness will be needed for State practice to be sufficiently dense to contribute to the creation of a customary norm on this matter. Moreover, when considering the right to self-determination in the context of decolonization to be a customary norm with a *jus cogens* character, the bar for amending this rule and stretching it to cover a right to remedial secession – thus a right beyond decolonization – will be high as well. As such, almost uniform and universal practice would be required accompanied by strong and clear *opinio juris*. At the same time, however, in view of the nature of the alleged norm, it is likely that there is relatively little activity by States in the matter.[145] While this observation justifies attaching more weight to verbal State practice, this is expressly not to say that a customary norm may be established in the complete absence of physical actions. Overall, it is to be concluded that under the contemporary interpretation of the conventional approach, the materialization of a customary right to remedial secession will not be assumed too easily.

Having outlined the contemporary interpretation of the conventional approach towards customary international law, the question arises as to the basis of which acts, expressions or otherwise the constituents of State practice – either physical or verbal – and *opinio juris* may be determined for the purposes of the present study. When

---

[145] This will be discussed in Chapter VI.

assessing the existence of a customary right to remedial secession, the presence of *opinio juris* will be derived from statements of States regarding the lawfulness of unilateral secession as a remedy in general. Such statements thus concern a general legal opinion, which is not aimed at a specific situation. When statements are issued by States concerning the legality of *specific* cases of unilateral secession as a remedy, these pronouncements will be regarded as verbal State practice. The content of such pronouncements often contain the general legal conviction of States – i.e. *opinio juris* – at the same time. In other words, the same act may provide evidence of both verbal State practice and *opinio juris* when reference is made to both general opinion and a specific case. As such, it may be difficult to disentangle these two elements. Finally, successful attempts at unilateral secession as a remedy will be considered as examples of physical State practice. In this connection, the close interrelationship between physical practice and verbal practice may be noted, as the success or otherwise of an attempt to secede unilaterally may to a certain extent depend upon the responses of already existing States to that particular effort, i.e. verbal practice.

Whatever the guidance which the approach set forth above can provide in assessing the existence of a norm of customary international law, it should be emphasized that the formation of custom is an ongoing process, lacking a clear starting point, as well as a clear tipping point at which a non-legal norm converts into a customary norm. As a result, the issue of crystallization of customary international law remains obscure to a certain extent. In this connection, the analogy with a path in the forest has been made: "there is no clear benchmark when the route transcends into a path, but viewing it at a given moment it is possible to note that it has become to exist as one".[146] Similarly, like a path in the forest may shift, transform, or even fade over time, customary norms may be amended or abandoned through developments in practice and *opinio juris*. As such, it may be argued that a clear end point is lacking in the formation process of customary international law as well.[147]

To conclude, while a contemporary interpretation of the conventional approach as outlined above will be guiding in the following analysis, the more progressive human rights approach with its emphasis on *opinio juris* over (physical) State practice and weight attached to considerations of morality or humanity has been and will be contemplated on a more subsidiary level. For, it may be interesting to see whether adherence to the conventional or progressive model will lead to diverging outcomes

---

[146] Arajärvi, *The Changing Nature of Customary International Law: Methods of Interpreting the Concept of Custom in International Criminal Tribunals* at p. 21, citing the references made in the work by Karol Wolfke. See K. Wolfke, *Custom in Present International Law* (2nd revised edn, Martinus Nijhoff Publishers, Dordrecht 1993) at pp. 54-55.

[147] See Arajärvi, *The Changing Nature of Customary International Law: Methods of Interpreting the Concept of Custom in International Criminal Tribunals* at p. 21. It should be noted, however, that the lack of a clear end point is by no means an exclusive attribute of customary international law. Other sources of international law may also develop over time, albeit in a different fashion than custom.

as to the question of whether a remedial right to unilateral secession does exist under contemporary international law.

5. CONCLUSIONS

The present Chapter has provided an introduction to the concept of customary international law for the purpose of enunciating the approach which will be utilized in the subsequent assessment of the existence of a customary right to remedial secession. In this respect, first, the two constituents of custom have been expounded, i.e. State practice and *opinio juris*. The first constituent is traditionally considered to be the core element for the materialization of customary international law, whereas the second serves as evidence of the belief that this practice is required by law. It was explained that, for the behaviour of States to contribute to the formation of custom, the resulting practice is to be sufficiently dense. In this connection, the factors of uniformity, extensiveness and representativeness, and duration have been elaborated upon as these may determine the density of the practice. In the context of explicating their role in the creation of customary international law, the contemporary interrelatedness of the two constituents of custom was revealed as well. As such, the close connection between the manifestations of verbal State practice and *opinio juris* and the trend to deduce *opinio juris* from the availability of general State practice under certain circumstances were addressed. These developments may be seen as a broadly accepted, contemporary interpretation of the conventional model.

Having discussed the traditional model, some progressive yet more contentious approaches towards ascertaining customary international law, such as the so-called sliding scale theory and the very liberal human rights approach, were elaborated upon. It was demonstrated that these progressive models reflect a different interpretation of the value attached to the two constituents of custom, as they generally prioritize *opinio juris* over State practice rather than vice versa. What is more, the progressive views clearly show a connection between the substantive importance of the norm and the readiness to balance or even neglect shortcomings in the traditional components of custom, in particular deficiencies as regards physical State practice. In this respect, under the progressive models, considerations of morality or humanity are assigned an important part in the formation process of customary international law.

In sum, this Chapter has shown that the concept of customary international law is an ambiguous one on which a great variety of views are presented and on which the final decision has not yet been taken. Accordingly, it appears that the particular model one adheres to may influence the approach to and outcome of an assessment of whether a customary right on a particular matter does exist. Since this remark also applies regarding the question of a (customary) right to unilateral secession, it was necessary to explicate which approach towards ascertaining norms of customary international law will be applied in the present study. While the progressive models admittedly hold great (moral and humanitarian) attraction, they do entail a number of serious objections on a conceptual, methodological and rather substantive level. Considering the most prominent critiques, it was submitted that the progressive approaches such as the human rights methodology stretch the nature of customary international law too far as they are able to find new customary norms whenever that is desirable from a moral or humanitarian point of view. As such, these approaches seem to confuse what international law is at present with what international law should ideally be. However, prudence is called for when presuming the existence of new customary norms, so it was argued. This Chapter therefore led to the conclusion that a contemporary interpretation of the conventional approach towards customary international law should be applied when assessing the existence of a customary right to remedial secession. In short, this approach still requires the presence of both State practice and *opinio juris* for a customary norm to emerge. While, according to this approach, State practice includes verbal practice, it was emphasized that some physical practice is also needed to establish a norm of customary international law so as to uphold the distinction between *lex lata* and *lex ferenda*. Using this approach, the following Chapter will be devoted to examining the existence of a customary right to remedial secession under contemporary international law.

CHAPTER VI
A CUSTOMARY RIGHT TO
REMEDIAL SECESSION?

"While the claim that there is a 'right of secession of last resort' has been supported by some writers and by a contrario *reasoning [...], it is without support in State practice. It has not emerged as a rule of customary law. It is not found in any treaty. And it has no support from the practice of the UN."*

The Republic of Cyprus*

1. INTRODUCTION

The previous Chapter provided an introduction to the concept of customary international law and, in this respect, outlined a basic model for assessing whether a customary norm has emerged regarding the concept of remedial secession. A contemporary interpretation of the conventional approach was put forward.

The present Chapter will involve a review of international responses to claims of unilateral secession outside the context of decolonization, in order to determine to what extent the indispensable elements of customary international law are present with respect to the concept of remedial secession. In doing so, the recognition (or, non-recognition) of newly proclaimed States will be considered, as recognition by the international community constitutes a significant element of State practice in response to the exercise of a right to external self-determination by means of unilateral secession.[1] While it should be noted with the Supreme Court of Canada that recognition does not "provide any retroactive justification for the act of secession",[2] it may positively give some insight in the international community's acceptance (or

---

* International Court of Justice, *Accordance with International Law of the Unilateral Declaration of Independence by the Provisional Institutions of Self-Government of Kosovo (Request for Advisory Opinion)*, Written Statement of the Republic of Cyprus, 3 April 2009, at para. 143.

[1] See C.W. Griffioen, *Self-Determination as a Human Right. The Emergency Exit of Remedial Secession* (Master's Thesis, Utrecht University 2009) at p. 108; D. Raič, *Statehood and the Law of Self-Determination* (Kluwer Law International, The Hague 2002) at pp. 426-427.

[2] Supreme Court of Canada, *Reference re Secession of Quebec*, [1998], 2 S.C.R. 217, at para. 155.

otherwise) of unilateral secession as a remedy in response to exceptional humanitarian circumstances.[3] In order to better understand the role of recognition in this context, this Chapter will commence with a brief introduction to the theory and practice of recognition.

In the analysis of this Chapter, Kosovo's attempt to secede from Serbia in 2008 will play a prominent part. As will be further explained below, the example of Kosovo may not only be seen as the test case for the present-day existence of an alleged remedial right to secession considering the circumstances giving cause to the declaration of independence, but also provides a meaningful insight into the contemporary views of States regarding a right to remedial secession. Alongside the case of Kosovo, a number of other attempts to secede will be addressed which have been invoked as demonstrating support for the existence of a right to remedial secession. The international responses to the various cases will be considered, thereby seeking to disclose the existence or otherwise of a customary right to remedial secession.

This Chapter will therefore end with a legal appraisal of the international practice assessed in view of the elements of customary international law. In this respect, first, a contemporary interpretation of the conventional approach towards customary international law will be used as framework for this assessment. On a subsidiary level, the more progressive human rights approach will be considered, which emphasizes *opinio juris* over (physical) State practice and takes review of arguments of morality or humanity. Finally, the question will be answered as to what extent a customary right to unilateral secession has emerged under contemporary international law. What is more, the twofold approach noted above will disclose whether adherence to the conventional or progressive model leads to different result with respect to this question.

2. THE RECOGNITION OF STATES: A BRIEF INTRODUCTION

When examining the practice of unilateral secession, it is vital to consider the concept of recognition as well, since the two are closely related. By granting (or withholding) international recognition, existing States may respond to attempts at unilateral secession, which aim at establishing a new, independent State. According to Shaw, the recognition of aspirant States by third States may be classified as "a method of accepting factual situations and endowing them with legal significance, but this relationship is a complicated one".[4] Indeed, as will be explained below, while the act of recognition is often based on non-legal considerations, it may positively have legal consequences on the international level.[5] Recognition involves more than a mere

---

[3]   See Raič, *Statehood and the Law of Self-Determination* at p. 88.

[4]   M.N. Shaw, *International Law* (5th edn, Cambridge University Press, Cambridge 2003) at p. 185.

[5]   See J. Vidmar, 'Explaining the Legal Effects of Recognition' (2012) 61 *International and Comparative Law Quarterly* 361 at p. 381.

precondition for the formal establishment of international relations between States. It will be contended hereafter that, in addition to this, individual recognition statements may reveal *opinio juris* or verbal State practice with respect to unilateral secession and an alleged right to remedial secession. For *opinio juris* or verbal State practice to be discerned, the explicit acknowledgement of such an entitlement is required. Moreover, (virtually) universal recognition practice may reflect the acceptance of a claim to unilateral secession and, in some disputed situations, it may even determine the ultimate success of such an attempt. It will also be stressed, however, that prudence is called for when deducing positive entitlements from recognition practice. In the context of the present Chapter, the granting of recognition to or withholding it from an aspirant State will therefore not be regarded as presenting conclusive evidence for the (non-)existence of a right to remedial secession. Rather, recognition practice may reflect the acceptance or otherwise of a claim to unilateral secession – that is not necessarily implying the existence of a legal right in this respect – which is important for assessing the value of cases which have sometimes been adduced as providing support for the acceptance of a right to remedial secession. In this connection, the line of argument presented in the present Chapter will be that merely instances of unilateral secession which have been broadly recognized by the international community as such may potentially constitute relevant (physical) State practice with respect to the existence of a right to remedial secession. If there is no unilateral secession, neither can there be remedial secession.

Although an elaborate assessment of the theory and practice regarding recognition is not required for the purpose of this study,[6] a concise review in this respect is indispensable in order to explain the relevance of recognition for the present purposes. Therefore, this Section will address the two main schools of thought regarding recognition, and, in doing so, touch upon the criteria for statehood. Subsequently, bearing in mind the objectives and consequences of recognition, its importance with respect to attempts to unilateral secession will be highlighted.

---

[6]   For a more elaborate and in-depth discussion of this matter, see, for instance, I. Brownlie, *Principles of Public International Law* (7th edn, Oxford University Press, Oxford 2008) at pp. 85-102; M.C.R. Craven, 'Statehood, Self-Determination, and Recognition' in M.D. Evans (ed.) *International Law* (3rd edn, Oxford University Press, Oxford 2010) at pp. 203-251; J.R. Crawford, *The Creation of States in International Law* (2nd revised edn, Clarendon Press, Oxford 2006) at pp. 3-36; J. Dugard and D. Raič, 'The Role of Recognition in the Law and Practice of Self-Determination' in M.G. Kohen (ed.) *Secession International Law Perspectives* (Cambridge University Press, Cambridge 2006) at pp. 94-137; M. Fabry, *Recognizing States. International Society and the Establishment of New States Since 1776* (Oxford University Press, New York 2010); T.D. Grant, *The Recognition of States: Law and Practice in Debate and Evolution* (Praeger, Westport/London 1999); H. Lauterpacht, *Recognition in International Law* (Cambridge University Press, Cambridge 1963); Raič, *Statehood and the Law of Self-Determination* at pp. 28-48; Shaw, *International Law* at pp. 367-408; C. Warbrick, 'Recognition of States' (1999) 41 *International and Comparative Law Quarterly* 473.

2.1. The Constitutive and Declaratory Approach

The question of the purpose and legal effect of recognition is much debated, as different approaches exist on this topic. In this discussion, often labelled as the 'great debate',[7] two approaches can be discerned: the constitutive and the declaratory.[8] These approaches towards recognition reflect the two main schools of thought concerning the establishment of States. In short, the constitutive approach contends that recognition is a *conditio sine qua non* for statehood. Put differently, recognition establishes or constitutes a State and grants it legal personality. Without recognition, an entity cannot be considered as a State under international law. The declaratory model, on the other hand, maintains that States may emerge independent of recognition. According to this view, an entity will become a State as a subject of international law as soon as it meets the criteria of statehood, while recognition merely formally acknowledges or declares this situation. In other words, under the declaratory view, "[r]ecognition is *evidence* that a state has come into being, but it is in no way an instrument of that creation".[9] The criteria determining whether an entity actually is a State are stipulated in the 1933 Montevideo Convention on the Rights and Duties of States (hereafter: Montevideo Convention). Article 1 of this Convention lists four requirements for an entity to acquire statehood, which are generally seen to constitute customary international law:[10] a permanent population, a defined territory, an effective government and the capacity to enter into relations with other States.[11] In addition, a number of other requirements have been suggested over time.[12] As will be further explained hereafter in the context of the emergence of the successor States to the Socialist Federal Republic of Yugoslavia, the Guidelines on the Recognition of New States in Eastern Europe and in the Soviet Union, which were drafted by the European Community in 1991, intended to make the recognition of States subject to *inter alia* their democratic establishment, respect for the right to self-determination, human rights, minority

---

[7]   See Crawford, *The Creation of States in International Law* at p. 19.

[8]   See, for instance, Craven, 'Statehood, Self-Determination, and Recognition' at pp. 241-243; Dugard and Raič, 'The Role of Recognition in the Law and Practice of Self-Determination' at p. 97; Grant, *The Recognition of States: Law and Practice in Debate and Evolution* at p. xx; Raič, *Statehood and the Law of Self-Determination* at pp. 28-33; Shaw, *International Law* at p. 369.

[9]   Grant, *The Recognition of States: Law and Practice in Debate and Evolution* at p. xx.

[10]   See, for instance, Raič, *Statehood and the Law of Self-Determination* at p. 24; C. Ryngaert and S. Sobrie, 'Recognition of States: International Law or Realpolitik? The Practice of Recognition in the Wake of Kosovo, South Ossetia, and Abkhazia' (2011) 24 *Leiden Journal of International Law* 467 at p. 470. Despite their customary nature, these criteria have frequently been criticized, for instance for not being accurate and for lacking clarity. For a critical view in this respect, see for instance, Craven, 'Statehood, Self-Determination, and Recognition' at pp. 221-229.

[11]   *Montevideo Convention on the Rights and Duties of States*, 26 December 1933, 165 LNTS 19.

[12]   For a more elaborate analysis of this development, see Ryngaert and Sobrie, 'Recognition of States: International Law or Realpolitik? The Practice of Recognition in the Wake of Kosovo, South Ossetia, and Abkhazia' at pp. 474-484.

rights and the inviolability of frontiers.[13] As such, it may be said that the normative framework for recognition involves factual elements (enshrined in the Montevideo Convention) as well as moral considerations (stemming from the EC Guidelines).[14]

While it is beyond the scope of the present study to extensively discuss the advantages and flaws of both aforementioned approaches towards recognition, for the sake of clarity, some remarks deserve to be made here. The constitutive approach has been mainly criticized for leading to uncertainty. First, this conception of recognition grants a broad discretionary competence to States in their decision to recognize or not to recognize, which arguably involves the risk of arbitrariness. Secondly, and in connection to this, when an entity is recognized by some States, but not by others, the status of that particular entity remains obscure under the constitutive view, as it would be a State and a non-State at the same time.[15] The question thus arises as to how many and which States need to recognize an entity before it actually emerges as a State.[16] Needless to say, such uncertainty would be highly inexpedient. What is more, it cannot be denied that in practice, the decision to recognize or not to recognize may be strongly influenced by non-legal considerations.[17] In fact, "[t]he reality is that in many cases recognition is applied to demonstrate political approval or disapproval".[18]

---

[13] European Community, 'Declaration on Yugoslavia and on the "Guidelines on the Recognition of New States in Eastern Europe and in the Soviet Union in Eastern Europe and in the Soviet Union"', 16 December 1991, 31 *International Legal Materials* 1485 (1992). See also Section 3.2.4 of the present Chapter.

[14] It should be noted, however, that the precise relationship between the criteria from the Montevideo Convention and those of the EC Guidelines remains uncertain. An important question which has remained unanswered to date is whether the latter set of requirements is an addition to or a replacement of the traditional criteria. See Ryngaert and Sobrie, 'Recognition of States: International Law or Realpolitik? The Practice of Recognition in the Wake of Kosovo, South Ossetia, and Abkhazia' at pp. 477-478. Notwithstanding this question, it may be interesting to note that similar moral considerations as included in the EC Guidelines have been reflected in what is commonly referred to as the Copenhagen criteria, which enunciate standards for European Union membership. In addition to geographic and economic criteria, these standards involve political and moral requirements which need to be met before a State may accede to the European Union: "Membership requires that the candidate country has achieved stability of institutions guaranteeing democracy, the rule of law, human rights, respect for and protection of minorities [...]". See European Council, *Presidency Conclusions: Copenhagen European Council*, 21-22 June 1993, SN 180/1/93 REV 1, 22 June 1993, at para. 7(1)(iii).

[15] Shaw, *International Law* at p. 369.

[16] See Ryngaert and Sobrie, 'Recognition of States: International Law or Realpolitik? The Practice of Recognition in the Wake of Kosovo, South Ossetia, and Abkhazia' at p. 469; J. Vidmar, 'Remedial Secession in International Law: Theory and (Lack of) Practice' (2010) 6 *St Antony's International Review* 37 at pp. 378-381.

[17] Shaw, *International Law* at pp. 373-374. See also Craven, 'Statehood, Self-Determination, and Recognition' at pp. 243-244.

[18] See Shaw, *International Law* at p. 373. The United States, for example, refused to extend recognition to both North Korea and the People's Republic of China for years. This refusal was not because it

In view of the political nature of the recognition process, the declaratory approach appears to be more in conformity with reality, as an entity which fulfils the criteria of statehood may become a State notwithstanding the act of recognition.[19] This outlook was endorsed by the Badinter Arbitration Committee in one of its opinions as well, since it stated that "the existence or disappearance of the State is a question of fact; [and] that the effects of recognition by other States are purely declaratory".[20] More specifically, it held that:

> such recognition, along with membership of international organizations, bears witness to these state's conviction that the political entity so recognized is a reality and confers on it certain rights and obligations under international law.[21]

Support for the declaratory view may be also found in the Montevideo Convention, as Article 3 provides that "[t]he political existence of the State is independent of recognition by the other States" and Article 6 stipulates that "[t]he recognition of a State merely signifies that the State which recognizes it accepts the personality of the other with all the rights and duties determined by international law".[22]

Even though today, the declaratory approach towards recognition predominates both in practice and in literature,[23] a problem with this view is that it disregards the circumstances under which an entity has met the criteria for statehood. Consequently, it would be possible for an entity to become a State through serious breaches of international law. This possibility under the declaratory theory does not correspond to international practice, as States generally respond to such events with non-recognition, either on their own record or by order of the UN Security Council after having condemned the situation.[24] An example in this respect is the non-recognition in the

---

considered those entities lacking the criteria for statehood, but rather because the United States did not wish the (legal) consequences of recognition to follow. See Shaw, *International Law* at p. 368.

[19]   Dugard and Raič, 'The Role of Recognition in the Law and Practice of Self-Determination' at p. 98. See also Brownlie, *Principles of Public International Law* p. 88; Shaw, *International Law* at p. 369.

[20]   Conference on Yugoslavia, Arbitration Commission, *Opinion No. 1*, 29 November 1991, reprinted as: International Conference on the Former Yugoslavia, 'Opinions No. 1-3 of the Arbitration Commission of the International Conference on Yugoslavia' (1992) 3 *European Journal of International Law* 182 at pp. 182-183, para. 1a.

[21]   Conference on Yugoslavia, Arbitration Commission, *Opinion No. 8*, 4 July 1992, reprinted as: International Conference on the Former Yugoslavia, 'Opinions No. 4-10 of the Arbitration Commission of the International Conference on Yugoslavia' (1993) 4 *European Journal of International Law* 74 at pp. 87-88, para. 2.

[22]   *Montevideo Convention on the Rights and Duties of States*, 26 December 1933, 165 LNTS 19.

[23]   See Craven, 'Statehood, Self-Determination, and Recognition' at p. 243; Crawford, *The Creation of States in International Law* at p. 25; Dugard and Raič, 'The Role of Recognition in the Law and Practice of Self-Determination' at pp. 98-99; Vidmar, 'Remedial Secession in International Law: Theory and (Lack of) Practice' at p. 41.

[24]   An obligation of non-recognition may be seen to be included in Article 41(2) of the Draft Articles on the Responsibility of States for Internationally Wrongful Acts, which reads as follows: "No State shall

case of Southern Rhodesia, which was created in violation of the right to self-deter-mination.[25] Another drawback of the declaratory approach is that controversy exists on the question of whether an entity which has been recognized by none or very few States only can actually claim statehood. On the one hand, Malcolm N. Shaw has argued that while entities remaining completely unrecognized by other States will probably have difficulties in exercising their rights and duties, this does not neces-sarily prevent them from claiming statehood.[26] On the other hand, it has been argued that the question phrased above must be answered in the negative, as entities which remain unrecognized are unable to demonstrate their capacity to enter into inter-national relations with other States, therefore failing to meet one of the traditional criteria for statehood.[27] In a similar vein, the Canadian Supreme Court has observed that even when assuming that recognition is not a prerequisite for statehood, "the viability of a would-be state in the international community depends, as a practical matter, upon recognition by other states".[28] If one accepts this view, the recognition by existing States does play a certain part in the creation of new States even under the declaratory theory, thus introducing some sort of constitutive dimension to this approach.[29] This will be further explained hereafter.

Whatever the ongoing debate on the adequacy of the two approaches towards rec-ognition, it is clear from the above that the recognition of aspirant States is – to say the least – significant for their viability within the international community, as the abil-ity to enter into international relations with other States as well as the acknowledge-ment of various rights and duties will depend upon it. Practice has demonstrated that neither of the two theories on recognition is applied absolutely, but rather, that prac-tice seems to have adopted a middle course.[30] The strict distinction between the two

---

recognize as lawful a situation created by a serious breach, nor render aid or assistance in maintaining that situation." On non-recognition following the creation of States in violation of international law, see, for instance, Ryngaert and Sobrie, 'Recognition of States: International Law or Realpolitik? The Practice of Recognition in the Wake of Kosovo, South Ossetia, and Abkhazia' at p. 473; Crawford, *The Creation of States in International Law* at pp. 128-131.

[25] See UN Security Council Resolution 216 (1965) (*Southern Rhodesia*), UN Doc. S/Res/216 (1965), 12 November 1965, at para. 2. On the example of Southern Rhodesia, see also Crawford, *The Creation of States in International Law* at pp. 129-131.

[26] Shaw, *International Law* at p. 371.

[27] See, for instance, Dugard and Raič, 'The Role of Recognition in the Law and Practice of Self-Deter-mination' at p. 98.

[28] Supreme Court of Canada, *Reference re Secession of Quebec*, [1998], 2 S.C.R. 217, at para. 155.

[29] M.C.R. Craven, 'What's in a Name? The Former Yugoslav Republic of Macedonia and Issues of Statehood' (1995) 16 *Australian Year Book of International Law* 199 at p. 208; Dugard and Raič, 'The Role of Recognition in the Law and Practice of Self-Determination' at p. 99.

[30] For a similar conclusion, see Shaw, *International Law* at p. 369. See also Ryngaert and Sobrie, 'Rec-ognition of States: International Law or Realpolitik? The Practice of Recognition in the Wake of Kosovo, South Ossetia, and Abkhazia' at p. 471.

approaches thus can be said to be of limited importance for practical purposes.[31] As Ian Brownlie noted, "to reduce, or to seem to reduce, the issues to a choice between the two opposing theories is to greatly oversimplify the legal situation".[32]

2.2. Recognition and Unilateral Secession

Although the debate on the exact nature and consequences of recognition appears to be ongoing,[33] the relevance of recognition in the context of attempts to unilateral secession should not be underestimated. In general, recognition is regarded as a precondition for formally establishing international relations with other States.[34] Through recognition, States express their willingness to enter into international relations with the claimant State. As such, it may be said that recognition is a political act which primarily attaches practical significance to the concept of statehood. In the context of unilateral secession, however, the importance of recognition is more comprehensive. For the present purposes, this significance may be said to be twofold.

First, the individual recognition statements may disclose the motives – both legal and non-legal – for States to recognize. Where these motives are legal in nature, the presence of verbal State practice or *opinio juris* with respect to the permissibility of unilateral secession and, possibly, with respect to a right to remedial secession under international law might be discerned. Yet, to find verbal State practice or *opinio juris* supporting the thesis that a right to remedial secession does exist under contemporary international law, explicit reference to such an entitlement is to be made. This will be seen in the analysis hereafter.[35]

Secondly, as will be explained below, the recognition practice of the international community as a whole may impact the process of the creation of States, as it may shed light on the general acceptance of a claim to unilateral secession and, in some cases, even determine the success of such an attempt. This is explicitly not to say that recognition generally creates or constitutes States. Obviously, that would be irreconcilable with the predominance of the idea that recognition is declaratory rather than constitutive as was explained previously. Indeed, in situations in which the proclamation of a new, independent State is uncontested – that is when the criteria for statehood are met and the parent State does not oppose the proclamation by claiming, for instance, territorial integrity – recognition is to be viewed as a primarily declaratory

---

[31] See Craven, 'What's in a Name? The Former Yugoslav Republic of Macedonia and Issues of Statehood' at p. 208; Crawford, *The Creation of States in International Law* at p. 28.

[32] Brownlie, *Principles of Public International Law* at p. 88.

[33] See, for instance, Vidmar, 'Explaining the Legal Effects of Recognition'.

[34] See Craven, 'What's in a Name? The Former Yugoslav Republic of Macedonia and Issues of Statehood' at p. 208.

[35] See Section 3.1.1. of the present Chapter.

act,[36] thus formally acknowledging that the entity meets the conditions for statehood. However, as was noted by Matthew Craven, particularly in situations in which the status of an entity is disputed or remains ambiguous, acts of recognition "can have the effect of providing crucial evidence of an entity's status".[37] In this regard, widespread recognition may be said to have a 'corrective effect' in the sense that it may contribute to the success of a claim to independent statehood, even when the criteria in this respect – in particular the requirement of an *effective* government – may not have been met (yet).[38] The view that widespread recognition may actually resolve uncertainties regarding the status of claimant State seems to have been supported by the Supreme Court of Canada, as it observed in its *Reference re Secession of Quebec* that "[t]he ultimate success of [an attempt at] secession would be dependent on recognition by the international community".[39] For the present purposes, it should be noted that the significance of recognition as stipulated above especially holds for attempts to secede in which the consent of the parent State is lacking, i.e. cases of *unilateral* secession. In those circumstances, the virtually universal recognition of the aspirant State by already existing States may be said to comprise compelling evidence for the statehood of the former, notwithstanding the opposition of the parent State.[40] Conversely, the failure of attempts to unilateral secession may be "evidenced by the absence of recognition on the part of a sufficient number of States".[41] As such, the corrective or constitutive effect of widespread recognition may have a bearing on the emergence of State practice on the matter. For, it was contended in the previous Chapter that successful attempts to unilateral secession may constitute relevant State practice for the present purposes.[42]

Some caveats are called for in this respect. It was already noted that the corrective or constitutive effect outlined above is not to say that widespread recognition actually creates States. In addition, it should be emphasized that such recognition does not simultaneously imply the recognition of a (remedial) right to unilateral secession,

---

[36] See Vidmar, 'Remedial Secession in International Law: Theory and (Lack of) Practice' at p. 41; Vidmar, 'Explaining the Legal Effects of Recognition' at p. 370.

[37] Craven, 'What's in a Name? The Former Yugoslav Republic of Macedonia and Issues of Statehood' at p. 208.

[38] See A. Nollkaemper, *Kern van het internationaal publiekrecht* (5th edn, Boom Juridische Uitgevers, Den Haag 2011) at p. 94. See also Crawford, *The Creation of States in International Law* at p. 93.

[39] Supreme Court of Canada, *Reference re Secession of Quebec*, [1998], 2 S.C.R. 217, at para. 155.

[40] For an elaborate discussion of this issue, see in particular Vidmar, 'Explaining the Legal Effects of Recognition' at pp. 374-381. When accepting that virtually universal recognition following attempts at unilateral secession may have constitutive effects, an inevitable yet unanswered question, again, is "how many and whose recognitions are necessary for collective recognition to be seen as a State creation" (p. 378).

[41] Dugard and Raič, 'The Role of Recognition in the Law and Practice of Self-Determination' at p. 111. For a similar position, see Craven, 'What's in a Name? The Former Yugoslav Republic of Macedonia and Issues of Statehood' at p. 208, and Crawford, *The Creation of States in International Law* at p. 27.

[42] See Chapter V, Section 4.

even though that has sometimes been suggested.[43] In view of the role which non-legal considerations may play in the decision to recognize or not to recognize, it would go too far to contend that, as a rule, the mere recognition or non-recognition of a claimant State implies the acknowledgement or rejection of an entitlement to unilateral secession. As will be seen hereafter in the context of Kosovo, it may very well be that recognition is prompted by (geo-)political or other reasons rather than by the purported existence of an enforceable right to independence through unilateral secession.[44] For similar reasons, the existence of a right to remedial secession cannot simply be inferred from recognition practice. It would be particularly incorrect to deduce such existence from the absence or lack of recognition in a particular case, for instance by arguing that recognition remained forthcoming since the criteria for a right to remedial secession were not met.[45] Such a line of reasoning already presupposes the acceptance of such a right in general, while this matter is still open to question. Thus, while acts of recognition may in some situations determine the success of an attempt to secede in the absence of the consent of the parent State, and as such, be relevant for State practice, it should be emphasized that restraint is called for when inferring positive entitlements from recognition practice if no clear reference is made to the acceptance thereof.

Having explained the relevance of recognition in the context of attempts at unilateral secession, the following Section will now turn to an assessment of the actual responses of States to attempts at unilateral secession beyond decolonization.

3. ACKNOWLEDGEMENT OF A RIGHT TO REMEDIAL SECESSION IN PRACTICE?

Beyond the context of decolonization, there have been various cases in which the right to external self-determination has been exercised by means of secession. Most of these instances, however, have occurred with the (ultimate) approval of the parent State. As was explained earlier in this study, such cases of consensual secession are generally seen to be unproblematic under international law.[46] Nevertheless, a number of attempts to secede in the post-colonial era have been unilateral and may arguably be regarded as supporting the doctrine of remedial secession.

The present Section will seek to disclose the contemporary stance of States towards the existence or otherwise of a right to remedial secession. As such, it will examine whether practice indeed evidences the elements of customary international law – i.e. *opinio juris* and State practice – on this issue. Two questions will be guiding in this respect. First, has the attempt to secede unilaterally from the parent State

---

[43]   See, for instance, Raič, *Statehood and the Law of Self-Determination* at pp. 426-427.

[44]   See Section 3.1.1. of the present Chapter.

[45]   Such argument seems to be made by David Raič. See Raič, *Statehood and the Law of Self-Determination* at pp. pp. 426-427.

[46]   See Chapter III, Section 4.1.3.

been generally recognized as such by the international community of States? And secondly, which arguments did States advance for either supporting or opposing the attempt at unilateral secession?

In this analysis, a key role will be granted to Kosovo's attempt to secede from Serbia through the issuing of its unilateral declaration of independence on 17 February 2008 and the international responses thereto. As has been observed by commentators and was also pointed out by some States, in view of the specific circumstances preceding the 2008 declaration, the case of Kosovo may be regarded as the test case or experimental plot for the present-day validity of a perceived right to remedial secession.[47] What is more, many States have reacted to Kosovo's unilateral declaration of independence, both in general and in the context of the advisory proceedings before the International Court of Justice.[48] The case of Kosovo consequently provides a unique opportunity to gain an insight in the contemporary stance of the international community as to attempts at unilateral secession and, more specifically, the concept of remedial secession. Put differently, it may reflect *opinio juris* and (verbal) State practice on the matter. For these reasons, the international responses to Kosovo's declaration of independence will constitute the pith of the analysis below.

In addition to the case of Kosovo, a number of other situations will be addressed. These are the cases of Bangladesh, Eritrea, the Baltic Republics (and other successor States to the USSR) and, finally, Croatia and Slovenia (and the other successor States to the SFRY). This selection of cases is justified by the reference of some of these instances in the advisory proceedings on the legality of Kosovo's declaration of independence, as these attempts at unilateral secession were put forward in the context of substantiating arguments regarding the existence of a right to remedial secession. Moreover, these examples have been invoked in literature as supporting the doctrine of remedial secession and therefore merit closer analysis below.

3.1. The Case of Kosovo

As was noted before, Kosovo's unilateral declaration of independence of 17 February 2008 combined with the territory's history of oppression, gross human rights violations and international administration, have led a considerable number of commentators to contend that Kosovo was an eligible candidate for a right to remedial

---

[47] See, for instance, A. Tancredi, 'A Normative "Due Process" in the Creation of States through Secession' in M.G. Kohen (ed.) *Secession International Law Perspectives* (Cambridge University Press, Cambridge 2006) at pp. 187-188.

[48] See UN General Assembly Resolution 63/3 (*Request for an Advisory Opinion of the International Court of Justice on Whether the Unilateral Declaration of Independence of Kosovo is in Accordance with International Law*), UN Doc. A/Res/63/3, 8 October 2008; International Court of Justice Press Release, *Accordance with International Law of the Unilateral Declaration of Independence by the Provisional Institutions of Self-Government of Kosovo (Request for Advisory Opinion). Public hearings to be held from 1 December 2009*, No. 2009/27, 29 July 2009.

secession. The background of Kosovo's attempt to secede from Serbia has already been dealt with previously in the context of a discussion of the International Court of Justice's Advisory Opinion on the Accordance with International Law of the Unilateral Declaration of Independence by the Provisional Institutions of Self-Government of Kosovo.[49] Therefore, the background of the case will not be expounded here again. What should be examined here, however, are the international responses to Kosovo's unilateral declaration of independence for the purposes of assessing the existence of a customary right to remedial secession. To this end, the general responses to Kosovo's unilateral declaration of independence will be addressed first. These responses include statements presented during the relevant debates in the UN Security Council and General Assembly, as well as recognition statements. Subsequently, this section will turn to the submissions by States during the written and oral proceedings before the International Court of Justice.

3.1.1. General Responses to Kosovo's Declaration of Independence

Being two of the most prominent bodies of the United Nations, the Security Council and the General Assembly have acted as important fora for discussing the situation regarding Kosovo. One day after Kosovo issued its unilateral declaration of independence, the Security Council convened in response to the requests of the permanent representatives of Serbia and Russia to bring the recent developments in Kosovo to the attention of the Security Council.[50] In 2008, five further meetings were held in order to discuss the developments in Kosovo and its future.[51] Moreover, the General Assembly convened early October 2008 to vote on the request for an advisory opinion of the International Court of Justice, which was initiated by Serbia.[52] During these debates, the Members of both the Security Council and the General Assembly put forward their views with respect to Kosovo's attempt at unilateral secession through the issuing of its declaration of independence. The records of the debates show that while States did not make explicit reference to the questions of external self-determination, unilateral secession and remedial secession, the statements do provide useful insights in the views of States with respect to these matters. Broadly speaking, three

---

[49]   See Chapter IV, Section 3.3.6.1.
[50]   See UN Security Council, *Letter dated 17 February 2008 from the Permanent Representative of Serbia to the United Nations to the President of the Security Council*, UN Doc. S/2008/103, 17 February 2008; UN Security Council, *Letter dated 17 February 2008 from the Permanent Representative of the Russian Federation to the United Nations to the President of the Security Council*, UN Doc. S/2008/104, 17 February 2008; Security Council, 5839th meeting, UN Doc. S/PV.5839, 18 February 2008.
[51]   UN Security Council, 5850th meeting, UN Doc. S/PV.5850, 11 March 2008; UN Security Council, 5871st meeting (closed), UN Doc. S/PV.5871, 21 April 2008; UN Security Council, 5917th meeting, UN Doc. S/PV.5917, 20 June 2008; UN Security Council, 5944th meeting, UN Doc. S/PV.5944, 25 July 2008; UN Security Council, 6025th meeting, UN Doc. S/PV.6025, 26 November 2008.
[52]   UN General Assembly, 22nd plenary meeting, UN Doc. A/63/PV. 22, 8 October 2008.

categories may be discerned in the international responses of States: the first includes States which argued that Kosovo's unilateral declaration of independence constituted a violation of international law, the second class of States took the position that the parties involved should recommence their political negotiations to resolve the conflict, and finally, the third group responded to the declaration by formally recognizing Kosovo as a sovereign and independent State.[53] These categories will be addressed below. Arguably, a fourth category may be added to this in the sense that some States wished to remain neutral on the matter. Ultimately, some of these States could be classified under one of the first three categories as they did take a stance in the end. Examples in this respect are Burkina Faso and Panama, both of which did not take a clear position during the first Security Council debates, but nonetheless decided to recognize Kosovo after a while.[54] A number of other States from across the globe, however, have refrained from taking a position to date.[55] Since one may only speculate on the reasons for this silence,[56] this possible fourth category is of less relevance for the present purposes and will not be expounded upon below.

As noted above, the first category of responses comprises those States which contended that Kosovo's declaration of independence violated international law, as a consequence of which formal recognition was out of the question. The States involved primarily argued that the attempt to secede constituted a violation of the principle of respect for the territorial integrity of States as enshrined in the UN Charter. In addition to this, independence of Kosovo was considered to be a violation of UN Security Council Resolution 1244 (1999) as well. Serbia, for instance, declared that it would "not accept the violation of its sovereignty and territorial integrity" and noted that respect for these principles was called for by Security Council Resolution

---

[53] This categorization was also suggested by Helen Quane. See H. Quane, 'Self-Determination and Minority Protection after Kosovo' in J. Summers (ed.) *Kosovo: A Precedent? The Declaration of Independence, the Advisory Opinion and Implications for Statehood, Self-Determination and Minority Rights* (Martinus Nijhoff Publishers, Leiden/Boston 2011) at pp. 198-199.

[54] See UN Security Council, 5839th meeting, UN Doc. S/PV.5839, 18 February 2008 (Mr Kafando, Burkina Faso); UN Security Council, 5839th meeting, UN Doc. S.PV.5839, 18 February 2008 (The President, on behalf of Panama). For their recognition statements, see Burkina Faso, *Declaration de Reconnaissance de l'Etat du Kosovo*, 24 April 2008, retrieved via 'Who Recognized Kosova as an Independent State?', available at <http://www.kosovothanksyou.com>; Panama, *Comunicado de Prensa sobre Reconocimiento de la República de Kosovo*, 16 January 2009, available at <http://kosova.org/docs/independence/Panama.pdf >. Both websites last consulted on 24 September 2012.

[55] This category includes States from the African continent, as well as Latin America and Asia, including Bhutan, Botswana, Cambodia, Guyana, Mozambique, Nepal, Nicaragua, Rwanda, Suriname and Tajikistan.

[56] For possible explanations, see J. Almqvist, *The Politics of Recognition, Kosovo and International Law* (Working Paper, Real Instituto Elcano 2009) at pp. 11-12. It appears that a number of States which have not taken a position on the matter fear negative consequences for their domestic or regional situation or for the relationships with their allies.

1244 (1999).[57] Being one of the two States having requested the Security Council to meet the day after Kosovo's declaration of independence, Russia likewise held that:

> [t]he 17 February declaration by the local assembly of the Serbian province of Kosovo is a blatant breach of the norms and principles of international law – above all of the Charter of the United Nations – which undermines the foundations of the system of international relations. That illegal act is an open violation of the Republic of Serbia's sovereignty, the high-level Contact Group accords, Kosovo's Constitutional Framework, Security Council resolution 1244 (1999) – which is the basic document for the Kosovo settlement – and other relevant decisions of the Security Council.[58]

In somewhat more prudent wording, South Africa expressed its regret that Kosovo's unilateral decision was "not taken in conformity with a legal and political process envisaged by Security Council Resolution 1244 (1999)".[59] Even though the presence of legal considerations in these views is significant, this is certainly not to say that the opposition to Kosovo's declaration of independence should be seen as merely prompted by international law. In addition to the abovementioned arguments, the view was also presented that the recognition of Kosovo's independence would constitute a dangerous precedent, which would threaten regional and international peace, and stability. Serbia, for example, repeatedly adduced that:

> there are dozens of other Kosovo's in the world, and all of them are lying in wait for Kosovo's act of secession to become a reality and to be established as an acceptable norm. I warn Council members most seriously of the danger of the escalation of many existing conflicts, the flaring up of frozen conflicts and the instigation of new ones.[60]

Similar concerns were expressed by the Russian Federation[61] and Vietnam.[62] While not explicitly noted, it may be derived from the various statements that the States in this category did not consider a right to unilateral secession to exist. Rather, for this group of States, fundamental principles of international law such as State sovereignty

---

[57]   UN Security Council, 5839th meeting, UN Doc. S/PV.5839, 18 February 2008 (President Tadić, Serbia). See also UN Security Council, 5917th meeting, UN Doc. S/PV.5917, 20 June 2008 (President Tadić, Serbia).

[58]   UN Security Council, 5839th meeting, UN Doc. S/PV.5839, 18 February 2008 (Mr Churkin, Russian Federation). See also UN Security Council, 5917th meeting, UN Doc. S/PV.5917, 20 June 2008 (Mr Churkin, Russian Federation).

[59]   UN Security Council, 5839th meeting, UN Doc. S/PV.5839, 18 February 2008 (Mr Kumalo, South Africa).

[60]   *Ibid.*, (President Tadić, Serbia). See also UN Security Council, 5850th meeting, UN Doc. S/PV.5850, 11 March 2008.

[61]   See UN Security Council, 5839th meeting, UN Doc. S/PV.5839, 18 February 2008 (Mr Churkin, Russian Federation).

[62]   See *ibid.* (Mr Le Luong Minh, Vietnam).

and territorial integrity (combined with the fear for negative effects on peace and stability) were seen to exclude the acknowledgement of a right to unilateral secession.[63]

The second category of responses towards Kosovo's unilateral declaration of independence involved the view that Kosovo and Serbia should resume negotiations on Kosovo's final status. One of the States stressing the necessity of further dialogue was Vietnam. It urged the parties concerned:

> to engage [...] in good-faith dialogue and peaceful negotiations to resolve their differences and arrive at a durable comprehensive solution conforming to the fundamental principles of international law, the United Nations Charter and the provisions of Security Council resolution 1244 (1999), in the interest of peace and stability, not only in Kosovo, but also in the rest of the Balkans, in Europe and throughout the world.[64]

In similar terms, China expressed the hope that:

> all parties concerned will keep in mind the long-term interests of peace and security in the Balkan region, Europe and the world at large, and conduct candid negotiations and discussions for a constructive solution to the issue of Kosovo's status.[65]

In this connection, it also emphasized the need for a "mutually acceptable solution through political and diplomatic means".[66] Likewise, notwithstanding the declaration of independence, Indonesia called for a continued "dialogue and a negotiated solution", as that would "better guarantee peace and stability in the region".[67] This line of reasoning appears to be consistent with the conventional approach to the right to self-determination, which prioritizes the achievement of internal self-determination and excludes the option of secession as long as the consent of the parent State remains forthcoming. On a more practical level, the position that negotiations should be resumed would also reduce the risk of Kosovo serving as a precedent for entities with secessionist ambitions elsewhere in the world.[68]

Finally, the third class of responses towards Kosovo's unilateral declaration of independence concerns the formal recognition of Kosovo. The day after Kosovo's

---

[63] See Quane, 'Self-Determination and Minority Protection after Kosovo' at p. 198.

[64] UN Security Council, 5839th meeting, UN Doc. S/PV.5839, 18 February 2008 (Mr Le Luong Minh, Vietnam). See also UN Security Council, 5917th meeting, UN Doc. S/PV.5917, 20 June 2008 (Mr Le Luong Minh, Vietnam).

[65] UN Security Council, 5839th meeting, UN Doc. S/PV.5839, 18 February 2008 (Mr Wang Guangya, China).

[66] *Ibid.* See also UN Security Council, 6025th meeting, UN Doc. S/PV.6025, 26 November 2008 (Mr Li Kexin, China).

[67] UN Security Council, 5839th meeting, UN Doc. S/PV.5839, 18 February 2008 (Mr Natalegawa, Indonesia). See also UN Security Council, 6025th meeting, UN Doc. S/PV.6025, 26 November 2008 (Mr Kleib, Indonesia).

[68] See Quane, 'Self-Determination and Minority Protection after Kosovo' at p. 198.

declaration, during the 5839th Security Council meeting, several States announced that they had already recognized Kosovo or expressed their intension to do so in due course.[69] Since, Kosovo has been recognized as an independent State by 96 out of 193 UN Member States. These recognizing States include 22 EU Member States and three out of five permanent members of the UN Security Council, including the United States.[70] While this significant number of formal recognitions obviously cannot be ignored, it leaves the present-day legal status of Kosovo open to question. Previously in this Chapter, it was explained that although recognition is generally viewed as declaratory, it may be seen to have some constitutive effects in the case of attempts at unilateral secession. It was contended that if the parent State does not consent to the secession of part of its territory, virtually universal recognition by the international community of States may effectuate a successful secession. Kosovo has been recognized by a considerable number of States, but it arguably goes too far to contend that its recognition has been virtually universal. What is more, it has neither been admitted to the European Union nor the United Nations. As a consequence, it remains questionable whether Kosovo's attempt to secede from Serbia and create an independent, sovereign State has actually been successful. Put differently, the legal status of Kosovo remains ambiguous to date.[71] Despite these uncertainties, it is relevant to take a closer look at the recognition texts to see the justifications that States have adduced for granting recognition to Kosovo.[72] For the present purposes, it is of particular significance to assess whether the remedial secession doctrine – or elements thereof – has been invoked by recognizing States. In this respect, however, it should be noted that not all States have published their recognition statements and various States have not substantiated their decision to recognize, i.e. they merely noted that they formally recognized Kosovo as a sovereign and independent State.[73]

Of the States which gave reasons for the decision to recognize, it appears that most adduced political considerations, such as the need for stability, peace and security in

---

[69] See UN Security Council, 5839th meeting, UN Doc. S/PV.5839, 18 February 2008 (Mr Verbeke, Belgium); *ibid.* (Mr Urbina, Costa Rica); *ibid.* (Mr Ripert, France); *ibid.* (Mr Mantovani, Italy); *ibid.* (Sir John Sawers, United Kingdom); *ibid.* (Mr Khalilzad, United States of America).

[70] This was the state of affairs on 31 December 2012. See Ministry of Foreign Affairs of the Republic of Kosova, *Countries that have recognized the Republic of Kosova*, available at <www.mfa-ks. net/?page=2,33>, last consulted on 31 December 2012.

[71] See also Vidmar, 'Explaining the Legal Effects of Recognition' at pp. 378-381.

[72] Of the 96 States which have recognized Kosovo, the recognition statements of 49 States have been examined. That includes all recognition statements issued before 29 March 2008. After this date, statements were only considered occasionally, due to problems with the traceability of the documents. Moreover, some of the recognition statements concerned verbal acts, as a result of which no texts are available.

[73] See, for instance, Belgium, *Koninklijk besluit betreffende de erkenning van de Republiek Kosovo*, 24 February 2008, retrieved via 'Who Recognized Kosova as an Independent State?', available at <http://www.kosovothanksyou.com>; Malaysia, *Letter of Dr Rais Yatim to His Excellency Mr Skender Hyseni*, 30 October 2008, available at <http://kosova.org/docs/independence/Malaysia.pdf>. Both websites were last consulted on 24 September 2012.

the Balkans and beyond. It was frequently expected that the recognition of an independent Kosovo would have a positive effect on the situation in the region.[74] Turkey, for instance, emphasized in its recognition statement that it:

> attaches importance to advance the understanding of lasting peace in the Balkans which has suffered immensely in recent years and hopes that the independence of Kosovo will present an opportunity for the enhancement of stability and confidence among the countries in the region.[75]

Likewise, it was noted by another State that the recognition of an independent Kosovo would be "the only sustainable solution in the current situation which will provide the perspective of safety and stability in the region".[76] In a similar vein, the failure of protracted efforts to negotiate a peaceful settlement between Kosovo and Serbia led

---

[74] See, for instance, Austria, *Plassnik: Letter on Kosovo's Recognition Signed*, 27 February 2008, available at <http://www.bmeia.gv.at/en/foreign-ministry/news/press-releases/2008>; Bulgaria, Hungary and Croatia, *Joint Statement by the Governments of Bulgaria, Hungary and Croatia about the announcement of the recognition of Kosovo*, 19 March 2008, available at <http://www.mfa.hr/MVP.asp?pcpid=1640& tr=recognition+Kosovo>; Burkina Faso, *Declaration de Reconnaissance de l'Etat du Kosovo*, 24 April 2008, retrieved via 'Who Recognized Kosova as an Independent State?', available at <http://www.koso-vothanksyou.com>; Canada, *Canada Joins International Recognition of Kosovo, Press Release No. 59*, 18 March 2008, available at <http://news.gc.ca> (archived content); Finland, *Finland Recognised the Republic of Kosovo*, 7 March 2008, available at <http://formin.finland.fi/public/default.aspx?contentid= 123797&nodeid=15146&contentlan=2&culture=en-US>; France, *Lettre du President de la Republique, M. Nicholas Sarkozy, Addressee sur President du Kosovo, M. Fatmir Sejdiu*, 18 February 2008, available at <http://www.mofa.go.jp/announce/announce/2008/3/0318.html>; Germany, *Cabinet Approves Recognition of Kosovo as Independent State under International Law*, 20 February 2008, available at <http:// www.deutsche-aussenpolitik.de/daparchive/anzeige.php?zaehler=11196>; Japan, *Statement by Foreign Minister Masahiko Koumura on the Recognition of the Republic of Kosovo*, 18 March 2008, available at <http://www.mofa.go.jp/announce/announce/2008/3/0318.html>; Korea, *Recognition of the Republic of Kosovo*, 28 March 2008, available at <http://www.mofat.go.kr/ENG/main/index.jsp>; Saudi Arabia, *Saudi Arabia Announces Recognition of the Republic of Kosovo*, 20 April 2008, available at <http://www. spa.gov.sa/English/print.php?id=656348>; Senegal, *Dakar reconnaît le nouvel Etat*, 19 February 2008, available at <http://www.aps.sn/articles.php?id_article=40531>; United States of America, *U.S. Recognizes Kosovo as Independent State, Statement of Secretary of State Condoleezza Rice*, 18 February 2008, available at <http://2001-2009.state.gov/secretary/rm/2008/02/100973.htm>. All websites last consulted on 24 September 2012. See also Almqvist, *The Politics of Recognition, Kosovo and International Law* at p. 8; G. Bolton and G. Visoka, 'Recognizing Kosovo's Independence: Remedial Secession or Earned Sovereignty?' (2010) St Antony's College, University of Oxford (Occasional Paper No. 11/10) at p. 20.

[75] Turkey, *Statement of H.E. Mr. Ali Babacan, Minister of Foreign Affairs of the Republic of Turkey, Regarding the Recognition of Kosovo by Turkey*, 18 February 2008, available at <http://www.mfa.gov. tr>, last consulted on 24 September 2012.

[76] Lithuania, *Seimas of the Republic of Lithuania, Resolution on the Recognition of the Republic of Kosovo*, No. X-1520, 6 May 2008, retrieved via 'Who Recognized Kosova as an Independent State?', available at <http://www.kosovothanksyou.com>, last consulted on 24 September 2012.

some States to conclude that there was "no other alternative but to recognize [an independent] Kosovo".[77] Another example in this respect is Germany, which stated that:

> [a]lthough no stone was left unturned in attempts to negotiate a settlement between Kosovo Albanians and Serbians, all such efforts remained in vain. The German government is convinced that after so many years, further negotiations would not have resulted in a breakthrough.[78]

Various other States also made reference to failed negotiations on the final status of Kosovo, which may be read as support for independence as a last resort option or remedy.[79] At the same time, many States granting recognition emphasized the *sui generis* nature of the case of Kosovo, thus seeking to limit its potential precedential value.[80] An illustrative example in this respect is the statement of the United States, which contended that:

> the unusual combination of factors found in the Kosovo situation – including the context of Yugoslavia's break-up, the history of ethnic cleansing and crimes against civilians in Kosovo, and the extended period of UN administration – are not found elsewhere and therefore make Kosovo a special case. Kosovo cannot be seen as a precedent for any other situation in the world today.[81]

---

[77] Malta, *Malta Recognizes Kosovo as an Independent State*, 22 August 2008, available at <http://www.foreign.gov.mt/default.aspx?MDIS=21&NWID=68>, last consulted on 24 September 2012.

[78] Germany, *Cabinet Approves Recognition of Kosovo as Independent State under International Law*, 20 February 2008, available at <http://www.deutsche-aussenpolitik.de/daparchive/anzeige.php?zaehler=11196>, last consulted on 24 September 2012.

[79] See, for instance, Bulgaria, Hungary and Croatia, *Joint Statement by the Governments of Bulgaria, Hungary and Croatia about the announcement of the recognition of Kosovo*, 19 March 2008, available at <http://www.mfa.hr/MVP.asp?pcpid=1640&tr=recognition+Kosovo>; Canada, *Canada Joins International Recognition of Kosovo*, Press Release No. 59, 18 March 2008, available at <http://news.gc.ca> (archived content); Costa Rica, *Costa Rica se pronuncia por la independencia de Kósovo, Comunicación Institucional (Costa Rica Kósovo-1143)*, 17 February 2008, available at <www.rree.go.cr>; Iceland, *The Government of Iceland formally Recognizes Kosovo*, 5 March 2008, available at <http://www.mfa.is/news-and-publications/nr/4135>; Luxembourg, *Le Luxembourg reconnaît formellement le Kosovo*, 21 February 2008, available at <http://www.gouvernement.lu/salle_presse/actualite/2008/02-fevrier/20-asselborn-kosovo/index.html>; Macedonia, *Macedonia Recognizes Kosovo*, 9 October 2008, available at <http://www.mia.com.mk/default.aspx?vId=57722300&lId=2>; Slovenia, *Slovenia Recognizes Kosovo*, 5 March 2008, available at <http://kosova.org/docs/independence/Slowenien.pdf>. All websites last consulted on 24 September 2012.

[80] For a similar observation, see Quane, 'Self-Determination and Minority Protection after Kosovo' at p. 199; Ryngaert and Sobrie, 'Recognition of States: International Law or Realpolitik? The Practice of Recognition in the Wake of Kosovo, South Ossetia, and Abkhazia' at pp. 480-481.

[81] United States of America, *U.S. Recognizes Kosovo as Independent State, Statement of Secretary of State Condoleezza Rice*, 18 February 2008, available at <http://2001-2009.state.gov/secretary/rm/2008/02/100973.htm>, last consulted on 24 September 2012.

Positions of the same kind were expressed by various other States.[82] Ryngaert and Sobrie noted that such "emphasis on the *sui generis* character of the recognition of Kosovo diminishes the international-law relevance of such a recognition".[83] Indeed, stressing the uniqueness of the case of Kosovo as a justification for the decision to recognize its independence rather than adducing legal arguments in this respect prevents entitlements from being deduced from the recognition statements as well as limits the precedential value of the events regarding Kosovo.

It is striking that in their decision to recognize Kosovo, only few States appear to have relied upon international law – at least to a certain extent. While some States made mention of the fulfilment of the normative criteria for statehood,[84] the human rights violations on the territory,[85] and the legal framework created by Security Council Resolution 1244 (1999), the Rambouillet Accords and the Ahtisaari Plan,[86]

---

[82] See, for instance, Canada, *Canada Joins International Recognition of Kosovo, Press Release No. 59, 18 March 2008*, available at <http://news.gc.ca> (archived content); UN General Assembly, *Request for an advisory opinion of the International Court of Justice on whether the unilateral declaration of independence of Kosovo is in accordance with international law*, UN Doc. A/63/PV.22, 8 October 2008, (Mr Ripert, France); Latvia, *Announcement by Minister of Foreign Affairs of Republic of Latvia on Recognition of Kosovo's Independence*, available at <http://www.mfa.gov.lv/en/news/press-releases/2008/february/20-february/>; Peru, *Perú decide reconocer independencia de Kósovo*, Comunicado Oficial 002-08, 22 February 2008, retrieved through <http://www.kosovothanksyou.com/>; Poland *Government has Recognized the Independence of Kosovo*, 26 February 2008, available at <http://www.premier.gov.pl/en/press_centre/news/government_has_recognised_the_,2220/>; Slovenia, *Slovenia Recognizes Kosovo*, 5 March 2008, available at <http://kosova.org/docs/independence/Slowenien.pdf>; Sweden, *Sweden Recognises the Republic of Kosovo*, 4 March 2008, available at <http://www.sweden.gov.se/sb/d/10358/a/99714>; Switzerland, *Statement by the President of the Swiss Confederation*, 27 February 2008, available at <http://www.sweden.gov.se/sb/d/10358/a/99714>. All websites last consulted on 24 September 2012.

[83] Ryngaert and Sobrie, 'Recognition of States: International Law or Realpolitik? The Practice of Recognition in the Wake of Kosovo, South Ossetia, and Abkhazia' at p. 481.

[84] See, for instance, Burkina Faso, *Declaration de Reconnaissance de l'Etat du Kosovo*, 24 April 2008, retrieved via 'Who Recognized Kosova as an Independent State?', available at <http://www.kosovothanksyou.com>; Canada, *Canada Joins International Recognition of Kosovo, Press Release No. 59*, 18 March 2008, available at <http://news.gc.ca> (archived content); Costa Rica, *Costa Rica se pronuncia por la independencia de Kósovo, Comunicación Institucional (Costa Rica Kósovo-1143)*, 17 February 2008, available at <www.rree.go.cr>; Dominican Republic, *Posición de la Republica Dominicana sobre Kosovo*, 11 July 2009, retrieved via 'Who Recognized Kosova as an Independent State?', available at <http://kosovothanksyou.com>; United States of America, *U.S. Recognizes Kosovo as Independent State, Statement of Secretary of State Condoleezza Rice*, 18 February 2008, available at <http://2001-2009.state.gov/secretary/rm/2008/02/100973.htm>. All websites last consulted on 24 September 2012.

[85] See, for instance, Canada, *Canada Joins International Recognition of Kosovo, Press Release No. 59*, 18 March 2008, available at <http://news.gc.ca> (archived content); Costa Rica, *Costa Rica se pronuncia por la independencia de Kósovo, Comunicación Institucional (Costa Rica Kósovo-1143)*, 17 February 2008, available at <www.rree.go.cr>; Ireland, *Minister for Foreign Affairs Dermot Ahern TD Announces Ireland's Recognition of the Republic of Kosovo*, 29 February 2008, available at <http://foreignaffairs.gov.ie/home/index.aspx?id=42938>.

[86] See, for instance, Costa Rica, *Costa Rica se pronuncia por la independencia de Kósovo, Comunicación Institucional (Costa Rica Kósovo-1143)*, 17 February 2008, available at <www.rree.go.cr>;

they generally did so without giving much detail. More significant for the present purposes is that a mere handful of States noted the will of the people[87] and the right to – or principle of – self-determination, yet again without further elucidation. Albania, for example, merely noted that "[t]he Government of Albania considers the creation of the State of Kosovo as a historical event, sanctioning the right of Kosovo citizens for self-determination".[88] In a similar vein, Burkina Faso reaffirmed *"l'importance de l'égalité entre les peuples et de leur droit naturel a disposer d'eux-mêmes"*[89] and the United Arab Emirates found that the recognition of Kosovo as an independent and sovereign State was "[i]n accordance with its firm support for the principle of the legitimate right of people to self-determination".[90] It is important to note that none of these States elaborated on these arguments and none of them actually made such reference in the context of a presumed right to remedial secession or external self-determination otherwise. Rather, they made mention of the right to self-determination in conjunction with various other considerations primarily being non-legal in nature. The recognition statement issued by Slovenia exemplifies this. In this declaration, it was explained that the decision to recognize Kosovo was based on, *inter alia*, the:

Denmark, *Denmark Recognizes Kosovo as an Independent State*, 21 February 2008, available at <http://kosova.org/docs/independence/Denmark.pdf>; Estonia, *Estonia Recognizes Republic of Kosovo*, 21 February 2008, available at <http://www.vm.ee/?q=en/node/682>; Finland, *Finland Recognised the Republic of Kosovo*, 7 March 2008, available at <http://formin.finland.fi/public/default.aspx?contentid=123797&nodeid=15146&contentlan=2&culture=en-US>; United States of America, *U.S. Recognizes Kosovo as Independent State, Statement of Secretary of State Condoleezza Rice*, 18 February 2008, available at <http://2001-2009.state.gov/secretary/rm/2008/02/100973.htm>.

[87]   See, for instance, Afghanistan, *The Statement of Islamic Republic of Afghanistan on the Recognition of Independence of Kosovo*, 18 February 2008, available at <http://kosova.org/docs/independence/Afghanistan.pdf>; Australia, *Australia Recognises the Republic of Kosovo*, 19 February 2008, available at <http://www.foreignminister.gov.au/releases/2008/fa-s034_08.html>; Costa Rica, *Costa Rica se pronuncia por la independencia de Kósovo, Comunicación Institucional (Costa Rica Kósovo-1143)*, 17 February 2008, available at <www.rree.go.cr>; Ireland, *Minister for Foreign Affairs Dermot Ahern TD Announces Ireland's Recognition of the Republic of Kosovo*, 29 February 2008, available at <http://foreignaffairs.gov.ie/home/index.aspx?id=42938>; Saudi Arabia, *Saudi Arabia Announces Recognition of the Republic of Kosovo*, 20 April 2008, available at <http://www.spa.gov.sa/English/print.php?id=656348>; Slovenia, *Slovenia Recognizes Kosovo*, 5 March 2008, available at <http://kosova.org/docs/independence/Slowenien.pdf>. All websites last consulted on 24 September 2012.

[88]   Albania, *Statement of Prime Minister of Albania Mr. Sali Berisha on Recognition of Independence of Kosova*, 18 February 2008, available at <http://keshilliministrave.al/index.php?fq=brenda&m=news&lid=7323&gj=gj2>.

[89]   Burkina Faso, *Declaration de Reconnaissance de l'Etat du Kosovo*, 24 April 2008, retrieved via 'Who Recognized Kosova as an Independent State?', available at <http://www.kosovothanksyou.com>.

[90]   United Arab Emirates, *UAE Recognises Kosovo*, 14 October 2008, retrieved via 'Who Recognized Kosova as an Independent State?', available at <http://www.kosovothanksyou.com>, last consulted on 24 September 2012.

specific historical circumstances, such as the status of an autonomous province within Yugoslavia given to Kosovo by the 1974 constitution, the systematic repression of Kosovo Albanians and the years of international administration of Kosovo.

Moreover, it took into consideration that the protracted negotiations between Kosovo and Serbia on Kosovo's final status had remained fruitless. For Slovenia, these "were circumstances that made Kosovo a 'unique' case" and [...] suggested that 'no alternative solutions were possible or realistic'". In addition, Slovenia's decision was also guided by the fact that the declaration of independence was adopted by the Kosovo Assembly "as a legitimate expression of the will of the majority of Kosovo's population"[91] and in view of:

> the right of peoples to self-determination, the concern for the stability of Kosovo and the region, as well as the conclusions of the February EU General Affairs and External Relations Council meeting.[92]

Having regard to this conjunction of factors other than self-determination, it seems legitimate to raise the question as to whether the States concerned would have considered the right to self-determination *an sich* to constitute a sufficient basis warranting Kosovo's secession from Serbia.[93]

In sum, it appears that States generally did not deem international law to be a determining factor in their decision to formally recognize Kosovo, not to mention that they presumed a right to remedial secession to underlie this choice. Rather, it seems that States first and foremost felt "the need to assess the case in light of political considerations",[94] thus confirming the political nature of recognition practice.

3.1.1.1. Recapitulation

Having considered the general responses of States to Kosovo's unilateral declaration of independence, involving both statements issued during the debates in the Security Council and General Assembly and recognition statements, three common approaches towards the matter have been disclosed. First, various States opposed

---

[91] Slovenia, *Slovenia Recognizes Kosovo*, 5 March 2008, available at <http://kosova.org/docs/independence/Slowenien.pdf >, last consulted 24 September 2012. For a similar reference to the will of the majority, see the recognition statement of Ireland, in which it was noted that "more than 90% of Kosovo's population wants independence". See Ireland, *Minister for Foreign Affairs Dermot Ahern TD Announces Ireland's Recognition of the Republic of Kosovo*, 29 February 2008, available at <http://foreignaffairs.gov.ie/home/index.aspx?id=42938>, last consulted 24 September 2012.

[92] Slovenia, *Slovenia Recognizes Kosovo*, 5 March 2008, available at <http://kosova.org/docs/independence/Slowenien.pdf >, last consulted on 24 September 2012.

[93] See also Quane, 'Self-Determination and Minority Protection after Kosovo' at p. 204.

[94] Almqvist, *The Politics of Recognition, Kosovo and International Law* at p. 9.

Kosovo's attempt to secede from Serbia by designating the declaration of independence as a violation of international law. In doing so, reference was generally made to the principles of State sovereignty and respect for the territorial integrity of States as stipulated in the UN Charter and to the (legal) framework created by UN Security Council Resolution 1244 (1999). Secondly, a group of States repudiated the issuing of Kosovo's unilateral declaration of independence by calling for the resumption of political negotiations on the final status of Kosovo. It was observed that both approaches towards Kosovo's proclamation of independence arguably reflect the conventional view on the right to self-determination, with respect for State sovereignty and territorial integrity being prioritized and external self-determination being ruled out as long as the consent of the parent State is absent.

Finally, a third group of States responded to the declaration of independence more positively by formally recognizing Kosovo as an independent State. From the various recognition texts, however, it followed that legal considerations seem to have played only a very marginal role in the decision to grant recognition to Kosovo. The traditional (normative) criteria for statehood and the right to self-determination were scarcely referred to, and even where States did so, this clearly did not constitute their principal argument for recognition. Instead, it was seen that States appeared to be primarily guided by political considerations, such as the promotion and preservation of peace and stability in the region and the fact that sustained negotiations to reach a peaceful settlement between the parties continued to be to no avail. In view of this, it may not come as a surprise that references to the notion of remedial secession – or an entitlement to unilateral secession otherwise – were not made in the various statements. Nevertheless, it was seen that some States did consider the grave human rights abuses on the territory and the failed negotiations on the final status of Kosovo in their decision to recognize, both of which may be linked to attributes of the remedial secession doctrine.[95] It may be questioned, however, whether these grounds actually stemmed from the acceptance of a right to remedial secession, or merely arose from concerns pertaining to peace and stability in the region. Considering the lack of other clear references to the concept of remedial secession or elements thereof, and in view of the emphasis on other (non-legal) factors, one may argue that the latter line of reasoning seems more likely. Moreover, bearing in mind the fact that many recognizing States stressed the *sui generis* nature of the case of Kosovo, thereby arguing that it could thus not be regarded as a precedent, may also be seen as an indication that these States did not consider a legal entitlement to be applicable to Kosovo.

---

[95] For the right to remedial secession in doctrine, see Chapter IV, Section 2.2.

3.1.2. The Advisory Proceedings before the International Court of Justice

In contrast to the general responses to Kosovo's declaration of independence as addressed above, reference to the concept of remedial secession was made during the advisory proceedings before the Court. As the statements submitted during the advisory proceedings dealt with legal issues more elaborately, they provide for valuable insights on the contemporary stance of States regarding the existence of an entitlement to remedial secession. In this respect, a number of positions become apparent when studying the submissions of States. Broadly speaking, the submissions can be classified in two categories. The first category comprises those States which expressed support for the existence of a right to remedial secession in their statements. In contrast, the second class includes a greater number of States, which opposed the existence of a right to remedial secession. The views of States categorized under these classes will be discussed below in the abovementioned order.[96]

3.1.2.1. Support for the Existence of a Right to Remedial Secession

During the proceedings before the Court and against the backdrop of the specific case of Kosovo, a number of States expressed their support for the existence of a right to remedial secession under contemporary international law in general as well. In addition to the Authors of the Unilateral Declaration of Independence (Kosovo), these States were Albania, Estonia, Finland, Germany, Ireland, Jordan, the Netherlands, Poland, Slovenia, Switzerland and the Russian Federation. Some of these States merely touched upon the acknowledgement of such a right or even accepted it rather implicitly, but most commented on the matter at length. Bearing in mind the question of the existence of a customary right to remedial secession, these views and arguments deserve to be considered here one by one.[97] In doing so, where possible, particular attention will be paid to the sources the States adduced for the existence of a right to remedial secession and the conditions listed for the lawful exercise of such an entitlement.

3.1.2.1.1. Views and Arguments Supporting a Right to Remedial Secession

As it might seem self-evident that the Authors of the Unilateral Declaration of Independence (Kosovo) (hereafter: the Authors) claimed a right to remedial secession for the purpose of justifying the issuing of their declaration, it is worth noting that it was

---

[96] It should be noted that since the aim of the present Chapter is to examine the existence of a customary norm, it would be beyond the scope of the present analysis to critically consider the different arguments presented by the States participating in the advisory proceedings and comment upon the accuracy of their position from other angles.

[97] The State submissions will be addressed in alphabetical order.

not before the Written Comments that this concept was (implicitly) put forward and claimed to be applicable in the case at hand "given the massive human rights violations perpetrated and the systematical denial of the right to self-determination by the FRY/Serbia".[98] Initially, the Authors held the view that the question which was put before the Court in Resolution 63/3 could be answered "without passing upon whether the people of Kosovo were authorized by international law to exercise a right of self-determination by seeking independence".[99] It was only due to the many States which had touched upon this question that the Authors felt compelled to briefly deal with this issue as well, while in essence, they still considered it unnecessary.[100] The Authors submitted that the Friendly Relations Declaration's safeguard clause clearly:

> recognizes that independence may be an appropriate choice in the case where a State does not conduct itself in compliance with the principle of equal rights and self-determination of peoples. In those particular circumstances, the State concerned not only forfeits the benefit of the safeguard clause [...], but also the right to invoke its sovereignty against the will of a people deprived of its right of self-determination. As Professor Tomuschat put it: "Within a context where the individual citizen is more regarded as a simple object, international law must allow the members of a community suffering structural discrimination – amounting to grave prejudice affecting their lives – to strive for secession as a measure of last resort after all other methods employed to bring about change have failed."[101]

In addition to these references to the Friendly Relations Declaration and an eminent scholar, the Authors briefly adduced the decision of the Canadian Supreme Court in the *Reference re Secession of Quebec*, before they linked this support to the specific case of Kosovo.[102] Considering the "decade of deliberate exclusion from governing institutions and violation of basic human rights, culminating, in 1998-1999, in massive crimes against humanity and war crimes", it was concluded that the people of Kosovo were entitled to exercise their right to self-determination through declaring

---

[98] International Court of Justice, *Accordance with International Law of the Unilateral Declaration of Independence by the Provisional Institutions of Self-Government of Kosovo (Request for Advisory Opinion)*, Further Written Contribution of the Authors of the Unilateral Declaration of Independence (Kosovo), 17 July 2009, at para. 4.33.

[99] International Court of Justice, *Accordance with International Law of the Unilateral Declaration of Independence by the Provisional Institutions of Self-Government of Kosovo (Request for Advisory Opinion)*, Written Contribution of the Authors of the Unilateral Declaration of Independence (Kosovo), 17 April 2009, at para. 8.41. See also International Court of Justice, *Accordance with International Law of the Unilateral Declaration of Independence by the Provisional Institutions of Self-Government of Kosovo (Request for Advisory Opinion)*, Further Written Contribution of the Authors of the Unilateral Declaration of Independence (Kosovo), 17 July 2009, at para. 4.31.

[100] *Ibid.*, at para. 4.32.

[101] *Ibid.*, at para. 4.39.

[102] *Ibid.*, at para. 4.40.

independence form Serbia.[103] The fact that there have been various developments on the territory from 1999 onwards does not alter this entitlement, as the new situation did not involve a substantial improvement as regards the right to self-determination for the people of Kosovo, so the Authors contended.[104] In view of this and considering the "long but ultimately fruitless" negotiation process, they deemed the declaration of independence to be "a last recourse to effectively exercise their right".[105]

Being the kin-State of the Kosovo Albanian population, it may not come as a surprise that Albania claimed the existence of a right to remedial secession and its applicability in the case of Kosovo. In this respect, it observed that declarations of independence have traditionally been justified following oppression by the parent State.[106] More specifically, Albania acknowledged a right to remedial secession by reference to the safeguard clause of the Friendly Relations Declaration and emphasized that:

> this paragraph clearly recognizes secession where no government representing the whole people belonging to the territory without distinction as to race, creed or colour exists.[107]

Albania subsequently referred to the Vienna Declaration and Programme of Action and the Canadian Supreme Court's decision in the *Reference re Secession of Quebec*, in which a right of secession in case of oppression was clearly recognized, so it said.[108] In its Written Comments, Albania additionally argued that legal literature contains "strong support" for the existence of such a right to remedial secession, "though applicable under exceptional circumstances".[109] With respect to a right to remedial secession, Albania regarded Kosovo as a case in point in view of what it called the "institutionalized policy of repression and gross and widespread human rights violations against Kosovar Albanians"[110] by the Serb authorities and the fact that "[a]ll possible means were used before the Kosovar authorities declared the independence

---

[103] *Ibid.*, at para. 4.40. For an account of these past injustices, see also paras 3.29-3.58.

[104] *Ibid.*, at paras 4.50-4.52.

[105] *Ibid.*, at para. 4.52.

[106] International Court of Justice, *Accordance with International Law of the Unilateral Declaration of Independence by the Provisional Institutions of Self-Government of Kosovo (Request for Advisory Opinion)*, Written Statement of Albania, 14 April 2009, at para. 86.

[107] *Ibid.*, at para. 81.

[108] *Ibid.*, at paras 82-83.

[109] International Court of Justice, *Accordance with International Law of the Unilateral Declaration of Independence by the Provisional Institutions of Self-Government of Kosovo (Request for Advisory Opinion)*, Written Comments of Albania, 17 July 2009, at para. 59.

[110] International Court of Justice, *Accordance with International Law of the Unilateral Declaration of Independence by the Provisional Institutions of Self-Government of Kosovo (Request for Advisory Opinion)*, Written Statement of Albania, 14 April 2009, at paras 86-92.

of the country".[111] From this, it follows that Albania recognized two general preconditions for the exercise of an entitlement to remedial secession, i.e. a policy of repression and gross and widespread violations of human rights and the exhaustion of all options for a negotiated solution.

Estonia also contended that "the application of the principle of self-determination can under certain circumstances lead to declaration of independence and to secession".[112] It clearly did not consider the right to self-determination to involve an unconditional right to secede unilaterally. Rather, Estonia stressed the point that "secession should normally not be considered and self-determination should be enjoyed inside the existing States. In some cases, however, self-determination may exceptionally legitimize secession".[113] According to Estonia, international law accepts an entitlement to unilateral secession for a subjugated group when two cumulative conditions are fulfilled. First, there must be "suffering from a severe and long-lasting refusal of internal self-determination by the State in which a group is living", and secondly, all "other possible ways to resolve the situation must be exhausted".[114] In other words, secession is seen as an *ultima ratio* means. While it found that the events in Kosovo met both conditions for the exercise of a right to secession, Estonia subsequently observed that the option to exercise such a right ceases to exist when the requirements are no longer satisfied. In this respect, it noted that one may contend "that since for several years in Kosovo there was no violence from the side of the Serbian government, in 2008 the time had lapsed to make use of the right to secession".[115] Nonetheless, Estonia submitted that following the oppression and atrocities, a protracted negotiation process was started, which sought to find a solution acceptable for both parties. Only when that process proved to be unsuccessful, could the possibility to use secession be considered as an *ultima ratio* means.[116] Finally, Estonia found that the *sui generis* character of the case of Kosovo ultimately determined the legality of its unilateral secession.[117]

While Finland acknowledged that "[i]n post-1945 law, self-determination is accompanied by a strong rule in favour of the territorial integrity of existing States",[118] it also argued that this latter principle is not absolute and may be pushed

---

[111]   *Ibid.*, at para. 96. See also paras 93-95.
[112]   International Court of Justice, *Accordance with International Law of the Unilateral Declaration of Independence by the Provisional Institutions of Self-Government of Kosovo (Request for Advisory Opinion)*, Written Statement of Estonia, 13 April 2009, at para. 2.1.
[113]   *Ibid.*, at para. 2.1.
[114]   *Ibid.*, at paras 2.1.1-2.1.2.
[115]   *Ibid.*, at para. 2.1.3.
[116]   *Ibid.*, at para. 2.1.3.
[117]   *Ibid.*, at para. 2.2.
[118]   International Court of Justice, *Accordance with International Law of the Unilateral Declaration of Independence by the Provisional Institutions of Self-Government of Kosovo (Request for Advisory Opinion)*, Written Statement of Finland, 16 April 2009, at para. 6.

aside under exceptional circumstances. In the opinion of Finland, this option was already expressed in the *Åland Islands* case and was subsequently reflected by the safeguard clause of the Friendly Relations Declaration and the decision of the Canadian Supreme Court on the right of Quebec to secede unilaterally from Canada.[119] In this respect, Finland observed:

> The rationale invoked in these cases points to a distinction between normal situations and those of abnormality, or rupture, situations of revolution, war, alien subjugation or the absence of a meaningful prospect for a functioning internal self-determination regime.[120]

According to Finland, the situation of Kosovo could be regarded as 'abnormal' due to the concurrence of five factors: the violent break-up of the Socialist Federal Republic of Yugoslavia, the unilateral changes in Kosovo's constitutional status, the persecution of the Kosovo Albanians in 1989-1999, the international recognition of the special nature of the situation through UN Security Council Resolution 1244 (1999), and the failure by the Serb authorities to provide a credible framework for internal self-determination.[121] Against this background, the legality of Kosovo's declaration of independence was to be determined, Finland held. In this connection, it recalled the observation of the Commission of Rapporteurs in the *Åland Islands* case:

> The separation of a minority from the State of which it forms a part and its incorporation in another State can only be considered as an altogether exceptional solution, a last resort when the State lacks either the will or the power to enact and apply just and effective guarantees.[122]

In the opinion of Finland, such a right to remedial secession applied to the situation of Kosovo. From its reasoning in the specific case of Kosovo, it follows that Finland considered two criteria to be relevant for the exercise of such a right in general, that is, the suppression of the right to (internal) self-determination and the absence of other realistic solutions.[123]

Germany discussed its position concerning the legality of declarations of independence, the right to self-determination and remedial secession at length. It first noted that:

---

[119]   *Ibid.*, at paras 7-8.
[120]   *Ibid.*, at para. 9.
[121]   *Ibid.*, at para. 10.
[122]   *Ibid.*, at para. 11.
[123]   *Ibid.*, at para. 12.

[t]here is considerable authority for the proposition that a declaration of independence leading to a secession and secession itself are of an entirely factual nature and that international law in general is silent as to their legality.[124]

Germany referred to various expert opinions for the Supreme Court of Canada's *Reference re Secession of Quebec*, such as those of James R. Crawford, Thomas M. Franck and Malcolm N. Shaw, to underpin this argument.[125] Alternatively, Germany held that "given the very special situation of Kosovo, international law would not object to Kosovo's independence". Aware of the importance of the principle of territorial integrity in this context and its vexed relationship with self-determination, Germany noted the relevance of the Friendly Relations Declaration and the Helsinki Final Act. It asserted that:

[i]t clearly emerges from both these documents that the principle of self-determination is recognized as being on the same level as, and by no means subservient to, the principle of sovereignty, the sovereign equality and the territorial integrity of States.[126]

Against the backdrop of the distinction between the internal and external dimension of the right to self-determination, Germany argued in favour of a right to external self-determination outside the colonial context. It found that the denial of such an entitlement would even render the right to internal self-determination futile in practice:

There would be no remedy for a group which is not granted self-determination that may be due to it under international law. The majority in the State could easily and with impunity oppress the minority, without any recourse being open to that minority.[127]

This is not to say, however, that Germany considered a right to secession to be a broad right which can be invoked by any group at any time. Without making reference to any specific sources, Germany concluded that while the right to self-determination should as a rule be exercised internally, the same right "may exceptionally legitimize secession if this can be shown to be the only remedy against a prolonged and rigorous refusal of internal self-determination".[128] Thus, such an entitlement to remedial secession would merely come into play under the two criteria that were also stated in the submissions addressed above. Germany explained that although the condition

---

[124] International Court of Justice, *Accordance with International Law of the Unilateral Declaration of Independence by the Provisional Institutions of Self-Government of Kosovo (Request for Advisory Opinion)*, Written Statement of Germany, 15 April 2009, at para. VI.1 (p. 27).

[125] *Ibid.*, at para. VI.1 (pp. 27-29).

[126] *Ibid.*, at para. VI.2 (p. 32).

[127] *Ibid.*, at para. VI.2 (p. 34).

[128] *Ibid.*, at para. VI.2 (p. 34).

of "exceptionally severe and long-lasting refusal of internal self-determination" will usually go hand in hand with gross violations of human rights, it is the lack of internal self-determination which is decisive for the legality of secession, in combination with the requirement of *ultimum remedium*.[129] As regards this latter condition, Germany stressed that although time has lapsed since the oppression and atrocities suffered by the Kosovo Albanian population, it would "be both illogic and unjust" to hold "that this lapse of time made the right of external self-determination disappear before it could even be used". Thus, it seems that for Germany, there is no time factor involved in the requirement of unilateral secession being an *ultimum remedium*. The fact that the "very legacy of the conflict" makes other (less far-reaching) solutions of the conflict impossible would be sufficient to stand this test.[130] All in all, Germany found that the case of Kosovo met the threshold for the lawful secession from Serbia. First, it held that the history of Kosovo represents an obvious example of "prolonged and severe repression and denial of all internal self-determination" and secondly, it considered it to be clear that "there have been negotiations in several formats over a considerable period of time", but all remained fruitless. In consequence, Germany alleged that the route to external self-determination was open.[131]

Ireland commenced its submission by noting "that international law contains neither a general right nor a general prohibition on unilateral declarations of independence". It adduced the writings of several authors and the judgment of the Supreme Court of Canada in its *Reference re Secession of Quebec* as providing support for this view.[132] Despite the alleged neutrality, Ireland recognized that an attempt to secede unilaterally may be illegal in the case that the action constitutes a violation of peremptory norms of international law or when the UN Security Council declares the action illegal.[133] Since both exceptions were not applicable to the case of Kosovo, its unilateral declaration of independence was not in violation of international law, Ireland submitted.[134] Further or alternatively, Ireland asserted that Kosovo's declaration of independence was not contrary to international law as it concerned the exercise of the right to self-determination following gross human rights violations. While it rejected the existence of a "unilateral *right* of secession by constituent parts of existing States",[135] Ireland contended that by way of an exception, a right to secession may be warranted under extreme circumstances. In this respect, reference was made to

---

[129] *Ibid.*, at para. VI.2 (p. 35).
[130] *Ibid.*, at para. VI.2 (p. 36).
[131] *Ibid.*, at para. VI.2 (p. 35).
[132] International Court of Justice, *Accordance with International Law of the Unilateral Declaration of Independence by the Provisional Institutions of Self-Government of Kosovo (Request for Advisory Opinion)*, Written Statement of Ireland, 17 April 2009, at paras 18-21.
[133] *Ibid.*, at paras 22-23.
[134] *Ibid.*, at paras 24-26.
[135] *Ibid.*, at para. 28 (emphasis original).

the *Åland Islands* case and the judgment in the *Reference re Secession of Quebec*.[136] Ireland shared the view uttered in this latter ruling that such a qualified right to secession in the event of gross human rights violations "arises in only the most extreme of cases and, even then, under carefully defined circumstances" and as a remedy of last resort.[137] More specifically, Ireland considered a right to secession:

> to arise "only when a people had been subject to such repression by the majority within a State that separation was the only feasible alternative", or where a people is "discriminated against in such a way that remaining in the State cannot be demanded any longer".[138]

According to Ireland, these elements are cumulative, thus requiring serious human rights violations to involve "an element of discrimination" and the absence of other remedies or feasible alternatives before a right to secession may arise.[139] With respect to the case of Kosovo, Ireland found five factors to be of particular importance for judging the legality of Kosovo's unilateral declaration of independence: the withdrawal of Kosovo's autonomy by the regime in Belgrade, the sustained period of international administration of the territory, the grave and extensive human rights violations by the Serb authorities, the desire for independence of 90 per cent of Kosovo's population and the non-existence of other remedies and realistic alternatives in view of the extensive international negotiation process.[140] Considering these circumstances, Ireland concluded that the case of Kosovo constituted a *"sui generis* case representing an exercise of self-determination in the context of gross or fundamental human rights abuses".[141]

Being the first non-Western State expressing its support for the existence of a right to remedial secession, Jordan opposed the argument that the principle of territorial integrity is absolute and constitutes a barrier to external self-determination.[142] Adducing the Friendly Relations Declaration's safeguard clause, Jordan asserted that this paragraph implies that a State's territorial integrity ceases to exist if a State violates the right to self-determination of its population. According to Jordan, this applied to the case of Kosovo:

---

[136] *Ibid.*, at paras 29-30.
[137] *Ibid.*, at para. 30.
[138] *Ibid.*, at para. 30.
[139] *Ibid.*, at para. 32.
[140] *Ibid.*, at para. 33
[141] *Ibid.*, at para. 34.
[142] International Court of Justice, *Accordance with International Law of the Unilateral Declaration of Independence by the Provisional Institutions of Self-Government of Kosovo (Request for Advisory Opinion)*, Oral Statement of Jordan (Al Hussein), CR 2009/31, 9 December 2009, at paras 29-31.

> When a State revokes the status of a territory as autonomous, denies its people their acquired right under such autonomy, engages in a policy of ethnic cleansing against such people, and commits grave breaches of international humanitarian law, systematic human rights violations and crimes against humanity against them, then such people's right to self-determination has been violated by the State. And in such circumstances, that State can no longer claim a right of territorial integrity.[143]

Jordan found additional support for this restriction of the scope of territorial integrity in the Vienna Declaration and Programme of Action and the ruling of the Canadian Supreme Court in the *Reference re Secession of Quebec*.[144] This latter judgment ultimately led Jordan to voice its support for a right to secession following the "total frustration of internal self-determination or blocking [of] its meaningful exercise" and "after all negotiating avenues were exhausted".[145] In view of the "consistent denial and revocation of the Kosovo's people's right to self-determination" and considering the exhaustion of "all negotiating avenues", Jordan contended that in the case of Kosovo, this high threshold was certainly met.[146]

The Netherlands also expressed strong support for the right to remedial secession, but did so on grounds which deviate somewhat from the lines of reasoning presented above. Therefore, these pleadings will be dealt with at greater length. The Netherlands first submitted that "the right to political self-determination may evolve into a right to external self-determination in exceptional circumstances".[147] In this respect, it adduced an *a contrario* interpretation of the safeguard clause of the Friendly Relations Declaration as most of the other States also did. Yet, it is noteworthy that the Netherlands subsequently remarked that while "there is an abundance of literature on the law of self-determination" which certainly is informative, it did not consider it to be authoritative as "[t]he divergence of views in doctrine prevents, in our view, its use as a source of international law under Article 38 of the Statute of the Court".[148] Therefore, it asserted that in addition to treaty provisions, legal opinions and State practice on the matter needed to be examined.[149] In this connection, the Netherlands explained why there are only few examples of lawful attempts at unilateral secession beyond situations concerning non-self-governing territories or foreign occupation. A first explanation is that the right to external self-determination beyond decolonization

---

[143] *Ibid.*, at para. 35.

[144] *Ibid.*, at paras 36-37.

[145] *Ibid.*, at para. 38.

[146] *Ibid.*, at para. 38.

[147] International Court of Justice, *Accordance with International Law of the Unilateral Declaration of Independence by the Provisional Institutions of Self-Government of Kosovo (Request for Advisory Opinion)*, Written Statement of the Netherlands, 17 April 2009, at para. 3.6.

[148] International Court of Justice, *Accordance with International Law of the Unilateral Declaration of Independence by the Provisional Institutions of Self-Government of Kosovo (Request for Advisory Opinion)*, Oral Statement of the Netherlands (Lijnzaad), CR 2009/32, 10 December 2009, at para. 9.

[149] *Ibid.*, at para. 9.

developed only relatively recently, namely in the second half of the twenty-first century. Secondly, since the conditions for the exercise of a right to secession are strict, situations in which such a right was claimed often failed to meet the threshold and therefore could not lawfully exercise a right to external self-determination. Yet, in the opinion of the Netherlands, the creation of Bangladesh and Croatia are examples of situations in which the international community has accepted the exercise of such a right.[150] Furthermore, it is striking that the Netherlands founded part of its argument in favour of an entitlement to remedial secession on the doctrine of State responsibility and the definitions proposed in the respect by the International Law Commission.[151] More specifically, in the submissions of the Netherlands, it was argued that a denial of fundamental human rights and the absence of a government representing the whole population belonging to the territory amount to a violation of the right to self-determination, which constitutes a peremptory norm of international law.[152] As the Articles on Responsibility of States for Internationally Wrongful Acts prescribe, a "serious breach" of such a peremptory norm has particular consequences.[153] According to the Netherlands, unilateral secession may be seen as such a consequence, provided that "all effective remedies [...] have been exhausted to achieve a settlement".[154] Considering the events in Kosovo, it was argued that these two cumulative criteria were met in this specific case.[155] First, a government representing the whole people of the Socialist Federal Republic of Yugoslavia was lacking and fundamental human rights in Kosovo were systematically denied.[156] According to the Netherlands, this amounted to a "serious breach of the obligation to refrain from any forcible action which deprives peoples of their right to self-determination in Kosovo".[157] Secondly, it was submitted that all options to achieve a negotiated solution on Kosovo's status were exhausted.[158] In this connection, the Netherlands expressly noted that Kosovo's right to remedial secession had not ceased as a result of the passage of time since the serious breach of the right to self-determination. Rather,

---

[150] *Ibid.*, at para. 10.

[151] International Court of Justice, *Accordance with International Law of the Unilateral Declaration of Independence by the Provisional Institutions of Self-Government of Kosovo (Request for Advisory Opinion)*, Written Statement of the Netherlands, 17 April 2009, at para. 3.9.

[152] *Ibid.*, at para. 3.10.

[153] International Court of Justice, *Accordance with International Law of the Unilateral Declaration of Independence by the Provisional Institutions of Self-Government of Kosovo (Request for Advisory Opinion)*, Written Comments of the Netherlands, 17 July 2009, at para. 3.10.

[154] International Court of Justice, *Accordance with International Law of the Unilateral Declaration of Independence by the Provisional Institutions of Self-Government of Kosovo (Request for Advisory Opinion)*, Written Statement of the Netherlands, 17 April 2009, at para. 3.11.

[155] *Ibid.*, at paras 3.12-3.14.

[156] *Ibid.*, at para. 3.12.

[157] *Ibid.*, at para. 3.13.

[158] *Ibid.*, at para. 3.14.

the time has been used to satisfy the procedural condition for the exercise of the right to external self-determination, namely the exhaustion of all effective remedies to achieve a settlement on the status of Kosovo.[159]

Finally, while acknowledging the controversy surrounding the right to external self-determination and its application to the case of Kosovo, the Netherlands made a firm stand and submitted that Kosovo's proclamation of independence was justified on the basis of the right to external self-determination.[160]

On the basis of the Friendly Relations Declaration, Poland discerned four groups of peoples entitled to the right to self-determination, including:

people inhabiting states that infringe the right to self-determination and, thereby, being prevented form effective exercise of that right (which could, in particular, take the form of those people being represented in the host state's government that would reflect, in a not discriminatory manner, the whole of a given state population).[161]

With respect to this category, Poland adduced that their right to self-determination may under particular circumstances be lawfully exercised through secession.[162] As such, it accepted the existence of a remedial right to secession in situations of a State gravely violating the international human rights of the people inhabiting its territory, for instance by committing "genocide, crimes against humanity, war crimes and other massive violations of human rights and humanitarian law".[163] Moreover, Poland emphasized that an entitlement to remedial secession may only arise as an option of last resort to protect a people from the "wrongful acts" committed by the authorities of the State in which they live.[164] In this connection, reference was made to the Friendly Relations Declaration, which, according to Poland reflected the idea that in certain circumstances, the right to self-determination is not subordinated by the principle of territorial integrity.[165] While Poland did not further substantiate its claim for a right to remedial secession with references to other sources, it did deem Kosovo to be entitled to exercise such a right in view of the specific circumstances.[166] It emphasized that:

---

[159] *Ibid.*, at para. 3.15.
[160] *Ibid.*, at paras 3.16-3.22.
[161] International Court of Justice, *Accordance with International Law of the Unilateral Declaration of Independence by the Provisional Institutions of Self-Government of Kosovo (Request for Advisory Opinion)*, Written Statement of Poland, 14 April 2009, at para. 6.1.
[162] *Ibid.*, at para. 6.3.
[163] *Ibid.*, at para. 6.5.
[164] *Ibid.*, at para. 6.7.
[165] *Ibid.*, at paras 6.8-6.9.
[166] *Ibid.*, at para. 6.10-6.6.12.

the exercise of the right to self-determination of Kosovo's people in Serbia was not longer possible and unattainable. That conclusion is validated by the scale of violations of human rights and humanitarian law by Serbia. In such a situation Kosovo could legitimately exercise its remedial right of secession from Serbia in order to protect and preserve most fundamental rights and interests of its people. Therefore, the territorial integrity of Serbia – in the consequence of its own wrongful acts against Kosovo – eroded and was undermined already in 1999.[167]

Consequently, Poland argued that Serbia could no longer invoke the principle of respect for the territorial integrity of States as a shield against the exercise of a right to remedial secession by the people of Kosovo.[168]

The Russian Federation also voiced support for the existence of a right to remedial secession. It noted that an attempt at secession, such as in the case of Kosovo, is *"prima facie*, contrary to the requirement of preserving the territorial integrity" of the parent State.[169] In this context, the Russian Federation contended:

> that the principles of international law are to be applied in the light of each other, in a way that would produce a most harmonious interpretation of the various principles in a given situation.[170]

With regard to the principles of territorial integrity and self-determination, it therefore adduced the safeguard clauses of the Friendly Relations Declaration and the Vienna Declaration and Programme of Action, which, according to the Russian Federation, suggests that a State respecting the rights of the peoples on its territory enjoys the prerogative of territorial integrity. Moreover, by reference to the Supreme Court of Canada, it noted that the right to self-determination "has evolved within a framework of respect for the territorial integrity of States" and that the internal exercise of this right is preferred.[171] Nevertheless, the Russian Federation raised the question of whether the possibility of secession exists under particular circumstances.[172] It acknowledged the existence of a right to remedial secession, albeit in extreme situations only, as was phrased by the Canadian Supreme Court in the *Reference re Secession of Quebec*.[173] The Russian Federation therefore emphasized that it:

---

[167] *Ibid.*, at paras 6.11-6.12.

[168] *Ibid.*, at para. 6.12

[169] International Court of Justice, *Accordance with International Law of the Unilateral Declaration of Independence by the Provisional Institutions of Self-Government of Kosovo (Request for Advisory Opinion)*, Written Statement of the Russian Federation, 16 April 2009, at para. 76.

[170] *Ibid.*, at para. 82.

[171] *Ibid.*, at paras 83-85.

[172] *Ibid.*, at para. 86.

[173] *Ibid.*, at para. 87.

is of the view that the primary purpose of the "safeguard clause" is to serve as a guarantee of territorial integrity of States. It is also true that the clause may be construed as authorizing secession under certain conditions. However, those conditions should be limited to truly extreme circumstances, such as an outright attack by the parent State, threatening the very existence of the people in question. Otherwise, all efforts should be taken in order to settle the tension between the parent State and the ethnic community concerned within the framework of the existing State.[174]

Thus, while acknowledging that secession may only be warranted in exceptional situations and that it is a remedy of last resort, it is to be noted that the Russian Federation did not consider the denial of internal self-determination to be a precondition for the exercise of a right to remedial secession. On the basis of the criteria adduced to the case of Kosovo, it was concluded that no right to remedial secession was warranted at the moment Kosovo's unilateral declaration of independence was issued. Although the Russian Federation even questioned whether such an entitlement had emerged in the 1990s, it assertively found that the situation in 2008 had improved to such an extent that it could by no means be qualified as 'extreme circumstances' triggering a right to remedial secession.[175]

Slovenia accepted the existence of a right to remedial secession rather implicitly. Not only did it refrain from naming the concept of remedial secession, it also remained obscure which conditions Slovenia considered to be applicable in this respect and on which particular sources or developments in practice it founded its argument. In its submissions, Slovenia primarily focused on the correlation between the peoples' right to self-determination on the one hand, and the principle of respect for the territorial integrity of States on the other. In doing so, it contended that the latter principle is not absolute and must even be earned by the State. Slovenia recalled that over recent decades, the right to self-determination has evolved and "has been given precedence over the principle of respect for the territorial integrity of States".[176] More specifically, it held that:

> [i]f a State does not respect the right to self-determination and its government does not enjoy representativity or if the latter is lost, it cannot count on having its territorial integrity assured. In such circumstances, demand for independent statehood to the disadvantage of territorial integrity of a common State might be the only way to realize the right to free determination of political status of people forming part of the population of the common State [...].[177]

---

[174] *Ibid.*, at para. 88.

[175] *Ibid.*, at paras 89-103.

[176] International Court of Justice, *Accordance with International Law of the Unilateral Declaration of Independence by the Provisional Institutions of Self-Government of Kosovo (Request for Advisory Opinion)*, Written Statement of Slovenia, 17 April 2009, at para. 2.

[177] International Court of Justice, *Accordance with International Law of the Unilateral Declaration of Independence by the Provisional Institutions of Self-Government of Kosovo (Request for Advisory*

For these reasons, Slovenia stressed the importance of the specific circumstances of each case in considering whether a right to external self-determination may arise.[178] As such, it might be argued that Slovenia acknowledged the existence of a right to remedial secession, albeit in not so many words. Nevertheless, it did not consider the possible applicability of such an entitlement with respect to the situation in Kosovo, as a result of which Slovenia's true intentions may be questioned.

Being the last State uttering its support for the existence of a right to remedial secession under contemporary international law, Switzerland first observed that "[t]he actual extent of the right to self-determination remains a matter of dispute".[179] In this connection, it plainly posed that:

> a States territorial integrity is not protected to an unlimited extent if its government does not represent the whole population, arbitrarily practices discrimination against certain groups, and thus clearly violates the right of peoples to self-determination.[180]

According to Switzerland, in such situations, an attempt at unilateral secession by a people comprising a part of the population of the territory may be in conformity with the principle of territorial integrity and international law in general.[181] Switzerland substantiated its argument by referring to the *Åland Islands* case and the ruling of the Canadian Supreme Court in its *Reference re Secession of Quebec*, in which the right of a people to secede unilaterally was not ruled out.[182] Moreover, Switzerland noted that "prevailing doctrine" also acknowledged such an entitlement by way of exception and shared this view.[183] In sum, it voiced the following opinion:

> respect for territorial integrity is undoubtedly an important principle of international law. However, it is not isolated from other fundamental principles of international law, and in particular it cannot be called on for the purpose of excluding a right to secession under all circumstances. A right to secession based on the right of peoples to self-determination *can* exist, but may only be exercised in exceptional circumstances, when all other means of exercising the right to self-determination have failed or have to be regarded as futile due to grave and systematic violations of human rights. In other words, the proclamation of an independent State distinct form the former must remain a solution of last resort in order for a population to be able to exercise its right to self-determination internally, and enjoy the human rights and the rights of members

---

Opinion), Written Comments of Slovenia, 17 July 2009, at para. 8.

[178] *Ibid.*, at para. 8.

[179] International Court of Justice, *Accordance with International Law of the Unilateral Declaration of Independence by the Provisional Institutions of Self-Government of Kosovo (Request for Advisory Opinion)*, Written Statement of Switzerland, 25 May 2009, at para. 58.

[180] *Ibid.*, at para. 63.

[181] *Ibid.*, at para. 63.

[182] *Ibid.*, at paras 64-65.

[183] *Ibid.*, at para. 66.

of minorities that are guaranteed by international law. In such extreme situations, the right of a people to separate itself from a State through a unilateral declaration of independence has to be defined as an *ultima ratio* solution.[184]

Thus, Switzerland accepted the existence of a right to remedial secession under exceptional circumstances and only "after the exhaustion of all possible avenues aiming to restore a situation in which human rights are respected, including the right to internal self-determination".[185] Based on these theoretical views, Switzerland concluded that the strict conditions for a right to remedial secession were fulfilled in the case of Kosovo: the people of Kosovo had a right to self-determination, it had suffered from grave and systematic violations of human rights, and independent statehood through unilateral secession was the last resort option for this people to exercise its right to self-determination.[186] In this respect, Switzerland did not consider the lapse of time and the improved circumstances on the territory to raise a barrier for a right to remedial secession. For, the declaration of independence was issued "once it had become clear that the process that had been pursued since 10 June 1999 [...] could not come to a consensual solution".[187]

3.1.2.1.2. Recapitulation

All in all, it can be concluded that, in addition to the Authors of the declaration of independence, eleven States have expressed their support for the existence of a remedial right to unilateral secession under contemporary international law and its applicability to the case of Kosovo. Most of them have done so by actually naming the concept of remedial secession. Moreover, the States concerned generally substantiated their claims by adducing the safeguard clauses of the Friendly Relations Declaration and the Vienna Declaration and Programme of Action, the decisions in the *Åland Islands* case and the relevant paragraphs of the ruling of the Canadian Supreme Court in its *Reference re Secession of Quebec*. The interpretations by the various States of these particular sources were, on the whole, similar. In addition, a few States also referred to scholarly literature, albeit generally without specifying which writings they deemed relevant in this respect. What is also striking is that virtually no

---

[184] *Ibid.*, at para. 67 (emphasis original).

[185] International Court of Justice, *Accordance with International Law of the Unilateral Declaration of Independence by the Provisional Institutions of Self-Government of Kosovo (Request for Advisory Opinion)*, Written Comments of Switzerland, 17 July 2009, at para. 7.

[186] International Court of Justice, *Accordance with International Law of the Unilateral Declaration of Independence by the Provisional Institutions of Self-Government of Kosovo (Request for Advisory Opinion)*, Written Statement of Switzerland, 25 May 2009, at paras 68-97.

[187] International Court of Justice, *Accordance with International Law of the Unilateral Declaration of Independence by the Provisional Institutions of Self-Government of Kosovo (Request for Advisory Opinion)*, Written Comments of Switzerland, 17 July 2009, at para. 95.

State claimed that the existence of a right to remedial secession is rooted in practice. Even where this was asserted, the validity of this claim was hardly underpinned. For example, in the submissions of the Netherlands, it was held that the establishment of Bangladesh and Croatia can be seen as cases in point, yet without further explanation. From the very limited number of references to practice, it may be deduced that States do not consider international practice to provide for strong support for the existence of a right to remedial secession, possibly even due to the (presumed) absence of State practice which is both relevant and sound in this respect.

Whatever the accuracy of the arguments addressed above, from the written and oral pleadings of States supporting a right to remedial secession, it further becomes clear that a general or automatic right to secession for peoples is out of the question. Rather, this concept is commonly regarded as a qualified right which may emerge under exceptional circumstances only. While the (number of) conditions for the exercise of this right and the formulations put forward in the State submissions differ to a certain extent, they may be reduced to at least two cumulative prerequisites – one being substantive and the other being procedural. The substantive requirement is that the people at issue suffer from a persistent refusal of internal self-determination by the central authorities of the State in which the group is living. The presence of gross human rights violations is viewed either as an expression – if not the ultimate expression – of this denial of internal self-determination, or as an additional requirement. Once it is established that the substantive prerequisite is met, the procedural element requires that any other viable peaceful options to resolve the situation are absent, i.e. remedial secession operates as an *ultimum remedium*.

There appears to be disagreement, however, on whether there would be a kind of time factor included in the prerequisites for remedial secession. On the one hand, a couple of States seemed to imply that the passage of time may have a negative effect on the existence of a right to remedial secession in a particular case: the possibility of unilateral secession would be excluded as soon as the human rights violations and oppression of the people concerned has ended, as that would arguably mean that the criteria for a right to remedial secession are no longer fulfilled. On the other hand, some other States did not consider the elapse of time to be problematic in this respect. To put it even more strongly, it was argued by the Netherlands that the passage of time may contribute to the fulfilment of the procedural condition for the exercise of a right to remedial secession, which is the requirement of the exhaustion of all effective and realistic remedies to settle the conflict. Put differently, it may be contended that a certain period of time needs to go by before one can conclude that all effective and realistic remedies have indeed been exhausted and there is no prospect for a negotiated settlement. All in all, it seems that there is too much divergence on the question of a time factor to draw clear conclusions in this respect.

The conditions outlined above and the specific circumstances in Kosovo up to the adoption of its declaration of independence has led most States under the present category to conclude that the case of Kosovo meets the requirements of a right to remedial secession. They generally contended that the oppression of the Kosovo Albanian population during the 1990s combined with the absence of any prospect to the exercise of meaningful self-determination within the framework of the existing State – despite sustained negotiations on the international level – gave rise to such a right. In this respect, Estonia, Finland and Ireland referred to the exceptional nature of the situation as being 'abnormal' or '*sui generis*'. Only two States, i.e. Russia and Slovenia, concluded that the conditions for a right to remedial secession were not met in the specific circumstances of the case of Kosovo.

The support for the existence of a right to remedial secession as discussed above needs to be weighed against the submissions of States which did not hold the same opinion on this matter. For this purpose, the following sub-section will address the opposition to the existence of an entitlement to remedial secession as voiced during the advisory proceedings.

3.1.2.2. Opposition to the Existence of a Right to Remedial Secession

While there has been a non-negligible body of support for the existence of a right to remedial secession under contemporary law, the majority of State submissions did oppose this outlook during the advisory proceedings before the Court, including the submissions of Argentina, Azerbaijan, Belarus, Bolivia, Brazil, Burundi, China, Cyprus, Egypt, France, Iran, Japan, Libya, Norway, Romania, Serbia, Slovakia, Spain, the United Kingdom, the United States, Venezuela and Vietnam. In general, it is possible to discern two broad lines of arguments explicitly opposing a right to remedial secession: the alleged lack of evidence for the existence of such a right under positive international law, and the prioritization of the principle of respect for the territorial integrity of States over the exercise of the peoples' right to self-determination. Some States have concentrated on either of these two lines of reasoning, while others have combined both arguments in their pleadings. Besides these two broad lines of argument, a third yet minor reasoning may be discerned which touches upon the perceived neutrality of international law as regards attempts to secede. The observations which are most illuminating for the various lines of argument will be discussed below.

3.1.2.2.1. Views and Arguments Opposing the Existence of a Right to Remedial Secession

Argentina's submissions may be addressed here first, as they combine both lines of arguments opposing the existence of a right to remedial secession: they prioritized the principle of respect for the territorial integrity of States and argued that there is no support for an entitlement to remedial secession under positive international law. As to the first argument, Argentina alleged that the principle of respect for the territorial integrity of States is a principle firmly founded in international law, which is essential for upholding the international legal system.[188] In this regard, Argentina considered the principle of territorial integrity to apply "not only to States and international organisations, but also to other international actors, particularly those involved in internal conflict threatening international peace and security".[189] It asserted that various UN Security Council resolutions in the context of internal conflicts or attempts at secession show evidence of this broad scope of application of the principle of respect for territorial integrity. For, these resolutions – for instance concerning the situations in the Federal Republic of Yugoslavia, Croatia, Georgia and Sudan – call upon both State and non-State entities to comply with this principle.[190] With respect to the second line of reasoning, Argentina submitted that the theory of remedial secession "is nothing more than an argument made in doctrine, and which has not received any legal consecration". In this respect, it recalled the Supreme Court of Canada, which had noted that it remains questionable whether the concept of remedial secession "actually reflects an established international law standard".[191] Argentina subsequently held that while the safeguard clause of the Friendly Relations Declaration has been interpreted *a contrario* as legitimizing unilateral secession where the State lacks a government representing the whole people of the territory, "[i]t has never been interpreted in such a way by any competent body". Moreover, Argentina found that neither the *travaux préparatoires* nor practice permits such an inverted interpretation.[192] It therefore concluded that this doctrinal interpretation is flawed and that the right to self-determination of peoples does not provide support for an entitlement to unilateral secession.[193] Unfortunately, Argentina did not further elaborate on this argument. Based on *inter alia* the views expounded above and having considered the specific circumstances in the case of Kosovo, Argentina concluded that Kosovo's unilateral declaration of independence was not in accordance with international law.[194]

In a similar vein, China combined two lines of reasoning. China commenced its plea by stressing the point that the "right of self-determination recognized by

---

[188] International Court of Justice, *Accordance with International Law of the Unilateral Declaration of Independence by the Provisional Institutions of Self-Government of Kosovo (Request for Advisory Opinion)*, Written Statement of Argentina, 17 April 2009, at para. 69.

[189] *Ibid.*, at para. 75.

[190] *Ibid.*, at paras 75-80.

[191] *Ibid.*, at para. 85.

[192] *Ibid.*, at para. 97.

[193] International Court of Justice, *Accordance with International Law of the Unilateral Declaration of Independence by the Provisional Institutions of Self-Government of Kosovo (Request for Advisory Opinion)*, Written Comments of Argentina, 15 July 2009, at para. 59.

[194] International Court of Justice, *Accordance with International Law of the Unilateral Declaration of Independence by the Provisional Institutions of Self-Government of Kosovo (Request for Advisory Opinion)*, Written Statement of Argentina, 17 April 2009, at para. 132.

international law has its specially defined content and scope of application". It observed that the situations in which the right to self-determination was exercised either involved situations concerning the colonial context, alien subjugation or foreign occupation, or were endorsed by the General Assembly, Security Council or International Court of Justice.[195] Beyond such situations, the exercise of a right to (external) self-determination is more controversial. While some States have invoked a right to remedial secession, China pointed out that it did "not believe there is such a right under international law".[196] Three arguments were presented to substantiate this position. China's first and third arguments concerned the lack of proof for the existence of a right to remedial secession. China first held that the *travaux préparatoires* of the Friendly Relations Declaration disclose that the purpose of the safeguard clause was to ensure the respect for the sovereignty and territorial integrity of States rather than granting a "remedial right" to ethnic groups thus encouraging those sub-State entities to attempt to secede unilaterally.[197] Further, China argued that the *a contrario* interpretation of the Friendly Relations Declaration's safeguard clause:

> contravenes the objective and purpose of the Friendly Relations Declaration. Up to this day, no authoritative international legal bodies have ever adopted such a reading. No support can be found either in State practice or *opinio juris* for such an alleged right under customary international law.[198]

In essence, China's second argument involved the prevalence of the principle of territorial integrity over the right to self-determination. It contended that an entitlement to remedial secession is incompatible with the principles of State sovereignty and respect for territorial integrity. In this respect, it found that "if such a claim were permitted under international law, as it concerns the fundamental interests of States, there should have been positive and explicit provisions to that effect".[199] Since such a provision is lacking under international law, the principles of sovereignty and territorial integrity prevail over a purported right to unilateral secession. Bearing this in mind, and having assessed UN Security Council Resolution 1244 (1999),[200] China was of the opinion that the unilateral declaration of Kosovo was not in accordance with international law.

Cyprus adduced similar arguments, contending that there is insufficient proof for the present-day acknowledgement of a right to remedial secession. In this respect, it

---

[195] International Court of Justice, *Accordance with International Law of the Unilateral Declaration of Independence by the Provisional Institutions of Self-Government of Kosovo (Request for Advisory Opinion)*, Oral Statement of China (Xue), CR 2009/29, 7 December 2009, at para. 21.

[196] *Ibid.*, at para. 23.

[197] *Ibid.*, at para. 24.

[198] *Ibid.*, at para. 26.

[199] *Ibid.*, at para. 25.

[200] *Ibid.*, at paras 2-11.

first noted that an alleged right to remedial secession is sometimes inferred from an inverted reading of the safeguard clauses of the Friendly Relations Declaration and the Vienna Declaration and Programme of Action.[201] Cyprus made out a case against this interpretation:

> First, such a major right as this would require a positive source, rather than a mere *a contrario* reasoning. Second, the overwhelming majority of States participating in the drafting of the Declaration did not agree that peoples might have a right of secession from an existing State. Third, the provision refers back to the right of self-determination as set out in the 1960 Declaration, which, as we have noted, largely to colonial situations and does not refer to minorities within a State. Fourth, even if the provision does not rule out secession there are plenty of international principles that do [...]. In short, the provision does not recognize a right to secession. On the contrary, and at the most, it affirms the right of internal self-determination.[202]

While acknowledging that the claim that a remedial right to secession does exist has found some support in scholarly writings and in the abovementioned *a contrario* interpretation, Cyprus contended that such a claim is not reflected in State practice.[203] In this regard, it made reference to the ruling of the Supreme Court of Canada in the *Reference re Secession of Quebec*, in which it was concluded that it remains questionable whether the concept of remedial secession "actually reflects an established international law standard".[204] Moreover, it recalled the attempted secessions from Georgia by South Ossetia and Abkhazia, which were generally criticized as being violations of the principle of territorial integrity rather than viewed as examples of the lawful exercise of an entitlement to secession.[205] Further, Cyprus rejected the case of Bangladesh as supporting a claim of remedial secession.[206] All in all, Cyprus concluded that there is no right to secession as a last resort under contemporary international law. Having considered the relevant circumstances and applicable *lex specialis*, Cyprus accordingly submitted that the declaration of independence of Kosovo was inconsistent with international law.[207]

Romania's arguments opposing the existence of a right to remedial secession are illustrative for the present purposes as well. In its pleadings, it recognized that:

---

[201] International Court of Justice, *Accordance with International Law of the Unilateral Declaration of Independence by the Provisional Institutions of Self-Government of Kosovo (Request for Advisory Opinion)*, Written Statement of Cyprus, 3 April 2009, at paras 140-142.

[202] *Ibid.*, at para. 142.

[203] *Ibid.*, at para. 143.

[204] *Ibid.*, at para. 143.

[205] *Ibid.*, at para. 144.

[206] *Ibid.*, at para. 145.

[207] *Ibid.*, at para. 193.

there is a constant need and endless search for a balanced solution between the principles of sovereignty and territorial integrity, on the one hand, and the principles of equal rights and self-determination of peoples, on the other.[208]

Bearing in mind this balancing exercise, Romania observed that doctrine has formulated the concept of remedial secession, which applies to "parts of existing States in exceptional circumstances, in case those specific parts are denied a meaningful exercise of the right to self-determination".[209] In this respect, it noted that various sources have been adduced as supporting the theory of remedial secession, such as the safeguard clause of the Friendly Relations Declaration and the decision of the Supreme Court of Canada in the case on the secession of Quebec. Nevertheless, Romania argued that the theory of remedial secession "is not yet fully established in international law and is still wanting of meaningful State practice".[210] During its oral pleadings before the Court, Romania reiterated this position and adduced the:

continuing uncertainty in doctrine and case law as to the existence and scope of an exception to the rule concerning application of the principle of self-determination in the case of existing States.[211]

According to Romania, most authors still hold that a right to remedial secession "does not form part of international law as it stands".[212] It is noteworthy that, despite its rejection of the present-day existence of an entitlement to remedial secession, Romania subsequently set out the theory as formulated in literature and applied this to the case of Kosovo. In this respect, it came to the conclusion that Kosovo did not meet the requirements of the theory of remedial secession when it declared independence.[213]

Unsurprisingly, Serbia opposed the existence of a right to remedial secession in its submissions before the Court, as this position is obviously tailored to its own interests and aimed at self-preservation. Nevertheless, the arguments it set out to explain what it called "the flawed character of the purported justification of so-called 'remedial secession'" deserve to be addressed here due to their specificity. First, Serbia sought to demonstrate that the safeguard clause "is part of a firm practice of guaranteeing the

---

[208] International Court of Justice, *Accordance with International Law of the Unilateral Declaration of Independence by the Provisional Institutions of Self-Government of Kosovo (Request for Advisory Opinion)*, Written Statement of Romania, 14 April 2009, at para. 64.

[209] *Ibid.*, at para. 132.

[210] *Ibid.*, at para. 138.

[211] International Court of Justice, *Accordance with International Law of the Unilateral Declaration of Independence by the Provisional Institutions of Self-Government of Kosovo (Request for Advisory Opinion)*, Oral Statement of Romania (Aurescu), CR 2009/32, 10 December 2009, at para. 22.

[212] *Ibid.*, at para. 23.

[213] *Ibid.*, at paras 24-26.

preservation of the political unity and territorial integrity of independent States".[214] For this purpose, it referred to paragraph 6 of Resolution 1514 (XV) and analysed the safeguard clause of the Friendly Relations Declaration. Serbia held that the inclusion of this clause stemmed from the wish of various States to make explicit reference to the respect for the territorial integrity of States in connection to the principle of equal rights and self-determination of peoples.[215] Moreover, it advanced that both the safeguard clause and the relevant paragraph of Resolution 1514 (XV) exemplify an established practice of emphasizing the territorial integrity of States. In this respect, it referred to the international responses to the secessionist attempts by Katanga and Biafra.[216] Apart from the argument set out above, Serbia adduced a second argument, contending that an *a contrario* interpretation of the Friendly Relations Declaration's safeguard clause is not corroborated by "the terms of the paragraph, its context, its object and purpose, the *travaux préparatoires* and subsequent practice".[217] As Serbia alleged,

> [t]hose who read the safeguard clause as recognizing "remedial secession" adopt an erroneous interpretation of General Assembly resolution 2625 (XXV) by reading the paragraph backwards and implying a meaning that is not present in the text. The Declaration on Principles of International Law contains a positive statement: that there must be respect for the political unity and the territorial integrity of "States *conducting themselves* in compliance with the principle of equal rights and self-determination of peoples". It does not say that "States that do not conduct themselves in compliance with the principle of equal rights and self-determination of peoples could be the object of an action that would dismember or impair, totally or in part, their territorial integrity or political unity".[218]

An inverted reading of the safeguard clause is not only incompatible with a good faith interpretation of that paragraph, in addition, such reading conflicts with what follows from the *travaux préparatoires*, so Serbia stated. From these preparatory works, it follows that the safeguard clause was not intended to amend the scope of the principle. Rather, its purpose was "to expressly state or reaffirm something clearly, in order to avoid confusion or an incorrect interpretation of this right at issue".[219] Put differently, according to Serbia, the safeguard clause was intended to safeguard the territorial integrity and political unity of States in relation to the principle of equal rights

---

[214] International Court of Justice, *Accordance with International Law of the Unilateral Declaration of Independence by the Provisional Institutions of Self-Government of Kosovo (Request for Advisory Opinion)*, Written Statement of Serbia, 17 April 2009, at para. 589.

[215] *Ibid.*, at paras 590-594.

[216] *Ibid.*, at paras 595-600.

[217] *Ibid.*, at para. 589.

[218] *Ibid.*, at para. 604.

[219] *Ibid.*, at para. 606.

and self-determination of peoples, and not to provide for an entitlement to secession under circumstances.[220] In addition, Serbia argued that an *a contrario* interpretation of the Friendly Relations Declaration's safeguard clause is not supported by State practice either:

> To date there has not been a single instance where a State has been successfully created by the secession of territory from an existing State in circumstances where the secession was officially justified on the basis of the exercise of the right to self-determination by "remedial secession".[221]

While the cases of Bangladesh and Eritrea are sometimes adduced as successful examples of remedial secession, Serbia held that these cannot be regarded as such due to the consent of the parent States.[222] In its Written Comments, Serbia subsequently sought to refute the arguments adduced by those States supporting a right to remedial secession.[223] In sum, Serbia was of the firm opinion that:

> [t]hose States advancing the "remedial secession" doctrine have been unable to justify their position in legal terms, and have simply taken the doctrine for granted and have failed to explain how this doctrine forms part of positive international law. The simple reason for this is that it does not.[224]

Yet, even when assuming that a right to remedial secession does exist under international law, it would not be applicable to the case of Kosovo since the alleged requirements for such a right were no met, so it was argued. First, Serbia viewed the Kosovo Albanians not to constitute a 'people' entitled to self-determination.[225] Secondly, Serbia found that as the Kosovo Albanian population decided to create its own governmental institutions within Serbia, parallel to the apparatus at the central level, their right to internal self-determination could not be considered to have been violated by Serbia.[226]

A similar view regarding the lack of evidence for a right to remedial secession under positive international law was – albeit less extensively – presented by Azerbaijan. This State adduced that there is no evidence that contemporary international law

---

[220] *Ibid.*, at paras 607-608.

[221] *Ibid.*, at para. 613.

[222] *Ibid.*, at para. 613.

[223] International Court of Justice, *Accordance with International Law of the Unilateral Declaration of Independence by the Provisional Institutions of Self-Government of Kosovo (Request for Advisory Opinion)*, Written Comments of Serbia, 15 July 2009, at paras 342-349.

[224] *Ibid.*, at para. 312.

[225] International Court of Justice, *Accordance with International Law of the Unilateral Declaration of Independence by the Provisional Institutions of Self-Government of Kosovo (Request for Advisory Opinion)*, Written Statement of Serbia, 17 April 2009, at paras 570-588.

[226] *Ibid.*, at paras 639-649.

acknowledges a right to secession by way of sanction or remedy. It held that support for this stance was found in "both the textual analysis of the existing provisions on territorial integrity and self-determination and [in] State practice demonstrating the absence of any successful application of the so-called 'remedial secession'".[227] While it did not refer to the Friendly Relations Declaration explicitly, it seems that Azerbaijan rejected an *a contrario* interpretation of the safeguard clause in this document. In view of this, Azerbaijan noted that "one should be seriously concerned about the attempted unilateral solution of the Kosovo problem through the declaration of independence by its Provisional Institutions of Self-Government".[228]

A number of other States have principally focused on the argument concerning the incompatibility of an entitlement to secession – whether remedial or not – with the principle of respect for the territorial integrity of States. While this argument was generally substantiated less extensively in the submissions before the Court than the argument concerning the lack of evidence for a right to remedial secession under positive international law, some States have elaborated on this particular position as well. Spain, for instance, asserted that "international law has not recognized a general right of peoples unilaterally to declare secession from a State"[229] and emphasized the fundamental and absolute character of the principle of respect for State sovereignty and territorial integrity. After an analysis of the relevant provisions of the UN Charter and the Friendly Relations Declaration, Spain stated that this principle is part of what it called the "essential, non-derogable core of the basic principles of international law" as recorded in these documents.[230] In addition, Spain recalled the acknowledgement of sovereignty and territorial integrity as fundamental principles of the international system as stated in other international instruments, such as the Helsinki Final Act, the Charter of Paris and the Treaty of the European Union.[231] Subsequently, it made reference to the practice of the Security Council, in the context of internal armed conflicts during which serious breaches of human rights and humanitarian law were committed by the parties involved.[232] Spain found that "the Security Council has repeatedly and constantly maintained a position of unequivocal support and

---

[227] International Court of Justice, *Accordance with International Law of the Unilateral Declaration of Independence by the Provisional Institutions of Self-Government of Kosovo (Request for Advisory Opinion)*, Oral Statement of Azerbaijan (Mehdiyev), CR 2009/27, 3 December 2009, at para. 40.

[228] International Court of Justice, *Accordance with International Law of the Unilateral Declaration of Independence by the Provisional Institutions of Self-Government of Kosovo (Request for Advisory Opinion)*, Written Statement of Azerbaijan, 17 April 2009, at para. 27.

[229] International Court of Justice, *Accordance with International Law of the Unilateral Declaration of Independence by the Provisional Institutions of Self-Government of Kosovo (Request for Advisory Opinion)*, Written Statement of Spain, 14 April 2009, at para. 24.

[230] *Ibid.*, at para. 25.

[231] *Ibid.*, at para. 26.

[232] *Ibid.*, at paras 30-33.

respect for the sovereignty and territorial integrity of the State".[233] In this connection, it emphasized that:

> secessionist tensions, the ethnic and religious dimension of some of the serious viola-
> tions of human rights against the civilian population committed during the mentioned
> conflicts, or even the intervention of the International Criminal Court and other inter-
> national tribunals in these internal armed conflicts, all these have not altered the firm
> practice of the Security Council aimed at preserving the sovereignty and territorial
> integrity of the States concerned.[234]

In view of the strong support for the principle of respect for sovereignty and territorial integrity of States, both in theory and in practice, Spain held that this principle
cannot be "subservient to the exercise of an alleged right to self-determination exercised via a unilateral act".[235] In its Written Comments, Spain further elaborated on its
position regarding the right to self-determination of peoples. In this respect, it noted
that this right can be exercised through a variety of ways and should not simply be
equated with independence.[236] In the specific case of Kosovo, Spain considered the
right to self-determination to have been guaranteed internally, i.e. through the establishment of the international administration regime on the territory which guarantees
a system of self-governance for Kosovo. Therefore,

> [b]earing in mind this remedy fashioned by the international community in 1999,
> Spain considers that no other form of reaction or remedy is legally defensible, much
> less so through the secession-as-sanction or secession-as-remedy formulas, which [...]
> have no proper basis in international law, this being of particular bearing on the case
> of Kosovo.[237]

Strongly emphasizing the principle of territorial integrity, Iran argued that even in the
case of large-scale violations of human rights and humanitarian law, the territorial
integrity of States is to be observed and has always been observed in comparable situations. In this connection, Iran made reference to several resolutions of the UN Security Council in which the principle of territorial integrity was upheld. Thus, for Iran,

> the right to self-determination for minorities is an internal one and means their entitle-
> ment to democracy and human rights and does not involve any right to secession. This

---

[233] *Ibid.*, at para. 34.
[234] *Ibid.*, at para. 34.
[235] *Ibid.*, at para. 24.
[236] International Court of Justice, *Accordance with International Law of the Unilateral Declaration of Independence by the Provisional Institutions of Self-Government of Kosovo (Request for Advisory Opinion)*, Written Comments of Spain, 17 July 2009, at paras 7-8.
[237] *Ibid.*, at para. 8.

means that the right of self-determination is not a principle of exclusion or separation but a principle of inclusion.[238]

From this, it may be deduced that Iran considered the unilateral declaration of independence of Kosovo to infringe the territorial integrity of Serbia rather than to be an expression of the right to self-determination of the Kosovo Albanian population.

Likewise, in the opinion of Venezuela, the principle of respect for the sovereignty and territorial integrity of States is absolute. It asserted that it is clear from the Friendly Relations Declaration "that the right of peoples to self-determination cannot go against the territorial integrity of sovereign States".[239] Therefore, minorities within a State can merely exercise their right to self-determination internally, not externally through unilateral secession.[240] According to Venezuela, such external self-determination may only be exercised by territories which have been "subject to a regime of colonization" or are independent republics. Obviously, these conditions were not met in the case of Kosovo.[241] Thus, as the right to self-determination could not provide for a lawful basis for Kosovo's unilateral declaration of independence and this attempt at secession violated Serbia's territorial integrity, Venezuela considered it to constitute a breach of international law.[242]

In addition to the two (principal) lines of argument set forth above, a third line of argument may be discerned. A few States expressed their opposition to the existence of a legal entitlement to remedial secession in less unequivocal terms, adducing what may be called the 'legal neutrality argument'. In this context, the submissions of Burundi, the Czech Republic, France, the United Kingdom and the United States may be mentioned. According to these States, international law remains 'neutral' as regards the issue of secession as it does neither explicitly permit, nor explicitly prohibit it. Under this view, an attempt to secede through a declaration of independence is considered to be a matter of fact rather than of law. As the Czech Republic aptly summarized this line of argument:

> [i]t is widely recognized in doctrine that contemporary international law does not know any rule prohibiting a declaration of independence or, more generally, a secession. International law neither prohibits nor promotes secession; it does, however, take new

---

[238] International Court of Justice, *Accordance with International Law of the Unilateral Declaration of Independence by the Provisional Institutions of Self-Government of Kosovo (Request for Advisory Opinion)*, Written Statement of Iran, 17 April 2009, at para. 4.1.

[239] International Court of Justice, *Accordance with International Law of the Unilateral Declaration of Independence by the Provisional Institutions of Self-Government of Kosovo (Request for Advisory Opinion)*, Oral Statement of Venezuela (Fleming), CR 2009/33, 11 December 2009, at para. 22.

[240] *Ibid.*, at para. 25.

[241] *Ibid.*, at para. 26.

[242] *Ibid.*, at paras 38-40.

factual situations into account and accepts the political reality of a successful secession. In that sense, secession is considered "a *legally neutral act* the consequences of which are regulated internationally".[243]

Similar views were presented by Burundi,[244] France[245] and the United Kingdom.[246] The United States likewise referred to the neutrality of international law towards situations concerning attempts to secede through declarations of independence. It noted that international law does not regulate those situations,[247] save those cases in which international law becomes relevant due to the specific circumstances which amount to a violation of a peremptory norm of *jus cogens*. Examples in this respect are the establishment of an apartheid regime through the declaration of independence, or cases in which the attempt at secession involves the threat or use of armed force by a third State.[248] While sharing the viewpoint that international law "does not regulate the creation of states as regards the exercise of the right to self-determination", Burundi went one step further and argued that violations of peremptory norms still have:

---

[243] International Court of Justice, *Accordance with International Law of the Unilateral Declaration of Independence by the Provisional Institutions of Self-Government of Kosovo (Request for Advisory Opinion)*, Written Statement of the Czech Republic, 14 April 2009, at p. 7 (emphasis added).

[244] International Court of Justice, *Accordance with International Law of the Unilateral Declaration of Independence by the Provisional Institutions of Self-Government of Kosovo (Request for Advisory Opinion)*, Oral Statement of Burundi (Barankitse), CR 2009/28, 4 December 2009, at para. 2.1.2: "The creation of a State is a matter of fact and cannot be the object of a judgment of validity".

[245] International Court of Justice, *Accordance with International Law of the Unilateral Declaration of Independence by the Provisional Institutions of Self-Government of Kosovo (Request for Advisory Opinion)*, Written Statement of France, 7 April 2009, at para. 2.8: "[W]hile is entirely clear that there is no right to secession in international law, it is equally apparent that international law does not prohibit secession, nor, consequently, a declaration of independence by part of a State's population".

[246] International Court of Justice, *Accordance with International Law of the Unilateral Declaration of Independence by the Provisional Institutions of Self-Government of Kosovo (Request for Advisory Opinion)*, Written Statement of the United Kingdom, 17 April 2009, at para. 5.13: "It is not surprising that existing States have generally felt an aversion to secession. This aversion has sometimes led them to adopt language suggesting the unlawfulness of secession as a matter of international law. Of course attempts at secession may well – as already noted – be contrary to the municipal law of the State concerned. [...] But, from the standpoint of international law there was, and is, no prohibition *per se* of secession".

[247] International Court of Justice, *Accordance with International Law of the Unilateral Declaration of Independence by the Provisional Institutions of Self-Government of Kosovo (Request for Advisory Opinion)*, Written Comments of the United States of America, 17 July 2009, at p. 13: "It is true that the international community is very cautious about secessionist attempts, especially when the situation is such that threats to international peace and security are manifest. Nevertheless, as a matter of law the international system neither authorises nor condemns such attempts, but rather stands *neutral*. Secession as such, therefore, is not contrary to international law."

[248] *Ibid.*

no consequence as regards validity, only as regards responsibility, for example with respect to the obligation not to recognize [...]. This is confirmed by practice, as the case of Rhodesia illustrates. Moreover, it is because international law does not validate the creation of States that secessions are almost always regarded, in doctrine, as pure questions of fact which are not subject to any judgment of validity as regards international law.[249]

Notwithstanding their subtle distinctions, as in the views of the aforementioned States, international law is considered to neither authorize nor proscribe secession, their 'legal neutrality argument' is tantamount to the implicit rejection of the existence of a positive right to remedial secession. Therefore, it is classified under this heading. Nevertheless, it is noteworthy that in contrast to the States which had explicitly opposed such a right, these States eventually concluded that Kosovo's declaration of independence and accompanying attempt to secede was *not* in violation of international law.[250] For, viewed at from this perspective, international law is generally considered to stand aloof in this respect.

3.1.2.2.2. Recapitulation

To sum up, two principal lines of argument were presented in the submissions opposing a right to remedial secession. With respect to the argument concerning the purported shortage of proof for the existence of a right to remedial secession under positive international law, the *a contrario* interpretation of the Friendly Relations Declaration's safeguard clause was primarily criticized on the basis of various well-established interpretation methods, thus considering the terms of the clause, its context, object and purpose, and drafting history. Moreover, the absence of State practice supporting the theory of remedial secession was put forward as an argument for repudiating the existence of such an entitlement. It was contended that there have been no instances in which a State was either successfully established through unilateral

---

[249] International Court of Justice, *Accordance with International Law of the Unilateral Declaration of Independence by the Provisional Institutions of Self-Government of Kosovo (Request for Advisory Opinion)*, Oral Statement of Burundi (Barankitse), CR 2009/28, 4 December 2009, at para. 2.1.2.

[250] See International Court of Justice, *Accordance with International Law of the Unilateral Declaration of Independence by the Provisional Institutions of Self-Government of Kosovo (Request for Advisory Opinion)*, Written Statement of the Czech Republic, 14 April 2009, at p. 12; International Court of Justice, *Accordance with International Law of the Unilateral Declaration of Independence by the Provisional Institutions of Self-Government of Kosovo (Request for Advisory Opinion)*, Written Statement of France, 7 April 2009, at para. 2.82; International Court of Justice, *Accordance with International Law of the Unilateral Declaration of Independence by the Provisional Institutions of Self-Government of Kosovo (Request for Advisory Opinion)*, Written Statement of the United Kingdom, 17 April 2009, at para. 6.72; International Court of Justice, *Accordance with International Law of the Unilateral Declaration of Independence by the Provisional Institutions of Self-Government of Kosovo (Request for Advisory Opinion)*, Written Statement of the United States of America, 17 April 2009, at p. 90.

secession which was justified on the basis of a right to remedial secession, or attempts at unilateral secession which remained unsuccessful due to the fact that the situation did not meet the requirements of a (perceived) right to remedial secession.

The argument regarding the prevalence or even absolute character of the principle of respect for the territorial integrity of States over the right to self-determination of peoples was generally substantiated less extensively. Nevertheless, those States which explained their argument did so by reference to the various documents in which the principle of territorial integrity is firmly established (e.g. the UN Charter and the Friendly Relations Declaration) and the fundamental nature and status of the principle within the international (legal) system. Moreover, a couple of States adduced the practice of the UN Security Council, which has clearly and consistently established and preserved the territorial integrity of States so far, even in the context of internal and secessionist conflicts. As such, the view that the principle of respect for the territorial integrity is merely applicable to the relationships between States was brushed aside. Argentina, for example, expressly argued that this fundamental principle is also applicable to international actors other than States.

In addition, a distinct yet minor line of argument was presented by a few States claiming the neutrality of international law *vis-à-vis* attempts to secede. Since international law neither expressly prohibits nor expressly permits secession, these States contended that international law remains 'neutral' towards the matter. This argument boils down to the implied denial of any right to remedial secession under contemporary international law.

On a general level, the arguments presented by the States in the present (i.e. second) category provided for a substantial counterweight against the position that a right to remedial secession does exist. With respect to the specific case of Kosovo, the arguments rejecting the existence of a right to remedial secession as set out above led most States in this class to designate Kosovo's unilateral declaration of independence and its attempt to secede as a violation of international law.

3.1.3. Conclusions on the International Responses to Kosovo's Declaration of Independence

This sub-section was devoted to a study of the international responses to Kosovo's unilateral declaration of independence with a view to examining the emergence of a customary right to remedial secession. To this end, the general responses of States were explored first. It was seen that the debates in the UN Security Council and General Assembly as well as the recognition texts overall did not disclose support for the existence of a right to remedial secession. Hardly any reference to the right to (external) self-determination was made and where this was done, it was done so only very summarily. Rather, the statements presented generally reflected an unaltered strong adherence to the traditional prerogatives of States, such as State sovereignty and territorial integrity, and stressed the need for a negotiated solution, thereby ruling out attempts at unilateral secession. Moreover, it was seen that States were primarily governed by political considerations rather than legal motives. Most States expected (the recognition of) a sovereign and independent Kosovo to promote and preserve peace and stability in the Balkans, and did not adduce an alleged right to self-determination or remedial secession as justification for their decision to recognize Kosovo. Thus, instead of revealing the acknowledgement of a right to remedial secession, the general responses to Kosovo's unilateral declaration of independence seem to reflect the traditional interpretation of the right to self-determination, within which the Westphalian concepts of State sovereignty and respect for the territorial integrity of States take precedence and the consent of the parent State is needed for secession to become permissible.

In contrast to these general responses, the written and oral proceedings before the International Court of Justice on Kosovo's unilateral declaration of independence demonstrated that there actually is some support for the thesis of remedial secession amongst States. Such a right has been clearly advocated by the Authors of the declaration of independence and by eleven States. They contended that contemporary international law acknowledges an entitlement to remedial secession on the basis of an *a contrario* interpretation of the safeguard clauses included in the Friendly Relations Declaration and Vienna Declaration and Programme of Action, the *Åland Islands* case and the ruling of the Canadian Supreme Court in its well-known *Reference re Secession of Quebec*, and some support in scholarly literature. These States argued that it follows from these sources that such a right to unilateral secession is warranted as *ultimum remedium* in cases where the central authorities of the State deny a people their right to internal self-determination. By contrast, other States rejected the presence of a right to remedial secession under positive international law. They generally did so on the basis of a purported lack of evidence for such a right and/or the supposed predominance of the principle of respect for the territorial integrity of States. Only a few States implicitly opposed the existence of a right to remedial secession by claiming the neutrality of international law towards the issue of secession.

Whatever the appraisal of the lines of arguments set out above, it should be noted that the positions of some States may be motivated by their own (geo-political) interests. A considerable number of States opposing the existence of a right to remedial secession were States which are dealing with secessionist entities on their respective territories as well. Examples in this respect are Argentina (Falkland Islands), Azerbaijan (Nagorno-Karabach), China (Taiwan, Tibet), Cyprus (Northern Cyprus) and Spain (Basque Country, Catalonia). As such, it may well be that their positions are motivated by self-interest rather than by true rejection of a legal entitlement to remedial secession.[251] Other States have special ties with sub-State groups aiming

---

[251] This was also observed by K. Caluwaert, *De toekomst van onafhankelijkheidsbewegingen en het recht op zelfbeschikking* (Master's Thesis, Ghent University 2010) at para. 128.

to secede and therefore may be more inclined to support such an entitlement. An example in this respect is the Russian Federation, maintaining strong ties with the secessionist movements in Georgia, or Albania, being the kin-State of the Kosovo Albanian population. While these national interests may well explain the responses of States to Kosovo's unilateral declaration of independence, they do neither diminish nor increase the weight which is to be attached to these particular responses when examining the existence of a customary norm.

Furthermore, it is noteworthy that the 43 States which participated in the written and oral proceedings before the Court predominantly concerned Western (or even: European) States. Only a limited number of States which had submitted their views were of Asian, African or Latin-American origin and only one non-Western State (i.e. Jordan) adduced a right to remedial secession.[252] A greater participation from non-Western States would most likely have increased the opposition to the existence of an entitlement to remedial secession.[253] This deficit in the representativeness of the submissions in the advisory proceedings and the supposed effect thereof may also play a role in considering the views of States and weighing them for the purpose of determining a norm of customary international law.

3.2. Other Cases

As has been explained before, the case of Kosovo is of importance for the present study in different respects. In addition to the case of Kosovo, some other instances beyond the context of post-colonial State creation might be seen to be relevant with respect to the question of the emergence of a customary right to remedial secession. A few cases have sometimes been suggested as disclosing State practice on this matter, in particular the creations of Bangladesh and Croatia.[254] These instances were

---

[252] The participating States were: Albania, Argentina, Austria, Azerbaijan, Belarus, Bolivia, Brazil, Bulgaria, Burundi, China, Cyprus, Croatia, Czech Republic, Denmark, Egypt, Estonia, Finland, France, Germany, Iran, Ireland, Japan, Jordan, Latvia, Libya, Luxembourg, Maldives, the Netherlands, Norway, Poland, Romania, Russian Federation, Saudi Arabia, Serbia, Sierra Leone, Slovakia, Slovenia, Spain, Switzerland, United Kingdom, United States of America, Venezuela and Vietnam. In addition to these States, the Authors of the Unilateral Declaration of Independence (Kosovo) participated in the proceedings. While Bahrain and the Lao People's Democratic Republic had expressed their intention to participate in the proceedings as well, they did not present their position before the Court.

[253] See also J. Summers, 'Kosovo: From Yugoslav Province to Disputed Independence' in J. Summers (ed.) *Kosovo: A Precedent? The Declaration of Independence, the Advisory Opinion and Implications for Statehood, Self-Determination and Minority Rights* (Martinus Nijhoff Publishers, Leiden/Boston 2011) at p. 44.

[254] See, for instance, Dugard and Raič, 'The Role of Recognition in the Law and Practice of Self-Determination' at pp. 120-130; Raič, *Statehood and the Law of Self-Determination* at pp. 332-333; C. Ryngaert and C.W. Griffioen, 'The Relevance of the Right to Self-Determination in the Kosovo Matter: In Partial Response to the Agora Papers' (2009) *Chinese Journal of International Law – Advance Access* at paras 24-27.

also mentioned during the advisory proceedings on Kosovo's declaration of independence, albeit without any further elaboration.[255] Some other examples which have occasionally been referred to as situations endorsing the doctrine of remedial secession are the emergence of Eritrea and the successor States of the former Soviet Union (USSR) and Socialist Federal Republic of Yugoslavia (SFRY). While these cases may ostensibly seem relevant for the present purposes, these latter instances will not be further considered here, as they are not sound examples of successful unilateral secession in the first place. This will be contended below.[256]

3.2.1. Bangladesh

The separation of Bangladesh (otherwise known as East Pakistan) from Pakistan (West Pakistan) in 1971 is frequently mentioned as an example of remedial secession and is sometimes even regarded as evidence for the existence of a right in this respect.[257] This case therefore merits closer examination. In 1947, the State of Pakistan was created out of the provinces which had previously belonged to British India and the Indian States with a majority Muslim population.[258] Geographically, Pakistan's territory was divided into two parts, with India situated in between. Moreover, East Pakistan and West Pakistan were worlds apart in historical, ethnic, cultural and linguistic respects as well. As Pavković and Radan aptly put it, "[t]he only aspect of social life which the two populations shared was that of Islam".[259] Further, in the decades following the creation of Pakistan, the East experienced an increasing domination of its politics and economy by the central government in the West.[260] As East Pakistan "suffered relatively severe and systematic discrimination" from the authorities in Islamabad,[261] tensions between both parts of Pakistan built up. The elections for the National Assembly of Pakistan held in December 1970 led to an overwhelming victory of the Bengali Awami League in East Pakistan, while the Pakistan People's Party won in the West. The election programme of the Awami League aimed at

---

[255] See International Court of Justice, *Accordance with International Law of the Unilateral Declaration of Independence by the Provisional Institutions of Self-Government of Kosovo (Request for Advisory Opinion)*, Oral Statement of the Netherlands (Lijnzaad), CR 2009/32, 10 December 2009, at para. 10.
[256] The cases will be addressed in chronological order.
[257] See, for instance, Dugard and Raič, 'The Role of Recognition in the Law and Practice of Self-Determination' at pp. 120-123; Griffioen, *Self-Determination as a Human Right. The Emergency Exit of Remedial Secession* at pp. 123-124; Raič, *Statehood and the Law of Self-Determination* at pp. 340-342; Ryngaert and Griffioen, 'The Relevance of the Right to Self-Determination in the Kosovo Matter: In Partial Response to the Agora Papers' at para. 24.
[258] A. Pavković and P. Radan, *Creating New States: Theory and Practice of Secession* (Ashgate Publishing, Aldershot 2007) at p. 103.
[259] *Ibid.* at p. 104.
[260] V.P. Nanda, 'Self-Determination Outside the Colonial Context: The Birth of Bangladesh in Retrospect' (1979) 1 *Houston Journal of International Law* 71 at p. 72.
[261] Crawford, *The Creation of States in International Law* at p. 140.

introducing a federal structure in Pakistan, thus granting full autonomy to the East. However, due to fear of a majority in the National Assembly and the federalization of Pakistan, the central government suspended the National Assembly's inaugural session in March 1971. Mass demonstrations from the side of the Bengali population in the East followed and soon the wish for mere autonomy converted into a desire of full independence.[262] The central authorities subsequently responded with large-scale military actions to crush the resistance and "initiated a reign of terror throughout East Pakistan",[263] which according to some even culminated in (selective) genocide.[264] On 10 April 1971, the Awami League proclaimed the independence of East Pakistan while still being in armed conflict with the military forces of the central government. As the violence and repression of the Bengalis continued and about ten million refugees crossed the border with neighbouring India, India eventually intervened early December 1971 to fight the forces of Pakistan's central government in both East and West Pakistan. The UN General Assembly soon adopted Resolution 2793 (XXVI), which *inter alia* called for the withdrawal of Indian forces, but did not make any reference to the right to self-determination or an entitlement to secession of the East.[265] After two weeks of war, the Pakistani forces in the East surrendered and India proclaimed a ceasefire in the West.[266] Meanwhile, India and Bhutan had already recognized the new State of Bangladesh. As soon as it became clear that the governmental forces were defeated, more States expressed the recognition of Bangladesh, even though the Indian military did not leave the territory until the end of March 1972. Most States, however, only recognized Bangladesh after Pakistan had granted its recognition on 22 February 1974.[267] Bangladesh was admitted to the UN in September of that same year.[268]

---

[262] See Nanda, 'Self-Determination Outside the Colonial Context: The Birth of Bangladesh in Retrospect' at pp. 73-74; Pavković and Radan, *Creating New States: Theory and Practice of Secession* at pp. 105-108.

[263] Nanda, 'Self-Determination Outside the Colonial Context: The Birth of Bangladesh in Retrospect' at p. 74.

[264] See, for instance, Crawford, *The Creation of States in International Law* at p. 141; Pavković and Radan, *Creating New States: Theory and Practice of Secession* at p. 108 (noting that news reports on genocide "proved to be much exaggerated"). For an elaborate documentation of the atrocities, see International Commission of Jurists, 'East Pakistan Staff Study' (1972) 8 *International Commission of Jurists Review* 23 at pp. 26-41.

[265] UN General Assembly Resolution 2793 (XXVI) (*Question considered by the Security Council at its 1606th, 1607th and 1608th meetings on 4, 5 and 6 December 1971*), UN Doc. A/Res/2793 (XXVI), 7 December 1971. The resolution was adopted by 104 votes in favour, 11 against, and 10 abstentions.

[266] See Crawford, *The Creation of States in International Law* at p. 141; Nanda, 'Self-Determination Outside the Colonial Context: The Birth of Bangladesh in Retrospect' at p. 74; Pavković and Radan, *Creating New States: Theory and Practice of Secession* at p. 108; Vidmar, 'Remedial Secession in International Law: Theory and (Lack of) Practice' at p. 43.

[267] Pavković and Radan, *Creating New States: Theory and Practice of Secession* at p. 108.

[268] See UN UN Security Council Resolution 351 (1974) (*New Member: Bangladesh*), UN Doc. S/Res/351 (1974), 10 June 1974; UN General Assembly Resolution 3203 (XXIX) (*Admission of the*

In view of the events outlined above, it appears that the breakaway of Bangladesh from Pakistan initially constituted a case of unilateral secession as the consent of the parent State was obviously lacking. But while the circumstances leading to the declaration of independence involved oppression and gross human rights violations, it remains open to question whether it can actually be classified as a case in which a right to remedial secession was accepted. Several arguments may be adduced in this respect. First, it has been argued that the Indian army's defeat of Pakistan "merely produced a *fait accompli*, which in the circumstances other States had not alternative but to accept".[269] Put differently, had the Indian military not intervened and ousted the forces of Pakistan's central government from the territory of Bangladesh, it is unlikely that other States would have recognized it.[270] In a similar vein, it should be noted that although the human rights violations in East Pakistan and the news reports of genocide may be said to have led to international sympathy for the declaration of independence, it did not lead to recognition.[271] In fact, most States only appeared willing to grant recognition to the newly proclaimed State after Pakistan had eventually recognized it.

In view of this and considering the silence as regards the existence of any legal entitlement to unilateral secession, it appears that the resignation and acknowledgement of the situation by the parent State were decisive for the international community's decision to recognize instead of the mere fact of oppression and gross human rights violations taking place on the territory. Thus, while in view of the circumstances, the case of Bangladesh arguably had the potential of becoming an example of remedial secession,[272] it was not recognized as a case of unilateral secession by the international community and does not provide for unequivocal support for the thesis that a right to remedial secession does indeed exist. Rather, the case of Bangladesh seems to suggest that the international community did not consider such an entitlement to exist at that time.[273]

People's Republic of Bangladesh to membership in the United Nations), UN Doc. A/Res/3203 (XXIX), 17 September 1974.

[269] Crawford, *The Creation of States in International Law* at p. 393.

[270] Pavković and Radan, *Creating New States: Theory and Practice of Secession* at p. 108.

[271] *Ibid.* at p. 108.

[272] Yet, even when assuming that a right to remedial secession did exist at that time, it remains unlikely that the case of Bangladesh fulfilled the preconditions for the exercise of such a right. For, it is highly questionable whether the secession from Pakistan could be regarded as an *ultimum remedium*, since no (international) negotiation process was pursued to settle the dispute internally and implement the right to self-determination through means short of secession.

[273] See also Vidmar, 'Remedial Secession in International Law: Theory and (Lack of) Practice' at p. 43. For a different conclusion, see Griffioen, *Self-Determination as a Human Right. The Emergency Exit of Remedial Secession* at pp. 123-124.

3.2.2. Eritrea

The secession of Eritrea from Ethiopia in 1993, to start with, presented an example of *consensual* secession rather than *unilateral* secession. Eritrea's struggle for independence is to be seen against the backdrop of a colonial history.[274] Eritrea had been a colony of Italy since 1890, after which Eritrea was administered by the United Kingdom under a trusteeship. After World War II, the victors were to decide on the disposition of the colonies of the defeated powers. As they could not come to an agreement, the matter was referred to the United Nations, which therefore created an Ethiopian/Eritrean federation in 1952 as an attempt to meet Eritrea's demand for self-determination.[275] However, Ethiopia's Emperor Haile Selassie unilaterally dissolved the federal structure after a decade and annexed Eritrea. In response to this act, the Eritrean Liberation Front (ELF) and the Eritrean People's Liberation Front (EPLF) were formed.[276] When in 1974 Emperor Haile Selassie was ousted during a coup, a Marxist military regime came to power in Ethiopia, led by Menghistu Haile Mariam. The ELF and the EPLF continued their struggle for independence, yet international recognition remained absent.[277] As Menghistu's regime was unable to control these movements, armed forces were sent into the country to terrify the population. Villages were burnt down or bombed, major offensives were initiated against the independence movements, and even incendiary devices were used during the conflict.[278] In 1991, however, the EPLF assisted an Ethiopian movement in overpowering the forces of Menghistu's regime in Eritrea. The Ethiopian transitional government which was established after the fall of Menghistu's regime acknowledged that the people of Ethiopia were entitled to self-determination and consented to the organization of a referendum on Eritrea's independence. The referendum, which was held in April 1993, was monitored by the UN and resulted in an overwhelming majority of 99.8 per cent of the Eritrean population opting for independence.[279] Consequently, Eritrea proclaimed its independence from Ethiopia without opposition by the Ethiopian

---

[274] For an in-depth discussion of the creation of Eritrea and its preceding struggle for independent State-hood, see R. Iyob, *The Eritrean Struggle for Independence: Domination, Resistance, Nationalism 1941-1993* (Cambridge University Press, Cambridge/New York 1995).

[275] See A. Cassese, *Self-Determination of Peoples. A Legal Reappraisal* (Cambridge University Press, Cambridge 1995) at p. 219; Crawford, *The Creation of States in International Law* at p. 402.

[276] See Raič, *Statehood and the Law of Self-Determination* at p. 315, footnote 31.

[277] Crawford, *The Creation of States in International Law* at p. 402.

[278] See, for instance, Human Rights Watch, *Ethiopia: "Mengistu has Decided to Burn us Like Wood" – Bombing of Civilians and Civilian Targets by the Airforce*, 24 July 1990, available at <http://www.hrw.org/reports/pdfs/e/ethiopia/ethiopia907.pdf>, last consulted on 21 September 2012.

[279] See Crawford, *The Creation of States in International Law* at p. 402; Raič, *Statehood and the Law of Self-Determination* at p. 315, footnote 31.

authorities. Within about a month, Eritrea was admitted to the United Nations with the support of Ethiopia's government.[280]

As such, the secession of Eritrea in 1993 cannot be seen as an example of unilateral secession, but rather as a case of secession with the consent of the parent State.[281] Accordingly, the concept of remedial secession cannot be seen to be applicable to the present case, even though the Eritrea's claim of independence was preceded by the oppression of and atrocities towards the Eritrean population and serious human rights violations on the territory.

3.2.3. The Baltic Republics (and the Other Successor States to the USSR)

As was noted elsewhere in the present study, the disintegration of the former Soviet Union in 1991 is generally regarded as a case of dissolution rather than secession. While some of the events leading to the break-up of the Soviet Union have been addressed previously,[282] it may be worth briefly recalling and emphasizing some features for the present purposes.[283] The disintegration of the Soviet Union can be seen as a two-phase process.[284]

The first phase involved the regaining of independence of the Baltic republics, which had been sovereign States during the inter-war period and, in that capacity, had been members of the League of Nations. However, as a consequence of the secret Molotov-Ribbentrop Pact, Estonia, Latvia and Lithuania were forcibly occupied and annexed by the Soviet Union in 1940.[285] While the annexation was never recognized *de jure*, most Western States accepted the Baltic republics as *de facto* constitutive republics of the Soviet Union.[286] In 1990, Lithuania unilaterally proclaimed independence, asserting a constitutional right to secede.[287] In early 1991, the Soviet Union attempted to force Lithuania to withdraw its declaration of independence, but

---

[280] See UN General Assembly Resolution 47/230 (*Admission of Eritrea to membership in the United Nations*), UN Doc. A/Res/47/230, 28 May 1993.

[281] See Cassese, *Self-Determination of Peoples. A Legal Reappraisal* at pp. 218-222; Crawford, *The Creation of States in International Law* at p. 402; Raič, *Statehood and the Law of Self-Determination* at p. 315, footnote 31.

[282] See Chapter III, Section 4.1.1, footnote 214.

[283] See, for instance, Cassese, *Self-Determination of Peoples. A Legal Reappraisal* at pp. 258-268; Crawford, *The Creation of States in International Law* at pp. 393-395; Raič, *Statehood and the Law of Self-Determination* at pp. 290-291 (footnote 261); Vidmar, 'Remedial Secession in International Law: Theory and (Lack of) Practice' at pp. 43-45.

[284] See Vidmar, 'Remedial Secession in International Law: Theory and (Lack of) Practice' at p. 43.

[285] Crawford, *The Creation of States in International Law* at pp. 393-394. For background information on the situation in the Baltic republics and the run-up to their proclamations of independence, see for instance, Pavković and Radan, *Creating New States: Theory and Practice of Secession* at pp. 131-135.

[286] See Cassese, *Self-Determination of Peoples. A Legal Reappraisal* at p. 262.

[287] Constitution of the Union of Soviet Socialist Republics, adopted on 7 October 1977, Article 72. See also Chapter III, Section 4.1.4.

to no avail: in a (retrospective) referendum held in February 1991, an overwhelming majority of more than 90 per cent of the votes were cast in support of independence from the Soviet Union.[288] Following a period of negotiations with the Soviet Union and referenda held amongst their respective populations, Estonia and Latvia declared independence in August 1991.[289] On 6 September of that same year, the State Council of the Soviet Union voted unanimously for the recognition of the three Baltic States. It may be observed that while this recognition was granted almost immediately after the declarations of independence of Estonia and Latvia, this recognition was only received eighteen months after Lithuania had proclaimed independence.[290] Be that as it may, the UN Security Council subsequently recommended the admission of these States to the UN.[291] In this respect, it was emphasized that their restoration of independence on the one hand, and the consent of the parties involved on the other:

> The independence of the Republic of Estonia, the Republic of Latvia and the Republic of Lithuania was regained peacefully, by means of dialogue, with the consent of the parties concerned, and in accordance with the wishes and aspirations of the three peoples. We can only welcome this development, which obviously represents progress in respecting the principles of the Charter of the United Nations and in attaining its objectives.[292]

According to James R. Crawford, the consent of the parent State was deemed crucial in this respect, as the admission of the Baltic States to the UN was not considered before the Soviet Union recognized them, even though the States had been illegally occupied and annexed.[293] Admittedly, a few States had recognized the independence of the Baltic States before the Soviet Union did so.[294] Likewise, the European Community collectively recognized the three States on 27 August 1991.[295] With regard to the responses of individual States, it was generally emphasized that "since the independence of the Baltic States had been unlawfully suppressed, they had the right

---

[288] Crawford, *The Creation of States in International Law* at p. 394.

[289] See *ibid.* at p. 394.

[290] See Vidmar, 'Remedial Secession in International Law: Theory and (Lack of) Practice' at p. 44.

[291] See UN Security Council Resolution 709 (1991) (*New member: Estonia*), UN Doc. S/Res/709 (1991), 12 September 1991; UN Security Council Resolution 710 (1991) (*New member: Latvia*), UN Doc. S/Res/710 (1991), 12 September 1991; UN Security Council Resolution 711 (1991) (*New member: Lithuania*), UN Doc. S/Res/711 (1991), 12 September 1991.

[292] See the statement of the President of the Security Council on behalf of the Member States: Security Council Official Records, UN Doc. S/PV/3007, 12 September 1991.

[293] Crawford, *The Creation of States in International Law* at p. 394.

[294] However, most States were reluctant to do so. According to Antonio Cassese, "[t]he reluctance on the part of Western States to [immediately] provide strong support for the Baltics undoubtedly stemmed from the widely held belief that a unified democratic Soviet Union was in the interest of the international community". See Cassese, *Self-Determination of Peoples. A Legal Reappraisal* at p. 264.

[295] See Vidmar, 'Remedial Secession in International Law: Theory and (Lack of) Practice' at p. 44.

of self-determination".[296] However, this right was not regarded as an entitlement to unilateral secession, but rather as a right "to resolve their future status through free negotiation with the Soviet authorities", thereby taking into consideration the rights and interests of both parties involved.[297] All in all, while this first phase of the disintegration of the Soviet Union might indeed be seen as a series of secessions – which ultimately resulted in the dissolution of the USSR – and while the unlawful suppression involved arguably raises the question of remedial secession, the independence of the Baltic States cannot be regarded as separate instances of successful unilateral secession. Such a conclusion is precluded by the fact that the Baltic States were not recognized by the international community until the Soviet Union consented to the independence of all three States.[298] Accordingly, this initial stage of the Soviet Union's disintegration does not show situations of successful unilateral secession which provide support for the existence of an entitlement to remedial secession.

The second phase of the disintegration of the Soviet Union concerned the breakaway of the twelve remaining (constituent) republics, which was motivated by the political crisis at the central level of the Soviet Union in the early 1990s.[299] For this reason, it has been suggested that it should be regarded as a primarily political process, rather than a process inspired by legal grounds such as a right to self-determination.[300] Before proclaiming independence, most of the twelve republics held referenda to consult their respective populations on the question of whether or not to separate from the Soviet Union.[301] Subsequently, the republics – Georgia excluded – held a couple of meetings during which declarations were adopted with the purpose of forming a Commonwealth of Independent States (CIS) and discontinuing the USSR.[302] The first meeting in this respect was the tripartite meeting of the Russian Federation, Ukraine and Belarus, held in Minsk on 8 December 1991 and resulting in the signing of the Agreement on the Establishment of the Commonwealth of Independent States.[303] This so-called Minsk Agreement was supplemented with the adoption of a protocol on 21 December 1991, by which the remaining republics of the Soviet Union (except for Georgia, which joined in 1993) accepted the extension of the CIS to their territories.[304] Later that day, the eleven republics adopted the Alma

---

[296] Crawford, *The Creation of States in International Law* at p. 394.

[297] See *ibid.* at pp. 394-395.

[298] See also Vidmar, 'Remedial Secession in International Law: Theory and (Lack of) Practice' at p. 44.

[299] See, for instance, Pavković and Radan, *Creating New States: Theory and Practice of Secession* at pp. 138-141.

[300] See Cassese, *Self-Determination of Peoples. A Legal Reappraisal* at p. 266.

[301] See *ibid.* at p. 266.

[302] See Vidmar, 'Remedial Secession in International Law: Theory and (Lack of) Practice' at p. 45.

[303] 'Agreement on the Establishment of the Commonwealth of Independent States', 8 December 1991, (1992) 31 *International Leal Materials: Current Documents* 143.

[304] 'Protocol to the Agreement on the Establishment of the Commonwealth of Independent States', 21 December 1991, (1992) 31 *International Legal Materials: Current Documents* 147.

Ata Declaration, which stated that "[w]ith the establishment of the Commonwealth of Independent States, the Union of Soviet Socialist Republics ceases to exist". Moreover, it was declared that the eleven newly established States would support the Russian Federation taking over the membership of the Soviet Union within the United Nations.[305] Accordingly, the continuity of the legal personality of the State was recognized and it is in view of this that it has sometimes been argued that the eleven republics had seceded from the Soviet Union rather than the latter having dissolved.[306] More importantly however, the course of events as outlined above demonstrates that the break-up of the Soviet Union and the creation of the various successor States were, first and foremost, the result of a consensual process. What is more, it appears that the international community of States found this consensual element to be of fundamental importance, as it readily recognized both the newly established States and the Russian Federation as continuing the Soviet Union's legal personality.[307] The European Community responded to the events by the prompt issuing of a Declaration on the "Guidelines on the Recognition of New States in Eastern Europe and in the Soviet Union",[308] which made reference to the principle of self-determination and formulated five conditions for recognition.[309] With these criteria – stressing *inter alia* commitment to the rule of law, democracy, human rights and guarantees for minority rights – it may be said that international recognition of the newly established States was made contingent upon the presence of internal self-determination.[310]

In sum, even though different conclusions might be drawn from a political perspective, when seen through a legal lens, the disintegration of the Soviet Union was

---

[305] 'Alma Ata Declaration', 21 December 1991, (1992) 31 *International Legal Materials* 148. See also Crawford, *The Creation of States in International Law* at p. 395, footnote 8.

[306] See Chapter III, Section 4.1.1.

[307] It is to be noted that the view that the Russian Federation is the 'continuator State' of the Soviet Union is generally accepted, albeit not unanimously. On this issue, see A. Nussberger, 'Russia' in R. Wolfrum (ed.) *Max Planck Encyclopedia of Public International law* (Oxford University Press, New York 2009) at paras 89-108.

[308] European Community, 'Declaration on Yugoslavia and on the "Guidelines on the Recognition of New States in Eastern Europe and in the Soviet Union in Eastern Europe and in the Soviet Union"', 16 December 1991, 31 *International Legal Materials* 1485 (1992).

[309] The five conditions listed in the Declaration were the following: "respect for the provisions of the Charter of the United Nations and the commitments subscribed to in the Final Act of Helsinki and in the Charter of Paris, especially with regard to the rule of law, democracy and human rights; guarantees for the rights of ethnic and national groups and minorities in accordance with the commitments subscribed to in the framework of the CSCE; respect for the inviolability of all frontiers which can only be changed by peaceful means and by common agreement; acceptance of all relevant commitments with regard to disarmament and nuclear non-proliferation as well as to security and regional stability; commitment to settle by agreement, including where appropriate by recourse to arbitration, all questions concerning State succession and regional disputes".

[310] For a similar observation, see Cassese, *Self-Determination of Peoples. A Legal Reappraisal* at pp. 267-268.

ultimately a consensual process.[311] As such, it cannot be regarded as a (successful) example of unilateral secession – not to mention remedial secession.

3.2.4. Croatia and Slovenia (and the Other Successor States to the SFRY)

The fragmentation of the SFRY is regularly noted in the context of the doctrine of remedial secession. The complexity of this multifaceted and violent process merits a more elaborate discussion of the events involved. In doing so, two important points will be made. First, it will be demonstrated that in the context of the collapse of the SFRY, merely the independence of Croatia and potentially also Slovenia may be seen to have constituted examples of unilateral secession. Secondly, it will be contended that while these cases of secession may have been remedial in character in view of the context in which they took place, they have not unequivocally been recognized as such by the international community. Therefore, they cannot be considered as cases providing conclusive support for the existence of a customary right to remedial secession.

The demise of the SFRY is generally seen to have started in 1990 and may be said to have ended with the Dayton-Paris Peace Agreement of 14 December 1995. While the background and context of these events are too complex to put in a nutshell, it should be observed that the break-up of the SFRY should be seen against the back-drop of economic decline and changes in power relations on the one hand, and an increased sense of nationalism and separatism by the population on the other. Hatred between three major ethnic groups within the SFRY – i.e. Muslims, Serbs, and Croats – grew stronger and turned into a bloody civil war involving gross human rights violations. Ultimately, these events culminated in the collapse of the SFRY.[312]

The first phase of the process of disintegration may be seen to involve the declarations of independence of Croatia and Slovenia on 25 June 1991. The withdrawal of the constitutional autonomy of both Kosovo and Vojvodina by the Milošević government in Serbia in 1989 combined with the establishment of a pro-Serb government in Montenegro led to an increasingly strong position of Serbia within the federation. In fact, this position made it possible for Serbia to outvote Croatia and Slovenia, as well as Macedonia in decision-making processes on the federal level. Combined with other factors, such as the "over-representation of Serbs in the federal civil service and army", and the "exploitation of the more wealthy republics of Croatia and

---

[311] See Vidmar, 'Remedial Secession in International Law: Theory and (Lack of) Practice' at p. 45.

[312] See Cassese, *Self-Determination of Peoples. A Legal Reappraisal* at pp. 268-269; S. Oeter, 'Dissolution of Yugoslavia' in R. Wolfrum (ed.) *Max Planck Encyclopedia of Public International Law* (fully updated online edn, Oxford University Press, New York 2011) at paras 10-33; Pavković and Radan, *Creating New States: Theory and Practice of Secession* at pp. 133-153; Raič, *Statehood and the Law of Self-Determination* at pp. 342-356.

Slovenia for the purpose of providing welfare benefits for Serbia",[313] this resulted in a call by Croatia and Slovenia for more autonomy within the federal structure of the SFRY.[314] This call met with fierce opposition on the part of Serbia, whose Communist government aimed at centralizing the federation rather than decentralizing it. Serbia and Montenegro's refusal to install the Croatian candidate for the post of federal President in May 1991 induced both Croatia and Slovenia to proclaim independence. Subsequently, aiming to put down the uprising, the Yugoslav National Army (YNA) invaded the two insurgent territories. The YNA withdrew from Slovenia shortly after, which may arguably be interpreted as the acquiescence in the emergence of an independent Slovenian republic.[315] In Croatia, however, troops remained active to support the Serb minority there. Extensive diplomatic efforts on the part of the European Community eventually led to the conclusion of the so-called Brioni Accord on 7 July 1991.[316] This provisional agreement involved a cease-fire, suspended the proclamations of independence of both Croatia and Slovenia for a period of three months, and included a commitment to start negotiations on the future of the Federation during this period. These undertakings were to be supervised by EC observers.[317] In spite of the conclusion of the Brioni Accord, the situation in Croatia soon escalated and developed into a full-scale civil war with the YNA and the Serb minority on Croatian territory fighting against the Croatians.[318] Consequently, serious crimes were reported, such as:

> widespread violations of human rights, including denial of the right to life, the destruction of towns and villages as well as of cultural and religious objects, and the 'ethnic cleansing' of Croats and other nationalities inhabiting the areas of Croatia in which Serbs constituted a majority or a substantial minority.[319]

Furthermore, in the autumn of 1991, YNA started bombarding the city of Dubrovnik. Due to the culmination of events, approximately 600,000 people in Croatia were

---

[313] Dugard and Raič, 'The Role of Recognition in the Law and Practice of Self-Determination' at pp. 123-124.

[314] See also M. Weller, 'The Self-Determination Trap' (2005) 4 *Ethnopolitics* 3 at p. 181; M. Weller, 'The International Response to the Dissolution of the Socialist Federal Republic of Yugoslavia' (1992) 86 *American Journal of International Law* 569 at pp. 569-570.

[315] See, for instance, Raič, *Statehood and the Law of Self-Determination* at pp. 332-333.

[316] *Joint Declaration of the EC Troika and the Parties Directly Concerned with the Yugoslav Crisis*, 7 July 1991, reproduced in: S. Trifunovska (ed.), *Yugoslavia Through Documents: From its Creation to its Dissolution* (Martinus Nijhoff Publishers, Dordrecht 1994) at pp. 311-315.

[317] Dugard and Raič, 'The Role of Recognition in the Law and Practice of Self-Determination' at p. 124; Oeter, 'Dissolution of Yugoslavia' at paras 15-16; Pavković and Radan, *Creating New States: Theory and Practice of Secession* at p. 148.

[318] Oeter, 'Dissolution of Yugoslavia' at para. 17.

[319] Dugard and Raič, 'The Role of Recognition in the Law and Practice of Self-Determination' at pp. 124-125 (and the sources referred to there).

displaced.[320] In early October 1991, Serbia, Montenegro, Vojvodina and Kosovo conducted a *coup* against the collective Presidency, as a result of which decisions within the Presidency would be taken on the basis of the votes of these four republics only and certain tasks were transferred from the Federal Parliament to the Presidency. In practice, this implied that the other republics were excluded from political participation within the Federation and virtually all power was usurped by Serbia and Montenegro. In response to these developments, practically immediately after the moratorium enshrined in the Brioni Accord had lapsed, Croatia reissued its declaration of independence on 8 October 1991.[321]

The proclamations of independence by Croatia and Slovenia and the subsequent ferocious war may be seen to have triggered the second phase of the process of disintegration as other constituent republics proclaimed their independence as well. In mid-October 1991, Bosnia-Herzegovina declared itself a sovereign State and in November of that year, Macedonia adopted a new constitution in which it claimed independence, thus bringing about the break-up of the SFRY.[322]

Having explained the two-phased collapse of the SFRY, the question arises as to how to evaluate these events in terms of the concept of remedial secession. For this purpose, it is important to consider international responses to the events outlined above. The international community primarily responded to the crisis on the territory through the Peace Conference on Yugoslavia, which was founded by the European Community (EC) on 27 August 1991 and chaired by Lord Carrington. The principal aim of this Conference was to draft a comprehensive treaty amongst the constituent republics of the SFRY for the purpose of terminating the conflict. This also implied the objective of seeking an accord on the "constitutional re-design of Yugoslavia".[323] Additionally, as part of the Conference, an arbitration committee presided by Robert Badinter was established for the purpose of giving advice on legal issues in connection with the Yugoslav crisis.[324] It is important to note that the reports of this so-called Badinter Arbitration Committee appear to have guided the stance of both the Member States of the European Community as regards the emergence of the successor States of the SFRY and, in the end, also of many Member States of the United Nations.[325] In its first report, Opinion No. 1, the Badinter Arbitration Committee was asked to answer the question of whether the declarations of independence by the Yugoslav republics which had already been issued or which would be issued in the future, should be regarded as States established as a consequence of secession or dissolution. The Badinter Arbitration Committee responded by concluding that the SFRY was "in

---

[320] *Ibid.* at p. 125.
[321] *Ibid.*
[322] Crawford, *The Creation of States in International Law* at p. 396.
[323] Pavković and Radan, *Creating New States: Theory and Practice of Secession* at p. 148.
[324] See also Chapter III, Section 4.1.4.
[325] Crawford, *The Creation of States in International Law* at p. 401.

the process of dissolution".[326] As has been contended previously in the present study, however, the contention that the SFRY had dissolved does not necessarily imply that the notion of secession is out of the question. Rather, it has been argued that as they did not involve consensual acts, the declaration of Croatia and possibly also Slovenia may be viewed as attempts at unilateral secession, which eventually led to the dissolution of the SFRY.[327] In this respect, it should be noted, however, that the unilateral character of the secession of Slovenia is more equivocal, as the SFRY may be said to have acquiesced in its separation. Moreover, the arguments the Badinter Arbitration Committee adduced for the view that the SFRY was dissolving were twofold: first, the Commission noted that four of the six constitutive republics had declared their independence, and secondly, that "[t]he composition and workings of the essential organs of the Federation [...] no longer met the criteria of participation and representatives inherent in a federal state".[328] This latter argument appears to refer to a lack of internal self-determination, as a consequence of which one might argue that the Badinter Arbitration Committee implicitly deemed the concept of remedial secession applicable to the situation at hand. In this context, however, it is to be emphasized that the Badinter Arbitration Committee had not acknowledged a prior right to independence for the constituent republics, for instance on the basis of a right to (external) self-determination. More correctly, from the arguments presented, it is to be deduced that the Badinter Arbitration Committee considered the break-up of the SFRY to be an irreversible process, as a consequence of which various independent republics emerged. The early recognition of these republics should be seen against the backdrop of the (political) facts on the ground rather than on the basis of a legal right to secession for each of the constituent republics.[329] This will be explained below.

Following Opinion No. 1 of the Badinter Arbitration Committee, the EC adopted the Guidelines on the Recognition of New States in Eastern Europe and in the Soviet Union on 16 December 1991.[330] These Guidelines stipulated several requirements for the recognition of the successor States of the SFRY and USSR, so as to ensure a

---

[326] Conference on Yugoslavia, Arbitration Commission, *Opinion No. 1*, 29 November 1991, reprinted as: International Conference on the Former Yugoslavia, 'Opinions No. 1-3 of the Arbitration Commission of the International Conference on Yugoslavia' at pp. 182-183, para. 3. It may be noted that in its Opinion No. 8, the Badinter Arbitration Committee considered the process of dissolution to be complete, as a result of which the SFRY had ceased to exist. See Conference on Yugoslavia, Arbitration Commission, *Opinion No. 8*, 4 July 1992, reprinted as: International Conference on the Former Yugoslavia, 'Opinions No. 4-10 of the Arbitration Commission of the International Conference on Yugoslavia' at pp. 87-88, at para. 4.

[327] See Chapter III, Section 4.1.4.

[328] Conference on Yugoslavia, Arbitration Commission, *Opinion No. 1*, 29 November 1991, reprinted as: International Conference on the Former Yugoslavia, 'Opinions No. 1-3 of the Arbitration Commission of the International Conference on Yugoslavia' at pp. 182-183, at paras 2(a) and 2(b).

[329] See Crawford, *The Creation of States in International Law* at p. 401.

[330] European Community, 'Declaration on Yugoslavia and on the "Guidelines on the Recognition of New States in Eastern Europe and in the Soviet Union in Eastern Europe and in the Soviet Union"', 16 December 1991, 31 *International Legal Materials* 1485 (1992).

coordinated process of recognition. Not only did the Guidelines make reference to "the normal standards of international practice" on State recognition, the document also introduced respect for the principle of self-determination, minority rights and existing boundaries as relevant criteria in this respect.[331] The newly proclaimed States were subsequently invited to submit an application for recognition in conformity with the terms of the Guidelines,[332] and with the exception of Serbia and Montenegro, all four constituent republics did do so.[333] Accordingly, these applications were forwarded to the Badinter Arbitration Committee, which issued opinions so as to advise the EC Member States on the question of whether or not to extend recognition to the newly declared States. After the Guidelines were issued, however, Germany announced that it would recognize both Croatia and Slovenia, notwithstanding whether or not the Badinter Arbitration Committee would recommend doing so. Yet, the Badinter Arbitration Committee was of the opinion that Croatia did not meet all requirements enshrined in the Guidelines.[334] It nonetheless decided – most likely influenced by the decision of Germany – to advise positively on recognition, provided that Croatia would take the necessary steps.[335] As a consequence, the European Community collectively recognized both Slovenia and Croatia on 15 January 1992,[336] leading to the subsequent recognition by many other States and, ultimately, the admission to the United Nations.[337] It has often been contended that the recognition of Croatia was premature since its government arguably did not exercise effective control over the whole territory, hence failing to meet the 'traditional' criteria for statehood as stipulated in the Montevideo Convention.[338]

---

[331] *Ibid.*

[332] European Community, 'Declaration on Yugoslavia and on the "Guidelines on the Recognition of New States in Eastern Europe and in the Soviet Union in Eastern Europe and in the Soviet Union"', 16 December 1991, 31 *International Legal Materials* 1485 (1992).

[333] Crawford, *The Creation of States in International Law* at p. 397.

[334] According to the Badinter Arbitration Committee, the Constitutional Act adopted by Croatia insufficiently safeguarded the protection of human rights and minority rights.

[335] Conference on Yugoslavia, Arbitration Commission, *Opinion No. 5 on the Recognition of the Republic of Croatia by the European Community and its Member States,* 11 January 1992, reprinted as: International Conference on the Former Yugoslavia, 'Opinions No. 4-10 of the Arbitration Commission of the International Conference on Yugoslavia' at para. 3. For the Badinter Arbitration Committee's (positive) advice on the recognition of Slovenia, see Conference on Yugoslavia, Arbitration Commission, *Opinion No. 7 on the Recognition of the Republic of Slovenia by the European Community and its Member States,* 11 January 1992, reprinted as: International Conference on the Former Yugoslavia, 'Opinions No. 4-10 of the Arbitration Commission of the International Conference on Yugoslavia' at pp. 80-84.

[336] European Communities, *Statement by the Presidency on Recognition of Yugoslav Republics,* EPC Press Release 9/92, 15 January 1992.

[337] See UN General Assembly Resolution 46/236 (*Admission of the Republic of Slovenia to membership in the United Nations*), UN Doc. A/Res/46/236, 22 May 1992; UN General Assembly Resolution 46/238 (*Admission of the Republic of Croatia to membership in the United Nations*), UN Doc. A/Res/46/238, 22 May 1992.

[338] See, for instance, Shaw, *International Law* at pp. 383-384.

What may be deduced from the above is that Croatia's attempt to secede indeed constituted an example of unilateral secession and may be seen to have been remedial in character due to the gross human rights violations committed on the territory by the parent State. Whether Slovenia's attempt may also be qualified as such is less obvious due to the SFRY's acquiescence in the situation. As noted before, if there is no unilateral secession, there can be no remedial secession either. In any event, the subsequent emergence of Croatia and Slovenia as independent States, however, was not accepted by the international community because of their remedial character and, thus, the acknowledgement of a right to remedial secession. Rather, it appears that both States were primarily recognized since their respective secessions and the disintegration of the SFRY as a whole were considered as a *fait accompli* and the criteria for statehood and recognition as incorporated in the Montevideo Convention and the EC Guidelines were met.[339] In sum, it is clear that these cases do not constitute conclusive evidence for the existence of a customary norm on remedial secession.[340]

3.2.5. Conclusions on the International Responses to Other Cases

While at times, the emergence of some particular States has been suggested as supporting the thesis of a right to remedial secession, the above review has demonstrated that State practice beyond decolonization does not disclose unequivocal support in this respect. Several points were made in this regard. First, a number of instances of State creation have been rejected as being accurate examples of unilateral secession. This includes the creations of Eritrea and the Baltic Republics and the other successor States to the USSR. The argument runs that if there is no situation of unilateral secession in the first place, there can be no case of remedial secession either,[341] these cases cannot be seen as providing support for the existence of a right to remedial secession. Secondly, the creation of Bangladesh and that of Croatia and Slovenia were considered more elaborately. It was found that it is questionable whether Slovenia could qualify as an example of unilateral secession in the first place, because of the central authorities' acquiescence in the situation. In contrast, both Bangladesh and Croatia positively constituted examples of unilateral secession, for the consent of the respective parent States was clearly lacking. While both had suffered from gross human rights violations committed by the parent State, and as such may be said to have been 'remedial' in character, it appeared that these claimant States were not accepted by the international community for this reason. Thus, although the emer-

---

[339] See also Crawford, *The Creation of States in International Law* at p. 401.

[340] For a similar conclusion, see Vidmar, 'Remedial Secession in International Law: Theory and (Lack of) Practice' at p. 47. For a contrasting view, see, for instance, Griffioen, *Self-Determination as a Human Right. The Emergency Exit of Remedial Secession* at p. 126.

[341] For a similar observation, see Vidmar, 'Remedial Secession in International Law: Theory and (Lack of) Practice' at p. 47.

gence of both Bangladesh and Croatia may potentially be understood on the basis of the doctrine of remedial secession, it would be going too far to contend that these cases present convincing evidence for the existence of an entitlement to remedial secession. In sum, it is to be concluded that – also beyond the case of Kosovo – the post-decolonization practice of State creation does not reflect obvious support for a right to remedial secession being rooted in State practice.

4. LEGAL APPRAISAL OF INTERNATIONAL RESPONSES TO ATTEMPTS AT UNILATERAL SECESSION: STATE PRACTICE AND *OPINIO JURIS*

Having explored the international responses to attempts at unilateral secession, it now becomes possible to assess to what extent a customary right to remedial secession has emerged. First and foremost, this will be done on the basis of the contemporary interpretation of the conventional approach towards customary international law as outlined previously in this respect. Subsequently, on a more subsidiary level, the human rights approach will be briefly considered in order to demonstrate whether adherence to this more progressive model will lead to a different conclusion regarding the existence of a customary norm. As was contended before, the essence of the contemporary interpretation of the conventional approach towards customary international law is that both State practice and *opinio juris* are required for the creation of a customary norm and that both elements are, in principle, considered to be equally important. Both constituents will be considered below, starting with State practice and subsequently addressing *opinio juris*.

4.1. State Practice

As was explained in the previous Chapter, both physical and verbal acts are generally acknowledged as manifestations of State practice. It was also noted that while these two manifestations are by no means completely interchangeable, the relative shortage with respect to the one manifestation may be counterbalanced by the strength of the other. How much weight is to be attributed to each of these is to be considered against the backdrop of the level of activity in the matter at hand.[342] In the present context, successful attempts at unilateral secession (as a remedy) are considered to constitute physical State practice, while verbal State practice is seen to include statements issued by States regarding the lawfulness of specific attempts at unilateral secession.[343] As such, physical and verbal acts are strongly related. It may even be argued that with respect to the practice of unilateral secession, verbal acts are a precondition

---

[342]   See Chapter V, Section 2.1.
[343]   By contrast, the existence of *opinio juris* may be derived from statements reflecting a *general opinion* on the lawfulness of unilateral secession.

for the emergence of physical acts. The significance of verbal State practice in this regard may also be seen to be confirmed by the fact that although there are dozens of secessionist movements worldwide, attempts – either successful or unsuccessful – to actually break away do not occur on a very regular basis. Therefore, since there is relatively little physical activity by States in the issue of unilateral secession, it is justified to attach more weight to verbal acts than to physical acts of States. The core question which needs to be answered now is whether this State practice is sufficiently dense for contributing to the establishment of a norm of customary international law. Put differently, is the available practice of States – both physical and verbal – virtually uniform as well as extensive and representative?[344] In view of the fact that a right to remedial secession would affect the sovereign prerogatives of States, it was argued that a high threshold is set in this respect.[345]

As was seen before, the creation of a number of States has sometimes been adduced as providing support for the thesis of a right to remedial secession: Bangladesh, Eritrea, the Baltic Republics, Croatia and Slovenia, and, most recently, Kosovo. It was found, however, that only three of these instances of State creation could be considered as sound examples of *unilateral* secession in the first place. These concerned the cases of Bangladesh, Croatia, and Kosovo. In addition to being unilateral, the secession of these entities could arguably be considered as 'remedial' in character due to their respective backgrounds of oppression and gross human rights violations which had taken place on their territories. By this line of reasoning, it may be contended that these instances constitute relevant physical State practice in the context of assessing the existence of a right to remedial secession.

It was also observed, however, that it could not be conclusively inferred from the responses of the international community that the success of these attempts to secede was actually a result of the acceptance and perceived applicability of an entitlement to remedial secession. Indeed, the international responses of States to Kosovo's unilateral declaration of independence have disclosed a certain body of verbal State practice in support of such a positive right to remedial secession. It was found that eight States contended that Kosovo's attempt to secede from Serbia was lawful on the basis of a right to secession as a remedy of last resort to the oppression and gross human rights violations to which the Kosovo Albanian population had been submitted under the regime of President Milošević.[346] Such verbal State practice, however, is very limited and has merely been reflected with respect to the case of Kosovo. In the context of other cases, no similar statements regarding the lawfulness of these attempts at unilateral secession were expressed. Rather, the international responses to the secessions of Bangladesh and Croatia appear to suggest that the international

---

[344] See Chapter V, Sections 2.1.1-2.1.4.
[345] See Chapter V, Section 4.
[346] These States comprised Albania, Finland, Germany, Ireland, Jordan, the Netherlands, Poland and Switzerland. See Section 3.1.2.1 of the present Chapter.

community of States sought to justify their recognition on different grounds than the existence of a right to remedial secession. As a consequence, it remains questionable whether there are any successful cases of remedial secession in practice to date.[347]

In view of the above, and considering the high threshold set in this respect due to the subject matter of the norm, it is evident that the practice of State creation beyond decolonization cannot be said to constitute dense State practice in support of a right to remedial secession. There is clearly too little convincing practice – both physical and verbal – to label it as being virtually uniform, extensive and representative. The shortage of relevant physical practice cannot be counterbalanced by the availability of verbal State practice on the matter either, as the latter is both insufficiently present and inconclusive as well. Thus, in sum, it is to be concluded that the available State practice does not meet the threshold of the contemporary interpretation of the conventional approach towards customary international law.

4.2. *Opinio Juris*

While it was seen there is no dense State practice in support of a right to remedial secession, it has sometimes been argued that "there is a substantial *opinio juris* on the lawfulness of remedial secession in the international community".[348] *Opinio juris*, being the general legal conviction of States, may in the present context be derived from the pronouncements of States regarding the lawfulness of remedial secession in general.[349] And indeed, the international responses by States to attempts at unilateral secession have reflected the belief of a number of States that present-day international law covers a right to unilateral secession as a remedy to persistent oppression and gross human rights violations. This observation particularly followed from the written and oral submissions of States during the advisory proceedings before the International Court of Justice on Kosovo's unilateral declaration of independence, which did not merely disclose the views of States with respect to the specific case of Kosovo – i.e. constituting verbal State practice – but also elaborated on the more general state of the law, or at least the state of the law as they perceived it. Against the background of the events regarding Kosovo, eleven States[350] (and the Authors of the Unilateral Declaration of Independence, i.e. Kosovo) expressed their support for the existence of a right to remedial secession under contemporary international law in general. Most of these States elaborated on the matter by explaining their arguments

---

[347] This is notwithstanding the question of whether Kosovo can, at present, be regarded as a State under international law in the first place. See Section 3.1 of the present Chapter.

[348] See, for instance, Ryngaert and Griffioen, 'The Relevance of the Right to Self-Determination in the Kosovo Matter: In Partial Response to the Agora Papers' at para. 27.

[349] See Chapter V, Section 2.2.

[350] The States concerned were Albania, Estonia, Finland, Germany, Ireland, Jordan, the Netherlands, Poland, Slovenia, Switzerland and the Russian Federation.

in this respect, but Slovenia seemed to accept the existence of a right to remedial secession rather implicitly and refrained from underpinning its position.[351] As such, the value of Slovenia's opinion may be questioned.

The question subsequently presents itself as to whether the views of these States actually constitute sufficiently strong and unequivocal *opinio juris* for the purpose of the creation of a customary norm on the lawfulness of remedial secession. Given the subject matter of such a norm – affecting the sovereign rights of states – a high degree of proof is required for determining *opinio juris*. In this regard, it is important to recall that despite the body of support for the acceptance of a legal entitlement to remedial secession, the majority of States participating in the advisory proceedings held the opposite view. Eighteen States explicitly rejected the existence of a right to remedial secession under positive international law, thereby clearly reacting against those States contending that such a right can be discerned at present.[352] As has been expounded previously, two broad lines of argument were frequently adduced by this group of 18 States. The first line of argument concerned the perceived lack of evidence for the present-day acceptance of such a right, while the second line of argument involved the prevalence of the principle of respect for the territorial integrity of States.[353] Moreover, a third yet minor line of reasoning concerned the perceived neutrality of international law towards attempts to secede – an argument which is tantamount to the (implicit) rejection of a right to remedial secession.[354]

In this connection, reference may also be made to various other sources, such as the statements made during the debates on Kosovo in the UN Security Council and General Assembly, the texts formally recognizing Kosovo as an independent State, and the international reactions – or perhaps the lack thereof – to other attempts at unilateral secession as discussed in the present Chapter. Although these responses have not indisputably expressed *opinio juris* opposing the existence of a right to remedial secession, they have by no means disclosed traces of a general legal conviction supporting a right of remedial secession either. Rather, it may be argued that most of these responses even appear to reflect a traditional outlook on the right to self-determination, strongly reinforcing Westphalian principles and excluding the possibility of secession absent the approval of the parent State.

When considering the above, it may be admitted that amongst States, there is indeed some support for the thesis that remedial secession currently exists as a legal entitlement. At the same time, however, it is to be concluded no strong and

---

[351] See Section 3.1.2.1 of the present Chapter.
[352] These States were Argentina, Azerbaijan, Belarus, Bolivia, Brazil, China, Cyprus, Egypt, Iran, Japan, Libya, Norway, Romania, Serbia, Slovakia, Spain, Venezuela and Vietnam. See Section 3.1.2.2 of the present Chapter.
[353] See Section 3.1.2.2.1 of the present Chapter.
[354] The legal neutrality argument was adduced by the Czech Republic, France, the United Kingdom and the United States.

unequivocal *opinio juris* can be determined in this respect. Particularly the submissions of States during the advisory proceedings before the International Court of Justice on Kosovo have demonstrated that opinions on the matter are mixed and most States even have expressed the contrary view, i.e. that such a right does not exist under contemporary international law. In sum, there can be no other conclusion than that, at present, no substantial manifestation of *opinio juris* on the existence of a right to remedial secession under international law can be found.

4.3. Taking Stock: A Customary Right to Remedial Secession?

The preceding sections have demonstrated that the practice of post-decolonization State creation neither discloses sufficiently dense State practice for ascertaining a customary right to remedial secession, nor a body of strong and unequivocal *opinio juris* in this respect. As was contended previously, the contemporary interpretation of the conventional approach towards customary international law requires the presence of the objective as well as the subjective constituent of custom and considers both elements to be equally important. Moreover, while it acknowledges that the importance of physical and verbal State practice is to be seen in relation to the level of activity in the issue, it emphasizes that physical actions may not be completely absent. In view of this and the serious shortcomings of both State practice and *opinio juris* with respect to an alleged right to remedial secession, it is to be concluded that, so far, no such right has materialized under customary international law.

It has been argued by some authors, however, that support for the existence of such a customary norm can be found when adopting a more progressive approach towards customary international law.[355] Therefore, it may be interesting to see whether adherence to the liberal yet contentious human rights method towards custom would indeed lead to different conclusions on the issue of remedial secession. As explained in the previous Chapter,[356] the human rights approach entails the more important the interests of morality and humanity, the more weight may be attached to the subjective constituent when ascertaining norms of customary international law. In essence, this implies that when strong and unequivocal *opinio juris* is present, some discrepancies in State practice may be overlooked.[357] It was noted, however, that under this approach as well, *opinio juris* is to be confirmed by the availability of a certain amount of State practice. As the physical practice of States in the field of human

---

[355] See, for instance, Ryngaert and Griffioen, 'The Relevance of the Right to Self-Determination in the Kosovo Matter: In Partial Response to the Agora Papers' at para. 14.

[356] See Chapter V, Section 3.1.

[357] See J. Wouters and C. Ryngaert, 'Impact on the Process of the Formation of Customary International Law' in M.T. Kamminga and M. Scheinin (eds) *The Impact of Human Rights Law on General International Law* (Oxford University Press, Oxford 2009) at p. 112.

rights and humanitarian law is often incoherent, unreliable or completely absent, the focus in this respect may be on verbal rather than physical State practice.[358]

Bearing this in mind, and considering the findings of the present Chapter so far, it is to be concluded that even under the human rights method of ascertaining customary international law, the existence of a customary norm of remedial secession cannot be determined. It was seen that there is an apparent shortage of physical State practice on the matter and although the focus may be on the verbal acts of States, it was demonstrated that verbal practice is limited as well and has only been reflected with regard to the case of Kosovo. No similar statements on the lawfulness of attempts at unilateral secession were found with respect to other cases. The principal obstacle for ascertaining the materialization of a customary norm, however, involves the element of *opinio juris*. Although some *opinio juris* on the existence of a remedial right to unilateral secession was found, it was also seen that this is by no means substantial, strong and unequivocal, and that a significant body of opposition to this view was revealed. Hence, the available *opinio juris* is insufficient for compensating for the relative lack of State practice on this matter, as a result of which no customary norm of remedial secession can be said to have crystallized under the human rights method either.

5. CONCLUSIONS

This Chapter has dealt with the international responses to attempts at unilateral secession, most prominently with respect to Kosovo's unilateral declaration of independence. In doing so, general responses to Kosovo's attempt to secede from Serbia were considered first, involving debates in the UN Security Council and General Assembly as well as recognition texts. It was seen that reference to the right to (external) self-determination was scarcely made, not to mention the existence of a remedial right to unilateral secession. In contrast, strong support for the Westphalian principles of sovereignty and territorial integrity was expressed and the need for a mutually consented solution was highlighted. What is more, it was seen that political considerations, including questions of peace and stability, were guiding for most States. Secondly, the submissions of States before the International Court of Justice in the advisory proceedings were scrutinized. While it was seen that a number of States explicitly contended that a right to remedial secession is part and parcel of contemporary international law, most States explicitly opposed the existence of such an entitlement, arguing that there is no evidence in this respect and emphasizing the dominance of the principle of respect for the territorial integrity of States. As such, it was held that the case of Kosovo did not constitute an indisputable example of remedial secession. The creation of Bangladesh, Eritrea, the Baltic Republics (and the other successor

---

[358] See *ibid.* at p. 115.

States to the USSR), and Croatia and Slovenia (and the other successor States to the SFRY) demonstrated that international practice before Kosovo's attempt to secede does not reveal conclusive evidence for the existence of a right to remedial secession either.

The second part of the present Chapter was devoted to assessing the existence of a customary right to remedial secession on the basis of the aforementioned findings. For this purpose, the contemporary interpretation of the conventional approach towards customary international law as outlined in the previous Chapter was utilized. Considering the relevant State practice and *opinio juris* with respect to an alleged right to remedial secession, it was concluded that no such right currently exists under customary international law. Neither sufficiently dense State practice nor a body of strong and unequivocal *opinio juris* in support of a right to remedial secession was found. Even under the more liberal human rights approach, the constituents of customary international law were insufficiently present to ascertain a customary norm in this respect. In view of the state of the art, it seems that there is still a long way to go before a fully fledged customary right to remedial secession will materialize under international law – if ever.[359]

---

[359] See Chapter VII, Section 3.2 for some reflections on the possible future development of a right to remedial secession against the background of the humanization of the international legal order.

CHAPTER VII
RECAPITULATION, CONCLUSIONS, AND FINAL REFLECTIONS

"The transformation from international law as a State-centred system to an individual-centred system has not yet found a definitive new equilibrium"

Christian Tomuschat*

1. INTRODUCTION

The present study has sought to shed light on the contemporary meaning of the peoples' right to self-determination and, more specifically, the question of external self-determination after serious injustices. To this end, the following research question has been considered:

To what extent has a legal entitlement to 'remedial secession', i.e. a right to external self-determination as a remedy to serious injustices, emerged under contemporary international law?

The purpose of this closing chapter is twofold. First, it is to offer a recapitulation, highlighting the main findings from the previous chapters and culminating into the final conclusion of this study. Secondly, the aim of this chapter is to provide some final reflections on the concept of remedial secession, its alleged effectuation through recognition and possible future development.

2. A RIGHT TO REMEDIAL SECESSION?

Having analysed the content and meaning of the right to self-determination and having examined the sources of international law, it has been concluded that so far, a

---

*   C. Tomuschat, 'International Law: Ensuring the Survival of Mankind on the Eve of a New Century: General Course on Public International Law' (1999) 281 *Collected Courses of the Hague Academy of International Law (Recueil des Cours)* 9 at p. 162.

right to external self-determination as a remedy to serious injustices has not emerged under contemporary international law. It was seen that, although some support for such a right does exist, its theoretical foundations are rather weak and, even more importantly, that its main flaw is the lack of acknowledgement in State practice. This section will recapitulate the main findings of this study, which have led to the above-mentioned conclusion.

2.1. The Development of the Right to Self-Determination

With a view to determining the core meaning of the right to self-determination and answering the question of its generally accepted, contemporary meaning, the point of departure of the present study has been the historical development of the notion of self-determination. In Chapter II, it was seen that its roots may be found in the theories and ideologies underlying and arising from the American and French revolutions.[1] Notwithstanding these early traces, it was not until the aftermath of World War I that the concept of self-determination first appeared on the international stage.[2] Most prominently, T. Woodrow Wilson propagated self-determination in his proposal for a post-war settlement in 1918. While it had not yet emerged into a legal entitlement, it was seen that, due to Wilson's efforts, the concept of self-determination had evolved into a political principle on the international plane. This development was also reflected in the creation of the League of Nations' Mandate System, which may be viewed as being founded on the principle of self-determination. For, its objective was to protect the inhabitants of formerly colonized territories and to promote their development, thus guiding them towards self-government. Notwithstanding the fact that the concept of self-determination was used as a political principle in the aftermath of World War I, it was applied rather randomly. It first gained legal significance in the *Åland Islands* case in 1920, which is often considered as a landmark case in the development of the right to self-determination. In this case, the Commission of Jurists and the Committee of Rapporteurs denied self-determination by means of the separation of part of a territory as being a (general) right under positive international law. At the same time, however, the possibility of secession as a last resort option in cases of extreme oppression seemed to be recognized.

Chapter II showed that the concept of self-determination entered the second stage of its evolution after World War II, when it was included in the Charter of the United Nations.[3] As the Charter introduced self-determination as one of its principal purposes, this was considered to be an important step in the development of self-determination. Yet, while Articles 1(2) and 55 of the Charter explicitly referred

---

[1] See Chapter II, Section 2.
[2] See Chapter II, Section 3.1.
[3] See Chapter II, Section 3.2.

to self-determination, the precise legal status and content of the notion remained unclear. Some light was shed on this in the context of decolonization, when self-determination became a legal entitlement for colonial peoples. UN General Assembly Resolution 1514 (XV) is generally regarded as one of the most important contributions in the decolonization process, as it proclaimed the necessity to end colonialism and contended that all (colonial) peoples have the right to self-determination. As such, the right to self-determination was seen to involve a right to create an independent State (or to freely associate or integrate with another State), so as to enable the people to "freely determine their political status and freely pursue their economic, social and cultural development". Thus, in the context of decolonization, the right to self-determination was mainly considered to be implemented externally, and was seen to be realized as soon as a colonial territory became independent from its colonizer. The significance and elementary character of this right was highlighted by the International Court of Justice in the *East Timor* case, as it determined that the right to self-determination had evolved into a norm *erga omnes*, thus involving an obligation owed towards the international community of States as a whole. In this case, the Court did not explicitly note that the right to self-determination constitutes a peremptory norm. Nonetheless, it is often contended that, with respect to dependent territories, the right to self-determination has attained the status of *jus cogens*, meaning that no derogation from such norm is permitted. It was against the backdrop of the decolonization process as well that the International Court of Justice pronounced the core meaning of the right to self-determination. In its advisory opinion in the *Western Sahara* case, the Court stressed that the "essential feature of the right of self-determination" is that its "application requires a free and genuine expression of the will of the peoples concerned".[4] Seen in this light, the right to self-determination took on a new meaning after the decolonization period.

2.2. The Contemporary Meaning of the Right to Self-Determination

Beyond the decolonization process, the development of the right to self-determination continued. In this respect, as was demonstrated in Chapter III, two important developments can be discerned.[5] The first development concerned the continuing evolution of the legal status of self-determination. As a consequence of various new international instruments including the right to self-determination, such as common Article 1 of the International Human Rights Covenants of 1966 (ICCPR and ICESCR), it evolved into a fundamental legal entitlement. The second development involved the crystallization and acknowledgement of the two dimensions of self-determination. While it

---

[4]   International Court of Justice, *Western Sahara*, Advisory Opinion, ICJ Reports 1975, p. 12, at para. 55.
[5]   See Chapter III, Section 2.

was seen in Chapter II that, during the decolonization period, the right to self-determination was primarily considered to be realized externally, over recent decades, an internal dimension has emerged in State practice and international legal documents.[6] With the advent of the internal manifestation of the right to self-determination, a different mode of implementation became increasingly relevant. Self-determination is no longer merely realized through the formation of new States, but in addition, it requires a continuous implementation within the framework of existing States, in the relationship between a people and its government. Chapter III showed that the core meaning of this internal dimension may be defined as "the need to pay regard to the freely expressed will of peoples".[7] This translates into two principal requirements, i.e. the presence of a government representing the people and popular participation in the political decision-making process of the State are required. In addition to this, special arrangements such as autonomy, federalism or complex power-sharing may sometimes be necessary in order to ensure the internal dimension of the right to self-determination for all inhabitants of the territory. For, it was seen that not merely entire populations of existing States, but also sub-groups within such States and indigenous peoples may also be considered as subjects of the right to internal self-determination.

Notwithstanding the relatively recent emergence of the internal dimension of the right to self-determination and the emphasis on this intra-State aspect in contemporary legal and political documents, the more traditional, external dimension of the right to self-determination has maintained relevance today.[8] As pronounced in the UN Friendly Relations Declaration, this external dimension may be implemented through the peaceful dissolution of a State, the (re)union or merger of one State with another State, or through secession. This latter mode of external self-determination was defined as the establishment of a new independent State through the withdrawal of an integral part of the territory of an existing State from that State, carried out by the resident population of that part of the territory, either with or without prior consent of the parent State or domestic constitutional authorization.[9] When exercised by the population of a State as a whole, or when it concerns either a consensual or constitutional secession, external self-determination is not considered to be problematic under international law. In cases of consensual or constitutional separation, the right to secede is even founded on national rather than international law. However, the lawfulness of unilateral secession – i.e. the separation of part of a territory by a segment of the population in the absence of such prior consent or constitutional arrangement – is much more controversial. Chapter III showed that several circumstances may explain this controversy. First, international legal documents contain neither an

---

[6]   See Chapter III, Section 3.
[7]   International Court of Justice, *Western Sahara*, Advisory Opinion, ICJ Reports 1975, p. 12, at para. 59.
[8]   See Chapter III, Section 4.
[9]   See Chapter I, Section 3.3.1.

explicit entitlement to unilateral secession, nor an express prohibition thereof. Secondly, the disruptive effect of this mode of external self-determination may explain the debate on the lawfulness of unilateral secession. For, there appears to be a conflict between the traditional international legal principles of State sovereignty and respect for territorial integrity – aiming at maintaining the territorial *status quo* – on the one hand, and an alleged right to unilateral secession – effectuating territorial change – on the other. Not only would a right to unilateral secession disrupt the traditional international legal system, it might also lead to the excessive fragmentation of States, hence possibly threatening international or regional peace and stability. In view of this controversy and obscurity, it was found that the state of the art with respect to the question of a right to unilateral secession and, more specifically, unilateral secession as a remedy to serious injustices, merits closer examination.

2.3. Traces of a Right to Remedial Secession in Contemporary International Law

For assessing to what extent a remedial right to unilateral secession has emerged under contemporary international law, Chapter IV turned to the classical method of examining the sources of international law. Article 38(1) of the Statute of the International Court of Justice and the sources listed therein provided a starting point in this respect. It was explained that customary international law merits separate discussion due to the significance of the international practice of States for the development of the right to self-determination in general. Moreover, the conclusion that the theoretical basis of a right to remedial secession is rather fragile made it even more important to examine the existence of a customary norm in this respect in detail.

First, international conventions were considered with a view to finding traces of a right to unilateral secession.[10] In this respect, it was seen that the UN Charter, the 1966 International Human Rights Covenants, the 1978 Vienna Convention on Succession of States in Respect of Treaties and the International Convention on the Elimination of All Forms of Racial Discrimination (ICERD) offer little guidance with respect to the question of the existence of a right to unilateral secession. Neither the texts of these international documents, nor the drafting history or context were conclusive on this matter.

Subsequently, doctrine was examined.[11] It was demonstrated that, following the scholarly writings of Lee C. Buchheit and Antonio Cassese, a considerable number of authors supported the thesis that a right to unilateral secession does exist under exceptional circumstances. The arguments in this respect were primarily founded on two international instruments, i.e. the UN Friendly Relations Declaration (1970) and

---

[10] See Chapter IV, Section 2.1.
[11] See Chapter IV, Section 2.2.

the Vienna Declaration and Programme of Action (1993). Both documents contain a so-called safeguard clause, which affirms respect for the territorial integrity of States:

> conducting themselves in compliance with the principle of equal right and self-determination of peoples [...] and thus possessed of a government representing the whole people belonging to the territory without distinction as to race, creed or colour.[12]

Reading the safeguard clause *a contrario*, it might suggest that a State lacking a representative, non-discriminatory government would forfeit its right to territorial integrity. When interpreted as such, a right to unilateral secession would not be ruled out or, to put it even more strongly, the denial of a people's right to internal self-determination by the State would warrant a right to external self-determination by means of unilateral secession. In addition to the lack of internal self-determination, three parameters for the exercise of such remedial right to secession were frequently noted in literature, i.e. the presence of flagrant violations of fundamental human rights, structural discriminatory treatment and the exhaustion of all peaceful remedies. As such, unilateral secession is arguably considered to be a last resort remedy for such gross injustices committed by the mother State. Notwithstanding the relative consensus in this respect, it was also seen that those authors arguing in favour of a right to unilateral secession as a remedy are divided on the question of the subjects of such an entitlement. While remedial secession is generally considered to be a right of 'peoples', the detailed interpretation of this notion has remained problematic. In this respect, scholarship seems to be particularly divided on the question which minorities – numerical, linguistic, religious, ethnic, etc. – may be regarded as 'peoples' as the bearers of a right to unilateral secession. Furthermore, it should be recalled that, although indeed a substantial body of support for the existence of such a right to remedial secession was found in doctrine, it was also demonstrated that scholarship was equivocal on the matter. Particularly – though not exclusively – in the context of Kosovo's unilateral declaration of independence, it was seen that authors were rather reticent about claiming the present-day existence of a (remedial) right to unilateral secession, both in that specific case and more generally. In fact, various scholars have explicitly repudiated the thesis of such a right on a number of grounds. The inverted or *a contrario* reading of the safeguard clause, for instance, was rejected as being an inappropriate means of effectuating a fundamental change in the interpretation of one of the core principles of international law, i.e. that of territorial integrity. Most prominently, however, they opposed the existence of a right to unilateral or remedial secession by contending that authors have been unable to adduce adequate and convincing practical evidence for such a claim.

---

[12]   UN General Assembly Resolution 2625 (XXV) (*Declaration on Principles of International Law Concerning Friendly Relations and Co-operation Among States in Accordance with the Charter of the United Nations*), UN Doc. A/Res/2625 (XXV), 24 October 1970, Principle V, Para. 7.

Having concluded that a right to remedial secession has found significant – but by no means conclusive – support in doctrine, Chapter IV turned to an assessment of the decisions and opinions from both national and international judicial bodies.[13] It was demonstrated that, in various cases, reference was made to the acknowledgement of a right to remedial secession to a certain extent. Most of these decisions and opinions did not dwell at great length on the precise circumstances under which a right to unilateral secession may be lawfully exercised. Yet, some common features were discerned in this respect, i.e. the presence of massive human rights violations and the denial of the meaningful exercise of the right to internal self-determination. Notwithstanding the support expressed for the thesis that a right to remedial secession does exist under contemporary international law, some important points were made. First, it was observed that, in some cases, the judges relied on a tendency they had derived from literature instead of expressing their own opinion on the question of whether a right to unilateral or remedial secession exists under international law. The judgment of the Canadian Supreme Court in its *Reference re Secession of Quebec* constituted a clear example in this respect. Secondly, it was recalled that most courts have used very cautious language when claiming the existence of a right to unilateral or remedial secession under contemporary international law. In the *Reference re Secession of Quebec*, for instance, after identifying a trend in scholarly writings on the matter, the Canadian Supreme Court noted that it remains uncertain whether this alleged entitlement is actually rooted in positive international law. Restraint was also exercised by the International Court of Justice in its advisory opinion on Kosovo's unilateral declaration of independence, as it stressed that the opinions of States differed on this issue. Moreover, in the case of the *Katangese Peoples' Congress v. Zaire*, it was seen that the African Commission on Human and Peoples' Rights did not make explicit reference to a right to unilateral or remedial secession. Only when reading the decision of the African Commission *a contrario* could its argument possibly be interpreted as acknowledging a right to unilateral secession as a remedy to severe human rights violations and the denial of internal self-determination. Thirdly and finally, it was emphasized that no judicial body has actually granted a people the right to secede unilaterally in view of the circumstances at hand. As such, it was contended that the judicial acknowledgement of a remedial right to unilateral secession has remained theoretical only. In sum, it was concluded that judicial opinions and decisions remain rather ambiguous on the matter.

Next, general principles of (international) law were explored.[14] In doing so, two categories of general principles were discerned. First, general principles which appear in the majority of the various systems of municipal law were considered, such as the principles of good faith, proportionality and equity. It was contended that such

---

[13] See Chapter IV, Section 2.3.
[14] See Chapter IV, Section 2.4.

principles are background principles which can merely play a subsidiary role, as they are used in interpreting existing norms of international law in a specific situation. The second category involved general principles developed in international law and applicable to the relationships among States. In this respect, primarily the principles of respect for the territorial integrity of States and *uti possidetis juris* were scrutinized, as it is often contended that these fundamental principles of the international legal order clash with an alleged right to unilateral secession. Close scrutiny of these principles, however, demonstrated that these concepts are not completely irreconcilable. As to the principle of respect for the territorial integrity of States, it was first submitted that secessionist groups may be viewed as (additional) addressees of this principle and, thus, are considered to be bound by it. Moreover, it was contended that the principle of territorial integrity is by no means absolute. Hence, balancing the demands of territorial integrity on the one hand and self-determination on the other does leave some scope for the thesis of a remedial right to unilateral secession. As regards the principle of *uti possidetis juris*, it was first seen that it remains open to question whether it would bear on all situations involving the establishment of a new, independent State, including instances in which the seceding entity is not connected to a territory which is delimited by some kind of internal borders. Subsequently, it was found that where the principle does indeed apply, *uti possidetis juris* primarily determines the geographical delimitations of the new State rather than prohibiting the creation of a new State in general. Put differently, it would merely put geographical restrictions to the exercise of the right to (external) self-determination, but not restrict its general exercise. In addition to the principles of respect for the territorial integrity of States and *uti possidetis juris*, self-determination was briefly addressed in its capacity as a general principle of international law. While encompassing the core meaning of self-determination, it was argued that the principle merely functions as a very loose and all-embracing standard, which is of only limited value with respect to far-reaching questions as that of a right to remedial secession. In sum, it was concluded that general principles of (international) law do not provide a conclusive answer to the question of a present-day entitlement to remedial secession: they neither disclose clear traces of such a right, nor an unequivocal prohibition thereof.

Finally, having examined the sources of international law as listed in Article 38(1) of the Statute of the International Court of Justice – with the exception of custom, which was dealt with separately in Chapters V and VI – the final part of Chapter IV touched upon two supplementary (quasi-)sources of international law, that is the unilateral acts of States and acts of international organizations.[15] For the larger part, however, both sources were considered elsewhere in the present study. Unilateral acts of States relevant for the present purposes are formal recognition statements, which were addressed in the context of the international responses to attempts at unilateral

---

[15]   See Chapter IV, Section 2.5.

secession.[16] It was seen, however, that the statements recognizing Kosovo as an independent State did not disclose support for the existence of an entitlement to remedial secession. Rather, most States recognized Kosovo with a view to contributing to peace and stability in the region. The content of relevant acts of international organizations, such as the UN Friendly Relations Declaration and the Vienna Declaration and Programme of Action, were dealt with in the context of the development of the right to self-determination beyond decolonization and its contemporary meaning,[17] and against the backdrop of scholarly writings.[18] As such, it was seen that the safeguard clauses of these legally non-binding documents have sometimes been interpreted *a contrario* as recognizing a right to unilateral secession as a remedy to the denial of internal self-determination. Yet, considering the nature of the acts of international organizations, it was submitted that restraint is to be exercised in deriving legal norms from these acts, as they are frequently the result of political compromises and are generally not intended to create legally binding norms.[19]

In conclusion, Chapter IV demonstrated that contemporary international law shows some (theoretical) support for the existence of a remedial right to unilateral secession. It was seen that this support was primarily found in scholarly literature and, to a more limited extent, in judicial decisions and opinions. It was emphasized that, according to Article 38(1)(d) of the Statute of the International Court of Justice, these are subsidiary sources of international law and hence have supplementary rather than primary value. In addition, it was seen that the thesis of a right to remedial secession was first and foremost founded on an *a contrario* reading of the safeguard clause of the Friendly Relations Declaration and Vienna Declaration and Programme of Action. Such interpretation is not only rather progressive, but also controversial, primarily in view of the indeterminacy of the clause and its delicate relationship with the fundamental principle of territorial integrity. At this stage, it was concluded that the theoretical basis of a right to remedial secession is quite weak, making it even more pertinent to scrutinize whether the international practice of States reflects adequate and persuasive support for such an entitlement.[20] The subsequent Chapters were therefore devoted to answering the question as to what extent a remedial right to unilateral secession has emerged as a norm of customary international law.

---

[16] See Chapter VI, Section 3.1.1.
[17] See Chapter III, Sections 2.2. and 2.3.
[18] See Chapter IV, Section 2.2.
[19] See Chapter IV, Section 2.5.
[20] See Chapter IV, Section 3.

2.4. Preliminary Remarks on Assessing the Existence of a Customary Right to Remedial Secession

Before assessing to what extent a customary right to remedial secession has materialized, the concept of customary international law was introduced in Chapter V. This Chapter first elaborated on the two traditional constituents of customary international law, i.e. State practice and *opinio juris sive necessitatis* and demonstrated how these elements have traditionally been interpreted by the International Court of Justice and literature.[21] It was seen that the constituent of State practice is traditionally considered to function as the key element for the creation of norms of customary international law, while *opinio juris* evidences the conviction that such practice is required by a legal obligation. Moreover, it was explained that the practice of States merely contributes to the materialization of customary international law when this practice is sufficiently dense. This density may be determined by three factors: the uniformity, the extensiveness and representativeness, and possibly also the duration of the practice. When explained as such, the two constituents are both clearly distinctive elements which require separate proof for ascertaining customary law. However, it was demonstrated that today, the two constituents have increasingly grown towards one another. This is the result of an inclusive approach towards State practice, not merely taking into account the physical acts (and omissions) of States, but also their verbal acts. These latter acts are closely linked to the subjective constituent of custom, i.e. *opinio juris*, as the content of verbal acts often simultaneously reflects the State's legal conviction. This interrelatedness makes it difficult – and arguably largely theoretical – to separate the two elements of custom. In this connection, it was observed that there is a general tendency to infer *opinio juris* from the presence of State practice, provided that the available practice is sufficiently dense and unequivocal. This was labelled as the contemporary interpretation of the conventional approach.

In addition to the conventional model, Chapter V critically considered some progressive yet more controversial approaches towards determining customary international law, such as the sliding scale theory and the human rights approach.[22] In contrast to the conventional model emphasizing State practice, these progressive theories generally prioritize *opinio juris* over (physical) State practice. Moreover, these conceptions show a relationship between the substantive significance of the norm on the one hand, and the willingness to balance or even neglect inadequacies in the traditional constituents of custom – in particular physical State practice – on the other. In this regard, it appeared that the progressive models are strongly inspired by considerations of morality or humanity. While such approaches may indeed be attractive from a moral or humanitarian perspective, some serious objections on a conceptual,

---

[21] See Chapter V, Section 2.
[22] See Chapter V, Section 3.

methodological and more substantive level were raised. Most importantly, it was contended that the progressive approaches – primarily the human rights approach – stretch the nature of customary international law too far as their methodologies allow for ascertaining new customary norms whenever that is considered desirable from a moral or humanitarian perspective. In this regard, it appeared that the progressive approaches confuse international law as it currently is with what international law should ideally look like.

Considering the critique on the very progressive theories on the one hand, and given the evolution witnessed by the traditional model of customary international law on the other, Chapter V concluded that a contemporary interpretation of the conventional approach deserved to be applied when examining whether a customary right to remedial secession does exist.[23] With a view to upholding the distinction between *lex lata* and *lex ferenda*, this approach first and foremost requires the availability of State practice as well as *opinio juris* for ascertaining new norms of customary law. It acknowledges that State practice covers both physical and verbal acts of States, and that the shortage with respect to the one manifestation may be counterbalanced by the strength of the other. However, it was emphasized that the two manifestations of practice are not fully interchangeable as a consequence of which physical acts could be completely absent. Rather, the contemporary interpretation of the conventional approach accepts that the relative importance of physical and verbal practice may be seen in relation to the level of activity in the matter at hand, but nevertheless requires that physical practice is needed for the formation of customary law.

2.5. A Customary Right to Remedial Secession?

On the basis of the abovementioned preliminary remarks and the approach enunciated, Chapter VI was devoted to the exercise of assessing the emergence of a right to remedial secession under customary international law. Before actually considering international responses to attempts at unilateral secession, however, the relevance of recognition for the present purposes was explained.[24] In this respect, the two main schools of thought towards recognition, the constitutive and declaratory theories, were addressed.[25] Subsequently, the significance of recognition in the context of attempts at unilateral secession was expounded. It was submitted that while recognition is generally seen to be declaratory in nature, in cases of unilateral secession, virtually uniform recognition of the aspirant State by already existing States may well determine the ultimate success of the attempt at unilateral secession and thus, comprise evidence for statehood. As such, widespread recognition may under

---

[23] See Chapter V, Section 4.
[24] See Chapter VI, Section 2.
[25] See Chapter VI, Section 2.1.

certain circumstances have some constitutive effects, thus having a bearing on the development of State practice with respect to unilateral secession. Moreover, it was explained that individual recognition statements may disclose *opinio juris* or verbal State practice on the existence of a right to remedial secession, provided that such reference is made explicitly.[26]

Chapter VI then turned to an examination of the international responses to attempts at unilateral secession.[27] In this analysis, a key role was granted to Kosovo's attempt to secede from Serbia in 2008 and the international responses thereto.[28] For, Kosovo was not only often referred to as a test case for the present-day existence of a remedial right to unilateral secession considering the circumstances preceding its declaration of independence, but also provides unique insights in the contemporary views of States regarding a right to remedial secession. First, the general responses of States to Kosovo's unilateral declaration of independence were explored. Neither the debates in the UN Security Council and General Assembly nor the recognition texts of individual States reflected the acknowledgement of a remedial right to unilateral secession. Very few references to the right to (external) self-determination were made and where such reference was made, this was done very briefly and did not constitute the main argument. Instead, the general responses to Kosovo's attempted secession primarily demonstrated strong support for the principles of State sovereignty and respect for the territorial integrity of States as enshrined in the UN Charter and the (legal) framework created by UN Security Council Resolution 1244 (1999). In this connection, the statements frequently called for a mutually consented settlement of the issue, thereby (implicitly) condemning attempts at unilateral secession. Furthermore, it was observed that first and foremost, the responses of States were guided by non-legal considerations. The majority of States expected the creation and recognition of an independent Kosovo to contribute to the promotion and preservation of peace and stability in the region, and did not advance a right to self-determination or remedial secession as justification for Kosovo's independence or the recognition thereof.

In addition to these general responses, the written and oral submissions of States before the International Court of Justice in the advisory proceedings on Kosovo's unilateral declaration of independence were examined. It was demonstrated that the submissions in this respect revealed that there is some support for the thesis of a remedial right to unilateral secession. Several States unambiguously expressed the view that international law acknowledges a right to remedial secession. In general, this vision was founded on an *a contrario* reading of the safeguard clauses of the Friendly Relations Declaration and the Vienna Declaration and Programme of

---

[26]   See Chapter VI, Section 2.2.
[27]   See Chapter VI, Section 3.
[28]   See Chapter VI, Section 3.1.

Action, the *Åland Islands* case, the decision of the Supreme Court of Canada in the *Reference re Secession of Quebec*, and the support found in doctrine. Given the fact that references to practice were virtually absent, it was suggested that States did not consider international practice to provide strong proof of the existence of a right to remedial secession. Moreover, it was seen that, for most of these States, unilateral secession operated as an *ultimum remedium* in cases where the authorities of the State deny a people the exercise of their right to internal self-determination. Gross human rights violations were mentioned as well, either as a reflection of the lack of internal self-determination, or as a separate and additional precondition. It was found, however, that the majority of States participating in the advisory proceedings opposed the existence of a right to remedial secession. Theses States primarily contended that there is insufficient proof for the existence of such a right and/or claimed the prevalence of the principle of respect for the territorial integrity of States. A minor line of reasoning involved the alleged neutrality of international law as regards secession.

In addition to the case of Kosovo, Chapter VI considered several other cases which are sometimes suggested as upholding the thesis of a right to remedial secession.[29] It was demonstrated that international practice beyond the context of decolonization does not reveal strong and unambiguous support in this regard. First, some cases of State creation were repudiated as being sound examples of unilateral secession in the first place. In this respect, the cases of Eritrea and the Baltic Republics (and the other successor States to the USSR) were adduced. It was contended that if there is no case of unilateral secession in the first place, the concept of remedial secession cannot be seen to be applicable either. Consequently, it was concluded that the cases of Eritrea and the Baltic Republics cannot be seen to provide evidence for the existence of a right to remedial secession. Secondly, the cases of Bangladesh, Croatia and Slovenia were examined. It was argued that the cases of Bangladesh and Croatia indeed involved examples of unilateral secession in view of the lack of consent by the respective parent States. Moreover, the respective secessions may be said to have been 'remedial' in character, as they ensued from situations of persistent oppression and gross human rights violations by the parent State. Nonetheless, it appeared that both aspirant States were not accepted by the international community as a consequence of an alleged right to remedial secession, but rather for other reasons. Therefore, the cases of Bangladesh and Croatia cannot be seen to represent convincing examples of remedial secession, supporting the thesis that such a legal entitlement currently exists.

Having addressed various attempts at unilateral secession and the international responses thereto, it became possible to answer the question as to what extent a remedial right to unilateral secession has emerged under customary international law.[30]

---

[29]   See Chapter VI, Section 3.2.
[30]   See Chapter VI, Section 4.

For this purpose, the elements of State practice and *opinio juris* with respect to such a right were assessed. With regard to the objective constituent of custom, it was contended that only a couple of attempts at unilateral secession may potentially be seen to constitute relevant physical State practice on remedial secession and that verbal practice on this matter was merely found in the context of the case of Kosovo and even there to a only limited extent. It was argued that it remains uncertain whether there are any successful cases of remedial secession in practice so far. As to the subjective element of *opinio juris*, it was submitted that there is some body of *opinio juris* supporting the thesis that a right to remedial secession has emerged. It was concluded, however, that this body of *opinio juris* was by no means strong and unequivocal. In sum, it was seen that both constituents of custom are insufficiently present for ascertaining a customary right to remedial secession under the contemporary interpretation of the conventional approach towards customary international law. Even when endorsing the more liberal and progressive (though contested) human rights approach, which allows for inconsistencies in State practice to be overlooked when strong and unequivocal *opinio juris* is present, it was found that no customary right to remedial secession could be determined either.

2.6. Conclusions on a Right to Remedial Secession *De Lege Lata* and *De Lege Ferenda*

On the basis of the analysis in the present study as recapitulated above, general conclusions can now be drawn. In doing so, this section will distinguish between a right to remedial secession *de lege lata* on the one hand, and a right to remedial secession *de lege ferenda* on the other.

2.6.1. A Right to Remedial Secession De Lege Lata

Considering all findings of this study, it is to be concluded that the concept of external self-determination after serious injustices has not (yet) emerged as a legal entitlement under contemporary international law. It was seen that some support for such a right is indeed reflected in several sources of international law, most notably in the subsidiary sources of doctrinal writings and judicial decisions and opinions. However, this was deemed to be insufficient – in scope, in weight, as well as in persuasion – for labelling it as a positive legal entitlement today. The theoretical basis of a right to remedial secession is thus relatively weak and seems to be primarily prompted by considerations of morality and necessity, while international practice does not evidence convincing support for such a right either. Even when adopting the progressive human rights approach towards customary international law, it was seen that insufficient State practice and *opinio juris* are available for reaching the conclusion that remedial secession has emerged as a customary norm. At present, the right to self-determination does not allow for unilateral secession, but rather focuses on its internal dimension and is limited by the traditional core principles of international law, such as sovereignty and territorial integrity of the State. Put differently, self-determination claims first and foremost are to be implemented internally, i.e. within the framework of the existing State, and based on consent of the parent State. This may be realized through, for instance, the introduction of autonomy arrangements or possibly even complex power-sharing. Beyond the context of decolonization, self-determination in its external manifestation may only be exercised by peaceful dissolution, merger, (re)union, constitutional secession or consensual secession.

As such, it may be contended that the present international legal framework does not provide for a collective remedy for peoples oppressed and victimized by their State – at least not by means of unilateral secession. This is not to say, however, that there are no remedies whatsoever available under international law. Affected individuals may still claim individual human rights as enshrined in various international human rights covenants and mechanisms of minority protection may be used for enforcing minority rights. But at present, no remedial right to unilateral secession can be claimed.

2.6.2. A Right to Remedial Secession De Lege Ferenda

While it was demonstrated that to date, there is insufficient evidence of the existence of a legal entitlement to remedial secession under positive international law, it was also seen in this study that several sources of international law do reflect traces of such a right. From these traces, it appeared that some consensus exists on the contours of a right to remedial secession *de lege ferenda*. So while it is to be emphasized that this still deserves further discussion, elaboration and, most importantly, widespread support by the international community of States, a tentative framework for the possible future development of a right to remedial secession may be drafted on the basis of the previous Chapters. The traces of a right to remedial secession found in the sources of international law generally involve remedial secession as a mode of exercising the right to (external) self-determination. As such, it would operate as a qualified right rather than a primary right: it is commonly viewed as a right which would only arise in exceptional circumstances and when certain requirements – both substantive and procedural – have been met.

The first substantive requirement concerns the persistent denial of internal self-determination on the part of the central authorities of the (parent) State. More specifically, it would at least be required that the State persistently refuses to grant the people at hand participatory rights and a representative government before remedial secession may be lawful. As such, a strong link between the internal dimension of the right to self-determination and its external dimension was demonstrated in doctrine as well as judicial opinions and State practice. However, there are strong indications that the mere lack of internal self-determination will not suffice for secession to be lawful. In addition to this substantive prerequisite, two other factors were frequently noted in the traces of a right to remedial secession as well: the presence of gross human rights violations and discriminatory treatment of a people. Both factors are related to the requirement of the denial of internal self-determination and, as such, some scholars have contended that the fulfilment thereof may be derived from the lack of participatory rights and representative government. In general, however, the existence of flagrant breaches of fundamental human rights is seen to constitute a separate condition, thus raising the bar for activating a right to remedial secession to a high level. This additional parameter was broadly reflected in doctrine and judicial opinions as well as the statements of States supporting the remedial secession doctrine. The essential touchstone for a right to remedial secession, however, is that of the denial of internal self-determination.

In addition to the substantive prerequisites outlined above, a procedural requirement is to be met, requiring that remedial secession actually operates as an *ultimum remedium*. Put differently, this procedural element would necessitate the exhaustion of all effective and realistic remedies to settle the conflict peacefully within the framework of the existing State, before secession as a remedy may be warranted. Obviously, this would have to be considered on a case-by-case basis. In fact, what would be considered as a last resort remedy in the one situation might not be considered as such in the other. In some instances, the special modalities of implementing the right to self-determination internally, ranging from autonomy arrangements to complex power-sharing,[31] would still be seen to offer a realistic and effective alternative to secession, while in other, more grave and disrupted situations, these modalities would no longer be considered to offer a reasonable solution. In any event, given the sensitivity of the issue on the one hand, and the high threshold set for remedial secession on the other, it seems that international involvement in seeking peaceful alternatives to settle the conflict would be required as well, before all effective and realistic remedies may be said to be exhausted. In this respect, one may think of international involvement in the negotiations between the parent State and the secessionist entity – for instance as a facilitator or mediator, as was seen in the case of Kosovo – or in the form of recourse to international organizations or (judicial) bodies. Only then would the way to unilateral secession be open.

When marking the contours of a right to remedial secession *de lege ferenda*, it is to be recalled that there are some exceptional circumstances preventing the lawfulness of the exercise of such a right. Even when the parameters for the exercise of a right to remedial secession as set forth above are present, secession may not be lawful when violating a norm of *jus cogens*, such as the prohibition of the threat or use of force. In those situations, the UN Security Council may declare a specific attempt at

---

[31]   See Chapter III, Section 3.1.1.

secession to be illegal in view of the circumstances at issue and call upon the international community of States for (collective) non-recognition.[32]

3. FINAL REFLECTIONS ON REMEDIAL SECESSION

Having highlighted the main findings of the present study and having presented its general conclusions, this Section will offer some final reflections on the concept of remedial secession. Elaborating on the previous Chapters, this Section will question whether the concept of remedial secession can be effectuated through recognition. Subsequently, the possible future development of such a right will be briefly considered against the backdrop of the process of what is often referred to as the humanization of the international legal order.

3.1. Effectuating Remedial Secession through Recognition?

Although it has been concluded that remedial secession is not rooted as an entitlement in present-day international law, this is not necessarily to say that the concept of remedial secession is merely a theoretical construct that is without any merit whatsoever or that the possibility of unilateral secession is by definition excluded under all circumstances. Bearing in mind the constitutive effects which extensive recognition may have with respect to attempts at unilateral secession,[33] it may be argued that when an entity seeks "to emerge as a State unilaterally, the only way of doing so [successfully] is through international recognition".[34] In this line of reasoning, it has been suggested by some authors that the concept of remedial secession may be given effect through widespread recognition of the aspirant State by already existing States. Put differently, while unilateral secession is by no means an entitlement, arguably, it may well be that States are willing to grant recognition to entities which have attempted to break away considering the sustained oppression of the people concerned and the gross human rights violations on the territory and, by doing so on a very large scale, determine the success of a claim to independent statehood. Particularly in situations in which it is questionable whether the criteria for statehood have been met and, thus, whether statehood has been obtained as a matter of fact, widespread recognition may have significant consequences in this respect.[35] A similar line of reason-

---

[32]   See Chapter VI, Section 2.1.
[33]   See Chapter VI, Section 2.2.
[34]   J. Vidmar, 'Explaining the Legal Effects of Recognition' (2012) 61 *International and Comparative Law Quarterly* 361 at p. 374.
[35]   See, for instance, J. Dugard and D. Raič, 'The Role of Recognition in the Law and Practice of Self-Determination' in M.G. Kohen (ed.) *Secession International Law Perspectives* (Cambridge University Press, Cambridge 2006) at pp. 134-137; M.N. Shaw, 'Peoples, Territorialism and Boundaries' (1997) 8 *European Journal of International Law* 478 at p. 483; Vidmar, 'Explaining the Legal Effects of Recognition' at pp. 375-376; J. Vidmar, 'Kosovo: Unilateral Secession and Multilateral State-Making'

ing was presented by the Supreme Court of Canada in its *Reference re Secession of Quebec*, suggesting that, in deciding whether or not to grant recognition, States take the parent State's treatment of the independence-seeking entity into account.[36] It should be emphasized, however, that this is not to say that recognition may actually create an entitlement to remedial secession, but rather that it may determine the success of an attempt at unilateral secession.

Given this largely hypothetical option, it is to be recalled that the international responses to Kosovo's unilateral declaration of independence painted a different picture. It was seen that States generally did not disclose such a causal link between human rights concerns on the one hand and their decision to recognize on the other. A few States only made reference to human rights violations on the territory as one of the various – primarily non-legal – factors that led to the decision to recognize. It thus remains to be seen whether States will actually use the concept of remedial secession as some sort of guiding principle when deciding on whether or not to grant recognition to a claimant State in the future. In view of the political discretion which is left to States in this respect and the political interests that are at stake, political considerations will continue to play a prominent – if not decisive – role in this area. Moreover, the hypothetical option outlined here raises a more pragmatic question as to how many and which States need to recognize an aspirant State before such recognition may have constitutive effects.[37] At present, however, no clear-cut answer to this question can be given. As was observed previously, both established recognition theories – the constitutive and the declaratory – appear to be inadequate to explain and appreciate cases in which the international community of States has remained divided and it is questionable whether a State has emerged as a matter of fact, such as the example of Kosovo. Needless to say, this is an undesirable situation, as it may leave the status of aspirant States uncertain.

3.2. Remedial Secession and the Humanization of the International Legal Order

The emergence of the doctrine of remedial secession may well be appreciated in the context of the process which is often referred to as the humanization of the international legal order – and so might the possible future materialization of a legal entitlement in this respect.[38] This notion refers to the development of international law

---

in J. Summers (ed.) *Kosovo: A Precedent? The Declaration of Independence, the Advisory Opinion and Implications for Statehood, Self-Determination and Minority Rights* (Martinus Nijhoff Publishers, Leiden/Boston 2011) at pp. 156-157; J. Vidmar, 'Remedial Secession in International Law: Theory and (Lack of) Practice' (2010) 6 *St Antony's International Review* 37 at pp. 50-51.

[36] Supreme Court of Canada, *Reference re Secession of Quebec*, [1998], 2 S.C.R. 217, at para. 155.

[37] See, for instance, Vidmar, 'Explaining the Legal Effects of Recognition' at pp. 378-381.

[38] Sometimes, the term constitutionalization is also used in this context. While both concepts are indeed related, it is submitted here that they are not synonymous. Rather, they may be seen as two sides of the same coin, as the constitutionalization involves the creation of a system with various institutions,

from a primarily State-centred system towards a human-centred system,[39] in which States are no longer the sole actors and which is increasingly aimed at respecting and promoting the interests of human beings – both as individuals and as groups, labelled as peoples, minorities and indigenous populations.[40] As such, this tendency affects some of the fundamental principles of the classical Westphalian system, most prominently the notion of State sovereignty and its corollaries. It was aptly noted by one author that the humanization of the international legal order may thus be regarded as the quest for a new equilibrium which does not neglect the interests of States, but by no means automatically attaches the highest value to these interests either.[41] While involving a kaleidoscopic process, in essence, the manifestation of this quest may be seen to be twofold: the rights and interests of the human being are being strengthened, while simultaneously the sacrosanct position of the State is being challenged.

The gradual transformation of the international legal system outlined above has been marked with the codification of international human rights in response to the scourges of World War II. Considerations of morality and, more specifically, humanity influenced the international agenda more and more. The advent of international organizations – most prominently the United Nations – and regional organizations

---

documents, and competences which have proven to be of significant importance for the acknowledgement, implementation and enforcement of key norms in the process of the humanization of international law. On the constitutionalization of the international legal order, see for instance, J. Klabbers, A. Peters and G. Ulfstein (eds), *The Constitutionalization of International Law* (Oxford University Press, Oxford 2009); E. de Wet, *The International Constitutional Order* (Vossiuspers UvA, Amsterdam 2005).

[39] Most writers use the term 'individual-centred system'. For the present purposes, however, the term 'human-centred system' is preferred, as the humanization of the international legal order does not merely focus on the interests of the individual, but on human beings in general, including groups such as peoples, minorities, and indigenous populations. Likewise, the term 'individual' seems to be avoided by Willem van Genugten. See W.J.M. van Genugten, 'Handhaving van wereldrecht. Een kritische inspectie van valkuilen en dilemma's' (2010) 85 *Nederlands Juristenblad* 44 at p. 46. In even more general terms, Anne Peters referred to the development towards a 'humanized system'. See A. Peters, 'Humanity as the A and Ω of Sovereignty' (2009) 20 *European Journal of International Law* 513 at p. 514.

[40] For similar definitions or characterizations, see, for instance, A.A. Cançado Trindade, *International Law for Humankind. Towards a New Jus Gentium* (Martinus Nijhoff Publishers, Leiden 2010) at p. 3 (referring to the development towards a new *jus gentium* rather than using the term humanization of international law); Van Genugten, 'Handhaving van wereldrecht. Een kritische inspectie van valkuilen en dilemma's' at p. 46; M.T. Kamminga, *De humanisering van het volkenrecht (inaugural lecture)* (Universitaire Pers Maastricht, Maastricht 2001) at p. 7; M.T. Kamminga, 'Final Report on the Impact of International Human Rights Law on General International Law' in M.T. Kamminga and M. Scheinin (eds) *The Impact of Human Rights Law on General International Law* (Oxford University Press, Oxford 2009) at p. 2; T. Meron, *The Humanization of International Law* (Martinus Nijhoff Publishers, Leiden/Boston 2006) at p. xi (Introduction); Tomuschat, 'International Law: Ensuring the Survival of Mankind on the Eve of a New Century: General Course on Public International Law' at p. 162.

[41] See Van Genugten, 'Handhaving van wereldrecht. Een kritische inspectie van valkuilen en dilemma's' at p. 46: "De humanisering van de internationale rechtsorde, als inhaaloperatie op zoek naar een nieuw evenwicht waarin de belangen van staten niet worden weggeredeneerd maar ook niet langer per definitie het zwaarste wegen".

– such as the Council of Europe (CoE) – greatly contributed to this development. In a variety of ways, ranging from the framing of authoritative legal and non-legal instruments and the establishment of specialized agencies to the creation of supervisory mechanisms and even international courts and tribunals, this stimulated a humanist vision of the international legal order. Consequently, recent decades have witnessed not only an increasing value attached to human rights and a proliferation of human rights instruments and mechanisms, but also a rising impact of human rights law and principles of humanity on various branches of general international law. Examples in this respect are the influence of the human rights discourse on the law of treaties, the law of war, international economic law, the doctrines of State responsibility and the immunity of heads of State, and as was seen previously in this study, even (scholarly thinking on) the formation process of customary international law.[42] While perhaps not revolutionary *per se*, the endorsement of the responsibility to protect – commonly referred to as RtoP or R2P – by the UN General Assembly during the 2005 World Summit[43] is generally regarded as a major step in the humanization process, as it arguably reflected a new – or at least revisited – outlook on the relationship between State sovereignty and human rights.[44] Indeed, the responsibility to protect is founded on the idea that sovereignty includes a responsibility, meaning that it has

---

[42] See Chapter V of the present study, critically considering the human rights approach towards customary international law. On the impact of human rights law and principles of humanity on the various branches of general international law, see Cançado Trindade, *International Law for Humankind. Towards a New Jus Gentium*; W.J.M. van Genugten, C. Homan, N.J. Schrijver and P.J.I.M. de Waart, *The United Nations of the Future: Globalization with a Human Face* (KIT-Publishers Amsterdam 2006); M.T. Kamminga and M. Scheinin (eds), *The Impact of Human Rights Law on General International Law* (Oxford University Press, Oxford 2009); Meron, *The Humanization of International Law*.

[43] See UN General Assembly Resolution 60/1 (*2005 World Summit Outcome*), UN Doc. A/Res/60/1, 16 September 2005, at paras 138-139: "[e]ach individual State has the responsibility to protect its populations from genocide, war crimes, ethnic cleansing and crimes against humanity. This responsibility entails the prevention of such crimes, including their incitement through appropriate and necessary means. We accept that responsibility and will act in accordance with it. The international community should, as appropriate, encourage and help States to exercise this responsibility and support the United Nations in establishing an early warning capability". See also, more recently, General Assembly, *Implementing the Responsibility to Protect: Report of the Secretary-General*, UN Doc. A/63/677, 12 January 2009.

[44] On the responsibility to protect, see, for instance, J. Genser and I. Cotler (eds), *The Responsibility to Protect: The Promise of Stopping Mass Atrocities in Our Time* (Oxford University Press, Oxford/New York 2012); C. Stahn, 'Responsibility to Protect: Political Rhetoric or Emerging Legal Norm?' (2007) 101 *American Journal of International Law* 99. In this respect, it should be noted, however, that the responsibility to protect as initially envisaged by the International Commission on Intervention and State Sovereignty (ICISS) was much more encompassing than the concept as ultimately adopted by the UN General Assembly. See International Commission on Intervention and State Sovereignty, *The Responsibility to Protect* (International Development Research Centre, Ottawa 2001), in particular paras 6.13-6.40. See also W.W. Burke-White, 'Adoption of the Responsibility to Protect' in J. Genser and I. Cotler (eds) *The Responsibility to Protect: The Promise of Stopping Mass Atrocities in Our Time* (Oxford University Press, Oxford/New York 2012) at pp. 17-29; Stahn, 'Responsibility to Protect: Political Rhetoric or Emerging Legal Norm?' at pp. 102-110.

to be exercised in a responsible way. Since sovereignty and human rights are two sides of the same coin, they are not mutually exclusive. Rather, sovereignty is perceived as implying a responsibility towards the inhabitants of the State. As a result of this responsibility, sovereignty does not necessarily preclude external intervention – through the UN Security Council – when the State radically fails to meet its responsibility and submits its inhabitants to gross human rights violations, or does not protect them from other avoidable catastrophe.[45] It is to be pointed out, however, that the responsibility to protect as adopted by the UN General Assembly is sometimes labelled as old wine in new bottles,[46] as it merely allows for external intervention with UN Security Council authorization, which was already permitted under Chapter VII of the UN Charter. Moreover, the actual implementation of the responsibility to protect has proved problematic.[47] Despite the explicit acknowledgement of the concept by the UN General Assembly in 2005, broad and solid support appears to be lacking in practice and the fear of misuse of the concept and opening a Pandora's Box generally seems to prevail amongst important players in the international arena. Admittedly, the responsibility to protect was applied in the case of Libya[48] and Côte d'Ivoire.[49] Focusing on Libya, the UN Security Council for the first time relied on the responsibility to protect to approve a no-fly zone and authorize military intervention to protect civilians from a despotic and brutal regime in Resolution 1973 (2011).[50] While both this Resolution and the subsequent NATO-led intervention in Libya can be regarded as milestones with respect to the responsibility to protect,[51] there has been fierce criticism on the implementation of the concept as well. For example, the intervention has been criticized for causing many civilian casualties. Moreover, it has been contended that NATO interpreted the authorization to use armed force for human protection purposes too extensively so as to include the overthrow of the *de*

---

[45] See International Commission on Intervention and State Sovereignty, *The Responsibility to Protect*, in particular at paras 2.7-2.15.

[46] See, for instance, Stahn, 'Responsibility to Protect: Political Rhetoric or Emerging Legal Norm?'; S.P. Marks and N. Cooper, 'The Responsibility to Protect: Watershed or Old Wine in a New Bottle?' (2010) 2 *Jindal Global Law Review.*

[47] See E.C. Luck, 'From Promise to Practice: Implementing the Responsibility to Protect' in J. Genser and I. Cotler (eds) *The Responsibility to Protect: The Promise of Stopping Mass Atrocities in Our Time* (Oxford University Press, Oxford/New York 2012), in particular at pp. 97-106; Marks and Cooper, 'The Responsibility to Protect: Watershed or Old Wine in a New Bottle?' at pp. 122-126.

[48] See A.J. Bellamy and P.D. Williams, 'The New Politics of Protection? Côte d'Ivoire, Libya and the Responsibility to Protect' (2011) 87 *International Affairs* 825 at pp. 838-846.

[49] See *ibid.* at pp. 829-838. For the authorization of the use of armed force, see UN Security Council Resolution 1975 (2011) (*Côte d'Ivoire*), UN Doc. S/Res/1975 (2011), 30 March 2011.

[50] UN Security Council Resolution 1973 (2011) (*Libya*), UN Doc. S/Res/1973 (2011), 17 March 2011, at paras 4 and 6. The Resolution was adopted with ten votes in favour and five abstentions.

[51] See M.S. Helal, 'Middle East' in J. Genser and I. Cotler (eds) *The Responsibility to Protect: The Promise of Stopping Mass Atrocities in Our Time* (Oxford University Press, Oxford/New York 2012) at p. 228.

jure regime. Such interpretation seems to blur the lines between the responsibility to protect on the one hand, and (pro-democratic) intervention on the other.[52] Arguably, the case of Libya underlines:

> the need to further elucidate and elaborate the scope and content of [the responsibility to protect], and determine the policies and procedures that best serve the underlying purpose of [the responsibility to protect], namely the protection of civilians from egregious violations of their fundamental human rights.[53]

More generally, the above has illustrated that, notwithstanding the shift in thinking that has been realized since its inception and the impact the humanization process has had on international legal practice to date, the humanization of the international legal order has by no means been accomplished. Rather, it involves a dynamic and multifaceted yet arduous process, which is ongoing.[54]

Whatever the present stage of this transition, it is against the background of the humanization of the international legal order that the debate on the question of a right to external self-determination after serious injustices and the emergence of the doctrine of remedial secession might be appreciated. The suggestion of an 'emergency exit'[55] for peoples being submitted to oppression and flagrant human rights abuses by their own State arguably fits well in the humanization tendency. With this idea of an 'emergency exit', it is attempted to introduce considerations of humanity as a significant counterweight to the rights and interests of the State. The twofold manifestation of the humanization process is reflected here as well: first, it is sought to consolidate and expand people's right to (external) self-determination beyond the context of decolonization, and secondly, it simultaneously challenges the inviolable position of the State by prioritizing the interests of the people over the sovereign prerogatives of the State, when they conflict. As such, some parallels with the responsibility to protect may be discerned. Similar to the responsibility to protect, the concept of remedial secession departs from a relative understanding of the traditional Westphalian legal order, suggesting that in the case of gross injustices, a State may forfeit its sovereignty and territorial integrity (thus clearing the way for unilateral secession as

---

[52] See, for instance, Bellamy and Williams, 'The New Politics of Protection? Côte d'Ivoire, Libya and the Responsibility to Protect' at p. 846; Helal, 'Middle East' at p. 229.

[53] See Helal, 'Middle East' at p. 230. For a similar observation with respect to Côte d'Ivoire, see Bellamy and Williams, 'The New Politics of Protection? Côte d'Ivoire, Libya and the Responsibility to Protect' at p. 838.

[54] See Van Genugten, 'Handhaving van wereldrecht. Een kritische inspectie van valkuilen en dilemma's' at p. 46. By contrast, Anne Peters has contended that the endorsement of the responsibility to protect has "definitely ousted the principle of sovereignty from its position as a *Letztbegründung* (first principle) of international law". See Peters, 'Humanity as the A and Ω of Sovereignty' at p. 514.

[55] See P.H. Kooijmans, 'Zelfbeschikkingsrecht. Naar een nieuwe interpretatie?' in N. Sybesma-Knol and J. van Bellingen (eds) *Naar een nieuwe interpretatie van het recht op zelfbeschikking?* (VUB Press, Brussels 1995) at p. 168.

a remedy). And similar to the rationale behind the responsibility to protect, this boils down to the idea of sovereignty (and territorial integrity) as a responsibility of the State towards its inhabitants. When viewed in this light, the idea of remedial secession – once accepted as an international legal norm or principle – may be seen as contributing to the gradual transformation from a State-centred system to a human-centred system.

However, given that, to date, the concept of remedial secession has not been endorsed by the international community of States at large, one may wonder whether the contemporary international stance towards unilateral secession demonstrates that the limits of the humanization of this particular field of international law have been reached. Over recent decades, the position of the human being has been strengthened, while simultaneously States (including their highest representatives) have lost their inviolable position and influence in various branches of international law. Yet when it comes to the right to (external) self-determination, attempts at unilateral secession and the success thereof through granting or withholding recognition, States continue to be the prime actors, demarcating their own playing field and the applicable rules of play. They may be viewed as the 'gatekeepers'[56] of the international legal order, deciding who will be admitted to their system. The current shortage of support for the concept of remedial secession by States and, for instance, the problematic implementation of the responsibility to protect are symptomatic of the conclusion that, as was observed by Christian Tomuschat, "the transformation from international law as a State-centred system to an individual-centred system has not yet found a new equilibrium".[57] Nonetheless, the quest for this new balance between the sovereign prerogatives of the State on the one hand and the interests of human beings will in all probability continue. In view of this ongoing development and the traces of a remedial right to unilateral secession which can be found at present, it is not impossible that, one day, such a right will indeed be part and parcel of positive international law.

---

[56] This term was also used by Cedric Ryngaert and Sven Sobrie. See C. Ryngaert and S. Sobrie, 'Recognition of States: International Law or Realpolitik? The Practice of Recognition in the Wake of Kosovo, South Ossetia, and Abkhazia' (2011) 24 *Leiden Journal of International Law* 467 at p. 489.
[57] Tomuschat, 'International Law: Ensuring the Survival of Mankind on the Eve of a New Century: General Course on Public International Law' at p. 162.

SAMENVATTING

1. EEN RECHT OP 'REMEDIAL SECESSION'?

In dit onderzoek stond de hedendaagse betekenis van het zelfbeschikkingsrecht van volkeren centraal en, meer in het bijzonder, het vraagstuk betreffende externe zelfbeschikking als een remedie tegen ernstig onrecht. Daarbij was de volgende onderzoeksvraag het uitgangspunt:

> In hoeverre is een recht op 'remedial secession', dat wil zeggen een recht op externe zelfbeschikking als een remedie tegen ernstig onrecht, tot stand gekomen onder het hedendaagse internationale recht?

De belangrijkste conclusie van deze studie is dat een recht op externe zelfbeschikking als remedie tegen ernstig onrecht nog niet tot ontwikkeling is gekomen onder het hedendaagse internationale recht. Hoewel enige steun voor het bestaan van een dergelijk recht bestaat, zijn de theoretische grondslagen hiervan vrij zwak, terwijl de voornaamste tekortkoming bestaat uit het gebrek aan erkenning van een recht op 'remedial secession' in de statenpraktijk. Hieronder zullen de belangrijkste bevindingen van deze studie, die hebben geleid tot bovengenoemde conclusie, worden samengevat.

2. DE OPKOMST VAN HET ZELFBESCHIKKINGSRECHT

Om de kernbetekenis van het zelfbeschikkingsrecht te kunnen vaststellen en de vraag naar de algemeen aanvaarde, hedendaagse betekenis van het recht te kunnen beantwoorden, is de historische ontwikkeling van het concept zelfbeschikking als uitgangspunt genomen. In Hoofdstuk II werd duidelijk dat de basis van het concept kan worden teruggeleid tot de theorieën en ideologieën die ten grondslag lagen aan en voortkwamen uit de Amerikaanse en Franse Revoluties. Ondanks deze vroege sporen, verscheen het concept van zelfbeschikking pas tijdens de nasleep van de Eerste Wereldoorlog op het internationale toneel. T. Woodrow Wilson propageerde zelfbeschikking in zijn voorstel voor een vredesakkoord in 1918. Hoewel nog niet uitgegroeid tot een positief recht, zorgden Wilsons inspanningen ervoor dat het concept van zelfbeschikking zich had ontwikkeld tot een politiek beginsel op internationaal niveau. Deze ontwikkeling werd tevens weerspiegeld in de instelling van mandaat-gebieden door de Volkenbond. Ondanks het feit dat het concept van zelfbeschikking vlak na de Eerste Wereldoorlog werd gezien als een politiek beginsel, was de toepassing ervan enigszins willekeurig. Het kreeg voor het eerst juridische betekenis in de Åland *Islands*-zaak uit 1920, die over het algemeen wordt beschouwd als een mijlpaal in de ontwikkeling van het zelfbeschikkingsrecht. In deze zaak ontkenden de Commissie van Juristen en het Comité van Rapporteurs van de Volkenbond het bestaan van een (algemeen) recht op zelfbeschikking door middel van de afscheiding van een deel van een territoir. Wel leek de mogelijkheid van afscheiding als laatste redmiddel in het geval van extreme onderdrukking te worden erkend.

Na de Tweede Wereldoorlog begon de tweede fase in de evolutie van het zelf-beschikkingsrecht, toen het concept werd opgenomen in het Handvest van de Verenigde Naties (hierna: VN-Handvest). Aangezien het VN-Handvest zelfbeschikking als een van de voornaamste doelstellingen van de organisatie introduceerde, werd dit beschouwd als een belangrijke stap in de ontwikkeling van het zelfbeschikkingsrecht. Hoewel de artikelen 1(2) en 55 van het Handvest expliciet verwijzen naar het concept van zelfbeschikking, bleven de precieze juridische status en inhoud van het begrip onduidelijk. Dit werd verduidelijkt tegen de achtergrond van het dekolonisatieproces, toen zelfbeschikking werd gezien als een recht voor koloniale volkeren. Resolutie 1514 (XV) van de Algemene Vergadering van de Verenigde Naties wordt over het algemeen gezien als een van de belangrijkste bijdragen aan het dekolonisatieproces, aangezien het de noodzaak tot het beëindigen van kolonialisme verkondigde en stelde dat alle (koloniale) volkeren het recht op zelfbeschikking hebben. Als zodanig werd het zelfbeschikkingsrecht gezien als een recht op een onafhankelijke Staat (of om zich te verenigen met of integreren in een andere Staat), zodat het volk vrijelijk zijn politieke status kan bepalen en vrijelijk zijn economische, sociale en culturele ontwikkeling kan nastreven. In de dekolonisatiecontext werd het zelfbeschikkingsrecht dus voornamelijk extern geïmplementeerd en werd het geacht te zijn verwezenlijkt zodra een koloniaal gebied onafhankelijk werd van zijn kolonisator. Het belang en het fundamentele karakter van dit recht werden benadrukt door het Internationaal Gerechtshof in de *East Timor*-zaak, waarin het Hof vaststelde dat het zelfbeschikkingsrecht is uitgegroeid tot een *erga omnes* norm, en daarmee een verplichting betreft ten opzichte van de gehele internationale gemeenschap. Het Hof stelde niet expliciet dat het zelfbeschikkingsrecht een norm van dwingend internationaal recht vormt. Toch wordt vaak gesteld dat het recht op zelfbeschikking met betrekking tot afhankelijke (koloniale) gebieden de status van *jus cogens* heeft bereikt, hetgeen betekent dat er onder geen enkele omstandigheid van mag worden afgeweken. Het was tegen de achtergrond van het dekolonisatieproces dat het Internationaal Gerechtshof de kernbetekenis van het zelfbeschikkingsrecht heeft vormgegeven. In zijn advies in de *Western Sahara*-zaak heeft het Hof benadrukt dat het essentiële kenmerk van het zelfbeschikkingsrecht is dat de toepassing ervan de vrije en oprechte uiting van de wil van het volk vereist. Als zodanig kreeg het zelfbeschikkingsrecht een nieuwe betekenis na de dekolonisatieperiode.

3. DE HEDENDAAGSE BETEKENIS VAN HET ZELFBESCHIKKINGSRECHT

Na het dekolonisatieproces zette de ontwikkeling van het zelfbeschikkingsrecht zich voort. In dit verband kunnen twee belangrijke ontwikkelingen worden onderscheiden. De eerste ontwikkeling betrof de (voortdurende) evolutie van de juridische status van zelfbeschikking. Als gevolg van de opname van bepalingen in diverse nieuwe internationale instrumenten, zoals het gemeenschappelijke Artikel 1 van de mensenrechtenverdragen van 1966 (het Internationaal Verdrag inzake Burgerlijke en Politieke Rechten en het Internationaal Verdrag inzake Economische, Sociale en Culturele Rechten), ontwikkelde het zelfbeschikkingsrecht zicht tot een fundamenteel, positief recht. De tweede ontwikkeling betrof het uitkristalliseren en de erkenning van de twee dimensies van het zelfbeschikkingsrecht. In Hoofdstuk II werd duidelijk dat het zelfbeschikkingsrecht tijdens de dekolonisatieperiode in de eerste plaats geacht werd extern te worden gerealiseerd. In de laatste decennia is in de praktijk en in internationaalrechtelijke documenten echter een interne dimensie opgekomen. Met de opkomst van deze interne manifestatie van het zelfbeschikkingsrecht werd een andere wijze van implementatie meer relevant. Het zelfbeschikkingsrecht wordt niet langer slechts gerealiseerd door de vorming van nieuwe, onafhankelijke Staten, maar daarnaast vereist het doorlopende implementatie binnen de grenzen van bestaande Staten, in de relatie tussen een volk en zijn regering. De kernbetekenis van deze interne dimensie kan worden gedefinieerd als de noodzaak om rekening te houden met de vrije wil van volkeren. Dit vertaalt zich in twee belangrijke vereisten, namelijk de aanwezigheid van een representatieve regering en participatie van de bevolking in het politieke besluitvormingsproces binnen de Staat. In aanvulling hierop kunnen speciale regelingen, zoals autonomie, federalisme, of 'complex power-sharing' soms noodzakelijk zijn om de interne dimensie van het zelfbeschikkingsrecht te verzekeren voor *alle* inwoners van de Staat. Immers, niet alleen de gehele bevolking van een Staat, maar ook subgroepen binnen een Staat en inheemse volkeren kunnen worden beschouwd als dragers of subjecten van het recht op interne zelfbeschikking.

Ondanks de vrij recente opkomst van de interne dimensie van het zelfbeschikkingsrecht en de nadruk op dit interne aspect in hedendaagse juridische en politieke documenten, blijft de meer traditionele, externe dimensie van het zelfbeschikkingsrecht ook vandaag de dag nog relevant. Zoals verklaard in de VN-Verklaring inzake Vriendschappelijke Relaties tussen Staten, kan deze externe dimensie worden geïmplementeerd door de vreedzame desintegratie van een Staat, de vereniging of fusie van een Staat met een andere Staat, of door secessie. Deze laatste modaliteit van externe zelfbeschikking kan worden gedefinieerd als de oprichting van een nieuwe, onafhankelijke Staat door de afscheiding van een integraal deel van het grondgebied van een bestaande Staat, hetzij met of zonder toestemming van deze staat of een constitutionele machtiging. Wanneer uitgeoefend door de bevolking van een Staat als geheel of wanneer het gaat om een consensuele of constitutionele secessie, wordt externe zelfbeschikking niet als problematisch gezien onder internationaal recht. In het geval van een consensuele of constitutionele secessie wordt het recht op afscheiding gebaseerd op nationaal in plaats van internationaal recht. De rechtmatigheid van unilaterale secessie – dat wil zeggen de afscheiding van een deel van een grondgebied door een deel van de bevolking van de Staat zonder toestemming of grondwettelijke regeling – is echter meer omstreden. Deze controverse kan verklaard worden door een aantal factoren. De eerste factor betreft het feit dat internationaalrechtelijke documenten een expliciete erkenning noch een uitdrukkelijk verbod op unilaterale secessie bevatten. De tweede factor betreft het risico van de ontwrichtende werking die deze modaliteit van externe zelfbeschikking kan hebben. Er lijkt immers een conflict te bestaan tussen de traditionele internationaalrechtelijke beginselen van staatssoevereiniteit en respect voor de territoriale integriteit – gericht op handhaving van de territoriale *status quo* – enerzijds, en een vermeend recht op unilaterale secessie – dat territoriale verandering teweegbrengt – anderzijds. Niet alleen zou een dergelijk recht op unilaterale secessie de traditionele internationale rechtsorde verstoren, het kan ook leiden tot vergaande fragmentatie van Staten en daarmee een mogelijke bedreiging vormen voor de internationale of regionale vrede en stabiliteit. Gelet op deze controverse en onduidelijkheid over het al dan niet bestaan van een recht op eenzijdige afscheiding, verdient de stand van het internationale recht met betrekking tot de vraag naar een recht op unilaterale secessie en, meer specifiek, unilaterale secessie als een remedie tegen ernstig onrecht, ook wel aangeduid als 'remedial secession', nader onderzoek.

4. SPOREN VAN EEN RECHT OP 'REMEDIAL SECESSION' IN HET HEDENDAAGSE INTERNATIONALE RECHT

Om te toetsen in hoeverre een recht op 'remedial secession' tot ontwikkeling is gekomen onder het hedendaagse internationale recht, werd in Hoofdstuk IV de klassieke methode van onderzoek naar de diverse bronnen van het internationale recht toegepast. Artikel 38(1) van het Statuut van het Internationaal Gerechtshof en de bronnen die hierin worden opgesomd vormden het uitgangspunt. Internationaal gewoonterecht verdiende separate behandeling vanwege het belang van de internationale praktijk van Staten voor de ontwikkeling van het zelfbeschikkingsrecht in het algemeen. De conclusie dat de theoretische basis van een recht op 'remedial secession' enigszins zwak is, maakte het bovendien nog belangrijker om het al dan niet bestaan van een gewoonterechtelijke norm gedetailleerd onder de loep te nemen.

Allereerst zijn internationale verdragen onderzocht om te bezien of hierin sporen van een recht op unilaterale secessie zijn te vinden. In dit verband werd duidelijk dat het VN-Handvest, de mensenrechtenverdragen van 1966, het Verdrag van Wenen inzake Statenopvolging met betrekking tot Verdragen (1978), en het Internationaal Verdrag inzake de Uitbanning van alle Vormen van Rassendiscriminatie (IVRD) nauwelijks handvatten bieden met betrekking tot de vraag naar het bestaan van een recht op unilaterale secessie. Noch de tekst van deze documenten, noch de ontstaansgeschiedenis of context boden een overtuigend antwoord op deze vraag.

Vervolgens is de doctrine onder de loep genomen. Als gevolg van de werken van Lee C. Buchheit en Antonio Cassese heeft een aanzienlijk aantal auteurs zich op het standpunt gesteld dat een recht op unilaterale secessie in uitzonderlijke omstandigheden bestaat. Zij baseren zich voornamelijk op twee internationale instrumenten, namelijk de VN-Verklaring inzake Vriendschappelijke Relaties tussen Staten (1970) en de Verklaring en het Actieprogramma van Wenen (1993). Beide documenten bevatten een clausule (de zogenoemde 'safeguard clause'), die respect voor de territoriale integriteit van Staten die zich gedragen overeenkomstig het beginsel van gelijke rechten en zelfbeschikking van volkeren en dus met een regering die representatief is voor de gehele bevolking, zonder onderscheid naar ras, geloof, of huidskleur, bevestigt.

Wanneer deze clausule *a contrario* wordt gelezen, zou deze kunnen suggereren dat een Staat zonder een representatieve, niet discriminerende regering geen recht op territoriale integriteit heeft. Een dergelijke interpretatie zou een recht op unilaterale afscheiding niet uitsluiten. Sterker nog, wanneer de Staat een volk het recht op interne zelfbeschikking ontzegt, zou dit het ontstaan van een recht op externe zelfbeschikking door middel van unilaterale afscheiding rechtvaardigen. Naast het gebrek aan interne zelfbeschikking worden drie andere parameters voor de uitoefening van een recht op 'remedial secession' veelvuldig genoemd in de literatuur, namelijk flagrante schendingen van fundamentele mensenrechten, structurele discriminatie en de uitputting van alle vreedzame middelen. Als zodanig wordt unilaterale secessie gezien als een laatste redmiddel voor dergelijke ernstig onrecht gepleegd door de Staat. Ondanks het feit dat er relatieve overeenstemming lijkt te bestaan over de omstandigheden waaronder een recht op 'remedial secession' zou ontstaan, zijn degenen die hiervoor pleiten verdeeld over de vraag naar de subjecten van een dergelijk recht. Al wordt 'remedial secession' over het algemeen gezien als een recht van 'volkeren', de nadere invulling van dit begrip blijft problematisch. Auteurs lijken vooral verdeeld over de vraag welke minderheden – numeriek, linguïstisch, religieus, etnisch, etc. – kunnen worden beschouwd als een 'volk' dat drager is van een recht op unilaterale secessie. Tevens dient te worden benadrukt dat, hoewel een aanzienlijk aantal auteurs heeft betoogd dat een recht op 'remedial secession' bestaat, de doctrine niet eenduidig is over deze kwestie. Vooral – maar niet uitsluitend – in het kader van Kosovo's eenzijdige onafhankelijkheidsverklaring kon worden vastgesteld dat auteurs enigszins terughoudend waren om het bestaan van een recht op unilaterale secessie te claimen, zowel in het specifieke geval van Kosovo als meer in het algemeen. Diverse rechtsgeleerden hebben een dergelijke stelling zelfs expliciet verworpen. De *a contrario* lezing van de zogenoemde 'safeguard clause' werd bijvoorbeeld afgewezen als een gerechtvaardigd middel om de interpretatie van een van de basisbeginselen van internationaal recht, namelijk het principe van territoriale integriteit, fundamenteel te wijzigen. Maar bovenal waren deze auteurs van mening dat er in de praktijk onvoldoende en overtuigend bewijs is voor het bestaan van een recht op 'remedial secession'.

Nadat was geconcludeerd dat een recht op 'remedial secession' aanzienlijke – maar zeker niet afdoende – steun geniet in de doctrine, richtte Hoofdstuk IV zich op de toetsing van de uitspraken en opinies van zowel nationale als internationale rechterlijke organen. Hieruit bleek dat deze organen in diverse gevallen hebben verwezen naar de erkenning van een recht op 'remedial secession'. In de meeste gevallen werd echter niet uitvoerig stilgestaan bij de precieze omstandigheden waaronder een recht op unilaterale secessie rechtmatig zou kunnen worden uitgeoefend. Toch kan in dit opzicht een aantal omstandigheden worden onderscheiden, namelijk het bestaan van ernstige mensenrechtenschendingen en het feitelijk ontzeggen van de uitoefening van het recht op interne zelfbeschikking. Ondanks de zekere mate van steun voor de stelling dat een recht op 'remedial secession' bestaat onder het huidige internationale recht, moeten enkele belangrijke kanttekeningen worden gemaakt. In de eerste plaats werd opgemerkt dat de rechters zich in sommige gevallen beriepen op een tendens die zij uit de literatuur hadden afgeleid en niet op hun eigen mening over de vraag of een recht op unilaterale afscheiding of 'remedial secession' bestaat onder internationaal recht. Het oordeel van het Canadese Hooggerechtshof in de *Reference re Secession of Quebec* is daarvan een duidelijk voorbeeld. Een tweede kanttekening betreft de voorzichtige bewoordingen die door de meeste rechterlijke instanties werden gebruikt wanneer zij stelden dat een recht unilaterale afscheiding of 'remedial secession' bestaat. In de *Reference re Secession of Quebec*, bijvoorbeeld, constateerde het Canadese Hooggerechtshof een trend in de doctrine wat betreft 'remedial secession', maar merkte het ook op dat het onzeker blijft of dit vermeende recht daadwerkelijk is geworteld in het positieve internationale recht. Ook het Internationaal Gerechtshof betrachtte terughoudendheid in zijn advies over Kosovo's eenzijdige onafhankelijkheidsverklaring, waarin het met name benadrukte dat de visies van Staten op dit punt uiteenliepen. De Afrikaanse Commissie voor de Rechten van Mensen en Volken refereerde in de zaak betreffende *Katangese Peoples' Congress v. Zaire* niet expliciet aan een recht op unilaterale afscheiding of 'remedial secession'. Slechts wanneer de uitspraak *a contrario* wordt gelezen, zou de redenering van de Afrikaanse Commissie kunnen worden geïnterpreteerd als een erkenning van een recht op unilaterale afscheiding als een remedie tegen ernstige mensenrechtenschendingen en het ontzeggen van interne zelfbeschikking. Een derde en laatste kanttekening betreft het feit dat geen enkele rechterlijke instantie een volk daadwerkelijk een recht op eenzijdige afscheiding heeft toegekend in het licht van de specifieke omstandigheden van het geval. Rechterlijke erkenning van een recht op 'remedial secession' is tot op heden slechts theoretisch gebleven. Geconcludeerd werd dan ook dat hoewel de uitspraken en opinies van rechterlijke organen sporen bevatten van de acceptatie van een recht op 'remedial secession', zij onvoldoende duidelijkheid bieden over deze materie.

Vervolgens zijn de algemene rechtsbeginselen bestudeerd. Daarbij werden twee categorieën onderscheiden. Ten eerste werden algemene rechtsbeginselen aangestipt die in de meerderheid van de nationale rechtssystemen voorkomen, zoals goede trouw, proportionaliteit en billijkheid. Gesteld werd dat dergelijke beginselen achtergrondbeginselen zijn die slechts een ondergeschikte rol kunnen spelen, aangezien zij gebruikt worden om bestaande internationaalrechtelijke normen in een specifieke situatie te interpreteren. De tweede categorie betrof algemene rechtsbeginselen die tot ontwikkeling zijn gekomen in het internationale recht en van toepassing zijn op de verhoudingen tussen Staten. In dit verband werden allereerst de beginselen van respect voor de territoriale integriteit van Staten en *uti possidetis juris* onder de loep genomen, aangezien vaak wordt gesteld dat deze fundamentele beginselen van de internationale rechtsorde botsen met een vermeend recht op unilaterale secessie. Nadere beschouwing van deze beginselen maakte echter duidelijk dat deze concepten niet volledig onverenigbaar zijn. Met betrekking tot het beginsel van respect voor de territoriale integriteit van Staten werd eerst aangevoerd dat separatistische groepen kunnen worden gezien als (additionele) subjecten van dit beginsel en hieraan dus gebonden zijn. Daarnaast werd betoogd dat het beginsel van territoriale integriteit geenszins absoluut is. Het wegen van het beginsel van territoriale integriteit enerzijds en het zelfbeschikkingsrecht anderzijds laat derhalve enige ruimte voor een recht op 'remedial secession'. Wat betreft het beginsel van *uti possidetis juris* werd eerst opgemerkt dat het nog twijfelachtig is of het van toepassing is op alle situaties waarin sprake is van de oprichting van een nieuwe, onafhankelijke staat, met inbegrip van die situaties waarin de separatistische entiteit niet verbonden is aan een gebied dat wordt begrensd door een soort interne grenzen, zoals provinciale of federale grenzen. Waar het beginsel wel van toepassing is, zou *uti possidetis juris* enkel geografische grenzen stellen aan de uitoefening van het recht op (externe) zelfbeschikking en niet de uitoefening van dit recht in zijn algemeenheid beperken. In aanvulling op de beginselen van respect voor de territoriale integriteit van Staten en *uti possidetis juris*, werd zelfbeschikking kort aangestipt in de hoedanigheid van een algemeen beginsel van internationaal recht. Als zodanig omvat het de kernbetekenis van zelfbeschikking. Toch functioneert dit beginsel alleen als een zeer losse en overkoepelende standaard, die slechts van beperkte betekenis is als het gaat om verstrekkende vragen als die met betrekking tot een recht op 'remedial secession'. Tot slot werd geconcludeerd dat algemene rechtsbeginselen niet voorzien in een sluitend antwoord op de vraag of een recht op 'remedial secession' vandaag de dag bestaat: de beginselen laten noch duidelijke sporen van een dergelijk recht, noch een eenduidig verbod daarop zien.

Tot slot, na bestudering van de bronnen van het internationale recht zoals opgenomen in Artikel 38(1) van het Statuut van het Internationaal Gerechtshof – met uitzondering van internationaal gewoonterecht, dat afzonderlijk werd behandeld in de Hoofdstukken V en VI – werden twee aanvullende bronnen van internationaal recht aangestipt, namelijk de eenzijdige rechtshandelingen van Staten en besluiten van internationale organisaties. Eenzijdige rechtshandelingen van Staten die met name relevant zijn voor deze studie zijn formele erkenningsverklaringen, die zijn bestudeerd in het kader van de internationale reacties op pogingen tot unilaterale secessie. Daarbij werd echter duidelijk dat de verklaringen waarin Kosovo als een onafhankelijke Staat werd erkend, geen recht op 'remedial secession' ondersteunen. Integendeel, de meeste Staten erkenden Kosovo met het oog op vrede en stabiliteit in de regio. De inhoud van de relevante VN-documenten, zoals de VN-Verklaring inzake Vriendschappelijke Relaties tussen Staten en de Verklaring en het Actieprogramma van Wenen, werden behandeld in het kader van de ontwikkeling van het recht op zelfbeschikking na de dekolonisatieperiode en de hedendaagse betekenis ervan, en tevens tegen de achtergrond van de doctrine. Daarbij werd vastgesteld dat de zogeheten 'safeguard clauses' van deze juridisch niet-bindende documenten *a contrario* zijn uitgelegd als een erkenning van een recht op unilaterale secessie als een remedie voor het gebrek aan interne zelfbeschikking. Toch werd, gelet op de aard van deze documenten, gesteld dat terughoudendheid moet worden betracht bij het afleiden van juridische normen uit deze stukken, aangezien zij vaak het resultaat zijn van politieke compromissen en over het algemeen niet zijn bedoeld om juridisch bindende normen in het leven te roepen.

Samenvattend werd in Hoofdstuk IV aangetoond dat in het hedendaagse internationale recht een zekere mate van (theoretische) steun bestaat voor het bestaan van een recht op 'remedial secession'. Deze steun werd in de eerste plaats gevonden in wetenschappelijke literatuur en, in beperktere mate, in de uitspraken en opinies van rechterlijke organen. Benadrukt werd dat deze bronnen volgens Artikel 38(1) van het Statuut van het Internationaal Gerechtshof subsidiaire bronnen zijn en dus slechts van aanvullende in plaats van primaire waarde zijn. Daarnaast werd vastgesteld dat het bestaan ven een recht op 'remedial secession' eerst en vooral is gebaseerd op een *a contrario* lezing van de 'safeguard clauses' van de VN Verklaring inzake Vriendschappelijke Relaties tussen Staten en de Verklaring en het Actieprogramma van Wenen. Een dergelijke interpretatie is niet alleen vooruitstrevend, maar ook controversieel, vooral gelet op de onduidelijkheid van de clausule en de gevoelige verhouding met het fundamentele beginsel van respect voor de territoriale integriteit van Staten. Geconcludeerd werd dan ook dat de theoretische basis van een recht op 'remedial secession' erg zwak is. Met het oog op deze bevindingen is het belangrijk om te onderzoeken of de internationale praktijk van Staten wel voldoende en overtuigende steun voor een dergelijk recht weerspiegelt, nam hiermee toe. De volgende hoofdstukken waren daarom gericht op het beantwoorden van de vraag of een recht op 'remedial secession' bestaat als een norm van internationaal gewoonterecht.

5. INLEIDENDE OPMERKINGEN OVER HET TOETSEN VAN HET BESTAAN VAN EEN RECHT OP 'REMEDIAL SECESSION' ONDER INTERNATIONAAL GEWOONTERECHT

Alvorens te toetsen of een recht op 'remedial secession' zich heeft ontwikkeld tot een gewoonterechtelijke norm, werd het concept van internationaal gewoonterecht, inclusief de hedendaagse interpretaties daarvan, uitgewerkt in Hoofdstuk V. Opgemerkt werd dat praktijk van Staten traditioneel wordt beschouwd als het belangrijkste element voor de totstandkoming van gewoonterechtelijke normen, terwijl *opinio juris* blijk geeft van de overtuiging dat rechtens zo gehandeld behoort te worden. Daarbij werd opgemerkt dat de praktijk van Staten slechts onder voorwaarden bijdraagt aan de totstandkoming van internationaal gewoonterecht. Drie factoren zijn belangrijk in dit opzicht: de uniformiteit, de wijdverbreidheid en representativiteit, en mogelijk ook de duur van de praktijk. Tevens werd opgemerkt dat hoewel de beide componenten van gewoonterecht twee duidelijk te onderscheiden elementen zijn die afzonderlijk bewijs voor de vaststelling van gewoonterecht vereisen, zij steeds verder naar elkaar zijn toegegroeid. Dat is het gevolg van een inclusieve benadering van Statenpraktijk, waarbij niet alleen de fysieke handelingen (en omissies) van Staten, maar ook hun verbale handelingen relevant zijn. Deze verbale handelingen zijn nauw verbonden met de subjectieve component van gewoonterecht, *opinio juris*, aangezien de inhoud van verbale handelingen vaak ook de rechtsovertuiging van staten weergeeft. Deze verwevenheid maakt het moeilijk – en wellicht zelfs overwegend theoretisch – om de twee elementen van gewoonterecht te scheiden. In dit verband werd opgemerkt dat er een algemene tendens bestaat om *opinio juris* af te leiden uit de aanwezigheid van Statenpraktijk, mits de aanwezige praktijk voldoende 'dicht' en duidelijk is. Dit werd aangemerkt als de hedendaagse interpretatie van de traditionele benadering.

In Hoofdstuk V werden bovendien enkele progressieve maar meer controversiele benaderingen van het vaststellen van internationaal gewoonterecht kritisch onder de loep genomen, zoals de glijdende schaal-theorie en de mensenrechtenbenadering. In tegenstelling tot het conventionele model dat Statenpraktijk benadrukt, verkiezen deze benaderingen *opinio juris* boven de (fysieke) handelingen van Staten. Bovendien weerspiegelen deze opvattingen een relatie tussen de inhoudelijke betekenis van de norm enerzijds, en de bereidheid om tekortkomingen in de traditionele elementen van gewoonterecht tegen elkaar af te wegen of zelfs te negeren anderzijds. In dit verband werd gesteld dat de progressieve modellen van internationaal gewoonterecht sterk zijn ingegeven door morele of humanitaire overwegingen. Hoewel dergelijke benaderingen inderdaad aantrekkelijk kunnen zijn vanuit moreel of humanitair perspectief, werd een aantal serieuze bezwaren op zowel conceptueel, methodologisch en meer inhoudelijk niveau opgeworpen. Zo werd betoogd dat de progressieve modellen – voornamelijk de mensenrechtenbenadering – de aard van internationaal gewoonterecht te ver oprekken, omdat deze methoden het mogelijk maken om nieuwe gewoonterechtelijke normen vast te stellen wanneer dat wenselijk wordt geacht vanuit een moreel of humanitair perspectief. Als zodanig lijken de progressieve benaderingen internationaal recht zoals het momenteel is te verwarren met hoe internationaal recht er idealiter zou uitzien.

Gezien de kritiek op de zeer progressieve theorieën enerzijds, en gezien de evolutie die de traditionele benadering van internationaal gewoonterecht heeft doorgemaakt anderzijds, werd geconcludeerd dat de hedendaagse interpretatie van de traditionele benadering dient te worden gebruikt bij het toetsen of een recht op 'remedial secession' onder internationaal gewoonterecht tot stand is gekomen. Om het onderscheid tussen *lex lata* en *lex ferenda* te handhaven, werd een aanpak voorgesteld waarbij eerst en vooral de aanwezigheid van Statenpraktijk en *opinio juris* vereist zijn voor de vaststelling van nieuwe gewoonterechtelijke normen. Deze benadering erkent dat Statenpraktijk zowel fysieke als verbale handelingen van Staten omvat, en dat een tekort van de ene verschijningsvorm kan worden gecompenseerd door de kracht van de ander. Daarbij werd echter wel benadrukt dat de twee verschijningsvormen van Statenpraktijk niet volledig uitwisselbaar zijn als gevolg waarvan fysieke handelingen geheel afwezig zouden kunnen zijn. De hedendaagse interpretatie van de traditionele benadering staat toe dat het belang van fysieke en verbale praktijk wordt gezien in verhouding tot de hoeveelheid aanwezige activiteit op het betreffende gebied. Desalniettemin vereist deze benadering de aanwezigheid van fysieke praktijk voor de vorming van internationaal gewoonterecht.

6. 'REMEDIAL SECESSION' ALS EEN GEWOONTERECHTELIJKE NORM?

Op basis van het voorgenoemde kader richtte Hoofdstuk VI zich op de toetsing van het bestaan van een recht op 'remedial secession' onder internationaal gewoonterecht. Alvorens de internationale reacties op pogingen tot unilaterale secessie onder de loep te nemen, werd het belang van de erkenning van Staten voor deze studie uitgelegd. In dit kader kwamen de twee belangrijkste stromingen met betrekking tot erkenning aan de orde: de constitutieve en declaratoire theorie. Vervolgens werd de betekenis van erkenning in de context van pogingen tot eenzijdige afscheiding uitgelegd. Gesteld werd dat hoewel erkenning over het algemeen beschouwd wordt als declaratoir van aard, in het geval van eenzijdige afscheiding kan de vrijwel uniforme erkenning van de aspirant-Staat door al bestaande Staten het uiteindelijke succes van de poging tot unilaterale secessie bepalen en dus bewijs omvatten voor de positie als Staat ('statehood'). Als zodanig kan brede erkenning onder omstandigheden een zeker constitutief effect hebben, waardoor erkenning invloed kan hebben op de ontwikkeling van Statenpraktijk met betrekking tot een recht op 'remedial secession', mits een dergelijke verwijzing expliciet wordt gemaakt.

Vervolgens richtte Hoofdstuk VI zich op een analyse van de internationale reacties op pogingen tot eenzijdige afscheiding. In deze analyse werd een belangrijke rol toebedeeld aan Kosovo's poging om zich in 2008 af te scheiden van Servië en de internationale reacties daarop. Immers, Kosovo werd niet alleen vaak aangeduid als een test voor het bestaan van een recht op unilaterale secessie, maar geeft bovendien unieke inzichten in de hedendaagse opvattingen van Staten met betrekking tot een recht op 'remedial secession'. Eerst werden de algemene reacties van Staten met betrekking tot Kosovo's unilaterale onafhankelijkheidsverklaring onder de loep genomen. Noch de debatten in de VN-Veiligheidsraad en Algemene Vergadering, noch de erkenningsverklaringen van individuele Staten weerspiegelden echter de erkenning van een recht op 'remedial secession'. Verwijzingen naar het recht op (externe) zelfbeschikking werden nauwelijks gemaakt en waar een dergelijke verwijzing wel werd gemaakt, was deze kort en vormde zij bovendien niet het belangrijkste argument. Integendeel, de algemene reacties op Kosovo's poging tot afscheiding weerspiegelden voornamelijk sterke steun voor de soevereiniteit en respect voor de territoriale integriteit van Staten, zoals vastgelegd in het VN-Handvest en het (juridisch) kader dat VN-Veiligheidsraadresolutie 1244 (1999) biedt. In dit verband riepen de verklaringen vaak op tot een wederzijds erkende oplossing van de kwestie, waarmee pogingen tot eenzijdige afscheiding (impliciet) werden veroordeeld. Bovendien werden de reacties van Staten in de eerste plaats bepaald door niet-juridische overwegingen. De meerderheid van de Staten verwachtte dat de oprichting en erkenning van een onafhankelijk Kosovo zou bijdragen aan de bevordering en het behoud van de vrede en stabiliteit in de regio, en voerde geen recht op zelfbeschikking of 'remedial secession' aan als rechtvaardiging van Kosovo's onafhankelijkheid of de erkenning daarvan.

Behalve deze algemene reacties werden de schriftelijke en mondelinge opmerkingen van Staten bestudeerd die zij bij het Internationaal Gerechtshof inzonden dan wel presenteerden ten behoeve van de adviesprocedure inzake Kosovo's eenzijdige onafhankelijkheidsverklaring. Deze inzendingen bevatten enige steun voor het bestaan van een recht op 'remedial secession'. Diverse Staten waren van mening dat internationaal recht een recht op 'remedial secession' erkent. In het algemeen werd deze visie gebaseerd op een *a contrario* interpretatie van de zogeheten 'safeguard clauses' van de VN-Verklaring inzake Vriendschappelijke Relaties tussen Staten en de Verklaring en het Actieprogramma van Wenen, de Åland *Islands*-zaak, de beslissing van het Canadese Hooggerechtshof in de *Reference re Secession of Quebec*, en de steun die te vinden is in de doctrine. Gelet op het feit dat er vrijwel geen verwijzingen naar de praktijk werden gemaakt, werd geconcludeerd dat Staten de internationale praktijk niet beschouwden als sterk bewijs voor het bestaan van een recht op 'remedial secession'. De meeste van deze Staten zagen eenzijdige afscheiding als een *ultimum remedium* in gevallen waarin de autoriteiten van de Staat een volk het recht op interne zelfbeschikking ontzeggen. Ernstige mensenrechtenschendingen werden ook genoemd in deze context, ofwel als uiting van het gebrek aan interne zelfbeschikking, ofwel als afzonderlijke en extra voorwaarde. Deze Staten betoogden in de eerste plaats dat onvoldoende bewijs voorhanden is voor het bestaan van een recht op 'remedial secession' en/of beriepen zich op de voorrang van het beginsel van respect voor de territoriale integriteit van Staten. Een tweede (subsidiaire) redenering betrof de vermeende neutraliteit van internationaal recht ten opzichte van secessie.

Naast het geval van Kosovo werden enkele andere situaties bezien die soms worden aangevoerd als bevestiging van een recht op 'remedial secession'. Daarbij werd duidelijk dat de praktijk buiten de context van dekolonisatie geen sterke en duidelijke bevestiging van een dergelijk recht biedt. Eerst werden enkele gevallen van staatsvorming verworpen als zijnde zuivere voorbeelden van unilaterale afscheiding. Als zodanig werden Eritrea en de Baltische Republieken (en andere opvolgerstaten van de Sovjet-Unie) genoemd. Gesteld werd dat indien überhaupt geen sprake is van eenzijdige afscheiding, de term 'remedial secession' niet van toepassing is. Daarop werd geconcludeerd dat de gevallen van Eritrea en de Baltische Republieken niet kunnen worden gezien als bewijs voor het bestaan van een recht op 'remedial secession'. Vervolgens werden de gevallen van Bangladesh, Kroatië en Slovenië nader beschouwd. Aangevoerd werd dat de gevallen van Bangladesh en Kroatië (exclusief Slovenië) inderdaad voorbeelden van eenzijdige afscheiding betreffen, gelet op het ontbreken van de instemming van de betreffende Staat. Daarnaast zou gesteld kunnen worden dat deze afscheidingen een remedie vormden, aangezien zij voortkwamen uit situaties waarin de moederstaat de betreffende bevolking ernstig onderdrukte en onderwierp aan ernstige mensenrechtenschendingen. Toch bleek dat beide aspirant-Staten niet door de internationale gemeenschap werden erkend als gevolg van een vermeend recht op 'remedial secession', maar om andere redenen. De gevallen van Bangladesh en Kroatië kunnen daarom niet worden gezien als overtuigende voorbeelden van 'remedial secession' die bewijs vormen voor de stelling dat een dergelijk recht vandaag de dag bestaat.

Na diverse pogingen tot eenzijdige afscheiding en de internationale reacties daarop te hebben behandeld, werd het mogelijk om de vraag te beantwoorden of een recht op 'remedial secession' bestaat onder internationaal gewoonterecht. Daartoe zijn de elementen van Statenpraktijk en *opinio juris* met betrekking tot een dergelijk recht getoetst. Met betrekking tot het objectieve element van gewoonterecht werd gesteld dat slechts enkele pogingen tot eenzijdige afscheiding mogelijkerwijs kunnen worden gezien als fysieke Statenpraktijk wat betreft 'remedial secession' en dat verbale Statenpraktijk hierover enkel werd gevonden in het kader het geval van Kosovo en zelfs daar slechts in beperkte mate. Het blijft onzeker of er in de praktijk tot nu toe überhaupt succesvolle voorbeelden zijn van 'remedial secession'. Met betrekking tot het subjectieve element van *opinio juris* werd gesteld dat er een zekere mate van *opinio juris* bestaat wat betreft het bestaan van een recht op 'remedial secession'. Geconcludeerd werd echter dat deze *opinio juris* in geen geval sterk en eenduidig is. Kortom, beide componenten van gewoonterecht zijn in onvoldoende mate aanwezig om onder de conventionele benadering van internationaal gewoonte-recht, ook indien hedendaags geïnterpreteerd, het bestaan van 'remedial secession' te kunnen vaststellen. Zelfs wanneer de meer liberale en progressieve (maar omstreden) mensenrechtenbenadering – die het mogelijk maakt om onvolkomenheden in Statenpraktijk te negeren wanneer sterke en eenduidige *opinio juris* bestaat – zou worden gehanteerd, werd geconcludeerd dat een recht op 'remedial secession' niet bestaat als gewoonterechtelijke norm.

7. CONCLUSIES OVER EEN RECHT OP 'REMEDIAL SECESSION' *DE LEGE LATA* EN *DE LEGE FERENDA*

Op basis van de analyse in dit onderzoek zoals hierboven samengevat, zijn vervolgens algemene conclusies getrokken. Daarbij is een onderscheid gemaakt tussen een recht op 'remedial secession' *de lege lata* enerzijds en een recht op 'remedial secession' *de lege ferenda* anderzijds.

7.1. Een recht op 'remedial secession' *de lege lata*

Alle bevindingen uit dit onderzoek in overweging nemend, werd geconcludeerd dat het concept van externe zelfbeschikking als een remedie tegen ernstig onrecht vandaag de dag niet bestaat als een afdwingbaar recht onder het hedendaagse internationale recht. Vastgesteld werd dat in verschillende bronnen van internationaal recht inderdaad een zekere mate van steun voor een dergelijk recht weerspiegeld wordt, met name in de doctrine en rechterlijke uitspraken en opinies. Deze steun is echter onvoldoende – in omvang, in gewicht, en in overtuigingskracht – om het vandaag de dag een positief recht te noemen. De theoretische basis van een recht op 'remedial secession' is relatief zwak en lijkt vooral te worden ingegeven door morele overwegingen en vermeende noodzakelijkheid, terwijl de praktijk evenmin getuigt van overtuigende steun voor een dergelijk recht. Zelfs wanneer wordt uitgegaan van de progressieve mensenrechtenbenadering van internationaal gewoonterecht, werd duidelijk dat onvoldoende Statenpraktijk en *opinio juris* bestaan om tot de conclusie te komen dat 'remedial secession' zich heeft ontwikkeld tot een gewoonterechtelijke norm. Op dit moment behelst het zelfbeschikkingsrecht geen unilaterale secessie, maar richt het zich op de interne dimensie en wordt het beperkt door traditionele beginselen van internationaal recht, zoals soevereiniteit en respect voor de territoriale integriteit van de Staat. Met andere woorden, zelfbeschikking dient in de eerste plaats intern te worden vormgegeven, dat wil zeggen binnen het kader van de bestaande Staat en op basis van de instemming van deze Staat. Als zodanig kan zelfbeschikking worden gerealiseerd door middel van bijvoorbeeld het introduceren van vormen van autonomie. Buiten de dekolonisatiecontext kan zelfbeschikking in haar externe manifestatie alleen worden uitgeoefend door middel van vreedzame desintegratie, de

vereniging met of integratie in een andere Staat, secessie op basis van een constitutionele machtiging of met instemming van de Staat.

Als zodanig kan worden gesteld dat het huidige internationaalrechtelijke kader niet
voorziet in een collectieve remedie voor bevolkingsgroepen die door de Staat worden
onderdrukt en onderworpen aan ernstig onrecht – in elk geval niet door middel van
unilaterale secessie. Dat wil echter niet zeggen dat het internationale recht in geen
enkel rechtsmiddel voorziet. Individuen kunnen zich beroepen op individuele mensenrechten zoals vervat in diverse internationale mensenrechtenverdragen. Bovendien kunnen mechanismen voor minderhedenbescherming worden aangewend om de
rechten van minderheden in te roepen. Via deze mechanismen kunnen zij echter geen
aanspraak maken op een recht op 'remedial secession'.

7.2. Een recht op 'remedial secession' *de lege ferenda*

Hoewel is aangetoond dat onvoldoende bewijs voorhanden is om het bestaan van
een recht op 'remedial secession' aan te nemen, werd in dit onderzoek ook duidelijk dat diverse bronnen van het internationale recht sporen van een dergelijk recht
weerspiegelen. Uit deze sporen blijkt dat een zekere overeenstemming bestaat over
de contouren van een recht op 'remedial secession' *de lege ferenda*. Dus hoewel
benadrukt dient te worden dat dit nog verdere discussie, uitwerking en, belangrijker
nog, brede steun van de internationale statengemeenschap vereist, kan op basis van
de voorgaande hoofdstukken voorzichtig een kader worden geschetst voor de mogelijke toekomstige ontwikkeling van een recht op 'remedial secession'. De sporen van
een recht op 'remedial secession' in de bronnen van internationaal recht verwijzen
meestal naar een recht dat slechts ontstaat in uitzonderlijke omstandigheden en onder
bepaalde voorwaarden – zowel inhoudelijk als procedureel.

De eerste inhoudelijke voorwaarde betreft de aanhoudende ontzegging van
interne zelfbeschikking door de centrale autoriteiten van de Staat. Meer specifiek zou
minimaal vereist zijn dat de Staat herhaaldelijk weigert om de bevolkingsgroep rechten voor politieke participatie te verlenen en een representatieve regering te bieden
voordat 'remedial secession' rechtmatig kan zijn. In dat opzicht is een sterk verband tussen de interne dimensie van het zelfbeschikkingsrecht en de externe dimensie aangetoond in zowel de doctrine als in de rechtspraak en Statenpraktijk. Er zijn
echter sterke aanwijzingen dat enkel het ontbreken van interne zelfbeschikking niet
zal volstaan voor een rechtmatige afscheiding. Naast deze inhoudelijke voorwaarde
werden twee andere factoren vaak genoemd: de aanwezigheid van ernstige mensenrechtenschendingen en discriminatoire behandeling van een bevolkingsgroep. Beide
factoren houden verband met het vereiste van gebrek aan interne zelfbeschikking
en sommige auteurs hebben dan ook gesteld dat de aanwezigheid van deze factoren
kan worden afgeleid uit het ontbreken van politieke participatierechten en een representatieve regering. In het algemeen wordt het bestaan van flagrante schendingen

van fundamentele mensenrechten echter beschouwd als een separate voorwaarde, waardoor de lat voor het ontstaan van een recht op 'remedial secession' hoger wordt gelegd. Deze additionele parameter wordt breed gedragen in de literatuur en de rechtspraak, en wordt tevens weergegeven in de verklaringen van Staten die de doctrine van 'remedial secession' in beginsel ondersteunen. De belangrijkste toetssteen voor een recht op 'remedial secession' is echter de ontzegging van interne zelfbeschikking.

In aanvulling op de inhoudelijke voorwaarden hierboven beschreven, moet tevens aan een procedureel vereiste worden voldaan, namelijk dat 'remedial secession' daadwerkelijk een *ultimum remedium* is. Met andere woorden, dit procedurele vereiste maakt het noodzakelijk dat alle effectieve en reële middelen om het conflict op vreedzame wijze op te lossen zijn uitgeput voordat unilaterale afscheiding als remedie gerechtvaardigd zou zijn. Vanzelfsprekend dient per geval te worden bezien of aan dit vereiste is voldaan. Immers, wat in de ene situatie als een laatste redmiddel zou worden beschouwd, zal in de andere situatie niet als zodanig gelden. In sommige gevallen kunnen de modaliteiten om het zelfbeschikkingsrecht intern te implementeren, variërend van autonomie tot zogeheten 'complex power-sharing', nog een reëel en effectief alternatief voor afscheiding bieden, terwijl deze modaliteiten in een andere, meer ernstige en ontwrichtte situatie niet langer een redelijke oplossing kunnen bieden. In elk geval, gelet op de gevoeligheid van de materie enerzijds en de hoge drempel voor 'remedial secession' anderzijds, lijkt internationale betrokkenheid vereist. Die internationale betrokkenheid kan bijvoorbeeld vorm krijgen in de onderhandelingen tussen de Staat en de separatistische entiteit – bijvoorbeeld als gespreksleider of als mediator – of door hulp van internationale organisaties of andere (gerechtelijke) instanties. Slechts dan zou de weg naar unilaterale secessie open staan.

Bij het schetsen van de contouren van een recht op 'remedial secession' *de lege ferenda* dient benadrukt te worden dat een aantal uitzonderlijke omstandigheden in de weg staat aan de rechtmatige uitoefening van een dergelijk recht. Zelfs wanneer de parameters voor de uitoefening van een recht op 'remedial secession' zoals hierboven uiteengezet aanwezig zouden zijn, kan afscheiding onrechtmatig zijn wanneer daarmee een *jus cogens* norm wordt geschonden, zoals het geweldsverbod. In die situaties kan de VN-Veiligheidsraad gelet op de omstandigheden van het geval een poging tot afscheiding als illegaal bestempelen en de internationale gemeenschap oproepen de aspirant-Staat niet te erkennen.

8. ENKELE SLOTBESCHOUWINGEN OVER 'REMEDIAL SECESSION'

Aan het einde van het boek zijn enkele afsluitende beschouwingen over het concept 'remedial secession' gepresenteerd. Voortbordurend op de bevindingen uit de voorgaande hoofdstukken is eerst kort gereflecteerd op de vraag of het concept van 'remedial secession' kan worden geëffectueerd door middel van erkenning. Hoewel is geconcludeerd dat 'remedial secession' geen positief recht is onder het heden-daagse internationale recht, betekent dat niet noodzakelijkerwijs dat 'remedial seces-sion' niets meer is dan een theoretisch concept zonder enige praktische relevantie. Het betekent evenmin dat de mogelijkheid tot unilaterale secessie per definitie is uitgesloten. Gelet op de constitutieve effecten die brede erkenning kan hebben in het geval van pogingen tot unilaterale secessie, zou gesteld kunnen worden dat wan-neer een entiteit eenzijdig een Staat wil worden, dit feitelijk alleen mogelijk is door middel van internationale erkenning. Sommige auteurs hebben dan ook gesuggereerd dat het concept van 'remedial secession' kan worden geëffectueerd door middel van brede erkenning van de aspirant-Staat door al bestaande Staten. Met andere woor-den, hoewel 'remedial secession' geenszins een afdwingbaar recht behelst, zou het zo kunnen zijn dat Staten (meer) bereid zijn om entiteiten die zich vanwege onderdruk-king van een bevolking in kwestie en ernstige mensenrechtenschendingen op hun grondgebied proberen af te scheiden van de Staat te erkennen en door dit op grote schaal te doen, het succes van een claim op een onafhankelijke Staat bepalen. Dat betekent niet dat erkenning daadwerkelijk een recht op 'remedial secession' creëert, maar wel dat erkenning het succes van een poging tot unilaterale secessie sterk kan beïnvloeden. Met name in situaties waarin het twijfelachtig is of aan de criteria uit de Montevideo Conventie wordt voldaan, kan wijdverbreide erkenning in dit opzicht verstrekkende gevolgen hebben. Een soortgelijke redenering werd gebruikt door het Canadese Hooggerechtshof in de *Reference re Secession of Quebec*. In deze zaak suggereerde het Hooggerechtshof dat Staten bij de beslissing om al dan niet te erken-nen, de behandeling van de entiteit door de Staat laten meewegen. Gezien deze gro-tendeels hypothetische mogelijkheid moet benadrukt worden dat de internationale reacties op Kosovo's onafhankelijkheidsverklaring een ander beeld laten zien. Over het algemeen was een dergelijk causaal verband tussen mensenrechtenschendingen enerzijds en erkenning anderzijds niet zichtbaar. Slechts enkele Staten verwezen naar mensenrechtenschendingen op het grondgebied als een van de – voornamelijk niet-juridische – factoren die leidden tot de beslissing om te erkennen. Het blijft dus de vraag of Staten het idee van 'remedial secession' in de toekomst als een leidraad zullen gebruiken in de besluitvorming omtrent erkenning. In het licht van de poli-tieke beoordelingsvrijheid die Staten op dit gebied hebben en de politieke belangen die op het spel staan, zullen politieke overwegingen altijd een belangrijke – zo niet doorslaggevende – rol blijven spelen.

Vervolgens is, tegen de achtergrond van de ontwikkeling die vaak wordt aangeduid als de humanisering van de internationale rechtsorde, gereflecteerd op de mogelijk toekomstige ontwikkeling van een recht op 'remedial secession'. Met de humanise-ring van de internationale rechtsorde wordt verwezen naar de transformatie van het internationale recht van een voornamelijk Staat-gericht systeem naar een meer mens-gericht systeem, waarin Staten niet langer de enige actoren zijn en waarbij het accent in toenemende mate komt te liggen op het respecteren en bevorderen van de belangen en de rechten van de mens – zowel van individuen als groepen, aangeduid als volkeren, minderheden en inheemse volkeren. Als zodanig raakt deze ontwikkeling aan enkele kernbeginselen van het klassieke Westfaalse systeem, voornamelijk het concept van staatssoevereiniteit en de beginselen die hieruit voortvloeien. De humanisering van de internationale rechtsorde kan worden beschouwd als een zoektocht naar een nieuw evenwicht waarin de belangen van Staten niet worden genegeerd, maar evenmin per definitie het zwaarste wegen. Hoewel dit een caleidoscopisch proces betreft, wordt de kern ervan op twee manieren zichtbaar: de rechten en belangen van de mens worden versterkt, terwijl tegelijkertijd de onaantastbare positie van de Staat wordt betwist. Het is tegen de achtergrond van de humanisering van de internationale rechtsorde dat het debat over de vraag naar externe zelfbeschikking na ernstige mensenrechtenschendingen en de opkomst van het concept van 'remedial secession' kan worden begrepen. Betoogd werd dat de suggestie van een 'nooduitgang' voor volkeren die door de Staat worden onderworpen aan ernstig onrecht aansluit bij de humaniseringstendens. Met dit idee van een 'nooduitgang' worden humanitaire overwegingen opgeworpen als een belangrijk tegenwicht voor de rechten en belangen van de Staat. Ook hierin wordt de tweevoudige manifestatie van de humaniseringstendens weerspiegeld. Het idee van 'remedial secession' kan dus worden gezien als een bijdrage aan de geleidelijke transformatie van een Staat-gericht systeem naar een meer mens-gericht systeem. Het huidige gebrek aan steun voor het concept van 'remedial secession' door Staten is echter symptomatisch voor de conclusie dat de ontwikkeling van de internationale rechtsorde van een Staatgericht systeem naar een mensgericht systeem nog geen nieuw evenwicht heeft gevonden. De zoektocht naar een dergelijk evenwicht zal naar alle waarschijnlijkheid blijven doorgaan. Gelet op deze voortdurende ontwikkeling en de sporen van een recht op 'remedial secession' die op dit moment zichtbaar zijn, is het dan ook niet ondenkbaar dat een dergelijk recht op een dag deel zal uitmaken van het positieve internationale recht.

BIBLIOGRAPHY

ARTICLES, BOOKS, AND PAPERS

A

Abi-Saab, G., 'Report by George Abi-Saab: "The Effectivity Required of an Entity that Declares its Independence in Order for it to be Considered a State in International Law"' in A.F. Bayefsky (ed.) *Self-Determination in International Law Quebec and Lessons Learned* (Kluwer Law International, The Hague 2000)

Alfredsson, G., 'The Right to Self-Determination and Indigenous Peoples' in C. Tomuschat (ed.) *Modern Law of Self-Determination* (Martinus Nijhoff Publishers, Dordrecht 1993)

Allcock, J.B., 'Kosovo' in Encyclopædia Britannica (Encyclopædia Britannica Online edn 2010)

Almqvist, J., *The Politics of Recognition, Kosovo and International Law* (Working Paper, Real Instituto Elcano 2009)

Anaya, S.J., *Indigenous Peoples in International Law* (2nd edn, Oxford University Press, Oxford 2004)

Anghie, A., *Imperialism, Sovereignty and the Making of International Law* (Cambridge University Press, Cambridge 2007)

Arajärvi, N.J., *The Changing Nature of Customary International Law: Methods of Interpreting the Concept of Custom in International Criminal Tribunals* (European University Institute 2011)

Arajärvi, N.J., 'The Lines Begin to Blur? Opinio Juris and the Moralisation of Customary International Law' (2011) *SSRN Working Paper Series*

Arp, B., 'The ICJ Advisory Opinion on the Accordance with International Law of the Unilateral Declaration of Independence in Respect of Kosovo and the International Protection of Minorities' (2010) 11 *German Law Journal* 847

Aust, A., 'Advisory Opinions' (2010) 1 *Journal of International Dispute Settlement* 123

B

Barros, J., *The Aland Islands Question: Its Settlement by the League of Nations* (Yale University Press, New Haven 1968)

Bayefsky, A.F., 'Introduction' in A.F. Bayefsky (ed.) *Self-Determination in International Law. Quebec and Lessons Learned* (Kluwer Law International, The Hague 2000)

Bayefsky (ed.), A.F., *Self-Determination in International Law. Quebec and Lessons Learned* (Kluwer Law International, The Hague 2000)

Behiels, M.D., 'Quebec' in *Encyclopædia Britannica* (Encyclopædia Britannica Online edn 2010)

Bellamy, A.J., and P.D. Williams, 'The New Politics of Protection? Côte d'Ivoire, Libya and the Responsibility to Protect' (2011) 87 *International Affairs* 825

Bellinger, J.B., and W.J. Haynes, 'A US Government Response to the International Committee of the Red Cross study *Customary International Humanitarian Law*' (2007) 89 *International Review of the Red Cross* 443

Bianchi (ed.), A., *Non-State Actors and International Law* (Ashgate, Farnham 2009)

Blay, S.K.N., 'Territorial Integrity and Political Independence' in R. Wolfrum (ed.) *Max Planck Encyclopedia of Public International Law* (fully updated online edn Oxford University Press, New York 2010)

Blum, Y.Z., 'Russia Takes Over the Soviet Union's Seat at the United Nations' (1992) 3 *European Journal of International Law* 354

Bogdandy, A. von, and M. Rau, 'The Lotus' in R. Wolfrum (ed.) *Max Planck Encyclopedia of Public International Law* (fully updated online edn Oxford University Press, New York 2010)

Bolton, G., and G. Visoka 'Recognizing Kosovo's Independence: Remedial Secession or Earned Sovereignty?' (2010) St Antony's College, University of Oxford (Occasional Paper No. 11/10)

Borgen, C.J., 'Kosovo's Declaration of Independence: Self-Determination, Secession and Recognition' (2008) 12/2 *ASIL Insights*

Bosch, M. van den, and W.J.M. van Genugten, 'International Protection of Migrant Workers, National Minorities and Indigenous Peoples - Comparing Underlying Concepts' (2002) 9 *International Journal on Minority and Group Rights* 195

Bossuyt, M.J., *Guide to the "Travaux Préparatoires" of the International Covenant on Civil and Political Rights* (Martinus Nijhoff Publishers, Dordrecht 1987)

Brilmayer, L., 'Secession: A Theoretical Interpretation' (1991) 16 *Yale Journal of International Law* 177

Brownlie, I, *Principles of Public International Law* (7th edn, Oxford University Press, Oxford 2008)

Buchanan, A., *Justice, Legitimacy, and Self-Determination. Moral Foundations for International Law* (Oxford University Press, Oxford 2004)

Buchheit, L.C., *Secession: The Legitimacy of Self-Determination* (Yale University Press, New Haven 1978)

Burke-White, W.W., 'Adoption of the Responsibility to Protect' in J. Genser and I. Cotler (eds) *The Responsibility to Protect: The Promise of Stopping Mass Atrocities in Our Time* (Oxford University Press, Oxford/New York 2012)

Burri, T., 'The Kosovo Opinion and Secession: The Sounds of Silence and Missing Links' (2010) 11 *German Law Journal* 881

Butler, W.E., 'Territorial Integrity and Secession: The Dialectics of International Order' in J. Dahlitz (ed.) *Secession and International Law* (T.M.C. Asser Press, The Hague 2003)

Byers, M., *Custom, Power and the Power of Rules. International Relations and Customary International Law* (Cambridge University Press, Cambridge 1999)

C
Caluwaert, K., *De toekomst van onafhankelijkheidsbewegingen en het recht op zelfbeschikking* (Master's Thesis, Ghent University 2010)

Cançado Trindade, A.A., *International Law for Humankind. Towards a New Jus Gentium* (Martinus Nijhoff Publishers, Leiden 2010)

Cassese, A., *Self-Determination of Peoples. A Legal Reappraisal* (Cambridge University Press, Cambridge 1995)

Cassese, A., 'The International Court of Justice and the Right of Peoples to Self-Determination' in V. Lowe and M. Fitzmaurice (eds) *Fifty Years of the International Court of Justice Essays in Honour of Sir Robert Jennings* (Cambridge University Press, Cambridge 1996)

Cassese, A., *International Law* (Oxford University Press, Oxford 2001)

Castellino, J., *International Law and Self-Determination: The Interplay of the Politics of Territorial Possession with Formulations of Post-Colonial 'National' Identity* (Martinus Nijhoff Publishers, The Hague 2000)

Castellino, J., 'Territorial Integrity and the "Right" to Self-Determination: An Examination of the Conceptual Tools' (2008) 33 *Brooklyn Journal of International Law* 503

Cerna, C.M., 'Universal Democracy: An International Legal Right or a Pipe Dream of the West?' (1995) 86 *NYU Journal of International Law and Politics* 289

Cheng, B., 'United Nations Resolutions on Outer Space: 'Instant' International Customary Law?' (1965) 5 *Indian Journal of International Law* 23

Chernichenko S.V., and V.S. Kotliar, 'Ongoing Global Debate on Self-Determination and Secession: Main Trends' in J. Dahlitz (ed.) *Secession and International Law* (T.M.C. Asser Press, The Hague 2003)

Chesterman, S., *Just War or Just Peace? Humanitarian Intervention and International Law* (Oxford University Press, Oxford 2001)

Chesterman, S., *You, the People. The United Nations, Transitional Administration, and State-Building* (Oxford University Press, Oxford 2004)

Chodosh, H.E., 'Neither Treaty nor Custom: The Emergence of Declarative International Law' (1991) 26 *Texas International Law Journal* 87

Christakis, T., 'The ICJ Advisory Opinion on Kosovo: Has International Law Something to Say about Secession?' (2011) 24 *Leiden Journal of International Law* 73

Cismas, I., 'Secession in Theory and Practice: the Case of Kosovo and Beyond' (2010) 2 *Goettingen Journal of International Law* 531

Cobban, A., *The Nation State and National Self-Determination* (Collins, London 1969)

Cohen, H.G., 'Finding International Law: Rethinking the Doctrine of Sources' (2007) 93 *Iowa Law Review* 65

Coppieters, B., 'Introduction' in B. Coppieters and R. Sakwa (eds) *Contextualizing Secession Normative Studies in Comparative Perspective* (Oxford University Press, Oxford 2003)

Corten, O., *The Law against War* (Hart Publishing, Oxford 2010)

Corten, O., 'Territorial Integrity Narrowly Interpreted: Reasserting the Classical Inter-State Paradigm of International Law' (2011) 24 *Leiden Journal of International Law* 87

Craven, M.C.R., 'The European Community Arbitration Commission on Yugoslavia' (1995) 66 *British Yearbook of International Law* 222

Craven, M.C.R., 'What's in a Name? The Former Yugoslav Republic of Macedonia and Issues of Statehood' (1995) 16 *Australian Year Book of International Law* 199

Craven, M.C.R., 'Statehood, Self-Determination, and Recognition' in M.D. Evans (ed.) *International Law* (3rd edn Oxford University Press, Oxford 2010)

Crawford, J.R., 'Outside the Colonial Context' in W.J.A. Macartney (ed.) *Self-Determination in the Commonwealth* (Aberdeen University Press, Aberdeen 1988)

Crawford (ed.), J.R., *The Rights of Peoples* (Clarendon Press, Oxford 1988)

Crawford, J.R., 'Democracy and International Law' (1993) 64 *British Yearbook of International Law* 113

Crawford, J.R., 'Democracy and the Body of International Law' in G.H. Fox and B.R. Roth (eds) *Democratic Governance and International Law* (Cambridge University Press, Cambridge 2000)

Crawford, J.R., 'Report by James Crawford: "Response to Experts Reports of the *Amicus Curiae*"' in A.F. Bayefsky (ed.) *Self-Determination in International Law: Quebec and Lessons Learned Legal Opinions Selected and Introduced* (Kluwer Law International, The Hague 2000)

Crawford, J.R., 'The Right of Self-Determination in International Law: Its Development and Future' in P. Alston (ed.) *Peoples' Rights* (Oxford University Press, Oxford 2001)

Crawford, J.R., *The International Law Commission's Articles on State Responsibility. Introduction, Text and Commentaries* (Cambridge University Press, Cambridge 2002)

Crawford, J.R., *The Creation of States in International Law* (2nd revised edn, Clarendon Press, Oxford 2006)

Cunningham, F., *Theories of Democracy: A Critical Introduction* (Routledge, London/New York 2002)

D

Daes, E.-I.A., 'Some Considerations on the Right of Indigenous Peoples to Self-Determination' (1993) 3 *Transnational Law and Contemporary Problems* 1

Daes, E.-I.A., 'The Spirit and Letter of the Right to Self-Determination of Indigenous Peoples: Reflections on the Making of the United Nations Draft Declaration' in P. Aikio and M. Scheinin (eds) *Operationalizing the Right of Indigenous Peoples to Self-Determination* (Institute for Human Rights, Åbo Akademi University, Turku/Åbo 2000)

D'Amato, A.A., *The Concept of Custom in International Law* (Cornell University Press, London 1971)

DeLancey, M.W., 'Cameroon' in *Encyclopædia Britannica* (Encyclopædia Britannica Online edn 2010)

Dinstein, Y., 'The Degree of Self-Rule of Minorities in Unitarian and Federal States' in C. Brölmann, R. Lefeber and M. Zieck (eds) *Peoples and Minorities in International Law* (Martinus Nijhoff Publishers, Dordrecht 1993)

Dixon, M., *Textbook on International Law* (6th edn, Oxford University Press, Oxford 2007)

Doehring, K., 'Self-Determination' in B. Simma (ed.) *The Charter of the United Nations A Commentary* (2nd edn Oxford University Press, Oxford 2002)

Dugard, J., 'Secession: Is the Case of Yugoslavia a Precedent for Africa?' (1993) 5 *African Journal of International and Comparative Law* 163

Dugard, J., 'A Legal Basis for Secession: Relevant Principles and Rules' in J.

Dahlitz (ed.) *Secession and International Law* (T.M.C. Asser Press, The Hague 2003)

Dugard, J., and D. Raič, 'The Role of Recognition in the Law and Practice of Self-Determination' in M.G. Kohen (ed.) *Secession International Law Perspectives* (Cambridge University Press, Cambridge 2006)

Dumberry, P., 'Lessons Learned from the *Quebec Secession Reference* before the Supreme Court of Canada' in M.G. Kohen (ed.) *Secession International Law Perspectives* (Cambridge University Press, Cambridge 2006)

Duursma, J.C., *Fragmentation and the International Relations of Micro-States: Self-Determination and Statehood* (Cambridge University Press, Cambridge 1996)

E

Eide, A., 'The National Society, Peoples and Ethno-Nations: Semantic Confusions and Legal Consequences' (1995) 64 *Nordic Journal of International Law* 353

Eide, A., 'Territorial Integrity of States, Minority Protection, and Guarantees for Autonomy Arrangements: Approaches and Roles of the United Nations' (Local Self-Government, Territorial Integrity and Protection of Minorities 1996)

Eide, A., 'The Non-Inclusion of Minority Rights: Resolution 217C (III)' in G. Alfredsson and A. Eide (eds) *The Universal Declaration of Human Rights: A Common Standard of Achievement* (Martinus Nijhoff Publishers, The Hague 1999)

Eide, A., 'Rights of Indigenous Peoples. Achievements in International Law During the Last Quarter of a Century' (2006) 37 *Netherlands Yearbook of International Law* 155

Emerson, R., 'The Logic of Secession' (1980) 89 *Yale Law Journal* 802

Epps, V., *Evolving Concepts of Self-Determination and Autonomy in International Law: The Legal Status of Tibet* (Suffolk University Law School 2008)

F

Fabry, M., *Recognizing States. International Society and the Establishment of New States Since 1776* (Oxford University Press, New York 2010)

Fairhurst, J., *Law of the European Union* (8th edn, Pearson, Harlow 2010)

Falk, R., 'The Kosovo Advisory Opinion: Conflict Resolution and Precedent' (2011) 105 *American Journal of International Law* 50

Fiedler, W., 'Unilateral Acts in International Law' in R. Bernhardt (ed.) *Encyclopedia of Public International Law* (Elsevier, Amsterdam 2000)

Foster, C.E., 'Articulating Self-Determination in the Draft Declaration on the Rights of Indigenous Peoples' (2001) 12 *European Journal of International Law* 141

Fox, G.H., 'The Right to Political Participation in International Law' (1992) 17 *Yale Journal of International Law* 539

Fox G.H., and B.R. Roth (eds), *Democratic Governance and International Law* (Cambridge University Press, Cambridge 2000)

Francioni, F., 'Equity in International Law' in R. Wolfrum (ed.) *Max Planck Encyclopedia of Public International Law* (fully updated online edn Oxford University Press, New York 2010)

Franck T.M., and others, 'Expert Opinion Prepared in 1992 by T.M. Franck, R. Higgins, A. Pellet, M.N. Shaw and C. Tomuschat, "The Territorial Integrity of Québec in the Event of the Attainment of Sovereignty"' in A.F. Bayefsky (ed.) *Self-Determinaiton in International Law: Quebec and Lessons Learned* (Kluwer Law International, The Hague 1992)

Franck, T.M., 'The Emerging Right to Democratic Governance' (1992) 86 *American Journal of International Law* 46

Franck, T.M., 'Postmodern Tribalism and the Right to Secession' in C. Brölmann, R. Lefeber and M. Zieck (eds) *Peoples and Minorities in International Law* (Martinus Nijhoff Publishers, Dordrecht 1993)

Franck, T.M., 'Report by Thomas M. Franck: "Opinion Directed at Question 2 of the Reference"' in A.F. Bayefsky (ed.) *Self-Determination in International Law Quebec and Lessons Learned* (Kluwer Law International, The Hague 2000)

Frowein, J.A., 'Self-Determination as a Limit to Obligations Under International Law' in C. Tomuschat (ed.) *Modern Law of Self-Determination* (Martinus Nijhoff Publishers, Dordrecht 1993)

G

Gaja, G., 'General Principles of Law' in R. Wolfrum (ed.) *Max Planck Encyclopedia of Public International Law* (fully updated online edn Oxford University Press, New York 2010)

Genser J., and I. Cotler (eds), *The Responsibility to Protect: The Promise of Stopping Mass Atrocities in Our Time* (Oxford University Press, Oxford/New York 2012)

Genugten, W.J.M. van, 'Handhaving van wereldrecht. Een kritische inspectie van valkuilen en dilemma's' (2010) 85 *Nederlands Juristenblad* 44

Genugten, W.J.M. van, C. Homan, N.J. Schrijver and P.J.I.M. de Waart, *The United Nations of the Future: Globalization with a Human Face* (KIT-Publishers Amsterdam 2006)

Glazier, D.W., Wars of National Liberation' in R. Wolfrum (ed.) *Max Planck Encyclopedia of Public International Law* (Oxford University Press, New York 2010)

Graham, L.M., 'Self-Determination for Indigenous Peoples After Kosovo: Translating Self-Determination "Into Practice" and "Into Peace"' (2000) 6 *ILSA Journal of International and Comparative Law* 455

Grant, T.D., *The Recognition of States: Law and Practice in Debate and Evolution* (Praeger, Westport/London 1999)

Griffioen, C.W., *Self-Determination as a Human Right. The Emergency Exit of Remedial Secession* (Master's Thesis, Utrecht University 2009)

Guzman, A.T., 'Saving Customary International Law' (2005) 27 *Michigan Journal of International Law* 115

H

Hannum H., and R.B. Lillich, 'The Concept of Autonomy in International Law' (1980) 74 *American Journal of International Law* 858

Hannum, H., 'Rethinking Self-Determination' (1993) 34 *Virginia Journal of International Law* 1

Hannum, H., *Autonomy, Sovereignty, and Self-Determination. The Accommodation of Conflicting Rights* (2nd revised edn, University of Pennsylvania Press, Philadelphia 1996)

Hannum, H., 'The Advisory Opinion on Kosovo: An Opportunity Lost, or a Poisoned Chalice Refused?' (2011) 24 *Leiden Journal of International Law* 155

Hansen, N.G., *Modern Territorial Statehood* (Doctoral Thesis, Leiden University 2008)

Hasani, E., '*Uti Possidetis Juris*: From Rome to Kosovo' (2003) 27 *Fletcher Forum of World Affairs* 85

Henckaerts, J.-M., and L. Doswald-Beck, *Customary International Humanitarian Law* (International Committee of the Red Cross/Cambridge University Press, Cambridge 2005)

Henrard, K., *Devising an Adequate System of Minority Protection: Individual Human Rights, Minority Rights and the Right to Self-Determination* (Martinus Nijhoff Publishers, The Hague 2000)

Helal, M.S., 'Middle East' in J. Genser and I. Cotler (eds) *The Responsibility to Protect: The Promise of Stopping Mass Atrocities in Our Time* (Oxford University Press, Oxford/New York 2012)

Higgins, R., 'Postmodern Tribalism and the Right to Secession. Comments' in C. Brölmann, R. Lefeber and M. Zieck (eds) *Peoples and Minorities in International Law* (Martinus Nijhoff Publishers, Dordrecht 1993)

Higgins, R., *Problems and Process: International Law and How We Use It* (Oxford University Press, New York 1994)

Hilpold, P., 'Self-Determination in the 21st Century: Modern Perspectives for an Old Concept' in Y. Dinstein (ed.) *Israel Yearbook on Human Rights* (Nijhoff, Dordrecht 2006)

Hilpold, P., 'The Kosovo Case and International Law: Looking for Applicable Theories' (2009) 8 *Chinese Journal of International Law* 47

Hoffmeister, F., Cyprus' in R. Wolfrum (ed.) *Max Planck Encyclopedia of Public International Law* (fully updated online edn Oxford University Press, New York 2010)

I

International Commission of Jurists, 'East Pakistan Staff Study' (1972) 8 *International Commission of Jurists Review* 23

International Commission on Intervention and State Sovereignty, *The Responsibility to Protect* (International Development Research Centre, Ottawa 2001)

Iorns, C.J., 'Indigenous Peoples and Self-Determination: Challenging State Sovereignty' (1992) 24 *Case Western Reserve Journal of International Law* 199

Iyob, R., *The Eritrean Struggle for Independence: Domination, Resistance, Nationalism 1941-1993* (Cambridge University Press, Cambridge/New York 1995)

J

Jennings, W.I., *The Approach of Self-Government* (Cambridge University Press, Cambridge 1956)

Jennings, R.Y., 'The Identification of International Law' in B. Cheng (ed.) *International Law: Teaching and Practice* (Stevens, London 1982)

Jia, B.B., 'The Independence of Kosovo: A Unique Case of Secession?' (2009) 8 *Chinese Journal of International Law* 27

Joseph, S., J. Schultz and M. Castan, *The International Covenant on Civil and Political Rights: Cases, Materials, and Commentary* (Oxford University Press, Oxford 2000)

Judah, T., *Kosovo: What Everyone Needs to Know* (Oxford University Press, New York: 2008)

K

Kamenu, O.S., 'Secession and the Right of Self-Determination: An OAU Dilemma' (1974) 12 *Journal of Modern African Studies* 355

Kamminga, M.T., *De humanisering van het volkenrecht (inaugural lecture)* (Universitaire Pers Maastricht, Maastricht 2001)

Kamminga, M.T., and M. Scheinin (eds), *The Impact of Human Rights Law on General International Law* (Oxford University Press, Oxford 2009)

Kamminga, M.T., 'Final Report on the Impact of International Human Rights Law on General International Law' in M.T. Kamminga and M. Scheinin (eds) *The Impact of Human Rights Law on General International Law* (Oxford University Press, Oxford 2009)

Kelly, J.P., 'The Twilight of Customary International Law' (2000) 40 *Virginia Journal of International Law* 448

Kingsbury, B., 'Reconstructing Self-Determination: A Relational Approach' in P. Aikio and M. Scheinin (eds) *Operationalizing the Right of Indigenous Peoples to Self-Determination* (Institute for Human Rights, Åbo Akademi University, Turku/Åbo 2000)

Kirgis Jr., F.L., 'Custom on a Sliding Scale' (1987) 81 *American Journal of International Law* 146

Kirgis Jr., F.L., 'The Degrees of Self-Determination in the United Nations Era' (1994) 88 *American Journal of International Law* 304

Klabbers, J., and R. Lefeber, 'Africa: Lost Between Self-Determination and *Uti Possidetis*' in C. Brölmann, R. Lefeber and M. Zieck (eds) *Peoples and Minorities in International Law* (Martinus Nijhoff Publishers, Dordrecht 1993)

Klabbers, J., A. Peters and G. Ulfstein (eds), *The Constitutionalization of International Law* (Oxford University Press, Oxford 2009)

Knop, K., *Diversity and Self-Determination in International Law* (Cambridge University Press, Cambridge 2002)

Kohen, M.G., 'Introduction' in M.G. Kohen (ed.) *Secession International Law Perspectives* (Cambridge University Press, Cambridge 2006)

Kohen, M.G., and K. Del Mar, 'The Kosovo Advisory Opinion and UNSCR 1244 (1999): A Declaration of 'Independence from International Law'?' (2011) 24 *Leiden Journal of International Law* 109

Kolb, R., 'Selected Problems in the Theory of Customary International Law' (2003) 50 *Netherlands International Law Review* 119

Kooijmans, P.H., 'Zelfbeschikkingsrecht. Naar een nieuwe interpretatie?' in N. Sybesma-Knol and J. van Bellingen (eds) *Naar een nieuwe interpretatie van het recht op zelfbeschikking?* (VUB Press, Brussels 1995)

Kooijmans, P.H., 'Tolerance, Sovereignty and Self-Determination' (1996) 43 *Netherlands International Law Review* 211

Kumbaro, D., *The Kosovo Crisis in an International Law Perspective: Self-Determination, Territorial Integrity and the NATO Intervention* (2001)

L

Lansing, R., *The Peace Negotiations. A Personal Narrative* (Constable and Company, London 1921)

Lapidoth, R., *Autonomy: Flexible Solutions to Ethnic Conflicts* (United States Institute of Peace Press, Washington D.C. 1997)

Lauterpacht, H., *Recognition in International Law* (Cambridge University Press, Cambridge 1963)

Lauterpacht, H., *The Development of International Law by the International Court* (Cambridge University Press, Cambridge 1982)

Lauwers, G., and S. Smis, 'New Dimensions of the Right to Self-Determination: A Study of the International Response to the Kosovo Crisis' (2000) 6 *Nationalism and Ethnic Politics* 43

Lepard, B.D., *Customary International Law. A New Theory with Practical Applications* (Cambridge University Press, Cambridge 2010)

Letschert, R.M., 'Successful Integration While Respecting Diversity: 'Old' Minorities Versus 'New' Minorities' (2007) 18 *Helsinki Monitor* 46

Locke, J., *Two Treatises of Government [1689]* (Thomas Hollis edn, A. Millar et al., London 1764)

Luck, E.C., 'From Promise to Practice: Implementing the Responsibility to Protect' in J. Genser and I. Cotler (eds) *The Responsibility to Protect: The Promise of Stopping Mass Atrocities in Our Time* (Oxford University Press, Oxford/New York 2012)

M

Malanczuk, P., *Akehurst's Modern Introduction to International Law* (7th revised edn, Routledge, London/New York 1997)

Marks, S.P., and N. Cooper, 'The Responsibility to Protect: Watershed or Old Wine in a New Bottle?' (2010) 2 *Jindal Global Law Review*

McCorquodale, R., 'Self-Determination: A Human Rights Approach' (1994) 43 *International and Comparative Law Quarterly* 857

McCorquodale, R., 'An Inclusive International Legal System' (2004) 17 *Leiden Journal of International Law* 477

Meijknecht, A.K., *Towards International Personality: The Position of Minorities and Indigenous Peoples in International Law* (School of Human Rights Research Series, Intersentia/Hart, Antwerp/Groningen/Oxford 2001)

Meijknecht, A.K., 'Minority Protection System between World War I and World War II' in R. Wolfrum (ed.) *Max Planck Encyclopedia of Public International Law* (fully updated online edn Oxford University Press, New York 2010)

Mendelson, M.H., 'The Subjective Element in Customary International Law' (1996) 66 *British Yearbook of International Law* 177

Mendelson, M.H., 'The Formation of Customary International Law' (1998) 272 *Collected Courses of the Hague Academy of International Law (Recueil des Cours)* 155

Meron, T., *Human Rights and Humanitarian Norms as Customary Law* (Clarendon Press, Oxford 1989)

Meron, T., *The Humanization of International Law* (Martinus Nijhoff Publishers, Leiden/Boston 2006)

Miller, D.H., *The Drafting of the Covenant* (Putnam's, New York 1928)

Miller, R.A., 'Self-Determination in International Law and the Demise of Democracy?' (2003) 41 *Columbia Journal of Transnational Law* 601

Mills, K., *Human Rights in the Emerging Global Order. A New Sovereignty?* (Palgrave Macmillan, New York 1998)

Muharremi, R., 'Kosovo's Declaration of Independence: Self-Determination and Sovereignty Revisited' (2008) 33 *Review of Central and East European Law* 401

Muharremi, R., 'A Note on the ICJ Advisory Opinion on Kosovo' (2010) 11 *German Law Journal* 867

Müllerson, R., 'The Continuity and Succession of States by Reference to the Former USSR and Yugoslavia' (1993) 42 *International and Comparative Law Quarterly* 473

Müllerson, R., 'Precedents in the Mountains: On the Parallels and Uniqueness of the Cases of Kosovo, South Ossetia and Abkhazia' (2009) 8 *Chinese Journal of International Law* 2

Murswiek, D., 'The Issue of a Right of Secession - Reconsidered' in C. Tomuschat (ed.) *Modern Law of Self-Determination* (Martinus Nijhoff Publishers, Dordrecht 1993)

Musgrave, T.D., *Self-Determination and National Minorities* (Oxford University Press, Oxford 1997)

N

Nanda, V.P., 'Self-Determination Outside the Colonial Context: The Birth of Bangladesh in Retrospect' (1979) 1 *Houston Journal of International Law* 71

Nollkaemper, A., *Kern van het internationaal publiekrecht* (5th edn, Boom Juridische Uitgevers, Den Haag 2011)

Nolte, G., 'Secession and External Intervention' in M.G. Kohen (ed.) *Secession International Law Perspectives* (Cambridge University Press, Cambridge 2006)

Nussberger, A., 'Russia' in R. Wolfrum (ed.) *Max Planck Encyclopedia of Public International law* (Oxford University Press, New York 2009)

O

Oeter, S., 'Dissolution of Yugoslavia' in R. Wolfrum (ed.) *Max Planck Encyclopedia of Public International Law* (fully updated online edn Oxford University Press, New York 2011)

Oliver, P., 'Canada's Two Solitudes: Constitutional and International Law in *Reference re Secession of Quebec*' (1999) 6 *International Journal on Minority and Group Rights* 65

Orakhelashvili, A., *The Interpretation of Acts and Rules in Public International Law* (Oxford University Press, Oxford 2008)

Ouguergouz, F., and D.L. Tehindrazanarivelo, 'The Question of Secession in Africa' in M.G. Kohen (ed.) *Secession International Law Perspectives* (Cambridge University Press, Cambridge 2006)

P

Pavković, A., and P. Radan, *Creating New States: Theory and Practice of Secession* (Ashgate Publishing, Aldershot 2007)

Pellet, A., 'The Opinions of the Badinter Arbitration Committee: A Second Breath for the Self-Determination of Peoples' (1992) 3 *European Journal of International Law* 178

Pellet, A., 'Report by Alain Pellet: "Legal Opinion on Certain Questions of International Law Raised by the Reference"' in A.F. Bayefsky (ed.) *Self-Determination in International Law Quebec and Lessons Learned* (Kluwer Law International, The Hague 2000)

Peters, A., 'Humanity as the A and Ω of Sovereignty' (2009) 20 *European Journal of International Law* 513

Peters, A., 'Does Kosovo Lie in the *Lotus*-Land of Freedom?' (2011) 24 *Leiden Journal of International Law* 95

Petersen, N., 'Customary International Law. A New Theory with Practical Applications' (2010) 21 *European Journal of International Law* 795

Philpott, D., 'Self-Determination in Practice' in M. Moore (ed.) *National Self-Determination and Secession* (Oxford University Press, Oxford 2003)

Pomerance, M., *Self-Determination in Law and Practice* (Martinus Nijhoff Publishers, Dordrecht 1982)

Post, H., 'International Law Between Dominium and Imperium: Some Reflections on the Foundations of the International Law on Territorial Acquisition' in T.D. Gill and W.P. Heere (eds) *Reflections on Principles and Practices of International Law Essays in Honour of Leo J Bouchez* (Martinus Nijhoff Publishers, The Hague 2000)

Q

Quane, H., 'The United Nations and the Evolving Right to Self-Determination' (1998) 47 *International and Comparative Law Quarterly* 537

Quane, H., 'A Right to Self-Determination for the Kosovo Albanians?' (2000) 13 *Leiden Journal of International Law* 219

Quane, H., 'Self-Determination and Minority Protection after Kosovo' in J. Summers (ed.) *Kosovo: A Precedent? The Declaration of Independence, the Advisory Opinion and Implications for Statehood, Self-Determination and Minority Rights* (Martinus Nijhoff Publishers, Leiden/Boston 2011)

R

Radan, P., 'Post-Secession International Borders: A Critical Analysis of the Opinions of the Badinter Arbitration Commission' (2000) 24 *Melbourne University Law Review* 50

Radan, P., *The Break-Up of Yugoslavia and International Law* (Routledge, London/New York 2002)

Radan, P., 'The Definition of 'Secession'' (2007) *Macquarie Law Working Paper Series*

Raič, D., *Statehood and the Law of Self-Determination* (Kluwer Law International, The Hague 2002)

Ratner, S.R., 'Drawing a Better Line: *Uti Possidetis* and the Borders of New States' (1996) 90 *American Journal of International Law* 590

Rehman, J., 'The Concept of Autonomy and Minority Rights in Europe' in P. Cumper and S. Wheatley (eds) *Minority Rights in the 'New' Europe* (Martinus Nijhoff Publishers, The Hague/London/Boston 1999)

Reisman, W.M., 'Sovereignty and Human Rights in Contemporary International Law' in G.H. Fox and B.R. Roth (eds) *Democratic Governance and International Law* (Cambridge University Press, Cambridge 2000)

Roberts, A.E., 'Traditional and Modern Approaches to Customary International Law: A Reconciliation' (2001) 95 *American Journal of International Law* 757

Roberts, A.E., and S. Sivakumaran, 'Lawmaking by Nonstate Actors: Engaging Armed Groups in the Creation of International Humanitarian Law' (2012) 37 *Yale Journal of International Law* 107

Rodriguez Cedeno, V., and M.I. Torres Cazorla, 'Unilateral Acts of States in International Law' in R. Wolfrum (ed.) *Max Planck Encyclopedia of Public International Law* (fully updated online edn Oxford University Press, New York 2010)

Rosas, A., 'Internal Self-Determination' in C. Tomuschat (ed.) *Modern Law of Self-Determination* (Martinus Nijhoff Publishers, Dordrecht 1993)

Rousseau, J.-J., *The Social Contract and Discourses [1761]* (G.D.H. Cole edn, J.M. Dent and Sons, London/Toronto 1923)

Rozakis, C.L., 'Territorial Integrity and Political Independence' in R. Bernhardt (ed.) *Encyclopedia of Public International Law* (Elsevier, Amsterdam 2000)

Ryngaert, C., and C.W. Griffioen, 'The Relevance of the Right to Self-Determination in the Kosovo Matter: In Partial Response to the Agora Papers' (2009) *Chinese Journal of International Law - Advance Access*

Ryngaert, C., 'The ICJ's Advisory Opinion on Kosovo's Declaration of Independence: A Missed Opportunity?' (2010) 57 *Netherlands International Law Review* 481

Ryngaert, C., and S. Sobrie, 'Recognition of States: International Law or Realpolitik? The Practice of Recognition in the Wake of Kosovo, South Ossetia, and Abkhazia' (2011) 24 *Leiden Journal of International Law* 467

S

Salmon, J., 'Internal Aspects of the Right to Self-Determination: Towards a Democratic Legitimacy Principle?' in C. Tomuschat (ed.) *Modern Law of Self-Determination* (Martinus Nijhoff Publishers, Dordrecht/Boston/London 1993)

Sanders, D., 'Self-Determination and Indigenous Peoples' in C. Tomuschat (ed.) *Modern Law of Self-Determination* (Martinus Nijhoff Publishers, Dordrecht 1993)

Sands, P., and P. Klein, *Bowett's Law of International Institutions* (5th edn, Sweet & Maxwell, London 2001)

Schachter, O., 'Entangled Treaty and Custom' in Y. Dinstein (ed.) *International Law at a Time of Perplexity: Essays in Honour of Shabtai Rosenne* (Martinus Nijhoff Publishers, Dordrecht 1989)

Scharf, M.P., 'Earned Sovereignty. Juridical Underpinnings' (2004) 31 *Denver Journal of International Law and Policy* 373

Schoiswohl, M., *Status and (Human Rights) Obligations of non-Recognized De Facto Regimes in International Law: The Case of 'Somaliland'. The Resurrection of Somaliland Against All International 'Odds': State Collapse, Secession, Non-Recognition and Human Rights* (Martinus Nijhoff Publishers, Leiden 2005)

Schrijver, N.J., *Sovereignty over Natural Resources: Balancing Rights and Duties* (Cambridge University Press, Cambridge 2008)

Schrijver, N.J., 'Kosovo: dynamiek of dynamiet?' (2010) 85 *Nederlands Juristenblad* 1737

Sepúlveda, M., and others, *Human Rights Reference Handbook* (3rd revised edn, University for Peace, Ciudad Colon 2004)

Shaw, M.N., 'The International Status of National Liberation Movements' (1983) 5 *Liverpool Law Review* 19

Shaw, M.N., 'The Definition of Minorities in International Law' in Y. Dinstein (ed.) *The Protection of Minorities and Human Rights* (Martinus Nijhoff Publishers, Dordrecht/Boston/London 1992)

Shaw, M.N., 'Peoples, Territorialism and Boundaries' (1997) 8 *European Journal of International Law* 478

Shaw, M.N., 'Report by Malcolm N. Shaw: "Re: Order in Council P.C. 1996-1497 of 30 September 1996"' in A.F. Bayefsky (ed.) *Self-Determination in International Law Quebec and Lessons Learned* (Kluwer Law International, The Hague 2000)

Shaw, M.N., *International Law* (5th edn, Cambridge University Press, Cambridge 2003)

Shaw, M.N., 'The Role of Recognition and Non-Recognition with Respect to Secession: Notes on Some Relevant Issues' in J. Dahlitz (ed.) *Secession and International Law* (T.M.C. Asser Press, The Hague 2003)

Shelton, D., 'Self-Determination in Regional Human Rights Law: From Kosovo to Cameroon' (2011) 105 *American Journal of International Law* 60

Simma, B., and P. Alston, 'The Sources of Human Rights Law: Custom, Jus Cogens, and General Principles' (1988-1989) 12 *Australian Year Book of International Law*

Simma, B., 'NATO, the UN and the Use of Force: Legal Aspects' (1999) 10 *European Journal of International Law* 1

Simpson, G., *Great Powers and Outlaw States. Unequal Sovereigns in the International Legal Order* (Cambridge University Press, Cambridge 2004)

Sinclair, I.,'The Significance of the Friendly Relations Declaration' in V. Lowe and C. Warbrick (eds) *The United Nations and the Principles of International Law* (Routledge, London/New York 1994)

Smis, S., *A Western Approach to the International Law of Self-Determination: Theory and Practice* (Doctoral Thesis, Vrije Universiteit Brussel 2001)

Spijkers, O., *The United Nations, the Evolution of Global Values and International Law* (School of Human Rights Research Series, Intersentia, Cambridge/Antwerp/Portland 2011)

Stahn, C., 'Responsibility to Protect: Political Rhetoric or Emerging Legal Norm?' (2007) 101 *American Journal of International Law* 99

Sterio, M., *On the Right to External Self-Determination: "Selfistans", Secession and the Great Powers' Rule* (Working Paper, Cleveland State University 2009)

Summers, J., *Peoples and International Law: How Nationalism and Self-Determination Shape a Contemporary Law of Nations* (Martinus Nijhoff Publishers, Leiden/Boston 2007)

Summers, J., 'Kosovo: From Yugoslav Province to Disputed Independence' in J.

Summers (ed.) *Kosovo: A Precedent? The Declaration of Independence, the Advisory Opinion and Implications for Statehood, Self-Determination and Minority Rights* (Martinus Nijhoff Publishers, Leiden/Boston 2011)

Suski, M., 'On Mechanisms of Decision-Making in the Creation (and the Re-Creation) of States – with Special Reference to the Relationship between the Right to Self-Determination, the Sovereignty of the People and the *pouvoir constituant*' (1997) 3 *Tidsskrift for Rettsvitenskap* 426

Suski, M., 'Keeping the Lid on the Secession Kettle: A Review of Legal Interpretations Concerning Claims of Self-Determination by Minority Peoples' (2005) 12 *International Journal on Minority and Group Rights* 189

T

Tancredi, A., 'A Normative 'Due Process' in the Creation of States through Secession' in M.G. Kohen (ed.) *Secession International Law Perspectives* (Cambridge University Press, Cambridge 2006)

Tasioulas, J., 'Customary International Law and the Quest for Global Justice' in A. Perreau-Saussine and J.B. Murphy (eds) *The Nature of Customary Law: Philosophical, Historical and Legal Perspectives* (Cambridge University Press, Cambridge 2007)

Thio, L.-A., 'International Law and Secession in the Asia and Pacific Regions' in M.G. Kohen (ed.) *Secession International Law Perspectives* (Cambridge University Press, Cambridge 2006)

Thirlway, H., 'The Sources of International Law' in M.D. Evans (ed.) *International Law* (Oxford University Press, Oxford 2003)

Thornberry, P., 'The Democratic or Internal Aspect of Self-Determination with Some Remarks on Federalism' in C. Tomuschat (ed.) *Modern Law of Self-Determination* (Martinus Nijhoff Publishers, Dordrecht 1993)

Thornberry, P., *International Law and the Rights of Minorities* (Clarendon Press, Oxford 2001)

Thürer, D., *Das Selbstbestimmungsrecht der Völker: mit einem Exkurs zur Jurafrage* (Stämpfli, Bern 1976)

Thürer, D., and T. Burri, 'Secession' in R. Wolfrum (ed.) *Max Planck Encyclopedia of Public International Law* (fully updated online edn Oxford University Press, New York 2009)

Thürer, D., and T. Burri, 'Self-Determination' in R. Wolfrum (ed.) *Max Planck Encyclopedia of Public International Law* (fully updated online edn Oxford University Press, New York 2010)

Tilly, C., *Democracy* (Cambridge University Press, Cambridge 2007)

Tomuschat, C., 'Obligations Arising for States Without or Against their Will' (1993) 241 *Collected Courses of the Hague Academy of International Law (Recueil des Cours)*

Tomuschat, C., 'Self-Determination in a Post-Colonial World' in C. Tomuschat (ed.) *Modern Law of Self-Determination* (Martinus Nijhoff Publishers, Dordrecht 1993)

Tomuschat, C., 'International Law: Ensuring the Survival of Mankind on the Eve of a New Century: General Course on Public International Law' (1999) 281 *Collected Courses of the Hague Academy of International Law (Recueil des Cours)* 9

Tomuschat, C., 'Secession and Self-Determination' in M.G. Kohen (ed.) *Secession International Law Perspectives* (Cambridge University Press, Cambridge 2006)

Treves, T., 'Customary International Law' in R. Wolfrum (ed.) *Max Planck Encyclopedia of Public International law* (fully updated online edn Oxford University Press, New York 2010)

Trifunovska (ed.), S., *Yugoslavia Through Documents: From its Creation to its Dissolution* (Martinus Nijhoff Publishers, Dordrecht 1994)

Türk, D., 'Recognition of States: A Comment' (1993) 4 *European Journal of International Law* 66

V

Vashakmadze, M., and M. Lippold, '"Nothing But a Road Towards Secession"? The International Court of Justice's Advisory Opinion on Accordance with International Law of the Unilateral Declaration of Independence in Respect of Kosovo' (2010) 2 *Goettingen Journal of International Law* 619

Vidmar, J., 'International Legal Responses to Kosovo's Declaration of Independence' (2009) 42 *Vanderbilt Journal of Transnational Law* 779

Vidmar, J., 'Remedial Secession in International Law: Theory and (Lack of) Practice' (2010) 6 *St Antony's International Review* 37

Vidmar, J., 'Kosovo: Unilateral Secession and Multilateral State-Making' in J. Summers (ed.) *Kosovo: A Precedent? The Declaration of Independence, the Advisory Opinion and Implications for Statehood, Self-Determination and Minority Rights* (Martinus Nijhoff Publishers, Leiden/Boston 2011)

Vidmar, J., 'Explaining the Legal Effects of Recognition' (2012) 61 *International and Comparative Law Quarterly* 361

W

Ward, W., 'The Right to Free, Prior and Informed Consent: Indigenous Peoples Participation Rights within International Law' (2011) 10 *Northwestern Journal of International Human Rights* 54

Wagner, M., 'Non-State Actors' in R. Wolfrum (ed.) *Max Planck Encyclopedia of Public International Law* (fully updated online edn Oxford University Press, New York 2010)

Warbrick, C., 'Recognition of States' (1999) 41 *International and Comparative Law Quarterly* 473

Warbrick, C., 'Kosovo: the Declaration of Independence' (2008) 57 *International and Comparative Law Quarterly*

Watts QC, A., 'Nuclear Tests Cases' in R. Wolfrum (ed.) *Max Planck Encyclopedia of Public International Law* (fully updated online edn Oxford University Press, New York 2010)

Weller, M., 'The International Response to the Dissolution of the Socialist Federal Republic of Yugoslavia' (1992) 86 *American Journal of International Law* 569

Weller, M., 'The Self-Determination Trap' (2005) 4 *Ethnopolitics* 3

Weller, M., 'Settling Self-Determination Conflicts: An Introduction' in M. Weller and B. Metzger (eds) *Settling Self-Determination Dispute: Complex Power-Sharing in Theory and Practice* (Martinus Nijhoff Publishers, Leiden/Boston 2008)

Weller, M., 'Why the Legal Rules on Self-Determination Do Not Resolve Self-Determination Disputes' in M. Weller and B. Metzger (eds) *Settling Self-Determination Disputes: Complex Power-Sharing in Theory and Practice* (Martinus Nijhoff Publishers, Leiden/Boston 2008)

Weller, M., *Escaping the Self-Determination Trap* (Martinus Nijhoff Publishers, Leiden 2009)

Weller, M., *Contested Statehood: Kosovo's Struggle for Independence* (Oxford University Press, Oxford 2009)

Weller, M., 'Settling Self-Determination Conflicts: Recent Developments' (2009) 20 *European Journal of International Law* 111

Weller, M., 'Modesty Can Be a Virtue: Judicial Economy in the ICJ Kosovo Opinion?' (2011) 24 *Leiden Journal of International Law* 127

Wet, E. de, *The International Constitutional Order* (Vossiuspers UvA, Amsterdam 2005)

Wheatley, S., 'Minority Rights, Power Sharing and the Modern Democratic State' in P. Cumper and S. Wheatley (eds) *Minority Rights in the 'New' Europe* (Martinus Nijhoff Publishers, The Hague/London/Boston 1999)

Wheatley, S., 'Democracy in International Law: A European Perspective' (2002) 51 *International and Comparative Law Quarterly* 225

Wheatley, S., *Democracy, Minorities and International Law* (Cambridge University Press, Cambridge 2005)

Whelan, A., 'Wilsonian Self-Determination and the Versailles Settlement' (1994) 43 *International and Comparative Law Quarterly* 99

White, R.C.A., 'Self-Determination: Time for a Re-Assessment?' (1981) 28 *Netherlands International Law Review* 147

Wilde, R., 'International Decisions - Accordance with International Law of the Unilateral Declaration of Independence in Respect of Kosovo' (2011) 105 *American Journal of International Law* 301

Wildhaber, L., 'Territorial Modifications and Breakups in Federal States' (1995) 33 *Canadian Yearbook of International Law* 41

Wilson, G., 'Self-Determination, Recognition and the Problem of Kosovo' (2009) 56 *Netherlands International Law Review* 455

Wilson, J., 'Ethnic Groups and the Right to Self-Determination' (1996) 11 *Connecticut Journal of International Law* 433

Wilson, T.W., 'An Address to a Joint Session of Congress' in A.S. Link (ed.) *The Papers of Woodrow Wilson* (Princeton University Press, Princeton 1984)

Wolfke, K., *Custom in Present International Law* (2nd revised edn, Martinus Nijhoff Publishers, Dordrecht 1993)

Wouters, J., B. De Meester and C. Ryngaert, 'Democracy and International Law' in I.F. Dekker and E. Hey (eds) *Netherlands Yearbook of International Law* (T.M.C. Asser Press, The Hague 2003)

Wouters, J., and C. Ryngaert, 'Impact on the Process of the Formation of Customary International Law' in M.T. Kamminga and M. Scheinin (eds) *The Impact of Human Rights Law on General International Law* (Oxford University Press, Oxford 2009)

Wright, J., 'Minority Groups, Autonomy, and Self-Determination' (1999) 19 *Oxford Journal of Legal Studies* 605

X

Xanthaki, A., *Indigenous Rights and United Nations Standards. Self-Determination, Culture and Land* (Cambridge University Press, New York 2007)

Y

Yee, S., 'Notes on the International Court of Justice (Part 4): The *Kosovo* Advisory Opinion' (2010) 9 *Chinese Journal of International Law* 763

Z

Zyberi, G., 'Self-Determination through the Lens of the International Court of Justice' (2009) 56 *Netherlands International Law Review* 429

CASE LAW

African Commission on Human and Peoples' Rights

African Commission on Human and Peoples' Rights, *Katangese Peoples' Congress v. Zaire*, Comm. No. 75/92, 1995 (not dated)

African Commission on Human and Peoples' Rights, *Kevin Ngwanga Gumne et al. v. Cameroon*, Comm. No. 266/2003, 2009 (not dated)

Constitutional Court of the Russian Federation

Constitutional Court of the Russian Federation, *Republic of Tatarstan*, 13 March 1992, Decision No. 671

European Court of Human Rights

European Court of Human Rights, *Loizidou v. Turkey*, Application No. 15318/89, Judgment (Merits), 18 December 1996

Inter-American Court of Human Rights

Inter-American Court of Human Rights, *Case of the Saramaka People v. Suriname*, Series C No. 172, Judgment, 28 November 2007

International Court of Justice

International Court of Justice, *Corfu Channel (United Kingdom of Great Britain and Northern Ireland v. Albania)*, Merits, Judgment, ICJ Reports 1949, p. 4

International Court of Justice, *Asylum (Colombia v. Peru)*, Judgment, ICJ Reports 1950, p. 266

International Court of Justice, *Fisheries (United Kingdom v. Norway)*, Judgment, ICJ Reports 1951, p. 116

International Court of Justice, *Case Concerning the Temple of Preah Vihear (Cambodia v. Thailand)*, Merits, Judgment, ICJ Reports 1962, p. 6

International Court of Justice, *South West Africa cases (Ethiopia v. South Africa; Liberia v. South Africa)*, Second Phase, Judgment, ICJ Reports 1966, p. 6

International Court of Justice, *North Sea Continental Shelf (Federal Republic of Germany/Denmark; Federal Republic of Germany/Netherlands)*, Judgment, ICJ Reports 1969, p. 3

International Court of Justice, *Barcelona Traction, Light and Power Company, Limited (Belgium v. Spain)*, Second Phase, Judgment, ICJ Reports 1970, p. 3

International Court of Justice, *Legal Consequences for States of the Continued Presence of South Africa in Namibia (South West Africa) notwithstanding Security Council Resolution 276 (1970)*, Advisory Opinion, ICJ Reports 1971, p. 31

International Court of Justice, *Nuclear Tests (Australia v. France)*, Judgment, ICJ Reports 1974, p. 253

International Court of Justice, *Western Sahara*, Advisory Opinion, ICJ Reports 1975, p. 12

International Court of Justice, *Continental Shelf (Libyan Arab Jamahiriya/Malta)*, Judgment, ICJ Reports 1985, p. 13

International Court of Justice, *Case Concerning Military and Paramilitary Activities in and against Nicaragua (Nicaragua v. United States of America)*, Merits, Judgment, ICJ Reports 1986, p. 14

International Court of Justice, *Case Concerning the Frontier Dispute (Burkina Faso v. Republic of Mali)*, Judgment, ICJ Reports 1986, p. 554

International Court of Justice, *Border and Transborder Armed Actions (Nicaragua v. Honduras)*, Jurisdiction and Admissibility, Judgment, ICJ Reports 1988, p. 12

International Court of Justice, *East Timor (Portugal v. Australia)*, Judgment, ICJ Reports 1995, p. 90

International Court of Justice, *Legality of the Threat or Use of Nuclear Weapons*, Advisory Opinion, ICJ Reports 1996, p. 226

International Court of Justice, *Legal Consequences of the Construction of a Wall in the Occupied Palestinian Territory*, Advisory Opinion, ICJ Reports 2004, p. 136

International Court of Justice, *Sovereignty over Pedra Branca/Pulau Batu Puteh, Middle Rocks and South Ledge (Malaysia v. the Republic of Singapore)*, Judgment, ICJ Reports 2008, p. 1

International Court of Justice, *Accordance with International Law of the Unilateral Declaration of Independence in Respect of Kosovo*, Advisory Opinion, ICJ Reports 2010, p. 403

International Criminal Tribunal for the Former Yugoslavia

International Criminal Tribunal for the Former Yugoslavia, *Prosecutor v. Tadić*, Decision on the defence motion for interlocutory appeal on jurisdiction, ICTY-IT-94-AR72, 2 October 1995

International Criminal Tribunal for the Former Yugoslavia, *Prosecutor v. Kupreškić*, Trial Chamber Judgment, ICTY-IT-95-16-T, 14 January 2000

International Criminal Tribunal for the Former Yugoslavia, *Prosecutor v. Milutinović et al.*, Judgment (vol. 1), ICTY-IT-05-87-T, 26 February 2009

League of Nations International Commission of Jurists and Committee of Rapporteurs

Report of the International Commission of Jurists (Larnaude, Huber, Struycken), LNOJ Special Supplement No. 3 (October 1920)

Report of the International Committee of Rapporteurs (Beyens, Calonder, Elkens), 16 April 1921, LN Council Document B7/2I/68/106 [VII]

Permanent Court of International Justice

Permanent Court of International Justice, *Minority Schools in Albania*, Advisory Opinion, PCIJ Series A/B, No. 64, (1935)

Permanent Court of International Justice, *The Case of the SS Lotus (France v. Turkey)*, Judgment, PCIJ Series A, No. 10 (1927)

Supreme Court of Canada

Supreme Court of Canada, *Reference re Secession of Quebec*, [1998], 2 S.C.R. 217

UN Human Rights Committee

UN Human Rights Committee, *A.D. (the Mikmaq Tribal Society) v. Canada*, Communication No. 78/1980, UN Doc. Supp. No. 40 (A/39/40) at p. 200 (1984)

UN Human Rights Committee, *Kitok v. Sweden*, Communication No. 197/1985, UN Doc. CCPR/C/33/D/197/1985 (1988)

UN Human Rights Committee, *Ominayak and the Lubicon Lake Band v. Canada*, Communication No. 167/1984, UN Doc. Supp. No. 40 (A/45/40) at p. 1 (1990)

UN Human Rights Committee, *Apirana Mahuika et al. v. New Zealand*, Communication No. 547/1993, UN Doc. CCPR/C/70/D/547/1993 (2000)

UN Human Rights Committee, *J.G.A. Diergaardt et al. v. Namibia*, Communication No. 760/1997, UN Doc. CCPR/C/69/D/760/1997 (2000)

UN Human Rights Committee, *Gillot v. France*, Communication No. 932/2000, UN Doc. A/57/40 at p. 270 (2002)

DOCUMENTS OF INTERNATIONAL ORGANIZATIONS AND ASSOCIATIONS

Conference on Security and Co-operation in Europe / Organization for Security and Co-operation in Europe

Conference on Security and Co-operation in Europe, *Conference on Security and Co-operation in Europe Final Act*, Helsinki, 1 August 1975

Conference on Security and Co-operation in Europe, *Document of the Copenhagen Meeting of the Conference on the Human Dimension*, Copenhagen, 29 June 1990

Conference on Security and Co-operation in Europe, *Charter of Paris for a New Europe*, Paris, 21 November 1990

Conference on Security and Co-operation in Europe, *Document of the Moscow Meeting on the Human Dimension, Emphasizing Respect for Human Rights, Pluralistic Democracy, the Rule of Law, and Procedures for Fact-Finding*, Moscow, 3 October 1991

European Union

Council of the European Communities, *Declaration on Yugoslavia and on the "Guidelines on the Recognition of New States in Eastern Europe and in the Soviet Union"*, 16 December 1991, 31 *International Legal Materials* 1485 (1992)

European Communities, *Statement by the Presidency on Recognition of Yugoslav Republics*, EPC Press Release 9/92, 15 January 1992

European Council, *Presidency Conclusions: Copenhagen European Council*, 21-22 June 1993, SN 180/1/93 REV 1, 22 June 1993

International Law Association

International Law Association, Committee on the Formation of Customary (General) International Law, *Statement of Principles Applicable to the Formation of General Customary International Law*, London Conference (2000)

International Law Association, Committee on the Rights of Indigenous Peoples, *Interim Report*, The Hague Conference (2010)

International Law Association, Committee on the Rights of Indigenous Peoples, *Final Report*, Sofia Conference (2012)

International Law Association, Committee on the Rights of Indigenous Peoples, *Resolution No. 5/2012, Rights of Indigenous Peoples*, 75th Conference of the International Law Association held in Sofia, Bulgaria, 26-30 August 2012

Organization of African Unity / African Union

Organization of African Unity, *Resolution adopted by the first ordinary session of the Assembly of the Heads of State and Government held in Cairo, U.A.R., from 17 to 21 July 1964*, AHG Res. 1 – AHG. Res. 24 (1)

United Nations

International Court of Justice

International Court of Justice Press Release, *Accordance with International Law of the Unilateral Declaration of Independence by the Provisional Institutions of Self-Government of Kosovo (Request for Advisory Opinion). Filing of written statements and of a written contribution*, No. 2009/17, 21 April 2009

International Court of Justice Press Release, *Accordance with International Law of the Unilateral Declaration of Independence by the Provisional Institutions of Self-Government of Kosovo (Request for Advisory Opinion). Public hearings to be held from 1 December 2009*, No. 2009/27, 29 July 2009

International Court of Justice Press Release, *Accordance with International Law of the Unilateral Declaration of Independence by the Provisional Institutions of Self-Government of Kosovo (Request for Advisory Opinion). Conclusion of public hearings. Court ready to begin its deliberation*, No. 2009/34, 11 December 2009

International Law Commission

International Law Commission, 'Ways and means for making the evidence of customary international law more readily available', *Yearbook of the ILC*, 1950, vol. II

International Law Commission, 53rd session, 23 April – 1 June and 2 July – 10 August 2001, UN GAOR, 56th session, Suppl. No.10, A/56/10, *Draft Articles on Responsibility of States for International Wrongful Acts, with Commentaries*, UN Doc. A/CN.4/L.602/Rev.1, 26 July 2001

UN Commission on Human Rights

UN Commission on Human Rights, Sub-Commission on Prevention of Discrimination and Protection of Minorities, *The Right to Self-Determination: Implementation of United Nations Resolutions. Study Prepared by Héctor Gros-Espiell*, UN Doc. E/CN.4/Sub.2/405/Rev.1 (1980)

UN Commission on Human Rights, Sub-Commission on the Prevention of Discrimination and Protection of Minorities, *The Right to Self-Determination: Historical and Current Development on the Basis of United Nations Instruments. Study Prepared by A. Cristescu*, UN Doc. E/CN.4/Sub.2/404/Rev.1 (1981)

UN Commission on Human Rights, Sub-Commission on the Prevention of Discrimination and Protection of Minorities, *United Nations Sub-Commission on the Prevention of Discrimination and Protection of Minorities. Proposal Concerning a Definition of the Term 'Minority'. Report Submitted by Mr Jules Deschênes*, UN Doc. E/CN.4/Sub.2/1985/31 (1985)

UN Commission on Human Rights, Sub-Commission on Prevention of Discrimination and Protection of Minorities, *Study of the Problem of Discrimination Against Indigenous Populations, Final Report, submitted by the Special Rapporteur Mr. José R. Martínez Cobo*, UN Doc. E/CN.4/Sub.2/1986/7 (1986)

UN Commission on Human Rights, Sub-Commission on the Prevention of Discrimination and Protection of Minorities, *Study on the Rights of Persons Belonging to Ethnic, Religious and Linguistic Minorities. Study Prepared by F. Capotorti*, UN Doc. E/CN.4/Sub.2/384/Add.1-7 (1991)

UN Commission on Human Rights, Sub-Commission on the Prevention of Discrimination and Protection of Minorities, *Protection of Minorities, Possible Ways and Means of Facilitating the Peaceful and Constructive Solution of Problems Involving Minorities. Report Submitted by Asbjørn Eide*, UN Doc. E/CN.4/Sub.2/1993/34 (1993)

UN Commission on Human Rights, Sub-Commission on Prevention of Discrimination and Protection of Minorities (by E.-I.A. Daes, Chairperson of the Working Group on Indigenous Populations), *Discrimination against Indigenous Peoples: Explanatory Note Concerning the Draft Declaration on the Rights of Indigenous Peoples*, UN Doc. E/CN.4/Sub.2/1993/26/Add.1 (1993)

UN Commission on Human Rights, Sub-Commission on Prevention of Discrimination and Protection of Minorities, Working Group on Indigenous Populations, *Standard-Setting Activities: Evolution of Standards Concerning the Rights of Indigenous Peoples. Working Paper by the Chairperson-Rapporteur, Mrs. Erica-Irene A. Daes, on the concept of "indigenous people"*, UN Doc. E/CN.4/Sub.2-AC.4/1996/2 (1996)

UN Committee on the Elimination of Racial Discrimination

UN Committee on the Elimination of Racial Discrimination, *General Recommendation No. 21: Right to Self-Determination*, UN Doc. A/51/18 (1996), Annex VIII

UN Educational, Scientific and Cultural Organization

UNESCO, *International Meeting of Experts on Further Study of the Concept of the Rights of Peoples. Final Report and Recommendations*, Paris, 22 February 1990, SHS-89/CONF.602/7

UN General Assembly

UN General Assembly Resolution 217 (III) (*Universal Declaration on Human Rights*), UN Doc. A/Res/217, 10 December 1948

UN General Assembly Resolution 637 A-B-C (*The Right of Peoples and Nations to Self-Determination*), UN Doc. A/Res/637, 16 December 1952

UN General Assembly Resolution 742 (VIII) (*Factors Which Should be Taken into Account in Deciding Whether a Territory Is or Is not a Territory Whose People No Yet Attained a Full Measure of Self-Government*), UN Doc. A/Res/742 (VIII), 27 November 1953

UN General Assembly Resolution 1188 (XII) (*Recommendations Concerning International Respect for the Right of Peoples and Nations to Self-Determination*), UN Doc. A/Res/1188 (XII), 11 December 1957

UN General Assembly Resolution 1514 (XV) (*Declaration on the Granting of Independence to Colonial Countries and Peoples*), UN Doc. A/Res/1514, 14 December 1960

UN General Assembly Resolution 1541 (XV) (*Principles Which Should Guide Members in Determining Whether or Not an Obligation Exists to Transmit the Information Called for Under Article 73(e) of the Charter*), UN Doc. A/Res/1541 (XV), 15 December 1960

UN General Assembly Resolution 1815 (XVII) (*Consideration of Principles of International Law Concerning Friendly Relations and Co-operation Among States in Accordance with the Charter of the United Nations*), UN Doc. A/Res/1815 (XVII), 18 December 1962

UN General Assembly Resolution 1966 (XVIII) (*Consideration of Principles of International Law Concerning Friendly Relations and Co-operation Among States in Accordance with the Charter of the United Nations*), UN Doc. A/Res/1966 (XVIII), 16 December 1963

UN General Assembly Resolution 1966 (XVIII) (*Consideration of Principles of International Law Concerning Friendly Relations and Co-operation Among States in Accordance with the Charter of the United Nations*), UN Doc. A/Res/1966 (XVIII), 16 December 1966

UN General Assembly Resolution 2625 (XXV) (*Declaration on Principles of International Law Concerning Friendly Relations and Co-Operation Among States in Accordance with the Charter of the United Nations*), UN Doc. A/Res/2625 (XXV), 24 October 1970

UN General Assembly Resolution 2793 (XXVI) (*Question considered by the Security Council at its 1606th, 1607th and 1608th meetings on 4, 5 and 6 December 1971*), UN Doc. A/Res/2793 (XXVI), 7 December 1971

UN General Assembly Resolution 3203 (XXIX) (*Admission of the People's Republic of Bangladesh to membership in the United Nations*), UN Doc. A/Res/3203 (XXIX), 17 September 1974

UN General Assembly Resolution 46/236 (*Admission of the Republic of Slovenia to membership in the United Nations*), UN Doc. A/Res/46/236, 22 May 1992

UN General Assembly Resolution 46/238 (*Admission of the Republic of Croatia to membership in the United Nations*), UN Doc. A/Res/46/238, 22 May 1992

UN General Assembly Resolution 47/230 (*Admission of Eritrea to membership in the United Nations*), UN Doc. A/Res/47/230, 28 May 1993

UN General Assembly Resolution 48/153 (*Situation of human rights in the territory of the former Yugoslavia*), UN Doc. A/Res/48/153, 20 December 1993

UN General Assembly Resolution 48/121 (*World Conference on Human Rights*), UN Doc. A/Res/48/121, 14 February 1994

UN General Assembly, *Declaration on the Occasion of the Fiftieth Anniversary of the UN*, UN Doc. A/Res/50/49, 24 October 1995

UN General Assembly Resolution 60/1 (*2005 World Summit Outcome*), UN Doc. A/Res/60/1, 16 September 2005

UN General Assembly Resolution 61/295 (*United Nations Declaration on the Rights of Indigenous Peoples*), UN Doc. A/Res/61/295, 13 September 2007

UN General Assembly Resolution 63/3 (*Request for an Advisory Opinion of the International Court of Justice on Whether the Unilateral Declaration of Independence of Kosovo is in Accordance with International Law*), UN Doc. A/Res/63/3, 8 October 2008

UN General Assembly, 22nd plenary meeting, UN Doc. A/63/PV. 22, 8 October 2008

UN General Assembly, *Implementing the Responsibility to Protect: Report of the Secretary-General*, UN Doc. A/63/677, 12 January 2009

UN Human Rights Committee

UN Human Rights Committee, *General Comment No. 12: Article 1 (Right to Self-Determination), The Right to Self-Determination of Peoples*, UN Doc. HRI/GEN/1/Rev.1 (1994), 13 March 1984

UN Human Rights Committee, *Concluding Observations on Azerbaijan*, UN Doc. A/49/40, 3 August 1994

UN Human Rights Committee, *General Comment No. 25: Article 25 (Participation in Public Affairs and the Right to Vote), The Right to Participate in Public Affairs, Voting*

Rights and the Right to Equal Access to Public Service, UN Doc. CCPR/C/21/Rev.1/ Add.7 (1996), 12 July 1996

UN Permanent Forum on Indigenous Issues

Permanent Forum on Indigenous Issues, *Report on the International Workshop on Methodologies Regarding Free, Prior and Informed Consent and Indigenous Peoples*, UN Doc. E/C.19/2005/3, 17 February 2005

UN Secretary-General

UN Secretary-General, *An Agenda for Peace. Preventive Diplomacy, Peacemaking and Peace-keeping. Report of the Secretary-General pursuant to the statement adopted by the Summit Meeting of the Security Council on 31 January 1992*, UN Doc. A/47/277-S/24111, 17 June 1992

UN Security Council

UN Security Council Resolution 216 (1965) (*Southern Rhodesia*), UN Doc. S/Res/216 (1965), 12 November 1965

UN Security Council Resolution 351 (1974) (*New Member: Bangladesh*), UN Doc. S/Res/351 (1974), 10 June 1974

UN Security Council Resolution 541 (1983) *(On Cyprus)* UN Doc. S/ReS/541 (1983), 18 November 1983

UN Security Council Resolution 550 (1984) (*On Cyprus*), UN Doc. S/ReS/550 (1984), 11 May 1984

UN Security Council Resolution 709 (1991) (*New member: Estonia*), UN Doc. S/Res/709 (1991), 12 September 1991

UN Security Council Resolution 710 (1991) (*New member: Latvia*), UN Doc. S/Res/710 (1991), 12 September 1991

UN Security Council Resolution 711 (1991) (*New member: Lithuania*), UN Doc. S/Res/711 (1991), 12 September 1991

UN Security Council Resolution 1160 (1998) (*On the letters from the United Kingdom (S/1998/223) and the United States (S/1998/272)*), UN Doc. S/Res/1160, 31 March 1998

UN Security Council Resolution 1199 (1998) (*On the situation in Kosovo (FRY)*), UN Doc. S/Res/1199, 23 September 1998

UN Security Council, *Report of the Secretary-General pursuant to resolutions 1160 (1998) and 1199 (1998) of the Security Council*, UN Doc. S/1998/912, 3 October 1998

UN Security Council Resolution 1203 (1999) (*On the situation in Kosovo*), UN Doc. S/Res/1203, 24 October 1998

UN Security Council Resolution 1244 (1999) (*Kosovo*), UN Doc. S/Res/1244, 10 June 1999

UN Security Council, *Letter dated 26 March 2007 from the Secretary-General addressed to the President of the Security Council*, UN Doc. S/2007/168, 26 March 2007

UN Security Council, *Letter dated 17 February 2008 from the Permanent Representative of the Russian Federation to the United Nations to the President of the Security Council*, UN Doc. S/2008/104, 17 February 2008

UN Security Council, 5839th meeting, UN Doc. S/PV.5839, 18 February 2008

UN Security Council, 5850th meeting, UN Doc. S/PV.5850, 11 March 2008

UN Security Council, 5871st meeting (closed), UN Doc. S/PV.5871, 21 April 2008

UN Security Council, 5917th meeting, UN Doc. S/PV.5917, 20 June 2008

UN Security Council, 5944th meeting, UN Doc. S/PV.5944, 25 July 2008

UN Security Council, 6025th meeting, UN Doc. S/PV.6025, 26 November 2008

UN Security Council Resolution 1973 (2011) (*Libya*), UN Doc. S/Res/1973 (2011), 17 March 2011

UN Security Council Resolution 1975 (2011) (*Côte d'Ivoire*), UN Doc. S/Res/1975 (2011), 30 March 2011

UN Special Committee on Principles of International Law Concerning Friendly Relations and Co-operation Among States

UN Special Committee on Principles of International Law Concerning Friendly Relations and Co-operation Among States, *Report 6*, UN Doc. A/8018 (XXV)

UN World Conference on Human Rights

UN World Conference on Human Rights, *Vienna Declaration and Programme of Action*, adopted on 25 June 1993, UN Doc. A/CONF.157/23, 12 July 1993

Other UN Documents

UN Press Release, *Backing Request by Serbia, General Assembly Decides to Seek International Court of Justice Ruling on Legality of Kosovo's Independence*, UN Doc. GA/10764, 8 October 2008

SUBMISSIONS OF STATES BEFORE THE INTERNATIONAL COURT OF JUSTICE

Written Statements

International Court of Justice, *Accordance with International Law of the Unilateral Declaration of Independence by the Provisional Institutions of Self-Government of Kosovo (Request for Advisory Opinion)*, Written Statement of Albania, 14 April 2009

International Court of Justice, *Accordance with International Law of the Unilateral Declaration of Independence by the Provisional Institutions of Self-Government of Kosovo (Request for Advisory Opinion)*, Written Statement of Argentina, 17 April 2009

International Court of Justice, *Accordance with International Law of the Unilateral Declaration of Independence by the Provisional Institutions of Self-Government of Kosovo (Request for Advisory Opinion)*, Written Statement of Azerbaijan, 17 April 2009

International Court of Justice, *Accordance with International Law of the Unilateral Declaration of Independence by the Provisional Institutions of Self-Government of Kosovo (Request for Advisory Opinion)*, Written Statement of the Czech Republic, 14 April 2009

International Court of Justice, *Accordance with International Law of the Unilateral Declaration of Independence by the Provisional Institutions of Self-Government of Kosovo (Request for Advisory Opinion)*, Written Statement of the Republic of Cyprus, 3 April 2009

International Court of Justice, *Accordance with International Law of the Unilateral Declaration of Independence by the Provisional Institutions of Self-Government of Kosovo (Request for Advisory Opinion)*, Written Statement of Estonia, 13 April 2009

International Court of Justice, *Accordance with International Law of the Unilateral Declaration of Independence by the Provisional Institutions of Self-Government of Kosovo (Request for Advisory Opinion)*, Written Statement of Finland, 16 April 2009

International Court of Justice, *Accordance with International Law of the Unilateral Declaration of Independence by the Provisional Institutions of Self-Government of Kosovo (Request for Advisory Opinion)*, Written Statement of France, 7 April 2009

International Court of Justice, *Accordance with International Law of the Unilateral Declaration of Independence by the Provisional Institutions of Self-Government of Kosovo (Request for Advisory Opinion)*, Written Statement of Germany, 15 April 2009

International Court of Justice, *Accordance with International Law of the Unilateral Declaration of Independence by the Provisional Institutions of Self-Government of Kosovo (Request for Advisory Opinion)*, Written Statement of Iran, 17 April 2009

International Court of Justice, *Accordance with International Law of the Unilateral Declaration of Independence by the Provisional Institutions of Self-Government of Kosovo (Request for Advisory Opinion)*, Written Statement of Ireland, 17 April 2009

International Court of Justice, *Accordance with International Law of the Unilateral Declaration of Independence by the Provisional Institutions of Self-Government of Kosovo (Request for Advisory Opinion)*, Written Statement of the Netherlands, 17 April 2009

International Court of Justice, *Accordance with International Law of the Unilateral Declaration of Independence by the Provisional Institutions of Self-Government of Kosovo (Request for Advisory Opinion)*, Written Statement of Poland, 14 April 2009

International Court of Justice, *Accordance with International Law of the Unilateral Declaration of Independence by the Provisional Institutions of Self-Government of Kosovo (Request for Advisory Opinion)*, Written Statement of Romania, 14 April 2009

International Court of Justice, *Accordance with International Law of the Unilateral Declaration of Independence by the Provisional Institutions of Self-Government of Kosovo (Request for Advisory Opinion)*, Written Statement of the Russian Federation, 16 April 2009

International Court of Justice, *Accordance with International Law of the Unilateral Declaration of Independence by the Provisional Institutions of Self-Government of Kosovo (Request for Advisory Opinion)*, Written Statement of Serbia, 17 April 2009

International Court of Justice, *Accordance with International Law of the Unilateral Declaration of Independence by the Provisional Institutions of Self-Government of Kosovo (Request for Advisory Opinion)*, Written Statement of Slovenia, 17 April 2009

International Court of Justice, *Accordance with International Law of the Unilateral Declaration of Independence by the Provisional Institutions of Self-Government of Kosovo (Request for Advisory Opinion)*, Written Statement of Spain, 14 April 2009

International Court of Justice, *Accordance with International Law of the Unilateral Declaration of Independence by the Provisional Institutions of Self-Government of Kosovo (Request for Advisory Opinion)*, Written Statement of Switzerland, 25 May 2009

International Court of Justice, *Accordance with International Law of the Unilateral Declaration of Independence by the Provisional Institutions of Self-Government of Kosovo (Request for Advisory Opinion)*, Written Statement of the United Kingdom, 17 April 2009

International Court of Justice, *Accordance with International Law of the Unilateral Declaration of Independence by the Provisional Institutions of Self-Government of Kosovo (Request for Advisory Opinion)*, Written Statement of the United States of America, 17 April 2009

Written Comments

International Court of Justice, *Accordance with International Law of the Unilateral Declaration of Independence by the Provisional Institutions of Self-Government of Kosovo (Request for Advisory Opinion)*, Written Comments of Albania, 17 July 2009

International Court of Justice, *Accordance with International Law of the Unilateral Declaration of Independence by the Provisional Institutions of Self-Government of Kosovo (Request for Advisory Opinion)*, Written Comments of Argentina, 15 July 2009

International Court of Justice, *Accordance with International Law of the Unilateral Declaration of Independence by the Provisional Institutions of Self-Government of Kosovo (Request for Advisory Opinion)*, Written Comments of the Authors of the Unilateral Declaration of Independence (Kosovo), 17 July 2009

International Court of Justice, *Accordance with International Law of the Unilateral Declaration of Independence by the Provisional Institutions of Self-Government of Kosovo (Request for Advisory Opinion)*, Written Comments of the Netherlands, 17 July 2009

International Court of Justice, *Accordance with International Law of the Unilateral Declaration of Independence by the Provisional Institutions of Self-Government of Kosovo (Request for Advisory Opinion)*, Written Comments of Serbia, 15 July 2009

International Court of Justice, *Accordance with International Law of the Unilateral Declaration of Independence by the Provisional Institutions of Self-Government of Kosovo (Request for Advisory Opinion)*, Written Comments of Slovenia, 17 July 2009

International Court of Justice, *Accordance with International Law of the Unilateral Declaration of Independence by the Provisional Institutions of Self-Government of Kosovo (Request for Advisory Opinion)*, Written Comments of Spain, 17 July 2009

International Court of Justice, *Accordance with International Law of the Unilateral Declaration of Independence by the Provisional Institutions of Self-Government of Kosovo (Request for Advisory Opinion)*, Written Comments of Switzerland, 17 July 2009

International Court of Justice, *Accordance with International Law of the Unilateral Declaration of Independence by the Provisional Institutions of Self-Government of Kosovo (Request for Advisory Opinion)*, Written Comments of the United States of America, 17 July 2009

Written Contributions

International Court of Justice, *Accordance with International Law of the Unilateral Declaration of Independence by the Provisional Institutions of Self-Government of Kosovo (Request for Advisory Opinion)*, Written Contribution of the Authors of the Unilateral Declaration of Independence (Kosovo), 17 April 2009

International Court of Justice, *Accordance with International Law of the Unilateral Declaration of Independence by the Provisional Institutions of Self-Government of Kosovo (Request for Advisory Opinion)*, Further Written Contribution of the Authors of the Unilateral Declaration of Independence (Kosovo), 17 July 2009

Oral Statements

International Court of Justice, *Accordance with International Law of the Unilateral Declaration of Independence by the Provisional Institutions of Self-Government of Kosovo (Request for Advisory Opinion)*, Oral Statement of Serbia (Shaw), CR 2009/24, 1 December 2009

International Court of Justice, *Accordance with International Law of the Unilateral Declaration of Independence by the Provisional Institutions of Self-Government of Kosovo (Request for Advisory Opinion)*, Oral Statement of Azerbaijan (Mehdiyev), CR 2009/27, 3 December 2009

International Court of Justice, *Accordance with International Law of the Unilateral Declaration of Independence by the Provisional Institutions of Self-Government of Kosovo (Request for Advisory Opinion)*, Oral Statement of Burundi (Barankitse), CR 2009/28, 4 December 2009

International Court of Justice, *Accordance with International Law of the Unilateral Declaration of Independence by the Provisional Institutions of Self-Government of Kosovo (Request for Advisory Opinion)*, Oral Statement of China (Xue), CR 2009/29, 7 December 2009

International Court of Justice, *Accordance with International Law of the Unilateral Declaration of Independence by the Provisional Institutions of Self-Government of Kosovo*

(Request for Advisory Opinion), Oral Statement of Jordan (Al Hussein), CR 2009/31, 9 December 2009

International Court of Justice, *Accordance with International Law of the Unilateral Declaration of Independence by the Provisional Institutions of Self-Government of Kosovo (Request for Advisory Opinion)*, Oral Statement of the Netherlands (Lijnzaad), CR 2009/32, 10 December 2009

International Court of Justice, *Accordance with International Law of the Unilateral Declaration of Independence by the Provisional Institutions of Self-Government of Kosovo (Request for Advisory Opinion)*, Oral Statement of Romania (Aurescu), CR 2009/32, 10 December 2009

International Court of Justice, *Accordance with International Law of the Unilateral Declaration of Independence by the Provisional Institutions of Self-Government of Kosovo (Request for Advisory Opinion)*, Oral Statement of Venezuela (Fleming), CR 2009/33, 11 December 2009

RECOGNITION STATEMENTS

Afghanistan, *The Statement of Islamic Republic of Afghanistan on the Recognition of Independence of Kosovo*, 18 February 2008, available at <http://kosova.org/docs/independence/Afghanistan.pdf>

Albania, *Statement of Prime Minister of Albania Mr. Sali Berisha on Recognition of Independence of Kosova*, 18 February 2008, available at <http://keshilliministrave.al/index.php?fq=brenda&m=news&lid=7323&gj=gj2>

Australia, *Australia Recognises the Republic of Kosovo*, 19 February 2008, available at <http://www.foreignminister.gov.au/releases/2008/fa-s034_08.html>

Austria, *Plassnik: Letter on Kosovo's Recognition Signed*, 27 February 2008, available at <http://www.bmeia.gv.at/en/foreign-ministry/news/press-releases/2008>

Belgium, *Koninklijk besluit betreffende de erkenning van de Republiek Kosovo*, 24 February 2008, retrieved via 'Who Recognized Kosova as an Independent State?', available at <http://www.kosovothanksyou.com>

Bulgaria, Hungary and Croatia, *Joint Statement by the Governments of Bulgaria, Hungary and Croatia about the announcement of the recognition of Kosovo*, 19 March 2008, available at <http://www.mfa.hr/MVP.asp?pcpid=1640&tr=recognition+Kosovo>

Burkina Faso, *Declaration de Reconnaissance de l'Etat du Kosovo*, 24 April 2008, retrieved via 'Who Recognized Kosova as an Independent State?', available at <http://www.kosovothanksyou.com>

Canada, *Canada Joins International Recognition of Kosovo, Press Release No. 59*, 18 March 2008, available at <http://news.gc.ca> (archived content)

Costa Rica, *Costa Rica se pronuncia por la independencia de Kósovo,*
Comunicación Institucional (Costa Rica Kósovo-1143), 17 February 2008, available at <www.rree.go.cr>

Denmark, *Denmark Recognizes Kosovo as an Independent State*, 21 February 2008, available at <http://kosova.org/docs/independence/Denmark.pdf>

Dominican Republic, *Posición de la Republica Dominicana sobre Kosovo*, 11 July 2009, retrieved via 'Who Recognized Kosova as an Independent State?', available at <http://kosovothanksyou.com>

Estonia, *Estonia Recognizes Republic of Kosovo*, 21 February 2008, available at <http://www.vm.ee/?q=en/node/682>

Finland, *Finland Recognised the Republic of Kosovo*, 7 March 2008, available at <http://formin.finland.fi/public/default.aspx?contentid=123797&nodeid=15146&contentlan=2&culture=en-US>

France, *Lettre du President de la Republique, M. Nicholas Sarkozy, Addressee sur President du Kosovo, M. Fatmir Sejdiu*, 18 February 2008, available at <http://www.mofa.go.jp/announce/announce/2008/3/0318.html>

Germany, *Cabinet Approves Recognition of Kosovo as Independent State under International Law*, 20 February 2008, available at <http://www.deutsche-aussenpolitik.de/daparchive/anzeige.php?zaehler=11196>

Ireland, *Minister for Foreign Affairs Dermot Ahern TD Announces Ireland's Recognition of the Republic of Kosovo*, 29 February 2008, available at <http://foreignaffairs.gov.ie/home/index.aspx?id=42938>

Iceland, *The Government of Iceland formally Recognizes Kosovo*, 5 March 2008, available at <http://www.mfa.is/news-and-publications/nr/4135>

Japan, *Statement by Foreign Minister Masahiko Koumura on the Recognition of the Republic of Kosovo*, 18 March 2008, available at <http://www.mofa.go.jp/announce/announce/2008/3/0318.html>

Korea, *Recognition of the Republic of Kosovo*, 28 March 2008, available at <http://www.mofat.go.kr/ENG/main/index.jsp>

Latvia, *Announcement by Minister of Foreign Affairs of Republic of Latvia on Recognition of Kosovo's Independence*, available at <http://www.mfa.gov.lv/en/news/press-releases/2008/february/20-february/>

Lithuania, *Seimas of the Republic of Lithuania, Resolution on the Recognition of the Republic of Kosovo, No. X-1520*, 6 May 2008, retrieved via 'Who Recognized Kosova as an Independent State?', available at <http://www.kosovothanksyou.com>

Luxembourg, *Le Luxembourg reconnaît formellement le Kosovo*, 21 February 2008, available at <http://www.gouvernement.lu/salle_presse/actualite/2008/02-fevrier/20-asselborn-kosovo/index.html>

Macedonia, *Macedonia Recognizes Kosovo*, 9 October 2008, available at <http://www.mia.com.mk/default.aspx?vId=57722300&lId=2>

Malaysia, *Letter of Dr Rais Yatim to His Excellency Mr Skender Hyseni*, 30 October 2008, available at <http://kosova.org/docs/independence/Malaysia.pdf>

Malta, M*alta Recognizes Kosovo as an Independent State*, 22 August 2008, available at <http://www.foreign.gov.mt/default.aspx?MDIS=21&NWID=68>

Peru, *Perú decide reconocer independencia de Kósovo*, Comunicado Oficial 002-08, 22 February 2008, retrieved through <http://www.kosovothanksyou.com/>

Poland, *Government has Recognized the Independence of Kosovo*, 26 February 2008, available at <http://www.premier.gov.pl/en/press_centre/news/government_has_recognised_the_,2220/>

Saudi Arabia, *Saudi Arabia Announces Recognition of the Republic of Kosovo*, 20 April 2008, available at <http://www.spa.gov.sa/English/print.php?id=656348>

Senegal, *Dakar reconnaît le nouvel Etat*, 19 February 2008, available at <http://www.aps.sn/articles.php?id_article=40531>

Slovenia, *Slovenia Recognizes Kosovo*, 5 March 2008, available at <http://kosova.org/docs/independence/Slowenien.pdf>

Sweden, *Sweden Recognises the Republic of Kosovo*, 4 March 2008, available at <http://www.sweden.gov.se/sb/d/10358/a/99714>

Switzerland, *Statement by the President of the Swiss Confederation*, 27 February 2008, available at <http://www.sweden.gov.se/sb/d/10358/a/99714>

Turkey, *Statement of H.E. Mr. Ali Babacan, Minister of Foreign Affairs of the Republic of Turkey, Regarding the Recognition of Kosovo by Turkey*, 18 February 2008, available at <http://www.mfa.gov.tr>

United Arab Emirates, *UAE Recognises Kosovo*, 14 October 2008, retrieved via 'Who Recognized Kosova as an Independent State?', available at <http://www.kosovothank-syou.com>

United States of America, *U.S. Recognizes Kosovo as Independent State, Statement of Secretary of State Condoleezza Rice*, 18 February 2008, available at <http://2001-2009.state.gov/secretary/rm/2008/02/100973.htm>

OTHER WEB PAGES

Human Rights Watch, *Ethiopia: "Mengistu has Decided to Burn us Like Wood" – Bombing of Civilians and Civilian Targets by the Airforce*, 24 July 1990, available at <http://www.hrw.org/reports/pdfs/e/ethiopia/ethiopia907.pdf>

Human Rights Watch, *Under Orders: War Crimes in Kosovo*, available at <http://www.hrw.org/reports/2001/kosovo/>

Independent International Fact-Finding Mission on the Conflict in Georgia, *Report of the Independent International Fact-Finding Mission on the Conflict in Georgia* (2009), available at <http://www.ceiig.ch/Index.html>

Independent International Commission on Kosovo, *The Kosovo Report. Conflict, International Response, Lessons Learned*, available at <http://reliefweb.int>

International Labour Organization, *Indigenous and Tribal Peoples*, available at <http://www.ilo.org/indigenous/lang--en/index.htm>

Ministry of Foreign Affairs of the Republic of Kosovo, *Countries that have recognized the Republic of Kosova*, available at <www.mfa-ks.net/?page=2,33>

Ministry of Foreign Affairs of the Republic of Kosovo, *Kosovo Declaration of Independence*, available at <http://www.mfa-ks.net/?page=2,25>

Office of the United Nations High Commissioner for Human Rights, *Human Rights Committee, Status of Ratification, Reservations, Declarations*, available at <http://treaties.un.org/Pages/Treaties.aspx?id=4&subid=A&lang=en>

Southern Sudan Referendum 2011, *Southern Sudan Referendum Commission*, available at <http://southernsudan2011.com/>

U.S. Department of State, 'Timeline of U.S. Diplomatic History', *Bandung Conference (Asian-African Conference), 1955*, available at <http://history.state.gov/>

MISCELLANEOUS

'Agreement on the Establishment of the Commonwealth of Independent States', 8 December 1991, (1992) 31 *International Legal Materials: Current Documents* 143

'Opinions No. 1-3 of the Arbitration Commission of the International Conference on Yugoslavia' (1992) 3 *European Journal of International Law* 182

'Opinions No. 4-10 of the Arbitration Commission of the International Conference on Yugoslavia' (1993) 4 *European Journal of International Law* 74

'Protocol to the Agreement on the Establishment of the Commonwealth of Independent States', 21 December 1991, (1992) 31 *International Legal Materials: Current Documents* 147

INDEX

CURRICULUM VITAE

Simone F. van den Driest (Middelburg, 1984) studied International and European Public Law at Tilburg University. In 2008, she obtained a Master's degree in the specialization International and European Public Law (*cum laude*) and successfully completed the Research Master in Law at the same university (*cum laude*). Her Master's thesis 'Pro-Democratic Regime Change and the Right to Political Self-Determination: A Case Study of Iraq' was awarded with the Tilburg University Faculty of Law Master's Thesis Award 2008 and the Tilburg University Research Master's Thesis Award 2008. From 2008 to 2012, she was employed as a PhD researcher at the Department of European and International Public Law of Tilburg University. Besides working on her dissertation, she taught public international law and gave various guest lectures on the right to self-determination in international law and on Kosovo's unilateral declaration of independence. She also supervised students at both Bachelor's and Master's level during the writing of their theses. Moreover, she has been involved in various other activities, *inter alia*, as secretary and deputy chairperson of the PhD Council of Tilburg Law School, as a member of the editorial board of the Newsletter of the Netherlands School of Human Rights Research, as the coordinator of the Statelessness Summer Course (a joint effort of Tilburg University's Statelessness Programme and Open Society Justice Initiative) and as a member of the board of Tilburg Law School's alumni association, JUVAT.

SCHOOL OF HUMAN RIGHTS RESEARCH SERIES

The School of Human Rights Research is a joint effort by human rights researchers in the Netherlands. Its central research theme is the nature and meaning of international standards in the field of human rights, their application and promotion in the national legal order, their interplay with national standards, and the international supervision of such application. The School of Human Rights Research Series only includes English titles that contribute to a better understanding of the different aspects of human rights.

Editorial Board of the Series:
Prof. dr. J.E. Goldschmidt (Utrecht University), Prof. dr. D.A. Hellema (Utrecht University), Prof. dr. W.J.M. van Genugten (Tilburg University), Prof. dr. M.T. Kamminga (Maastricht University), Prof. dr. P.A.M. Mevis (Erasmus University Rotterdam), Dr. J.-P. Loof (Leiden University) and Dr. O.M. Ribbelink (Asser Institute).

For previous volumes in the series, please visit http://shr.intersentia.com.

Published titles within the Series:

52   Vera Vriezen, *Amnesty Justified? The Need for a Case by Case Approach in the Interests of Human Rights*
     ISBN 978-1-78068-075-0

53   Maite San Giorgi, *The Human Right to Equal Access to Health Care*
     ISBN 978-1-78068-081-1

54   Jeroen Blomsma, *Mens rea and Defences in European Criminal Law*
     ISBN 978-1-78068-104-7

55   Masha Fedorova, *The Principle of Equality of Arms in International Criminal Proceedings*
     ISBN 978-1-78068-111-5

56   Martine Boersma, *Corruption: A Violation of Human Rights and a Crime Under International Law?*
     ISBN 978-1-78068-105-4